Building Foundations

Building Foundations
Housing and Federal Policy

Edited by Denise DiPasquale
and Langley C. Keyes

upp

UNIVERSITY OF PENNSYLVANIA PRESS   Philadelphia

Library of Congress Cataloging-in-Publication Data

Building foundations : housing and federal policy / Denise DiPasquale
    and Langley C. Keyes, editors.
    p.   cm.
    ISBN 0-8122-8223-X. — ISBN 0-8122-1309-2 (pbk.)
    1. Housing policy—United States.   I. DiPasquale, Denise.
II. Keyes, Langley Carleton, 1938–   .
HD7293.B83   1990
363.5′8′0973—dc20   90-30442
                                                          CIP

Contents

Foreword

This book is being published at a critical time for housing in America. The paradox of the nation's housing has become increasingly clear. On the one hand, we have much to be proud of. We are a well-housed people. For most Americans, the goal of the 1949 Housing Act—a decent home and suitable living environment—has been achieved.

At the same time, for millions of Americans that goal is a frustrating fantasy. Homelessness is a national disgrace. Many working families are losing ground as their rents are rising faster than their incomes. The low-rent housing stock is an endangered species. Private units are being lost to conversion and abandonment; the subsidized stock is threatened by expiring use restrictions, withdrawal of federal production programs and the deterioration of public housing. After decades of steady progress, the homeownership rate has been falling since 1980, particularly among young families. High costs of home-ownership coupled with declining savings due, in part, to larger portions of income going to rent has made homeownership a dream deferred, if not abandoned.

A second paradox is emerging. There is growing recognition of the federal government's crucial role in providing leadership to meet the nation's housing needs. However, with declining federal funds for housing, there has been skepticism about the capacity of the federal government, especially the Department of Housing and Urban Development to meet the mounting housing challenges—a skepticism currently reinforced by the daily unraveling of the HUD scandals. Fortunately, the spirit and work of HUD Secretary Jack Kemp gives great hope that the problems at the agency will be resolved and that effective federal leadership in housing will be restored—a leadership that empowers the poor and encourages public-private partnerships to make decent and safe housing the legitimate expectation of all Americans.

For anyone engaged in formulating and implementing a new national housing policy, this book is essential. It carefully documents the central housing policy issues facing our nation today. Written by leading researchers and practitioners in the housing field, the papers in this volume represent much of the current wisdom on the fundamental issues that must be addressed in any consideration of national housing policy. Preliminary drafts of these papers were made available to the National Housing Task Force, which we chaired. The Task Force, a group of private individuals involved in every way with the problem of housing our citizens, was asked by Senators Alan Cranston and Alfonse D'Amato to design the blueprint for a revised national housing policy. Our work was significantly enhanced by both the papers themselves and our discussions with their authors.

It is time to reaffirm our commitment to a decent home for every American family. Achieving this goal requires the concerted efforts of not only the federal government but those sectors that have been the innovators in housing over the past decade—state and local governments, for-profit and non-profit developers, and community, civic, and religious groups. However, if they are to be a significant part of the delivery system for housing our people, the federal government must provide leadership and incentives.

We hope this book will inspire everyone interested in housing our citizens, just as the papers in it inspired us and our Task Force colleagues. The time for action is now.

James W. Rouse
Enterprise Foundation

David O. Maxwell
Fannie Mae

Preface

The seventeen papers included in this volume were written for the MIT Housing Policy Project which we directed. In establishing the agenda for the project, we gathered together practical researchers and thoughtful practitioners who were well versed in current policy in the housing field, knowledgeable about past initiatives, and cognizant of the issues to be addressed in any consideration of the federal role in housing. We did not try to assemble authors with similar views as to what the federal role ought to be. We sought people with experience, a reputation in the field, and the respect of their peers.

Our purpose was not to produce a policy document advocating a single set of recommendations. That was for the National Housing Task Force to do. Rather we saw our role as assembling the "state of the art" on those issues which lie at the heart of any reevaluation and reconsideration of federal policy.

Given the different perspectives of our authors, we wanted them to undertake their assignments with a shared sense of the project's purpose and a clear understanding of each other's tasks. We spent a day together in Washington in the summer of 1987 to accomplish these goals. We discussed the project's agenda, exchanged information, and explored common themes.

We met again in Washington in the late fall of 1987 when the drafts of the papers were written. In three day-long conferences the authors presented their work to a gathering of other authors, peers, and practitioners. Two readers, one from among the other writers and one "outside" commenter, provided critiques to each paper. We attempted to get readers whose points of view on the issue differed from that of the author so that the papers would be challenged not just endorsed. In most instances, we succeeded. The authors then returned to the drawing board, comments and critiques in hand, and produced final drafts which were published in a working paper series by the MIT Center for Real Estate Development in the spring of 1988. After we received a book contract, we went back to the authors one more time to edit the papers for final publication.

In a project of this magnitude, many people make significant contributions. It is important to us to acknowledge them. First and foremost, we would like to thank the authors of the papers who committed themselves to the project on extremely short notice and stayed the course through all the drafts and redrafts that followed. They maintained good humor while meeting the deadlines imposed and responding to our increasingly urgent phone calls. This is a cast we feel fortunate to be members of.

In addition to the authors, a group of people emerged who gave so generously of their time, special knowledge, and wisdom that we came to think of them as "friends of the project." These friends include Nancy Andrews, Doug Bibby, Don Campbell, Gordon Cavanaugh, Kent Colton, Cushing Dolbeare, Hilbert Fefferman, Tony Freedman, Harriet Ivey, Bruce Katz, Judy Kennedy, Jill Khadduri, Grace Morgan, Mort Schussheim, John Sidor, Steve Somers, Susan Wachter, and Barry Zigas.

This enterprise was generously financed by the Ford Foundation, the Fannie Mae Foundation, the Robert Wood Johnson Foundation, and Freddie Mac. Additional support was provided by the Joint Center for Housing Studies of Harvard University. The MIT Center for Real Estate Development furnished a gracious home for the project over the past three years.

Finally, we want to express our deep gratitude to our editor, colleague, and friend, Vivi Leavy. Her editorial capabilities, organizational skill, patience, and sense of humor were invaluable. It was our good fortune to work with her throughout this adventure.

Denise DiPasquale
Harvard University

Langley C. Keyes
MIT

Chapter 1
Housing Policy for the 1990s

Langley C. Keyes and Denise DiPasquale

As Congress considers legislation that would forge a new national housing policy, the appropriate role for the federal government is at the center of the policy debate. Over the last two decades, the view of that role has shifted considerably, from the image held in the late 1960s that the federal government should be the major actor in housing policy to the position in the early 1980s that the federal government should largely get out of the housing business.

This chapter has two goals: (1) to identify and analyze the critical issues that must be negotiated in the formulation of a new national housing policy; and (2) to assess the potential role of the federal government in that policy.

To this end, we rely heavily on the nineteen papers prepared for the MIT Housing Policy Project. However, this essay is not a summary of those papers. Given the diversity and breadth of views expressed, such an effort would be a compendium rather than an overview. Rather, ours is an interpretation of the policy agenda that must be negotiated as national legislation moves forward. That interpretation is, however, deeply indebted to the other authors in the project, and we call on their wisdom at many points throughout our discussion.

In order to frame the current housing debate, we also rely heavily on the history of national housing policy, particularly in the last two decades. This historical context is provided in large part by the reports of three blue ribbon commissions formed in the last twenty years to assess national housing policy: President Johnson's Committee on Urban Housing (the Kaiser Committee) in 1968, President Reagan's Commission on Housing (the President's Commission) in 1982, and the National Housing Task Force (Rouse/Maxwell) in 1988, part of a Congressional effort to set a new national housing agenda.

Taken together, the MIT Housing Policy papers and the reports of the three commissions point to four critical issues which represent the major points of tension in the current policy debate that must be resolved in order to formulate a new national housing policy. Collectively, these issues constitute the warp and woof of such legislation. The four issues are:

1. *Targeting federal resources.* Given the inevitable gap between need and available funding, who among the needy should receive those limited resources?
2. *The role of the existing stock.* How and to what extent should we preserve the existing private, subsidized private, and public low-income housing stock?
3. *Institution building and program design.* What are the appropriate roles for the federal, state, and local governments, the nonprofits, and the private sector in delivering housing programs?
4. *Public partnership.* How can housing programs be coordinated with related federal policies and programs, such as tax incentives, welfare assistance, and supportive services?

These issues encompass a number of themes that run through chapters in this book, themes that in some instances are new to debates about housing policy, such as expiring use restrictions and the homeless, and others that have long been on the table, such as troubled public housing projects, the appropriate way to subsidize low-income renters, and the role of the nonprofit sector.

We start the discussion with a brief overview of the three commission reports. This overview emphasizes the fundamental differences in perspective taken by the three groups, particularly on the role of the federal government in dealing with the nation's housing. We then proceed to discuss in more detail the four issues outlined above. For each, we define the concept, discuss its formulation by the commissions, and outline the parameters of the current debate surrounding the issue. Finally, we conclude with a discussion of the appropriate role of the federal government, particularly the Department of Housing and Urban Development, in future national housing policy.

A Tale of Three Commissions

President Johnson's Committee on Urban Housing, in its report *A Decent Home* (1968), assumed strong federal leadership in housing policy. The Kaiser Committee called for the construction or rehabilitation of six million low-income housing units by 1978 and was optimistic that this goal could be accomplished using federally subsidized programs. If economic times got tough and the resources more difficult to find, housing would simply have to be upgraded as a priority on the national agenda.

The Committee recognized that its production solution to the plight of low-income households called for "major efforts by the federal government, private enterprise, organized labor, and state and local governments in creative and affirmative partnerships."[1] The Committee believed that a public/private partnership could do the job, but if it were to fail, "we would then foresee the necessity for massive federal intervention, with the federal government becoming the nation's houser of last resort."[2] The Committee was convinced that the "housing problem" could and should be resolved with federal dollars.

Here, then, was a group of distinguished leaders, primarily from the private sector, proposing a highly specific policy by which to solve the low-income housing problem in America through the use of federal subsidy programs to create new and to rehabilitate old housing. While state and local governments and the private and nonprofit sectors were seen as key players in this crusade, there is no question who was in charge, setting the tone, creating the programs, and paying the bills.

From the vantage point of 1988, *A Decent Home* is a testament to a by-gone age, when the federal government bestrode low-income housing like the Colossus of Rhodes. Twenty years has witnessed an almost total transformation in how the federal government has defined its own role and that of others in solving the nation's housing problems.

In 1981, another president asked another group of prestigious individuals to form a commission to advise him on how to "formulate a housing policy consistent within itself and with (his) basic principles."[3] President Reagan's Commission on Housing gave its report to the President in April, 1982. Its view of the federal role in the low-income housing challenge presents a very different perspective from that of the authors of *A Decent Home*:

. . . the Kaiser Committee of 1967 . . . did its work at a time of high optimism about what government could accomplish in the economy. The numerical targets for housing production and expansive rhetoric of the Kaiser Report reflected a common belief that all problems would be solved if only the government would set the right goals and enforce the right policies.[4]

The Commission went on to characterize the programs emerging from the Kaiser Committee's recommendations in the 1968 Housing Act as contributing "to deterioration rather than renewal, to misery rather than comfort."[5] President Reagan's Commission, however, was optimistic about the future of housing, but only in a world which enabled "the genius of the market economy" to "escape the fetters of public regulation and policies."[6]

Despite its identification of the federal government as a major cause of the problem rather than a significant source of the solution to the low-income housing dilemma, the Commission did recognize "a continuing role for the federal government helping low-income households,"[7] not by the production of units, but rather by supplementing incomes to make it possible for people to rent in private developments.

The Commission was very clear to indicate that rent supplements should not be construed as an entitlement program. "The nation cannot afford yet another system of entitlements expanding endlessly out of effective control." [8] Grants should only be for families of very low income "living in inadequate housing and paying a large portion of their income for housing," [9] a number which the Commission calculated at roughly 1.1 million households. [10]

The Commission report did mention that there might be some locations in the country where the tightness of the housing market made a supply side approach urgent. But the existing federal Community Development Block Grant Program was seen as the appropriate vehicle for those few situations where new production or rehabilitation were the appropriate response to issues of affordability.

If there was a housing crisis in 1981, it was in the financing system, which was cluttered with regulation. From the Commission's perspective, "the sooner the government clears the way, the quicker the nation will gain the benefits of the homes a healthy system will provide." [11]

The Report of the National Housing Task Force, *A Decent Place to Live,* issued in March of 1988, is the work of the most recent prestigious national group established to comment on the state of the nation's housing and the role of the federal government in dealing with its problems. Unlike the previous two commissions, however, it was not established by the president, but rather "as part of a Congressional effort to . . . help set a new national housing agenda." [12]

The National Housing Task Force Report takes as its starting point "the paradox of housing in America . . . [that] the promise of 'a decent home and a suitable living environment,' set forth by the Housing Act of 1949, has become a reality for most of our citizens. But the 1949 commitment was 'for every American.' And for millions of our families, we have not only fallen short, but are losing ground." [13]

The Report focuses not on the "good news" about housing—the success stories for America's middle- and upper-middle-income families—but rather on "America's most pressing housing needs." Thus, the Report emphasizes the extent to which, in the past half decade, the number of households seeking low-rent housing has increased, and the number of units available to them has diminished. The double-edged sword of success in achieving higher standards is emphasized. As physical conditions improve, "there will be a price to be paid" and higher rents for improved housing will have to be subsidized. [14] Low-rent housing on the private market is becoming increasingly scarce, thus making even more valuable those units which the federal government has under contract through public housing or subsidized private rental housing. The Report also emphasizes that "all is not well for the American home-buyer." [15] For some, the dream is being deferred through the high cost of entry into that market.

Whereas the Kaiser Committee saw the federal government as the solution to the low-income housing problem and Reagan's Commission looked to the genius of the private market, the Rouse/Maxwell Task Force seeks a re-affirmation of federal commitment to a leadership role to "shape the national housing agenda." [16] But that leadership is not perceived as advocating a "made in Washington" approach to programmatic solutions. Rather, the Task Force Report emphasizes the collaboration of the federal government with public, private, and nonprofit partners engaged at the state and municipal levels, part-ners already at work representing a " 'new wave' of initiative and resource-fulness in meeting our critical housing needs." [17] Federal funds and federal leadership should leverage other investment—public and private—in the housing markets of the nation. The Report sees this leveraged use of federal dollars as the "key to the new partnership and a new element in federal hous-ing policy." [18]

Unlike the Kaiser Committee Report, the Rouse/Maxwell Report does not envision sufficient financial resources at the present time to "do away with" the low-income housing problem. It recognizes that "federal spending choices are severely limited." [19] But it does look to the year 2000 as a time when all Americans should have access to "fit, livable, and affordable housing." [20]

Targeting Federal Resources

Federal housing policy provides subsidies, direct or indirect, to a broad spec-trum of the population. Low-income households are served by direct subsi-dies, such as public housing and rental assistance. Higher income households are subsidized through the deductibility of mortgage interest and real estate taxes for federal income tax purposes. There is, however, a fundamental differ-ence between the subsidies provided to low-income households and those bene-fiting higher income households. Subsidies for the poor are made available through discretionary programs which have never been sufficiently funded to serve all eligible households. Recent estimates indicate that in 1987 only 28 percent of the nation's households with incomes below the poverty level re-ceived some type of housing assistance. [21] On the other hand, the subsidies provided through the homeowner income tax deductions are akin to an entitle-ment program—anyone who owns a home can claim a deduction for mort-gage interest and real estate taxes, and because of the progressive tax rate structure, the level of subsidy increases with income.

Apart from the equity concerns raised by a subsidy structure using dis-cretionary programs for the most needy in our society and an entitlement pro-gram for the more affluent, there is another problem often cited with this structure. Many moderate-income households have too much income to qual-ify for the direct subsidy programs and too little income to benefit from in-come tax deductions. Hence, these households often find themselves squeezed out of the housing subsidy system.

The reports of the Kaiser Committee, President Reagan's Commission, and the National Housing Task Force are strikingly consistent on the targeting issue in one important respect. All three maintain the subsidies to homeownership provided through the deductibility of mortgage interest and real estate taxes. However, the reports do differ on the targeting issue when considering direct subsidy programs for the low and moderate end of the income spectrum. Since the Kaiser Committee fundamentally saw housing as an entitlement for all Americans, targeting was not a concern. In contrast, President Reagan's Commission emphasized a narrowly targeted approach to housing assistance. Demand side vouchers, the major form of housing assistance recommended, were to be focused in the poorest households which the Commission estimated at roughly 1.1 million families. The National Housing Task Force favors a somewhat broader, highly structured distribution of subsidy. Under its recommendations, 80 percent of "Housing Opportunity Program" (HOP) funds would be designated for households at or below 80 percent of median income, with half of these funds for households below 50 percent of median. The remaining 20 percent of the HOP funds could go to households with incomes up to 120 percent of median. However, the Task Force implicitly envisions housing as an entitlement by the year 2000, a goal which, if realized, would again render the targeting issue moot.[22]

As was the case with these three prestigious commissions, homeownership subsidies through the federal income tax system are largely ignored in the current debates concerning allocation of federal assistance to housing. This is not to say that the issue is not raised by housing analysts. For example, in Chapter 3 of this book Downs argues that in determining how much money the federal government should spend on housing aid to low-income households, "Congress should recognize that (1) homeownership tax benefits cause much larger net costs to the federal government than the outlay costs of all direct forms of housing subsidies combined, and (2) middle- and upper-income groups receive the vast majority of all homeownership tax benefits." [23]

The targeting issue is generally framed in terms of direct federal budget outlays, a formulation which ignores tax subsidies to housing. This narrow approach results in a spectrum of concern for targeting housing resources that ranges only from homelessness at the low end to affordable homeownership (first-time homebuyers) at the high end.

Even if we accept this narrow spectrum as the definition of the possible target population for housing subsidy, the appropriate allocation of resources across this spectrum is open to debate. Downs argues that "the federal government should confine its direct housing assistance funding as much as possible to aiding low-income households . . . [It] should not provide significant housing assistance to non-low-income households—including first-time homebuyers—unless large amounts of federal funds are available for housing assistance of all types." [24]

At face value, it is difficult to argue with the view that government re-sources should be allocated to the most needy in our society. However, the realities of housing markets, program implementation, and politics suggest that this view may be too simplistic.

From a housing market perspective, it is difficult to isolate a specific tar-get population. It is true that the poor participate in a submarket of the overall housing market. However, there is no precise definition of *the* submarket serving the poor. Furthermore, the housing market is composed of a large number of interrelated submarkets and the problems found in one such sub-market can profoundly influence others. As Apgar points out in Chapter 2, "there is no single housing problem in America today but a series of intercon-nected problems that confront a wide range of households." [25]

For example, many argue that it is difficult to justify allocating resources to programs designed to open opportunities to moderate-income first-time homebuyers given the problems facing low-income renters. However, if po-tential first time homebuyers do not or cannot make the transition from renter to homeowner, they will stay in the rental market longer and drive rents higher. As a result, low-income households may find more and more of their incomes being absorbed by housing costs. Thus, the difficulties facing first-time homebuyers may create additional problems in the rental market.

On the supply side, the targeting issues are even more complex. Housing developments built solely for the poor have been criticized because they iso-late the poor both geographically and socially. If the development is to house only subsidized households, the incentives for the developer to be concerned with location and design are lost. Hence, low-income developments are often poorly designed and placed on marginal sites in problematic locations. In a mixed-income development, the developer must build for the market and go after the best sites and marketable designs. While some of the subsidy in mixed-income developments may go to higher-income households, these sub-sidy dollars may be viewed as purchasing better housing in better locations for low-income households. In addition, more affordable housing may actually be built because there may be less neighborhood opposition to mixed-income de-velopments. Finally, if one goal of the production program is to increase the overall supply of housing, the market rate units in the development help to achieve this end.

The arguments put forth above are not intended to suggest that the prob-lems facing first-time homebuyers and moderate-income renters or the goal of mixed-income production should dominate or even be put on equal footing with the problems facing the lowest income households when considering al-location of federal resources for housing. However, the arguments do suggest that there are good reasons to consider federal efforts to help alleviate these problems or promote mixed-income developments.

Such efforts may require only modest federal funding. For example, Di-

Pasquale suggests that if the target population for first-time homebuyer programs are moderate-income households requiring help over the initial hurdles of the downpayment and the carrying costs of the mortgage in the first few years, then many of these efforts may be self-financing to the extent that subsidies could be recaptured at some point in the future. In addition, to the extent that the initial hurdles could be cleared through existing federal insurance programs (FHA), the cost of these efforts may be relatively small.[26]

From an implementation perspective, even in an era of limited resources, targeting to the "poorest of the poor" poses some real operational challenges. Where do we draw the line below which households are eligible: 50 percent of median income, 80 percent of median, or some other percentage of median? How much flexibility should there be in making such determinations? As soon as a family's income reaches a threshold of say 50 percent of median should they be out of the system? How do we factor both the physical condition of their existing housing and the percentage of income paid for current rent into the determination of *which* of the eligible households in fact get the subsidy?

In examining eligibility criteria, Murray defines the "Law of Imperfect Selection" which states that "any objective rule that defines eligibility for a social transfer program will irrationally exclude some persons."[27] He argues that given this law the target populations of social programs continue to broaden over time.

No moral cost is incurred by permitting some undeserving into the program. A moral cost is incurred by excluding a deserving person. No one has a scalpel sharp enough to excise only the undeserving. Therefore it is not just a matter of political expedience to add a new layer to the eligible population rather than to subtract one. . . . It is also the morally correct thing to do.[28]

From a political perspective, it has been argued that success in passing housing legislation is tied to serving a broader constituency than the very poor. Friedman posits that "laws for the poor . . . are unlikely to be generated unless (a) the poor are a majority and have fair and adequate political representatives, or (b) on balance, proposed legislation serves the interest of some class larger and broader than the poor. The history of American housing law suggests that the second condition has been much more important in the genesis of housing policy than the first."[29]

In summary, the targeting issue is not as clear as it might appear at first glance. The narrow definition of the possible target population seems inappropriate given the level of subsidies being provided through the homeowner deductions. Even if we accept the narrow definition of the target population, the wisdom of an inflexible, very specifically targeted program must be questioned. The complexity of the housing market, with the interrelationships among the various submarkets, suggests that a broader look at the housing market is critical to any housing policy. Furthermore, on the supply side, there are benefits to mixed-income housing warranting consideration. Program experience suggests that very narrowly targeted programs are difficult to implement, run the risk of excluding deserving households, and isolate the poor. Finally, history indicates that housing legislation targeted at the very poor generates a weak and vulnerable political constituency.

The evidence implies that many complex tradeoffs must be assessed in targeting housing policy. In an era of scarce resources, the federal government must determine how to best leverage those resources to serve the most households. Even assuming that the lowest income households should be the primary beneficiaries of the nation's housing policy, they may be better served in the long term with a less narrowly targeted approach.

The Role of the Existing Stock: A Shifting Paradigm

A significant difference among the three commissions, which provides a key insight into the current housing situation, is their diverse view of the role and character of the existing housing stock.

The Kaiser Committee perceived the low-income housing challenge as one of supplying standard subsidized housing, either through new construction or rehabilitation of the existing substandard stock. Because the issue of physical adequacy dominated the Committee's thinking, existing housing was discussed primarily in terms of that percentage requiring either rehabilitation or clearance, a classic statement of the "problem" of the existing stock as one of physical adequacy.

Fourteen years later, the President's Commission transformed the image of the existing housing stock from one focused on structural inadequacies to one which pictured the existing stock in terms of a "growing and continued improvement in the quality of housing." [30] Where the Kaiser Committee had emphasized eliminating what was substandard, the President's Commission underlined the magnitude of improvements and the view that the central "existing stock" issue was no longer one of physical adequacy but "affordability (which) has clearly become the predominant housing problem among low-income Americans." [31] Through the "Housing Payments Program" recommended by the Commission, the existing private stock became the basis for insuring affordability rather than for a massive rehabilitation program.

The image of the existing stock is viewed in a very different light in the Rouse/Maxwell Report, where the issues of *adequacy* and *affordability* are replaced by a fundamental concern for the *availability* of supply. The existing stock is projected as an increasingly scarce commodity for low-income renters, a valuable resource becoming an endangered species.

The Kaiser Committee's and the President's Commission's reports take the existing stock as a given resource, one that needs to be rehabilitated or removed in the case of Kaiser and made affordable for low-income people in the case of the President's Commission. In Rouse/Maxwell, the existing stock is increasingly perceived as a source of loss—a loss which will make things worse for renters. Three central themes contribute to this image of increased scarcity: first, the loss of unsubsidized low-rent units to gentrification, to condominium conversion, and to the wrecker's ball has, in the last decade, diminished the supply of low-rent housing; second, the emergence of the expiring use restriction issue—the possibility that the low-income renting population will lose thousands of affordable subsidized private units; third, the aging of the existing supply of public housing. The nation's housing policy is thus perceived as having to expend resources and energy to keep the shelter situation of low-income renters from getting worse. The challenge is not simply how to better house more people but how to hang on to what we already have. For the first time the existing stock issue evokes an image of running hard to keep in place.

Apgar articulates this challenge. He identifies the loss of unsubsidized rental units and the rise in households needing such units. "Even with adjustment for inflation, the number of units renting for less than $300 per month dropped by 1.6 million between 1974 and 1985."[32] "In 1988, the number of poverty-level renter households stood at 7.7 million, slightly up from the 1985 figure of 7.2 million and well above the 1980 figure of 5.8 million."[33]

The picture is clearly focused as one of pressure at the bottom: more poor people chasing fewer lower priced rental units. But that pressure has two significant policy implications beyond the need for more resources to maintain the status quo for low-income renters. The first is the overall impact on the housing market of scarcity at the bottom. The second is the impact of shrinking supply on the current demand side subsidy strategy of the federal government.

In terms of overall market impact, Apgar points out that:

The growth of low-income rental households in the face of rapidly increasing real rents is a clear prescription for trouble. . . . There can be little doubt that the stock of low cost rental housing is declining. . . . The loss of low-rent units involves two distinct dynamics: some have fallen into disrepair and been removed from the stock; others . . . have been upgraded to attract higher-income tenants.[34]

Apgar takes the upward pressure image one step further when he posits that: "Low incomes . . . shrink the pool of potential first-time homebuyers. . . . Unable to secure a home of their own, many young households remain renters and bid up the price of rental housing."[35]

Thus, concomitant with the increased scarcity of low-rent housing is the dynamic which makes rental housing "increasingly the home of the nation's lower-income households, while higher-income households increasingly choose to own a home. . . . The growth in the number of low-income renter households has widened the income gap between owners and renters."[36] Yet, to hang on to their units, unassisted low-income tenants are forced to pay higher and higher percentages of their income for rent. Growing scarcity at the bottom of the existing stock of rental housing units has had a ratchet effect felt further up the housing chain. Apgar's image of America as "two nations, a nation of housing 'haves,' . . . and a nation of housing 'have nots' " derives in large measure from the dynamics of shrinking supply at the low-rent end, putting pressure on units and therefore households at higher rent levels. Consequently, these households have become the "have less" if not the "have nots." From a policy perspective, then, it is important to recognize the degree to which scarcity at the bottom of the stock has implications not only for renters at more moderate-income levels but also for potential homebuyers.

The shrinking low-rent housing stock impacts the demand side subsidy strategy that lies at the heart of the current administration's housing policy. As Clay and Wallace frame the issue:

. . . The essence of the HUD response has been to offer direct assistance (certificates and vouchers) to a few needy tenants. This policy does not expand the inventory of housing units *permanently* available to the poor and fails to solve the housing problem of many applicants because they are unable to locate a qualifying unit.[37]

Clay and Wallace's criticism of the "HUD response" (certificates and vouchers) surfaces the long-standing debate about the efficiency and cost-effectiveness of demand and supply side housing programs. In his detailed examination of the "voucher/production debate" for this book, John Weicher concludes that "neither vouchers nor production programs are a panacea," and that "no program works well in tight markets, at least in the short run." While acknowledging that "vouchers will not result in new housing construction," Weicher goes on to state that vouchers "may help preserve the stock of existing decent housing."[38] It is the impermanency of such preservation that Clay and Wallace highlight. They are concerned not only with the limitation of a demand side strategy in a tight housing market when applicants have difficulty locating a qualifying unit, but also the degree to which assisted units stay in the subsidized pool. A central consideration in the supply vs. demand side debate may well turn out to be which approach most readily lends itself to guaranteed long-term occupancy by low- and moderate-income people.

The expiring use restrictions on thousands of HUD-financed private rental dwellings has heightened concern for the permanency issue. Twenty years ago when the HUD developments were put under contract, the end of the use restriction period seemed far in the future. But that future has arrived in some instances and is on the horizon in many more. The detailed exploration by Clay and Wallace of 645,000 units about to emerge from use restriction suggests that, if events run their course with no federal intervention, "only 19 percent of the 645,000 units are predicted to remain in the subsidized housing stock . . . 43 percent are predicted to default and 38 percent to prepay."[39] Clay and Wallace estimate that it will cost $18.6 billion to preserve all of the units at risk, which, as they point out, is a substantial financial commitment.

Like its counterparts in the private markets, the existing public housing stock has come to be perceived as a valuable resource requiring conservation. The reframing of the public housing image across the three commission reports demonstrates how the existing stock issue has come into focus at the center of public housing's current portrait.

In keeping with its production orientation, the Kaiser Committee said nothing about public housing already in the ground. Rather, it directed its attention to how the private sector could help local housing authorities build and manage more units. The condition of the existing public housing supply was of concern to the President's Commission in 1982, but only in the context of alternative strategies for public housing's future—most of which centered on extricating the federal government from involvement in the program. Rouse/ Maxwell, on the other hand, takes preservation of the existing stock as the central public housing issue. "Public housing projects must be restored and upgraded if they are to continue to furnish satisfactory low-income housing into the next century." [40] The Task Force Report goes on to estimate the costs of such restoration at $10 billion. While recognizing that the figure is a large one, the Report justifies it as a cost effective approach to the long-term provision of low-income housing, because it "will preserve this inventory and keep it permanently for low-income use." [41]

Stegman's view is very much in keeping with the direction set forth by Rouse/Maxwell. While recommending that "Congress establish a modest annual goal to construct 20,000 new public housing units," he states that "although more costly than other forms of subsidized new production, public housing's permanence and proven record of housing the most difficult low-income families warrants its continuation as an important component of our national housing policy." [42]

As the numbers indicate, there are significant costs attached to preserving the existing public and subsidized private stock. It must be emphasized that these "costs" are not for net additions to the supply of housing available to low-income people, but simply the price to be paid to keep those units from being lost. Policy issues emerging from the discussion of the existing stock can be grouped into three categories: (1) the significance of permanency, (2) budgetary strategy and (3) local institutional mechanisms for preservation.

The expiring use crisis has confronted policy makers with an issue new to the housing debate. Given the programmed demise of subsidized stock, how do we insure that there will continue to be a pool of units in the private market which are affordable to low-income households?

Some have looked at the expiring use issue and concluded that the only way out of the bind is to have nonprofit or public entities own the housing in the first place. Others, more optimistic about incentive systems, envision mechanisms that will keep private owners involved in low-income housing in perpetuity. Emerging legislation must deal with this debate to ensure that there are incentives for public, private, and nonprofit institutions to stay in the low-income housing business.

The figures quoted by Clay and Wallace and by Rouse/Maxwell for preservation of the existing stock of subsidized rental and public housing are, no matter how creatively handled, "deep pocket items." While both documents argue that the expenditure, if handled intelligently, is "cost effective," the bottom line is that new budgetary authority is being spent to maintain the status quo. In a constrained fiscal environment, it is inevitable that such maintenance will be perceived as competitive with new efforts to make more units available to needy households. Those concerned with an expansion of resources for additional units must work to keep the expiring use issue and public housing modernization from being seen as part of a zero sum game in which resources allocated to those two arenas take away from increases elsewhere in the housing budget.

The thrust of the Rouse/Maxwell Report reflected in the Clay-Wallace and Stegman papers is that the specifics of expiring use work-outs and public housing administration need to be implemented at the local level. Wallace and Clay argue that "there is an important role for state and local government in designing and implementing preservation plans for their jurisdictions. . . . Project specific solutions are preferable to general ones."[43] Rouse/Maxwell looks to states and localities to help out local housing authorities: "As federal efforts increase, so must state and local responsibility."[44] Thus, beyond the funding issue, how the existing stock is preserved for low-income use depends on the capacity of public, private, and nonprofit institutions at the local level to initiate and/or maintain housing stock for low-income use.

Institution Building and Program Design

The housing programs developed by the federal government to meet its housing objectives over the past twenty years have been predicated on shifting views as to the capacity of different agents—public, private, and nonprofit—to carry out those programs. Whether grant-in-aid, block grant, mortgage insurance, supply or demand side, these housing programs either presume a set of institutions that have the capabilities necessary for their execution or are designed to help develop that institutional capacity.

Taking a long view of the federal government's handling of the institutional issue, we identify two separate thrusts: one directed at creating a national finance system to facilitate the flow of capital into the housing sector; the other focused on reinforcing and strengthening institutional actors—developers, the nonprofit sector, and the federal, state and local governments—in their roles of administering subsidy programs or getting housing built.

In both primary and secondary mortgage markets, the federal role in creating a national housing finance system has been substantial. The federal government has created a number of institutions that are either part of the federal bureaucracy or linked to the federal government. The Federal Savings and Loan Insurance Corporation (FSLIC), the Federal Home Loan Bank system (FHLB), and the Federal Housing Administration (FHA) are at the center of the primary market. These institutions were created in the 1930s to enhance the confidence of the public in thrift institutions and, in the case of FHA, to support investor confidence in mortgages as assets. Even with the current problems facing FSLIC which is technically bankrupt, these institutions are important participants in the primary market today.[45] Fannie Mae, also created in the 1930s, was designed to provide a secondary mortgage market to increase liquidity in the mortgage market. Today, the federal credit agencies, Fannie Mae and Freddie Mac, both chartered by Congress, and Ginnie Mae, which is housed in HUD, are dominant players in the secondary market.

In creating these successful institutions, the federal government has established a national financial market for mortgages—the product of hundreds of local housing markets. The federal government took the view that while housing markets are inherently local in nature, the mortgage market which finances housing need not be. The national primary and secondary mortgage system provides the means of moving capital for housing from weak to strong local markets. The system is thus able to respond to the unique demands of local markets while at the same time maintaining standardization of the mortgage instrument, which enhances the attractiveness of mortgages to investors.

The Kaiser Committee supported the presence of the federal government and its institutions in the mortgage market. It envisioned securitization of mortgages as the concept that was to revolutionize the secondary mortgage market. The level of activity in mortgage-backed securities in the 1980s surely must exceed even the Committee's vision of its importance. According to Lea, there has been "an explosion in the growth of the agency securitized secondary market. Agency issues of mortgage related securities rose from $133 billion in 1985 to over $280 billion in 1986, and their share of new originations rose from 47 percent to 56 percent."[46]

The 1982 President's Commission, in its efforts to sweep the board clear of government regulation and competition with the private sector, proposed that parts of this system—notably FHA and Fannie Mae—should be privatized. Moves in this direction have been consistently rejected by Congress.

The Rouse/Maxwell Report, in generally extolling the existing housing finance system as "an efficient mechanism for linking the mortgage market with domestic and international capital markets . . . finds no reason for change in the basic housing finance system."[47]

The second "institutional thrust" addressed by the federal government focuses on the roles of various actors—developers, nonprofits, federal, state, and local governments—in actually carrying out federal housing programs.

The three commissions handle the relationship between institutions and programs that provide direct subsidies or actually get housing built in significantly different ways.

The Kaiser Committee evolved a highly structured, centralized, deep subsidy set of supply side programs with which to meet the explicit objective of six million new or rehabilitated housing units in ten years. The exhortation to forge public-private partnerships was really encouragement to the private sector to respond to the lure of tax benefits and insured mortgages. The underlying presumption was that the private institutional capacity existed to meet this ambitious goal. The federal role was to provide the necessary incentives; financially rewarding but fairly specific programs would generate the desired private institutional response. HUD was in charge of program design and implementation and little attention was given to how state and local governments could participate.

Despite the fact that the President's Commission turned with scorn from deep subsidy supply side programs, it too focused on the role of the private sector as the central institutional force in carrying out the now limited federal housing role. In addition, clearing the playing field of public regulatory hurdles would enable the financial markets to respond to private initiatives. The federal program was a demand side subsidy built on existing private capacity. The federal government was to rely on private institutions or—as in the case of FHA and other aspects of the federally supported finance system—to turn them over to the private sector as soon as possible. "Institution-building" meant clearing away the regulatory mechanisms which were impeding the private sector from solving the problem.

In its formulation of the low-income housing agenda, Rouse/Maxwell focuses on the role of the federal government as an institution builder. This time the focus is not the finance system or private producers but rather:

. . . a new delivery system (that) . . . has taken root and has grown over the last decade. It has emerged from the community level in response to local needs and dwindling federal support. It is marked by vigorous new efforts by state and local governments and nonprofit developers and has enlisted the strength and experience of for-profit developers. Local financial institutions, the business community, and religious organizations are all important players in this "new wave" of local initiatives.[48]

Rouse/Maxwell sets the states, local governments, and nonprofit developers at center stage, in roles that neither of the previous commissions envisioned. States are barely mentioned in the Kaiser report, and the President's Commission viewed states and localities as sources of a multiplicity of regulations that blocked the capacity of the private development community to act efficiently.

The theme developed in Rouse/Maxwell of utilizing federal programmatic funds in a flexible way to reinforce and develop institutions at the state and local level is shared by Terner and Cook who call for block grants "thus allowing states (and localities) to exercise maximum flexibility in the implementation of housing policy."[49] That programmatic flexibility must be tempered by "strong incentives for state involvement . . . to leverage state funding, financing, and/or regulatory responses."[50] In recounting the ways a significant number of states have moved into programmatic initiatives, housing finance, and land use regulation, Terner and Cook recognize that "the federal government also needs to find ways to encourage less committed and competent state governments to become involved, as well as to adopt safeguards that will ensure that state involvement is in fact positive."[51]

From the institution building perspective, a central concern for Washington is how to involve state governments that currently have neither the will nor the capacity to engage in housing programs, particularly programs directed at low-income households. One approach to this challenge is to argue that states with a housing problem are by definition the ones that have been forced to take the initiative during the past seven years. Massachusetts, New York, Connecticut, and New Jersey, for example, have had to confront the housing agenda in their own backyards; they have set institutional mechanisms in motion and, as Terner and Cook emphasize, simply need financial resources from Washington to fuel their existing machinery. While this argument may be true in some cases, there remain states with serious housing problems in their cities or rural areas which because of financial, institutional, or political limitations have not put the housing issue on the state agenda.

Downs focuses on potential tension between federal housing objectives and those of states and localities when he posits that:

The greater the flexibility and discretion permitted to lower-level program administrators, the more likely it is that the money will be used in ways closely adapted to local conditions, and in close accordance with local goal priorities. However, local priorities often differ greatly from the objectives Congress had in mind when it appropriated the money.

Thus all arrangements for administering federal funds involve trade-offs between (1) closely adapting the uses of those funds to local needs and purposes, and (2) closely pursuing federal policy objectives.[52]

Despite this tension, Downs goes on to argue for local decision-making; because of the unique character of housing markets, national housing policies "will not be well adapted to actual conditions in many areas if a single strategy is required throughout the nation, or even throughout each state."[53]

The role of the nonprofit sector, the second major actor in the new delivery system described in Rouse/Maxwell, is emphasized in Mayer's analysis of "how federal programs can and should be structured to facilitate and take advantage of nonprofit involvement."[54] While optimistic about the capacity of the nonprofit sector, he recognizes the challenge both in scaling up examples of successful nonprofit institutions and in developing them where they currently do not exist. The challenge for the nonprofits is similar in some respects to that posed by Terner and Cook for the states: how to direct federal programmatic funds to help local institutions grow and flourish. Where Terner and Cook emphasize flexible programs combined with incentives as the means of promoting an institutional response, Mayer emphasizes set-asides and technical assistance to the nonprofit sector to expand their capacity.

The tension between local and national needs seems to have been effectively resolved in terms of housing finance. The federal government has played a central role in building institutions to create a national mortgage market where once there was a collection of local markets. That tension is still central at the programmatic level: how to design national housing programs which develop the institutional mechanisms most effective in dealing with local housing markets. The best of the current state and nonprofit programs represent an opportunity for federal initiatives to interact synergistically with local institutions in the nation's housing markets. The challenge is to build such local institutions throughout the country so that national housing goals can be achieved using them as the primary delivery systems.

Public Partnership: Coordination at the Policy and Implementation Levels

The need for more effective coordination between the federal housing agenda and other federal policies and programs impacting on that agenda is widely recognized. Three areas are set forth in which the theme of coordination is a critical issue: 1. tax incentives, 2. welfare assistance, and 3. supportive services. Housing and taxation need to be connected in the legislative arena. Welfare and housing have connections to be made at both the legislative and implementation levels. The domain of housing and supportive services is essentially an issue of implementation, that is, coordinating existing programs.

Perhaps the most critical coordination issue at the legislative level is that between housing policy and tax incentives. As Clancy points out, the time may be ripe for such a move:

Although the Congressional committee structure and budgetary process make this kind of coordination difficult, the potential for the kind of effective coordination that has not existed in either the design or implementation of housing programs and investment incentives for affordable housing over the past twenty years may now exist. The intense effort of the tax committees in the development of the Tax Reform Act of 1986 to understand housing programs and production and to design an effective investment incentive can be seen as a critical first step. Involving those individuals in the effort being initiated by the housing committees, though facing jurisdictional complexities, is clearly both possible and essential to designing future federal housing efforts as the kind of balanced combination of housing programs and investment incentives they need to be.[55]

The issue of coordination between the housing and welfare systems occurs at two levels. The most fundamental one is that raised by Newman and Schnare in their discussion of the "two-pronged approach to housing assistance" characterizing the current situation in which housing subsidy and welfare assistance programs are run separately, thereby producing a disjointed and inequitable distribution of federal resources.[56] The structural blending of welfare and housing dollars, what might be called "reform with a capital R," is a concept that has lurked below the surface of the Washington policy agenda since the mid-1970s' heated discussion about the possibility of "cashing out" the housing demand side subsidy programs and putting the money into the welfare budget.

While the Newman/Schnare analysis points vividly to the inequitable consequences of the "two-pronged system" which may result in double benefits for a portion of the eligible population while others get nothing, there is little indication in the paper or elsewhere as to how to craft a political strategy to bring about an equitable and efficient blending of the two systems. None of the welfare reform proposals recently debated in Congress addressed the issue. While the logic of such coordination and perhaps integration is impeccable, the political and institutional logistics for getting there are yet to be devised.

On the other hand, welfare and housing reform with a "small r," or at the implementation level, seems a reasonable challenge to address. "Small r" reform focuses on those ways in which housing programs and welfare administration can better reinforce each other at the local level.

In his discussion of the homeless, Keyes describes ways in which the Emergency Assistance program of the Public Welfare Department could be better used to prevent homelessness and argues that "the institutional refocusing necessary to carry off such a self-conscious shift in federal policy warrants serious exploration."[57] In addition, the chapter posits that a better working relationship between local public housing authorities and welfare offices could "create a better 'early warning system' for potential homelessness among the public housing population."[58]

The issue of connecting housing and services is explored by Newman and Struyk. In their analysis of the frail elderly and the chronically mentally ill, Newman and Struyk are explicit in their view that "although much greater communication and coordination between HUD and relevant mental health agencies are absolutely essential . . . HUD should be allowed to do what it does best, namely administer federal housing policy."[59] In other words, HUD should not get itself into the service delivery business. Given that focus, Newman and Struyk see the issue of coordination as one of linkage between Washington and the states in which "the existing system lends itself to a sharing of responsibility by the federal and state governments since there is a fairly clear division of functions and financing for housing (primarily federal) versus services (primarily state). But it is also this separation of functions and resources that creates the need for coordination."[60]

There are clearly other areas in which the issue of "coordination" is a critical one for the future of federal housing policy: the relationship between HUD and Farmers Home, for example, and between HUD and the major actors in the secondary mortgage market.

Carrying out the coordination in the areas described above requires work on the part of the committees drafting housing legislation in the first instance—that is, the Senate Subcommittee on Housing and Urban Affairs and the House Subcommittee on Housing and Community Development. Some of this communication seems to be occurring. For example, the Senate Subcommittee is reaching out to the Senate Finance Committee to ensure its participation in the housing legislation currently being drafted by the Subcommittee.

The degree to which coordination efforts are undertaken at the implementation level depends on: (1) the extent to which the Administration sees them as critical and (2) the capacity of the Department of Housing and Urban Development to take an aggressive role in coordination.

The plea for coordination at the programmatic level has always been problematic for the Department of Housing and Urban Development. There is a deep seated skepticism among federal policy veterans as to the efficacy of any such plea given the realities of legislation and bureaucratic life as they impinge on that agency. There is a long history of failed efforts to bring about coordination through HUD. In 1966, President Lyndon B. Johnson assigned the Secretary of the Department of Housing and Urban Development, Robert Weaver, "the leadership for urban matters." [61] Secretary Weaver assured the Senate Subcommittee on Intergovernmental Relations that HUD was "in a better position than ever before to make this mission as federal coordinator of urban issues a meaningful part of policy-making and administrative practice." [62] History was to demonstrate how difficult that coordination role was.

In the past two decades, the bold optimism of the HUD secretary that he could impose coordination on the host of programmatic initiatives impacting urban areas has been tempered by the bureaucratic realities of life. While the recently enacted McKinney Homeless Assistance Act provides a leadership role for HUD in coordinating other federal agencies, that role has been difficult to fulfill, not only because of Congressional budget cuts but also because of the diffidence of the Administration that had the Act forced upon it by Congress. Ultimately, the issue of coordination of housing with other programs will rest upon the will and capacity of HUD, backed by the will and capacity of the Administration.

The Federal Role and the Future of HUD

The issue of the federal presence in housing is not the same as the issue of HUD's role in that housing agenda. HUD is but one of a number of federal organizations having an impact on the nation's housing. Yet, since its creation in 1966, HUD has been the focal point of the nation's housing policy. And the role it is asked to play in the future says a good deal about the seriousness of the federal initiative.

HUD rests at the center of the Kaiser Committee report, the lead agency in the federal charge to eliminate all substandard housing. HUD is asked to play a more modest role in the President's Commission report, symbolic of the disengagement of the federal government from housing. Rouse/Maxwell makes a strong statement for a federal presence and particularly for the Department of Housing and Urban Development, which is seen as dealing with the "expiring use" issue; remedying the most troubled public housing projects; and implementing the report's centerpiece—the Housing Opportunity Program.

We conclude that the themes raised in this discussion also point to a strong HUD presence. Essentially, we are driven to this conclusion, but not because of any preconceived idea that HUD ought to be put at the center of a reinvigorated federal presence in housing. Several of the authors in the project expressed significant skepticism about HUD's ability to transcend its traditional conflicts and current low profile status. The current HUD scandals support this skepticism. Yet, whatever one's doubts, HUD has to play a lead role in dealing with the expiring use issue, preserving public housing stock, providing programs with incentives to build institutions at local and state levels, grappling with the targeting issue, and coordinating housing and social services.

In their paper for the MIT Housing Policy Project, Kaplan and James conclude an analysis of HUD with the following remarks.

Congressional commitment to the national housing policies, defined earlier, would lead to a more focused HUD mission and set of programs. . . . Its production-oriented programs, if converted to housing block grants and managed increasingly by state and local governments, would essentially be free of federal criteria and involvement—except for ground rules regarding targeting the grants to low- and moderate-income households and how they should be used in tight market situations. Similarly, its new housing allowance initiative, by definition, would be directed at low- and moderate-income households and not at specific jurisdictions. . . . The key distributors of HUD's programs would be state and local governments. . . . HUD, in this context, could well become a key instrument in carrying out new national housing policies.[63]

$*$ $*$ $*$ $*$

In 1949, the goal of a decent home and a suitable living environment for every American was set forth in national legislation. Today, no thoughtful observer of American housing would argue that we have reached the aspiration of 1949. But in the years since the declaration of intent was made, very different views have been expressed as to the magnitude of the distance between the nation's housing and the goal expressed in 1949.

The Kaiser Committee not only took the goal seriously but also embraced the central role of the federal government—its resources and its programs—in reaching that goal. It gave HUD a central role in running the massive Washington-based initiative. Fifteen years later, the President's Commission was impressed by how far the nation had moved toward the goal and worked creatively to reduce the federal role while extending that of the private market in making up the remaining difference.

1968 looks to have been the high water mark of federal commitment of resources to housing and reflective of another era. Yet, the minimal federal role articulated in 1982 seems equally dated in today's world of homelessness, expiring use restrictions, and a declining percentage of young homebuyers. Rouse/Maxwell reflects the tenor of the times in that it paints a picture of serious federal leadership in the nation's housing policy while recognizing that budgetary and political realities as well as the changing nature of program sponsorship at the local level preclude a return to the model of the 1960s.

The four themes that we have examined in this paper presuppose a federal housing policy world which looks much like that articulated in Rouse/Maxwell. What is critical is the emergence of a federal commitment to building a housing delivery system which can be expanded when, if, and as resources for housing become available. That system must deal with enhancing the institutional framework within which low-income housing is preserved; targeting resources in the most leveraged way; carrying out programmatic initiatives that enhance institutional development; and coordinating housing efforts with tax and social service policies. Energizing that system requires a reinvigorated Department of Housing and Urban Development: its mandate to lead the federal engagement in housing made explicit; its sense of public entrepreneurship in an era of budgetary austerity enhanced. These are ambitious aspirations for an agency that has been asked to preside over its own disengagement. But moving aggressively toward the goals of the 1949 Housing Act—that decent home and suitable living environment for all Americans—calls for no less.

Notes

1. *Report of the President's Committee on Urban Housing*, Edgar F. Kaiser, chair (Washington: USGPO, 1969) 5.
2. Kaiser, *Committee*, 5.
3. *Report of the President's Commission on Housing*, William F. McKenna, chair (Washington: USGPO, 1983) iii.
4. *President's Commission*, xvii.
5. *President's Commission*, xvii.
6. *President's Commission*, xvii.
7. *President's Commission*, xxii.
8. *President's Commission*, xxiii.
9. *President's Commission*, xxiv.
10. *President's Commission*, xxiv.
11. *President's Commission*, xxxv.

12. *A Decent Place to Live: The Report of the National Housing Task Force,* James W. Rouse, chair (available from the Task Force, 1625 Eye St., Washington, DC) ii.

13. *National Housing Task Force,* 1.

14. *National Housing Task Force,* 7.

15. *National Housing Task Force,* 8.

16. *National Housing Task Force,* 9.

17. *National Housing Task Force,* 10.

18. *National Housing Task Force,* 16.

19. *National Housing Task Force,* 17.

20. *National Housing Task Force,* 17.

21. Joint Center for Housing Studies, Harvard University, *The State of the Nation's Housing, 1988* (Cambridge: JCHS, 1988) 18.

22. "The Task Force recommends that Congress commit to providing sufficient rent assistance so that by the end of the century, in combination with an increased supply of affordable housing, no household that seeks fit, liveable, and affordable housing will lack the opportunity to obtain it." *National Housing Task Force,* 44.

23. A. Downs, Chapter 3, 107–108.

24. Downs, 107–108.

25. W. C. Apgar, Chapter 2, 26.

26. D. DiPasquale, Chapter 6.

27. C. Murray, *Losing Ground* (New York: Basic Books, 1984) 211.

28. Murray, *Losing Ground,* 212.

29. L. M. Friedman, *Government and Slum Housing* (New York: Arno Press, 1978) 191.

30. *President's Commission,* 9.

31. *President's Commission,* 12.

32. Apgar. Chapter 2, 44.

33. Apgar, 49.

34. Apgar, 44.

35. Apgar, 45.

36. Apgar, 49.

37. P. L. Clay and J. E. Wallace, Chapter 12, 313, emphasis added.

38. J. C. Weicher, Chapter 10, 287–288.

39. Clay and Wallace, Chapter 12, 324–325.

40. *National Housing Task Force,* 37.

41. *National Housing Task Force,* 37.

42. M. Stegman, Chapter 13, 346, 339.

43. Clay and Wallace, Chapter 12, 329.

44. *National Housing Task Force,* 38.

45. M. Lea, Chapter 7, 188.

46. Lea, 192.

47. *National Housing Task Force,* 52.

48. *National Housing Task Force,* 19.

49. I. D. Terner and T. Cook, Chapter 4, 131.

50. Terner and Cook, 131.

51. Terner and Cook, 135.

52. Downs, Chapter 3, 94.

53. Downs, 95.

54. N. Mayer, Chapter 14, 364.

55. P. E. Clancy, Chapter 11, 309.

56. S. Newman and A. Schnare, Chapter 15, 389.

57. L. Keyes, Chapter 16, 428.

58. Keyes, 428.

59. S. Newman and R. J. Struyk, Chapter 17, 457.

60. Newman and Struyk, 458.

61. *Creative Federalism,* hearings before the Senate Subcommittee on Intergovernmental Relations, Committee on Government Operations, 89th Congress, second session, November, 1966, 91.

62. *Creative Federalism,* 92.

63. M. Kaplan and F. James, "Institutional Roles, Relevance, and Responsibilities," Working Paper HP #3 (Cambridge: MIT Center for Real Estate Development, 1988) 33–34.

Chapter 2
The Nation's Housing: A Review of Past Trends and Future Prospects for Housing in America

William C. Apgar, Jr.

America is increasingly divided into two nations: first a nation of housing "haves," and second a nation of housing "have-nots." Most Americans are well housed and enjoyed the benefits of continued economic growth, but the prosperity of these Americans does not reflect the plight of the growing number of low- and moderate-income households.

Historically, improved housing conditions have been an important component in the overall improvement of the standard of living in the United States. For many, moving from renter to owner housing is a key step on the path to financial security. For those without sufficient income to make this step, obtaining good quality, affordable rental housing has been an equally worthy goal. Finally, housing assistance programs have long sought to provide minimally adequate housing to those on the bottom of the economic ladder—housing that can serve as the foundation upon which to build a better future for themselves and their families.

The growing number of housing "have-nots" suggests that this housing progress has stalled in recent years. Homeownership rates have declined sharply since 1980 and the supply of low-cost rental housing continues to shrink as units are lost to abandonment or are upgraded for higher income occupancy. For the growing number of low-income families, rents as a percent of income have increased steadily—a major factor in the rise of homelessness in America, particularly among young single-parent families.

Each housing problem identified in this chapter is in some sense distinct, but in many important respects the nation's housing problems are interrelated. Unable to secure a home of their own, many young households remain renters and bid up the price of rental housing. Rising rents have led to an increasing share of households paying 30, 40, or even 50 percent of their incomes for rents, if they can secure housing at all. High rents in the private nonsubsidized marketplace make it difficult for households to move out of existing subsidized units. The result is growing waiting lists for the limited available supply of subsidized housing. Those families least able to cope with high rent burdens all too frequently never get into a subsidized unit and end up in homeless shelters or on the street.

As these comments suggest, there is no single housing problem in America today, but a series of interconnected problems that confront a wide range of households. This chapter seeks to document these diverse housing problems and to provide a sound empirical foundation for what appears to be an emerging debate concerning the future direction of national housing policy.

Trends in Housing Costs

The cost of housing and other basic needs are key determinants of the standard of living for any family or individual. This section presents indices of housing costs for representative owner and renter housing units with fixed characteristics. By estimating housing costs for dwelling units of fixed attributes, these indices distinguish between changes in housing expenditures that result from changes in the type of housing consumed and those that reflect increases or decreases in the price of a housing unit of given characteristics.

Developing a Measure of the Cash Cost of Homeownership

Table 2.1 presents estimates of the after-tax cash cost of owning and operating a modest single-family home during the first year of occupancy measured in inflation adjusted 1988 dollars. For these calculations, a modest single-family home is defined as the median-valued home purchased in 1977 by a first-time buyer aged 25–29. The after-tax cash cost is the sum of several ongoing expenses (including outlays for mortgage interest payments, fuel and utility costs, maintenance and repairs, real estate taxes, and insurance) less the income tax savings associated with owning a home.

The estimates presented in Table 2.1 depict the annual cost of owning and operating a home of given characteristics. This approach is distinct from measures based on the price of homes actually sold each year. Such alternative measures can present a distorted view of cost trends, especially to the extent that the composition of home sales varies from year to year. To avoid these complications, a representative first-time buyer home was selected and the sales price of this home was indexed by the Department of Commerce, Construction Reports, Constant Quality Home Price Index. The result is an index of first-time buyer home purchase price for a home with similar characteristics to the home actually purchased in 1977.

In addition to the sales price, other elements of the cost index include

TABLE 2.1   Total Homeownership Costs
(1988 Dollars)

Year	Mortgage payments	Other costs	Before-tax cash cost	Tax savings	After-tax cash cost	Amortization of fees and closing cost	Opportunity cost of down-payment	Expected equity buildup	Total cost
1967	$3,501	$2,607	$6,107	$306	$5,801	$56	$508	$1,588	$4,777
1968	3,709	2,603	6,311	379	5,932	64	596	2,164	4,428
1969	4,103	2,628	6,732	489	6,242	73	765	2,993	4,087
1970	4,195	2,645	6,840	564	6,276	74	714	2,454	4,610
1971	4,038	2,743	6,781	398	6,383	59	523	2,564	4,401
1972	4,102	2,830	6,932	409	6,523	64	551	2,960	4,178
1973	4,347	2,806	7,153	370	6,783	84	826	3,898	3,795
1974	4,684	2,811	7,494	428	7,066	98	903	4,429	3,638
1975	4,858	2,823	7,681	500	7,181	100	753	5,086	2,948
1976	4,957	2,857	7,814	537	7,277	99	677	4,968	3,084
1977	5,236	2,936	8,172	154	8,018	108	745	6,063	2,807
1978	5,905	2,948	8,853	385	8,468	135	1,087	7,470	2,220
1979	6,723	2,836	9,560	565	8,995	171	1,418	8,267	2,317
1980	7,709	2,857	10,566	894	9,672	235	1,587	7,554	3,941
1981	8,650	2,897	11,547	1,200	10,347	297	1,892	6,229	6,308
1982	8,508	2,963	11,471	1,110	10,361	302	1,542	3,674	8,532
1983	7,130	2,968	10,098	858	9,240	260	1,206	2,237	8,469
1984	6,955	2,994	9,949	821	9,128	284	1,353	2,069	8,696
1985	6,507	2,967	9,473	732	8,741	258	1,056	1,935	8,120
1986	6,001	2,910	8,912	611	8,301	212	840	2,411	6,942
1987	5,561	2,843	8,404	409	7,995	201	869	2,146	6,917
1988	5,376	2,800	8,176	196	7,980	186	935	1,086	8,015

Source: Joint Center for Housing Studies, Harvard University, *The State of the Nation's Housing 1989,* Appendix 1.

mortgage rate and out-of-pocket expenses. The mortgage rate was set equal to the Federal Home Loan Bank Board Contract Mortgage Rate for all home loans. Mortgage payments were calculated for a 25-year mortgage with a 20 percent downpayment. Other cost components were estimated for 1977 using data from the Annual Housing Survey. Each expenditure component was then indexed by the comparable component of the consumer price index to form estimates of the cost for each year from 1967 to 1988.

Since mortgage interest rate and property tax payments are deductible expenses under federal tax law, the cash costs of homeownership are reduced on an after-tax basis. The amount of this tax savings depends on the income of the representative first-time buyer household, the number of personal exemptions, the amount of other allowable deductions, the allowable standard deduction, and the appropriate marginal tax rate for the homeowner in question. In this report, tax savings are based on the excess of housing deductions (mortgage interest and real estate taxes) plus non-housing deductions over the standard deduction. Non-housing deductions are set at 5 percent of income through 1986. Since the Tax Reform Act of 1986 limited the range of allowable non-housing deductions, non-housing deductions were assumed to decrease to 4.25 percent of income in 1987 and to 3.5 percent of income in 1988.[1]

Total Cost of Homeownership

The decision to buy a home involves both investment and consumption considerations. As indicated in Table 2.1, total cost equals the after-tax cash cost of homeownership plus the opportunity cost of downpayment, amortization of fees and closing costs, less expected equity buildup. Closing costs on a home, in addition to the assumed 20 percent downpayment, were set equal to the Federal Home Loan Bank Board estimate of fees and closing costs, amortized over a seven-year period at an interest rate assumed to equal the One-Year Treasury Bill Rate as reported by the Federal Reserve Bank.

Downpayment also imposes an annual cost on the homebuyer. This cost is assumed to equal earnings lost, or opportunity cost, of funds tied up in the home in the downpayment. Downpayment is assumed to equal 20 percent of the purchase price. Lost earnings on this downpayment are estimated using the One-Year Treasury Bill Rate as reported by the Federal Reserve Bank.

Each of these costs is offset by increases in homeowner equity. Anticipated equity buildup for any year is assumed to equal a weighted average of equity buildup over the past three years. The most recent year is weighted most heavily (weight = 50 percent), while the next most recent year receives a small weight (33 percent), and the first year of the series is weighted least (17 percent). The weighting pattern reflects the assumption that estimated price changes are sensitive to recent events, but that interpretation of recent events is tempered by knowledge of longer term housing price trends.[2]

While the total cost measure presented in Table 2.1 is more inclusive, the after-tax cash cost measure is the more relevant measure for assessing the ability of first-time buyers to purchase a home. In qualifying for a mortgage loan, banks and other lending institutions will compare the before-tax cash costs of homeownership with household income to determine if the prospective homeowner can "afford" to make the required mortgage payments. The potential for equity buildup may encourage households to seek to become homeowners, but unless a first-time buyer can accumulate the required downpayment and qualify for a mortgage to purchase a home, the potential for equity buildup is hypothetical. Total cost is a better measure of housing cost conditions of households already owning a home and therefore already enjoying the benefits of equity buildup.

Recent Trends in Homeowner Costs

Figure 2.1 depicts how both the after-tax cash and total costs of owning and operating a modest single-family home during the first year of occupancy have changed over the last 21 years. Measured in inflation adjusted 1988 dollars, the after-tax cash cost of homeownership reached a peak of $10,361 in 1982. Although it fell to $7,980 in 1988, the after-tax cash cost is still higher than the average recorded in the 1960s and the early 1970s.

The persistently high after-tax cost in recent years results in part from the fact that homeownership no longer offers the same tax advantages that it once did. As indicated in Table 2.1, the estimated tax savings for the representative first-time buyer fell from $1,200 in 1981 to $196 in 1988. Tax incentives are linked to nominal (as opposed to inflation-adjusted) interest rates; as a result the tax advantages of homeownership are greatest when mortgage interest rates are high. The Tax Reform Act of 1986 also reduced the tax advantages of homeownership by reducing marginal tax rates and raising the available standard deduction. Under tax reform, for example, married couples filing a joint return now receive a standard deduction of $5,000, up from $3,650 in 1986. Since moderate-income first-time buyers typically have few non-housing deductions to itemize, only a portion of their combined mortgage interest and property tax deduction will exceed the standard deduction. Since 1986, the effect of tax reform has been to moderate what otherwise would have been a greater improvement in the after-tax cash cost of homeownership.[3]

Similarly, the total cost of homeownership (including the foregone earnings on homeowner's equity and an allowance for price appreciation) also remains high by historical standards. Following a period of steady decline in the 1970s, in 1979 total costs began to move up sharply. By 1982, higher home prices, interest rates, and utility costs—together with smaller gains from appreciation—had boosted the total annual costs of owning a home to $8,532. Though falling from this peak until 1987, as a result of slower house price

Figure 2.1 Homeowner Costs
(in 1988 dollars)

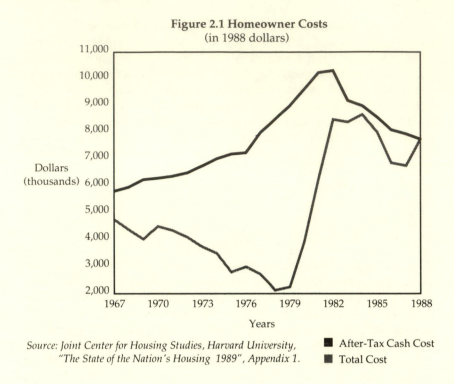

Dollars
(thousands)

Years

*Source: Joint Center for Housing Studies, Harvard University,
"The State of the Nation's Housing 1989", Appendix 1.*

■ After-Tax Cash Cost
■ Total Cost

appreciation and associated lower expected equity buildup, the total annual cost measure rose in 1988 to $8,015, a figure that is well above the average for the past 20 years.

There is little reason to expect a marked improvement in homeownership costs in the years ahead. The median price of the representative first home in 1988 approached $66,000, up more than 22 percent in inflated adjusted 1988 dollars from the $54,000 figure for 1967. Rising prices are a double-edged sword: while they make homeownership a good investment for those who already own, they also force young first-time buyers to make larger downpayments and/or larger monthly mortgage payments. The legacy of the rapid home price inflation of the 1960s and 1970s is the continuing high home sale prices, and the high after-tax cash costs of homeownership.

Renter Costs: Biased Data Distort Historical Analysis

Numerous studies of housing trends over the past two decades examine the residential rent component of the Consumer Price Index (CPI) prepared by the Bureau of Labor Statistics (BLS) and conclude that real rents are rising modestly now, but have yet to return to the peak levels achieved in the late 1960s.[4] Despite a sophisticated data collection effort and equally sophisticated series of adjustments performed by the BLS, CPI data present a distorted view of recent rent trends. As first noted by Ira S. Lowry of the RAND Corporation, the CPI rent component is derived from information obtained for a sample of residential dwelling units, which are resurveyed each year. For units continuing in the sample, adjustments are made only for major changes in the level of services provided by the property owner, or changes in the level of rent subsidy or discount. As a result, minor changes attributable to depreciation of the dwelling unit are not accounted for, nor are cost increases on utilities paid directly by the tenant.[5]

The failure to adjust the CPI rent index for depreciation produces a downward bias in the estimate of residential rent relative to the prices of other components of the CPI. A true price index tracks the price of a particular good or service of constant quality and characteristics. In 1988, the BLS introduced a series of adjustments to correct for the deficiencies mentioned above, but the Bureau has yet to adjust the historical data on residential rent. Based on review of the work of Lowry and others, this paper assumes that deterioration or obsolescence reduces the amount of housing services provided by the property owner by three quarters of one percent (.0075) per year and uses this assumption to estimate a revised residential rent series for the period of 1967 to 1988.[6]

Revised Estimates of Real Rents

Figure 2.2 presents estimates of real gross and contract rents for a representative unit with the characteristics of the median-priced rental unit in 1977. Contract rent is the monthly payment to the property owner for housing services. Gross rent includes not only contract rent but also payments for fuel, water, sewerage, and other utilities.

Real rents (that is, adjusted for inflation in other goods and services) tend to move with the business cycle, falling during cyclical downturns and rising during expansions. After a sharp increase in 1981–86, real rent increases slowed somewhat in the last two years. Nevertheless, since 1981 contract rents have increased 16.6 percent faster than the rate of inflation and now stand at their highest levels in more than two decades. Gross rents, while increasing somewhat more modestly due to the slowdown in energy price inflation, have still risen 13.6 percent between 1981 to 1988.

Gross rent is seemingly the more comprehensive measure, but changes in contract rent have considerable analytical significance. Gross rent, for example, can change as a result of shifting energy prices or other factors that have little to do with the long-run cost of housing capital. Policy analysts should note, however, that the persistent increase in contract rent during a pe-

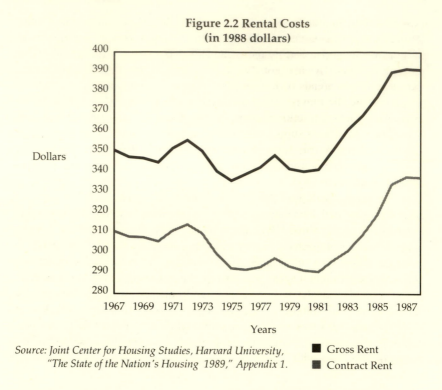

**Figure 2.2 Rental Costs
(in 1988 dollars)**

Dollars

Years

*Source: Joint Center for Housing Studies, Harvard University,
"The State of the Nation's Housing 1989," Appendix 1.*

■ Gross Rent
■ Contract Rent

riod of substantial new construction suggests that there has been a long-term increase in the rental price of housing capital. Unlike a runup of energy costs, such a long term trend is not quickly reversed. Over the past 7 years, the cost of supplying rental housing appears to have drifted upward, a movement that can only point to continuing high rent levels in the years ahead.

Rental Vacancies and Rent Trends

The rapid growth of rents seems inconsistent with the recent growth in residential vacancies, but this reflects the fact that there is no simple relationship between average or median rents and rental vacancy rates. Housing markets are distinctly local by nature, and within any local housing market there will be distinct housing submarkets defined both in terms of the type of housing provided and the characteristics of the households served. While these various submarkets are linked in the sense that households and units can move from one submarket to the next, they are not perfectly linked. Thus it is quite possible at any one point in time to have an excess supply of dwelling units in one submarket in an area (e.g., newer efficiency apartments in large multi-family structures) and an excess demand for units of another type (e.g., three bedroom apartments in smaller, wood frame structures).[7]

With these caveats in mind, some generalizations do explain the broad patterns of rent trends over the past two decades. For much of the 1960s and early 1970s, the movement of population and jobs away from large central cities and the construction of numerous subsidized rental units in these cities resulted in an excess supply of rental housing in many urban neighborhoods. This is especially true for low quality housing submarkets serving low- and moderate-income households. As a result, for much of this period, increases in real rents were modest, and disinvestment and abandonment of low-cost existing rental stock was high.

Despite high levels of apartment construction, median real rents have moved up sharply since 1981. In explaining the phenomenon of growing vacancies and rising rents, it is important to note that much of the increase in vacant units is concentrated in selected housing submarkets. Thus, the most rapid buildup in rental vacancies has been in the South. In addition, vacancies have tended to cluster in new housing units as opposed to older units, and larger apartment complexes, as opposed to those with five or fewer apartments. Since 1981 rental vacancies have grown from 1.53 million to 2.75 million. Of this increase, 64 percent has been the result of increased vacancies of units in structures with 5 or more units, while 75 percent have been in units built since 1970.

In theory, submarkets with high vacancies may draw households away from other submarkets, equalizing the vacancy rate across submarkets. Evidence suggests that rather than reduce rents in order to expand occupancy, many vacant newly constructed rental units remain on the market at relatively high rents. This is confirmed by data depicted in Table 2.2. Measured in inflation adjusted dollars, from 1981 to 1987, the bulk of the growth of rental housing has been concentrated in the upper end of the rent distribution. During this period, increases in the number of units renting for more than $300 accounted for all of the growth in total housing stock and 73 percent of the growth in vacant units.

These data confirm that the high rate of new construction of apartment units in the past several years has done little to add to available vacant units at low or moderate rents. Moreover, available data suggest that the growth in median rents understate the rent increases experienced at the low end of the market. New construction and major rehabilitation have added to housing supply at the upper end of the market, while housing disinvestment and abandonment continue to drain units away from the bottom. The result is a pattern for most market areas of modest rent increases for the best quality housing, but substantial rent increases at the low end of the market.[8]

TABLE 2.2   Number of Total and Vacant Rental Units with Rent Specified: 1981 and 1987

	1981: RENT SPECIFIED			1987: RENT SPECIFIED		
Contract rent[a]	Total (1000s)	Vacant (1000s)	Rate (%)	Total (1000s)	Vacant (1000s)	Rate (%)
0–150	5,045	193	3.8	4,632	165	3.6
150–300	11,463	537	4.7	10,690	859	8.0
300–400	6,158	307	5.0	7,483	651	8.7
400–500	3,146	152	4.8	4,276	351	8.2
500+	2,299	173	7.5	4,276	436	10.2
Total rent specified	28,111	1,363	4.8	31,357	2,462	7.9
Rent not specified	2,489	167	6.7	4,279	287	6.7
Total	30,600	1,530	5.0	35,636	2,749	7.7
Median contract rent	281	286	NA	304	330	NA

[a]Estimates are in 1987 constant dollars. Price adjustment done with CPI-U All Items. Source: William C. Apgar, Jr., "Recent Trends in Rental Vacancies," Working Paper W89-3, Joint Center for Housing Studies, Harvard University.

Demographic Trends to the Year 2000

Assessment of longer term trends in the demographic composition of the population provide a useful benchmark against which to view recent and likely future events in the nation's housing market. This section begins by considering factors likely to constrain household growth in the years ahead, followed by a discussion of the effect of demographic change on the composition of household growth. This discussion touches briefly on the possible implications of these changes for the market demand for housing in the years ahead, as well as the effect of demographic factors on the composition of the nation's low-income population.

The Decline of Household Growth

After a decade of record growth, household formation is now on a long-term decline that will last for the balance of the century. In the 1970s, the household growth averaged 1.7 million per year. In the early 1980s, the weak national economy and the high cost of housing combined to lower the average annual growth of households to close to 1.2 million. With the economic recovery of 1983–1988, household growth has rebounded somewhat, but remains erratic.

Despite this recent volatility, it seems clear that the aging of the baby boom and the arrival of the baby bust generation into household formation ages will slow household growth for the rest of the century. The 1990s will see the baby boom replaced by the baby bust as the prime engine of household formation. The baby boom generation is that large cohort of individuals born in the years 1946 to 1964. In 1965, birth rates turned down sharply, and total births declined steadily until 1975 when births started to move up again modestly. Since baby boomers are now between the ages of 25 and 43, the majority have already passed the household formation ages of 20 to 29. As baby boom is replaced by baby bust, household formation will inevitably slow.

The decline in the rate of growth of households is further exacerbated by continued housing affordability problems that confront many households. Many factors influence the propensity of individuals to form an independent household, but the recent decline in the proportion of individuals forming independent households seems to result largely from the high and rising housing costs that were documented earlier.

In combination, high housing costs and slower growth of the adult population will constrain household growth for much of the rest of the century. George Masnick and John Pitkin project that household growth will average 1.45 million per year from 1985 to 1990, before slowing further to 1.21 million per year in the early 1990s and to 1.08 million per year in the late 1990s.[9]

Changing Demographics and the Housing Market Outlook

In the short term, housing construction activity and housing consumption patterns are most sensitive to changes in mortgage interest rates, employment trends, and other economic factors. Over the longer term, demographic factors are a major determinant of the level and composition of housing industry activity.

While total household growth will slow in the years ahead, the aging of the baby boom will result in considerable growth in the number of households aged 35 to 44 in the late 1980s and early 1990s. Growth continues in this group into the 1990s, but by then the baby boom bubble will have moved on to the next higher age group, and the sharpest increases will be for households with heads aged 45 to 54 (Table 2.3).

Following the aging of baby boomers, the substantial growth in the number of single-person households represents the next most important demographic trend for the rest of the century. Increased life expectancy implies that the number of single-person elderly households will grow sharply in the years

TABLE 2.3 Households by Age and Type: 1980 to 2000

Age and household type	1980	1985	Proj. 1990	Proj. 1995	Proj. 2000
Household head under 25					
Single	1,644	1,323	1,243	1,227	1,259
Married with children	1,446	1,139	825	668	789
Married without children	1,370	976	670	553	601
Single parent with children	727	756	722	687	717
Other households	1,235	1,244	1,100	966	938
Total	6,422	5,438	4,560	4,101	4,304
Household head 25–34					
Single	3,364	3,905	4,479	4,601	4,354
Married with children	8,887	8,541	8,562	7,457	6,159
Married without children	2,732	2,950	2,655	2,278	1,986
Single parent with children	2,193	2,811	3,017	2,977	2,710
Other households	1,302	1,805	1,988	1,802	1,559
Total	18,478	20,012	20,701	19,115	16,768
Household head 35–44					
Single	1,531	2,323	3,338	4,063	4,542
Married with children	8,590	9,541	10,749	11,732	11,929
Married without children	1,352	1,953	2,330	2,571	2,627
Single parent with children	1,859	2,583	3,151	3,420	3,549
Other households	645	1,081	1,462	1,627	1,700
Total	13,977	17,481	21,030	23,413	24,347

ahead. Add to this the continued large number of younger households choosing to remain single and the result is a sharp increase in the number of one-person households.

The aging of the baby boom generation points to continued strong demand for good quality, single-family detached homes in the years ahead. Baby boom trade-up activity should also bode well for renovation and repair

TABLE 2.3   (*Continued*)

Age and household type	1980	1985	Proj. 1990	Proj. 1995	Proj. 2000
Household head 45–64					
Single	4,535	4,939	5,582	6,886	9,025
Married with children	6,038	4,637	4,962	5,637	6,234
Married without children	11,238	12,120	12,173	13,266	15,024
Single parent with children	1,216	974	1,178	1,482	1,785
Other households	2,204	3,026	3,250	3,654	4,404
Total	25,231	25,696	27,145	30,925	36,472
Household head 65 or older					
Single	7,087	8,110	9,607	10,955	11,933
Married with children	315	97	172	229	230
Married without children	7,029	7,893	8,560	8,903	8,869
Single parent with children	144	32	60	86	104
Other households	1,636	2,021	2,212	2,354	2,462
Total	16,211	18,153	20,611	22,527	23,598

Source: George S. Masnick, "U.S. Household Trends: The 1980s and Beyond," Working Paper W89-1, Joint Center for Housing Studies, Harvard University.

markets. In the past several years, renovation and repair activities have moved up sharply, in part the result of baby boomers satisfying their urge to improve their housing situation by repairing or adding to an existing good quality single family home.[10]

A key factor in this hopeful outlook is the fact that more than half of all baby boom families already own a first home. The rapid growth of house prices in the Northeast is well documented, but even in other regions of the country, baby boomers have accumulated significant home equity. Many baby boomers purchased their homes in the late 1970s, and hence shared at least a portion of the rapid growth of house prices that occurred in all regions of the country in the 1970s.

Not only did the 1980s see many baby boom families move into the child rearing phase of their life cycle, but also into their peak earning years. Typically, earned income increases steadily until an individual reaches age 40 to

45, then flattens out. The earning potential of baby boom households is further enhanced by the growing number of two-worker households. The greater incidence of multi-earner families and the high earning potential of well educated baby boom workers should result in a substantial increase in the number of upper-income households with the head of household aged 30 to 50. These trends should stimulate strong housing demand in the latter part of the 1980s and well into the 1990s.

Unlike the growth of baby boom families, however, the growth of single-person households should have a decidedly less pronounced effect on long term housing construction trends. First, single-person elderly households account for much of the growth of all single-person households, but this group will have a limited effect on housing trends. Elderly households have high rates of homeownership and low rates of mobility. Most elderly households, especially those in their sixties or older, are unlikely to move to a new unit. The growth of elderly households may stimulate considerable demand for new home health care and other services, but their effect on housing construction trends will be limited.[11]

Younger single-person households are more active in the housing market than their elderly counterparts, but they too will cause little stir in the housing market in the years ahead. The key to this element is that the housing vacated by baby boom households that trade up will accommodate a substantial share of the growth of single-person and other young households. Thus baby boom trade-up will generate increased demand for larger single-family detached housing, but these same baby boomers will leave behind numerous apartments, condos, townhouses, and other smaller units suitable to house many of the next generation of smaller households.

Demographic Trends and the Growth of Low-Income Households

The past 20 years have witnessed pronounced changes in the composition of the nation's low-income population, changes that result from a complex series of demographic, social, and economic causes. Rapid growth of the young adult population in the 1970s checked wage growth for many entry-level jobs. Rising divorce and increased incidence of teenage pregnancy have added to the number of economically disadvantaged single-parent households. The high inflation of the 1970s further eroded the real incomes of those with limited skills. Similarly, over the past decade, income transfer programs benefiting young families and individuals have lost ground to inflation.

Measured in real terms, today's young households have lower incomes than their counterparts of 1974. As indicated in Table 2.4, from 1974 to 1988, the real income of households with heads aged less than 25 fell by 27.5 percent from $17,896 to $12,969, while the income of households with heads aged 25 to 34 fell by 5.7 percent from $27,357 to $25,795. By contrast, the

TABLE 2.4   Households and Household Income by Age and Type

Age and household type	HOUSEHOLDS (1000s)			MEDIAN INCOME ($1988)		
	1974	1988	Change (%)	1974	1988	Change (%)
Household head under 25						
Single	1,136	1,245	9.60	11,665	11,224	−3.78
Married with children	1,709	917	−46.34	20,518	19,528	−4.83
Married without children	1,825	860	−52.88	23,461	26,059	11.07
Single parent with children	540	822	52.22	7,181	6,113	−14.87
Other households	833	1,383	66.03	13,177	11,689	−11.29
Total	6,043	5,228	−13.49	17,896	12,969	−27.53
Household head 25–34						
Single	1,810	4,019	122.04	20,609	21,216	2.95
Married with children	8,368	8,588	2.63	29,636	31,358	5.81
Married without children	2,268	2,947	29.94	35,215	38,851	10.33
Single parent with children	1,603	2,952	84.15	12,311	11,161	−9.34
Other households	623	2,077	233.39	22,125	22,083	−0.19
Total	14,672	20,583	40.29	27,357	25,795	−5.71
Household head 35–44						
Single	963	2,837	194.60	20,158	21,622	7.26
Married with children	8,217	10,031	22.08	35,621	40,655	14.13
Married without children	1,055	2,299	117.91	36,476	47,071	29.05
Single parent with children	1,416	2,787	96.82	16,095	17,586	9.26
Other households	414	1,369	230.68	22,797	24,555	7.71
Total	12,065	19,323	60.16	32,372	35,200	8.74
Household head 45–64						
Single	4,046	5,105	26.17	12,539	14,529	15.87
Married with children	6,662	4,690	−29.60	36,590	42,952	17.39
Married without children	10,363	12,398	19.64	33,102	37,424	13.06
Single parent with children	1,109	976	−11.99	16,916	17,837	5.44
Other households	2,141	3,308	54.51	22,797	24,050	5.50
Total	24,321	26,476	8.86	32,372	30,088	−7.06

TABLE 2.4   (*Continued*)

Age and household type	HOUSEHOLDS (1000s)			MEDIAN INCOME ($1988)		
	1974	*1988*	*Change (%)*	*1974*	*1988*	*Change (%)*
Household head 65 or older						
Single	5,884	8,683	47.57	6,917	7,896	14.15
Married	6,194	8,579	38.51	15,437	19,305	25.06
Other households	1,676	2,193	30.85	14,590	16,306	11.76
Total	13,754	19,456	41.46	10,943	12,662	15.71

Source: Joint Center for Housing Studies, Harvard University, *The State of the Nation's Housing 1989*, Appendix 9.

income of somewhat older households continued to advance, with the sharpest gains recorded by households with heads aged 65 or older.

The drop in income for young households is largely the result of the alarming situation of single-parent families with children. These households constitute both a growing share of young households and a growing share of the nation's poverty population. Since 1974, the number of single-parent households with heads aged 25 to 34 increased by 84 percent. In 1988, the median income for households in this group was a meager $11,161, 9.3 percent below the figure recorded for similar households in 1974. For single-parent households with heads aged less than 25, median income in 1988 was but $6,113, down 14.9 percent from the 1974 figure of $7,181.[12]

Trends in Housing Cost Burden

The relatively slow income growth for young households has important implications for housing in America. Low incomes not only limit the ability of many households to secure adequate and affordable housing in the nonsubsidized private marketplace, they also shrink the pool of potential first-time homebuyers. With the incomes of young households failing to keep pace with inflation, the construction and sales of housing targeted to first-time buyers will suffer. In addition, unable to secure a home of their own, many young households remain renters and bid up the price of rental housing.

Homeowner Cost Burden

Table 2.5 presents estimates of homeowner cost burden for potential first-time buyers and renter cost burden for all renter households. Homeowner cost burden is the after-tax cash cost or total cost as a percent of potential first-time buyers' annual income, proxied, in turn, by the median family income of married couple renters aged 25–29, depicted in Table 2.5 as "Young Renter."

Though down from peak levels of the early 1980s, the after-tax cost of homeownership remains high relative to the income of potential first-time buyers. Nationwide, the after-tax cash cost of owning a typical starter home in 1988 was 32.8 percent of the median income of potential first-time buyers in the 24–29 age group. As indicated in Table 2.5, this is some 50 percent higher than the share of income going to pay for a typical starter home in the early 1970s.

Although young married-couple renters earn more than other renters, their incomes have not kept pace with homeownership costs. For the representative first-time buyer, the after-tax cash cost of homeownership rose steadily from 23 percent of income in 1970 to 45 percent in 1982. The cash cost burden has declined since 1982, but remains well above the levels averaged during the late 1960s and early 1970s. Total homeownership costs as a percent of income have also fallen since 1982 but remain high by historical standards.

Recognizing the existence of numerous, seemingly similar housing affordability indices, it is useful to review the key elements of the housing cost burden measure presented here. First, the data in Table 2.5 refer to the situation of potential first-time buyers. To the extent that actual homeowners (as opposed to potential homebuyers) have, by definition, the incomes necessary to purchase a home, a measure based on the income of actual homebuyers would tend to understate cost burden.

Next, the measure of homeowner cost burden presented in this paper controls for the type of home being purchased. Rather than measure the costs of homes actually purchased, the measure presented here is for a home of constant quality. Again, to the extent that housing costs force households to purchase a home of lower quality, measures that use actual home sale data will tend to understate the homeowner cost burden.

Finally, it is important to note that housing affordability is a relative concept. In the face of higher housing costs, some households may choose to purchase a smaller home or one with fewer amenities. High housing costs may force others to delay or abandon their efforts to purchase a first home entirely. Whatever the response, the figures presented in Table 2.5 demonstrate that young households are less able to purchase a home of given standards today than 15 or 20 years ago. In this sense, housing is less affordable to potential first-time buyers than in the past.

Rental Cost Burden

Table 2.5 also presents estimates of the rental cost burden for a unit of constant quality, where rent burden is the annual contract or gross rent as a

TABLE 2.5 Income and Housing Costs, U.S. Totals, 1967–1988 (1988 dollars)

| | INCOME | | | OWNER COSTS | | | RENTER COSTS | | | COST AS PERCENT OF INCOME | | | | |
| | | | | | | | | | | FIRST-TIME BUYERS | | ALL RENTERS | |
Year	Total owner	Total renter	Young renter	After tax cash	Total cost	Contract rent	Gross rent	Cash burden	Total burden	Contract rent burden	Gross rent burden
1967	$26,731	$17,277	$26,079	$5,801	$4,777	$311	$351	22.2%	18.3%	21.6%	24.4%
1968	$26,643	$17,239	$26,016	$5,932	$4,428	$309	$348	22.8%	17.0%	21.5%	24.2%
1969	$27,467	$17,205	$25,958	$6,242	$4,087	$309	$348	24.0%	15.7%	21.6%	24.3%
1970	$27,737	$18,015	$27,165	$6,276	$4,610	$308	$346	23.1%	17.0%	20.5%	23.0%
1971	$27,626	$18,233	$27,349	$6,383	$4,401	$313	$353	23.3%	16.1%	20.6%	23.2%
1972	$28,590	$18,437	$27,789	$6,523	$4,178	$316	$356	23.5%	15.0%	20.6%	23.2%
1973	$28,837	$18,054	$26,831	$6,783	$3,795	$311	$351	25.3%	14.1%	20.7%	23.3%
1974	$29,179	$17,553	$27,127	$7,066	$3,638	$300	$341	26.0%	13.4%	20.5%	23.3%
1975	$28,602	$16,615	$25,868	$7,181	$2,948	$293	$336	27.8%	11.4%	21.1%	24.3%

Year											
1976	$28,822	$16,299	$25,045	$7,277	$3,084	$294	$340	29.1%	12.3%	21.6%	25.0%
1977	$29,975	$16,486	$24,917	$8,018	$2,807	$296	$345	32.2%	11.3%	21.5%	25.1%
1978	$29,603	$16,387	$25,374	$8,468	$2,220	$300	$350	33.4%	8.7%	21.9%	25.6%
1979	$29,243	$15,980	$24,289	$8,995	$2,317	$294	$344	37.0%	9.5%	22.1%	25.8%
1980	$28,559	$15,145	$23,511	$9,672	$3,941	$291	$343	41.1%	16.8%	23.1%	27.2%
1981	$28,655	$14,985	$23,266	$10,347	$6,308	$290	$345	44.5%	27.1%	23.2%	27.6%
1982	$28,756	$14,626	$22,806	$10,361	$8,532	$297	$355	45.4%	37.4%	24.3%	29.1%
1983	$29,029	$14,752	$23,080	$9,240	$8,469	$303	$364	40.0%	36.7%	24.7%	29.6%
1984	$29,749	$15,501	$23,936	$9,128	$8,696	$308	$369	38.1%	36.3%	23.9%	28.5%
1985	$30,616	$15,969	$24,449	$8,741	$8,120	$318	$378	35.8%	33.2%	23.9%	28.4%
1986	$31,627	$16,083	$24,611	$8,301	$6,942	$333	$391	33.7%	28.2%	24.8%	29.2%
1987	$31,867	$15,933	$24,369	$7,995	$6,917	$337	$392	32.8%	28.4%	25.3%	29.5%
1988	$32,300	$15,900	$24,300	$7,980	$8,015	$338	$392	32.8%	33.0%	25.5%	29.6%

Source: Joint Center for Housing Studies, Harvard University, *The State of the Nation's Housing 1989*, Appendix 1.

percent of the median income of renter households. As was true with the homeowner burden measure, the renter cost burden measure used here is for a unit with constant characteristics. To the extent that high renter costs force households to select units of lower quality, tracking actual rent burden (that is actual rent paid divided by household income) will understate the growth in rent burden.

The constant quality rental cost burden—measured as either annual gross rent or contract rent for the representative unit as a percent of median renter income—also remains relatively high (Table 2.5). The gross rent burden fell slightly from 1967 to 1974, but has moved up sharply since that time. What is striking is that the strong economic recovery that began in 1982 did nothing to alleviate the renter cost burden: increases in real rents have steadily outweighed growth in real income.

The growth of low-income rental households in the face of rapidly increasing real rents is a clear prescription for trouble. Surprisingly there has been much controversy about the extent of rental housing crisis. There can be little doubt that the stock of low cost rental housing is declining. Even with adjustment for inflation, the number of units renting for less than $300 per month dropped by 1.6 million between 1974 and 1985; the number of units with rents above $500, in contrast, increased by 5.7 million to 8.8 million. The loss of low-rent units involves two distinct dynamics: some have fallen into disrepair and been removed from the stock; others—especially those located in the stronger housing markets of the Northeast and West—have been upgraded to attract higher-income tenants.[13]

Despite these facts, there persists a sense that the rental housing problem is overstated. For example, as recently as 1982, the Report of the President's Commission on Housing concluded that rental cost burdens had not increased dramatically in the period from 1974 to 1981. The Commission argued that real rents had declined in the past decade. Any growth in rental payments had to represent, in the opinion of the President's Commission, the fact that households were choosing to consume rental units of better quality. High rent burdens were not the result of higher costs for a unit of given quality, but rather the result of higher levels of housing consumption.[14]

By developing a methodologically sound measure of the share of income required to rent a unit of constant quality, this report demonstrates that indeed rental payments burdens have grown sharply in the past decade. In 1988, the median rent burden stood at 30 percent, the standard widely recognized in current housing assistance programs as an appropriate level of rental payment. As a median figure, this implies that half of all renters (or some 16 million renter households) pay more than 30 percent of their income for housing.

In addition to using a refined measure of renter costs, the measure of renter costs presented in this report was also designed using data available on a more timely basis. The President's Commission employed data from the

American Housing Survey, data that are released with a significant time delay. By the spring of 1989, available AHS data covered only the years 1973 to 1985. By estimating incomes from the Current Population Survey (CPS) and rental cost from a combination of AHS and the adjusted annual residential rent component of the BLS's CPI, the rental cost burden measure presented in this chapter breaks new ground, providing an empirically valid, yet timely measure of the relationship between rents and incomes.

The Changing Composition of Owner and Renter Households

The problems facing renter households are obviously related to the decline in homeownership opportunities discussed in the previous section. Unable to secure a home of their own, many young households remain renters and bid up the price of rental housing. The result is growing financial pressure on those households least able to cope with the rising rent burden. This section will document the changing characteristics of the low-income renter population, and the growing rental payments burden that these households face.

Trends in Homeownership

Continued high housing costs have resulted in a steady decline in the homeownership rate since 1980, particularly among young households. The percent of households owning their own homes did increase nationwide from 1973 to 1980, but this share has since fallen—from 65.6 percent in 1980 to 63.9 percent in 1988. The sharpest declines were recorded among young households. For households aged 25 to 34, the homeownership rate fell from 52.3 percent in 1980 to 45.0 percent in 1988. Households aged 35 to 44 suffered similarly sharp declines (Table 2.6).

By contrast, the homeownership rate for older households continued to increase during the 1980s, as improved health and growing real incomes increased the ability of older homeowners to remain in their homes or to purchase a retirement home. Without this increase in elderly homeownership, the decline in homeownership among young households would have had an even more pronounced effect on the total homeownership rate.

While the data in Table 2.6 present a relatively clear picture of homeownership trends, it is important to realize that tracing trends in homeownership over the past 20 years is not a simple matter. The key difficulty stems from the inconsistency of various sources of information concerning homeownership. Much was made about the apparent rapid growth of homeownership during the 1970s. The 1970 Census set the homeownership rate at

TABLE 2.6   Homeownership by Age and Family Type (percent)

Age and family type	1973	1976	1980	1983	1988
Household head under 25					
Single	7.7	7.8	11.5	10.9	10.4
Married with children	38.9	34.5	38.8	32.7	29.4
Married without children	26.1	30.9	33.6	30.5	22.6
Single parent with children	13.7	8.2	10.1	7.9	7.2
Other households	7.6	8.5	9.9	11.1	11.8
Total	23.4	21.0	21.3	19.3	15.5
Household head 25–34					
Single	18.0	16.0	24.8	24.1	24.3
Married with children	66.8	69.8	71.1	64.7	62.7
Married without children	45.4	49.2	58.3	53.5	53.5
Single parent with children	31.7	28.7	31.8	24.5	23.8
Other households	18.0	25.3	29.4	29.1	29.7
Total	51.4	52.2	52.3	47.0	45.0
Household head 35–44					
Single	28.0	28.5	36.8	37.5	39.0
Married with children	81.0	83.0	85.4	83.2	81.2
Married without children	66.8	67.2	75.2	74.0	76.3
Single parent with children	48.2	48.0	50.1	49.6	47.0
Other households	51.5	50.8	53.9	48.1	47.6
Total	70.7	71.4	72.3	69.6	67.1

62.9 percent, while the 1974 Annual Housing Survey placed the rate at 64.6, but nearly all of this increase was the result of the differing data collection methods involved. Measured on a consistent basis, the Bureau of the Census estimates that the homeownership rate did increase slightly in the early and mid 1970s (from 64.2 percent in 1970 to 64.8 percent in 1976), and somewhat more rapidly from 1976 to 1980 (from 64.8 percent in 1976 to 65.6 percent in 1980).[15]

TABLE 2.6   (*Continued*)

Age and family type	1973	1976	1980	1983	1988
Household head 45–64					
Single	50.7	48.5	51.6	54.2	54.6
Married with children	85.7	87.0	87.7	86.9	86.0
Married without children	83.7	86.1	88.4	89.1	88.5
Single parent with children	61.4	61.7	64.5	57.2	58.5
Other households	66.8	66.9	68.0	68.1	67.3
Total	75.9	77.3	78.5	78.8	77.8
Household head 65 or older					
Single	57.8	56.8	59.2	62.0	60.7
Married	81.5	83.1	85.0	87.3	89.1
Other households	69.3	73.5	73.6	75.9	76.2
Total	69.8	70.6	72.3	74.8	75.0

Source: Joint Center for Housing Studies, Harvard University, *The State of the Nation's Housing 1989,* Appendix 13.

Tracing the extent of the recent decline in homeownership rates also severely taxes available data. Since 1980, the Census has implemented three broad sets of changes that could influence estimates of homeownership rates as they are presented in the CPS, or in the closely related Housing Vacancy Survey and American Housing Survey. These changes include 1) the introduction of a new sampling frame based on the 1980 Census; 2) the development of a new ratio adjustment procedure to make the CPS conform to independent monthly estimates of population controls; and, 3) the introduction of new procedures for estimating the effect on CPS estimates of higher levels of undocumented in-migration, especially among Hispanics. Preliminary results of an ongoing Joint Center study of the effect of these changes suggests that collectively they have served to overstate slightly the likely decline in homeownership rates that has occurred in recent years.[16]

Despite need for further detailed study of the effect of changing data collection procedures on homeownership trends, it seems unlikely that the observed decline in homeownership, particularly among young households, is totally the result of changes in data collection procedures. Notice that the homeownership rate is falling for a wide range of households, including young married couples with children, a group that historically has maintained high levels of homeownership. Even allowing for the changing demographic composition of households, the decline in age and household specific homeownership rates resulted in two million fewer young homeowners in 1988 than there would have been if the homeownership rates had been maintained at the 1980 level.

Given the lack of detailed time series data on homeownership rates, especially data cross-classified by type of household and region, it is difficult to make precise pronouncements as to the underlying cause of the observed decline in homeownership rates. Analysis of Current Population Survey data indicates that the decline in homeownership is not concentrated in any single area of the country. From 1983 to 1987, declines in the homeownership rate for households aged 25 to 29 were recorded in seven of the nine Census divisions. Only in the Mid-Atlantic and South Atlantic States did the rate of homeownership for this age group remain constant or move up slightly.

The decline in homeownership is also widespread for households aged 30 to 34. Of the nine Census Divisions, only in the South Atlantic Division did the homeownership rate for households aged 30–34 increase, and this increase was statistically insignificant. For all other divisions, the homeownership rate for households aged 30 to 34 declined from 1983 to 1987, with particularly sharp declines noted in the East North Central, West North Central, and Mountain Divisions.

These data are consistent with the view that it is the downpayment and cash costs constraint that limit first-time buyer access to new homes. For example, since 1983, housing costs have moved up sharply in New England, adding substantially to actual and expected equity accumulation. These increases have served to lower the total cost burden of owning a home, where again total costs include the expectation of capital gains. By contrast, the total cost burden of housing in the Pacific region remained high during the period, the result primarily of the more moderate price increases and the limited potential for equity buildup.

Yet despite the difference between the total cost trends for the two areas, each division experienced declines in the homeownership rate for households in the first-time buyer age groups. Only cash costs, which are uniformly high relative to income across the various regions, can explain the tendency for the rate of homeownership for young households to decline in most regions of the country. Price increases in New England may reduce the total housing cost burden for those households able to assemble the downpayment and meet the initial payments burden of a mortgage. For those households not able to make such downpayments or not able to secure a mortgage on terms that are within their financial reach, growing house prices simply make homeownership an even more distant goal.

Characteristics of Owner and Renter Households

Rental housing is increasingly the home of the nation's lower-income households, while higher-income households increasingly choose to own a home. Since 1974, the homeownership rate fell sharply for households with incomes less than $10,000 (again measured in 1988 dollars). By comparison, the number of homeowners with real incomes above $50,000 grew by 5.5 million over this period and the homeownership rate increased from 86.5 to 88.5 percent (Table 2.7).

The growth in the number of low-income renter households has widened the income gap between owners and renters. Between 1972 and 1982, the median income of renters fell by 21 percent, from $18,437 to $14,626 (Table 2.5). With the economic expansion of the mid-1980s the median renter income did improve slightly, but not enough to reduce poverty among renter households. In 1988, the number of poverty-level renter households stood at 7.7 million, up slightly from the 1985 figure of 7.2 million and well above the 1980 figure of 5.8 million. By 1988, 66 percent of all poverty-level households lived in rental housing.[17]

As a group, renter households, then, are younger and poorer, while homeowners are older and richer. From 1974, the median income of renters aged 25 to 34 fell by 12.8 percent (Table 2.8), while the median income of renters aged 25 or less was 22.8 percent lower than real incomes of young renters in the mid-1970s. Rental housing is also increasingly becoming the

TABLE 2.7   Household Income and Homeownership

Household income ($1000, 1988)	Number of households (1000s)		Percent homeowner	
	1974	1985	1974	1985
Under 10	13,804	17,843	46.9	41.2
10–20	15,337	18,229	54.3	52.4
20–30	15,163	17,531	64.2	62.2
30–50	17,276	19,521	76.9	75.7
Over 50	9,299	15,299	86.5	88.5
Total	70,879	88,424	64.7	63.5

Source: Joint Center tabulations based on U.S. Department of Housing and Urban Development Annual Housing Survey, 1974 & 1985.

TABLE 2.8 Households and Household Income by Age, Tenure, and Household Type

Age and household type	OWNER								RENTER							
	Number (1000s)		Median income ($1988)						Number (1000s)		Median income ($1988)					
	1974	1988	1974	1988					1974	1988	1974	1988				
Household head under 25																
Single	81	130	13,124	19,802					1,055	1,116	11,535	10,231				
Married with children	658	270	22,804	22,029					1,051	647	18,473	17,763				
Married without children	507	194	27,357	32,643					1,318	667	22,797	22,037				
Single parent with children	48	59	11,399	12,738					492	763	7,167	5,846				
Other households	83	156	19,834	10,183					750	1,227	11,855	12,109				
Total	1,377	809	23,025	22,176					4,666	4,420	15,958	12,315				
Household head 25–34																
Single	300	978	25,031	27,666					1,510	3,041	20,518	19,639				
Married with children	5,695	5,384	31,916	35,968					2,673	3,204	24,393	22,859				
Married without children	1,073	1,576	39,211	46,217					1,195	1,371	31,932	28,560				
Single parent with children	446	703	16,870	18,169					1,157	2,249	10,906	8,699				
Other households	116	616	29,212	27,797					507	1,461	20,668	21,081				
Total	7,630	9,257	31,916	35,170					7,042	11,326	22,341	19,474				
Household head 35–44																
Single	269	1,107	25,077	27,674					694	1,730	19,378	19,457				

Married with children	6,765	8,141	37,397	44,409	1,452	1,889	27,357	26,294
Married without children	723	1,754	38,687	48,372	332	546	30,822	40,598
Single parent with children	692	1,309	22,831	27,434	724	1,478	12,618	11,858
Other households	204	652	29,408	30,361	210	717	17,098	22,623
Total	8,653	12,963	36,156	41,541	3,412	6,360	22,091	20,308
Household head 45–64								
Single	1,955	2,788	13,587	16,836	2,091	2,317	11,399	11,486
Married with children	5,750	4,031	38,755	47,128	912	659	25,136	26,573
Married without children	8,771	10,973	34,196	39,466	1,592	1,424	27,266	22,950
Single parent with children	688	571	21,730	25,471	421	405	11,900	9,374
Other households	1,426	2,228	23,253	28,445	715	1,081	15,958	16,837
Total	18,590	20,591	31,939	35,459	5,731	5,886	18,238	16,460
Household head 65 or older								
Single	3,312	5,273	7,560	8,858	2,572	3,410	6,324	6,758
Married	5,070	7,648	38,778	44,621	1,124	931	24,712	26,157
Other households	1,211	1,672	27,913	22,254	464	521	20,634	14,945
Total	9,593	14,593	12,657	14,669	4,160	4,862	7,897	7,686

Source: Joint Center tabulations based on U.S. Department of Housing and Urban Development 1974 Annual Housing Survey and U.S. Department of Commerce 1988 Current Population Survey.

home of the nation's children. Between 1974 and 1988, the number of renter households with children grew more than four times faster than the rate for all households. In contrast, the number of young homeowners with children actually fell over the past decade and a half.

Housing the Nation's Poor

Over the past two decades, slower real income growth and higher real housing costs have exacerbated the problems of low- and moderate-income households. Gross rent as a share of income rose sharply from 1974 to 1988 and remains at historically high levels. Even paying a large share of their incomes for rent, many households still live in poor-quality housing. Moreover, most of these households must face the growing rental payments burden alone: available rental assistance is simply inadequate in light of the growing number of low-income renter households.

Rental Payments Burden by Family Type

The incidence of high rental burdens has increased, particularly among the young. In 1974, the gross rent burden (estimated as the ratio of median rent to income) for households with heads aged 25 to 34 was 20.1 percent; by 1988, the burden had reached 26.0 percent (Table 2.9). Households with heads under the age of 25 experienced even sharper increases.

As noted earlier, rental housing is increasingly becoming home to low- and moderate-income families with children, especially single-parent households. From 1974 to 1988, the number of married couples aged 25–34 with children who rented their housing increased from 2.7 million to 3.2 million (Table 2.8). At the same time, the number of single-parent families (primarily women with children) nearly doubled from 1.2 million to 2.2 million.

Table 2.9 makes clear why the rental payments burden is increasingly a problem for young households: the median income of young single-parent renter households with children fell 20 percent from $10,906 in 1974 to $8,699 in 1988. With shrinking incomes and growing rents, the increase in rent burden for this type of family is unavoidable. The rent burden for young single-parent families with children thus increased from 37.9 percent to 53.6 percent over this period.

Moreover, since the homeless are not counted as households by the Census Bureau, the data in Table 2.9 may actually understate the current payments problem. While there are no reliable national figures on the homeless, their number appears to have grown in recent years, especially among families with children. While further investigation into the causes of homelessness is clearly warranted, the data in Table 2.9 should leave little doubt that the rising rental payments burden is a major factor.

TABLE 2.9   Rent Burden by Age and Family Type

Age and household type	Median income ($1988)		Gross rent ($1988)		Gross rent burden	
	1974	1988	1974	1988	1974	1988
Household head under 25						
Single	11,535	10,231	310	350	32.2%	41.0%
Married with children	18,473	17,763	315	355	20.5%	24.0%
Married without children	22,797	22,037	355	401	18.7%	21.8%
Single parent with children	7,167	5,846	301	339	50.4%	69.7%
Other households	11,855	12,109	396	447	40.1%	44.3%
Total	15,958	12,315	337	380	25.3%	37.1%
Household head 25–34						
Single	20,518	19,639	357	404	20.9%	24.7%
Married with children	24,393	22,859	371	419	18.3%	22.0%
Married without children	31,932	28,560	412	465	15.5%	19.6%
Single parent with children	10,906	8,699	344	388	37.9%	53.6%
Other households	20,668	21,081	426	481	24.7%	27.4%
Total	22,341	19,474	374	422	20.1%	26.0%
Household head 35–44						
Single	19,378	19,457	351	396	21.7%	24.4%
Married with children	27,357	26,294	392	442	17.2%	20.2%
Married without children	30,822	40,598	387	437	15.1%	12.9%
Single parent with children	12,618	11,858	344	388	32.7%	39.3%
Other households	17,098	22,623	351	396	24.6%	21.0%
Total	22,091	20,308	370	416	20.1%	24.6%
Household head 45–64						
Single	11,399	11,486	277	314	29.2%	32.8%
Married with children	25,136	26,573	375	424	17.9%	19.2%
Married without children	27,266	22,950	378	427	16.6%	22.3%
Single parent with children	11,900	9,374	334	378	33.7%	48.4%

TABLE 2.9 (*Continued*)

Age and family type	Median income ($1988)		Gross rent ($1988)		Gross rent burden	
	1974	1988	1974	1988	1974	1988
Other households	15,958	16,837	317	357	23.9%	25.5%
Total	18,238	16,460	330	373	21.7%	27.2%
Household head 65 or older						
Single	6,324	6,758	219	247	41.6%	43.8%
Married	24,712	26,157	326	368	15.8%	16.9%
Other households	20,634	14,945	277	314	16.1%	25.2%
Total	7,897	7,686	257	291	39.0%	45.4%

Source: Joint Center tabulations based on U.S. Department of Housing 1974 Annual Housing Survey and U.S. Department of Commerce 1988 Current Population Survey.

Low-Income Housing Assistance

Housing assistance efforts have done much in the past to improve the housing situations of low-income households. It is surprisingly difficult, however, to obtain estimates of the characteristics of households actually served by these programs. HUD data suggest that in 1987, there were approximately 4.3 million units of public or otherwise federally subsidized rental housing, but provides no demographic data describing the characteristics of those living in these units. Lacking detailed HUD data, this discussion utilizes survey based estimates that differ slightly from the HUD estimates of total households served but that provide needed information on the characteristics of the households living in subsidized rental units.[18]

By any measure, the Housing and Community Development Act of 1974 sparked a major expansion in the number of households receiving rental assistance. According to the 1985 American Housing Survey, 4.2 million households lived in public housing or rental housing otherwise subsidized by the federal government (Table 2.10). While this growth has virtually stopped in the past several years, the 1985 figure is up nearly 95 percent from the figure of 2.1 million recorded by the 1974 Annual Housing Survey.

Much of the increase in housing assistance resources has gone to aid households at the lowest end of the income distribution. Among renter households with real incomes at or below the poverty level, the number living in subsidized housing more than doubled between 1974 and 1985. Nevertheless, existing programs serve only a small fraction of eligible low-income households. According to American Housing Survey data, just 13.9 percent of all renter households received housing assistance. Even among poverty households, less than one-third received subsidies.

Whether or not these data reflect appropriate targeting of resources is, of course, a political judgment. It is clear, however, that the growth of housing assistance has failed to keep pace with the growth of poor households. In 1974, 3.5 million renter households with incomes at or below federally established poverty thresholds received no housing assistance. By 1985, this pool of eligible but unassisted poor renter households had grown to nearly 5 million.

Without a housing subsidy program, the majority of poor renter families have nothing to protect themselves from the rapid run-up in rents that has occurred in the past decade. From 1974 to 1985, the median real gross rent paid by poverty renter households increased by 34 percent from $251 to $336. Rent payments were lower, of course, for those poverty households fortunate enough to secure subsidized units. Rent increases, nevertheless, were substantial even for subsidized renters, reflecting in large measure the fact that most programs now require a tenant to pay 30 percent of income for rent, up from the 25 percent norm in the 1960s and 1970s. The high rent burden for the poor is not a

TABLE 2.10   Subsidy Status of Renter Households (1000s)

	1974	1985	Change (%)
Non-poverty			
Subsidized	1,289	1,961	52.1
Unsubsidized	17,411	20,901	20.0
All non-poverty renters	18,700	22,864	22.3
Poverty			
Subsidized	856	2,219	159.2
Unsubsidized	3,539	4,971	40.5
All poverty renters	4,396	7,189	63.5
Total renters			
Subsidized	2,145	4,181	94.9
Unsubsidized	20,950	25,873	23.5
All renters	23,095	30,054	30.1

Source: Joint Center for Housing Studies, Harvard University, *The State of the Nation's Housing 1989*, Exhibit 21.

statistical artifact, but results from the growth in the number of non-subsidized households and the progressive tightening at the low end of the market.

Spatial Variation in Availability of Housing Assistance

The spatial distribution of current housing assistance resources reflects a complex history of program activity over the past 50 years. Current population statistics suggest that a relatively high share of renter households in the Northeast (14.8 percent) receive assistance. Each of the other regions trails behind the Northeast, though there is considerable variation across states within a region. In Kentucky in 1987, some 26.8 percent of all renters lived in public housing or other subsidized rental housing. By contrast, in Florida, only 10.5 percent of renter households lived in public or other subsidized rental housing. Numerous factors help explain the difference. Unlike Florida, Kentucky has a relatively large stock of public housing serving both large central cities and smaller cities and towns. The legacy of the housing resources built up over the past 50 years in the state continues to serve poor Kentucky households at a level not possible in Florida.

Variation across states is but one dimension of the geographic variation in the availability of rental assistance. A program such as the Section 8 Existing Housing Assistance obviously works better in areas with an active rental market and a set of landlords willing to lease units to subsidized tenants. Programs that require involvement of county or local governments work best in places that have strong local housing agencies and a tradition of aggressively seeking out funding for new housing initiatives. Finally, programs that rely on the involvement of active community-based organizations, competent private sector builders or developers, or responsible local financial institutions naturally work best where these resources are available.

With, at best, only 4.3 million assisted renter housing units available, changes in the targeting of assisted renter housing alone will be insufficient to deal with the housing problems of the renter households living in poverty; there simply are more low-income households than assisted rental units. Moreover, there are nearly 4.4 million poverty-level owner households. Housing problems for this group are especially acute in low-density rural areas where the lack of a well-developed rental housing market results in high shares of households owning substandard housing.

Although more careful targeting could make better use of existing housing assistance resources, the development of new program initiatives and expansion of national housing assistance resources is needed if the nation is to improve the housing conditions of both low-income owners and renters. For this expansion to reach poverty-level households in all regions, special effort must be made to address the housing problems in those states and regions that currently are under-represented in existing housing programs.

Conclusion

With the development of new national housing legislation at least a possibility in the near future, it is useful to consider the role of empirical analysis in policy formation. First, empirical analysis can focus public attention on important housing problems. As this report documents, there has been much controversy about the extent of the nation's housing problems, controversy fueled by a combination of inadequate data and an unwillingness on the part of many to recognize the growing problems of the housing "have-nots." Failure to assess carefully the decline in homeownership has led some to discount the significance of this trend. Flawed measures of rental housing cost have led many to dismiss the growing rental payments problem of the nation's most disadvantaged citizens. Having not carefully analyzed housing assistance efforts some have concluded that there is an adequate supply of subsidized housing. Hopefully information presented in this chapter will put some of these empirical controversies to rest.

Empirical analysis, of course, will not resolve the many political controversies that inevitably surround any domestic policy debate. While "housing need" studies abound, there is no scientific method for correctly determining the appropriate level of homeownership for any particular group, or for determining at what price housing becomes unaffordable. Whether or not the homeownership rates or the housing cost burdens depicted in this chapter are appropriate is a decidedly political judgment. But careful assessment of the factors that are causing the observed housing trends can at least suggest the broad outlines of the needed policy response. Thus, the decline in homeownership should not be viewed as an event unto itself, but rather should be viewed in the context of a broader housing market process. High housing costs force potential first-time homebuyers to remain in the rental housing market, bidding up the price of rental housing. This, in turn, further limits the homeownership opportunities of young renters, as increased rents reduce the ability of these households to save for a downpayment on a home.

This chapter also notes that the growing rental costs inevitably will have the most adverse impact on those least able to compete for the dwindling supply of low-cost housing. The decline in household formation and the growing homeless population are the result of a complex set of social and economic forces, but high housing costs must be viewed as a major factor.

In short, this paper argues that the nation faces a set of distinct, yet decidedly interconnected housing problems stemming from the combination of lagging income growth and continued high housing costs. Addressing these problems will require the concerted efforts of all levels of government to deal with a range of issues that confront both owners and renters. Development of a comprehensive national policy must build on a sound understanding of past trends and future prospects for housing in America. The problems facing the nation's low- and moderate-income households merit such special attention.

Notes

1. This chapter presents housing cost information initially presented in the report of the Joint Center for Housing Studies, Harvard University (Cambridge: JCHS, 1988) entitled *The State of the Nation's Housing 1988*, as updated in the most recent report, *The State of the Nation's Housing 1989* (Cambridge: JCHS, 1989).

2. For a discussion of how households form housing price expectations see J. Edwards, "The Formation of Housing Price Expectations," Working Paper W87-3 (Cambridge: Joint Center for Housing Studies, Harvard University, 1987).

3. For further discussion of the effect of tax reform on homeownership see Denise DiPasquale, "Homeowner Deductions and First-Time Homebuyers," Working Paper W89-2 (Cambridge: Joint Center for Housing Studies, Harvard University, 1989).

4. For a summary of these studies see J. C. Weicher, K. Villani, and E. A. Roistacher, eds., *Rental Housing: Is There a Crisis?* (Washington: Urban Institute Press, 1981).

5. For further discussion see I. S. Lowry, "Inflation Indexes for Rental Housing," Working Note N-1832-HUD (Santa Monica, California: Rand Corporation, 1982). See also W. C. Apgar, Jr. with R. Peng and J. Olson, "Recent Trends in Real Rents," Working Paper W87-5 (Cambridge: Joint Center for Housing Studies, Harvard University, 1987).

6. For further discussion see W. C. Randolph, "Estimation of Housing Depreciation: Short-Term Quality Change and Long-Term Vintage Effects," *Journal of Urban Economics* 23 (1988) 162–178,.

7. For a formal model of housing price dynamics see J. F. Kain and W. C. Apgar, Jr., *Housing and Neighborhood Dynamics* (Cambridge: Harvard University Press, 1985).

8. See W. C. Apgar, Jr., "Rental Housing in the United States," Working Paper W88-1 (Cambridge: Joint Center for Housing Studies, Harvard University, 1988); and W. C. Apgar, Jr. et al., "Recent Trends in Real Rents."

9. See J. R. Pitkin and G. S. Masnick, "Households and Housing Consumption in the United States, 1985 to 2000: Projections by a Cohort Method," Research Report RJ86-1 (Cambridge: Joint Center for Housing Studies, Harvard University, 1986); see also G. S. Masnick, "U. S. Household Trends: The 1980s and Beyond," Working Paper W89-1 (Cambridge: Joint Center for Housing Studies, Harvard University, 1989).

10. See W. C. Apgar, Jr. with J. Shannon and J. Olson, "The Determinants of Renovation and Repair Activity," Working Paper W87-7 (Cambridge: Joint Center for Housing Studies, Harvard University, 1987).

11. For further discussion see W. C. Apgar, Jr., "Home Sweet Home to Stay," *Mortgage Banking* (September 1987).

12. Income estimates were developed using data from the 1974 and 1985 Annual Housing Survey and 1986 and 1988 Current Population Survey. Income figures were deflated by the CPI-UX, a measure of inflation for all urban consumers. See also Congressional Budget Office, *Trends in Family Income: 1970–1986* (Washington: USGPO, 1988).

13. Joint Center for Housing Studies, *State of the Nation's Housing 1989*, Appendix Table 7. The finding concerning the decline in the stock of low rent units has been confirmed by a number of analysts. See, for example, Cushing N. Dolbeare, "Low-Income Housing Needs," Report Prepared for the National Low-Income Housing Coalition, Washington, 1987.

14. See *Report of the President's Commission on Housing,* William F. McKenna, chair (Washington: USGPO, 1983), Chapter 5, "The Dynamics of the Private Housing Market," and Chapter 7, "Rental Housing."

15. For discussion see U.S. Bureau of the Census, *Annual Housing Survey* (Washington: USGPO, 1980) Part A.

16. G. Masnick, "Changes in the Current Population Survey since 1984 Affecting Estimate of Homeownership Rates," Working Note (Cambridge: Joint Center for Housing Studies, Harvard University, 1988).

17. Joint Center for Housing Studies, *State of the Nation's Housing 1989*, Exhibit 10 and Appendix Table 6.

18. See Congressional Budget Office, *Current Housing Problems and Possible Federal Responses* (Washington: USGPO, 1988). For a discussion of trends in the number of HUD assisted rental dwelling units see the report by the National Low-Income Housing Coalition/Low-Income Housing Information Service; and the Center for Budget Priorities report, "A Place to Call Home: The Crisis in Housing for the Poor."

Chapter 3
A Strategy for Designing a Fully Comprehensive National Housing Policy for the Federal Government of the United States

Anthony Downs

This chapter presents an overview of key issues relevant to formulating a comprehensive national housing policy for the federal government of the United States. It is designed to serve as a background resource to persons developing a proposed Housing Act of 1989, which would embody, or at least be based upon, such a comprehensive national housing policy.

This chapter seeks to be broad enough to serve as a unifying background to often more detailed chapters in the book, but specific enough to deal clearly and directly with the key issues involved. It adopts as factual and objective a perspective as possible. But it also discusses certain issues that are inherently value-laden, and therefore cannot be dealt with in a purely scientific manner. In those cases, the chapter either describes alternative viewpoints reflecting different underlying values or describes a single viewpoint clearly labelled as that of the author. In fact, I have deliberately built great flexibility into this whole approach to creating a comprehensive national housing policy. Hence anyone can use it to define such a policy in conformity with his or her own values and policy judgments.

Basic Definitions and Housing Goals

Basic Definitions

Certain terms àre used in this paper in ways that may differ from their use elsewhere. For clarity, they are defined as follows:

Housing goals are the ultimate objectives concerning housing conditions in the United States that federal housing-related policies are designed to achieve.

All the housing goals used in this analysis have been officially adopted by Congress in past acts of legislation. However, Congress has attached time-tables, deadlines, or schedules to very few of them.

Key housing issues are policy questions that require choosing among alternative courses of action in order to pursue housing goals. In many cases these courses of action are mutually exclusive. In most cases, such choices are likely to be controversial.

Housing policies are general guidelines concerning how the federal government or other key housing-related actors ought to behave, in order that the nation may most effectively attain its housing goals. Each policy embodies a specific resolution of some key housing issue. Most housing policies depend heavily upon subjective value judgments made by the persons formulating them; hence there are no "purely objective" or "totally scientific" ways of designing such policies. Congress has officially adopted some specific housing policies. But many others required to round out a relatively comprehensive set of such policies have not been officially adopted.

A fully comprehensive national housing policy is an overall set of specific housing policies that, taken together, is designed to meet all the nation's housing goals to the maximum degree its formulators consider possible at the time they create it. Few fully comprehensive national housing policies have ever been explicitly stated by anyone, even just as proposals. Neither the Congress, nor any Administration, nor most private interest groups have ever done so.

The main reasons are that such a policy is very difficult to formulate; starting it explicitly would require clearly resolving extremely controversial issues that most elected officials would rather not confront publicly; and carrying out any such a policy would cost more money than most Congresses or Administrations have been willing to spend on housing problems.

It is not necessary for a national housing policy to be fully comprehensive in order to be significant and meaningful. A policy adopted by any relevant level of government—or key private agencies—that encompassed many of the issues described in this study and dealt with them decisively would represent a big improvement over most past approaches to the nation's housing problems. However, this study sets forth a fully comprehensive set of housing policy issues in order to provide a relatively complete overview of this subject.

Housing programs are specific sets of actions to be undertaken by the federal government and other key housing-related actors to achieve the nation's housing goals in accordance with its housing policies. Federal housing programs are usually spelled out in detail in legislation adopted by Congress, and then administered by the Department of Housing and Urban Development.

Housing programs have typically been modified over time, as experience with them indicates which of their elements are successful and which are not. Thus, the formulation, implementation, and amendment of specific housing programs should be perceived as a dynamic and evolutionary trial-and-error process based upon learning from experience, rather than as just the execution of laws adopted once and for all.

Key housing actors are organizations or persons whose behavior does or could significantly affect how well the nation achieves its housing goals. They include Congress, the current federal Administration in general, the Department of Housing and Urban Development (HUD), the Federal Reserve Board, state governments, local governments, the homebuilding industry and specific firms therein, unions engaged in homebuilding, the real estate brokerage industry and specific firms therein, federally-linked credit agencies, the savings and loan industry and specific associations therein, mortgage banking firms, the Federal Home Loan Bank Board, non-profit agencies engaged in housing activities, and many others.

Appropriate housing roles are specific social functions that each type of housing actor ought to carry out, in the opinion of the person defining such roles. These roles are derived from housing goals. But roles refer to the social functions that actors ought to perform, rather than to the results of performing such functions, which are the subjects of housing goals.

Low-income households are those with annual money incomes below 80 percent of the median household incomes in the metropolitan or other areas where they reside. They are further divided into two sub-groups: very-low-income households have annual money incomes below 50 percent of the median household incomes in their areas; moderately-low-income households have annual money incomes from 50 percent to 80 percent of the median household incomes in their areas.

Moderate-income households have annual money incomes from 80 percent to 120 percent of the median household incomes in their areas. Households with incomes over 120 percent of the median household incomes in their areas are either middle-income or upper-income households. However, no specific income borderline between these two groups is used in this paper.

Officially Adopted Housing Goals

Analysis of past Congressional statements about housing policy objectives reveals the following as primary target goals:[1]

> "Realization as soon as feasible of . . . a decent home and a suitable living environment for every American family."[2]

- This central housing goal of national housing policy was set forth by Congress in the Housing Act of 1949.

Providing housing assistance to low-income households by:

- Enabling those now living in physically adequate units but paying "excessive" fractions of their incomes for housing to reduce those fractions to desirable levels.
- Enabling those now living in physically inadequate units to occupy "decent" quality units.
- Enabling those now living in overcrowded units to occupy units that are not overcrowded.

Providing similar housing assistance to numerous specific groups, including the elderly, Indians, disabled veterans, persons displaced by government actions, etc.

Encouraging homeownership among households, regardless of their incomes.

Increasing the total available supply of decent-quality housing units of all types and at all price levels.

Eliminating racial and ethnic discrimination in housing markets.

Stimulating the economy by increasing construction activity in the housing industry.

Improving the quality of deteriorated neighborhoods.

Reducing the concentration of low-income households in poverty areas.

These goals and their relationships to other elements of a comprehensive national housing policy are discussed later in this chapter.

Criteria of Desirability for a Comprehensive National Housing Policy

Both in formulating a comprehensive national housing policy, and in evaluating alternative versions of such a policy, it is necessary to use some guidelines concerning what such an overall policy should be like. These guidelines are criteria of desirability. They describe the particular characteristics that the entire set of policies within the comprehensive national policy should exhibit as a whole. I suggest the following criteria:

Internal consistency. Specific policies within the comprehensive national housing policy should not conflict with each other in ways that will greatly reduce their effectiveness.

Completeness. The comprehensive policy should contain specific policies that pursue all the nation's housing goals appropriately dealt with primarily as housing matters.

Minimal contents. The comprehensive policy should *not* contain specific policies pursuing non-housing goals, or pursuing housing goals that are more appropriately dealt with primarily as *non-housing* matters.

Affordability. The total federal cost of all specific policies contained in the comprehensive national housing policy should be within the current financial capabilities of the federal government, given the rest of the federal budget and national economic conditions.

Realistic role assignment. Specific housing policies should be based upon realistic assumptions about how each of the actors involved will actually behave, given the incentives facing them and their normal goals and objectives.

Consistency with other federal policies. Specific housing policies should not conflict with other federal policies in ways that will greatly reduce the effectiveness of either.

Political feasibility. The specific housing policies that must be adopted by governmental agencies should have at least some slight chance of being so adopted under current political conditions.

Political Feasibility and the Educational Impact of a National Housing Policy

This study is aimed at several different audiences, each of which has somewhat different characteristics, knowledge, needs for information, and capabilities for action. One important audience consists of government officials capable of adopting those elements of a national housing policy requiring legislation, including members of the U.S. Congress and their staffs. Most such officials are not specialists in housing affairs, but they are quite sensitive to current political forces in the nation. This creates a problem concerning how key housing issues should be presented in this study.

On the one hand, it would be desirable to set forth a broad spectrum of possible perceptions of housing issues and potential public policies concerning them. Some, for example, believe that the nation faces an immediate and acute "housing crisis," while others believe our housing problems are minor. Many of these viewpoints would be considered by most practical politicians to be politically unfeasible under today's conditions.

Likewise, if the study proposed many possible government actions considered by most Americans so "radical" as to be politically unacceptable, members of this key governmental audience might dismiss the study's entire contents as impractical. For example, some housing experts claim the nation faces an acute "housing crisis" requiring immediate provision of federal assistance for many more than the 400,000 units per year achieved in 1972 and 1973—by far the highest number of units so funded in U.S. history. I do not agree with their assessment. Moreover, if this study reflected such a "radical" viewpoint throughout, I believe it would be regarded by the very people to whom such appeals must be addressed—members of Congress and their staffs—as totally impractical. To avoid that outcome, I have tried to follow a balanced approach to national housing policy that combines a relatively broad analysis of key issues, with some sensitivity to the political feasibility of specific policy recommendations.

Identifying Major Housing Problems and Key Housing Issues

I have divided what I believe to be the nation's most significant housing problems, as of 1987, into two groups. The first group is consumer-oriented; that is, it views housing from the perspective of the households who occupy it. The second group is industry-oriented; that is, it views housing from the perspective of the industry that produces it and maintains and operates it (in the case of rental housing)—including all aspects of that industry. The key problems in each of these groups are briefly described below. This analysis focuses mainly upon urban housing problems, with very little emphasis upon rural housing problems. More detailed analyses of these problems and quantification of their actual extent in the United States, will be presented in other chapters.

Consumer-Oriented Housing Problems

1. There are eight main types of low-income housing problems.

Affordability. Many low-income households have such low incomes they cannot occupy decent quality units without paying excessive fractions of their incomes for housing (that is, more than about 30 percent, according to current federal definitions of this problem). Most of these households are already living in decent-quality housing. Hence what they need most is either higher incomes or lower prices for the same housing, rather than physically-improved housing units.

Physical inadequacy. Many low-income households live in units that have deteriorated or that lack facilities considered essential for decent housing, such as adequate plumbing.

Overcrowding. Some low-income households live in units that have too many persons per room for decent quality living. Units with more than 1.0 persons per room or 2.0 persons per bedroom are considered overcrowded.

An increasing shortage of low-rent housing units. The total supply of relatively low-rent housing units has been shrinking because of rising rents, dem-olitions and conversions of older units, and very little construction of new subsidized units. As a result, the supply of such units is becoming less and less adequate to meet the number of households who can only afford to pay relatively low rents.

Poor-quality neighborhoods. Many low-income households live in neighbor-hoods that are unsafe, inadequately provided with public services and facili-ties, or otherwise undesirable.

Homelessness. Thousands of very poor persons across the nation do not have any permanent dwellings at all, but reside in streets, parks, or other outdoor locations. They are concentrated in large cities.

Desubsidization. Thousands of now-subsidized housing units occupied by low-income households may cease being subsidized because their owners are eligible to remove them from such status, or they are in dire financial straits. In either case, their removal from subsidized status threatens to sharply raise housing costs for the low-income households now occupying them.

Inadequate coordination of governmental housing and welfare policies. Fed-eral, state, and local governments spend almost as much on housing assistance through all welfare programs—including Aid to Families with Dependent Children (AFDC), Supplemental Security Income (SSI), and General Assis-tance—as the Department of Housing and Urban Development (HUD) spends on assisted housing. However, many welfare housing payments do not cover the cost of providing standard-quality housing; hence, their recipients live in substandard units, even though those units receive government support. This results in government provision of inadequate housing for millions of low-income households, and immense regional disparities in assisted housing quality for such households.

2. Racial and ethnic discrimination in housing markets is much more common than most people think. It is a key obstacle to the effective use of housing vouchers by black households in many cities. Its most common form is "steering" of white households seeking dwellings into all-white neighbor-hoods, and black or minority households seeking dwellings into mostly black or minority neighborhoods.

3. First-time buyer affordability problems arise when households seeking homeownership for the first time cannot afford either to purchase homes with-out spending excessive fractions of their incomes on monthly payments, or to make the downpayments necessary to purchase those homes on which they could afford to make monthly payments. These are similar to affordability

problems among low-income households, but first-time-buyer households normally do not have low incomes.

4. Excessively costly local government regulations raise the cost of building new housing units far above both what is necessary to provide decent, safe, and sanitary dwellings and what many moderate-income and nearly all low-income households can afford to pay without spending excessive fractions of their incomes for housing, if then.

5. Regional or sub-regional housing exclusion occurs when large portions of a metropolitan area have such high housing costs that many moderate-income and nearly all low-income households cannot afford to live there without spending inordinately high fractions of their incomes for housing, if then. Such exclusion results from a combination of excessively costly local government regulations and high land costs caused by strong demands for land in economically growing areas.

Industry-Oriented Housing Problems

1. Insolvency and financial instability in the thrift industry threaten that industry's ability to continue financing home ownership. This problem has been the focus of recent major legislation by Congress.

2. Volatility of overall housing demand raises housing costs and causes great instability within the homebuilding industry. Housing construction has always been highly cyclical because of the dependence of housing demand upon interest rates, which move up and down during the general business cycle. The resulting instability of total housing demand causes periodic shrinkage in the number of firms engaged in housing construction during housing "slumps," followed by rapid expansion during housing "booms." This cycle raises the average cost of new housing above what it would be if demand were much more stable over time.[3]

3. Volatility of home mortgage interest rates affects the ability of potential homebuyers to borrow the money necessary for such purchases. This volatility results from the linkage of interest rates to the general business cycle. When interest rates in general are relatively high, so are mortgage interest rates. Hence the number of households who can afford to borrow to buy homes falls. Conversely, that number rises when interest rates are low. This volatility affects not only new home construction, but the sales of existing homes.

4. Creation of avoidable uncertainties affecting homebuilding through constant changes in governmental policies related to housing. These policies include federal tax laws and regulations, local zoning ordinances and building codes, specific forms of federal housing subsidy programs, levels of funding for such programs, and methods of administering them. The resulting uncertainties raise the costs of building new homes and diminish both the ability of and the incentives for private builders to create both additional market-rate housing and additional assisted housing.

Key Housing Issues That Should Be Resolved

For purposes of this analysis, thirteen key housing issues can be defined. All of them should at least be considered in the formulation of any fully comprehensive national housing policy. However, an organization's national housing policy can be both fruitful and effective even if it takes into account only some issues. These issues have been divided into four groups, each discussed in a subsequent section of this chapter. The discussions present the main arguments concerning different possible resolutions of the issue, then make specific recommendations either there or in the final section. Each recommendation is a specific housing policy that I believe would effectively move the nation towards achieving its housing goals, in a manner consistent with my own social values.

I have presented as cogently as I can the reasons why I recommended each specific policy. Nevertheless, since it is impossible to define such policies without making value judgments, these policies clearly embody my own subjective value judgments. Many are likely to be controversial. I urge readers to define their own policies for each key issue.

Issues Concerning Basic Housing Roles and Responsibilities

Dealing effectively with the nation's many housing problems requires a concerted effort of thousands of key actors across the nation. Each actor must perform one or more specialized roles in accordance with its capabilities and opportunities. In fact, one of the most crucial steps in creating an effective comprehensive national housing policy is deciding what roles each major actor should perform.

Deciding what roles are "appropriate" for each key actor is inescapably controversial; there is no "purely objective" way to do it. In this section, I have assigned specific roles to each major actor in ways that I believe will result in the most effective overall attainment of the housing goals described earlier. Where practical, I have presented justifications for the role assignments shown, especially concerning those likely to be the most controversial.

Why the Federal Government Should Be Concerned with Housing

During much of American history, the federal government did not play any significant direct role concerning housing. It assumed each individual household would provide its own shelter as best it could and ignored any resulting deficiencies. But the Great Depression of the 1930s produced a threat of massive financial foreclosures on home mortgages. To prevent this outcome, the federal government launched a multi-faceted set of policies concerning housing. This approach resulted from the federal government's belief that housing has special characteristics differentiating it from other consumer goods and warranting special federal and other government interest. Most important, owning one's own home had become a central desire of nearly all American households. It symbolized both economic and personal success and participation in the responsibilities of citizenship. Homeowners tended to maintain their homes and neighborhoods better than renters, and to participate more fully in civic life. Therefore, homeownership deserved governmental encouragement. Yet homeownership required long-term commitment by individual households of large amounts of capital—far more than they could finance out of their current incomes.

Hence homeownership could not become widespread unless appropriate financial institutions existed for gathering capital out of society's savings. Those institutions also had to remain viable and to have strong incentives to lend their capital to homebuyers. Supporting, regulating, and stimulating such institutions in the depressed economic conditions of the 1930s required direct federal policy intervention.

Both the construction and financing of housing are large-scale activities. Hence, they are of vital importance to the federal government in its role of helping to keep society economically prosperous. In addition, access to adequate shelter is a necessity for all citizens. Yet many poor households cannot afford decent quality housing because it is the most expensive single item in most households' budgets. This fact puts it in a class different from most other requirements of life. Therefore, the federal government has an interest in helping such persons find shelter as part of its promotion of the general welfare.

Finally, housing has a community aspect because, in highly urbanized societies, the nature of each dwelling and what goes on there has "spillover" effects that influence the quality of life nearby. The quality of community life is an important concern of governments, since they must regulate many aspects of that life and provide services for it. This community aspect is mainly a concern of local and state governments. However, there are immense financial disparities among communities across the nation; so the federal government has an interest in making opportunities geographically more equal, based upon its promotion of the general welfare. Also, many communities and their local governments exhibit racial discrimination, segregation, and other prejudices that violate the individual rights of minority and other groups. The federal government has a responsibility for protecting the rights of such groups.

Thus, a number of federal concerns have evolved during the past six decades that justify the federal government's taking an active interest in developing and carrying out an effective national housing policy.

Appropriate Housing-Related Roles for the Federal Government

The main housing-related roles I believe appropriate for the federal government are set forth below. All have already been declared by Congress or previous Administrations to be appropriate federal activities and performed by the federal government at some time or other.

Federal Role Number 1: Financial Housing Subsidies

The federal government should finance a major portion of all resource-redistributive housing and other aids to low-income households. This includes various forms of housing and income subsidies that are considered appropriate, including housing vouchers and subsidies for the construction of new housing units.

Discussion. I believe a key role of the federal government is that of financing all public activities requiring major redistributions of economic resources from middle- and upper-income households to low-income households. Most large-scale solutions to low-income housing and poverty problems require such redistribution. Effective attacks on physically inadequate housing, over-crowding, homelessness, and desubsidization will also require provision of money by someone other than the households benefiting from those attacks.

Why couldn't state and local governments provide the required funds? If such governments attempt to tax their middle- and upper-income residents so as to provide greater assistance for their low-income residents, many of the former will move to other jurisdictions to escape taxation. This is especially likely with small local governments, such as those in most suburbs. Residents of such communities can usually find similar housing nearby quite easily without having to change jobs. Even state governments may find some of their residents moving to nearby states to escape high redistributive taxes, as many New Yorkers have moved to Connecticut and New Jersey. Only the federal government can impose such taxes upon its middle- and upper-income residents without much fear that they will move to some other nation.

That is why I believe an appropriate role for the federal government is to provide funding for resource-redistribution, though not necessarily to administer those funds. This role is especially crucial in reducing the extent of low-income housing problems, because what most low-income households need is more income, rather than better housing.

Federal Role Number 2: Maintaining a General Economic Climate Favorable to Housing Transactions

Through appropriate monetary and fiscal policies, the federal government should help create and maintain a general economic climate conducive to high-level construction and sales of new housing units; high-level financing and sales of existing housing units; and adequate job opportunities and income levels for households.

Discussion. This role implies maintaining a general economic climate marked by relatively low nominal interest and inflation rates, and steady but not extremely high rates of real economic growth (since very high rates of real economic growth would probably generate rapid inflation and high interest rates). Of course, the federal government cannot and should not influence general economic conditions so as to serve only the interests of housing consumers and the housing industry. Rather, it must consider the welfare of all other sectors, and take account of the inherently cyclical nature of the national and world economies.

Because housing production and sales levels are so heavily influenced by interest rates, this role of the federal government is one of the most important of all from the viewpoints of both housing consumers and housing producers.

Federal Role Number 3: Regulating and Supporting Housing Finance Institutions.

The federal government should regulate and support existing institutions engaged in both primary and secondary financing of home mortgages so they can remain economically viable and thereby make adequate funds available to households who want to buy or refinance homes. This includes providing credit guarantees for certain types of housing finance.

Federal Role Number 4: Encouraging Maximum Feasible Private-Sector Actions Regarding Housing.

The federal government should encourage efficient use of resources in housing by maximizing the roles performed in housing markets by private firms as opposed to public agencies. Specifically, it should encourage homeownership among all types of households and encourage maximum use of private firms to plan, finance, build, and operate subsidized housing.

Federal Role Number 5: Attacking Racial Discrimination in Housing.

The federal government should vigorously enforce all federal laws against racial and other ethnic discrimination in housing markets. It should take an active role in "testing" for the presence of discriminatory practices, and in bringing suit against those engaging in such practices. It should also encourage state and local governments to increase their enforcement efforts.

Discussion. Repeated experience in explicit field tests and in the Experimental Housing Allowance Program indicates that racial discrimination is still prevalent in housing markets and greatly reduces the housing choices of minority-group members. Use of such programs as housing vouchers will not be nearly as effective in markets which discriminate as in those which do not. Hence, the federal government has a vital interest in attacking such discrimination all across the nation.

Federal Role Number 6: Setting General Housing Quality Standards.
The federal government should set general standards of acceptable housing quality for units subsidized with federal funds. But it should leave detailed standards for such quality to be determined by local authorities (possibly subject to periodic federal review).

Federal Role Number 7: Developing a Comprehensive National Housing Policy.
The federal government should develop a comprehensive national housing policy from combinations of specific policies that effectively reduce low-income and other housing problems. But it should also constrain total federal spending on housing assistance within limits related to reducing the federal budget deficit.

Appropriate Housing-Related Roles for Other Key Actors

This section describes what I believe are appropriate housing-related roles for key actors other than the federal government whose behavior affects housing problems. However, this chapter is written primarily for, and from the perspective of, the federal government, so this section merely lists important housing-related roles for these other actors without detailed discussions or justifications of such role assignments.

State governments should

(1) Finance infrastructures.
(2) Help finance more low-income housing.
(3) Press for lower-cost housing regulations.
(4) Encourage scattering of low-income housing.
(5) Enforce anti-discrimination laws.
(6) Politically support federal low-income housing aids.
(7) Act as an arbiter among local governments and as a forum for discussion among them concerning low-income housing issues.

Local governments should

(1) Protect local property values.
(2) Permit "balanced" mixtures of local housing.
(3) Reduce local obstacles to lower-cost housing.
(4) Strengthen local tax bases.
(5) Enforce anti-discrimination laws.
(6) Encourage development of, and supporting, public-private partnerships aimed at providing more housing for low-income households.

Private sector components of the housing industry

Homebuilding firms should

(1) Construct housing.
(2) Rehabilitate housing.
(3) Participate in housing subsidy programs.
(4) Politically support federal low-income housing aids.

Nonprofit, housing-oriented organizations should

(1) Construct new housing units for low-income households.
(2) Rehabilitate existing housing units in distressed neighborhoods.
(3) Encourage residents of low-income neighborhoods to improve their own areas through self-help efforts.
(4) Develop housing for homeless persons.

Realtors and realtor firms should

(1) Sell and rent homes fairly.
(2) Politically support federal low-income housing aids.
(3) Press for lower-cost housing regulations.

Financial institutions engaged in enabling households to buy, sell, and own housing include commercial banks, savings banks, savings and loan associations, mortgage bankers, secondary mortgage market firms, federally-linked housing credit agencies (such as GNMA, FHLMC, and FNMA), and pension funds that buy mortgages and mortgage-backed securities. These institutions should combat housing problems by

(1) Providing adequate and affordable mortgage credit.
(2) Politically supporting federal low-income housing aids.
(3) Developing local below-market-rate programs.
(4) Pressing for lower-cost housing regulations.

Responsibility for Funding Housing Assistance

Another major housing policy question is which public or private actors should be responsible for funding the following: (1) housing-oriented assistance for low-income households; (2) housing-oriented assistance for non-low-income households; (3) creation, repair, or maintenance of housing-related infrastructures, such as highways, streets, and water systems; and (4) credit-cost-reduction programs designed to make housing finance easier for households of any income.

Resolution of the funding issue depends upon what roles each of the major actors relevant to housing policies is presumed to perform. The following sections briefly describe where responsibility for each of these types of funding ought to lie.

Funding housing assistance for low-income households. The federal government should exercise primary responsibility for such funding. As pointed out earlier, only the federal government can raise substantial tax revenues to be used in redistributing resources from non-poor to poor households without providing strong incentives for the former to leave its area of tax jurisdiction.

That does not mean that state and local governments cannot or should not provide any funding for low-income housing. State governments can do so—at least to some extent—with much less risk of driving high-income residents from their boundaries than local governments would incur. Hence, states can and should supplement federal funding to a limited extent. But local governments should be expected to provide very little funding.

Funding housing assistance for non-low-income households. State or local governments which provide housing assistance for non-poor households run much less risk of driving high-income residents out of their areas of jurisdiction than those which provide such aid to poor households. An example is the use of state powers of condemnation and land-value write-down to assemble urban renewal parcels on which developers subsequently build high-rent apartments. The federal government, therefore, should confine its direct housing assistance largely to low-income households, leaving it up to individual states and localities to fund housing assistance programs aimed at the non-poor.

Two counter-arguments were raised against this recommendation by reviewers of this study. One is that federal subsidies encouraging creation of mixed-income rental projects containing, say, 80 percent market-rent and 20 percent low-rent units provide these key benefits: they make it easier to locate subsidized housing in suburban neighborhoods that oppose mainly-low-income projects, thereby scattering more poor households in desirable environments outside concentrated poverty areas; and they impose market discipline on the quality of construction and level of costs incurred by developers of low-income housing units, because those units must be part of market-oriented projects. A second counter-argument is that including federal aid to first-time homebuyers—who do not have low incomes—in any overall federal housing strategy would increase the political feasibility of getting that strategy passed.

Federal housing aid hardly seems focused on the poor when the tax benefits of homeownership accrue largely to middle- and upper-income households. The potential tax revenues sacrificed by the Treasury each year because of such benefits are much larger than the direct expenditure costs of *all* housing subsidies to low-income households combined.[4]

Consequently, in theory, an excellent way to fund housing assistance for low-income households would be to reduce the existing tax benefits received by relatively high-income households. In 1981, 73.5 percent of total tax benefits from mortgage interest deductions went to taxpayers with incomes of $30,000 or more, although they were only 18.8 percent of all taxpayers. Conversely, 63.4 percent of taxpayers had incomes under $20,000, but they received only 7.6 percent of all the tax benefits from mortgage interest deductions.

Thus, homeownership tax benefits provide enormously disproportionate aid to high-income taxpayers, even though they need such aid least. Reducing only partly the amount of assistance they receive would make substantially more funds available for housing assistance to low-income taxpayers without increasing federal deficits. It would also increase the equity of housing assistance considered as a whole. By reducing homeownership tax benefits less than 20 percent—and taking almost all of that reduction from high-income households—the United States government could probably pay for a housing voucher entitlement program serving all eligible very-low-income renter households who applied.[5] Those potential recipients need federal housing assistance far more than the affluent homeowners whose tax benefits would be reduced by such a policy. Moreover, this policy would considerably decrease housing affordability problems among very-low-income households.[6]

However, experience shows that Congress has not been willing to touch existing homeownership tax benefits, even when drafting and adopting an overall Tax Reform Act in 1986. In fact, few, if any, elected officials in the United States are willing to oppose, or even to suggest reducing, current homeownership tax benefits. The main reason is that nearly two-thirds of all U.S. households own their own homes.[7] Moreover, the asset values of their homes usually represent their largest investments; so they want to preserve the current advantages they get from homeownership tax benefits. Therefore, recommending that Congress adopt such a policy is likely to prove futile. Nevertheless, that is my recommendation, because I believe adopting it would be more just, more effective, and more efficient than present policies.

Funding creation, repair, or maintenance of housing-related infrastructures. In the past, four different types of actors have contributed to this type of funding. Local governments traditionally financed streets, water systems, and sewer systems for new residential developments within their own boundaries, usually with general revenue bond issues. Until recently, the federal government also provided substantial funds for highways, sewage treatment plants, and some sewer and water systems. However, federal funding for all these purposes other than highways has been greatly reduced in the 1980s. State governments also funded highways, and still do. They sometimes assisted in financing other types of infrastructure too.

Very recently, local governments constrained by limits on their property taxing ability have shifted many infrastructure costs to private developers. Some localities require developers to dedicate land to streets, schools, and parks; and to build streets, sewer systems, water systems, schools, and recreational facilities serving their own projects. In some areas, local governments even require developers to build facilities serving projects not being created by those developers themselves, in order to get building permits for their own projects.

This chapter is not the proper place to debate the wisdom of shifting infra-structure costs from local governments to developers—and therefore to occupants of newly-developed subdivisions. Given the federal budget deficit, it makes sense for the federal government to leave infra-structure financing to other levels of government and to private parties. Only in those cases where local housing infrastructure requirements result from standards mandated by federal law is there much rationale for federal financing. That applies mainly to some sewage treatment and other pollution control facilities. Also, the federal government should probably maintain the Interstate Highway System, since that was a federally-funded project initially justified on grounds of national defense.

But for the most part, financing housing infrastructure should be a responsibility of state and local governments and private developers. Exactly how those actors should divide this responsibility is an issue beyond the scope of this discussion.

Funding credit-cost reduction programs for housing finance. Insofar as the reduction of housing credit costs is done directly and is intended to benefit low-income households, it is a housing subsidy for low-income households. Therefore, financing it should be the responsibility of the federal government, for reasons stated earlier.

However, there are indirect ways of reducing housing credit costs, too—and their benefits do not flow only to low-income households. For example, the federal government provides deposit insurance for savings accounts of up to $100,000 at banks and savings and loans. This insurance enables those institutions to raise funds from households at lower interest rates (paid to savers) than would otherwise be possible. Hence those institutions can make mortgage loans to homebuyers at lower rates than they could if they did not have such federal insurance. Most of the borrowers who gain from such lower mortgage interest rates are not low-income households, but middle- or upper-income ones.

Provision of this insurance has two possible costs to the federal government. One is a higher cost of federal borrowing generally. In theory, since bank and thrift savings accounts up to $100,000 are just as secure as Treasury securities, the Treasury has to pay slightly higher interest rates on its bonds and notes to attract funds than it would if that were not the case. However, no one knows how much higher these rates are.

The second cost is very large; it results from the recent bankruptcy of the Federal Savings and Loan Insurance Corporation (FSLIC).

It is reasonable to conclude that if reducing housing credit costs requires public funding, responsibility for such funding should lie with the federal government. That is precisely why Congress is paying billions to preserve the savings and loan industry.

The Level of Federal Funding for Housing Assistance Programs

As noted earlier, only federal funding can overcome on a large scale the income deficiencies of low-income households. The amount of money the federal government spends on housing assistance each year is probably the single most important variable determining the nature of any comprehensive housing policy strategy.

Annual federal spending on housing assistance can be divided into two types: continued support for already-assisted units and support for adding more assisted units to the present inventory. Therefore, careful distinctions must be made between outlays and budgetary authority in discussing levels of federal funding.

The federal government already assists about five million households in occupying housing. That assistance absorbs large federal outlays (current spending) each year. However, the budgetary authority (authorization to spend in the future) for providing such assistance was granted in the past, and is not part of current outlays. Moreover, the annual outlays resulting from past contractual obligations cannot be reduced without breaching the contracts concerned.

Consequently, the issue of how much the federal government should spend on housing assistance each year should be divided into two sub-issues: (1) how much must it spend currently on supporting already-assisted housing to meet its contractual obligations? and (2) how much additional assistance should it obligate itself to spend in the future on more assisted units?

For convenience of discussion, I have arbitrarily defined four alternative levels of federal funding on assisted housing as follows:

(1) Minimal federal funding: Continuing existing outlays but requesting no budgetary authority for additional assistance.
(2) Moderate federal funding: Continuing existing outlays and requesting enough budgetary authority to add 200,000 households per year to the total number being assisted. That is about one-half the number added during the years of maximum additions (the early 1970s under the Nixon Administration and the late 1970s under the Carter Administration).
(3) High-level federal funding: Continuing existing outlays and requesting enough budgetary authority to add 400,000 households per year to the total number being assisted. That is about the maximum number ever added in any one year. However, it equals only about 1 per-

cent of all low-income households in the U.S. and about 2.6 percent of all low-income households who are suffering from some housing problem and not now receiving federal housing assistance. Hence it would take over 35 years of such additional assistance each year to aid all those households.

(4) Maximal federal funding: Continuing existing outlays and requesting sufficient budgetary authority to add enough households per year to the total number being assisted so as to aid within 15 years all 20 million low-income households that in 1983 were suffering from some type of housing problem, as defined earlier. About 15 million low-income households were suffering from some type of housing problem in 1983 but not receiving any federal housing aids. But an estimated 3.7 million of these households received welfare assistance of some type, presumably including some shelter allowances.[8] Hence this standard implies funding aid to an additional 11.3 million households in 15 years, or about 753,000 more each year. That is 88 percent more than received federal funding in the highest previous year ever (1972). (In order to attain the same target in 10 years, the annual increment would have to be 1.13 million households, or almost triple the previously highest level.)

Under current budgetary conditions, these four alternatives not only cover but go well beyond the whole spectrum of practical possibilities. However, the exact amount of money required for each of these levels would vary, depending upon the specific forms of aid chosen, as discussed later.

Which of these four federal funding levels should be incorporated into a comprehensive national housing policy? The answer is clearly a matter of subjective judgment. I believe the moderate federal funding level represents a desirable target that Congress should try to reach in the near future. It may be unable to raise funding of federal housing assistance to that level immediately, because of the constraint imposed by large current overall federal budget deficits. But it should begin gradually moving from present minimal federal funding to this higher—but still moderate—funding level.

This recommendation will be considered grossly inadequate by those who believe the nation now faces a catastrophic "housing crisis." But I believe funding at either of the two higher levels described above is not politically feasible in the near future under present budgetary circumstances.

The Level of State and Local Funding

During the 1980s, because of a sharp decline in annual *additional* federal housing assistance, state and local funding has become much more important to reducing low-income housing problems. Moreover, state and local governments are not bound by federal regulations concerning how they use their own funds (unless they combine those funds with federal funds). So state and local money should be used in more flexible ways, and can be better adapted to local conditions.

However, funding levels for such money can differ in each state and locality; so it is not practical to define overall levels for the entire nation based upon aggregating regional variations. Actors in each state and locality can therefore define the alternatives for this issue most relevant to the communities in which they operate.

The Level of Private-Actor Commitment

Any private-sector firm, non-profit organization, or other organization desiring to help overcome low-income housing problems must make some initial decision about roughly how many resources it is prepared to use in such an effort. The resources involved could include time, money, materials, and attention from its top leadership. This initial decision will help focus its attention upon tactics that would require about that level of resources. After analyzing possible tactics and other elements of its potential strategy, the organization should select those it believes are best for itself. Then it can refine its initial estimate of the resources required.

An immense variety of tactics related to low-income housing problems could be fruitfully carried out by an equally immense diversity of private actors. Therefore, it is impossible to become more specific here about how such actors should determine what size or type of commitments they ought to make, and exactly how they should proceed. Each actor must make such determinations for itself.

Issues Concerning the Allocation of Federal Resources

Several key aspects of a comprehensive national housing policy deal with how those federal resources to be used for housing assistance should be allocated among different activities. These issues are discussed in this section. Not all can be resolved satisfactorily, even in theory. However, their most salient aspects are at least addressed, and specific recommendations are made where possible.

Relating Federal Housing Aids to Other Federal Low-Income Assistance

One of the most complicated and intractable issues connected with federal housing-oriented assistance is its relationship to other forms of federal aid, especially to low-income households. Such other forms include direct income assistance (such as Aid to Families with Dependent Children and Supplemental Security Income) and in-kind assistance (such as food stamps and health care assistance).

The nature of federal assistance. Most such assistance is designed to raise the effective incomes of poor or other low-income households.[9] This can be done either by paying them money, or by providing them with in-kind benefits. Housing assistance can be of either type. Housing vouchers pay recipients money directly, though the recipients are required in return to live in decent-quality housing units. Other housing subsidies reduce the costs to the recipients of occupying decent-quality housing units; hence, they are essentially in-kind benefits.

Why coordinating different forms of federal assistance is desirable. For several reasons, it would be highly desirable to coordinate all forms of federally-funded aid to low-income households. First, some forms of aid are more efficient than others; hence, there is an a priori case for using more of the former and less of the latter. For example, housing vouchers cost less than half as much per household aided per year as new construction subsidies.

Moreover, direct cash payments to households without any requirements that the recipients live in decent-quality housing would be even more efficient than housing vouchers. This would be true because annual administrative costs per household of "no-strings" cash payments would be lower and the percentage of eligible households who actually use the aid would be higher. In addition, direct cash payments with "no strings" permit the recipients to do whatever they want with the money. In contrast, housing vouchers require the recipients to spend enough on housing to allow them to occupy decent-quality units.

On the other hand, experience with federally-funded welfare programs shows that millions of households receiving relatively "no strings" forms of aid live in substandard housing units, or pay very high fractions of their incomes to occupy standard units, as noted earlier. This has caused some expert analysts to recommend offering low-income households two levels of housing aid: a relatively high level per household for households occupying standard quality units, and a lower level for those who choose to occupy substandard units.[10] However, such a "two-tier" system would perpetuate two existing conditions that the same analysts complain about: federally supporting occupancy of substandard units by households receiving welfare, and maintaining many housing quality standards among similar households receiving welfare in different localities and regions.

A second reason for coordinating different forms of federally-funded aid to the poor would be to minimize negative impacts upon the nation's labor supply. Direct payments of cash to low-income persons reduce their incentives to work harder. Such reductions in incentives also occur from in-kind benefits, though they are probably smaller.

Large-scale social experiments conducted in the United States show that providing low-income households with enough cash beyond what they earn themselves to bring their incomes up to the poverty level tends to reduce their work effort by between 5 and 10 percent.[11] This reduction is concentrated in the work effort of secondary earners, especially women, rather than primary earners. Nevertheless, it is surely a significant social cost of providing such assistance.

Moreover, the adverse labor-supply effects of federal aid are aggravated when several aid programs impose separate "implicit income tax rates" upon benefit recipients. An implicit income tax rate exists when a household that raises its earned money income thereby reduces the benefits it can receive from some assistance program. This drop in benefits offsets some of the gains from having earned a higher income; hence, it can be perceived as an implicit tax on that income.

For example, a housing voucher program may provide a household with the difference between 30 percent of its annual earned income and a standardized average cost of a decent-quality housing unit. If the household increases its income by $1,000 per year, it thereby loses benefits equivalent to 30 percent of that increment. That amounts to a 30 percent marginal tax rate upon any increases in its income—above and beyond legal federal income tax rates.

If a household is receiving several different types of federally-funded assistance, each one of them may impose a different implicit income tax rate upon any increase in the household's earned income. These rates can add up to very high combined rates at the margin.[12] That results in a diminished incentive for members of the household to earn more income directly.

Two other reasons to coordinate federally-funded assistance programs are to reduce overlapping and to increase consistency of treatment. If eligibility rules for one form of aid do not require households to report other forms of aid as part of their incomes, they will be considered poorer than they really are by administrators of the first form of aid. Hence, they may receive more assistance than Congress intended them to have. Also, when different programs have varying eligibility rules, persons in the same circumstances may receive widely-varying amounts of federal assistance, depending upon which specific forms of aid they receive.

Using housing vouchers vs. "no strings" cash income supplements. A high fraction of housing voucher assistance really acts as a direct income supplement unrelated to housing. The Experimental Housing Allowance Program showed that households receiving vouchers used most of the added money to increase their spending on things other than housing.[13] This is perfectly consistent with the purpose of housing vouchers, which is to reduce the economic burden of housing costs upon low-income households.

But if what most low-income households really need to overcome housing affordability problems is more money income, why not just pay them directly? Why link their receipt of this added income to housing, at all? Two advantages would accrue from abolishing such linkages. The administrative costs of "pure" income maintenance programs are notably lower than those of a housing voucher program. Also, the percentage of eligible households who actually participate in "pure" income maintenance programs is much higher than the percentage who participate in housing voucher programs. Voucher recipients must live in housing certified to be of decent quality; whereas recipients of "pure" income maintenance do not need to meet this requirement. Yet meeting such a housing quality requirement often takes considerable effort, such as moving or repairing one's housing unit.

Therefore, some economists argue that housing vouchers should be replaced by a combination of "pure" income maintenance subsidies and new construction subsidies.[14] The former should not even be administered by HUD, but by the Department of Health and Human Services (HHS), which administers most other federal direct income assistance programs.

Many members of the homebuilding industry have attacked housing vouchers with opposite motives. They recognize that much of the funding used for housing vouchers is not spent on housing; therefore, it does not benefit the homebuilding industry. Hence, they want nearly all housing assistance money to be used for new construction subsidies. But they would also oppose shifting housing assistance funding from HUD to HSS or other federal departments concerned with "pure" income maintenance.

Theoretical ways of integrating diverse forms of federal assistance. Many past studies have been made of the problems of coordinating diverse forms of federal assistance. In summarizing a book on this subject that she edited, Irene Lurie identified the following possible solutions: (1) merging all existing forms of federal assistance to low-income households into a single program, such as a negative income tax; (2) consolidating different federal assistance programs into a smaller number of programs by merging those most closely related; (3) dividing the beneficiaries of all such programs into different categories, and providing a separate program to aid each category; (4) redesigning programs so that their benefits increase with earned income or with the number of hours worked, so as to end negative work incentives; (5) converting some programs into forms of insurance; and (6) having each program take better account of other benefits, for example, by counting them as income when computing its own level of support.[15] Only the first alternative—replacing all present forms with a single cash payment system—truly solves all problems of coordination generated by the interrelationships of such programs. However, this alternative has other difficulties; moreover, Congress has rejected this approach several times in the past.

Taking account of political realities. Another important aspect of this issue involves the difficulties of obtaining political support for any federal programs that tax a majority of citizens (those with moderate, middle, and upper incomes) to benefit a minority (those with low incomes). One way to increase such political support is to tie the benefits received by the low-income minority to specific products, such as food, housing, and health care. By giving low-income households such "in-kind" or "tied" benefits instead of cash, the federal government increases the demand for those particular products. That benefits the industries creating those products, whose members therefore gladly support such programs. Experience shows that Congress is far more willing to pass appropriations for such industry-supported forms of aid than it is for "pure" income maintenance. Therefore, anyone who wants to aid low-income households as much as possible should support several in-kind benefit programs, rather than one all-cash program—in spite of the theoretical superiority of the latter.

Conclusion. There is no "ideal" resolution of this issue. My own views are essentially identical to those put forward by Henry Aaron, from whom I therefore quote the following passage:

As an analyst, I would conclude that the federal government should not institute a general program of housing allowances or rapidly expand existing construction-related subsidies.[16] Instead, I would urge that, at the margin, resources should be directed at reforming the system of unconstrained cash assistance (in other words, welfare programs) and to continuing programs of modest scale to meet the housing needs of particular groups. I would also emphasize the desirability of project-grant authority to assist in restoring or preventing decay in particular neighborhoods with new construction or demand subsidies, as the particular needs of diverse communities dictate. . . .

As a policy maker, I would judge the foregoing findings and conclusions as incomplete and oversimplified. . . . As a policy analyst interested in giving more help to low-income households, I would support a link between construction-related subsidies and demand subsidies similar to housing allowances. In short, I would support a program with the same elements as the section 8 program—a combination of construction-related subsidies and demand subsidies in one program. I would try to make the part of the program devoted to allowances as large as possible, certainly larger than the part devoted to construction.[17]

Relative Emphasis on Specific Forms of Housing Aid

Once the federal government has decided how much money to spend on housing assistance in any given year, it must also decide how to allocate those funds among several alternative forms of housing assistance. There are four main forms:

(1) Increasing the housing purchasing power of low-income households to help them pay for whatever types of housing units they choose to occupy. This can be done either by supplementing their incomes through housing vouchers or by reducing their rental costs, paying

owners of the units they occupy, and thus reducing the rents charged to such households. Rent supplement programs are of this type.

(2) Encouraging the construction of new housing units for occupancy by low-income households through various subsidies. These units can be either owned by public authorities, as in past public housing projects, or owned by private parties, as in Section 8 units.

(3) Encouraging the rehabilitation of existing housing units for occupancy by low-income households or perhaps by other types of households. These units can also be either owned by public housing authorities or owned by private parties.

(4) Maintaining now-subsidized units in subsidized status, rather than having them shifted to non-subsidized status by their owners.

In reality, deciding how much to spend altogether for housing aids is not independent of deciding what forms those aids should take. That is true because some forms of housing aid (such as housing vouchers) cost much less per household aided per year than other forms (such as building new public housing units). Hence decisions about total spending and about how to allocate funds among specific forms of aid are usually made simultaneously. Or they are made through an iterative process of going back and forth between these two issues until some mutually consistent results are arrived at concerning both. However, in this analysis, these two issues are considered separately.

In allocating total federal housing aids, it is reasonable to devote the greatest number of resources to forms of aid that will deal most effectively with the most serious and widespread housing problems. The housing problem affecting by far the greatest number of households concerns affordability. The most direct and effective means of coping with that problem is increasing the housing purchasing power of low-income households. Hence they are best aided through housing vouchers or rent supplements of some type.[18]

This reasoning leads to what can be called a demand-side subsidy strategy. It emphasizes either housing vouchers paid directly to very-low-income households, and perhaps to moderately-low-income households or rent supplements paid to their landlords. Housing vouchers permit the beneficiaries themselves to look for their own housing. Hence, this strategy delivers housing assistance directly and immediately to those households who need it most. Almost all observers believe this is the best strategy in metropolitan areas that already have "loose" rental housing markets, as Houston did in 1987.

But this strategy might not work well in metropolitan areas with very "tight" rental markets. There the supply of vacant rental units available to voucher recipients is small; an example is the Boston metropolitan area in 1987. It might be necessary to subsidize construction of additional rental units to reduce low-income housing problems in such areas. That means using a supply-side subsidy strategy.

Shortages of vacant rental units are not the only reason why a purely demand-side strategy might not work in some areas. Experience in both the Experimental Housing Allowance Program and the Section 8 existing program indicates that the main reason housing voucher recipients have difficulty finding available rental units is racial discrimination against minority households. This was often a much more important factor than any absolute shortage of vacant rental units. The percentage of voucher recipients who were unable to find acceptable units has almost always been highest among black households looking for housing in mainly-white areas. Hence, rigorous enforcement of anti-discrimination laws may be just as important to the success of low-income housing strategies as adding to the available supply of rental units.

New construction subsidies may also be needed to provide certain types of units not normally furnished by the market, such as those for very large families. Finally, unlike housing vouchers, new construction subsidies allow locational targeting of housing assistance to specific areas. One example is that of building low-income housing in very high-cost areas like Montgomery County, Maryland, to provide better job and school opportunities to low-income households, and to ease local labor shortages.

An important consideration is that housing vouchers have typically cost about one-half as much per year for each household aided as most new construction subsidies. Hence, the same amount of public spending per year can aid twice as many households if used as vouchers than if used to build new units. However, this may not be true in those metropolitan areas such as Boston where real rents have been rising quite rapidly.

Subsidy costs for building new units are much lower if shallow (small per household) subsidies are used, rather than deep (large per household) ones. Yet only the latter enable very low-income households to live in newly-built units. Shallow subsidies on new units can be used only for moderately-low-income households, and perhaps not even for them, because such subsidies do not bring rents down very far below market rents. On the other hand, shallow subsidies permit creating more new units per million dollars of public funds spent than deep subsidies.

The above discussion omits two other forms of housing aid cited above: rehabilitation and preventing now-subsidized units from becoming desubsidized. Both seek to maintain or improve the usefulness of existing housing units as shelter for low-income households, rather than adding to the existing supply. However, rehabilitation does add to the existing supply of good-quality units by upgrading poor-quality ones. Past rehabilitation programs have been divided into three types, depending upon the amount of work done on each unit. Substantial rehabilitation requires major renovation; it is usually just as costly as new construction. Moderate and minor rehabilitation cost less per unit than new construction, but more than housing vouchers. Moreover, they add to the supply of good-quality units, whereas housing vouchers usually do not.[19] Hence, rehabilitation should be considered a supply-side tactic, along with new construction. In fact, these four tactics should be considered close substitutes for each other on the supply side of the market.

How much of the federal housing aid going into any metropolitan area should be used for rehabilitation rather than building new units depends upon specific conditions in that area. Rehabilitation has the advantage of causing far less public resistance from nearby residents than the construction of new subsidized housing units for low-income occupancy. On the other hand, sometimes the rents charged for rehabilitated units are much higher than those formerly charged for the same units. That may cause some displacement of low-income households. This can generate major local resistance among poor households likely to be displaced.

This discussion emphasizes a conclusion to be reinforced later in another section: in theory, a separate strategy for allocating federal housing resources among alternative forms of aid ought to be developed within each metropolitan area to suit specific market conditions there.

It is not possible to make sensible recommendations at this time concerning how many federal resources ought to be devoted to preventing desubsidization. Not enough is known about how many now-subsidized units are likely to be taken out of that status during each year in the near future, or where those units are located, or what it would take to prevent such desubsidization. Hence, comments on these subjects must await development of more information about potential desubsidization. See Chapter 12 in this volume by Clay and Wallace.

Relative Emphasis on Aiding Low-Income Households

In the past, not all public funds used for housing assistance have aided low-income households. Many households who used federally-tax-exempt bond funding for their home mortgages had incomes far above their area medians. The tax shelters built into past subsidies for rental housing development benefited high-income investors, while providing units occupied by low-income households. In many rental projects aided by federal subsidies, only 20 percent of the units were occupied by low-income households; the rest paid market rents. Either they or the developers therefore gained from such subsidies.

Another aspect of this issue involves tax benefits received by homeowners. These tax benefits are not exactly comparable to those received from the direct expenditure of public funds. Tax benefits prevent the loss of income through taxes; whereas public spending makes available additional income raised from other people by taxes. Yet both certainly increase the well-being of their recipients. Moreover, as pointed out earlier, the annual revenues "sacrificed" by the U.S. Treasury through homeowner tax benefits are much larger than the annual public costs of all direct housing subsidies paid to low-income households. Furthermore, most homeowner tax benefits are received by relatively high-income households. Thus, the nation's present overall housing policy—including homeowner tax benefits—confers much larger publicly-financed benefits upon upper-income households than upon very-low-income households or even upon all low-income households.

So one crucial aspect of this issue is: to what extent should the housing aids provided by public funds—or other benefits generated by public policies—be focused upon low-income households as compared to moderate-, middle-, and upper-income households?

A second crucial aspect is: among low-income households, to what extent should housing subsidies be focused upon very-low-income households, as compared to moderately-low-income households? The former presumably have more acute needs, but also require larger subsidies per household aided. This raises the question of shallow vs. deep housing subsidies, which is discussed below, along with the next issue.

Where to Insert New Subsidized Housing Units into the Existing Supply

Understanding this issue requires a brief explanation of how the "trickle-down" process works.[20] That process has always been the major source of housing for the vast majority of low-income households in the United States, and still is. Most new housing units of all types are built on vacant land at the periphery of already-built urban areas. In the United States, building and zoning codes require that all such new housing be of relatively high quality; hence, most low-income households cannot afford to occupy new units. Instead, upper-income and middle-income households move into new units as they are built on the urban periphery.

As these units age, they become less attractive to relatively affluent households, especially if they deteriorate. Even if they are well-maintained, they become functionally obsolete compared to newer units built farther out on the periphery. Hence the most affluent households move out farther to still newer units. Other households move into these no-longer-new units, which may still be in excellent condition. These other households are somewhat lower on the income distribution than the original occupants. Yet they have high enough incomes to keep the units in good shape.

More time passes, and these same units become even more functionally obsolete and probably somewhat deteriorated. So their occupants move on to newer units, and other households still farther down in the income distribution move in. This process repeats itself until the once-brand-new housing units have "trickled down" through the income distribution to low-income households. By that time, the units may be 20 to 30 years old or even older. Many are in rather poor physical condition. That is one reason why even very-low-income households can afford to occupy them. In this way, the "trickle-down" or "filtering" of privately-owned housing units provides homes for households of all income groups, including the poorest. It has been the major source of housing for the poor throughout American history.

With this analysis as background, consider the question posed by this strategy issue: where in the "trickle-down" process should public funds be used to insert additional housing units so as to benefit low-income households? Any such "insertion" amounts to a supply-side subsidy strategy because it involves creation of additional housing units (in contrast to a pure demand-side strategy like using only vouchers). There are four main alternative supply-side subsidy strategies:

(1) The no-direct-subsidy supply-side strategy. The only public funds used to influence the housing supply are tax benefits provided to homeowners. These encourage middle- and upper-income households to buy new homes, thereby adding to the total supply. This strategy inserts new housing units into the supply only at the top of the process.

(2) The deep-subsidy supply-side strategy. Directly-subsidized new units are built for occupancy by very-low-income households. This requires large subsidies per household and amounts to inserting new subsidized housing units at the bottom of the "trickle-down" process.

(3) The shallow-subsidy supply-side strategy. Directly-subsidized new units are built for occupancy by moderately-low-income or even moderate-income households. This amounts to inserting new subsidized units in the middle of the "trickle-down" process.

(4) The two-sided subsidy strategy. Very shallow subsidies are used on the supply side of the market—so shallow only moderate-income households can afford the subsidized rents. But the money saved through smaller subsidies per household permits building enough new subsidized units to add significantly to the overall supply. That lowers rents throughout the market, including in previously-existing rental units. Then housing vouchers are provided to low-income households, enabling them to occupy "decent" older units, which now have lower rents.

Each of these alternatives has major advantages and disadvantages, as described below.

No-direct-subsidy supply-side strategy. When no direct housing subsidies are used on the supply side of the market, improvements in low-income housing must come entirely through either operation of the "trickle-down" process or demand-side subsidies, such as housing vouchers. For purposes of analysis, it will be assumed that no demand-side subsidies are used either. Hence, this overall approach eliminates the cost of direct housing subsidies and avoids conflicts over where to locate new subsidized units.

But the "trickle-down" process only benefits low-income households in a given area when total new housing production exceeds net new household formation there by large absolute amounts for several years. Then an "excess supply" accumulates that "loosens" the entire market substantially. Downward pressure appears on rents and housing prices, especially in the most deteriorated neighborhoods. In fact, extensive housing abandonment may occur there, as in the late 1960s and early 1970s. At least the balance of supply and demand becomes more favorable to tenants.

Unfortunately, there are many imperfections in the "trickle-down" process. By the time older housing units become available to very-low-income households, those units are often deteriorated and undesirable. Also, the process often does not work well across racial lines, and there are racially-divided housing markets in many metropolitan areas. And it does not work at all whenever new housing starts fall low relative to the total of net new household formations and removals of housing from the inventory. The most recent such period was in the early 1980s.

Finally, this process compels most very poor households to live together in the oldest and most deteriorated neighborhoods in each metropolitan area. In many places, these neighborhoods become dominated by undesirable conditions often associated with extreme poverty. Examples are high rates of unemployment, crime, delinquency, mental illness, broken homes, arson, and physical decay.

Deep-subsidy supply-side strategy. Providing brand new housing units for occupancy by very-low-income households is a vastly superior strategy for those households who receive the required deep housing subsidies. It gives public assistance directly and immediately to the households with the greatest housing needs. It also permits achieving various locational objectives, because subsidized new units can be placed on specific sites, as discussed earlier.

However, such a deep-subsidy supply-side strategy has three major drawbacks. First, deep subsidies are so costly that only a small number of households can be aided by them per million dollars of public funds spent. This means that the overall percentage of income-eligible households who will actually receive such subsidies is likely to be quite low.

Also, this strategy does not add to the total housing supply as much as a shallow-subsidy supply-side strategy would with the same total expenditure. This provides a smaller spillover gain to those low-income households who do not receive direct subsidies than would creating a larger net addition to the total rental supply.

A spillover gain from new subsidized units occurs when the number of such units built is so large, in relation to the entire market, that the overall balance between supply and demand is perceptibly altered. Total supply expands faster than total demand within a given period. This exerts downward pressure on the rents of all nearby units throughout that income-segment of the market, including unsubsidized units.[21] Thus, construction of new subsidized units can aid many low-income households besides those who live in the new units themselves. Since most low-income households do not live in subsidized housing, spillover effects that benefit them are important. Those effects might even be larger in the aggregate than the direct benefits received by households living in new subsidized units.

However, beneficial spillover effects only occur when the number of new subsidized units is very large, as in the early 1970s. Then those effects were enormous. They actually helped cause massive housing abandonment in the poorest neighborhoods of many big cities, because there was such an overall surplus of housing. In contrast, if only a few new subsidized units are built each year, as in the past few years, their spillover effects are insignificant.

The second drawback of deep subsidies is that they provide very-low-income households with brand new units that are often of better quality than the housing occupied by the taxpayers who are paying for the deep subsidies. This seems quite unfair to the latter.

The third disadvantage of deep supply-side subsidies is that they generate intense controversies about where to locate the new subsidized units. Most non-low-income households do not want very-low-income households as neighbors.

Shallow-subsidy supply-side strategy. Compared to a deep-subsidy supply-side strategy, a shallow-subsidy one has several advantages. First, it creates more new units for low-income households per million dollars of public funds spent. Second, shallow subsidies tend to generate less intense locational controversies. Nearby residents are likely to object less vehemently to new moderately-low-income neighbors than to new very-low-income ones. Therefore, it is easier to mix the former type of households into projects where a majority of units are at market rents.

Finally, shallow subsidies permit creation of larger overall increases in the total housing supply per million dollars spent on subsidies. This can produce larger positive spillover effects benefiting unsubsidized low-income households living nearby. However, such spillover effects are significant only if the number of new subsidized units is quite large, relative to the previous local housing supply affordable by low-income households.

The biggest drawback of shallow subsidies is that they do not concentrate public aid on those households with the greatest need.

Two-sided subsidy strategy. This approach has two major parts. One is using subsidies to stimulate as large an increase in the total rental housing supply as possible, without regard to who occupies the new units. This can best be done with very shallow supply-side subsidies. Only moderate-income households— not low-income ones—can afford the subsidized rents. If the resulting total increase in the rental supply is big enough, it will put downward pressure on rents throughout the market, via the spillover effects described earlier.

The second part of this dual strategy is to provide low-income households with housing vouchers so they can occupy previously existing decent-quality rental units. The rents of such units will have fallen because of the big spillover impact of the new shallow-subsidy units on the overall market.

In theory, this combination could provide the greatest overall benefit to low-income households. It aids both those who receive housing vouchers and those who occupy previously-existing units in which rents have fallen. But in practice, this strategy is effective only if a huge number of new subsidized units are built each year. Otherwise the spillover effects are too small to reduce rents very much in surrounding unsubsidized units.

Only rarely has total production of new subsidized units been large enough to make this strategy work for the nation as a whole. However, it has worked in a few specific markets where very large numbers of new subsidized units were built in a short time, compared to the total size of those local markets.

Mixing supply-side strategies. In practice, it is possible to combine deep and shallow subsidies in various mixtures, rather than focusing exclusively upon one or the other. Hence mixed supply-side strategies are often used. Designing such mixtures means accepting a "balanced compromise" of some type combining the advantages and disadvantages of each major strategy discussed above.

The optimal geographic scale for housing strategies. Since all housing markets are metropolitan-area-wide or smaller in scope, rather than national or even statewide, the most appropriate geographic scale at which to apply any of these strategies is the metropolitan-area level. This means the optimal overall housing policy strategy would permit designing a different specific housing strategy for each metropolitan area, rather than using a single strategy in all such areas nationwide. That conclusion has a direct bearing upon how federally-funded housing programs should be administered.

Issues of Intergovernmental Relationships in National Housing Policy Implementation

Several key issues relevant to a comprehensive national housing policy concern how the programs it contains should actually be carried out "in the field." But the execution of housing programs is always done in places that lie within jurisdictions both other than, and in addition to, that of the federal government—namely, state and local government. Such governments are inescapably involved in the implementation of all federal housing policies.

Appropriate Administrative Arrangements

Designing the most appropriate arrangements for administering federally-funded programs within a comprehensive national policy requires answering three key questions:

(1) At what governmental level should specific housing programs be administered?

(2) Through what specific funding devices should federal funds be supplied?

(3) How should administration of various federal housing assistance programs be allocated among federal agencies, specifically the Department of Housing and Urban Development and the Department of Agriculture, which contains the Farmers' Home Administration (FMHA)?

The answers to these questions are closely interrelated, because the specific funding devices appropriate to a given program will vary, depending partly upon at what level that program is administered. Although some of the answers have already been discussed in earlier sections, these questions are discussed further below.

Specific administrative levels and funding devices available. Housing subsidies for low-income households are best funded by the federal government, but the funds involved do not have to be administered in detail from the federal level. They could also be administered at the following levels: (1) multi-state regions, (2) states, (3) counties, (4) metropolitan areas, (5) multi-county regions within states, (6) specialized functional agencies serving any of the above, (7) local governments, and (8) private firms. Several different specific funding devices are possible, each usually associated with certain particular levels of administration. These devices are listed below, in descending order of the degree of discretion each allows to the state or other governments or private parties involved in spending the money:

Revenue sharing occurs when the federal government allocates specific amounts directly to lower-level governments in accordance with a basic formula, and permits those governments to do whatever they wish with the money. It provides the greatest degree of discretion to those bodies. The allocation formula normally involves local characteristics such as population, real income levels, and amount of tax effort.

Flexible block grants also involve the federal government's allocating specific amounts directly to lower-level governmental bodies in accordance with a basic formula. The receiving agencies can be at the state, regional, local, or metropolitan-area levels. Each receiving agency has great discretion over what is done with this money, but must conform to purposes set forth by very broad guidelines. The allocation formula is usually based upon local conditions concerning variables relevant to the purposes of the grant, such as population, percentage of residents in poverty, average age of housing, and so forth.

Narrowly-defined block grants are similar to flexible ones, but require the receiving agencies to spend the money within relatively narrowly-defined parameters set by the federal government.

Categorical programs require lower-level governments or private actors to prepare project proposals and apply to a federal agency (such as HUD) for funding. The agency evaluates all such proposals in accordance with specific criteria furnished in advance to potential applicants. This arrangement by-passes state and local governments, except insofar as project sponsors must receive local permission for constructing new buildings, etc.

Matching grants can be used in connection with any of the above devices, but require that the lower-level body spending the money raise a certain amount of funds from its own sources in order to qualify for receipt of federal funds. Different matching formulas can be used, in which the amount of locally-raised funds required to receive each dollar of federal funds varies. In some cases, the local agencies can use in-kind services as part or all of their own contributions. Matching grants create incentives for the lower-level agencies spending federal money both to take responsibility for meeting some program costs themselves, and to use all the funds they spend more efficiently—since some of them are their own.

The greater the flexibility and discretion permitted to lower-level program administrators, the more likely it is that the money will be used in ways closely adapted to local conditions, and in close accordance with local goal priorities. However, local priorities often differ greatly from the objectives Congress had in mind when it appropriated the money.

Thus, all arrangements for administering federal funds involve trade-offs between (1) closely adapting the uses of those funds to local needs and purposes, and (2) closely pursuing federal policy objectives. No arrangement maximizes attainment of both these goals simultaneously.

Selecting the levels and devices most appropriate for administering federal housing assistance. It is especially important to permit great low-level discretion concerning the administration of federal funds for low-income housing. This is true because housing markets operate at metropolitan-area-wide levels or even smaller jurisdictional levels rather than state-wide, region-wide, or nationally. Hence, housing policies should often be quite different in different metropolitan areas, or even in sub-portions of a single metropolitan area. Those policies will not be well adapted to actual conditions in many areas if a single strategy is required throughout the nation, or even throughout each state.

Unfortunately, there are very few strong governmental agencies at the metropolitan-area level. Hence federal policy-makers are in a dilemma: should they entrust discretion over federal housing-related funds to the state level—which is too big geographically—or the local level—which is usually too small and is often plagued by narrow parochial perspectives? There is no satisfactory answer to this question. Instead, many federal programs target a portion of their funds at states and another portion at individual communities.

Another approach would be for the federal government to ask state governments to create new, special regional administrative agencies to handle federal housing assistance funds at appropriate geographic levels. These agencies would have jurisdiction over entire metropolitan areas or entire multi-county rural regions within each state. The Economic Development Administration, for example, has created Economic Development Districts in parts of some states. However, such an approach is not likely to be very effective in administering federal housing assistance funds.

For one thing, existing laws and regulations governing housing markets are now mainly made by local governments. Hence no new subsidized housing can be built within the boundaries of any community without permission of its local government. Few local governments, if any, will be willing to yield that authority to some new regional decision-making body. Those governments least likely to yield such authority are precisely the ones controlling areas where it would be most desirable to place at least some new subsidized units—that is, middle- and upper-income suburban communities.

Another problem would be determining how the members of the new regional housing agencies would be selected, and whether they would perceive of themselves as representatives of their own local governments, or representatives of the region as a whole. Thus, if the members were appointed by mayors or other leaders in lower-level governments, they would be likely to act as representatives of those governments. If they were elected at large, or appointed without reference to local government officials, they might perceive themselves as representing the entire region. In that case, local government officials would be highly unlikely to cooperate closely with the new agency.

Past experience with new regional agencies of this type suggests that they are not likely to be very effective, unless the facilities they are funding are obviously regional in nature because of the spatially-extensive technology involved. That is true of regional highway systems, some water systems, some sewer systems, communications systems, and population control systems. But it is not true of housing. All the housing markets within a single metropolitan area are both economically and sociologically related to each other, and somewhat interdependent. But they are not technologically linked; hence, governments likely to gain from treating their own markets as totally separate from all others are technically able to do so.

For these reasons, I do not believe the federal government should mandate the creation of new, regional agencies at the metropolitan-area level for the administration of federal housing assistance funds.

Using a two-level federal block grant. Rather, I tentatively suggest that the federal government allocate specific funding amounts to each metropolitan area or rural region, but leave it up to state governments to determine exactly what agencies ought to administer those funds. This arrangement would require some type of block grants. The formula for allocating funds to those grants should not be based upon population alone, but should also take account of other relevant factors. They might include the age of each metropolitan area's housing stock, the property tax burden its governments place upon local residents (the higher the burden, the greater the effort they are making themselves; hence, the more federal funds they should receive as a positive incentive to making such efforts); the percentage of households living in poverty there; and the percentage of housing units in substandard condition there.

This approach would have the advantage of tying total housing assistance funding to genuine housing markets, since a certain amount of money would be potentially allocated to each metropolitan area or rural region. It would also have the advantage of shifting actual administration closer to genuine housing markets, since presumably each state would allocate funds to lower-level agencies in those markets. And it would take the federal government out of the detailed fund-allocation business by leaving those decisions up to state governments.

Such an arrangement could be combined with a state or local fund-matching requirement. That would avoid having local fund administrators view federal housing funds as entirely "free money" that could be spent with much-less-than-maximum regard for efficiency or effectiveness. However, imposing a fund-matching requirement makes it hard for the poorest areas to participate in federal housing assistance programs as easily as less poor areas, even though the former need the help more.

Technical problems in funding a two-level block grant. The block-grant approach suggested above raises a key technical problem. No Congress can bind the future decisions of later Congresses; hence, the only way a specific Congress can set up a block grant program to run longer than its own political lifetime is to appropriate a large amount of federal budget authority in one year that can be used to fund annual federal outlays over many later years. This tactic was used in the urban renewal program in the 1960s. But it tends to distort federal financing by lumping in one year's budget a large sum intended to be spent over many years. Thus, Congress is likely to resist this tactic under present stringent budgetary conditions.

Furthermore, such "front-loaded" funding limits the alternative forms of housing aid that state and local governments can offer with these federal funds. Many types of housing subsidies require annual payments of small amounts of subsidy over long periods: housing allowances and interest-rate subsidies, for example. But transferring federal funds appropriated in a single year to lower-level governments to be parceled out by them over many years raises technical difficulties under current laws governing disbursement of federal money. There might be much less flexibility in what state and local governments could do with these block grant funds than is implied by the analysis justifying this overall approach. No fully satisfactory resolution of this problem can be offered by this study.

Allocating housing assistance functions among federal agencies. At present, two different federal departments—HUD and the Department of Agriculture—both administer housing assistance programs. The latter does so through its Farmers' Home Administration (FMHA). It administers programs very similar to those run in the past by HUD, but directs them at rural areas rather than urban areas. From the viewpoints of both administrative neatness and development of a single coherent and comprehensive national housing policy, this schizophrenic arrangement makes little sense. In fact, the main reason for perpetuating it is that the Department of Agriculture has typically had much more political support and power than HUD. Therefore, some housing assistance programs run by FHMA have survived longer and been better funded than similar programs run by HUD. If administration of those programs were transferred to HUD, they might soon be cut back even more than they have been up to now.

Nevertheless, in the long run, it would be sensible to administer all housing assistance programs within a single federal department, rather than in two departments. Hence, the activities of the Farmers' Home Administration should be transferred into the Department of Housing and Urban Development.

Pursuing Locational Objectives with Housing Assistance Funds

A purely demand-side housing subsidy strategy for attacking low-income housing problems might never encounter any locational issues. Eligible households within each market area could be given vouchers and permitted to find accommodations wherever they wanted to and could. When such a household found and occupied a housing unit, its neighbors would not need to know either that the household was receiving a housing subsidy or that it was a low-income household.

However, any housing strategy that involves constructing new subsidized units for low-income households cannot avoid locational issues. There is no escaping the question: "Where will those units be built?" Moreover, all new subsidized units are highly visible, and local governments must give explicit permission in advance for their construction. Thus, everyone in the vicinity will know they are subsidized units, and where they will be built, long before construction begins.

As a result, housing strategies involving the construction of many new subsidized units must deal with the first locational question listed below, and may deal with the others. These questions are:

Can locations be found for these new units someplace where all local objections can be overcome and permission therefore received to build them?

Can the new units be located so as to reduce existing poverty concentration in the metropolitan area as a whole?

Can these new units be used to demonstrate physical improvement in deteriorated neighborhoods?

Can the new units be used to increase economic and other opportunities for low-income households in neighborhoods that are mainly moderate-, middle-, or upper-income, and thereby reduce shortages of labor there?

These questions are discussed in turn below.

Getting local permission. The first question is crucial. Persons living near sites proposed for new subsidized units who do not want low-income households as neighbors can object to the creation of those units in the early planning stages. In fact, residents in hundreds of neighborhoods across the nation have successfully rejected the proposed creation of new subsidized units in or near them. This is a variant of the "NIMBY syndrome": "Not In My Back Yard!" Thus, working out acceptable accommodations with the local government and nearby neighborhood groups is essential to any strategy involving construction of new subsidized housing.

Reducing poverty concentration. Because so many communities have resisted new subsidized housing, most such units have been located in or near low-income neighborhoods within large cities. Residents of such areas are less likely to object to having new low-income neighbors than are residents of middle- or upper-income neighborhoods. Hence, construction of new subsidized units often increases the concentration of low-income households within already-poor neighborhoods, or at least within big cities with higher-than-average portions of low-income residents.[22] Such increases are socially undesirable; so it is usually preferable to place new subsidized units away from existing low-income neighborhoods. This is most easily done when the units are scattered on several sites, with only a few on each site. That minimizes neighborhood perceptions of being "invaded" or "overwhelmed" by low-income newcomers. However, scattered-site placement also increases per-unit construction and management costs.

Upgrading deteriorated areas. Where low-income neighborhoods have become deteriorated and blighted, it may be desirable to reverse the preceding strategy by deliberately placing new subsidized units *within* such areas. This upgrades these areas with brand new housing, improving both the quality of local structures and the areas' general appearance. It also demonstrates public commitment to making these areas better places to live.

Increasing outlying economic opportunities. Another locational tactic is to place new subsidized units in fast-growing suburban areas far from most existing low-income neighborhoods. This has the dual advantage of providing better job and educational opportunities to the low-income residents, and relieving shortages of unskilled workers often found in far-out suburban areas. However, it requires persuading suburban governments to accept such units. That is probably done most easily when the new units to be occupied by low-income households are supported politically and partly financed by a state housing agency; integrated into a project containing a majority of market-rent units; and located in small clusters rather than in one big project.

Should the federal government try to pursue locational objectives with its housing assistance funds? In the past, federal attempts to pursue locational objectives through its administration of housing assistance funds have not been very effective. In some cases, federal administrators strongly discouraged locating new subsidized housing units for low-income occupants in or near existing low-income areas. But such efforts usually resulted in very few new subsidized units being built at all. Local residents and local governments in non-poor neighborhoods usually vehemently resisted placement of new subsidized units there.

Similar resistance by suburban communities has made it difficult to locate new subsidized units for low-income households in fast-growth suburban areas where job opportunities were expanding most rapidly. Hence, the only locational strategy objective that federal authorities have succeeded in attaining has been helping to up-grade deteriorated areas. I believe the federal government can best pursue these locational objectives by delegating their attainment to state governments, especially to state housing agencies. This would be part of transferring the administration of federal housing assistance funds to state or lower-level agencies. If Congress expresses these locational objectives in its legislation, federal authorities can put pressure on state administrators to pursue those goals. The most notable successes at doing so in the past have been accomplished by state housing agencies anyway, such as the one in Massachusetts.

However, this approach means that state housing agencies should be required to put pressure on local governments to accept low-income housing units in order to qualify for other benefits, such as having their residents eligible to receive mortgage funds obtained through selling tax-exempt state bond issues. The state housing agency in Massachusetts has developed a number of instruments and incentives for accomplishing this goal.

The Level of Quality Standards and Local Regulations

A crucial influence upon housing costs consists of local government regulations determining what quality standards, building methods, and densities are required for new units. Many local governments have adopted requirements that raise the per-unit costs of housing far above the minimum necessary to meet basic health and safety standards. They have done so in response to pressures from their residents to maintain high-quality residential environments. But such regulations also raise housing costs far beyond what many households can afford—including many moderate-income ones and almost all low-income ones.

Legal control over such regulations rests with local governments. Experience shows that it is almost impossible for the federal government to exert much influence over suburban communities that deliberately use such regulations to exclude low-income households. Federal officials have little leverage in changing such behavior.

State governments have more leverage upon local governments. States have constitutional power over localities, and usually fund more local services in many suburbs than does the federal government. However, most state governments have been reluctant to pressure suburban governments to change their local land-use regulations. In most states, all suburbs combined contain more voters than any other type of jurisdiction. Hence elected state officials are not anxious to antagonize suburban officials.

Furthermore, federal regulations themselves impose relatively costly building requirements upon subsidized housing units. One is the Davis-Bacon requirement that builders pay locally-prevailing union wage rates. Most private residential builders today use non-union labor at much lower wage rates. Moreover, builders of subsidized units must go through much longer and more complicated administrative and application procedures than builders of non-subsidized units. As a result, extensive experience shows that new housing units built under federally-subsidized programs—no matter who builds them—typically cost 20 to 35 percent more than similar units built by private developers without subsidies. That is one reason why housing vouchers cost so much less per household aided than subsidized new construction programs.

One way to reduce such costs would be to build smaller housing units for low-income households than typical of market-rate units. Another would be to use inexpensive mobile homes for low-income households. Up to now, both these tactics have been strongly opposed by some low-income groups themselves as discriminatory. Many believe they deserve to live in the same quality units as moderate- or middle-income households, even though they cannot afford to pay for such quality. Their opposition has been reinforced by most local governments, which are unwilling to lower quality standards for low-income units built within their boundaries.

As a result, few formulators of housing strategies have made much progress at lowering housing construction costs by altering existing local housing or zoning regulations. Therefore, the federal government should not place high priority upon trying to change local regulations of this type through its administration of housing assistance funds. Rather, it should express making such changes as a desired goal, and delegate to state governments the responsibility for accomplishing them.

Summary of Recommended Specific Housing Policies

Earlier sections of this chapter have presented discussions of key housing policy issues. In the course of these discussions, many recommendations have been made concerning specific housing policies that I believe ought to be incorporated into a comprehensive national housing policy. These recommendations are listed below. Each is linked to the particular key issue it is designed to resolve. In a few cases, I have included specific recommendations here that were not spelled out explicitly in earlier discussions. However, those added recommendations are consistent with earlier discussions.

This set of recommendations comes as close as I can get to framing a comprehensive national housing policy. How well it meets the criteria of desirability for such a policy is discussed at the end of this section.

These recommendations represent my own views about what specific policies should be incorporated into a comprehensive national housing policy. Many other people will have very different views, and will therefore prefer other specific policy recommendations. However, I believe that any persons or organizations wishing to formulate a fully comprehensive national housing policy must make at least some recommendations about all the issues set forth below.

This conclusion does not mean that all organizations seeking to create a national housing policy appropriate to their own purposes must make it as comprehensive as the one set forth in this study. An organization could develop what it could legitimately refer to as a "national housing policy" appropriate for its own purposes by dealing with only some relevant subset of all the issues discussed below. Exactly which issues such a policy must include in order to be considered a truly "national" policy I leave to the reader's judgment.

Specific Housing Policy Recommendations

Issue Number 1. What housing-related roles is it appropriate for the federal government to perform?

> *Financing housing subsidies for low-income households.* The federal government should finance a major portion of all resource-redistributive housing and other aids to low-income households, including housing vouchers and subsidies for the construction of new housing units.

> *Maintaining a general economic climate favorable to high levels of housing transactions.* Through appropriate monetary and fiscal policies, the federal government should help create and maintain a general economic climate conducive to high-level construction and sales of new housing units, high-level financing and sales of existing housing units, and adequate job opportunities and income levels for households.

> *Regulating and supporting housing finance institutions.* The federal government should regulate and support existing institutions engaged in both primary and secondary financing of home mortgages so they can make adequate funds available to households who want to buy or refinance homes, and so they remain economically strong and viable. This includes possible provision of federal credit guarantees where necessary.

> *Encouraging maximum feasible private-sector actions regarding housing.* The federal government should encourage efficient use of resources in housing by maximizing the roles performed in housing markets by private firms as opposed to public agencies. Specifically, it should encourage homeownership among all types of households and encourage maximum use of private firms to plan, finance, build, and operate subsidized housing.

> *Attacking racial discrimination in housing.* The federal government should vigorously enforce all federal laws against racial and other ethnic discrimination in housing markets. It should take an active role in "testing" for the presence of discriminatory practices, and in bringing suit against those engaging in such practices. It should also encourage state and local governments to increase their enforcement efforts.

> *Setting general housing quality standards.* The federal government should set general standards of acceptable housing quality for units subsidized with federal funds, including maximum quality standards. But it should leave detailed standards for such quality to be determined by local authorities.

Developing a comprehensive national housing policy. The federal government should develop overall housing strategies from combinations of specific tactics that effectively reduce low-income and other housing problems, but also constrain total federal spending on housing assistance within limits related to reducing current high levels of federal budget deficits.

Issue Number 2. What housing-related roles is it appropriate for other key actors to perform?

Setting their own agendas. The federal government should encourage states, localities, and private actors to undertake any and all housing-related roles that will help the nation meet its housing goals.

Issue Number 3. What public or private actors should be primarily responsible for funding the following?

Housing-oriented assistance for low-income households. The federal government should have primary responsibility for funding such assistance. However, state governments can also make significant contributions to this funding.

Housing-oriented assistance for non-low-income households. State governments and private actors—especially the households themselves—should have primary responsibility for funding such assistance. The federal government should finance as little such assistance as possible, unless it adopts a strategy requiring a mixture of shallow-supply-side subsidies and market-rate units in the same projects to maximize total increases in the rental housing supply.

One equitable source of federal financing of housing assistance for low-income households would be a partial reduction of the size of federal homeownership tax benefits now received by high-income households.

Creation, repair, and maintenance of housing-related infrastructures. State and local governments should have primary responsibility for funding such activities, with two exceptions. The federal government should have primary responsibility for building and maintaining the Interstate Highway System and for financing facilities to meet environmental quality standards which federal legislation has mandated.

Credit-cost reduction programs designed to make housing finance easier. The federal government should have primary responsibility for formulating and carrying out policies specifically designed to reduce housing credit costs to existing and potential homeowners. The private sector, including savings and loan associations, mortgage banking firms, banks, and secondary mortgage market firms, should also have significant responsibility for creating and operating such programs.

Issue Number 4. How much money should the federal government spend on housing-oriented assistance?

Moderate federal funding. The federal government should have as a spending "target" enough annual outlays and budgetary authority to add 200,000 households per year to the total number being assisted. That is about one-half the number added during the years of maximum additions (the early 1970s under the Nixon Administration and the late 1970s under the Carter Administration). However, because of the stringent budgetary situation that exists when federal deficits are large, it may be desirable for federal housing expenditures to rise gradually over time from their 1987 level to this higher "target" level.[23]

Issue Number 5. How much money should state and local governments and key private actors spend on housing-oriented assistance?

Setting their own spending levels. The federal government should not attempt to determine the spending levels appropriate to state governments, local governments, and private actors concerning housing. Rather, it should encourage them to undertake any and all housing-related roles that will help the nation meet its housing goals, when combined with responsible performance by the federal government of the federal roles described above. Such encouragement could take the form of providing matching grants for funds from state and local governments and even from private actors.

Issue Number 6. How should federally-funded housing assistance programs be related to other forms of federally-funded assistance to low-income households, such as welfare and food stamps?

Relating federal housing-oriented assistance to welfare reform. Specifically, the following alternatives should be considered:

If welfare reform and expansion are adopted: The federal government may adopt significant welfare spending reforms that result in non-housing assistance providing a much higher level of income support to poor households than was the case in 1987. In that case, federal emphasis upon housing assistance should be relatively restrained. The housing affordability problems of many low-income households would then be remedied by higher welfare spending or income derived from jobs related to welfare programs.

In that case, federal housing assistance should emphasize new-construction-oriented housing subsidies, since the income-support function of housing vouchers would already be taken care of by higher levels of welfare spending.

If welfare reform and expansion are not adopted: The federal government may not adopt welfare spending reforms like those described above. In that case, federal emphasis upon housing assistance should reach the levels of spending described in the discussion of Issue Number 4 above.

In that case, federal housing assistance should emphasize both housing vouchers and new-construction-oriented housing subsidies, but primarily the former, since vouchers are more effective at remedying housing affordability problems.

Issue Number 7. What proportions of all the federal government resources used for direct housing aid (that is, excluding tax benefits) should be spent for (1) income supplementation (as with housing vouchers), (2) constructing new housing units for low-income occupancy, (3) rehabilitating existing privately-owned units, (4) rehabilitating existing public housing, and (5) maintaining now-subsidized units in subsidized status?

Dependence on welfare reform. To some extent, the proper policy concerning this issue depends upon whether welfare reform and higher levels of welfare spending are adopted, as discussed concerning Issue Number 6 above. However, the remaining discussion of this issue set forth below assumes that no major welfare reform or higher levels of welfare spending will be adopted in the near future.

Dependence on desubsidization research. To some extent, the proper policy concerning this issue also depends upon further research about the magnitude and nature of potential desubsidization—that is, the removal of now-subsidized units from subsidy status. Three possible policy responses are described below; which should be chosen depends upon the results of further research.

(1) If that research indicates that many thousands of now-subsidized units are likely to be desubsidized in the near future, and that this could be avoided by federal spending per unit similar to that required for a housing voucher program, then using federal funds to avoid such desubsidization should have very high priority among the five forms listed above. It should even take precedence over using housing vouchers outside of existing subsidized projects, since retaining households in such projects avoids disruptive relocation.

(2) If that research indicates that many thousands of now-subsidized units are likely to be desubsidized in the near future, but that avoiding this result would require spending more per unit than housing vouchers, but less than new construction, then using federal funds to avoid such desubsidization should have only moderate priority among

the five forms listed above—probably lower priority than housing vouchers, but higher than new construction subsidies.

(3) If that research indicates that not many now-subsidized units will be desubsidized in the near future, or that preventing such units from becoming desubsidized would be more costly per unit than building new units, then using federal funds to avoid desubsidization should have very low priority among the five forms listed above.

Transferring resolution of this allocation issue to lower levels of government. Ideally, decisions about which of these specific forms federally-funded housing assistance should take should be made at the metropolitan-area level in urbanized areas and the regional housing market level in rural areas. Then, different mixtures of forms could be designed to suit particular conditions in each metropolitan or regional area. In order for this to occur, federal funding for housing assistance would have to take the form of some type of block grant of undifferentiated funds, made to each state or each metropolitan or rural regional area, to be used within that state or area as the decision-making authorities there thought best. That would require allocating federal funds among states or metropolitan and rural regional areas in accordance with some type of formula based upon relevant factors.

Thus, resolution of this issue is closely interrelated to resolution of the "appropriate administrative arrangements" issue. If it is possible to transfer decisions about how to allocate federally-funded housing aid among the above forms to lower levels of government, and still be confident that those lower levels would pursue federal housing goals, such a shift would be desirable. If it is not possible to transfer such allocation decisions to lower levels of government, then the considerations set forth below should be determining.

Resolving this allocation issue at the federal level. If resolution of this allocation issue cannot be transferred to lower levels of government, it will have to be done at the federal government level. How it should be resolved there depends heavily upon the total resources available for all these forms of housing assistance, as follows:

(1) If only relatively small amounts of federal funds are available for housing assistance, nearly all those funds should be used in the form of housing vouchers for very-low-income households. Housing vouchers address housing affordability problems more effectively than any other forms (except perhaps reducing desubsidization, if that costs no more per unit than housing vouchers). Moreover, housing vouchers cost about one-half as much per year per household aided as other subsidies. In this case, it would be necessary to use a

demand-side subsidy strategy, because not enough funds would be available to permit using them to augment existing housing supplies.

(2) If moderately-large amounts of federal funds are available for housing assistance (though much more than in 1987), a mixture of different forms should be used, though vouchers should receive considerably more than all other forms combined. All forms used should predominantly aid low-income households, with emphasis upon very-low-income households. In this case, it might be possible to use a deep-subsidy supply-side strategy, which concentrates new construction subsidies on units for immediate occupancy by very-low-income households.

(3) If very large amounts of federal funds are available for housing assistance, those funds should be more evenly divided between housing vouchers and all other forms of assistance, though vouchers should receive no less funding than all other forms combined.

In the third case, it might be possible to use a shallow-subsidy supply-side strategy or a two-sided subsidy strategy. In those strategies, shallow new construction subsidies would be used to maximize the total number of new units built per dollar of federal aid. That number would be large enough to affect the market prices of nearby non-subsidized rental units, thereby aiding non-subsidized low-income households. Housing vouchers would be used to insure that an appropriate share of those new units were occupied by very-low-income households. Under this strategy, many housing vouchers would be tied to specific housing units.

Issue Number 8. What proportion of all the federal government resources used for housing aid should be spent directly to aid low-income households, as compared to aiding moderate-, middle-, or upper-income households?

Concentration on low-income households. The federal government should confine its direct housing assistance funding as much as possible to aiding low-income households. The only exception would be using such assistance to maximize the total number of additional rental units built under a shallow-subsidy supply-side strategy or a two-sided subsidy strategy, in which federal assistance is used to support rental projects occupied by a mixture of low-income and other households.

Taking homeownership tax benefits into account. In deciding how to allocate federal funds for housing assistance among different income groups, Congress should take account of homeownership tax benefits and how they are distributed among income groups. This could assume two forms.

Congress should recognize that (1) homeownership tax benefits cause much larger net costs to the federal government than the outlay costs of all direct forms of housing subsidies combined, and (2) middle- and upper-income groups receive the vast majority of all homeownership tax benefits. These facts provide a solid moral basis for concentrating all direct federal housing assistance on aiding low-income households.

In order to increase housing aid to low-income households without raising federal spending, Congress should also consider a partial reduction of homeownership tax benefits—especially those now going to upper-income households. This could be done while still preserving most existing homeownership tax benefits, and therefore without attacking the basically sound idea of encouraging homeownership.

Making aid to non-low-income households dependent on the total amount of federal housing assistance funds available. The federal government should not provide significant housing assistance to non-low-income households—including first-time homebuyers—unless large amounts of federal funds are available for housing assistance of all types.

Issue Number 9. Where in the "trickle-down" process—that is, at what income level—should federal funds for housing aid be used to insert additional new housing units into the existing inventory?

Interdependence of this issue with others. Proper policies concerning this issue are closely interrelated with policies adopted concerning other issues, especially issues number 4, 7, and 8 discussed above and issues 11 and 12 discussed below. In particular, the answer to this question depends heavily upon the total amount of federal assistance available for housing, discussed under issue number 4.

All federal housing policies will encourage insertion of most newly-built housing units—which are unsubsidized—at relatively high-income levels as long as homeownership tax benefits are concentrated at those levels. In fact, such "high-level" insertion of new units would also be dominant even if no homeownership tax benefits existed. Higher-income households will always be more easily able to afford newly-built units—which are relatively expensive—than other income groups; so most new units will always be occupied by higher-income households. Hence the "trickle-down" process is almost sure to remain the principal means by which low-income households are supplied with housing, even if federal housing assistance expands to much higher levels than its present level.

However, in addition:

If only a small amount of federal housing assistance is available, it should be used mainly to finance housing vouchers. Such vouchers would enable low-income households to occupy existing units, rather than new ones; so federal housing aids would be concentrated on inserting new units at relatively high income levels, though homeowner tax benefits.

If a large amount of federal housing assistance is available, it should also be used to finance construction of a significant number of new units to be occupied directly by low-income households. Then federal housing aids would be concentrated on inserting new units at both low-income levels through such new building and at high-income levels through continuation of homeowner tax benefits.

If large enough amounts of federal housing assistance are available to use either a shallow-subsidy supply-side or a two-sided subsidy strategy, some of that assistance would help create market-rent units to be occupied by middle- and moderate-income households in projects where low-income units were also mixed in. Then federal housing aids would be inserting new units at relatively low-income levels by using vouchers for those low-income units, at moderate- and middle-income levels for the market-rent units in those projects, and at high-income levels through continuation of homeowner tax benefits.

Issue Number 10. How should federal housing assistance be related to needs among occupants of federally-assisted housing units for receiving other social services, such as home health care, personal counseling, and job training?

Non-treatment of this issue in this chapter. This issue is not analyzed here; hence no policy recommendations are presented about it.

Issue Number 11. How should federal funds for low-income housing be administered? At what governmental level should detailed fund allocation decisions be made? What specific mechanisms should be used to make such administration effective?

Resolution of this issue was already dealt with under Issue 7.

Issue Number 12. Should federal housing assistance be used to further specific locational objectives (such as avoiding further concentration of poor households in deteriorated neighborhoods)? If so, which ones, and to what extent?

Shifting pursuit of locational objectives to lower administrative levels. The federal government should declare the desirability of using federal housing assistance funds to achieve certain locational objectives. These would include generally avoiding further concentration of low-income households in poor neighborhoods; upgrading such neighborhoods physically in a few cases; and locating subsidized housing for low-income households in areas that both lack such housing and are experiencing rapid job growth. The federal government should encourage lower-level agencies to pursue these locational objectives to the maximum extent feasible, periodically review their efforts to do so, and use their success in doing so as one criterion for deciding what agencies will receive future federal housing assistance funds.

Issue Number 13. What housing quality standards should be required in federally-assisted housing? Should federally-funded housing assistance programs aim at reducing construction costs required by local government regulations that seem excessive?

Housing quality standards in federally-assisted programs. The federal government should usually require that all housing units its funds assist meet prevailing local minimum quality standards concerning health and safety wherever that housing is situated. It should not impose additional quality standards upon such units under normal conditions.

Attempting to reduce "excessive" quality standards set by local governments. The federal government should establish maximum housing quality standards for health and safety, and initially require that no locality impose quality standards beyond those maximum standards on federally-assisted units. Probably the most effective way to do this would be to set maximum permissible cost amounts per unit, rather than by dealing with detailed physical specifications. If this approach results in very few federally-assisted housing units being located outside low-income neighborhoods, it should be modified to avoid that outcome.

* * * *

The views in this paper are solely those of the author, and not necessarily those of the Brookings Institution, its Trustees, or its other staff members.

Notes

1. This list of Congressionally-defined objectives is taken from Anthony Downs, *Federal Housing Subsidies: How Are They Working?* (Lexington, MA: Lexington Books, 1973) 1–2. Another set of secondary target goals taken from past legislation is also presented there. One of those secondary goals has been elevated to primary status here, because Congress officially adopted it in 1974. It is: "Reducing the concentration of low-income households in poverty areas." The primary target goals stated here are virtually identical with the eight major housing goals cited by Henry Aaron in "Policy Implications: A Progress Report," in K. L. Bradbury and A. Downs, eds., *Do Housing Allowances Work?* (Washington: Brookings Institution, 1981) 70–76.

2. From Section 2 of the National Housing Act of 1949. Taken from Committee on Banking, Currency, and Housing of the House of Representatives, *Basic Laws and Authorities on Housing and Community Development, Revised through July 31, 1975* (Washington: 94th Congress, 1st Session, July 31 1975) 1.

3. This situation causes a serious problem from the viewpoint of the housing construction industry, but may not be a problem from the viewpoint of the welfare of the nation as a whole. The nation's economy benefits from having a large industry capable of both rapid expansion and rapid contraction in total output, without serious diminution of its long-run productive capacity. Housing construction is such a flexible sector. Hence, what is a problem of cyclical instability from the viewpoint of the housing construction industry, is an advantage of counter-cyclical activity from the viewpoint of the nation as a whole.

4. See Congressional Budget Office, *The Tax Treatment of Homeownership: Issues and Options* (Washington: CBO, September 1981) especially p. 7.

5. See A. Downs, *Rental Housing in the 1980s* (Washington: Brookings Institution, 1983) 144.

6. Such a housing voucher entitlement program would not fully eliminate housing affordability problems among very-low-income households, even though these households would all be eligible for assistance. The reason is that not all eligible households actually apply for and receive housing vouchers, as shown by the Experimental Housing Allowance Program. Some refrain because the vouchers they are eligible for would be too small to justify all the required "red tape"; others because they oppose receiving any federal "handouts"; others because racial discrimination makes it hard for them to find housing that has enough quality to qualify for voucher payments; and others for unknown reasons. Altogether, about 50 percent of those eligible in the Supply Experiment failed to participate. See Bradbury and Downs, eds., *Housing Allowances*, 131–141.

7. In 1978, among the 50.9 million taxpayers who owned their own homes, 38.9 percent claimed the mortgage interest deduction, 23.4 percent had mortgages but did not claim the deduction, and 36.9 percent did not have mortgages. The percentage who claimed this deduction rose steadily along with the incomes of the homeowners filing. See Congressional Budget Office, *Tax Treatment*, 10.

8. This total was calculated by multiplying the 4.6 million households who received welfare assistance but no federal housing aids times the 80 percent of such households suffering from housing problems. These figures were taken from S. J. Newman and A. B. Schnare, *Reassessing Shelter Assistance in America, Volume 1: Analysis and Findings* (Washington: Urban Institute, November 1986).

9. Social security payments are not confined to low-income households; hence they have not been included in the above list. However, social security payments are the largest single form of income supplementation made by the federal government, in terms of total expenditures. Therefore, coordinating or integrating housing assistance with social security payments is also important.

10. Newman and Schnare propose at least considering such an arrangement. See Newman and Schnare, *Reassessing Shelter Assistance*.

11. A. Rees, "The Labor Supply Results of the Experiment: A Summary," in H. W. Watts and A. Rees, eds., *The New Jersey Income Maintenance Experiment, Volume II: Labor Supply Effects* (New York: Academic Press, 1977) 31.

12. Combined marginal tax rates of this type as high as 86 percent for a negative income tax were calculated by Leonard Hausman, including in-kind benefit programs. See I. Lurie, "Integrating Income Maintenance Programs: Problems and Solutions," in I. Lurie, ed., *Integrating Income Maintenance Programs* (New York: Academic Press, 1975) 6–9.

13. Henry Aaron summarized this experience as follows: "Based on evidence from the housing allowance experiment, housing allowances are 3 to 8 percent housing program and 92 to 97 percent income maintenance." Aaron, "Policy Implications," in Bradbury and Downs, eds., *Housing Allowances*, 79.

14. For a discussion of this argument, see Aaron, "Policy Implications," 83–87, 93–96.

15. Lurie, "Integrating Income Maintenance Programs," 14–17.

16. The term "housing allowances" as used by Aaron is virtually identical in meaning with the term "housing vouchers" as used in the rest of this chapter.

17. Aaron, "Policy Implications," 95–96.

18. However, housing vouchers have substantial disadvantages compared to other forms of federal housing aid. These are pointed out later in the text.

19. The Experimental Housing Allowance showed that a significant percentage of existing units that ultimately qualified for vouchers had been rehabilitated to some extent. In the Supply Experiment, among units that did not meet required standards when their occupants were initially granted vouchers, over 75 percent were repaired enough to qualify—though this usually required relatively minor expenditures. See Edwin S. Mills and Arthur Sullivan, "Market Effects," in Bradbury and Downs, eds., *Housing Allowances,* 256–260.

20. For an in-depth analysis of the "trickle-down" process and its relation to metropolitan area development, see A. Downs, *Neighborhoods and Urban Development* (Washington: Brookings Institution, 1981) especially chapter 4.

21. Rents in those nearby subsidized units may not actually decline because of such pressure. However, they will be lower than they would have been in its absence.

22. One exception occurs where state housing agencies have been successful in locating some subsidized units in suburban areas, as in Massachusetts. This is usually done through projects in which all units benefit from some form of subsidy (such as low-interest tax-exempt bond financing), but only some units are actually occupied by low-income households (often 20 percent of the total). Hence the local community perceives such projects as predominantly market-oriented, and the developer has a strong incentive to use such subsidies.

23. Although no specific recommendation was made on this issue in my previous discussion of it, this is my recommendation. It is proposed more as a basis of discussion than as a result of any careful consideration of all the implications of this level of federal spending on housing assistance.

Chapter 4
New Directions for Federal Housing Policy: The Role of the States

Ian Donald Terner and Thomas B. Cook

The role of the states in the arena of national housing policy has been likened to that of a spectator at a tennis match, sitting at the net watching the action fly back and forth between the players.[1] The federal government has been poised on one side of the court, controlling the nation's major housing programs, interest rates, and housing tax benefits. On the other side of the court, local government and the private sector have controlled land use and development. Until recently, the states had been watching from the sidelines, offering various health and safety regulations, and only a few minor housing programs.

In the last few years, however, many states have ventured out onto the court to take an active part in the game, on both sides of the net. On one side, they have begun filling the void left by a "no-show" federal government, which has systematically dismantled its role as housing policy-maker and provider of major housing programs.

On the other side of the net the states have been pushing themselves back into the arena once occupied exclusively by local government. Some states are reclaiming for themselves some of the land use and other regulatory powers which they had formerly delegated to cities and towns. Too often states had seen local housing developments, especially subsidized affordable projects, become engulfed in the passions of local neighborhood disputes over land use and growth. The results of such opposition were often smaller or more costly projects—or no projects at all.

There is great variability among the fifty states in the move from housing spectator to player. In general the activist states pursue variations of three basic strategies: (1) The state as an *innovator/manager* of housing policy and programs; (2) The state as a *provider* of housing finance mechanisms; and (3) The state as a *regulator* of local residential land use decisions. The three strategies of policy and program innovator, financier, and regulator are discussed in the three sections which follow.

The states with the largest demonstrated commitment to housing are generally considered to be Massachusetts, New York, Connecticut, Maryland, New Jersey, and California. Although much attention has been placed on these six, at least 21 additional states have also taken strong steps toward an activist policy. These include, alphabetically: Alabama, Alaska, Colorado, Delaware, Florida, Illinois, Kentucky, Michigan, Minnesota, Mississippi, Missouri, Ohio, Oregon, Pennsylvania, Rhode Island, Texas, Vermont, Virginia, Washington, West Virginia, and Wisconsin. Most of the remaining states have at least issued a modest number of bonds for housing, and many have adopted targeted housing programs. Undoubtedly, several states not mentioned by name might well be included in this second-tier classification.

The enduring legacy of this period of state activism may be a permanently enlarged role for the states in targeting housing programs to their own particular needs and priorities; innovation in response to those needs; and coordinating many resources and diverse players in the housing arena. Such a combination of roles will enable states to achieve the greater efficiency of a decentralized delivery system which is closer and more sensitive to the constituencies served.

Thus, while the 50 states in general, and even the most aggressive housing "activist" states, may never attain a primacy in the funding or finance area relative to the potential of the federal government, their period of activism during the federal retreat establishes many of them as powerful and constructive partners. This will be particularly true if under HUD Secretary Jack Kemp there is to be a reconstituted federal housing effort. Such an activist role is in no way assured for all of the states, some of which are still on the sidelines waiting for the federal government to resume the game. Others may fall short of the role of active or constructive partner, because of lack of political leadership and/or institutional competence. In a worst-case situation a few states may present a clogged or superfluous layer of bureaucracy, threatening the flow of funds and aid from federal funding sources to local government and private sector implementors.

Given this range of current and future responses, this discussion will focus on states which have shown commitment and growing capacity to undertake major housing initiatives. Further, we argue that such commitment is indicative of the kinds of roles that a majority of the states could play if provided with incentives by the federal government with a reinvigorated commitment to a national housing agenda.

The State as an Innovator of Housing Programs

With the retreat of the federal government from its housing programs in the late 1970s and early 1980s, the states—many lacking a track record in the complex financing and regulatory operations of housing programs—were faced with a significant challenge.[2] To replace the activism of the Department of Housing and Urban Development (HUD), each state needed to identify and research its own housing problems, devise policies and programs to address those problems, and then find ways to implement the policies and fund the programs.

In an impressive flowering of innovations, initiatives, and institutions, many states responded to the challenge presented by the federal withdrawal. They became major players in housing finance, devised and operated new housing programs, and used regulatory powers not available to the federal government to achieve a wide range of housing goals.

All but two of the 50 states now have housing finance agencies which have collectively financed the purchase of more than 900,000 homes, predominantly for first-time buyers, and the construction of almost 650,000 new apartments. In the last six years, states have also responded with the adoption of more than 300 new housing programs which run the gamut from emergency homeless shelters to rural housing rehabilitation to builder incentives for affordable rental housing. Numerous states have also exercised their regulatory powers to shape local land use decisions, building practices, and residential lending in order to address statewide housing issues. While the extent and success of state housing initiatives vary, the wide range of responses demonstrates a willingness on the part of the states to undertake and maintain housing programs.

Through analysis of current state housing program activities, this section examines three state capacities: 1. the ability of states to target resources, 2. the ability of states to innovate, and 3. the ability of states to coordinate diverse resources and players in the operation of housing programs.

Targeted Allocation of Resources

America's housing problems are many, and they vary with geography. Nationally, we face the serious issues of homelessness, decaying and vacant public housing units, the lack of affordable rental units for the poor, declining rates of homeownership, and the loss of low-income housing units because of expiring federal subsidies.

However, the magnitude and manifestations of our problems are different from place to place. The Connecticut suburb is plagued by a shortage of single-family housing affordable to first-time buyers. Rural California lacks farmworker housing. Residential development in Florida overwhelms local infrastructure and spawns growth control measures. And industrial cities in Michigan face housing deterioration, abandonment and segregation. Clearly, the nation must deal with a variety of housing needs.

The broad range of housing programs, financing methods, and regulatory approaches adopted by the states demonstrates the diversity of the nation's housing problems. Based on the particular needs of the states—and in light of their unique market, institutional, financial, and political realities—state governments can best design programs to address those problems of greatest importance.

For example, compare two states with active housing programs: California and Maryland. California has targeted its efforts to provide emergency shelter for the homeless, to construct rental housing, to support nonprofit acquisition of residential hotels, to aid self-help groups in building new homes, to protect mobile home owners, and to increase the amount of farmworker housing. Maryland, on the other hand, has concentrated on rehabilitation, addressing both owner-occupied and rental housing for low- and moderate-income families. Maryland has also focused on upgrading substandard housing to meet state codes, constructing low-cost rental housing, and supporting nonprofit housing development. With a large stock of older homes, Maryland concentrates much of its energy on improving habitability and affordability within a variety of existing structures. With its generally newer housing stock, California's major rehabilitation concern is largely limited to residential hotels. The state also directs substantial resources toward mobile homes and farmworker housing, issues not of great relevance in Maryland. However, both states are faced with shortages of low-cost rental housing and both operate programs to support its construction.

A review of state housing programs shows that most states make careful decisions about how, where, and to whom to target their housing assistance. For instance, Alaska has directed the majority of its efforts toward increasing homeownership and has spent very little to increase its stock of rental housing. More urban states, such as New York and Massachusetts, have undertaken major efforts to build rental housing, as well as sponsoring programs to assist first-time homebuyers.

States address a wide range of special population groups with their housing programs. Virginia has earmarked funds for the homeless, Pennsylvania has initiated aid for the preservation of single room occupancy (SRO) housing, Maryland has subsidized transitional housing for women, and Ohio has funded the development of shared housing for seniors. Massachusetts runs three separate programs targeted at special needs: elderly housing, handicapped housing, and family housing. Florida has one of the most geographically targeted approaches with its Pocket of Poverty Program, a pilot project to build and upgrade housing in one poor Florida community.

While this targeting of specific populations may be scattered and uneven, it illustrates the differences in housing issues from state to state. Further evidence is found in the choices states make between programs which support new construction and those which encourage rehabilitation. States with a short supply of housing and strong demand—such as California, Nevada, and (until the decline in oil production) Alaska, Colorado, and Texas—have emphasized new construction programs. Other states with larger stocks of older housing have sponsored rehab programs. Maryland, as noted, supports housing preservation, the promotion of livability standards, and special rehabilitation such as indoor plumbing provision and lead paint removal. Minnesota, where cold weather places a great burden on low-income tenants, operates a low-interest rehabilitation loan program to improve the energy conservation and habitability of rental housing. West Virginia provides financing for the rehabilitation of housing in older cities as part of downtown revitalization programs. And Michigan, with a healthy supply of available housing, has chosen to redirect its tax-exempt bond authority away from the financing of new construction, to a mortgage credit certificate program to improve affordability for first-time homebuyers.

New Jersey demonstrates the ability of a state to target its housing programs during a period of change. Since the mid-1970s, the state's Department of Community Affairs (DCA) has operated a very successful rehabilitation program in the older parts of New Jersey. Following the second Mt. Laurel decision in 1983 mandating the geographic expansion of low-income housing opportunities, the DCA began a program to subsidize the construction of affordable housing in New Jersey suburbs. The DCA was able to use its expertise in the management of the rehabilitation program to quickly and effectively initiate a construction program.

Innovation in Housing Programs

In addition to targeting resources to state needs, state control of housing programs allows for innovation and creativity in the design and delivery of housing assistance. Housing markets vary from state to state depending on regional economies. Agencies and administrations vary with the structure of state governments. Political feasibility varies with the constituent groups in power.

While this diversity presents a challenge to the designers of federal housing programs who must try to fashion all-encompassing national programs, it presents opportunities for state programs. Each state can assess its market, institutional, and political landscape to determine the most effective approach for achieving a housing policy objective. For example, a state with strong community development corporations may find success with a program which encourages nonprofit housing construction, but in another state without nonprofit capacity a program which allocates funding to private builders may be more effective. In fact, in an increasing number of states, innovative delivery systems are taking advantage of nonprofit capacity. New York spends $100 million a year on housing programs through some 350 nonprofits; about 20 percent of these funds support administrative costs. Maryland runs a similar program. For 20 years Connecticut has provided low-cost financing to community housing development corporations, and recently the state added programs to support nonprofit sponsorship of limited equity co-ops, mutual housing associations, and land trusts. The Wisconsin Partnership for Housing Development, a nonprofit group now supported by corporate, foundation, and municipal loans and grants, was spawned by the state with a one-time grant.

A more common approach to nonprofit development is taken by Colorado, Delaware, Oregon, Rhode Island, California, Massachusetts, Florida and several other states which provide small predevelopment loans to nonprofit organizations, enabling these organizations to assemble land, financing, subsidies, and the approvals necessary to build affordable housing. While the federal government has made its subsidy programs available to nonprofits, the state programs show a much greater cognizance of the opportunity, and have designed specific programs to involve them.

While some states have demonstrated innovative collaborations with nonprofits, others emphasize local governments, the entities with land use powers which are closest to the delivery of housing services. Pennsylvania, for instance, provides predevelopment loans only to local governments and redevelopment agencies. Further, a new $5 million annual program provides transitional rental housing, and is operated through counties.

Massachusetts has an innovative Homeownership Opportunity Program which is designed to gain local support for state-sponsored construction of mixed-income, for-sale housing. The state provides below-market mortgages from its housing finance agency with additional state funds to buy down mortgage payments for low- and moderate-income buyers. While the actual development is carried out by either nonprofit or for-profit developers, the local governments are required to make contributions to the projects in the form of fee waivers, density bonuses, donations of land and/or direct subsidies.

In other cases, states have developed programs which tap into the development skills and financial strength of private homebuilders. New York, a supporter of nonprofit rental housing, operates a first-time homebuyers program utilizing for-profit developers. In this program, the state takes advantage of private builders who are supplying market-rate single-family homes by providing minor subsidies to reach potential buyers otherwise shut out of the market.

With the shortage of federal housing funds, some states—most notably New York, Massachusetts, Connecticut, and California—have allocated general fund revenues for housing programs. However, in most states redirection of general revenues to housing programs has been difficult. Thus, several states have instead created housing trust funds supported by dedicated revenues. Examples include a transfer tax on real estate transactions in New Jersey and Maine. Washington earmarks interest on escrow accounts; Kentucky uses surplus reserves from its mortgage bond program; and California utilizes tideland oil revenues. These innovative revenue sources have produced hundreds of millions of dollars.

Another innovation has focused on land. In California, where urban areas are chronically short of buildable sites, the state has aggressively pursued this policy. State law requires that public entities, when disposing of surplus land, first make it available to housing agencies, local governments, or nonprofit organizations for affordable housing. In addition, the state must inventory and make available a list of its surplus lands, and local governments are required by the state to take note of surplus sites in their general plans. Other state laws and executive orders give preference to housing uses on surplus properties. With the active involvement of nonprofit builders and local housing agencies, hundreds of sites, many of them surplus schools in infill locations in expensive suburbs, have been developed with affordable housing. The extent to which California has designated the use of its surplus public lands for housing and the process by which it has undertaken that designation, may serve as a model to the federal government and other states.

Coordinated Approaches to Housing

One of the key roles that states can play is the coordination of federal programs, state resources, local land use planning, and private initiatives. In the past, affordable housing development consisted primarily of negotiating the terms of a single federal program with a designated subsidy program at the center of the transaction. However, now a developer often must combine a wide variety of resources such as local land use concessions, predevelopment loans, low interest construction and permanent financing, federal block grant funds, and private investments and contributions. Each project requires the careful crafting of many pieces.

Successfully combining these resources has required nonprofit organizations, local governments, and private builders to be skillful real estate and political entrepreneurs. State governments must be equally knowledgeable in designing housing programs that maximize the leverage of these funds, and that help creative developers coordinate the necessary pieces.

Examples of this integration of resources at the state level include the Connecticut Municipal Housing Trust Fund which provides matching grants to local governments to magnify the power of other resources. The Wisconsin Housing Partnership combines private investments with state and local support to leverage federal funding, and Rhode Island combines state bond financing and no-interest second mortgages to make the federal low-income housing tax credit viable. Colorado, Alaska, and Indiana have taken federal housing programs for the elderly or Native Americans and added their own resources to extend benefits.

Massachusetts has initiated a well-coordinated housing program, the State Housing Assistance for Rental Production (SHARP), to bring together several programs into one. SHARP builds upon tax-exempt bond financing provided by the Massachusetts Housing Finance Agency. Then it takes the benefits of reduced interest rates a step further with state-funded loan subsidies to private or nonprofit sponsors. These loans are for a 15-year period, after which the project must be self-supporting. In exchange, the developer agrees to rent at least 25 percent of the units to low-income households. Coordinating yet other programs, Massachusetts provides either federal Section 8 certificates or state Chapter 707 housing certificates to the low-income tenants to assure the cash flow for the developer. Finally, the developer is encouraged to take advantage of federal Community Development Block Grant (CDBG) funds and other state and local assistance.

State-sponsored predevelopment loans and grants mentioned earlier also point to state success in coordinating housing programs. These programs give crucial early support to nonprofits or local governments to enable them to package federal subsidy requests. For example, Florida's Farmworker Housing Assistance Trust Fund has made available $3.8 million in loans and grants for site acquisition and other predevelopment costs, yielding a tenfold return in federal funds.

The record of state housing activity is one of responsiveness to particular problems, creativity and coordination. Cut adrift by the retreat of the federal government, many states, often without past experience, identified particular housing needs and addressed them. Often this involved the artful combination of state, federal, and local entities teamed up with private builders and community development corporations.

The State Role in Housing Finance

Not only have the states responded to the federal housing withdrawal by creating innovative programs, but also by expanding their role in housing finance as both a fiduciary and a regulator.[3] States have financed home purchases for almost a million first-time buyers, and more than 650,000 rental apartments. Most of this activity has taken place since 1980.

While state actions may appear minor when compared to national and international market forces affecting interest rates and the supply of mortgage capital, states have moved in to fill at least part of the void. And although state programs are small compared to the Federal Housing Administration or the Veteran's Administration, state finance programs have performed a significant service.

The 1980s have seen an era of unprecedented change in the home mortgage and construction-finance market. After decades of relatively stable interest rates, tight federal rules governing financial institutions and ever-present federal housing finance agencies, these institutions moved backstage. Mortgage interest rates shot up into double digits, while banking deregulation brought Wall Street and a host of other new players onto the scene. In this setting the states gained a much more important role in housing finance.

The states got their start in the 1960s and 1970s when they provided financing for federally-subsidized rental housing. The provision of mortgage capital to privately-built low-income housing helped leverage federal funds. This may have been one of the first demonstrations of the ability of states to maximize federal housing programs.

With the formation of housing finance agencies in the 1960s and 1970s, many states were in a position to expand their operations into the tumultuous 1980s. Multi-family housing bonds issued by the states between 1980 and 1987 surpassed the total number of bonds issued in the decades beforehand (see Table 4.1); between 1980 and 1987 more than 400,000 new apartments were financed by state agencies.

While the rental track record of the states has been notable, the biggest increase in activity has been in ownership financing. Over 80 percent of the mortgage revenue bonds issued by the states came after 1980. More than 600,000 home purchases were made possible by state housing finance institutions between 1980 and 1987 (see Table 4.1).

In addition, more than half of the states set aside some of their bond authority to issue mortgage credit certificates, an innovative method to bolster homeownership through the use of a federal income tax credit.

Finally, in addition to boosting rentals and homeownership with a high volume of bond activity, state housing finance agencies have also engaged in some special targeting. Like their programmatic counterparts, housing finance agencies have also emphasized such populations as the elderly, the handicapped, and farm workers.

Mortgage Revenue Bonds: Homeownership

In order to increase homeownership opportunities, 48 states have issued more than $48 billion in mortgage revenue bonds (MRBs). In order, Alaska, New York, California, Virginia, and Connecticut have mounted the largest programs. As noted, over 80 percent of the activity took place since 1980. Starting with no background in 1980, the states of Alabama, Florida, Mississippi, Ohio, Pennsylvania, and Texas each issued more than $1 billion in MRBs through 1987.

MRBs helped spur new production in areas where strong demand created a need for affordable ownership, such as California, and in Alaska and Texas before the oil crash. However, for the most part MRBs assisted in the purchase of existing, usually less costly, homes. Of all loans made through 1985, over 60 percent were for the purchase or rehabilitation of existing homes.

The chief criticism of MRBs was that middle- and upper-income groups were the primary beneficiaries. However, in 1985, the biggest year on record for MRBs, the average purchase price on an MRB loan was about $54,000, with an average annual borrower income of under $27,000. During this same

TABLE 4.1   Industrial Development Bonds (IDBs) and Mortgage Revenue Bonds
(MRBs) Issued by State Housing Finance Agencies (through 1987, in millions of
dollars)

State	IDBs	Percent since 1980	MRBs	Percent since 1980
Alabama	$322.3	100	$1,049.9	100
Alaska	na	na	3,618.8	70
Arizona	na	na	0.0	0
Arkansas	222.0	100	633.3	100
California	703.6	77	2,368.0	82
Colorado	529.2	78	837.1	71
Connecticut	634.0	54	1,978.0	62
D.C.	263.8	100	100.0	100
Delaware	136.8	72	392.8	87
Florida	1,160.3	100	1,002.0	100
Georgia	10.4	100	490.1	80
Hawaii	35.8	100	501.0	100
Idaho	65.3	2	415.4	67
Illinois	1,185.5	49	832.0	100
Indiana	28.3	100	875.0	100
Iowa	179.7	81	481.2	60
Kansas	na	na	na	na
Kentucky	267.6	82	869.7	41
Louisiana	231.4	100	550.0	100
Maine	178.0	35	524.5	76
Maryland	1,091.1	62	952.0	83
Massachusetts	2,084.4	44	1,027.9	98
Michigan	974.4	22	906.4	73
Minnesota	621.9	17	1,210.4	64
Mississippi	0.0	0	977.7	100
Missouri	401.7	34	799.3	85

TABLE 4.1 (*Continued*)

State	*IDBs*	*Percent since 1980*	*MRBs*	*Percent since 1980*
Montana	24.4	8	761.5	71
Nebraska	189.8	82	980.9	100
Nevada	171.4	82	662.0	63
New Hampshire	131.0	93	738.1	63
New Jersey	1,627.3	33	1,645.0	89
New Mexico	111.0	73	1,000.0	56
New York	na	na	2,559.4	91
North Carolina	290.7	100	626.3	91
North Dakota	23.9	100	266.7	100
Ohio	222.8	100	1,164.0	100
Oklahoma	273.0	91	893.7	100
Oregon	196.0	57	529.0	68
Pennsylvania	775.0	40	1,010.0	100
Rhode Island	374.1	31	1,384.8	57
South Carolina	262.0	100	712.2	64
South Dakota	91.2	45	990.0	64
Tennessee	51.8	0	1,159.8	69
Texas	320.2	100	1,147.0	100
Utah	84.2	85	953.9	79
Vermont	1,946.0	36	474.1	70
Virginia	735.7	45	2,144.0	75
Washington	425.2	100	455.4	100
West Virginia	511.9	26	568.0	71
Wisconsin	426.1	20	912.4	90
Wyoming	0.8	100	855.9	71
U.S. TOTAL	$20,592.0	56	$48,396.4	81

Source: National Council of State Housing Agencies

period the median home price on the sale of an existing home was over $75,000 and the median buyer income was over $41,000. Clearly, while the beneficiaries of MRBs were not primarily low-income households, the program did reach many first-time buyers who earned less than the average homebuyer.

Despite the increase of homeownership opportunities, concern about the efficiency of the inherent federal subsidy in MRBs and criticism about the lack of targeting requirements in MRB programs led to the introduction of new restrictions in the Tax Reform Act of 1986. A cap on total bond volume was set for each state and new targeting requirements were imposed. However, the majority of the states were aware of the need to target assistance before the federal government could respond and had already imposed their own income and price limitations.

Industrial Development Bonds: Rental Housing

Industrial development bonds (IDBs) have been the primary tool of the states in providing financing for rental housing. Many states were already familiar with the financing of apartment construction from their earlier involvement with federal subsidy programs, and they used IDBs to encourage new rentals. States have issued over half of their IDBs between 1980 and 1987, and the total amount loaned exceeded $20 billion in 1987 (see Table 4.1).

By volume of bonds issued, the leading states were New York, Massachusetts, Vermont, New Jersey, Illinois, Florida, and Maryland, each of which passed the $1 billion mark. Of particular note were Florida, Washington, Texas, North Carolina, South Carolina, and Oklahoma which had no prior experience in rental finance, and issued more than $250 million in IDBs between 1980 and 1987. Not recounted here, but also of importance to state financing, was the issuance of IDBs by local governments, which is regulated by the states.

Contrasted with MRBs, IDBs have been used almost exclusively to add to the stock of rental housing. Well over 95 percent of multi-family IDBs have been used to fund new construction and substantial rehabilitation of apartments. Much of this financing came at a crucial time to revive apartment construction which is highly cyclical. In the early 1980s interest rates were high, mortgage money was scarce, and rental housing was not being built. As vacancy rates fell and rent levels rose much faster than inflation, developers, nonprofit builders, and public agencies turned to IDBs to reverse the downturn. In 1985, state and local governments responded in force with more than $16 billion in bonds and restarted the rental housing market in many parts of the country.

This countercyclical role of tax-exempt bonds should not be underestimated. In California, for example, IDBs financed most of the new apartment projects in 1984. In 1985, more than 75 percent of all rental housing production was publicly financed. More than 100,000 apartments were built in California in that year alone, and rents stabilized as vacancy rates rose.

Again, criticism has been strong of the use of IDBs for apartments because of the loss of federal revenues from tax-exempt bonds. The Tax Reform Act of 1986 responded to these charges by limiting the number of bonds each state could issue and by setting tougher affordability standards. Prior to 1986, developers using IDBs were required to set aside 20 percent of the units for low-income families earning less than 80 percent of the area median income. The 1986 tax changes now require more low-income units in rental projects financed with tax-exempt bonds.

However, as with MRBs, 29 states had already instituted their own income limits on IDB programs prior to the passage of tax reform. And the record shows that 35 percent of the rental units built in 1985 using state-issued IDBs served low-income families, although the law only required 20 percent. Furthermore, developer interest in IDBs waned as the market softened and as large institutional lenders began to invest in rental housing.

Special Programs by Housing Finance Agencies

Although most states have concentrated their financing efforts on MRBs and IDBs, many state housing finance agencies have undertaken special programs to target particular housing needs, respond to an opportunity, or take advantage of their reserve funds. A tally by the National Council of State Housing Agencies has identified more than 200 housing programs run by the nation's 48 housing finance agencies. States instituted many of these programs in the past few years, building upon the development experience and knowledge gained in financing thousands of units of ownership and rental housing.

While programs run by state finance agencies are as diverse as those run by state housing and community development departments, a few examples are worthy of mention. Oregon has financed the construction of more than 2,000 housing units for the elderly and disabled, Connecticut has made available $20 million in reverse annuity mortgages to enable cash-poor seniors to recover the equity in their homes, and Maine has offered one percent mortgage loans to finance homeless shelters.

In some states, such as Michigan and Minnesota, the housing finance agency is the primary institution for state support of housing and the agency runs a wide variety of programs to serve diverse needs. In other states, the housing finance agency works in concert with other state departments. In Massachusetts, the Executive Office of Communities and Development uses the state housing finance authority in combination with its own subsidy programs. In California, the housing finance agency leverages local resources by conditioning some of its financing on a contribution from a local entity. State housing finance agencies have also brought new money to bear on state housing problems. Rhode Island, Virginia, Wisconsin, and Maryland have set aside loan reserves, created revolving trust funds, and combined resources with other departments to support new programs. In sum, housing finance agencies play a broader role than that of financier, and in many states are an important contributor to the range of state housing initiatives.

While an important policy decision needs to be made (and was with the Tax Reform Act of 1986) about the efficiency of the inherent federal subsidy in tax-exempt bonds, states should be given credit for making good use of one of the few opportunities available to encourage affordable housing. Further, the data show that states made homeownership available to those for whom conventional financing would not have served and exceeded federal targeting requirements.

Besides being a vehicle for the delivery of housing assistance, IDBs and MRBs also provided financial training for state and local governments. With the knowledge and expertise gained in housing finance and development, state finance agencies were able to expand their activities to better address housing needs and make better use of other public and private resources.

To preserve and expand an important weapon in the state housing arsenal new federal housing policy should recognize and promote the ability of the states to finance both ownership and rental housing. States should be given the flexibility to tailor bond programs to meet their needs, and the federal government should reward those states which run efficient and effective programs.

State Regulatory Powers

Perhaps the most powerful and enduring role for state involvement in the provision of housing is as the ultimate regulator—and in some cases arbiter—of local land use decisions.[4] Land use regulation is a role that only the state can play. The U.S. Constitution, outside of protection against the uncompensated taking of private property, reserves to the states the right to regulate the use of land. Most states have delegated this authority to local governments, but states inherently maintain the prerogative to enact laws to guide how local entities control land development.

The complete delegation to local governments of land use control has not always served the cause of housing. Land use restrictions enacted by many local governments—large-lot zoning, growth limits, and specific project denials—deter the construction of low- and moderate-income housing. To overcome these exclusionary practices, some states have asserted their primacy over the regulation of land use. These pro-active measures have frequently met with resistance from towns, cities, and counties, but they have had a fundamental impact on land use decisions made by local governments. Massachusetts has made judicious use of its regulatory powers to encourage the construction of low- and moderate-income housing. It has selectively limited the power of local government to deny or prohibit specific subsidized housing development through Chapter 774 of the Acts of 1969. It then furthered its promotion of low- and moderate-income housing by creating a strong incentive for local governments to participate in state and federal housing subsidy programs through Executive Order 215. These initiatives are discussed by Michael Wheeler elsewhere in this volume. The combination of state housing programs with land use regulatory powers has helped make each more effective. Examples follow from Oregon and California of state involvement in local land use planning and the encouragement of affordable housing.

Oregon: Housing as a Part of Comprehensive Planning

Unlike Massachusetts, where the state has wielded its regulatory power over land use in a targeted way, Oregon has asserted its land use authority in a more general way with the passage of the Land Conservation and Development Act of 1973. Adopted primarily to limit urban sprawl and environmental degradation, the Act set forth 19 state goals to which the plans of local governments must conform. The Act also created an appointed body, the Land Conservation and Development Commission (LCDC), to enforce implementation. In short, Oregon has created a statewide comprehensive planning program with housing as one of its basic goals.

The tenth of the 19 goals requires local governments to inventory all buildable land for residential use and adopt plans that "shall encourage the availability of adequate numbers of housing units at price ranges and rent levels which are commensurate with the financial capabilities of Oregon households." While there was some question at first as to the exact meaning of this goal, the LCDC clearly articulated its position in 1978 when it refused to approve the general plan of a Portland suburb because its land use policies did not give "any consideration to low-cost housing needs of its own residents and workers, much less those of the region."[5]

Thus, while created primarily as an environmental protection agency, the LCDC has become an enforcer of a state requirement that local government plans address regional housing needs. The LCDC has consistently encouraged cities and counties to increase planned densities, revise subdivision and building standards in order to allow for manufactured housing, and grant density bonuses for the provision of low- and moderate-income housing. Furthermore, the state law prevents the local adoption of growth moratoria or numerical limits on housing development. The grafting of these pro-active housing requirements onto environmental legislation has created an unusual coalition of homebuilders and environmental groups who both support the state law.

While it has typically given local governments a fair amount of flexibility in how they meet the state goals, including the housing goal, the LCDC can, and has, issued enforcement orders requiring a locality to take specific steps to allow for the development of housing. Most observers agree that state involvement has increased the density of residentially zoned land throughout the state. It has, however, also restricted the expansion of urban areas, and this may leave somewhat limited housing opportunities.

Despite support from homebuilders and housing advocates, the LCDC's efforts to encourage land use plans which allow for affordable housing development has not guaranteed that such development takes place. The state only requires that local land use regulations allow for a range of housing; nothing requires that the locality be pro-active in the provision of housing. Furthermore, after the LCDC has approved a locality's general plan, there are few opportunities for review and enforcement.

While the state's exercise of land use authority is not coordinated with other state or federal efforts to provide assistance in the construction of low- and moderate-income housing as it is in Massachusetts, Oregon's inclusion of housing in its statewide land use law has been a positive factor. Furthermore, Oregon has successfully demonstrated how a state can use its regulatory powers as a tool in the implementation of housing policy.

California: A Diversity of Housing Laws

California has probably enacted more pro-housing laws than any other state. Hit in the late 1970s with strong growth pressures and significant increases in the cost of housing, a powerful coalition of interests successfully sought the adoption of numerous laws that attempted to rearrange the local planning process in order to encourage the development of housing, particularly low- and moderate-income housing.

California was also one of the first states to pass legislation requiring local governments to adopt comprehensive land use plans. Furthermore, the state dictated in some detail what issues the plans had to address, and how they should be implemented. As part of these overall requirements, California has required cities and counties to incorporate a "housing element" into their general plans, articulating how they intend to meet their "responsibility to use the powers vested in them to facilitate the improvement and development of housing to make adequate provision for the housing needs of all economic segments of the community." [6]

The housing requirements are detailed in setting out how each locality will assess current housing conditions, land availability, and government constraints to housing production. In addition, cities and counties must affirmatively detail their housing programs and quantify their objectives for residential development in the coming five years. These requirements were made a part of state law in 1980 with the passage of a comprehensive housing bill, AB 2853.

Perhaps the most controversial aspect of California's housing element law is the regional "fair-share" housing obligations articulated for every community. The appropriate regional agency, or, for rural areas, the California Department of Housing and Community Development (HCD), determines how many units of housing, and at what affordability levels, are needed region-wide. This total is then distributed on a "fair-share" basis to each municipality or county within the region, which then must affirmatively plan for reaching these goals.

While ambitious in its commitment to the provision of affordable housing, and pro-active in the requirement that HCD review and certify for compliance each of the 400 housing elements throughout the state, the goals of AB 2853 have not been fully realized because of the lack of enforcement mechanisms. Although the state is required to review and comment on every housing element, and each locality is required to consider the state's comments, in the end the state's findings are only advisory to the local government. Unlike Oregon, California does not have the power to require specific changes in a locality's housing element or land use plan.

This does not mean, however, that AB 2853 is not without influence or effect. A local government that does not have a housing element certified to be in compliance with state law, does not have a valid general plan. The jurisdiction is open to legal challenge from injured parties such as consumers, or developers unable to build low-income housing. The most common form of judicial action in cases regarding inadequate plans is to suspend a locality's authority to issue building permits for any use. While such a remedy does not directly promote housing, the reality (and even the threat) of suspending all building permits, including commercial and industrial, is an inducement to compliance.

The state has also used some of its limited power to penalize local governments which have not adopted a housing element in compliance with state guidelines. The state controls its own programs, as well as a small amount of CDBG funds for rural communities (most cities in the state receive their federal funds directly). California has, on occasion, denied funding to localities with inadequate housing elements. This experience suggests that if the state had more discretionary funds to disperse, as Massachusetts does, it would be better able to enforce compliance with the provisions of state law.

However, as it is, California's housing element law has not been as successful in influencing local land use decisions as initially hoped. The exercise of completing a housing element does not force a local government to implement its provisions. However, the preparation of the housing element itself does force a community to confront regional housing responsibilities, review its regulatory practices, and assess its housing needs and conditions. While this review has proved beneficial to the development of low- and moderate-income housing, California has not been able to realize all of its housing goals.

Concurrent with passage of the housing element law, the state passed several other laws that attempted to modify local land use planning with regard to affordable housing. The state required that cities and counties:

zone adequate land with appropriate standards to allow for residential development to meet growth and employment projections;

not limit residential growth without making specific findings about the overriding public welfare need to do so;

not decrease the number of units in a residential project if it is consistent with the underlying zoning, unless the development poses a critical threat to the public welfare;

grant developers additional density in housing developments if a portion of the units are for low- and/or moderate-income households;

allow for the development of manufactured housing at the same standards as other forms of residential construction; and

permit the addition of secondary ("in-law") units, to single-family homes.

This cluster of state laws was passed to address specific shortcomings in the local planning process, and these laws have brought about reforms on the local government level. Although highly indicative of a statewide commitment to housing, all these laws suffer somewhat from fragmentation and the lack of potent enforcement mechanisms. The state has not orchestrated its housing and land use laws as comprehensively as Oregon has, nor has it used them as part of a coordinated housing program as Massachusetts has. This is in part due to a lack of state funding. Still, the diversity of laws in California demonstrates the many areas in which states can play a role in local land use and housing affairs. And, were it given control over significant federal resources, California shows a great potential for correcting many of the local land use restrictions which have added to the exceedingly high cost of housing in the state.

The case studies outlined above provide successful examples of state intervention in the regulatory arena to encourage the provision of housing. Numerous other states have also exercised their authority in land use and other matters to encourage local government support for affordable housing development. New Jersey, for instance, overhauled statewide building codes to encourage lower-cost construction. Many states have instituted preemptive manufactured housing standards, and several have prohibited local governments from enacting local residential rent controls. The State of New York continues to set rent control policies in its largest city.

The record indicates that states, when they choose to do so, can have a significant impact through the exercise of their regulatory powers. Oregon has made the development of lower-cost rental and manufactured housing a real possibility in almost every community in the state. Massachusetts has artfully applied its land use powers as part of its comprehensive approach to housing. And California, by forcing each locality to recognize the state's housing problems, has brought about significant reforms in several local land use practices and has encouraged the development of affordable housing throughout the state.

The positive results of state exercise of land use authority should be encouraged by the federal government, and those states willing to employ their power to aid in the development of housing should be rewarded. A demonstration of pro-active state regulation should be counted by the federal government as equivalent to a financial contribution when allocating matching funds. This will further the effectiveness and efficiency of federal housing assistance and programs. States which allow local governments to enact overly restrictive, exclusionary, or discriminatory land use regulations should not be given priority in the awarding of federal housing grants. Instead, the federal government should use the carrot of housing assistance to encourage state and local governments to reform local land use practices.

Federal Incentives for State Activism: The Future

Given the demonstrated ability of many states to initiate and manage housing programs, the challenge to federal housing policy, when and if a renewed national commitment is at hand, will be to structure a relationship whereby states will be given the opportunity to participate in a meaningful way, perhaps even to administer entire federal programs, as states can now do with the Small Cities Community Development Block Grant Program and the Rental Rehabilitation Program. The successes of many states in effectively administering these programs, as well as implementing their own policies, suggests that renewed federal housing aid be offered in a block grant format, rather than in a categorical format, thus allowing states (and localities) to exercise maximum flexibility in the implementation of housing policy.

The concept of a federal block grant program springs from the success of at least half the states in implementing housing policies, the responsiveness of states to past and present block grant programs, and the desire of Washington to maximize effectiveness with limited federal dollars. Thus, a block grant program must contain some strong incentives for state involvement in housing to leverage state funding, financing, and/or regulatory responses.

For example, the Council of State Community Affairs Agencies (COSCAA) has suggested that 55 percent of a proposed federal block grant for housing be allocated by need, but released only after states meet some threshold requirement of state-sponsored funding or financing; that 20 percent of the funds be a bonus to states which exceed minimum requirements for state involvement; that 20 percent be distributed solely as an entitlement based on need; and that the remaining five percent be used as a discretionary fund.

The key assumption behind a federal block grant program is that it would not only leverage state funds and thus improve the efficiency of federal funding, but also through the matching and bonus provisions spur additional state activism on the housing front. The lure of federal funding would make it easier for state legislators to justify state housing expenditures to cost-conscious or uninterested constituencies. The argument that "federal money is available to our state, but will leak away and go elsewhere unless we act," can be a powerful incentive to commit state resources.

While the specific size and allocation process of a block grant program needs to be decided on the federal level, states should have the freedom to decide the specific end uses to which such funds are allocated. The degree of success by numerous states in the implementation of policy and the administration of programs in the housing field, and in several other areas, strongly suggests that states be given a large degree of flexibility in the application of federal funds.

However, even in the case where the federal government chooses to retain a categorical grant format, state and local grantees which have demonstrated their abilities to operate successful programs should be selectively permitted to exert greater operating flexibility. Some new federal initiatives begin to embrace the notion of a flexible targeting and tailoring role for the states. Needed, however, are ways to prevent clogged, incompetent, or obstructive states from impeding the flow of federal resources.

The federal government should also support state activism in the area of housing finance. All but two of the states have issued bonds to assist new homebuyers and/or construct new rental housing. The success of tax exempt bonds to restart housing markets and to provide more affordable shelter, demonstrates the need for, and wisdom of, extending this authority. States with proven track records ought to be afforded greater flexibility in tailoring bond programs to their particular needs and circumstances, and should be rewarded for effective bond programs with grant funds or additional bond authority.

Another enduring, and perhaps growing, aspect of current state activism is in the land use arena, whereby states are intervening, and trying to inject the vision of state housing policy into the affairs of local governments. Those states which have reclaimed in part their constitutional power to regulate land use have had success in counteracting negative local policies. Any future federal housing policy should encourage states to correct those local land use practices which are anti-housing, and reward those which support the development of affordable housing.

The Appropriate Level of Government

The activist states in the 1980s have blazed a trail of positive initiatives and now serve as models for their peers. This positive view of state government may surprise students of political science who were taught that states are the "backwaters of government." Writing in the *New York Times,* Richard Nathan of Princeton University and Martha Derthick of the University of Virginia observed that the common perception of states is of a government

made reactionary by having territorial jurisdictions that are small and hopelessly irrational, by having legislatures that are too large and too rarely in session, or by having agencies that are poorly staffed, inexpert and readily captured by special interests.[7]

However, the two professors of government go on to report a new surge of state activism in a wide variety of sectors, including housing. In order to spur their own economic development, states are reforming social welfare and health systems, investing more in public works and education, and undertaking numerous initiatives. Nathan and Derthick cite census data showing an annual average increase of 5.6 percent in state aid to localities from 1983 to 1986, reversing decades of constant or declining state assistance. "The increased activism of state governments is likely to be one of the most important legacies of the Reagan years," they conclude.[8]

State-implemented federal housing policy would not only take advantage of the increased activism and ability of state governments, it would also direct housing assistance to the most appropriate level of government.

In formulating a new national housing policy, one must face the issue of who should implement that policy, that is, design and manage programs, review proposals, and allocate funds. On the one hand, housing is a very local issue, with land use decisions, small homebuilders, community groups, and particular market conditions taken into consideration. To respond and adapt to these local realities, subsidy programs should be managed by a governmental agency able to understand the local market.

In the best of all possible worlds, federal resources and credit derived from the broadest national base would flow directly to the smallest units of local government, which would efficiently, creatively, and wisely solve the problems at hand. They would have the greatest sensitivity to needs, while sharing the broader responsibilities of the larger community, region, and marketplace.

However, the imperfections of the real world and the narrow parochialism of some local governments argues against local control of federal housing programs. Many cities and counties have very little expertise or very little interest in—and sometimes opposition to—the provision of affordable housing. Secondly, the realization of many housing goals—eliminating housing segregation for instance—requires a level of government able to take a larger view of housing problems and opportunities. Finally, although housing development is a very local issue, housing markets tend to work not on a city level, but on a metropolitan or regional level.

In the preceding chapter of this volume, Anthony Downs argues that the optimal level of government for the administration of housing programs is the metropolitan level, where decision-makers are close enough to housing problems and realities to understand local particulars and peculiarities, yet can maintain a broader, regional view than the city or county. We agree with Downs in theory, but unfortunately, very few functioning metropolitan governments exist. Further, the creation of new regional entities is fraught with political and bureaucratic obstacles. For these reasons, Downs shares our view that states are generally at the best level to manage the allocation of federal housing funds.

States are at the mid-point between the local and federal level, possess some of the information and resources of both, and have powers not available to either. Like the federal government, states have the political and administrative machinery to study, debate, and define housing policies. Similarly, they have experience in public finance, the management of programs, and the allocation of funds between competing claims. However, states also have an understanding of and sensitivity to local housing issues, as well as offering a more direct avenue for input from constituent groups. Finally, states also possess regulatory powers over local land use, subdivision, and building decisions which are constitutionally prohibited from the federal government.

In sum, states are generally in the best position, from a policy perspective, to allocate federal funds and implement housing policy, but they also possess some unique attributes which make them solely suited to address the nation's housing problems.

The ability of the states to occupy this middle ground clearly depends on their size, their wealth, the quality of their political leadership, the competence of their bureaucracies, their political boundaries with respect to housing markets and metropolitan regions, and a host of other factors. Their *need* to occupy this middle ground depends on the severity of their housing problems and the behavior of the federal and local entities at the top and bottom layers of the governmental sandwich. Because of these compounding variables, the housing record of the states spans the full gamut, from highly competent and engaged to incompetent and disengaged.

Many examples of state activism in the housing field have been presented to demonstrate the willingness and ability of states to take on a larger implementation role in federal housing policy. These examples are representative of the three main arenas of state housing activity: housing programs, housing finance, and state regulation of local land use policy. The record shows a growing level of sophistication and effectiveness by state governments in all three.

We believe that federal housing policy will best be implemented at the state level. Given the special position of state governments to understand local realities yet pursue larger objectives, to coordinate funding and regulation, and to bring their own and other resources to bear, a state-level plan for the enactment of federal policies and programs will generally be most efficient and most cost-effective. The challenge to federal policy-makers is to design an approach that gives states enough freedom to meet their own housing needs in the manner best suited to each state. At the same time, the federal government also needs to find ways to encourage less committed and competent state governments to become involved, as well as to adopt safeguards that will ensure that state involvement is in fact positive.

* * * *

The authors wish to thank Bradley Inman, Carl Reidy, John Sidor, and current and former employees of the California Department of Housing and Community Development for their suggestions, information and comments.

Notes

1. Portions of this chapter are adapted and paraphrased from California Department of Housing and Community Development (Director I. Donald Terner), *101 Steps to Better Housing: The California Housing Plan, 1982* (Sacramento: CDHCD, 1982). Additional material is drawn from Council of State Community Affairs Agencies, *Proposal for a Revitalized National Housing Policy* (Washington: COSCAA, 1987).

2. Some of the material in this section is drawn from the Council of State Community Affairs Agencies, *State Housing Initiatives: A Compendium* (Washington: COSCAA, 1986); and J. Sidor, *1987 Compendium Update* (Washington: COSCAA, 1987); and various issues of *Housing Update*.

3. Most of the data and background material for this chapter come from the National Council of State Housing Agencies, *Production Activities State Housing Finance Agencies, 1985 and Cumulative; Housing Initiatives of State Housing Finance Agencies;* and *Delivering the American Dream: The Challenges to the State Housing Finance Agencies* (Washington: NCSHA).

4. Background information for this chapter was drawn from J. Sidor, *Influencing Land Supply and Land Development for Affordable Housing: Massachusetts, California, and Oregon* (Washington: COSCAA, 1984); and C. LaCasse, "An Overview of Chapter 774: The Anti-Snob Zoning Law," Massachusetts Institute of Technology, Department of Urban Studies and Planning, 1987; and California Department of Housing and Community Development, Director Christine Diemer, *California Affordable Housing Legislation: A Study of Local Implementation* (Sacramento: CDHCD, 1984).

5. State of Oregon, Land Conservation and Development Commission, *Statewide Planning Goals and Guidelines* (Salem, March 1980).

6. State of California, Government Code, Sec. 65580(d), Article 10.6.

7. Richard P. Nathan and Martha Derthick, "Reagan's Legacy: A New Liberalism Among the States," *New York Times,* December 18, 1987.

8. Nathan and Derthick, "Reagan's Legacy."

Chapter 5
Federal Fair Housing Policy: The Great Misapprehension

George C. Galster

Martin Luther King fell to an assassin's bullet on April 4, 1968. One week later an omnibus civil rights bill passed Congress, after languishing for years in committees. Title VIII of this bill prohibited discrimination against those who would rent or purchase homes on the basis of race, sex, creed, nationality, or religion. Federal fair housing law figuratively was born out of King's casket.

The passage of federal fair housing statutes brought us a step closer to the goal of equal housing opportunities for all citizens. With twenty years of hindsight it appears to be but a baby step, however, in light of two salient facts. First, illegal acts of housing discrimination continue to be perpetrated at an alarming rate. Recent audits that have utilized interracial pairs of "testers" have found, on average, that black homebuyers face at least a one-in-five chance of being discriminated against each time they confront a housing agent.[1] The comparable figures for black and Hispanic apartment seekers are one-in-two and one-in-three, respectively. Second, a high level of racial residential segregation persists. On average, 79 percent of black households would need to move from their 1980 location in order to achieve complete integration of our larger metropolitan areas (where most blacks live). The comparable percentages are 48 and 43 for Hispanics and Asians, respectively.[2] Recent studies have found that the segregation of blacks within our large metropolitan areas has hardly changed since 1970. The isolation of Hispanics from Anglos has increased in areas with significant gains in Hispanic population.[3]

Why has federal fair housing policy apparently had such limited efficacy? I propose that federal fair housing policy has suffered from crucial misapprehensions over the *ends* of policy, the *means* of achieving these ends, and the *process* of implementing these means. Given the resulting lack of appropriate programmatic efforts, it is no wonder that the goals of Title VIII of the Civil Rights Acts of 1968 remain as elusive as ever.

In this chapter I first examine the current controversy about fair housing policy, which revolves around the seemingly contrary positions of "freedom of choice" and "stable racial integration." The analysis which follows of the ends, means, and process of implementing fair housing policy shows that a comprehensive federal fair housing policy that carefully specifies policy means that *expand* housing choices for all races, implemented through a metropolitan-wide process, can achieve *both* ends of freedom of choice and stable integration. In the next section I present the broad guidelines for national fair housing policy that follow from my analysis. The final section briefly considers the relationship between fair housing policy and other aspects of national housing policy.

The discussion which follows focuses on the racial aspects of the transactions involving the rental or sale of dwelling units in the private housing market. This focus is not meant to suggest that other related issues, such as lending and insurance redlining, do not warrant attention, or that housing discrimination based on non-racial characteristics is trivial.[4] Rather, racial access to housing opportunities has always been at the center of the national fair housing debate. Furthermore, much of my analysis is relevant to the broader range of fair housing issues, and the policy recommendations made herein would if executed have the effect of securing improved housing opportunities for all protected classes.

Fair Housing: Ends, Means, and Process

The controversy swirling around fair housing policy in the 1980s centers on the prospective pursuit of two goals. One goal can be labeled "freedom of choice," a situation in which any dwelling on the market is made equally available to any homeseeker of appropriate economic means, regardless of race, sex, ethnicity, religion, source of income, etc. The other goal can be labeled "stable racial integration," a situation where many, if not most, neighborhoods are characterized by substantial demand by majority and minority homeseekers that persist over time. The controversy centers on two questions. Is stable racial integration (hereafter SRI) an important goal? Is the pursuit of SRI consistent with the pursuit of freedom of choice (hereafter FOC)?[5]

The great misapprehension about fair housing policy is fundamentally due to a failure to disentangle ends, means, and process. It is conventional to believe that the ends of FOC and SRI are incompatible because particular means for achieving them are. Conflict over the appropriate means for achieving SRI frequently arises because the appropriate, metropolitan-area-wide frame of reference for comprehending desegregation processes is not taken. Careful consideration of the two ends of fair housing policy, the possible means for achieving these ends, and the process by which these means are implemented will reveal the fundamental complementarity between FOC and SRI. I argue that, in *principle,* true FOC is only possible in the presence of SRI, and that, in *practice,* an *appropriate* set of policies designed to promote SRI is *necessary* for the achievement of FOC.

Ends

It is beyond question that FOC should be a goal of fair housing policy. But what does FOC really mean? The conventional definition is that FOC means the ability of anyone of appropriate economic means to acquire any particular dwelling desired. This definition is based on an overly narrow and unreasonable conception of housing.

It is clear that FOC as a goal of Title VIII meant the expansion of potential housing choices of minority homeseekers outside traditional minority neighborh~ ds. Implicit in this view is the expansion of choices not only of dwelling type and quality, but also of neighborhood characteristics like schools, public services, physical environment, proximity to employment, and, presumably, racial composition.

This broader view of "housing" as a package consisting of both dwelling and neighborhood attributes has consistently rested at the foundation of federal policy since the Housing Act of 1946 articulated the goal of "a decent home *and a suitable living environment"* (emphasis mine) for all Americans.

It follows from this definition of housing as a package that FOC means the expansion of options for minority (as well as majority) households to live in stable, racially integrated neighborhoods.[6] But for FOC to be more than a sham, this presumes that there actually *are* such neighborhoods from which to choose. Unfortunately, given longstanding prejudices and institutional features, and the peculiar processes of racial tipping abetted by illegal acts which I shall discuss more below, SRI rarely occurs in metropolitan housing markets without active policy intervention. In our largest cities only about one-fifth of the census tracts may be classified as racially mixed, and of these only one-fourth remained mixed during the 1970–1980 period.[7] This means that the goal of FOC cannot be achieved *in principle* without simultaneously achieving the goal of SRI.

Means

The issue of "means" raises the question as to how society goes about pursuing SRI. Must it be done in such a way that, ironically, the very FOC which it seeks to expand is constricted? The oft-heard response of "yes" is based on a misapprehension about what means necessarily must be employed in the pursuit of SRI.[8]

There is no doubt that the use of racial quotas as a means of integration maintenance in a community or housing complex restricts the choices of minority homeseekers. Because it thereby imposes undue burdens on the protected class, its use has been adjudged illegal.[9]

Other frequently employed devices do not create serious limitations of choice. Restrictions on "for sale" signs and on solicitations by real estate agents, for example, have been upheld in Federal court.[10]

Still other means or attaining SRI are actually *choice-enhancing*. The provision of additional information (either through the various media or through first-hand tours of homes) to minority and majority homeseekers about housing options in neighborhoods in which traditionally they would not search clearly expands housing choices. Similarly, the provision of economic incentives to *all* homeseekers who make "pro-integrative" moves indirectly provides extra resources for defraying the higher housing market search costs which such non-traditional moves might entail.

Thus, although certain means for achieving SRI clearly restrict FOC, other means are neutral, and still others expand the range of choices. But we can go farther than this claim that the *means* of achieving SRI do not necessarily conflict with the *ends* of FOC. Achieving the *end* of SRI is in itself a crucial *means* of achieving FOC.

The crux of the argument is this. Because "equal-status" interracial residential contact is a fundamental means by which prejudices are eroded, and because prejudices of white real estate agents or their clientele are the root motivators for discriminatory acts in the housing market, attaining SRI becomes a means for promoting FOC. Social scientists have documented how whites' racial stereotypes have withered when they have the opportunity to live with minority neighbors of roughly equal socio-economic status—precisely the sort of goal sought by integration advocates.[11] Recent studies also have reached a consensus that most discriminatory behavior in the housing market is founded on either the personal prejudices of agents or their belief that it is in their financial interest to cater to the presumed prejudices of their white customers.[12] Thus, insofar as SRI can be achieved and such prejudices thereby reduced, the pursuit of FOC can be eased. But, unlike the current strategy that tries to eliminate discrimination through deterrence, this approach tries to eliminate it by removing its root cause. Empirical support for this contention has been provided by a recent study showing that, after controlling for other factors, metropolitan areas with less segregation evidence lower rates of housing discrimination.[13]

Not only does the end of SRI complement the means of achieving FOC, but the converse is true as well. Any individual community's task of securing a balance between housing demands of minority and majority homeseekers is abetted the greater the FOC among *all* communities in the metropolitan area. The more FOC is a reality *everywhere,* the less focused will be the influx of minority homeseekers *anywhere.* Similarly, the more widely minorities exercise their FOC, the fewer the "all-white havens" to which prejudiced whites in integrated communities can flee. In support of this claim, recent statistical analysis has shown that if discriminatory activity in a neighborhood is reduced from the incidence present in the average metropolitan area to that present in areas with the lowest measured incidence,[14] a decrease of neighborhood segregation by about one-third would result.[15]

In sum, the means of achieving SRI need not necessarily be antithetical to the end of FOC. On the contrary, the pursuit of either goal is fundamentally complementary to the achievement of the other.

Process

If the pursuit of the twin goals of FOC and SRI are as complementary as claimed, why have we not witnessed a more significant decline in segregation as communities have promulgated open housing policies? This common expectation stems from a misapprehension that fair housing is a local municipal problem demanding localized responses.

The federal government has never attempted to insure that *all* the distinct municipalities comprising the typical metropolitan area promptly and aggressively adopt the tenets of Title VIII. Attempts at area-wide coordination by private fair housing groups, such as the Cuyahoga Plan in Cleveland and the Leadership Council in Chicago, have produced only modest successes because they have not been backed by sufficiently strong legal, budgetary, or political pressures. As a result, individual local governments continue to have great latitude in enacting fair housing legislation, enforcing existing statutes, affirmatively marketing their community, and pursuing pro-integration strategies.

This local autonomy would not be so injurious to the cause of fair housing were it not for the idiosyncratic spatial features of the racially dual housing market. Historically, increments in the supply of housing needed by the minority community have occurred through the peripheral expansion of this community's boundaries into formerly all-white neighborhoods. Given the pervasive discriminatory barriers facing them in most white areas, minority homeseekers understandably concentrated their search in or near minority neighborhoods. No wonder, then, whenever a new area came to be perceived as "open" to minorities they flocked to occupy it. This surge of spatially concentrated minority demand, accompanied and abetted by unscrupulous "block-busting" and "steering" activities, often produced a "tipping" dynamic that exacerbated the flight of white households and led to the rapid resegregation of the area. The frequent repetition of this spatial dynamic reinforced white households' beliefs that residence in integrated areas was undesirable. The legacy of the dual housing market is that, even today, most minority homeseekers search only in traditional minority neighborhoods or in nearby ones which have clearly expressed an openness to them; and most white home-seekers eschew searching in neighborhoods containing more than trivial numbers of minorities.[16]

Given the lack of spatial coordination in the pursuit of fair housing and the spatial dynamics of resegregation and housing market search, each individual municipality faces powerful incentives to behave in ways that impede the attainment of either fair housing goal. Communities on the fringe of metropolitan areas can treat fair housing as a non-issue. After all, with a perceived demand only from white homeseekers, what is "the problem?" Communities nearer traditional areas of minority housing searches face a more urgent dilemma. On the one hand, such communities can backslide on providing open housing opportunities, thereby avoiding the putatively inevitable tipping of some of their neighborhoods but acquiring the stigma of bigotry. On the other hand, communities can aggressively market themselves as "open." But, especially if they are located adjacent to predominantly minority neighborhoods, they may find that choice-neutral and choice-enhancing techniques for promoting integration are inadequate to forestall the momentum of resegregation. Given these perverse incentives facing each municipality, it is no wonder that fair housing has often not been pursued vigorously and that its twin goals appear contradictory.

However, this apparent contradiction disappears if we take a coordinated, metropolitan area-wide perspective. If all metropolitan area governments simultaneously enacted programs to affirmatively market their communities, none would face the aforementioned dilemma. As housing searches of all homeseekers expanded into nontraditional neighborhoods, the concentration of demands by one race or the other would be spatially diffused. As a consequence, choice-neutral and choice-expanding types of pro-integration strategies would succeed in achieving SRI.

In sum, the conflict between FOC and SRI apparent at the municipal level is not inevitable. Rather the misapprehension is the product of a particular history of spatially uncoordinated fair housing efforts which has arisen out of localized policy perspectives.

Toward a National Fair Housing Policy

The foregoing analysis yields distinct implications for the formulation of future federal fair housing policy. First, guiding principles concerning FOC and SRI must be clarified so that the debilitating skirmishing over the appropriate ends of fair housing can cease. Efforts must be taken to provide both a legal framework and an adequate resource base so that the deterrent effect of Title VIII can be maximized. Policies promoting SRI directly should be initiated. Finally, the coordination of municipal fair housing activities within each metropolitan area must be encouraged.[17]

Clarification of Principles

The first goal of federal policy must be to state unambiguously the principles of national fair housing policy. Both programmatic goals *and* the appropriate (and inappropriate) means of achieving them must be spelled out.

Because SRI is a prerequisite to true FOC as well as a stimulant for its attainment, it is clear that the twin goals of FOC *and* SRI should be affirmed explicitly.[18] However, it is also clear that while certain means for attaining SRI (such as those described below) should be encouraged, other means (such as racial quotas) should be proscribed if they conflict with the FOC goal.

Establishment of a Legal Framework for Deterrence

Any law proscribing a certain activity is successful in eliminating that activity only insofar as it establishes a potent deterrent. In order to be effective, deterrence means that those who would commit illegal acts must perceive: (1) a high probability that their illegal acts will be detected; (2) a high probability that, once detected, their acts will be challenged and judged illegal; *and* (3) a high probability that, once convicted, they will incur a significant penalty. I argue that current federal law—even since the Fair Housing Amendments Act of 1988—does not provide an adequate deterrent.[19]

The legal framework provided by the Fair Housing Amendments Act focuses on the latter two components of deterrence above. It tries to increase the probability of conviction by, for example, lengthening the statute of limitations, providing court-appointed attorneys for plaintiffs, and increasing the speed of complaint resolution through the establishment of administrative law tribunals. It tries to increase the perceived penalties by raising the limitation on punitive damage awards from $1,000 to $50,000 for first offenders, and to $100,000 for second offenders.

Unfortunately, these particular amendments hold little promise for significantly abetting deterrence. Indeed, such is the prognosis for any legal framework that is premised on individual victim detection and initiation of legal redress: the enforcement process would be triggered by individuals subjected to housing discrimination complaining to HUD or the appropriate local authority, and then pursuing redress if, upon investigation, their complaint showed probable cause. In the case of housing discrimination, neither aspect of this premise can be relied upon in practice. Individuals typically cannot detect illegal acts and, even when they do, their prospective benefits from seeking redress often fall short of their prospective costs of doing so. Each aspect is considered in turn below.

The detection of discrimination. Relatively few individual victims of discrimination realize that they have been victimized. An ironic consequence of the passage of Fair Housing Laws is that discrimination has "gone underground"; discriminatory techniques have become more subtle precisely so as to avoid detection.[20] As a consequence, it now appears that *less than 1 percent* of the illegal acts of housing discrimination are complained about.[21]

In light of this subtle nature of the acts being legally proscribed, HUD's response has been curious indeed. Instead of concentrating on how to better detect illegal acts, HUD sought the voluntary elimination of these acts through the cooperation of the real estate industry. Illustrative was the first of several installments of the Voluntary Affirmative Marketing Agreement (VAMA) negotiated with the National Association of Realtors in 1972. In conjunction, Community Housing Resource Boards (CHRB), consisting of volunteer representatives of local fair housing groups and the real estate industry, were established to monitor compliance with VAMA.

The fatal flaws in this approach are well known. There are no incentives to participate in VAMA and actively pursue its guidelines. Given their lack of resources, the divided loyalties of their governing boards, and unfamiliarity with VAMA provisions, CHRBs have been ineffective in their monitoring efforts.[22] The smaller scale and less professional segments of the real estate industry, especially in the rental market, have been little affected. Certainly, securing the cooperation of major real estate interests in the pursuit of fair housing policy is a worthy aim. However, in the absence of comprehensive, industry-wide professional associations and strong incentives for self-policing of their members by these associations, to substitute voluntary compliance for detection emasculates effective deterrence. The proof is in the persistent plague of discriminatory acts cited above.

The pursuit of redress. Even when discriminatory acts are sufficiently blatant to arouse suspicion on the part of aggrieved individuals, typically there are strong disincentives which discourage their pursuit of legal redress. Complainants must bear the substantial time, inconvenience, psychological, and sometimes monetary costs of the investigation, conciliation, or litigation process. By contrast, their prospective compensatory damage awards appear quite modest, given the average settlements.[23] Furthermore, the desired dwelling in question may no longer be available. The result is an unwillingness of many who believe that they have been discriminated against to formally complain.

The recent fair housing amendments provide for plaintiff attorney fees and speedier investigation and adjudication processes, in an attempt to alter the relative balance of perceived costs and benefits. But there are inherent limitations in how far one can tip this balance so long as the *individual* is seen as the complainant. The individual must always seek an immediate resolution of the homeseeking problem, and will always perceive relatively high time, inconvenience, and psychological costs in the pursuit of relief, even when out-of-pocket expenses are reimbursed.

From individual to collective modes of enforcement. The fundamental flaw in the current federal legal framework for achieving FOC is its purely individualistic premise. What is required are legal modifications that affirm and expand the role of organizations and governments as collective vehicles of enforcement. A provision in the recent fair housing amendments that allows the Secretary of HUD to initiate complaints represents a step in the right direction. But further steps should be taken. Given the aforementioned unambiguous statement of the twin fair housing goals of FOC and SRI, the expansion of collective enforcement mechanisms could mean the inclusion of such entities as neighborhood associations and local governments who seek SRI. Because housing discrimination interferes with the achievement of SRI, such organizations working for SRI will thereby gain clear legal standing to obtain redress for such practices.[24]

Such a collective viewpoint offers two advantages over the individualistic one. First, collective investigations hold more promise of detecting illegal acts. Second, collective resources are likely to be superior to individual ones, thus enhancing the capabilities for pursuing legal redress.

Organizations have at their disposal a proven, legal means of detecting discrimination that individuals do not: testing.[25] Testing has been the conventional means of investigating complaints by bona fide homeseekers for many years. But if it is used solely in this capacity, it will be subject to the limitation of the individualistic approach above: most victims will not complain so as to trigger the testing mechanism.

Effective detection of housing discrimination *requires* that an *ongoing, comprehensive program of random testing* be conducted by one or more organizations throughout each metropolitan area.[26] Given the subtle nature of most discriminatory acts, testing is the only foolproof means of uncovering it. Given the pervasiveness of discrimination geographically and in both owner and rental sectors, testing must be comprehensive in scope. Given that all housing market agents must be convinced that there is a nontrivial chance that their activities will be checked, the testing must be ongoing and random. It is clear that only through a collective approach can such an "enforcement testing" policy be implemented, and redress for illegal acts that it uncovers be sought in the courts.

Although the evidence is limited, it appears that such collective enforcement techniques can create a potent deterrent. Cleveland Heights, Ohio, has undertaken a series of random tests in its community since the late 1970s. This program, coupled with efforts to educate the real estate industry about fair housing and well-publicized suits against major real estate brokerage firms,[27] has produced a dramatic decline in the observed incidence of discriminatory acts, as revealed by the tests themselves.[28] Similar efforts by the Kentucky Commission on Human Rights have returned comparable dividends.[29]

Given that court-worthy evidence has been provided through testing, the collective pursuit of legal redress would hold more promise for the attainment of significant remedies. Due to their comparatively limited resources, individual plaintiffs are more likely to settle suits for minimal compensatory damages. These settlements are unlikely to represent significant penalties to defendants, especially when damages are reimbursed though insurance and public disclosure of the settlement terms is proscribed. Organizations and governments, on the other hand, would tend to pursue punitive damages and affirmative relief, so as to alter the defendant's behavior in the future.

Establishing a legal framework for deterrence: a summary. To establish a legal structure that provides a credible deterrent to would-be discriminators, federal policy must move beyond its individualistic focus. So long as enforcement relies upon individual victims both recognizing that they have been victimized and then pursuing channels of legal redress, the two prerequisite components of deterrence, detection and conviction, will remain impotent. A legal framework for effective deterrence fundamentally must focus on collective enforcement. Organizations and governments must be empowered to employ comprehensive, random "enforcement testing," and a wider range of groups must be given legal standing to file suits on the basis of evidence so gathered.

Although this may seem like a radical approach for the enforcement of fair housing laws, there are ample precedents. In the case of toxic wastes and other pollutants, the federal government has deemed that it is unreasonable to expect individual citizens to file suit against potential polluters. After all, citizens often do not know that they are being harmed, and cannot easily muster sufficient resources to undertake a legal battle with suspected polluters. As a result, collective enforcement has been applied through the establishment of the Environmental Protection Agency. Other precedents have been established in the Mine Safety and Health Act of 1977 and the Occupational Safety and Health Act of 1979. Both empower the federal government to initiate warrantless administrative "spot" inspections so as to guard against health and safety violations in the workplace which otherwise might not be recognized by workers. Similar sorts of pro-active federal enforcement efforts occur in the realms of anti-trust, consumer and mail fraud, and bank examinations, for instance.

Commitment of Adequate Resources to Enforcement

It is painfully obvious that by its focus on individualistic enforcement, voluntary compliance, and "monitoring" by volunteer-staffed CHRBs the federal government has sought fair housing "on the cheap." Even a significantly revised legal framework as described above will do little to enhance deterrence if inadequate resources are committed to the enforcement testing effort. Two main questions arise about such a distribution of resources: To whom? How?

Recipients of resources. Several approaches are possible. The federal government could *directly* undertake the job of enforcement, or it could *indirectly* do so by commissioning other, more local entities. The former approach would mean the establishment of federal fair housing enforcement agencies (presumably an arm of HUD) in metropolitan areas across the country. Their task primarily would be to conduct enforcement testing programs and to initiate suits against violators.

The latter approach has predominated in the past. For example, federal funding has been directed to private, not-for-profit fair housing groups.[30] Expanding the efforts of these groups is appealing, given the substantial base of expertise and potential for private leveraging of public funds which these private groups offer.[31] Two concerns remain, however, about whether these groups should be the centerpiece of an expanded enforcement effort.

First, there is fear on the part of elements of the real estate industry that private groups would abuse their enforcement powers and use testing evidence as a means for extorting concessions from individual agents and the industry.[32] Any new legal framework that expands and codifies the central role of private groups in enforcement testing would need to reiterate the applicability of existing laws which specify strong penalties for any such attempts at extortion or harassment.

Second, sole reliance on existing private groups would result in uneven geographic law enforcement. The current network of six dozen or so private fair housing groups is most dense in the major metropolitan areas of the Northeast, North Central, and West Coast regions. Smaller cities in these regions, and even large cities in other regions, have no similar organizations. And it is questionable whether the federal government could supply sufficient blandishments to such areas that these groups could be formed. In the event that they could not be, comprehensive enforcement would imply that the federal government directly establish local HUD agencies in these areas, as described above.

Another mechanism of indirect enforcement would be to better utilize state or local government civil rights agencies.[33] The ability of these agencies to gain relief for complainants has improved markedly in the last decade.[34] Although geographic coverage would be less of a problem here, the uniformity of enforcement effort might well be. Vagaries in the local political climate likely would mean vast disparities in the willingness of local governments to serve as effective instruments of federal policy, as the history of the civil rights movement makes plain.

Mechanisms of resource transfer. Once the recipients of enforcement resources are identified, a means of transferring these funds must be established. Again, both direct and indirect mechanisms are possible. Direct mechanisms would include a conventional line item in the HUD budget for the local enforcement testing offices described above. Another form of direct support would be earmarked grants to qualifying local organizations or governments who were contracted to perform enforcement efforts, as is currently done under the Fair Housing Assistance Program.

Indirect forms of support could take a wider variety of forms. One strategy would be to provide financial "carrots and sticks" to lower levels of government so that *they* would directly provide support for the enforcement agencies. "Carrots" might consist, for example, of raising the current caps on the amount of revenue bonds that states could issue if they developed and implemented metropolitan-wide strategies for FOC and SRI. "Sticks" might consist of requiring states or local governments to actively support approved fair housing organizations in order to qualify for *any* sort of intergovernmental grant.[35] In order to represent a potent incentive these strings must be attached to funds that *all* local jurisdictions rely upon, not certain categorical grants that (especially affluent) communities can take or leave. Again, the precedent of the Environmental Protection Agency (EPA) is instructive. The EPA has tied compliance with particular clean air regulations to the receipt of federal highway funds.

Another strategy for indirectly supplying resources to enforcement organizations is through court-awarded compensatory damages. Current legal precedents suggest that only relatively modest awards are appropriate, and only under limited circumstances.[36] Although these funds undoubtedly would be insufficient to support fully the enforcement testing program envisioned, they potentially could provide an important source of supplementary resources which would be freed from public sector budgetary pressures.

Promotion of Stable Racial Integration

True FOC implies the presence of SRI. Furthermore, the movement toward SRI removes a major motivator for illegal discriminatory acts, thereby making the attainment of FOC more realistic. Finally, a racially segregated society imposes enormous social and economic costs on all citizens, minority and majority races alike.[37] For these reasons SRI should be established as an explicit goal of federal policy. It follows that federal policies should develop means to achieve SRI that go beyond merely hoping that it will occur as a byproduct of the effort to enforce Title VIII.

Indirectly the goal of SRI could be served by providing financial incentives to local governments to develop their own strategies for its attainment, similar to those suggested above in the context of enforcement. But federal policy could also move to directly encourage SRI.

One avenue, which has shown promise at the local level,[38] is to provide financial incentives to any households (regardless of race) who move in such a fashion that SRI is abetted. One comparatively simple mechanism for doing so at the federal level would be to provide an income tax credit through the Internal Revenue Service. Eligibility for the credit would need to be certified by the local fair housing agency into whose jurisdiction the applicant moved. Such eligibility presupposes that "neighborhoods" have been defined and their current racial composition monitored on a regular basis. But this should not prove an insurmountable task of appropriate, metropolitan-wide fair housing organizations were established and provided with adequate resources, as argued for below.

The principle of providing public tax incentives for undertaking particular activities deemed to involve overriding societal interests is well established. We have seen fit to offer tax credits to those who, among other things, renovate historical buildings, offer jobs to the hard-core unemployed, buy instead of rent a home, install energy conservation devices, and invest in the latest technology for their factories. Is SRI any less in the public interest?

Encouragement of Metropolitan Area-Wide Coordination

As explained above, SRI can only be accomplished through means which do not violate FOC if *all* local communities participate in fair housing activities. Thus, a prime component of any federal fair housing policy must be a mechanism for securing such metropolitan area-wide coordination of efforts in the combined pursuit of both FOC and SRI.

One obvious means for doing so is through the careful tailoring of the financial incentives to local governments described above. Federal funds to states might, for instance, be tied to the establishment and/or support of regional fair housing organizations (either public or private) that both enforce Title VIII so as achieve FOC and promote SRI in their major metropolitan areas. States might be especially effective "conveners" of confederations of municipalities with a region. Regional Planning Agencies (A-95 Boards) might also be considered as coordinating frameworks. Similarly, direct federal financial aid to municipalities might be made contingent upon their formal cooperation with such a regional organization. Regardless of the particular mechanism, however, it should be recognized that the overwhelming majority of local governments must be induced to actively support fair housing, if the twin goals of FOC and SRI are to be attained in that region.

Fair Housing and Other Housing Policies

Pursuit of the goals of fair housing should be considered in the context of a broader set of potential federal housing policies. Analysis of the interrelationships between fair housing policy and other housing policies reveals a great potential for symbiotic, mutually reinforcing arrangements. That is, the particular means of pursuing the broader housing goals of expanding homeownership, preserving decent homes and neighborhoods while revitalizing others, and providing lower-income households with the means to occupy appropriate dwellings, potentially can be tailored so as to abet the achievement of fair housing goals. In turn, the attainment of fair housing enhances the pursuit of these broader goals.

Expanding Homeownership

A variety of policies provide subsidies to *individual* homeseekers thereby making homeownership financially feasible. Such individualistic policies offer the opportunity for encouraging subsidy recipients to purchase dwellings in a pattern that promotes SRI. For example, the Ohio Housing Finance Agency has set aside a portion of its below-market interest rate mortgages for exclusive use by first-time homebuyers making pro-integrative moves.

Conversely, achievement of FOC in housing would go far to stimulate homeownership among minority households. Because of their discriminatory confinement in sectors of the urban housing market where single-family homes are relatively scarce, property appreciation rates are relatively low, and threats of fire and vandalism are relatively high, minorities evidence a 10 percentage-point lower propensity to own their own home, compared to otherwise identical whites.[39]

Preserving and Revitalizing Neighborhoods

Wherever the federal government offers financial incentives for the upkeep or rehabilitation of properties, potential leverage exists for the promotion of fair housing. Every sort of inducement, from tax breaks to direct rehabilitation subsidies could, in principle, be tied to explicit commitments from owners and developers to affirmatively market the affected properties. Portions of the stock of dwellings offered for urban homesteading could be set aside for those whose occupancy would further the aim of SRI.

Conversely, movement toward SRI would prove a boon to the effort to preserve decent-quality neighborhoods. Today the self-fulfilling prophecies associated with neighborhood racial tipping and resegregation provide strong disincentives for the adequate maintenance of properties in the affected areas.[40] On the other hand, statistical analysis reveals that homeowners in neighborhoods that are stably integrated reinvest in their homes no differently than those in segregated areas.[41]

Assisting Lower-Income Households

Demand-side subsidies aimed at enabling lower-income households to occupy decent-quality dwellings without paying a burdensome fraction of their income toward rent could be readily adapted to encourage SRI.[42] Owners of new or substantially rehabilitated Section 8 units are now required to affirmatively market, but enforcement has been minimal. Recipients of either Section 8 or rent voucher subsidies could be provided information and counseling about pro-integrative housing options. Perhaps the amount of the subsidy could be varied so as to provide an incentive for pro-integrative moves.

Conversely, enhanced FOC would improve the efficiency of any demand-side assistance program, by expanding the set of feasible housing choices. Studies of past assistance programs have revealed the limited mobility patterns of recipients and have drawn pessimistic inferences about the desegregating potential of such efforts.[43] But the primary reason for this limited mobility is the lack of information about non-traditional neighborhood options and the fear of confronting discrimination in such areas.[44]

Deconcentration of Lower-Income Households

One further housing policy option, the dispersal of lower-income households from central city neighborhoods into the suburbs (through the construction of scattered-site subsidized housing or the geographic expansion of Section 8 existing dwellings) offers less potential complementarity with a fair housing policy aimed at *racial* FOC and SRI. Even if such a deconcentration policy were successful in supplying significant numbers of subsidized dwellings in the suburbs and having them occupied by large numbers of minority households, without initiating the tipping phenomenon, the goals of racially fair housing would be served only modestly. At one level, SRI would have been achieved, and the life chances of the assisted residents undoubtedly would have been improved. But the sorts of social interactions between the original white residents and the new, lower-income minority residents will not be of the "equal-status" variety which are crucial for the erosion of prejudices.[45] Indeed, such a scheme might backfire if it strengthens whites' ascriptions of traits of a particular socioeconomic class to all racial minorities.

*   *   *   *

In summary, true freedom of choice *presupposes* the existence of many stable, integrated neighborhoods. The achievement of stable racial integration *enhances* the pursuit of freedom of choice in housing, and vice versa. This analysis suggests that a national fair housing policy must:

1. *Clarify principles.* The mutual goals of freedom of choice and stable racial integration should be affirmed. Particular choice-restricting components of pro-integration strategy should be proscribed.
2. *Establish a legal framework for deterrence.* The system of enforcement must move away from one based on victim-initiated complaints and voluntary cooperation from the real estate industry, to one based

on collective enforcement through public or private groups. An effective deterrent can only be generated by a comprehensive program of ongoing, random testing conducted throughout all metropolitan areas by public and/or private organizations. A wider range of organizations must be empowered to bring suit based on these tests, and to receive significant compensatory damages upon court findings in their favor.

3. *Commit adequate resources for enforcement.* Organizations capable of undertaking the aforementioned enforcement effort must be established where they do not exist, and financially supported where they do. Resources could be transferred directly to these organizations by the federal government. Or, financial incentives could be created to induce lower levels of government to provide support to such organizations. Supplementary resources would be provided by court-awarded damage claims.

4. *Promote stable racial integration.* Integration should be directly promoted by providing incentives either to local governments to develop their own pro-integration plans and/or to individuals who make pro-integrative moves.

5. *Encourage metropolitan area-wide coordination.* Financial incentives must be carefully tailored so that municipal governments have strong incentives to develop area-wide fair housing institutions and cooperate in both anti-discrimination and integration maintenance efforts.

The pursuit of fair housing goals is complementary to the pursuit of numerous other housing policy goals. Thus, fair housing policy is of central importance in the formulation of a comprehensive, national housing policy.

Notes

1. G. Galster, "Racial Discrimination in Housing During the 1980s: A Review of the Audit Evidence," paper presented at Urban Affairs Association Meetings, Baltimore, March 1989.

2. Reynolds Farley, "The Residential Segregation of Blacks from Whites," pp. 14–28 in U.S. Commission on Civil Rights, *Issues in Housing Discrimination* (Washington: USGPO, 1986). See also S. McKinney and A. Schnare, "Trends in Residential Segregation by Race, 1960–1980" (Washington: Urban Institute, October 1986).

3. D. Massey and N. Denton, "Trends in the Residential Segregation of Blacks, Hispanics and Asians: 1970–1980," *American Sociological Review* 52 (Dec. 1987) 802–25. Also see G. Tobin, ed., *Divided Neighborhoods: Changing Patterns of Racial Segregation* (Newbury Park, CA: SAGE Publications, 1987).

4. The focus is also not on public sector discriminatory policies, such as public housing authorities' tenant assignment procedures or municipalities' racially exclusionary zoning programs. These, too, are not trivial, but beyond the scope of this

paper. See O. Hetzel, "A Perspective on Legal Issues in Housing Discrimination," in U.S. Commission on Civil Rights, *Issues in Housing Discrimination,* vol. 1.

5. R. Lake, "Postscript: Unresolved Themes in the Evolution of Fair Housing," in John Goering, ed., *Housing Desegregation and Federal Policy* (Chapel Hill: University of North Carolina Press, 1986); O. Newman, "Fair Housing: The Conflict Between Integration and Non-Discrimination," in U.S. Commission on Civil Rights, *Housing Discrimination.*

6. The Supreme Court has held, for example, that white residents who were not directly harmed by a discriminatory policy nevertheless had standing to challenge such a policy because it denied them the benefits of interracial association; see Trafficante v. Metropolitan Life Insurance Co., 409 U.S. 205 (1972).

7. G. Galster, "Neighborhood Racial Change, Segregationist Sentiments, and Affirmative Marketing Policies," *Journal of Urban Economics,* forthcoming; B. Lee, "Racially Mixed Neighborhoods During the 1970s," *Social Science Quarterly* 66 (1985) 346–364.

8. See, e.g., W. North, *Passwords and Prejudices* (Chicago: NAR, 1986); National Assoc. of Realtors, *Statement of Policy* (Chicago: NAR, 1987) 12.

9. See A. Polikoff, "Sustainable Integration or Inevitable Resegregation: The Troubling Questions," in Goering, ed., *Housing Desegregation;* Mario et al. v. Starret City Assoc., 1979 (79 C. V. 3096: E.R.N.) and USA v. Starret City Assoc., 1984 (C.V. 84-2793). For summaries of the case, see Newman, "Fair Housing" and *TRENDS in Housing* 26, 1 (1987) 1.

10. Greater South Suburban Board of Realtors and NAR v. South Suburban Housing Center, 1984 (No. 83 C8149).

11. For a review of the evidence, see J. Yinger, "On the Possibility of Achieving Racial Integration Through Subsidized Housing" and R. Helper, "Success and Resistance Factors in the Maintenance of Racially Mixed Neighborhoods," both in Goering, ed., *Housing Desegregation.*

12. J. Yinger, "Measuring Discrimination Through Fair Housing Audits," *American Economic Review* 76 (1986) 881–893; G. Galster, "On the Ecology of Racial Discrimination in Housing," *Urban Affairs Quarterly* 23 (1987) 84–107.

13. G. Galster and M. Keeney, "Race, Residence, Discrimination, and Economic Opportunity," *Urban Affairs Quarterly* 24 (1988) 87–117.

14. As measured by the Housing Market Practices Survey; see R. Wienk, C. Reid, J. Simonson, and F. Eggers, *Measuring Racial Discrimination in American Housing Markets* (Washington: HUD, 1977).

15. G. Galster, "More Than Skin Deep," in Goering, ed., *Housing Desegregation;* Galster and Keeney, "Race, Residence, Discrimination."

16. D. Birch et al., *Behavioral Foundations of Neighborhood Change* (Washington: USGPO/HUD, 1979); R. Lake, *The New Suburbanites* (New Brunswick, NJ: CUPR/Rutgers University Press, 1981); A. Vidal, "Racial Differences in Housing Search Behavior," paper presented at Eastern Economics Association meeting, Boston, 1983.

17. I do not claim originality for all these proposals. Various elements have been suggested, e.g., by A. Downs, *Opening Up the Suburbs* (New Haven, CT: Yale University Press, 1973), and by the U.S. Civil Rights Commission, *The Federal Fair Housing Effort* (Washington: USGPO, 1979).

18. In Linmark Assoc. v. Township of Willingboro, 1977 (431 U.S. 85, 94) the Supreme Court recognized a national commitment to SRI implicit in Title VIII.

19. See, for instance, General Accounting Office, *Stronger Federal Enforcement Needed to Uphold Fair Housing Laws* (Washington: USGAO, 1978); U.S. Commission on Civil Rights, *Federal Civil Rights Commitments* (Washington: USCCR,

1983); Leadership Conference on Civil Rights, "Some Questions and Answers on the Fair Housing Amendments Act of 1983" (Washington: LCCR, 1983); Citizens' Commission on Civil Rights, *A Decent Home* (Washington: Center for National Policy Review, Catholic University, 1983); NCDH Exec. Dir. Martin Sloane, Testimony before Senate Subcommittee on the Constitution (April 7, 1987).

20. R. Wienk et al., *Measuring Racial Discrimination in American Housing Markets* (Washington: HUD/PR&R, 1979); H. Newburger, *Recent Evidence on Discrimination in Housing* (Washington: HUD/PD&R, 1985); W. Tisdale, Executive Director of Milwaukee Fair Housing Center, "Housing Discrimination: A New Technology," in U.S. Commission on Civil Rights, *A Sheltered Crisis* (Washington: USCCR, 1983).

21. HUD has been processing 4,000 to 5,000 complaints annually during the 1980s; see W. S. Davis, "Presentation," in U.S. Commission on Civil Rights, *Federal Commitments;* Antonio Monroig, handout at joint HUD-civil rights organizations meeting (Sept. 6, 1985). Local public and private fair housing authorities may have received a comparable number, though the estimates are imprecise. By contrast, HUD has conservatively estimated that approximately two million illegal acts of housing discrimination occur annually; see Monroig, Sept. 6, 1985 handout; J. Goering, "Minority Housing Needs and Civil Rights Enforcement," in Jamshid Momeni, ed., *Race, Ethnicity, and Minority Housing in the U.S.* (Westport, CT: Greenwood Press, 1986); and U.S. Dept. of HUD, *FY 1986 Budget: Summary* (Washington: USGPO, 1986) FHEO-7.

22. See J. James, *An Initial Study of the CHRB Program* (Washington: HUD-PDR, September 1985).

23. An average damage award of $500 was noted in J. Wallace et al., *An Evaluation of the Fair Housing Assistance Program* (Cambridge: Abt Associates report for HUD-PDR, June 1985), and Goering, "Minority Housing Needs."

24. Currently, individual homeseekers, private fair housing groups, and (under certain circumstances) individual testers have legal standing to sue. What is being suggested here is that damage awards be permitted for a wider range of groups that pursue SRI and FOC. For a review of legal precedents, see Assistant Secretary FHEO Antonio Monroig, "Justification Memo on HUD Enforcement Responsibilities and the Role of Private Fair Housing Councils" (Washington: HUD/FHEO, Dec. 5, 1984); and Hetzel, "Perspective on Legal Issues."

25. The generally accepted definition of testing may be found in National Committee Against Discrimination in Housing, *Guide to Fair Housing Law Enforcement* (Washington: NCDH/HUD, 1979), 39. The efficacy of testing as a means of detecting discriminatory acts is discussed in Wallace et al., *Evaluation of Fair Housing.*

26. Pilot projects for comprehensive, random testing will be undertaken under the auspices of the Fair Housing Initiatives Program in 1989.

27. Heights Community Congress v. Rosenblatt Realty 1975 (73 F.R.D. 1; N.D. Ohio); Heights Community Congress v. Hilltop Realty 1983 (C79-422; N.D. Ohio).

28. Heights Community Congress, *1985 Housing Availability Report* (Cleveland Heights, OH: HCC, Jan. 1986).

29. (Executive Director, Kentucky Commission on Civil Rights) G. Martin, testimony before Senate Subcommittee on Housing and Urban Affairs (June 18, 1986); Galster, "Racial Discrimination in Housing."

30. Funding has been provided through the Fair Housing Enforcement Demonstration and Fair Housing Assistance Programs, and is forthcoming as part of the Fair Housing Initiatives Program.

31. It has been shown that private groups leverage $2–3 for each federal dollar

received; see HUD, *The Fair Housing Enforcement Demonstration* (Washington: HUD-PDR-750, October, 1983).

32. See, e.g., (Vice-President of NAR) William North, testimony before Senate Subcommittee on Housing and Urban Affairs, June 6, 1986.

33. Currently the bulk of HUD's $5–6 million annual fair housing enforcement budget is allocated to states and localities having laws which are "substantially equivalent" to Title VIII.

34. Goering, "Minority Housing Needs."

35. This represents an extension of the principle applied under the "expected to reside" stipulations used in the past to qualify localities for CDBG funds. Analogously, modernization funds for local Public Housing Authorities have been tied to their desegregation activities.

36. The cases of Havens Realty Corp. v. Coleman 1982 (455 U.S. 363) and Davis v. Mansards 1984 (597 F. Supp. 334, N.D. IN) awarded compensatory damages to private fair housing groups, but only because the violation involved misrepresentation of housing market information and thereby interfered with the groups' mission of providing accurate information to homeseekers.

37. See, e.g., J. Yinger, G. Galster, B. Smith, and F. Eggers, "Status of Research into Racial Discrimination and Segregation in American Housing Markets," *HUD Occasional Papers* 6 (1979) 55–175; Leadership Council for Metropolitan Open Communities, *The Costs of Housing Discrimination and Segregation* (Chicago: LCMOC, 1987); G. Galster, "Residential Segregation and Interracial Economic Disparities," *Journal of Urban Economics* 21 (1987) 22–44; Galster and Keeney, "Race, Residence, Discrimination."

38. The Ohio Housing Finance Agency has set aside a portion of its below-market interest rate mortgage funds (raised by general obligation state bond issues) for use by homebuyers making pro-integrative moves. The cities of Shaker Heights and Cleveland Heights in the eastern Cleveland suburbs and the Fund for an Open Society in Philadelphia offer low-interest, deferred repayment loans to homebuyers making pro-integrative moves. The City of Oak Park, IL, is experimenting with a plan that provides financial incentives to apartment owners who maintain racially integrated buildings. For further details and discussion, see R. Silverman, "Subsidizing Tolerance for Open Communities," *Wisconsin Law Review* 19 (1977) 375–501, and A. Polikoff, Testimony before the House Subcommittee on Constitutional and Civil Rights, December 12, 1988.

39. See Yinger et al., "Research into Racial Discrimination," for a review of the evidence here.

40. See D. Varady, *Neighborhood Upgrading: A Realistic Assessment* (Albany, NY: SUNY Press, 1986); W. Grigsby, M. Baratz, D. Maclennan, and G. Galster, *The Dynamics of Neighborhood Change and Decline* (London: Pergamon, 1987).

41. G. Galster, *Homeowners and Neighborhood Reinvestment* (Durham, NC: Duke University Press, 1987) ch. 9.

42. For more on the relationship between vouchers and fair housing issues, see J. Palffy, "Housing Vouchers," in U.S. Commission on Civil Rights, *A Sheltered Crisis*.

43. J. Sutker, "Race and Residential Modality: The Effects of Housing Assistance Programs on Household Behavior," in Goering, ed., *Housing Desegregation*.

44. G. Weisbrod and A. Vidal, "Housing Search Barriers for Low Income Renters," *Urban Affairs Quarterly* 16 (1981) 465–482.

45. Yinger, "On the Possibility of Achieving Racial Integration."

Chapter 6
First-Time Homebuyers: Issues and Policy Options

Denise DiPasquale

The combination of rapidly rising housing prices and increasing mortgage interest rates in the late 1970s and early 1980s has generated much concern that homeownership is becoming less affordable, particularly to young, first-time homebuyers. The most often cited evidence of the decline in affordability is the recent decline in the national homeownership rate. From the end of World War II until 1980, the homeownership rate in the U.S. increased steadily. Since 1980, it has fallen every year.[1]

While the statement is shopworn, homeownership is a major part of the American dream. Many polls indicate that Americans view owning a home as a significant measure of success. In recent years, the media has given a great deal of attention to moderate- and middle-income households who are finding it increasingly difficult to join the ranks of homeowners; their plight has become a major political issue in many areas of the country.[2]

Over the past four decades, federal, state, and local policy has promoted homeownership. It has been argued that the benefits of homeownership go well beyond those provided to the household that actually buys the home. Homeownership is thought to contribute to the stability and quality of life in local neighborhoods and communities. In addition, homeownership is viewed as a way of preserving and enhancing the value of the existing housing stock.

Even with all the popular rhetoric on the virtues of homeownership, government intervention to provide assistance to first-time homebuyers is controversial. The issue is generally framed as the problem that young moderate-income households have in achieving homeownership. These households are not poor; they tend to have good jobs and make what most people would consider a good living. However, due to increases in the costs of homeownership, they have difficulty making the transition from renter to homeowner in what has become the traditional time frame, say between the ages of 25 and 35.

Critics of government assistance to first-time homebuyers argue that this is not the traditional target population of government subsidies. Such money should be allocated to the truly needy in our society. Proponents of government assistance to first-time homebuyers cite the long-term priority status of homeownership in the U.S. In addition, proponents argue that federal housing assistance has been focused on the poor through a variety of subsidy programs and on the affluent through the income tax deductions for mortgage interest and real estate taxes. There is a gap in this structure caused by the fact that moderate-income households have too much income to qualify for the subsidy programs and too little income to take advantage of the income tax deductions.

This chapter reviews the evidence on the affordability of homeownership for first-time homebuyers and examines the past, current, and proposed policy options for increasing affordability. In the next section, the first-time homebuyer issue is defined more explicitly. In the third section the determinants of affordability are examined. The fourth section reviews past, current, and proposed programs to provide homeownership opportunities at the federal, state, and-local levels. Finally, the potential role of the federal government is discussed.

The Nature of the Problem

A 1986 survey of buyers of new homes by the National Association of Homebuilders (NAHB) indicates that 72.6 percent of first-time buyers who bought new single family homes were between the ages of 25 and 34 with a median age of 30.8. The median income of these buyers was $38,100. Among first-time buyers who bought condominiums 66.1 percent were between 25 and 34; their median income was $34,400.[3]

While these statistics provide a useful description of households who purchased homes in 1986, there are no comparable statistics which provide a profile of potential first-time buyers who want to purchase a home but cannot afford to do so. In fact, the target population of concern in the first-time homebuyer question is somewhat elusive.

In practice, there are at least three definitions of first-time homebuyers used. The alternatives range from literal first-time homebuyers (households that have never owned a home) to households that have not owned a home recently (under the mortgage revenue bond definition, households that have not owned a home in the last three years), to any household which cannot afford homeownership. This broadened definition of first-time homebuyers seems to result from the fact that the central issue is really the affordability of homeownership. However, the issue is most often framed specifically in terms of young families trying to make the transition from renter to homeowner. This framing of the issue is not surprising since, in general, we expect young households that have never owned or do not currently own a home to have a difficult time achieving homeownership, given the upfront costs of buying a home and the income required to support monthly mortgage payments. In addition, this narrow framing of the issue permits a basis for analysis because a variety of data sources provide information on young renter households. For this reason, our analysis focuses on young renter households between the ages of 25 and 35. However, the policies discussed in this paper may apply to the broader definition of the first-time homebuyer.

There is a general sense that the high end of the target population is moderate-income households for whom homeownership is just beyond their grasp. However, there is also concern that lower-income households not be excluded from homeownership opportunities. How wide the income range should be when considering the first-time homebuyer issue remains an open question. From a policy perspective, the income level of the target population is an important issue. For moderate-income households, policies that provide short-term assistance to help households over the initial hurdles of the downpayment and monthly payments in the early months or years may be sufficient. Such policies may be "self-financing" in that these households may be expected to repay the subsidy in the future. On the other hand, for low-income households, homeownership policies may involve long-term assistance with less opportunity to recapture the subsidy.

Homeownership Rates

In 1980, the homeownership rate for the U.S. peaked with 65.6 percent of all households owning a home. In 1988, current estimates indicate that the rate has dropped to 63.9 percent. Table 6.1 provides estimates of the homeownership rate by age for the U.S. and the four census regions for 1973, 1976, 1980, 1983, and 1988. As expected, there are significant declines among younger households (ages 34 and younger) over the period. While the national homeownership rate for all households peaked in 1980, the rates reported in Table 6.1 indicate that the decline in homeownershp rates for young households began much earlier. The homeownership rate peaked in 1973 for households younger than age 25 and for those in the 25−29 age group. For households in the 30−34 age group, the homeownership rate peaked in 1976, with 62.4 percent of these households owning a home. However, in each of these groups, the most dramatic decline has occurred since 1980. It is often argued that the decline in homeownership rates nationally is driven by declines in rates in the higher cost regions such as the Northeast and the West, particularly California. However, the data conflict with this expectation. Across all age groups, the homeownership rate is lower in 1988 than in 1980 in the Midwest, South, and West, with the largest decline occurring in the Midwest. (Since 1983, the rate has risen slightly in the West.) The rate has increased somewhat in the Northeast since 1980. The increase in the Northeast may be due to the rapid house price appreciation over the period in the

TABLE 6.1   Homeownership Rates by Region and Age Group

Age group	Year	Nation	Northeast	Midwest	South	West
<25	1973	23.4%	17.4%	25.3%	29.9%	15.3%
	1976	21.0%	15.7%	24.4%	24.2%	15.1%
	1980	21.3%	14.5%	24.6%	25.0%	16.2%
	1983	19.3%	16.5%	21.8%	23.0%	11.6%
	1988	15.5%	13.0%	14.9%	19.8%	11.2%
25–29	1973	43.6%	36.2%	47.9%	47.6%	39.7%
	1976	43.2%	34.3%	48.6%	46.8%	39.0%
	1980	43.3%	35.9%	50.5%	46.4%	36.0%
	1983	38.2%	32.4%	43.5%	41.7%	31.4%
	1988	36.2%	35.9%	41.4%	37.9%	27.8%
30–34	1973	60.2%	51.3%	66.5%	62.1%	59.5%
	1976	62.4%	59.3%	68.6%	63.2%	56.9%
	1980	61.1%	55.0%	68.1%	63.4%	54.9%
	1983	55.7%	53.6%	63.0%	56.6%	48.2%
	1988	52.6%	50.8%	57.3%	53.8%	47.2%
35–39	1973	68.5%	62.2%	76.0%	68.7%	65.2%
	1976	69.0%	60.3%	77.5%	69.2%	67.5%
	1980	70.8%	65.8%	78.0%	71.7%	66.1%
	1983	65.8%	61.2%	74.0%	66.0%	60.5%
	1988	63.2%	63.7%	68.3%	62.9%	57.8%
40–44	1973	72.9%	69.2%	79.2%	71.5%	71.1%
	1976	73.9%	65.4%	81.3%	74.1%	72.6%
	1980	74.2%	66.0%	80.7%	76.3%	71.2%
	1983	74.2%	68.2%	81.6%	76.3%	67.9%
	1988	71.4%	70.1%	77.7%	72.1%	64.7%
45–54	1973	76.1%	72.2%	80.9%	76.1%	74.6%
	1976	77.4%	73.7%	81.1%	78.1%	75.4%
	1980	77.7%	72.7%	83.7%	79.1%	73.3%
	1983	77.1%	72.7%	82.6%	78.2%	73.2%
	1988	76.0%	72.5%	79.7%	77.2%	73.2%
55–64	1973	75.7%	69.8%	79.6%	77.9%	74.4%
	1976	77.2%	71.8%	82.4%	78.1%	75.7%
	1980	79.3%	74.0%	83.1%	81.7%	76.7%
	1983	80.5%	74.6%	85.0%	83.0%	76.9%
	1988	79.6%	74.1%	83.6%	81.9%	77.5%
65–74	1973	71.3%	60.1%	76.6%	75.9%	70.0%
	1976	72.7%	63.0%	77.6%	76.1%	71.4%
	1980	75.2%	67.4%	79.1%	78.2%	73.9%
	1983	76.9%	69.6%	81.6%	80.2%	73.7%
	1988	78.2%	72.3%	80.8%	80.2%	78.5%

TABLE 6.1   (*Continued*)

Age group	Year	Nation	Northeast	Midwest	South	West
>74	1973	67.1%	58.2%	71.8%	71.9%	62.2%
	1976	67.2%	57.5%	70.0%	72.2%	65.6%
	1980	67.8%	56.0%	69.0%	74.6%	67.7%
	1983	71.6%	61.2%	74.7%	77.4%	70.2%
	1988	70.4%	61.1%	68.2%	79.0%	70.6%
All ages	1973	64.4%	59.2%	69.1%	66.5%	60.6%
	1976	64.8%	59.8%	69.5%	66.4%	61.2%
	1980	65.6%	60.7%	70.3%	68.3%	60.5%
	1983	64.9%	61.4%	70.0%	67.1%	58.7%
	1988	63.9%	61.9%	67.0%	65.9%	58.9%

Source: Joint Center for Housing Studies, Harvard University, *The State of the Nation's Housing 1989*, pp. 12, 29.

region. This appreciation in house values provided a major incentive to buy for any household that could afford to get into the market.

Among the younger households in the 25 to 29 and 30 to 34 age groups, who are the focus of this analysis, there are declines in the homeownership rate since 1980 in all regions except the Northeast where there is an increase in the 25–29 age group in 1988. In the West, the homeownership rate has been falling for households in these two groups since 1973.

Determinants of Affordable Homeownership

In the late 1970s, the difficulties facing first-time homebuyers were often attributed to rapid house price inflation. By the early 1980s, the problems were more likely to be attributed to high mortgage interest rates. We need to be cautious in looking for a single determinant of affordability. Housing markets are local in nature and significantly different market conditions occur across regions. While housing prices may be relatively flat in a particular region there may still be an affordability problem due to relatively low incomes among the first-time buyer population. Similarly, in a region where incomes are rising rapidly when compared to other regions, there may still be an affordability problem if housing prices are rising faster than incomes.

In analyzing the affordability of homeownership, we must examine several factors. The house price, household income, upfront cash costs including the downpayment and closing costs, monthly housing expenses, mortgage interest rates, the type of mortgage instrument (fixed-rate versus an adjustable or graduated payment mortgage), and the mortgage underwriting guidelines jointly determine the affordability of homeownership.

TABLE 6.2 First Time Homebuyers' Median Housing Prices and Young Renters' Median Incomes

Year	NATION		NORTHEAST		MIDWEST		SOUTH		WEST	
	Sale price	Median household income	Sale price	Median household income	Sale price	Median household income	Sale price	Median household income	Sale price	Median household income
1972	$21,611	$10,400	$26,048	$10,300	$20,993	$10,700	$19,958	$9,800	$22,780	$10,500
1973	23,490	10,700	28,157	10,800	22,628	11,200	21,295	10,700	25,783	11,300
1974	25,682	11,900	30,673	12,700	24,460	12,000	22,988	11,400	29,086	11,800
1975	28,432	12,300	33,263	13,600	26,978	12,700	25,275	11,800	32,690	11,500
1976	30,868	12,600	34,632	13,700	29,397	12,900	27,057	12,000	36,293	12,200
1977	34,800	13,300	37,000	15,200	32,700	14,800	29,700	12,300	42,900	12,700
1978	39,846	14,400	41,107	15,900	37,376	15,100	33,323	14,000	50,837	13,300
1979	45,518	15,200	46,657	16,400	41,823	15,500	38,165	14,500	58,559	15,000
1980	50,530	16,300	51,245	16,500	44,276	16,700	42,857	15,700	66,152	16,400
1981	54,775	17,700	55,389	18,600	48,134	17,600	47,045	16,900	70,699	18,500

1982	56,202	18,400	58,201	20,100	50,162	18,000	48,975	18,800	71,386	19,300
1983	57,594	19,400	60,680	22,000	49,050	18,200	49,896	18,800	73,788	20,000
1984	59,821	20,000	67,044	22,600	51,503	20,100	51,619	20,200	73,359	22,800
1985	61,387	22,200	74,444	24,400	51,862	20,700	52,985	21,000	75,547	23,600
1986	64,067	22,800	88,282	26,100	54,282	21,500	54,113	21,300	78,293	24,400
1987	65,882	23,400	99,990	27,600	56,853	21,600	54,303	22,100	81,041	24,700
1988	65,949	24,300	103,154	29,300	59,767	21,900	53,987	23,100	79,627	25,700
Changes:										
1972–1980	133.82%	56.73%	96.73%	60.19%	110.91%	56.07%	114.74%	60.20%	190.40%	56.19%
1980–1988	30.51%	49.08%	101.30%	77.58%	34.99%	31.14%	25.97%	47.13%	20.37%	56.71%
1972–1988	205.16%	133.65%	296.02%	184.47%	184.70%	104.67%	170.50%	135.71%	249.55%	144.76%

Sources: Joint Center for Housing Studies, Harvard University, *The State of the Nation's Housing 1989*, pp. 22–24. All figures are converted to nominal dollars using the CPI-UXI index.

House Prices and Income

A standard measure of homeownership affordability is an index which compares median income with median housing prices such as the index published by the National Association of Realtors.[4] However, given our interest in potential first-time homebuyers, this standard measure seems inappropriate since these buyers often earn less than the median income and are expected to purchase homes priced below the median. For this analysis, we will examine trends in house prices and incomes using data constructed by the Harvard Joint Center for Housing Studies to reflect house prices paid and incomes earned by potential first-time homebuyers. The house price data reflect the price paid for a house with similar attributes and quality; the income data are median incomes for married couples between the ages of 25 to 29 who are renters.[5]

As shown in Table 6.2, the median house price for first-time buyers in the U.S. increased from $21,611 in 1972 to $65,949 in 1988, representing a percentage change of 205.2 percent. Over the same period the median income of young renters rose from $10,400 in 1972 to $24,300 in 1988, representing a percentage change of 133.7 percent. A large portion of the increase in median housing price occurred during the 1970s. The percentage change in median price was 133.8 percent for the 1972–1980 period and just 30.5 percent for the 1980–1988 period. Median incomes rose by 56.7 percent from 1972 to 1980 and 49.1 percent from 1980 to 1988. While incomes have increased faster than home prices in the 1980–1988 period, these increases in incomes do not begin to narrow the gap between incomes and prices created by the home price increases of the late 1970s.

Furthermore, the data presented in Table 6.2 indicate that changes in house prices have varied widely across regions. During the 1972–1980 period, the large increase in the national median house price paid by first-time homebuyers seems to be driven by the extraordinary increase in the West of 190.4 percent. During the same period, the Northeast lagged behind all other regions with a percentage change of 96.7 percent. The story changes dramatically during the 1980–1988 period. The largest increase in median price is seen in the Northeast with a 101.3 percent change while prices in the West only increased by 20.4 percent. There is much less variation in percentage change in income across regions. During the 1972–1980 period, the percentage change in income ranged from 60.2 percent in the Northeast and South to 56.1 percent in the Midwest and West. However, the percentage change in income lagged significantly behind the percentage change in median house price in all regions. For the 1980–1988 period, the change in income exceeded the change in median house price in the South and West. However, over the entire 1972 to 1988 period house prices have increased much more rapidly than income in all regions.

Mortgage Interest Rates

During the late 1970s and early 1980s, there was considerable volatility in mortgage interest rates. As shown in Figure 6.1, nominal interest rates on 30-year fixed-rate mortgages were relatively stable from 1975 until 1978 ranging between 8.8 percent and 9.4 percent. However, mortgage rates jumped to 10.7 percent in 1979 and continued to rise until they reached their peak at 14.8 percent in 1982. By 1987, nominal rates had fallen to 8.9 percent; in 1988, they rose slightly to 9.0 percent. As shown in Figure 6.1, real interest rates increased dramatically in the early 1980s. In recent years, while real rates have declined since the early 1980s, they remain at very high levels (in the 5.0 percent to 8.0 percent range) when compared to the levels during the 1970s (−2 percent to 4 percent range). High real mortgage rates increase the real costs of homeownership.

Homeownership Costs

Both the after tax cash costs and total costs are considered in examining the costs of homeownership. The after-tax cash costs of homeownership are defined as the mortgage payment for principal and interest, insurance, real estate taxes and utilities less the tax benefits from the deductibility of mortgage interest and real estate taxes. The major difference between the after-tax cash costs and total costs is that total costs of homeownership include the expected appreciation in the value of the house. The higher the expected appreciation in house prices, the lower the total costs of homeownership.

William Apgar, in Chapter 2 of this volume, presents estimates of the annual after-tax costs of homeownership and the total costs of homeownership for potential first time homebuyers in Figure 2.1. The after-tax costs of homeownership peaked in the early 1980s and have declined somewhat in recent years due to the decrease in mortgage interest rates. This decline has been dampened somewhat by the diminished tax savings for homeownership under the Tax Reform Act of 1986 due to the decrease in tax rates and the increase in the standard deduction.[6] The total costs of homeownership bottomed out in 1978 and 1979 and showed a dramatic increase in the early 1980s. This increase is due to the rise in interest rates and the decline in expected house price appreciation. While both the after tax and total costs of home owning have declined somewhat since the early 1980s, they remain high by historic standards.

The impact of inflation on the demand for housing and homeownership is an important issue. There are two arguments made in the literature which describe opposite effects on housing demand and homeownership. One argument posits that expected inflation decreases the after-tax cost of housing and hence increases both the quantity of housing demanded, as well as home-

Figure 6.1 Nominal and Real Mortgage Rates

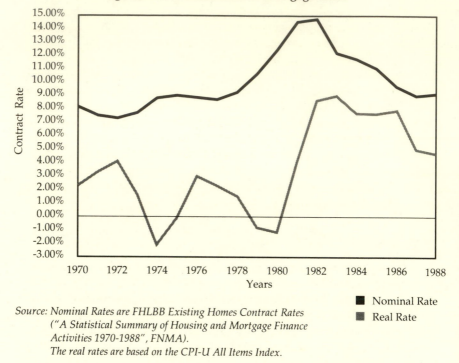

Source: Nominal Rates are FHLBB Existing Homes Contract Rates
("A Statistical Summary of Housing and Mortgage Finance
Activities 1970-1988", FNMA).
The real rates are based on the CPI-U All Items Index.

■ Nominal Rate
■ Real Rate

ownership rates. In other words, price appreciation increases the attractiveness of housing as an investment. Hence, households buy more housing (e.g., larger and/or higher quality houses), and more households make the transition from renter to homeowner. The alternative argument is that given the standard fixed-rate mortgage, house price inflation decreases the size of the mortgage loan that the household can qualify for and therefore decreases the quantity of housing demanded (e.g., households buy smaller houses), which may provide a barrier to renters in making the transition from renter to homeowner. The empirical evidence on the net impact of these two effects is mixed.[7]

The first argument outlined above has been used to explain trends in homeownership rates. It has been argued that the rise in homeownership in the late 1970s was the result of rising house prices, which made homeownership a good investment. Similarly, the decline in homeownership in the 1980s is explained by the decline in house price appreciation. While it is clear that rising prices make housing a good investment for those who can enter the market, rising prices also increase the downpayments and monthly payments required to purchase a home. These increases may serve as barriers to homeownership, particularly to young renter families. To illustrate the point, the house price data provided in Table 6.2 document the rapid house price appreciation in the West during the 1970s. However, a reexamination of the homeownership rates presented in Table 6.1 indicates that the homeownership rate for young households in the 25–29 and 30–34 age groups in the West has been falling since 1973. While housing was certainly a good investment in the West in the 1970s, the decline in homeownership among young households during that period may be due to the barriers to entry of large downpayments and monthly payments created by increasing house prices. In the 1980s, while house price inflation slowed throughout much of the country, except in the Northeast, house price levels remain high as a result of the rapid increases in prices of the 1970s. Hence, the upfront cash costs and initial monthly payments may still provide barriers to homeownership for young families.[8]

Alternative Mortgage Instruments

The rising interest rates of the early 1980s made it increasingly difficult for many households and particularly for many potential first-time homebuyers to afford homeownership. The market responded to this affordability problem by creating a series of new mortgage instruments. These instruments included the adjustable-rate mortgage, in which the interest rate for the initial period (usually 1, 3, or 5 years) is below market rates for 30-year fixed-rate mortgages. However, in subsequent periods the rate could adjust upward if interest rates are rising, or decline if interest rates are falling. The lower rate in the initial period is due to the decreased risk to the lender resulting from the ability to adjust the interest rate over the term of the loan.

The graduated payment mortgage is another mortgage instrument designed to increase the affordability of homeownership. In the initial period, the monthly payment is less than that which would be necessary to amortize the loan amount over the life of the loan. The shortfall in the monthly payment is added to the balance of the loan. Over the term of the loan, the monthly payments increase so that the principal and interest is fully paid by the end of the term of the loan.

While there were many other mortgage instruments marketed during the early 1980s, the adjustable rate and graduated payment mortgages were the most popular. However, they are not without their problems. The fundamental assumption underlying the adjustable rate mortgage when interest rates are rising and the graduated payment mortgage is that household incomes will grow over the term of the loan so that households will be able to afford larger monthly payments over time. If household incomes fail to rise fast enough to keep up with changes in monthly payments, the household may be at risk of default.

The graduated payment mortgage has the additional risk that the outstanding balance may rise to exceed the purchase price of the house. Hence, a homebuyer's equity in the house is depleted as the outstanding balance on the loan rises thereby increasing the risk of the homebuyer defaulting on the loan. As a result, lenders are somewhat reluctant to originate these loans.[9]

Underwriting Guidelines

Mortgage underwriting guidelines have a major impact on the ability of a household to purchase a home. The guidelines are designed to ensure that the costs of the mortgage appropriately relate to the borrower's ability to pay. The Federal National Mortgage Association (Fannie Mae) and the Federal Home Loan Mortgage Corporation (Freddie Mac) issue mortgage underwriting guidelines which are generally viewed as the industry standard.

Currently, Fannie Mae underwriting guidelines suggest that total monthly housing expenses cannot exceed 28 percent of gross monthly household income if the loan to value ratio (LTV) is .90 or less. Total monthly housing expenses are defined to include:

1. Monthly payment for principal and interest
2. Hazard insurance
3. Mortgage insurance
4. Real estate taxes
5. Homeowners' association dues
6. Payments required for subordinate financing

In addition, total monthly obligations which include monthly housing expenses, monthly payments on installment or revolving debt that extend beyond 10 months, and alimony and child support payments cannot exceed 36 percent of gross monthly household income. If the loan to value ratio is greater than .90, total monthly housing expenses cannot exceed 25 percent of gross monthly income and total montly obligations cannot exceed 33 percent of monthly income.[10] In addition, mortgage insurance is generally required on all mortgages where the LTV exceeds .80.

The current tighter guidelines for loans with LTVs greater than .90 were adopted in October 1985, a result of the higher default rates among high LTV mortgages originated in the early 1980s. Throughout the early 1980s prior to this change, Fannie Mae guidelines maintained the housing expense to income ratio at .28 and the total monthly obligation to income ratio at .36.[11] However, in response to rising interest rates and the resulting problems with qualifying for mortgages, many mortgage insurance companies were setting more flexible guidelines. By 1983, many firms had set the monthly housing expense to income ratio at .31 and the total monthly obligation to income ratio at .38. In fact, there were some companies that had set the housing expense to income ratio at .33. Again, with rising default rates, the mortgage insurance companies have moved back to a housing expense to income ratio of .28.[12]

The differences in these income guidelines have a major impact on the price of the house that a household can afford. In Table 6.3, we consider a household with gross annual income of $30,000. Given a 30-year fixed-rate mortgage at 10 percent, the maximum price the household could pay is calculated under different assumptions concerning the LTV ratio and the housing expense to income ratio.

In Case I in Table 6.3, a housing expense to income ratio of .25 is considered. In the first column of the table, a 30-year fixed-rate mortgage at 10 percent with a LTV ratio of .95 is assumed. In addition, real estate taxes are set at 1.5 percent of the purchase price, points at closing are set at 3 percent (1 percent as the origination fee and 2 percent in closing costs), and mortgage insurance and hazard insurance are assumed to be 0.375 percent and 0.6 percent, respectively. Given these assumptions, a household with gross annual income of $30,000 can afford a house priced at $60,190. The total upfront cash required at closing would be $4,725 (downpayment of $3009 plus closing costs of $1715).

If the LTV ratio is decreased to .90, the maximum house price that the household could afford increases to $62,944, but the total upfront cost at closing increases to $7,994. If the LTV ratio is decreased to .80, the maximum affordable house price increases to $71,261 with total upfront costs at closing of $15,962. In this case, it is assumed that no mortgage insurance is required.

The impact of increasing the housing expense to income ratio is demonstrated in Cases II through IV in the table. Assuming a housing expense to income ratio of .28 and LTV ratio of .95, .90, and .80 increases the maximum house price affordable to the household earning $30,000 to $67,413, $70,498, and $79,812, respectively. When the housing expense to income ratio is increase to .31 or .33 the range in maximum affordable house price is increased to $74,635 to $88,364 and $79,451 to $94,065 respectively, depending on the LTV ratio.

Clearly, these maximum affordable house prices are quite sensitive to changes in interest rates, as well. If, for example, the household chose an adjustable rate mortgage where the initial interest rate was 8 percent, the LTV ratio was .90, and the housing expense to income ratio was .28, the maximum affordable house price would be $81,064, up from $70,498. If, on the other hand, interest rates rose to 13 percent that same household could only afford to purchase a house priced at $58,396.

Summary

The evidence presented in this section suggests that the high house price levels resulting from the rapid price increases in the 1970s continue to cause high

TABLE 6.3 Simulating Price and Mortgage Cost under Different Underwriting Guidelines, Mortgage Rate: 10%

	Case I. Housing expense/income 0.25			Case II. Housing expense/income 0.28		
Assumptions						
Household income	$30,000	$30,000	$30,000	$30,000	$30,000	$30,000
Housing expense/income	0.25	0.25	0.25	0.28	0.28	0.28
Loan/value ratio	0.95	0.90	0.80	0.95	0.90	0.80
Term of the loan	360	360	360	360	360	360
Interest rate	10%	10%	10%	10%	10%	10%
Points at closing	3%	3%	3%	3%	3%	3%
Real estate tax rate	1.5%	1.5%	1.5%	1.5%	1.5%	1.5%
Mortgage insurance	0.375%	0.375%	0.0%	0.375%	0.375%	0.0%
Hazard insurance	0.6%	0.6%	0.6%	0.6%	0.6%	0.6%
Price and mortgage costs						
Housing price	$60,190	$62,944	$71,261	$67,413	$70,498	$79,812
Loan amount	$57,180	$56,650	$57,009	$64,042	$63,448	$63,850
Cash requirements at closing	$4,725	$7,994	$15,962	$5,292	$8,953	$17,878
Downpayment	$3,009	$6,294	$14,252	$3,371	$7,050	$15,962
Closing and other costs	$1,715	$1,699	$1,710	$1,921	$1,903	$1,915
Total monthly payments	$625	$625	$625	$700	$700	$700
Payments for P&I	$502	$497	$500	$562	$557	$560
Other payments	$123	$128	$125	$138	$143	$140

	Case III. Housing expense/income 0.31			Case IV. Housing expense/income 0.33		
Assumptions						
Household income	$30,000	$30,000	$30,000	$30,000	$30,000	$30,000
Housing expense/income	0.31	0.31	0.31	0.33	0.33	0.33
Loan/value ratio	0.95	0.90	0.80	0.95	0.90	0.80
Term of the loan	360	360	360	360	360	360
Interest rate	10%	10%	10%	10%	10%	10%
Points at closing	3%	3%	3%	3%	3%	3%
Real estate tax rate	1.5%	1.5%	1.5%	1.5%	1.5%	1.5%
Mortgage insurance	0.375%	0.375%	0.0%	0.375%	0.375%	0.0%
Hazard insurance	0.6%	0.6%	0.6%	0.6%	0.6%	0.6%
Price and mortgage costs						
Housing price	$74,635	$78,051	$88,364	$79,451	$83,087	$94,065
Loan amount	$70,904	$70,246	$70,691	$75,478	$74,778	$75,252
Cash requirements at closing	$5,859	$9,912	$19,793	$6,237	$10,552	$21,070
Downpayment	$3,732	$7,805	$17,673	$3,973	$8,309	$18,813
Closing and other costs	$2,127	$2,107	$2,121	$2,264	$2,243	$2,258
Total monthly payments	$775	$775	$775	$825	$825	$825
Payments for P&I	$622	$616	$620	$662	$656	$660
Other payments	$153	$159	$155	$163	$169	$165

Source: Author's calculations.

after-tax cash costs and total costs of homeownership. While real mortgage interest rates and the after-tax cash costs and total costs of homeownership are down from the peak levels achieved in the early 1980s, they remain high by historic standards. In addition, high mortgage default rates have resulted in a tightening of mortgage underwriting guidelines. The combination of these factors may explain at least part of the decline in homeownership among young households.

Policy Options

As a result of the long-standing priority status given homeownership in the United States, there are a variety of past, current and proposed methods of government intervention at the federal, state and local levels to open home-ownership opportunities. In this section, these efforts to provide homeowner-ship opportunities are reviewed in order to help shape future policy.

Two barriers to homeownership are generally discussed: the downpay-ment problem (upfront cash required at closing) and the monthly payment problem (ability to support the monthly payment). Clearly, these barriers are related since the size of the downpayment determines the size of the monthly payment. Recent work suggests that the downpayment is the toughest hurdle. An analysis of renter households in 1986 suggests that only 11.5 percent had both the income and savings necessary to purchase a typical starter home— 81.2 percent did not have the savings to make a 20 percent downpayment plus closing costs and 64.3 percent did not have the income required to qualify for the mortgage.[13]

While policies to promote homeownership tend to focus on either the downpayment or monthly payment problems, some programs address both by focusing on decreasing the price of the house. Programs targeted at the down-payment problem, the monthly payment problem, and the house price can be grouped into four categories. The programs either provide direct subsidies or loans, change local regulation, take on more mortgage risk, or provide tax incentives. These policy options are summarized in Table 6.4. While there is experience at the federal, state, and local levels with programs that provide direct subsidies or loans and tax incentives, most experience with changing local regulation is at the state and local level, and most experience with pro-grams that take on additional mortgage risk is at the federal level.

As shown in Table 6.4, direct subsidies or loans for downpayments may take the form of cash grants and various types of second mortgages. Such programs are provided by many state and local governments, and the number of these efforts has increased considerably in recent years. Historically, the method of alleviating the downpayment problem is the provision of high LTV loans. Such loans are generally considered high risk. The federal government absorbs this risk through its mortgage insurance program under the Federal

TABLE 6.4   Policy Options

	Subsidies/loans	Local regulation	Mortgage risk	Tax incentives
Downpayment	Cash grants Second mortgages		High LTV loans	IHA
Monthly payment	Effective interest rate buydown		Higher housing expense/income ratio	MRBs
			Alternative mortgage instruments	Mortgage interest deduction
House price	Cash grant Land contribution Price discount	Increased density		

Housing Administration (FHA) which offers high LTV mortgages. There also are proposals for providing preferential federal income tax treatment for savings accounts for downpayments (Individual Housing Accounts (IHA)). Contributions to such accounts as well as income earned on these accounts would be free from federal income tax.

Direct subsidies of monthly payments for principal and interest have been provided by the federal government and some state governments. The monthly payment problem may also be alleviated by using more flexible underwriting guidelines which permit a household to qualify for a mortgage when housing expenses as a fraction of income exceed the accepted guidelines. Again, these mortgages are viewed as higher risk. This type of risk, within limits, has been absorbed by the federal government through its FHA mortgage insurance program.

The tax exempt status of mortgage revenue bonds (MRB) and the deductibility of mortgage interest and real estate taxes from income for federal and some state income taxes have provided a substantial subsidy to homeownership. However, the deductibility of mortgage interest and real estate taxes provides only modest benefits to typical first time buyers who tend to purchase less expensive homes and have lower incomes. Given low marginal tax rates and the size of these deductions relative to the standard deduction, the tax savings have been small. With the increase in the standard deduction and decrease in marginal tax rates under Tax Reform, the tax benefits of homeownership to the typical first time buyer are even smaller.[14]

A number of state and local initiatives have been designed to decrease the house price including cash grants, land contributions, or changes in local regulations to increase density.

In the remaining portion of this section, specific government programs that absorb mortgage risk or provide direct subsidies to promote homeownership opportunities for first time buyers are reviewed in order to structure thinking about future policies. In addition, the proposed tax incentives for downpayment savings accounts and the tax exempt status of mortgage revenue bonds are investigated.

Section 235

The Section 235 Program of the Housing and Community Development Act of 1968 was established to promote homeownership opportunities among lower-income households. The program was targeted for households with incomes less than 80 percent of the median income in the local area.[15] Under the program, downpayments required were minimal and deep interest rate subsidies were provided. In fact, a subsidy was provided to bring a household's monthly housing expenses (payment for principal and interest, taxes, and insurance) to no more than 20 percent of the household's gross income as long as the subsidy did not bring the effective mortgage interest rate below 1 percent. The mortgages were FHA insured.

As the many evalutions of the program have pointed out, the subsidy formula had a somewhat perverse feature. If a household was receiving less than the maximum subsidy (e.g., the effective mortgage rate was greater than 1 percent when housing expenses were kept to 20 percent of income), additional subsidy could be provided if maintenance, taxes, insurance or other operating expenses increased. Hence, a lower income household receiving the maximum subsidy would be liable for any such increases while higher income households not yet receiving the maximum subsidy could receive additional subsidy to cover such increases until the maximum subsidy was reached.[16]

Default rates in the 235 program were high. In the existing home program, there were many allegations of fraud and bribery in the process of certifying that the units met program standards. In many instances, the eligible buyer found that the house needed major repairs shortly after purchase. If the buyer could not afford the repairs, default became an attractive option. In addition, if the household wanted to move within a few years of purchasing the home there was an incentive simply to default since the household had little if any equity in the home.[17]

The 235 program was modified in 1975. The maximum subsidy was limited to an effective buydown of the mortgage interest rate to 5 percent. In addition, larger downpayments were required.[18] Currently, the program is inactive.

FmHA Section 502

The Farmers Home Administration (FmHA) Section 502 program is designed to provide direct loans to homebuyers in rural areas for the purchase or rehabilitation of an existing home or the construction or purchase of a new home. The program design is somewhat similar to that of the Section 235 program. Under Section 502, households are required to pay 20 percent of their incomes for principal, interest, taxes, and insurance. The difference between the actual monthly payments and 20 percent of the household income is covered by the subsidy. Hence, the subsidy under the program is effectively an interest rate buydown. Household income is recertified every two years. At that time a change in income may result in a change in the interest rate on the loan. A household receiving an interest rate subsidy is required to repay the subsidy at sale if the house has appreciated in value. Under the program, no downpayment is required.[19]

The recertification of income and the recapture of the subsidy at resale are important features of this program. If the program only checked income eligibility when the home was purchased then a household whose income rose substantially would continue to receive the subsidy as long as the household remained in the home. With recertification of income, the household only receives the subidy as long as income levels warrant assistance. The recapture of the subsidy at resale limits the windfall to the household to the total appreciation of the property less the subsidy.

FHA Section 203(b) Program

The Federal Housing Administration was created in 1934. Under the Section 203(b) program, the FHA encouraged the use of long term, high loan to value ratio, fixed payment mortgages by providing insurance on these loans, thereby assuming the risk of default. The Government National Mortgage Association (Ginnie Mae) provides an active secondary market for FHA loans. As Weicher points out, the program is generally regarded as successful. The evidence of this success often cited is the dramatic increase in homeownership rates from the 1930s through 1980 and the fact that the program has been actuarially sound.[20] Even with the losses sustained during fiscal 1988, largely the result of defaults on loans in the oil producing states, estimates suggest that the program remains financially sound.

The purpose of the FHA insurance program is to provide access to homeownership for those who would be underserved by the private market. This mandate is generally defined to include lower income homebuyers, buyers with less equity with which to purchase a home, and first-time homebuyers. As a result, the program always had limits on the maximum mortgage amount. Prior to 1979, the same limit was imposed nationally. Since then, while the national limit has been set at $67,500, the limit can be raised to 95 percent of the local area median house price, up to a maximum of $101,250. In today's market, there are many areas where the $101,250 maximum loan amount seriously constrains the use of the FHA program.[21]

The FHA program has served to increase the affordability of home-ownership by insuring high LTV ratio loans, often in excess of .95, thereby reducing the cash required for a downpayment. In addition, the underwriting guidelines for the FHA program are somewhat more flexible than the industry guidelines discussed in the previous section. Current FHA guidelines suggest that total housing expenses should not exceed 38 percent of net income (net of federal income taxes) and total obligations should not exceed 53 percent of net income. FHA considers "compensating factors" such as credit history in applying its underwriting guidelines and may permit buyers to exceed both guidelines. In fact, for loans insured during the 1981–1983 period, both guidelines were exceeded for 30 percent of the loans.[22]

In a recent study of default experience in the FHA program, the housing expense to income and total obligation to income ratios appeared to have little impact on the default rate. Default rates tend to be higher with loans with high LTV ratios and in markets with low housing appreciation rates. In such cases, the buyer has little equity in the house because of a low downpayment and low appreciation in value and, hence, realizes little cost in defaulting.[23]

Since the early 1960s, private mortgage insurance has grown considerably. Private mortgage insurers have been able to compete effectively with FHA by insuring less than 100 percent of the loan amount. Private mortgage insurers tend to draw the lower risk households that in the absence of private insurers would have used FHA. In recent years there has been increased concern that FHA is competing directly with private insurers. The 1982 Report of the President's Commission on Housing recommended that "FHA should increasingly complement, rather than compete with, the private market . . . FHA should, however, continue to provide mortgage insurance for standard home loans (i.e., fixed-rate, level-payment mortgages) where the private market is unable or unwilling to do so."[24]

FHA certainly provides an opportunity to experiment with innovative mortgage instruments and underwriting practices. This is not to suggest that FHA take on undue risk, but rather provide a leadership role in mortgage design and underwriting guidelines for low- and moderate-income households. Some of these efforts could be targeted specifically at first-time homebuyers. However, the current loan limits would continue to make it difficult for FHA to serve high cost areas.

The Role of the Federal Credit Agencies

As stated earlier, Fannie Mae and Freddie Mac play a major role in setting industry standards for mortgages and underwriting guidelines. For example, in the early 1980s, a proliferation of adjustable rate and graduated payment mortgages was created to deal with the affordability problems resulting from high mortgage interest rates. Many of the early mortgages written provided deep discounts in the initial period which permitted buyers to purchase homes but the payment schedules increased dramatically. In many cases, increases in income did not keep up and the default rates on these mortgages were high.

Fannie Mae and Freddie Mac designed adjustable rate mortgages which offered yearly caps on the annual increase in payments and on the interest rate for the life of the loan. In the case of graduated payment mortgages limits were placed on the amount of negative amortization that could occur. These mortgages were designed to enhance the affordability of the mortgage but also limit the risk of default. These restrictions on adjustable-rate mortgages and graduated-payment mortgages have become standard in the industry.

In late 1987, both Fannie Mae and Freddie Mac announced that they would invest in conventional mortgages with no mortgage insurance premium paid at settlement. In other words, in high LTV loans with private mortgage insurance (generally loans with an LTV ratio greater than .80), the premium for mortgage insurance for the first year may be financed rather than paid at closing. For a $100,000 mortgage, this could reduce the cash required at closing by $500.[25] While this reduction is small when compared with the total upfront cash required at closing, this change in policy by Fannie Mae and Freddie Mac provides a useful example of how modification of current practice can enhance affordability.

Fannie Mae and Freddie Mac clearly play a leadership role in setting industry standards for mortgage products, underwriting guidelines, and general business practice. Both organizations serve a broad segment of the mortgage market; the current maximum loan amount that can be purchased by Fannie Mae and Freddie Mac is $186,700. Given their leadership position, there is an opportunity for Fannie Mae and Freddie Mac to examine current mortgage products, underwriting guidelines, and general business practice to assess other possible changes that enhance affordability. This is not to suggest that either organization adopt or promote unsound business practice, but rather to suggest that current practice be reevaluated.

Individual Housing Accounts

Traditionally, the concern over the ability of moderate-income young households to meet downpayment requirements has been met with mortgage insurance permitting high loan to value ratio loans. In the late 1970s and early 1980s, many analysts proposed individual housing accounts as a method of decreasing the length of time required to save for the downpayment.

While there are many formulations of the individual housing account notion, the basic idea is similar to that of an IRA. Deposits to an individual housing account, as well as interest on the account, would be exempt from income taxes. As with IRAs, there would be annual limits on the amount that could be deposited in these accounts. The funds in the account could only be used for a downpayment on a house; withdrawals for other purposes would be subject to penalties. Most advocates of this proposal limit program participation to first-time homebuyers. Some current proposals suggest permitting penalty-free withdrawals from IRAs for downpayments on homes, rather than setting up a separate account for housing. Essentially, homeownership would become an allowable investment under IRA rules. Using funds already in existing IRAs for a downpayment would cost the Treasury nothing. However, to the extent that permitting investment in homeownership encourages households to open new IRAs, there would be costs in terms of losses in tax revenues.

Critics of this proposal suggest that the program will tend to subsidize those households that would have purchased a home without the program. Estimates suggest that the tax benefits from the program are quite small and therefore would have a negligible impact on overall savings and the homeownership rate.[26]

Mortgage Revenue Bonds

Mortgage revenue bonds (MRBs) are tax exempt bonds that may be issued by state and local housing finance agencies to fund mortgages primarily to first-time homebuyers. For MRB purposes, first-time homebuyers are defined as buyers who have not owned a home in the previous three years. Because these bonds are tax exempt, the mortgages they fund are offered at below market interest rates. The interest rate on these mortgages are usually 200 to 250 basis points below the rate on conventional loans. The intent of this program is to provide homeownership opportunities to moderate-income households.

Earlier in this paper we considered a household earning $30,000 per year with a fixed-rate conventional mortgage at 10 percent and an LTV ratio of .90. Using an expense to income ratio of .28, we found that the household could afford a house priced at $70,498. If the mortgage was funded using a MRB and the mortgage rate dropped to 8 percent as a result, that same household could afford a house priced at $81,064. Effectively the MRB provides this household with a monthly subsidy of $104.91.

As Terner and Cook point out in their chapter in this volume, the MRB program has been criticized for not being targeted narrowly enough at low- and moderate-income households. Since the subsidy continues for the life of the loan, households whose income has risen substantially continue to receive the subsidy. In addition, MRBs are often viewed as an expensive and inefficient method of providing subsidies to homebuyers. Estimates of the cost of MRBs in terms of forgone federal and state tax revenue are four times the subsidy actually received by the homebuyer. It was estimated that over the life of all bond backed loans outstanding in 1982, the revenue loss to the government would be $2.6 billion. The same benefit could be provided to the homebuyers with an interest rate buy down subsidy at a total cost of $680 million.[27]

Tax Reform restricted the use of MRBs through tightening the eligibility criteria in order to target the program more towards moderate-income households. While state and local governments often imposed income limits for eligible households, prior to Tax Reform there were no federal income limits imposed. Under Tax Reform, 95 percent of the proceeds must be allocated to first-time homebuyers (except in targeted areas), the house price cannot exceed 90 percent (110 percent in distressed areas) of the average purchase price in the area and there is a federal limit on income of 115 percent of the state or local area median income whichever is higher.[28]

The largest impact of Tax Reform on the use of tax exempt financing for housing is the volume limitation on private use bonds. Prior to Tax Reform, there were volume limitations on the use of MRBs based on the level of mortgage activity in the state. Under tax reform, state use of tax exempt bonds for private purposes which includes MRBs is capped at $75 per capita or $250 million, whichever is greater, through 1988. After 1988, the volume is capped at $50 per capita or $150 million.

Under these volume limitations, MRBs are competing with other private uses of tax exempt bonds, such as multifamily housing, mass transit facilities, water facilities, solid waste disposal, and student loans, for state bond allocations. In many states, these limitations may be quite restrictive. In California, for example, the volume cap would be $1,977 million which is substantially less than the 1984 MRB issues of $2,193 million.[29]

While the MRB program has been criticized as inefficient and limited in use under tax reform, the program is widely used by state and local governments. From the perspective of state and local governments, the clear advantage of the MRB program over a direct subsidy provided by the federal government is that the MRB program is an implicit subsidy that does not depend on funding through the federal budget process. The MRB program is an important component of many innovative programs to promote affordable homeownership.

However, additional modificatons to the program should be considered to decrease its costs. A mechanism to recapture the subsidy at some point in the future, such as at sale of the house or as incomes rise, should be considered. In addition, to the extent that the program is serving moderate-income households requiring shorter term assistance in meeting monthly payments in the early years of the loan, the program could be redesigned to permit a phaseout of the subsidy over the course of the loan, so that as incomes rise, the subsidy does not continue. Finally, the relative merits of the MRB program with modifications versus a direct subsidy program should be assessed.

State and Local Initiatives

Many state and local initiatives are designed to promote homeownership opportunities for first-time homebuyers. A number of these programs are "self-financing" in that subsidies may be recaptured at some point in the future, often at sale of the property. In some cases, the subsidy takes the form of a low-interest or no-interest loan. State and local governments have used MRBs to provide mortgage interest rate subsidies to first-time homebuyers.

In some states such as Kentucky, Massachusetts, Minnesota, and North Carolina, additional interest rate buydowns are provided from state or, in the case of Kentucky, housing finance agency funds. These programs are similar in design to the Section 235 program.[30] In Massachusetts, for example, the Homeownership Opportunity Program provides an additional 3 percent interest rate buydown over the tax exempt rate for the first four years of the loan. This subsidy is subject to recapture when the property is sold.[31] Again consider our household earning $30,000 per year. An interest rate buydown of 3 percent beyond the tax exempt rate of 8 percent (interest rate of 5 percent for the first 4 years), results in the household being able to afford a house priced at $102,000, compared to $81,064 with just the tax exempt rate of 8 percent.

State and local programs have also been developed to provide assistance with the upfront cash costs of purchasing a home. In Connecticut, for example, the Downpayment Assistance Program provides second mortgages at below market interest rates for households with annual incomes up to $32,000–$55,000 depending on where the home is located.[32]

Some homeownership programs include "silent" second mortgages which are nonamortizing second mortgages with no principal and interest payments required as long as the buyer remains in the house. In some cases these mortgages are no-interest loans. They are liens which must be repaid when the house is sold. A "silent second" mortgage may be used to finance part of the downpayment or to bring down the purchase price of the home. The Nehemiah Plan in New York includes a silent no-interest second mortgage for a $10,000 grant from the City provided to each homebuyer.[33] In some cases, a local government will take back a silent second in return for land donated to an affordable housing project.

Finally, in some state and local programs, houses are sold at below market prices. Again, in the Massachusetts homeownership program, developers providing new houses under the program are required to provide a certain percentage of units below maximum prices set in the program. In return, developers receive a comprehensive zoning permit which allows increased density.[34] Often, this results in units being provided at substantially less than market prices. A 30 percent reduction in the price of a home can substantially reduce the income required to purchase that home, as well as the upfront cash costs required. In order to maintain the affordability of the unit over time, there is a deed restriction which limits the buyer's price at resale to the same fraction of market value for which the unit was originally purchased.

Recently, the incomes required for households to be eligible to participate in many affordable homeownership programs has been rising. Many of these programs require that the homebuyer have mortgage insurance. In addition, many housing finance agencies purchase pool insurance on the mortgages they hold. As a result, the mortgages provided under these programs must adhere to standard industry underwriting guidelines. As stated earlier in this paper, industry underwriting guidelines have tightened considerably. Most private mortgage insurers require housing expense to income ratios that do not exceed .28. Many of these programs were operating with ratios in the .31 to .33 range. Hence, with the tightening of these underwriting guidelines, lower-income households may no longer qualify for the program.

While it is certainly true that prudent underwriting standards should be followed to avoid undue risk to both the mortgage lender and the homebuyer, many of the affordable homeownership programs offered by state and local governments decrease the risks to the mortgage lenders but these decreases are not taken into account in underwriting the loans.

There are two components of the risk involved in writing a mortgage: the risk of having to go through a default process and the risk of realizing a loss at foreclosure. When an affordable housing program provides homeownership opportunities by providing houses at below market prices, there are often deed restrictions which limit the gain at resale. However, in general, all deed restrictions are void in the event of foreclosure. Hence, the risk of realizing a loss at foreclosure is substantially lower when the purchase price is below market value than if the house was purchased at market value. Since standard underwriting practice is to evaluate a loan by examining the loan amount with respect to the purchase price, the decrease in risk associated with purchase prices that are below market values is ignored.

As a result of the decrease in mortgage risk provided by some of these state and local initiatives, it may be prudent to use more flexible underwriting guidelines tailored to the specifics of some of these programs and thus increase the pool of eligible households. In fact, some housing finance agencies have adopted or are considering adopting self-insurance plans in order to use more flexible underwriting guidelines.

The Federal Role

There is a long-standing tradition of granting priority status to homeownership in the U.S. The commitment of the federal government to promoting homeownership, in general, was reaffirmed recently when the deductions for mortgage interest and real estate taxes were maintained under tax reform. However, the federal government also has had a strong commitment to opening homeownership opportunities to low- and moderate-income households for whom the federal income tax deductions often provide little if any benefit. The target population of these efforts varies from moderate-income households, for whom homeownership is just beyond their grasp, to lower-income households, for whom homeownership is a more distant goal. The evidence presented in this paper demonstrating the decline in homeownership rates, particularly among young families, and the high costs of homeownership suggests that it is time to reassess federal efforts to promote homeownership among first-time home buyers.

Federal efforts to promote affordable homeownership have focused on absorbing mortgage risk through the FHA program and the federally linked credit agencies, implicit tax subsidies through the mortgage revenue bond program, and direct subsidies/loans through the Section 235 and FmHA Section 502 programs. Through existing institutions and program experience, the federal government has many options available to enhance the affordability of homeownership. Existing institutions and program experiences may be refocused on the current realities of homeownership affordability. In particular, it is important that the efforts of the federal government support and encourage state and local initiatives to promote homeownership.

Through the FHA mortgage insurance program and the activities of the federally linked credit agencies, the federal government has a long history of providing leadership in terms of mortgage design and underwriting standards. Because the mortgage market is a national market, this is an area where state and local governments really have had little effect. While many of the existing features of the FHA 203(b) program address problems faced by first-time buyers, the program could be expanded to provide new mortgage instrument designs and more flexible underwriting guidelines.

To deal with the monthly payment problem the FHA 203(b) program should experiment with alternative mortgage designs, including ARMs and GPMs, targeted to first-time homebuyers. The downpayment problem could continue to be addressed by high LTV ratio loans offered under the FHA program. The maximum FHA loan limit of $101,250 would have to be raised if the programs are to reach first-time buyers in high cost areas. A maximum loan limit at 95 percent of the local median house price with no overall cap should be considered.

FHA should experiment with more flexible underwriting guidelines targeted at first-time homebuyers which permit higher housing expense to income and total obligations to income ratios. These guidelines should encourage state and local initiatives to provide affordable homeownership by taking into account those aspects of these programs which reduce the risk associated with the mortgage. For example, as pointed out earlier, there is less risk of loss at default in cases where the purchase price is less than market value due to the donation of a site by the local government, a requirement that developers offer certain units at below market prices or a silent second mortgage brings down the purchase price.

These recommendations concerning mortgage instruments and underwriting guidelines targeted to first-time buyers are not intended to suggest that the federal government should take on unlimited risk. Rather, the recommendation is that the federal government should take on the risk of innovation, of experimenting with mortgage instruments and underwriting guidelines to determine which methods would enhance affordability while maintaining acceptable levels of risk.

Fannie Mae and Freddie Mac serve a broader portion of the mortgage market than FHA and Ginnie Mae, given their higher loan limit. These organizations are industry leaders in setting industry standards for mortgage products, underwriting guidelines, and general business practice. They are well positioned to reevaluate current practices in order to identify opportunities to enhance affordability without taking on unreasonable risk.

The MRB program is an important component of state and local initiatives to provide affordable homeownership. However, modifications to the program to increase efficiency should be considered, including designing a mechanism to recapture the subsidy at some point in the future and/or a phase-out of the subsidy as income rises. In addition, the advantages and disadvantages of the MRB program with modifications versus a direct subsidy program should be assessed.

Designing mortgage instruments and underwriting guidelines for first-time buyers and providing shallow indirect subsidies through the MRB program will open the door for some moderate-income households. However, this approach will not bring in low-income households. If the goal of the federal government is to promote homeownership opportunities for low-income buyers, a direct subsidy program is required. The subsidy could take the form of upfront cash grants for downpayments, or monthly subsidies to help cover payments of principal and interest. If a monthly subsidy program is considered, income eligibility standards for exit from, as well as entrance to, the program should be adopted similar to those in the Section 502 program. In any of these subsidy programs, consideration should be given to designing mechanisms in order to recapture the subsidies, such as those used in many current state and local initiatives. However, the ability to recapture the subsidy will depend on the income of the household, as well as the value of the property over time.

The federal government currently has both the institutional framework and the program experience to promote affordable homeownership for first-time buyers. Programs designed to take on additional mortgage risk are less costly; such programs, however, can only be expected to reach moderate-income households which need assistance in clearing the initial hurdles of the upfront costs and monthly payments, but will ultimately carry the costs of homeownership. If the target population is lower-income households, then longer term direct subsidies are required and these are expensive. Given scarce resources, the tradeoffs of assisting low-income households with homeownership opportunities versus rental housing must be assessed.

*   *   *   *

I would like to thank William Apgar, Hilbert Fefferman, Langley C. Keyes, Marvin Siflinger, and John Weicher for helpful comments on an earlier draft of this paper, and Rena Mourouzi-Sivitanidou for expert research assistance.

Notes

1. Joint Center for Housing Studies of MIT and Harvard University, *Homeownership and Housing Affordability in the United States: 1963–1985* (Cambridge: JCHS, 1985) 6.

2. *New York Times,* "Owning a Home Recedes as an Achievable Dream" in "Real Estate Report," September 13, 1987; *Wall Street Journal,* "A Dream Deferred," February 5 1988, 1.

3. National Association of Home Builders, "1986 Profile of the New Homebuyer: Single Family Homes Condominiums" (Washington: NAHB, 1986) 3–5.

4. National Association of Realtors, "Existing Home Sales" (Washington: NAR, 1986).

5. For a more detailed discussion of these data see William Apgar, Chapter 2 in this volume.

6. For further discussion of the impact of tax reform on first-time homebuyers see Denise DiPasquale, "Homeowner Deductions and First-Time Homebuyers," Working Paper W89-2 (Cambridge: Joint Center for Housing Studies, Harvard University, 1989).

7. J. R. Follain, "Does Inflation Affect Real Behavior: The Case of Housing," *Southern Economic Journal* (January 1982) 570–582. Follain examines two arguments: (1) increases in expected inflation increase demand for owner-occupied housing and homeownership versus (2) increase in inflation reduces the size of the loan that a household can obtain and therefore decreases demand for housing and homeownership. Follain concludes that "inflation dampens housing demand and homeownership opportunity for most households even though inflation adjusted after-tax cost of owner-occupied housing declines as inflation heats up" (p. 570). As Follain points out, James Kearl ("Inflation, Mortgages and Housing," *Journal of Political Economy* 87 [1979] 1115–1138) concludes that inflation decreases housing demand; Thomas P. Boehn and Joseph A. McKenzie ("The Investment Demand for Housing," Federal Home Loan Bank Board Research Working Paper No. 99 [January 1981]) conclude that inflation decreases demand for housing and homeownership. Patric H. Hendershott and James D. Shilling ("The Economics of Tenure Choice, 1955–79," NBER Working Paper No. 543 [September 1980]) and Harvey S. Rosen and Kenneth T. Rosen ("Federal Taxes and Homeownership: Evidence from Time Series," *Journal of Political Economy* [1980] 59–75) provide results that indicate that inflation has a positive impact on homeownership (572).

8. Further research on the determinants of homeownership rates, especially attempting to explain the trends in homeownership rates over the last 15 years, is needed.

9. A. Downs, *The Revolution in Real Estate Finance* (Washington: The Brookings Institution, 1985) 163.

10. Fannie Mae Selling Guide, Sections 208.01 and 208.02.

11. Interviews with staff in Mortgage Operations at Fannie Mae.

12. Interviews with staff at the Massachusetts Housing Finance Agency.

13. Joint Center for Housing Studies, Harvard University, *The State of the Nation's Housing 1989* (Cambridge: JCHS, 1989) 13–14.

14. See DiPasquale, "Homeowner Deductions." For a complete discussion of the impact of Tax Reform on owner occupied housing by Patric Hendershott, Chapter 9 in this volume.

15. P. Clay, *Homeownership for the Poor: The Experience and Opportunities,* Working Paper #10 (Cambridge: MIT Center for Real Estate Development, May 1987) 32.

16. J. C. Weicher, "Urban Housing Policy," in P. Mieszkowski and M. Straszheim, eds., *Current Issues in Urban Economics* (Baltimore: Johns Hopkins University Press, 1979) 479; and National Association of Home Builders, *Low and Moderate Income Housing: Progress, Problems and Prospects* (Washington: NAHB, 1986) 26–27.

17. Weicher, "Urban Housing Policy," 479.

18. NAHB, *Low and Moderate Income Housing,* 27.

19. C. B. Meeks, "Rural Housing: Status and Issues," Working Paper HP #19 (Cambridge: MIT Center for Real Estate Development, April 1988) 12–14.

20. Weicher, "Urban Housing Policy," 473.

21. Department of Housing and Urban Development, Division of Policy Studies, Office of Policy Development and Research, "An Assessment of FHA's Section 203(b) Program" (March 1986) 1.4.

22. HUD, "Assessment," 2.5.

23. HUD, "Assessment," 5.7–5.10.

24. *The Report of President's Commission on Housing,* William F. McKenna, chair (Washington: USGPO, 1983) 163.

25. *Boston Globe,* October 4 1987.

26. R. B. Clemmer, and J. C. Weicher, "The Individual Housing Account," *AREUEA Journal* 11.2:221–230.

27. Clay, *Homeownership for the Poor,* 44. The source for these estimates is GAO, *The Costs and Benefits of Single-Family Mortgage Revenue Bonds: Preliminary Report* (Washington: USGAO, 1983).

28. National Association of Home Builders, *Home Building after Tax Reform: A Builder's Guide* (Washington: NAHB, 1986) 46.

29. NAHB, *Home Building after Tax Reform,* 43–46.

30. M. A. Stegman and J. D. Holden, *Nonfederal Housing Programs* (Washington: Urban Land Institute, 1987) 37–40.

31. See brochures for Massachusetts Homeownership Opportunity Program.

32. See brochure for Connecticut Downpayment Assistance Program.

33. NAHB, *Low and Moderate Income Housing,* 94.

34. See Michael Wheeler, Chapter 8 in this volume.

Chapter 7
Housing and the Capital Markets
Michael J. Lea

During the last 15 years, the U.S. mortgage market has progressed from a segmented domestic credit market, dominated by specialized lenders, into a major component of the global capital markets. Mortgages, in their securitized form, have developed into highly marketable commodities, with the domestic capital markets supporting almost $3 trillion in trades in both 1986 and 1987.[1] Japanese and European investors now invest in mortgage related securities backed by U.S. home mortgages and trade these securities on their domestic exchanges.

The mortgage market has been transformed from an unstable source of credit, subject to periods of severe funds shortage, to the purveyor of $443 billion in credit in 1986 alone. Mortgage credit has become plentiful, even at times of peak demand or high interest rates. The increased supply of funds has reduced mortgage rates relative to other interest rates, and increased competition has led to a better selection of mortgages and lower rates in many markets.

The mortgage instrument has also changed. As late as 1980, there was only one mortgage instrument originated in any volume: the fixed-rate, level-payment mortgage. Now there is a seemingly endless array of mortgages, including dozens of variations of adjustable-rate mortgages (ARMs), graduated payment mortgages (GPMs), biweekly payment mortgages, and adjustable-rate mortgages that convert into fixed-rate mortgages. These new instruments allow the tailoring of payments to individual circumstances, enhancing affordability, particularly during inflationary periods.

Several factors have contributed to the development of the U.S. mortgage market into a highly efficient source of credit to home buyers. Financial institution deregulation has enhanced competition and innovation in the primary market. Technological progress in the generation, processing, and dissemination of information has increased efficiency in all aspects of mortgage credit delivery. The unbundling of the basic functions of origination, servicing, and funding in the mortgage market has allowed firms to achieve economies of scale and facilitated more competition. The rise of the secondary mortgage market has increased the investor base in mortgages, improved marketability, and aided risk management by market participants.

The policies of the federal government have been crucial in the development and expansion of the U.S. mortgage market. Since the 1930s, the federal government has supported a variety of institutions in the mortgage market. Traditionally, it supported the thrift institutions that originated and invested in home mortgages. Most recently, secondary mortgage market enterprises were created to enhance the credit quality, and thus the marketability of mortgage instruments, thereby increasing their attractiveness to investors.

However, the recent development and expansion of the mortgage market has not been without controversy. The thrift industry has experienced difficulties in the aftermath of financial deregulation. The extraordinary rise of nominal interest rates in the early 1980s weakened the financial strength of many thrifts with mismatched asset and liability portfolios. Speculative real estate investments created large losses for a number of institutions. These factors, combined with the deterioration of several large regional economies, technically bankrupted the Federal Savings and Loan Insurance Corporation (FSLIC).[2] To date, the FSLIC crisis has not been resolved. And the extended debate about recapitalizing the FSLIC has raised questions about the likelihood of continued federal support for specialized housing lenders and increased the cost of deposits for thrift institutions. High and volatile mortgage rates have contributed to housing affordability concerns, particularly for first-time and moderate-income homebuyers.[3] Although nominal interest rates fell sharply in 1985 and 1986, real interest rates have remained at historically high levels. Financial market deregulation and global integration of the capital markets have contributed to increased interest rate volatility. This volatility has shifted to mortgage borrowers as a result of the integration of the domestic mortgage and capital markets. These financial factors may be partly responsible for the falling rate of homeownership in the early and mid-1980s.

Expansion of the secondary mortgage market has not only facilitated the growth in federally supported mortgage debt, it has also increased competition for mortgage assets. Depository institutions investing in mortgages now compete directly with originators who sell to the federally backed secondary mortgage market enterprises. This competition may be forcing traditional mortgage investors, such as thrift institutions, out of the mortgage market and undermining their attempts to restructure their asset portfolios through investment in ARMs.[4]

Finally, the rapid growth of the mortgage market, particularly that associated with the issuance of securities guaranteed by institutions with implicit or explicit government backing, has raised questions about the potential "crowding out" of private non-housing investment. Some critics of the government's role in the mortgage market have questioned whether the system has fostered too much housing, at the expense of business plant and equipment investment.[5]

Resolving these issues while maintaining the efficiency of mortgage credit delivery is of paramount concern to policy makers. In the short run, resolution of the FSLIC crisis is likely to have a significant effect on the cost of mortgage credit, the economy, and mortgage borrowers. Full recapitalization of the FSLIC will require many billions of additional dollars. If these funds come from the mortgage market, the cost of mortgage credit will rise. If the funds come from taxpayers, they will perpetuate and expand the subsidization of mortgage borrowers, at the expense of other borrowers in the economy.

Over a longer time horizon, resolution of the issues that currently exist in the mortgage market will almost inevitably change the structure of the mortgage finance system in the U.S. Solving individual institution failures through merger and acquisition will accelerate the breakdown of distinctions between thrifts and banks and the historic prohibitions against interstate deposit taking. Thrift institutions, suffering from increased competition and declining profits in the mortgage business, will increasingly turn to non-mortgage lines of business. Unless their growth is checked, the secondary mortgage market institutions will continue to expand their role in the mortgage market.

Policy makers dealing with these issues will have to reexamine the roles of the various federally supported institutions in the market place, roles that have changed significantly since the institutions were founded. In the course of this examination, it will be important to understand the origins of the current system and how market forces have affected change.

In the next section of this chapter, the history of federal involvement in the mortgage market is reviewed. The cost of funding of mortgages is analyzed in the following section. Rationales for and alternatives to federal involvement are reviewed, followed by a final section discussing policy options.

The principal conclusion of this study is that the bankrupt condition of the FSLIC is likely to force a significant change in the structure of the mortgage market in the near future. Tapping the Treasury for general revenues to fund the FSLIC would likely force a reorganization of the regulatory and insurance bodies for the thrift industry. If there are no changes in the status of the secondary market agencies, thrifts will continue to reduce their specialization in mortgage investment. An alternative approach to funding the FSLIC lies in taxing and/or restructuring the secondary mortgage market agencies. The advantage of this approach is that it would result in a reduction in the flow of resources directed to the housing market by federal policy and better targeting of the federal presence in the mortgage market, but at the expense of higher mortgage rates.

The Origins of Federal Involvement

The federal role in the mortgage market dates back to the Great Depression.[6] That period was characterized by collapse of the financial system caused in large part by a lack of liquidity in the financial markets, an erosion of confi-

dence in financial institutions and, in the mortgage market, a lack of understanding of asset default risk on the part of investors.

Congress created several institutions in the early 1930s to restore public
confidence and improve liquidity in the financial markets. In the mortgage
market, the Federal Home Loan Bank (FHLB) system was established in 1932
to provide regulatory oversight and liquidity to the nation's thrift institutions,
the most important provider of mortgage credit at that time. The FSLIC was
set up to insure deposits at thrift institutions, enhancing public confidence.

In return for the deposit insurance and ability to borrow from the FHLBs,
thrift institutions were subject to significant asset and liability regulation.
They were chartered as mutual organizations to make long-term home mortgage loans financed by short-term deposits attracted from "small savers."
Their mortgage lending activities were restricted to their local market. Furthermore, like banks, thrifts were not allowed to branch across state lines.

In 1934, the Federal Housing Administration (FHA) was created to insure mortgages, increasing investor confidence in mortgage assets, and foster-
ing the adoption of the long-term, self-amortizing mortgage instrument. In
order to promote adoption of this instrument and increase liquidity in the
mortgage market, Congress created the Federal National Mortgage Asso-
ciaton (Fannie Mae) to provide a secondary market for the originators of FHA
mortgages.

Until the 1960s, these institutions met the nation's housing credit needs
admirably. However, inflation and rising interest rates led to a succession of
new policies and institutions in the mortgage market. Increased competition
for deposits between thrifts and banks in an inflationary environment led to
the imposition of deposit rate ceilings, designed to protect the stability of the
system. Thrifts were allowed a small differential over banks in order to support housing. However, the combination of deposit rate ceilings and the lack
of alternative funding sources for mortgages led to shortages in mortgage
funds when market interest rates rose above deposit rate ceilings.[7] Continued
interest rate volatility produced recurrent credit crunches and severe housing
cycles. The lack of nationwide lending tended to increase the geographic severity of housing cycles, as growing regions with an excess demand for funds
had no way to tap the excess supply of funds in slower growth regions.

To relieve these problems, in 1968 Congress restructured the ownership
of Fannie Mae and allowed it to purchase conventional market rate mortgage
loans. Also in 1968, the Government National Mortgage Association (Ginnie
Mae) was created to provide an outlet for special assistance mortgage programs and to develop a national secondary market in FHA and VA mortgages.
In 1970, Congress chartered the Federal Home Loan Mortgage Corporation
(Freddie Mac) to develop a national secondary market in conventional mortgages for thrift institutions.

The creation of the secondary market enterprises was designed to improve the liquidity and standardization of mortgages, facilitating easier sale and trading. It was hoped that liquidity in mortgage assets, combined with the debt financing activities of the FHLBs, would reduce the severity of housing cycles, by facilitating the flow of funds between regions and increasing the supply of funds to the mortgage market.

However, the 1970s were plagued with the continuance of housing cycles. Fannie Mae and FHLB debt-financed lending may have dampened the severity of cycles, but they did not eliminate them. Some critics contended that the activities of these agencies simply supplanted private market provision of credit, affecting only the timing of the market's response to changes in the demand for credit, and not the ultimate supply of credit.[8]

During this time, the secondary mortgage market was only slowly developing. The securitization of FHA and VA mortgages by Ginnie Mae proceeded more rapidly than conventional mortgage securitization by Freddie Mac, in part because Ginnie Mae securities carried the full faith and credit guarantee of the U.S. government. Investor acceptance of conventional mortgage-related securities was also inhibited by their lack of liquidity and the fact that they had a structure different from bonds.[9] Originator acceptance of agency purchase programs was slowed by the need to develop uniform documentation and underwriting of loans being securitized. As a consequence, securitization had not reached a point in which it was competitive with depository funding, a below-market source of funds reflecting regulated deposit rates.

The 1980s ushered in a period of extraordinary volatility in interest rates and extensive financial institution deregulation. The Depository Institutions Deregulation and Monetary Control Act (DIDMCA) put in place the gradual removal of interest rate ceilings on deposits, allowing depository institutions to compete for funds more effectively, but also raising their cost of funds. Federally chartered thrift institutions were allowed to make adjustable-rate mortgages (ARMs) beginning in 1981, enabling them better to match their asset and liability maturities. The introduction of ARMs and GPMs enhanced affordability for borrowers in a high interest rate environment. However, they did so by transferring interest rate risk to mortgage borrowers, reducing the role of thrift institutions as maturity intermediators (i.e., transforming short-term deposits into long-term mortgages).

The Garn-St. Germain legislation in 1982 opened up new, non-residential investment opportunities for thrift institutions, allowing them to build more diversified asset portfolios. This legislation also paved the way for more mutual-to-stock ownership conversions, interjecting more of a profit motive in thrift operations. These actions signaled a move by the federal government away from maintenance of a specialized mortgage finance system.

The volatile economic environment of the 1980s also taxed the resources of the FSLIC by contributing to post-Depression record numbers of thrift institution failures. As interest rates soared in the early 1980s, many thrift institutions found themselves with severely eroded net worth and earnings performance, reflecting their historical asset-liability maturity mismatch in funding mortgages. This weakened condition led many institutions to adopt a "go-for-broke strategy" to grow out of their earnings problems.[10] Combined with a deterioration in some regional economies, this high-risk, high-return strategy resulted in a succession of thrift failures, technically bankrupting the FSLIC.

In the secondary market, Freddie Mac and Fannie Mae came of age during the 1980s. In 1981 they created the "swap" programs, wherein seasoned mortgages were exchanged for more liquid mortgage securities guaranteed by the agencies. These securities aided thrift institutions in restructuring their portfolios by providing more efficient collateral for borrowing. Saddled with portfolios of underwater loans, thrifts made heavy use of the swap programs, fueling a boom in conventional mortgage securitization. Although only 17 percent of conventional mortgages had been securitized prior to 1980, this share rose to 24.5 percent by the end of 1985, with 55 percent of the increase coming from the securitization of seasoned mortgages through the swap programs.

The swap activities added liquidity to the mortgage-related securities market and facilitated an enormous increase in the trading volume of mortgages, primarily through the mortgage security vehicle. The collateralized-mortgage-obligation (CMO), which divided mortgage pools into maturity classes, provided a better match between mortgage assets and investor preferences. Their introduction, combined with increased liquidity `in mortgage related securities, brought pension plans, insurance companies and foreign investors into the mortgage market.

1985 and 1986 were watershed years in the secondary mortgage market, as they represented a shift in agency secondary market activity away from the swap of seasoned mortgages for mortgage-backed securities towards funding of new mortgage originations. A major factor in this shift was the decline in long-term interest rates, beginning in September of 1985, fueling an unprecedented refinancing boom. As long-term interest rates declined, the popularity of fixed-rate mortgages surged. In a deregulated environment, thrift institutions could no longer afford to fund investment in long-term fixed-rate mortgages with short-term deposits. Faced with a declining share of ARMs to total originations, many thrifts turned to a mortgage banking mode of operation, originating fixed-rate mortgages for immediate sale into the secondary market. This environment led to an explosion in the growth of the agency securitized secondary market. Agency issues of mortgage-related securities rose from $133 billion in 1985 to over $280 billion in 1986, and their share of new originations rose from 47 percent to 56 percent.

This period of growth in the secondary mortgage market was accompanied by a decline in the importance of thrift institutions as suppliers of funds to the mortgage market. Although the (FSLIC insured) thrift share of conventional mortgage originations has remained at or above 50 percent since 1983, their holdings of outstanding one-to-four family mortgage debt fell from 48 percent in 1983 to 44 percent at the beginning of 1987. This decline reflected a shift in focus towards mortgage banking as well as increased portfolio diversification.

The 1987–1988 time period reflects a resurgence of ARM origination activity, an area still dominated by thrift institutions. The share of ARMs to total conventional 1–4 family originations rose from 23 percent in 1986 to 53 percent in 1988. The share of new originations securitized by the agencies fell to 42 percent in 1988. Private mortgage security issues rose sharply during this time period, rising from $14 billion in 1985 to $71 billion in 1988.

Federal Backing and the Cost of Mortgage Credit

Federal backing of institutions in the mortgage market affects their costs of raising funds as well as the risks and returns of the mortgage investment. Thrift institutions receive a variety of benefits as long as they remain primarily mortgage investors. To retain a thrift charter, institutions must keep at least 60 percent of their assets in the form of residential mortgages, cash or government securities. In addition, through 1986, if thrifts maintained 82 percent of their assets in this form, they received a substantial tax benefit—a 40 percent reduction in taxable income lowering their effective tax rate from 46 to 28 percent.[11]

In return for these constraints on investment, thrift institutions can raise funds with federal backing through FSLIC deposit insurance and have access to FHLB advances and lines of credit. In effect, they have a full faith and credit guarantee on the majority of their deposits, no matter what their financial condition or creditworthiness. In addition, FHLB advances allow thrifts to access the capital markets at agency rates, which are lower than corporate rates. The market perceives the FHLBs to be less risky because they have a line of credit to the U.S. Treasury.

Despite their federal backing, in recent years thrift institutions have consistently paid 50 to 150 basis points over comparable maturity Treasuries for their funds.[12] The magnitude of this spread is striking because both thrift deposits and Treasury securities enjoy federal payment guarantees. These spreads reflect the controversy over the financial condition of the FSLIC, competition for funds among insured institutions and a marketability premium relative to Treasuries.

Thrift institutions must pay for their federal backing. A special assessment to fund the FSLIC was added to the regular assessment in 1985, raising the all-in costs of deposit insurance from 8 to 21 basis points. Also, the Depository Institutions Deregulation and Monetary Control Act (DIDMCA) phased in reserve requirements for thrifts for retail deposits with maturities less than 18 months. Reserves must be kept in non-interest bearing accounts, raising retail deposit costs by an additional 5 basis points and wholesale deposit costs by 30 basis points.

Another factor affecting thrift cost of funds is the amount of capital they must use to fund their assets. A program to phase in increased capital requirements for thrifts was begun in 1986, and a proposal to adopt risk based capital requirements was put forth by the FHLBB at the end of 1988. This proposal would require thrifts to have a capital-to-assets ratio of 8 percent by the end of 1992, more than doubling their current requirement.[13] At a 15 percent targeted after-tax return on equity, institutions having to increase their capital to assets ratio from 4 percent to 8 percent would experience an increase in their overall cost-of-funds (over 1 year certificates of deposit) of 64 basis points.[14]

The rise of the secondary market has created an alternative delivery channel for mortgage credit. Mortgage bankers (or thrifts acting in a mortgage banking role) can originate mortgages for eventual funding by capital market investors such as mutual funds, pension plans and life insurance companies. The federal government supports this delivery channel through its backing of the secondary market agencies. Agency guarantees protect investors from mortgage default. In turn, Freddie Mac can have its securities guaranteed by the FHLBs, and Fannie Mae has a direct line of credit to the U.S. Treasury. This form of support reduces the perceived risk of the securities these agencies issue. Ginnie Mae uses a full faith and credit guarantee of the U.S. government on its securities, which are backed by government insured FHA and VA mortgages.

Agency securities also receive favorable treatment under security law and depository institution regulations. These securities are exempt from SEC registration and state "blue-sky" laws, lowering their issuance costs. They can be used as collateral for thrift borrowings; they are an eligible investment for ERISA regulated pension plans; and they can be used in connection with bad debt and liquid asset calculations for thrifts. These attributes increase the demand for agency securities, raising their price and lowering yield requirements relative to privately issued securites.

Because agency securities have implicit or explicit backing of the federal government and regulatory advantages, their securities can be issued at lower rates than comparable, privately backed issues. For example, the recent study of Freddie Mac by its Advisory Committee found that its mortgage securities traded on average 25–30 basis points below comparable AA non–agency backed pass-through securities.[15] Fannie Mae longer-term debt securities typically trade at yields 10–20 basis points lower than comparable maturity AAA-rated financial corporation bonds and 40–60 basis points higher than comparable maturity Treasuries, reflecting investor perceptions about the value of the implicit federal backing.[16]

While the cost of funds for thrift institutions has risen in recent years, the cost of securitization through the federally chartered secondary market agencies has fallen.[17] The rise in the volume of activity at the agencies has allowed them to achieve significant economies of scale in their pooling and securitization functions, lowering their average costs.[18] Competition between the agencies has lowered agency guarantee fees.[19] Increased volume of issuance has improved the marketability of mortgage securities, narrowing bid-ask spreads. The development of new forms of mortgage securities has brought new investors into the market, increasing the demand for agency securities and tightening option-adjusted mortgage-to-Treasury yield spreads.[20] The reduced cost of security issuance has allowed the government secondary market institutions to bid more aggressively for mortgages, putting downward pressure on mortgage rates.

The secondary mortgage market agencies do not pay a fee akin to deposit insurance for their federal backing. In addition, they are allowed to operate on a more highly leveraged basis than their financial service industry competitors and counterparts. At the end of 1988, Fannie Mae had an equity to assets ratio of 2 percent and Freddie Mac had an equity to assets ratio of 11.7 percent. However, these ratios understate the true leverage of the agencies because of the contingent liabilities the agencies acquire through their issuance of guaranteed securities. When Fannie Mae and Freddie Mac fund mortgages by selling securities with timely and/or ultimate payment guarantees, these are, in effect, insuring against default. Therefore, the investor has recourse back to the agency even though the mortgages are no longer on their balance sheet. If the contingent liabilities are included in the capital to asset calculations, both corporations have ratios less than one percent.[21] Higher leverage reduces the agency costs of funding mortgage purchases, increasing the returns on shareholder equity and, potentially, the risks of agency activity to the federal government.

It is likely that federal backing of thrift institutions and secondary mortgage market agencies lowers the cost of mortgage credit to homeowners, relative to a private sector delivery system. However, to date, conclusive evidence of the magnitude of the effect of federal backing is elusive, since the difficulty in valuing the borrower's prepayment option in the mortgage contract complicates analysis of the determinants of mortgage-to-Treasury yield spreads.

It is clear that federal backing currently favors the secondary mortgage market agencies relative to thrift institutions in the purchase of mortgage assets. As noted earlier, securitization by the secondary mortgage market agencies is cheaper than private sector credit enhancement, as evidenced by the fact that privately issued AA rated mortgage pass-throughs trade at 25 to 30 basis points higher than yields on comparable Freddie Mac or Fannie Mae pass-throughs.

In addition, the agencies can debt finance mortgages at lower cost than thrift institutions. As shown in Table 7.1, Fannie Mae was able to debt-finance mortgage purchases at 71 basis points less on average than a typical

TABLE 7.1 Relative Cost of Funds (percent)[a]

		Thrift institutions	Fannie Mae
(1)	Six month Treasury	8.76	8.76
(2)	Borrowing spread	1.10	0.60
(3)	Cost of federal backing	0.21	0
(4)	All-in debt cost	10.07	9.36
(5)	Cost of equity	33.33	33.33
(6)	Funding weights: debt	97	98
	equity	3	2
(7)	Weighted cost of funds	10.77	9.83

[a]Calculations as follows:

(1) Month end yield, December 1988.

(2) Average thrift 6 month brokered CD to 6 month Treasury spread net of commission, January 1987–December 1988; average Fannie Mae 6 month debt obligation to 6 month Treasury spread, 1987–88.

(3) Based on deposit insurance fee of 21 basis points for thrift institutions—including FSLIC special assessment.

(4) (1) + (2) + (3)

(5) A 20 percent after-tax return on equity was used in this calculation. This required return translates into a pre-tax cost of 33.3 percent at a 40 percent marginal tax rate.

(6) Based on proposed risk based capital requirements for mortgage investment by thrift institutions and current Fannie Mae equity to assets ratio. Although Fannie Mae's ratio of equity to assets plus contingent liabilities is less than one percent, the higher number was used as a target leverage ratio for new mortgage acquisitions.

(7) (4) × (debt weight in (6)) + (5) × (equity weight in (6)).

thrift institution in 1987 and 1988 (9.36 percent and 10.07 percent) before consideration of differences in capital costs. Not only is Fannie Mae's average borrowing spread to Treasury less than most thrifts, it also operates without paying a fee for its federal backing. In reality, the disparity is even larger because Fannie Mae can operate with a significantly higher leverage ratio. These factors contribute to the disparity in returns on shareholder equity earned by investors in thrifts and the agencies. Solvent thrift institutions have found their after-tax returns on equity falling from 14.3 percent in 1986 to 5.4 percent in 1988, compared to after-tax returns on equity ranging between 25 percent and 28 percent for Freddie Mac and Fannie Mae shareholders in 1987 and 1988.

The disparity in this competition for mortgage assets may erode the competitiveness of thrift institutions in the future. Ironically, this situation was envisaged as early as 1934 when representatives of the thrift industry questioned whether their institutions could compete with Fannie Mae.[22] These concerns were reiterated at the time Ginnie Mae was created and Fannie Mae was restructured in 1968.

Resolution of the FSLIC crisis may reduce this disparity by reducing thrift borrowing costs relative to Treasuries. However, unless the capital ratios are equalized and the agencies charged for their federal backing, thrifts will continue to operate at a competitive disadvantage.

Rationales for Federal Involvement

One of the guiding principles of the free market system is the reliance on private markets to allocate resources, with a minimal amount of government intervention. Following this line of reasoning, the federal backing of institutions in the mortgage market should be dictated in part by the presence of inefficiencies or breakdowns in the market allocation of resources. To a large extent, the government is involved in the mortgage market because concerns about credit risk have traditionally discouraged the private market from mortgage investment. (The creation of FHA is an excellent example). Mortgages are backed by the collateral of individual houses in local markets. Underwriting of these assets has to be done on a loan-by-loan basis, which is costly, particularly for third party investors not familiar with local housing markets. Maintenance of mortgage investment is also a costly endeavor, necessitating monthly monitoring of payment remittance and local market conditions.

It has been argued that, without perceived government backing, investors would shy away from assets backed by real estate, making mortgage funds more cyclical, less available, and more expensive. Institutions specializing in real estate investment need government support, the argument continues, because they are vulnerable to a nationwide decline in property values, which might be triggered by another depression.

Government support of depository institutions and secondary market institutions lessens the exposure of investors to the credit risk inherent in mortgage assets. Deposit insurance takes away the need for individual depositors to assess the credit quality of assets in a thrift portfolio. Explicit or implicit support of institutions that guarantee mortgage securities also lessens or removes the need for investors to assess the credit quality of the assets collateralizing the security.

Government backing of mortgages through agency residential mortgage security guarantees is a more targeted and less risky way to support the goal of reducing the credit risk in mortgages than is deposit insurance or federal backing of agency debt securities. Agency mortgage security guarantees insure timely or eventual repayment of principal but do not guarantee against asset value changes due to interest rate changes. Deposit insurance and the implicit federal backing of agency debt obligations exposes the government to the risk of the funding strategy. For example, if the value of the assets falls below the value of the liabilities by more than the amount of capital, as would happen with a sustained rise in short-term interest rates, the federal government may have to advance funds to repay the debt holders (depositors).

The securitization process may reduce the government's overall interest rate risk in the mortgage market. In the past, thrift institutions (and the FSLIC) absorbed interest rate risk as part of their maturity intermediation function. However, the shift in funding of FRMs to the secondary market and the increased use of ARMs has shifted interest rate risk in the market to other investors (FRMs) and mortgage borrowers (ARMs).

If fixed-rate mortgage securities are sold to investors other than financial institutions whose deposits are government insured, the degree of risk to which taxpayers are ultimately exposed may be significantly reduced. In effect, the securitization process shifts the burden of managing interest rate risk to the private sector. Interest rate risk is absorbed by private investors who are compensated by the risk premium embedded in mortgage-to-Treasury spreads. Even if fixed-rate mortgage securities remain within depository institutions, they may reduce the government's interest rate risk if they are used to collateralize longer maturity borrowings (e.g. advances, mortgage-backed bonds) that allow a better duration match with the underlying mortgages.

Adjustable-rate mortgages are relatively well matched with short-term deposits and therefore present little interest rate risk exposure for the FSLIC. To date, thrifts have been almost the exclusive investor in ARMs. Securitization of ARMs has proceeded slowly, reflecting the diversity in characteristics of individual instruments. However, increased securitization of ARMs would squeeze the credit and liquidity values out of ARM-to-Treasury spreads, exacerbating the profitability problems of thrift ARM investments.

Securitization may increase the risks that the FSLIC insures by creating an adverse selection problem for depository institutions and the insurance fund.[23] Lower risk loans tend to be securitized because they necessitate less credit enhancement and entail less cost to evaluate. Depository institutions in search of higher yields will invest in less standardized and higher risk assets. This activity adds value in the economy but will not support the number of thrift institutions that exist today (e.g., moving into commercial lending—an area dominated by the over 12,000 members of the commercial banking industry and suffering from competition by high yield corporate bond issuance—will not help since that area cannot sustain a large number of new entrants). In addition, securitization may skim off the cream, the highest quality assets, leaving depository institutions, backed by federal deposit insurance, with the riskier assets in their portfolios.

The most visible effect of federal backing of the mortgage market is on mortgage rates. Lowering mortgage rates enhances housing affordability but also can entail a substantial opportunity cost. Lower mortgage rates, along with favorable income tax treatment of owner-occupied housing, lowers the cost of homeownership and increases housing consumption. A lower relative cost of housing consumption can lead to over investment in owner-occupied housing (relative to a totally private market allocation) which comes at the expense of business plant and equipment investment. Over time, lower levels of business investment will reduce the productivity of American workers, lowering real wages and reducing the competitiveness of American firms in world markets. Recent studies have estimated that in the absence of preferential tax treatment and lower mortgage rates, the housing capital stock would be about 10 percent smaller than its current level.[24] Furthermore, the Tax Reform Act of 1986 increased the relatively favorable position of owner-occupied housing, which may increase capital reallocation towards housing.[25]

If the federal government is involved in the mortgage market in order to improve affordability and expand the consumption of owner-occupied housing, ideally its programs should be targeted towards enhancing homeownership opportunities for those groups that would be denied the opportunity to own by the private market. The activities of FHA and Ginnie Mae are focused on first-time and moderate-income home buyers. However, the charters of Freddie Mac and Fannie Mae allow them to purchase residential mortgages up $186,700, a limit that is well above the median house price in most areas in the country.[26] Although agency activities foster some increase in homeownership, existing homeowners are more likely to benefit from agency support of the mortgage market than are households who would not have otherwise purchased a house.

Alternatives to Federal Involvement

Federal support of mortgage market institutions arose partly in response to breakdowns in market allocation of credit for housing. However, in keeping with the fundamental theme of market allocation, it is appropriate to ask whether the private market has progressed to the point where federal involvement could be scaled back. There is evidence to suggest that the economics of securitization are powerful enough to sustain the activity, even if the federal role in this market was reduced. The volume of securitization of non-conforming mortgages has been rising in the last few years. Issues of non-agency mortgage backed securities totalled only $6.8 billion in 1986 but rose to $18.5 billion in 1987 and $20.7 billion in 1988. According to Freddie Mac estimates, between 10 and 20 percent of the non-conforming market has now been securitized.

In the non-conforming market, securities are rated by either the quality of the issuer or the underlying collateral. Highly rated issuers (e.g., Sears, Citicorp, Residential Funding Corporation) have issued rated securities without credit enhancement. Issuers with lower ratings have used a variety of methods to enhance the credit quality of the securities they issue. Pool insurance can be obtained from mortgage insurers and letters of credit can be obtained from commercial banks or the FHLB. Senior-subordinated security structures, in which the credit risk of a pool of assets is concentrated in a subordinated or junior interest security, can be used to create an A or AA rated security. The subordinated interest in that pool can be sold separately or retained by the issuing institution. Over-collateralized issues, in which the value of the assets backing a security issue exceeds the par value of the issue, can safeguard investors from a decline in value of the assets backing the security.

The emergence of alternatives to agency credit enhancement has spawned private competitors of the agencies. Several large thrifts and Wall Street firms have set up their own conduit and securitization activities. These entities have supported reductions in agency loan limits, in order to expand their market access. However, small thrifts have supported expansion of agency loan limits because of their perception that they would get better pricing from the agencies than from private players. This debate has polarized the discussion of agency roles within the thrift industry and clouded the distinction between the roles of thrifts and the agencies in the mortgage market.

If the private mortgage market has developed to the point that it can supply a sufficient flow of funds to the mortgage market to meet borrower demand, then federal involvement could be scaled back. Continued expansion of the market accessible by the agencies may retard or preclude further development of the private market—and continue to foster over-consumption of housing at the expense of other goods and services. It has been argued that continuation of substantial federal support of the mortgage market is necessary to reduce uncertainty about the availability and cost of mortgage credit in distressed markets, such as the Texas market during the last two years. However, continuance of the FHA and Ginnie Mae programs could serve this function. Scaling back the current level of federal support for Freddie Mac and Fannie Mae would allow for further development of the private market without removing the government safety net from the mortgage market.

Policy Options

A confluence of events has created the need for reevaluting federal support of institutions in the mortgage market. The bankruptcy of the FSLIC has led to questions about the future role of thrift institutions. The development of the secondary mortgage market has lessened the need for federal backing of specialized depository investors in mortgages. And private market solutions to the high cost of assessing credit quality in mortgages have been created, reducing the need for direct federal involvement in credit enhancement.

Resolution of the FSLIC funding problem is likely to be the catalyst that forces change in the nature of federal support for the mortgage market. Because resolution is likely to be accompanied by regulatory changes, it is an appropriate time to ask questions about the future role and need for support by the federal government of thrifts and the secondary market agencies.

There is general agreement that the FSLIC will need a substantial ($40 to $80 billion) infusion to deal with the problems of the thrift industry. The FSLIC must have more funds in order to take more timely action to close bankrupt institutions. This would reduce the federal government's long-run cost in supporting depository institutions in two ways. First, early closure of non-viable institutions would truncate the government's losses. Second, recapitalization of the FSLIC and provision of solutions for bankrupt institutions before their situations hit the press would lower thrift deposit-to-Treasury spreads, enhancing their profitability and capital resources.

The revenues for FSLIC to close currently insolvent institutions must come either from general tax revenues or from mortgage borrowers. They cannot come from the industry alone, as the tangible net worth of GAAP solvent thrift institutions at the end of 1988 was only $33.7 billion. Furthermore, it would be counterproductive to reduce the capital buffer for FSLIC's future obligations in order to provide funds to pay for its current obligations. If funds for the FSLIC are to come from the taxpayer in general, policy makers will have to provide assurances that the current situation will not be repeated.

Do We Need Thrifts?

The federal government implicitly decided that specialized depository investors in mortgages were no longer necessary when it embarked on its program of deregulation in 1981. Since that time, the distinctions between banks and thrifts have been reduced. The regulations governing the degree of specialization in mortgages necessary to maintain a thrift charter have been liberalized. The tax incentives for thrift specialization in mortgages have been sharply reduced, and the threshold necessary to obtain the deduction has been reduced. A further move in this direction would be a merger of the regulatory bodies and insurance funds for all financial institutions. All financial institutions would be subject to the same regulations and capital requirements. This approach would enhance the perceived strength of the deposit insurance funds, and thus the competitiveness of insured institutions. However, a capital infusion to the FSLIC before a merger would be necessary to obtain support from the banking industry.

It is clear that thrift institutions are a vital part of the mortgage delivery system in the U.S., providing origination, servicing, and investment services. However, the development of the secondary mortgage market has lessened the need for federally backed depository institutions *restricted* in large part to the delivery mortgage credit services. A merger of the regulatory and insurance functions of banks and thrifts would create a level playing field for all depository institutions, and would let firms specialize in those functions in which they have a comparative advantage—without government interference in the market allocation of resources.

A transition towards a less specialized thrift industry could be accomplished without a major disruption to the mortgage market. If the secondary mortgage market agencies are kept intact, mortgage rates will continue to be less than other rates, although capital would continue to be allocated to owner-occupied housing and away from business plant and equipment investment. However, this approach would face the political hurdle of having to raise taxes or increase the deficit in order to fund the recapitalization.

Do We Need the Agencies?

An alternative to taxpayer funding of FSLIC liabilities would be to tax institutions in the industry and mortgage borrowers. If the federal government reduced its support of the secondary mortgage market institutions, thrift competitiveness and profitability would be enhanced, allowing these markets to contribute more to the FSLIC. Although it is likely that this approach would result in increasing mortgage rates, it would result in a more market-based allocation of capital, benefitting other borrowers, and a more targeted federal presence in the mortgage market.

There are at least three ways the federal government could restructure its presence in the secondary mortgage market: privatizing Freddie Mac and Fannie Mae; increasing the targeting of the federal secondary mortgage market presence; and imposing user fees on agency activities.

Agency privatization. The federal presence in the secondary market could be reduced by privatizing Freddie Mac and Fannie Mae. This approach would reduce the competitive pressures on the thrifts and reduce the allocation of resources going to owner-occupied housing. The federal government could take over the liquidation of Fannie Mae's portfolio and continue to provide indirect support of existing mortgage securities issued by both institutions. This support could mean continuing a Treasury line of credit supporting past guarantees but providing no federal support of new security issuance. If implemented over a relatively short period of time, the existing value of these firms to their stockholders could be retained, relative to a solution that led to their eventual phase-out through lower loan limits.

It is likely that Freddie Mac and Fannie Mae could continue to provide their conduit and securitization functions without implicit federal backing. The study of Freddie Mac by its Advisory Committee suggested that if privatized, it would obtain a AA rating as a mortgage insurer. Although Fannie Mae is not as well capitalized, if its mortgage securitization function were split from its portfolio management function and privatized, it is likely that it could be a viable private sector competitor.[27]

The advantages of this option would be an increase in the resources of the FSLIC through enhanced profitability of thrift institutions and a reduction in the subsidization of homeownership and housing consumption for middle- and upper-income households. Because the agencies could be viable as private entities, securitization would likely continue to dominate the mortgage market and be enhanced by increased competition from thrifts and other players.

The major cost of this approach takes the form of higher fixed-rate mortgage rates. Estimates of the current Freddie Mac/Fannie Mae advantage over private securities suggest that privatization would raise rates 25 to 30 basis points. Even if the impact is initially larger because of market uncertainty about the competitiveness of the "private" Freddie Mac and Fannie Mae, it would have far less of an impact on home buyers today than 15 years ago because of the alternative mortgage instruments now available. In fact, it is likely that the increase in fixed-rate mortgage rates would not be very visible. Volatility in these rates has caused mortgage rate movements of as much as 50 basis points in one day, which would swamp the effects of agency privatization. However, in the short run, every increase in mortgage rates would be blamed on privatization.

Targeting. A number of proposals have been offered to restrict Fannie Mae's and Freddie Mac's powers. Demands to reduce or freeze their loan limits, restrict their securitization activities to pass-through securities, and restrict their purchase activities to FRMs have been voiced.[28]

Reduction of loan limits would enhance the competitiveness of thrifts and private conduits in a larger segment of the mortgage market. Loan limits could be regionalized to reflect house price differences and maintain competitive balance on a national basis. While the current use of one limit for the entire country may be necessary to satisfy affordability concerns in high cost areas, the limit subsidizes higher real income homeowners in lower cost areas. Lowering the loan limit in lower cost areas would distribute the benefits of agency involvement more equitably. Also, this approach would reduce the proportion of the population affected by higher mortgage rates, relative to total privatization.

Restriction of agency purchase limits also would benefit private competitors in the mortgage market. These competitors could engage in conduit activities, create derivative securities on their own, and reduce the potential for monopoly pricing in the market. A cessation in the indexation of the loan limits would also aid private competitors. Currently, indexation of the loan limit ensures that mortgages only slightly above current limits will fall within agency purchase guidelines in succeeding years. The prospect of agency purchase eligibility in the near future may induce originators to hold their mortgages until they qualify, rather than sell them to private conduits for non-agency securitization.

It has been suggested that agency loan limits be reduced to the Ginnie Mae limits, which vary based on housing costs in local markets. However, this would emasculate Freddie Mac and Fannie Mae because they would be unable to compete with Ginnie Mae. Not only does Ginnie Mae have a superior guarantee, it places its guarantee directly on pools formed in the primary market and has lower costs of pooling and issuing securities. This approach would be inequitable for existing agency shareholders and damaging to the agencies' ability to attract and retain high quality personnel.

Restriction of agency purchases to FRMs would benefit thrift institutions, allowing them to continue earning current credit and liquidity spreads on their investment. This action would leave the thrift presence in the mortgage market mainly in ARMs, which would generate less interest rate risk exposure for the FSLIC than thrift investment in FRMs. The principal costs of this alternative are to Freddie Mac's and Fannie Mae's stockholders, for it limits a potentially profitable area of business. Also, this restriction could reduce standardization and marketability of ARMs at a time in which there is still an excess demand for ARMs by thrifts in many parts of the country.

User fees. A third alternative that has been discussed at length is the concept of user fees. The federal budget has proposed agency user fees of varying magnitude on debt and pass-through securities since 1982. User fees on Freddie Mac, Fannie Mae and the FHLBs would raise revenue and reduce the federal budget deficit, level the playing field between government and non-government backed entities in the mortgage market, and reduce the subsidy to owner-occupied housing investment. User fees on government backed institutions would increase the competitiveness of private players in the mortgage market. And user fees could be used to fund the FSLIC—in effect, taxing mortgage borrowers to solve the funding crisis.

Furthermore, if risk-based, user fees could be a tool to control the government's risk exposure in the mortgage market.[29] Higher risk activities, such as mismatched debt financing, could be discouraged if subject to higher user fees. The imposition of risk-based user fees would also be extended to deposit insurance. By charging premiums that vary with risk, the FSLIC could better manage its risk exposure in extending deposit insurance.

Earlier user fee proposals have not received substantial support. Politically, the perception that user fees would increase mortgage rates, reducing the government's visible support of homeownership and housing demand, has stymied their adoption. Substantively, the fees proposed have never borne a relationship to risks or costs of federal backing. Furthermore, if user fees were not completely passed on in the form of higher mortgage rates, the fees would reduce the profitability of the secondary market institutions and FHLBs, in effect taxing their shareholders.

Each of these approaches would reduce the federal backing of the secondary mortgage market agencies. However, only privatization is fully consistent with the goal of market-based resource allocation. If the agencies were privatized they could continue to provide the same services to the mortgage market—perhaps more effectively if private competitors were able to enter the market. Private secondary market firms combined with a healthier thrift industry would continue to support a highly developed mortgage market to allocate mortgage credit, and a targeted federal presence through GNMA and FHA would continue to address distributional issues.

Conclusion

There is no easy answer to the issue of the proper federal role in the mortgage market. Discussion often breaks down into politically charged rhetoric about the sanctity of homeownership. Furthermore, the discussion is complicated, because there are no precise estimates of the costs and benefits of government involvement. However, the FSLIC problem will not go away. Funding from the most recent recapitalization of the insurance fund will be exhausted in one to two years, and further funding will be required. The resources of the industry are limited—and undermining the profitability of thrift institutions to fund the FSLIC could prove counter-productive by creating more problems than it solves.

We must recognize that there are insufficient resources to pay for FSLIC recapitalization in the thrift industry, and that these funds will have to come from other sources. In the end, the political question will be whether to raise taxes in general or increase the deficit to fund FSLIC—a direct but highly visible means of support—or to raise mortgage rates by imposing user fees on government sponsored agencies and/or restricting their powers. The latter approach would be only slightly less visible and contentious than the former.

An answer to who pays to recapitalize the FSLIC will also have a major impact on the federal presence in the mortgage market. In effect, Congress can choose between increasing federal support of the mortgage market through continued backing of specialized thrifts and the secondary market agencies or reducing that support, recognizing that the mortgage market has "come of age" and that mortgage borrowers can effectively compete for capital without specialized institutions with extensive federal backing.

A reduction in federal support of the mortgage market may be the preferable solution if Congress believes that the private market should be primarily responsible for resource allocation and has progressed to the point at which it can supply sufficient funds to meet borrower demand. Although this action may raise mortgage rates, reduction in and a better targeting of the resources directed to the housing market by federal policy can provide enhanced overall welfare.

However, economic and political goals do not always coincide. Mortgage borrowers are a more concentrated and politically active constituency than taxpayers in general. In the end the resolution will be politically determined, with the outcome depending on the lobbying strengths of the affected parties.

*   *   *   *

The author wishes to thank Patric Hendershott, Leland Brendsel, Robert Buckley, Denise DiPasquale, John Tucillo, Robert Van Order, and John Weicher for their helpful comments.

Notes

1. Unless otherwise noted, the mortgage market data in this paper have been obtained from Federal Home Loan Mortgage Corporation, "Database," *Secondary Mortgage Markets* 5.3 (Fall 1987).

2. U.S. Government Accounting Office, *Thrift Industry: Forbearance for Troubled Institutions, 1982–1986* (Washington: USGPO, May 1987).

3. See Denise DiPasquale,Chapter 6 in this volume.

4. D. Jacobe, "Trading Places (Will the Secondary Market Become the Primary Market?)," U.S. League of Savings Institutions, April 1986; M. Lea, "Dueling Guarantees," *Secondary Mortgage Markets* 3.3 (Fall 1986) and "The Direct Approach," *Secondary Mortgage Markets* 3.4 (Winter 1987) and J. Tucillo, "Will Housing and Thrifts Still be a Natural Fit?" in *The Future Role of Thrift Institutions: Papers and Proceedings* (April 1987).

5. P. Hendershott, "Tax Changes and Capital Allocation in the 1980s," in M. Feldstein, ed., *The Effects of Taxation on Capital Formation* (Chicago: University of Chicago Press, 1987) and Edwin S. Mills, "Has the U.S. Overinvested in Housing?" *AREUEA Journal* 15.1 (Spring 1987).

6. K. Vallani, "The Federal Forecast: A Change in the Air," *Secondary Mortgage Markets* 2.1 (Spring 1985). Also, see J. Weicher, "The Future Structure of the Housing Finance System," presented at the American Enterprise Institution Conference on Restructuring the Financial System, Washington, November 1987, for a more detailed discussion of the institutions created during this period.

7. See the articles in Board of Governors of the Federal Reserve System, *Ways to Moderate Fluctuation in Housing Construction,* Staff Report (Washington, 1972).

8. See F. Arcelus and A. Meltzer, "The Markets for Housing and Housing Services," *Journal of Money, Credit and Banking* 5 (February 1973) and P. Hendershott and K. Villani, *Regulation and Reform of the Housing Finance System* (Washington: American Enterprise Institute, 1977).

9. Bonds are typically non-amortizing with semiannual interest payments. They may have a call feature permitting earlier than stated maturity redemption at stated prices. Mortgages amortize over the stated maturity, pay interest monthly, and are subject to early redemption at the discretion of the borrower.

10. For a discussion of these incentives, see E. Kane, "S&Ls and Interest Rate Reregulation: The FSLIC as an In-Place Bail Out Program," *Housing Finance Review* 1.3 (July 1982) and J. Guttentag, "Recent Changes in the Primary Home Mortgage Market," *Housing Finance Review* 3.3 (July 1984).

11. The Tax Reform Act of 1986 scaled back the thrift bad debt deduction from 40 to 8 percent of taxable income. As a result, the federal marginal income tax rate for

thrift institutions has risen from 28 to 32 percent, while that for other taxable corporations has fallen from 46 to 34 percent. Unlike the secondary mortgage market agencies, thrift institutions are subject to state income taxes.

12. Source: Imperial Corporation of America. Spreads represent the difference between 6 month broker-obtained insured certificates of deposit (CDs) and comparable maturity Treasury securities from January 1986 through December 1988. These CDs are marketed to retail customers in amounts under $100,000—yields are net of broker commission. This series was selected because it represents a continuous, secondary market-insured deposit rate and is often the marginal source of funds for large thrifts. Thrift institution branch-originated CDs may have lower quoted yields but also entail an incremental cost in origination and vary over time by maturity depending on the strategy and funding needs of individual institutions.

13. Currently, thrift institutions must maintain a 6 percent ratio of regulatory capital to FHLB liabilities, but can receive a credit of up to 2 percentage points if well matched in their funding. The proposed regulations also create a more restrictive definition of capital.

14. Specifically, at a 40 percent combined federal-state marginal tax rate, the pre-tax equity cost rises from 100 to 200 basis points as the capital to assets ratio rises from 4 to 8 percent. The net increase in the cost of funds is only 64 basis points assuming the increased equity substitutes for 1 year debt with an all-in cost of 9 percent.

15. See Freddie Mac Advisory Committee, Task Force, Report II, unpublished, February 1987. Part of the spread between agency and private securities may be a liquidity premium reflecting the relatively small volume of private pass-throughs issued to date. This component of the spread would fall with increased volume of issuance. Also, the CBO study of Sallie Mae Congressional Budget Office, *Issues and Options for the Student Loan Marketing Association* (Washington: USGPO, 1986), found that between 1982 and 1984 their debt, which is implicitly backed by the federal government, traded, on average, 30 basis points below AAA corporate debt.

16. Technically the value of the federal backing of thrift institutions and secondary market agencies varies with the interest rate environment and their methods of financing (see Lea, "Dueling Guarantees"). The value of federal backing of the thrift industry and Fannie Mac was much larger in the 1982–1984 period, when interest rates were high and these institutions had negative net worth, than it is in the current interest rate environment. For more detail, see E. Kane and C. Foster, "Valuing and Eliminating Subsidies Associated with Conjectural Government Guarantees of FNMA Liabilities" (New York: Salomon Brothers Center for the Study of Financial Institutions, May 1986).

17. It can be argued that the imposition of federal income tax on Freddie Mac in 1986 may have increased the costs of securitization. However, competition with Fannie Mae limited the degree to which this cost could be passed on to mortgage borrowers. Also, the federal corporate income tax is a profits tax on Freddie Mac's guarantee fee income stream from past purchases. Thus, tax payments are relatively invarient to the volume of new activity.

18. For example, Freddie Mac's average general and administration expenses fell from 12.5 basis points in 1980 to 7.1 basis points in 1987 as the volume of securities issued rose from $16.9 billion to $214.5 billion. Data from *Freddie Mac Annual Report* (Washington: Federal Home Loan Mortgage Corporation, 1986, 1988).

19. Guarantee fees on Freddie Mac's highly competitive swap programs, which are negotiated directly with lenders, fell from over 30 basis points in the early 1980s to 22 basis points by early 1987. This fall in fees is not necessarily related to a decline in costs. Because Freddie Mac and Fannic Mac constitute a duopoly in the conforming secondary mortgage market, price setting in this market may not be directly deter-

mined by their cost of funds, but rather by market share considerations subject to a minimum profit constraint.

20. The term option-adjusted yield spread refers to the spread between mortgage and Treasury securities net of the value of the borrowers' prepayment option; remaining differences in yield will reflect differences in perceived credit risk, marketability, and taxation.

21. For more information on the capital adequacy of Freddie Mac, see the report of the Freddie Mac Advisory Committee. Capital information obtained from *Freddie Mac Annual Report,* and *Fannie Mae 1988 Annual Report, The USA's Housing Partner* (Washington: Federal National Mortgage Association, 1988).

22. See Section 1 in M. Sener et al., "Evolution of Federal Legislative Policy in Housing," *Housing in the Seventies Working Papers 1,* National Housing Policy Review (Washington: USGPO, 1972).

23. S. Greenbaum, "Securitization, Asset Quality and Regulatory Reform" in Federal Home Loan Bank of New York, *The Future Role of Thrift Institutions: Papers and Proceedings of the First Annual Bryce Curry Conference.* (April 1987).

24. See Hendershott, "Tax Changes."

25. See Patric Hendershott,Chapter 9 in this volume.

26. For mortgages delivered after January 1, 1989. See M. Lea, "Raising the Roof," *Secondary Mortgage Markets* 3.4 (Winter 1987) for a discussion of the loan limit formula.

27. See S. Woodward, "Privatization Alternatives for FNMA," paper presented at the 13th Annual Conference of the Federal Home Loan Bank of San Francisco, December 1987, for a more detailed analysis of privatization options for Fannie Mae.

28. For this analysis, see the report of the Freddie Mac Advisory Committee.

29. See Villani, "Federal Forecast," and R. Van Order, "User Fees and Mortgage Markets," *Housing Finance Review* 6.2 (Summer 1987).

Chapter 8
Resolving Local Regulatory Disputes and Building Consensus for Affordable Housing

Michael Wheeler

Local land use and environmental regulations determine what housing gets built, where it goes, what it looks like, and even who lives in it. Whatever federal, state, and private resources are pumped into housing construction are ultimately filtered, directed and—sometimes—blocked by local regulation.

The argument that zoning, subdivision, and related ordinances add to the cost of housing is familiar; so is the contention that deregulation is the answer to the affordable housing problem. This chapter, however, challenges the view that the problem lies with the substance of local regulation. Instead it argues that greater attention must be given to innovative negotiation and mediation processes which can overcome regulatory deadlocks and build consensus for affordable housing.

Properly conceived, local regulation could provide the setting for bringing together housing advocates, private and nonprofit developers, municipal agencies, neighbors, and other affected citizens to create policies and projects that meet their particular needs. The forging of such partnerships requires not merely good intentions but government support, particularly at the state level. Administrative procedures modeled on the adversary system of our courts leave little room for creative problem solving; ad hoc attempts at compromise work in some instances, but are highly risky. Fortunately, approaches like negotiated design, negotiated investment strategy, and mediated negotiation—among others sketched later in this chapter—offer promising alternatives to the conventional regulatory process and the contention that it breeds. In an era of limited federal funding it is especially important to fashion new processes in which public and private entities can efficiently pool their resources to build more housing.

Local affordable housing disputes have to be understood as representing just one specific manifestation of broader conflicts over land use development policy. Techniques that have been used to form public-private partnerships for rebuilding downtown commercial areas, linkage programs that tie office construction to residential development, and even statutes that guide the siting of hazardous waste plants all offer important lessons for those who want to see more low- and moderate-income housing.

The following section of this chapter reviews the traditional analysis of the costs of local regulation. The next section describes the critical differences between local regulations as they appear in the books and as they are actually practiced. It is followed by a short catalog of ways in which negotiation can be formalized. The final portion of the chapter considers the initiatives the federal government can take in a domain which, for the most part, admittedly belongs to states and municipalities. The goal throughout is not merely to find ways to reduce regulatory friction, but to identify procedures that will encourage people aggressively to attack and solve local problems of housing affordability.

Coping with the Cost of Regulation

Local Regulation and Housing Costs

Local land use regulations drive up housing costs in six significant ways.

> Minimum lot size requirements mean that more land has to be acquired for each unit of housing that can be built.

> Regulations restricting housing to specified zones reduce the overall supply of developable land and thus drive up its price.

> Prohibitions against multi-family and accessory uses may result in inefficient use of space.

> Running the regulatory gauntlet among a variety of municipal (and sometimes regional and state) agencies is a costly and time-consuming process.

> Even when all agency approvals are granted, citizen groups and other third parties may have legal standing to institute lengthy and expensive legal challenges.

> The complexity and uncertainty of the approval process may scare away some potential builders and thus reduce competition on the supply side.

These impacts are not mutually exclusive, of course. Any one of them may be more or less important in a given case, but cumulatively their impact can be important.

During the last decade the greatest impact on housing costs has been felt in the Northeast and on the West Coast where local growth controls are the most stringent, and where much of the national population is concentrated.

Market forces there have already driven up the price of raw land and labor—and with them the cost of new housing. Resulting concern about the negative impacts of accelerated growth, in turn, has prompted stricter environmental standards which have pushed housing prices even further from the reach of average families. In such parts of the country, affordable housing has not been singled out for opposition; rather, development of any kind has become increasingly controversial.

Other parts of the country, of course, have seen relatively less development and are not as hostile to new growth. Even in these areas, however, local zoning and related requirements add measurably to the cost of housing. For people whose incomes are already stretched, any added cost is deeply felt. Well-intended municipal boards are often inattentive to the market impacts of their regulations. People are almost never explicitly zoned out of a community; rather they are priced out. Unfortunately there are also instances in which environmental arguments are cynically used to mask racial or class bigotry; even otherwise good-hearted people may get defensive if half-way houses for the mentally ill or handicapped are proposed for their neighborhoods.

Estimates of actual cost impacts depend on the local market, the nature and extent of the regulations, and perhaps, who is doing the calculation. According to Douglas W. Kmiec, there is "overwhelming empirical evidence that when zoning is out of control, it is at a cost borne largely by the housing consumer. The most recent Urban Policy Report states that the cost of excessive regulation is as much as 25 percent of the final unit price of a home." [1] Kmiec also cites econometric studies that blame land use regulation for 27 percent of the increase in real housing prices in California during the period of 1972 to 1979, as well as a study that suggests that housing costs in Boulder, Colorado, went up 25 percent from 1976 to 1979 (as against 11 percent in nearby communities) because of that city's growth control measures. A similar case was persuasively made in Bernard Frieden's *The Environmental Protection Hustle*.[2] Examining experience in northern California in the 1970's, Frieden notes that local regulations not only drive up prices, but significantly limit the variety and location of housing options.[3]

Not everyone agrees on the precise cost of regulation, however. Horror stories of projects requiring scores of permits and taking years to build are not hard to find, but they may not be wholly representative. Cost impacts undoubtedly vary from place to place as well. Nevertheless, there is no disputing that housing costs can be reduced by increasing density and expediting the permit process.

The Backlash Against Local Land Use Control

A chorus of somewhat strange political bedfellows has joined voices to call for a major cut-back in local land use regulatory power.[4] Among them are the housing advocates who for decades now have identified exclusionary zoning and related practices as a substantial problem. They have been reinforced more recently by free market defenders of private property rights, some of whom contend that regulation has actually prevented housing supply from efficiently meeting housing demand, while others seem to regard any regulation as an impermissible intrusion on personal liberty. Even environmentalists have expressed their frustration with local regulation. Growth control, they have learned, is hard to manage on a piecemeal basis; problems of groundwater protection, air pollution, and open space preservation often transcend municipal boundaries. At least some regulation, they conclude, could be done more cost effectively at a regional level.

An influential group of scholars has seconded the general motion with its members advocating everything from major decontrol of land use to the complete abolition of zoning.[5] This sentiment was clearly in harmony with the anti-regulatory politics that were in highest national ascendance in the first half of the 1980s.

This anti-regulatory attitude was manifested in the President's Commission on Housing's 1982 recommendation that cities and towns be stripped of their traditionally broad zoning powers. Specifically, the Commission concluded that "all state and local legislatures should enact legislation providing that no zoning regulations denying or limiting the development of housing should be deemed valid unless their existence or adoption is necessary to achieve a *vital and pressing governmental interest.*"[6] If this standard were adopted, a significant part of local regulation would be eliminated.[7]

The False Promise of Deregulation

Stripping local government of land use control is the obvious solution to the problem of zoning and housing costs. It is also the wrong one. It is profoundly wrong, first, because it defines the problem in zero-sum terms. Gains in the availability of housing can come, it postulates, only by attacking local autonomy and those environmental interests which that autonomy has thus far protected. Seen in these terms, the reduction of the costs of land use regulation necessarily means parting with some of its benefits as well. The strategy of fighting existing regulations largely defines away the search for new local land use control mechanisms that would both promote more housing and guard environmental values, perhaps even more effectively.

Second, the call for local deregulation is wrong in pragmatic terms, because it is doomed to fail. Even some deregulation advocates seem to sense this. A report entitled "Meeting America's Housing Needs," recently published by the National Institute of Building Science, noted that "Many studies done by the Kaiser Committee and the Douglas Commission reports of the 1960s and the President's Commission Report in the 1980s have all stated that over-regulation needlessly adds to the cost of low-income housing and causes delays. But strangely, over-regulation remains."[8]

In the same vein, Orlando Delogu—who has called local land use controls "an idea whose time has passed"—has observed that "It is ironic that as courts, commentators, and land use experts become more dissatisfied with . . . local land use prerogatives, the popular perception of many citizens and locally elected officials of an almost inherent right to exercise land use control powers at the local governmental level grows unabated." [9] Delogu himself appears optimistic that the deregulation movement will prevail, but in any forthcoming battle between his "courts, commentators, and land use experts" on one side and "many citizens and locally elected officials" on the other, the political odds on the revisionists succeeding seem long indeed.

Granted, there can be some value in documenting inefficiency and unintended consequences of regulatory actions. For example, the drafters of "Meeting America's Housing Needs" urge measuring "the impact of the zoning on a number of cities. Sheer numbers will build a strong case for rehabilitation and for residential reuse." [10] Lobbyists for deregulation will be better armed if they have current, objective information, but realistically, the gains from such efforts are likely to be at the margin.

Stricter land use and environmental concerns have emerged, after all, in response to deeply felt needs to protect the *status quo*. Some of the loudest local advocates for growth control measures are those who have recently fled densely populated cities and who do not want the crowds to follow on their heels. This is, moreover, an era of heightened environmental awareness. Lay people who ten or fifteen years ago could not have spelled aquifer now make knowledgeable presentations at conservation commission and planning board hearings when they fear groundwater protection is threatened.

There are far too many instances in which environmental concerns are invoked as a cover for private selfish motives, but many local land use regulations really do protect legitimate interests. The very words *over*-regulation and *excessive* regulation beg the fact that whether a regulation is *over* or *excessive* depends largely on the eye of the beholder. Cost-benefit analysis of regulation is of limited value when people can reasonably disagree about the calculation of costs and benefits and when, moreover, those costs and benefits inevitably fall unevenly on the population.

In advocating a major revocation of local land use power, writers like Delogu and Kmiec are swimming upstream against much more formidable political currents. All politics are local, as former Speaker of the House Thomas P. O'Neill was fond of reminding his colleagues. It seems highly unlikely that state and national leaders will want to take on the issue of home rule, even in the name of affordable housing. [11] At the most, states may be able to reclaim some veto or override power in carefully defined circumstances. If reducing the cost of local regulation depends on the wholesale curtailment of local land use powers, that battle is lost before it can ever begin.

Third, attacking local regulation in hopes of reducing housing costs is misdirected because in targeting formal procedures and substantive requirements, it ignores the reality that most important development approvals are granted through an informal process of multi-party negotiation. Proponents of affordable housing in particular often seek rezonings or special permits that increase density and reduce per unit land costs, and thus they inevitably get involved in the negotiation process. State enabling acts, local ordinances, and court decisions merely provide a loose legal context for such bargaining.[12] Often developers, regulatory agencies, and citizen groups reach agreements that bear little resemblance to what the law requires. A developer may "voluntarily" agree to make linkage payments, even though none is set forth in the ordinance, in order to win favorable treatment on discretionary issues. A municipality, in turn, may waive certain site design criteria if a proposed development serves important community needs. Neighbors likewise may agree not to challenge the grant of a variance, even if it is issued on shaky legal grounds, if the developer can satisfactorily mitigate local traffic or visual impacts.

Housing advocates need to better appreciate that the opposition cry of "not-in-my-backyard" is heard not only when affordable housing is proposed, but also when commercial development is planned and when controversial state facilities must be sited. Some see such development disputes as broadly betraying a breakdown in our planning process; still there is cause for cautious optimism. Commercial development disputes have been studied to some degree, and the techniques that researchers and practitioners have fashioned for resolving these problems clearly are relevant to affordable housing controversies. For example, the public-private partnerships which have been formed to revitalize economically depressed downtowns offer models for bringing together disparate parties to deal with local housing problems. Likewise, the fact that mediation has sometimes been successful in resolving protracted environmental battles suggests possibilities in the housing arena. Indeed, there have already been encouraging examples of local consensus building around affordable housing in which a variety of interest groups have managed to deal with their differences and pool their resources to mutual advantage.

In an era of sharply diminished federal aid, it is particularly important to promote new ways of bringing together people and institutions who can advance the production of housing only by acting collectively. The problem, in short, is not simply one of finding more efficient ways of reducing the costs of development disputes, but also of developing proactive mechanisms that will bring together local lenders, employers, regulators, and traditional housing advocates so that government subsidies can be stretched and packaged with local contributions of land, density increases, and even sweat. Such efforts are not within the scope of the traditional administrative system, but can be crucial in expediting the approval process.

In sum, these considerations—the fallacy of characterizing regulation as a zero-sum problem; the futility of trying to wrest much land use control from local authorities; and the myopia of focusing on formal regulations when development approvals so often are negotiated—make the strategy of simple deregulation one of little value. If this point has been belabored here, it is only because deregulation has so long been the only response housing advocates have mustered. The problem is still very real. If more pragmatic solutions are not found, local barriers may severely inhibit state and federal initiatives.

From Formal Regulation to Ad Hoc Negotiation

The Context: A Capsule History of Local Land Use Authority

Local land use regulation establishes the context in which development approvals are negotiated. The substance and content of municipal controls strongly affect the distribution of bargaining power among developers, abutters, local boards, and other groups. Recent Supreme Court decisions have altered that distribution of power, though in ways that are not yet fully apparent. What follows is the briefest of summaries of the evolution of local land use controls as they are applied in practice. Much of it should be familiar. It is intended to serve as a framework for connecting negotiated development generally to the specific problem of local affordable housing controversies.

There is a wide gap between the original theory of local land use regulation and its current practice. Early planners saw zoning as a tool for segregating incompatible uses: industry would be located in one section of town, shops in another, and housing in a third. Courts, in response to contentions that zoning is an unconstitutional infringement of property rights, rationalized its validity on the premise of predictability. The value of property, they reasoned, is protected, even enhanced, if property owners can invest in improvements in land without worrying that neighbors might subsequently establish some detrimental use. In *Euclid v. Ambler* and succeeding cases, courts were willing to leave largely to local legislatures the determination of what restrictions were appropriate for their communities.[13]

The neat zoning categories that separated residential, commercial, and industrial uses were doomed virtually from the start. The authors of the first zoning ordinances had assumed that most nonconforming uses, once ruled out of place, would wither away; instead, stores and businesses given a guaranteed monopoly (no new competition would be allowed) often flourished in areas zoned residential. Local boards also soon found that drawing zoning boundaries was inevitably an arbitrary exercise. Zones that made sense for the most part still could work hardships on some property owners. As a matter of constitutional law and of basic fairness, such owners had to be given variances. These variances and nonconforming uses often meant neighborhoods were much more diverse than the zoning maps indicated.

Local zoning authorities soon had to confront the complexity of guiding urban development. Differentiating not just uses, but density and bulk, meant that even small towns and cities could have many districts. Furthermore, because it was difficult to predict the shape and direction of growth, rezoning became necessary. Courts in some states were hostile to zone changes on the ground that they undercut the very predictability on which zoning is justified, but even these jurisdictions had to allow modifications where local circumstances had changed or mistakes had been made.

Over time, city councils and planning boards relied increasingly on special permitting procedures which required case-by-case review of certain development plans rather than simply allowing them as a matter of right. Instead of adopting an exhaustive zoning ordinance which included every conceivable use, a municipality could employ the special permit device to make ad hoc determinations if and when a problem arose.[14] Some communities "land banked" substantial tracts, creating large lot zones for the time being, so they would have the option in the future to say yes or no to projects that would need rezoning for increased density.

These flexibility devices evolved and grew out of practical necessity. Skepticism about the social and planning implications of *Euclidean* zoning grew as well. Rigid zoning requirements were blamed for cookie-cutter subdivisions; people also had second thoughts about the wisdom of segregating work, residence, and the marketplace. Although zoning and most other land use regulations still rest on *Euclid,* the planning concepts on which that case was based have been largely repudiated.

Flexibility Devices and the Inevitability of Negotiation

If land use regulation simply involved the application of immutable, quantitative standards, it would offer no opportunity for deal making. In practice, however, the availability of variances, special permits, and rezonings have essentially made the approval process one of negotiation. Negotiation can be around issuance of permits for a particular project, or can be part of a broader political process to establish general regulatory standards; indeed, specific projects often prompt a reexamination of general policy. Uses and structures which are legally permissible often do not maximize the development potential of property. For private and public developers alike downzoning and relaxation of other controls can produce significant gain. In all but the most trivial cases, submitted development proposals go through a process of review and revision before approvals are ultimately granted; in important cases, the process can be long and the revisions significant.

A developer who seeks to build multi-family housing, for example, may want a rezoning to allow greater density or a variance from dimensional requirements. To win the votes of politically responsive city councilors (or to insulate a permit from a legal challenge) the developer will likely have to meet concerns of abutters who fear negative impacts. Scaling down the project may prove necessary; in other instances mitigating measures, such as buffer strips and infrastructure improvements, may assuage the opposition. Even if most of what a developer plans to do is as of right, his need for discretionary approvals on specific issues will mean that everything is on the negotiation agenda. A planning board, for example, can use its power to waive stringent road width requirements as leverage to get a developer to agree to create somewhat larger lots, even though his original plan meets the minimum requirements. A developer who refuses to make such concessions runs the political risk that discretion will be exercised against him. (As we shall see shortly, however, the Supreme Court's recent land use decisions may have diminished the bargaining clout of local regulatory boards.)

By contrast, the strategy of some private and not-for-profit developers is to acquire tightly regulated parcels and to create added value by seeking upzonings which allow greater density. A ten-acre parcel previously zoned for one unit an acre becomes much more valuable if through rezoning it now can support six units an acre. If the municipality rezones but does nothing else, of course, the property owner gets a substantial windfall. Given local concerns about increased traffic and other environmental effects, there may be little incentive for zoning authorities to increase density. The political calculus changes, however, if a nonprofit developer can guarantee that the upzoning windfall will be redistributed to consumers. By being able to sell more market rate units, such a developer can use that profit to bring down the cost of other units. The amount of subsidy depends on several factors: the overall increase in density (and, hence, land value), the proportion of market and affordable units, and the amount and duration of the discount. All of these considerations will be on the bargaining table when rezoning is proposed. Not-for-profit firms like BRIDGE in San Francisco have been successful in persuading local agencies to upzone in cases in which private developers would never prevail.

Negotiation works in both directions, of course. Communities that want to foster certain kinds of development (typically projects that add to the tax and job base) offer zoning incentives in the form of intensity of use bonuses. In such instances, rezoning is often on the table along with other municipal carrots such as favorable tax assessment and provision of services. Communities try to fashion a package that is sufficiently attractive to bring in needed development without giving away the store.

Some state courts have been hostile to "contract zoning"—rezoning that responds to the needs and promises of a particular developer—but in cases that are negotiated to all the parties' satisfaction, no one brings a legal challenge. Negotiators thus have to look over their shoulders to statutory and case law to determine who has standing to bring a suit and must therefore be mollified. Nevertheless, it is clear that municipalities, in giving to and taking from developers, routinely go beyond their ostensible authority.

Characterizing the local development approval process as one of negotiation is not to say it is easy by any means. The developer (be it a private firm, a nonprofit organization, or a public agency) typically finds itself negotiating with a number of local boards, each with its own responsibilities and agenda; to compound matters, these boards often have conflicting visions of their jurisdiction. The developer must deal as well with a variety of ad hoc citizen groups, some of which may have banded together just to oppose this project; such groups may be unfamiliar with the approval process and distrustful of both the developer and the municipal authorities. It may not be clear who speaks for whom or who has authority to make a binding settlement. Much of this interaction takes place, moreover, in formal administrative hearings that mimic the adversary process and offer little haven for joint problem-solving.

Given these obstacles and more, it is remarkable that many land use disputes are ultimately negotiated successfully. If as much attention were given to improving this ad hoc process as has been given to revising the substance of land use regulations, the equity and efficiency of development negotiations would surely be improved.[15]

Exactions and Linkage

Courts have consistently upheld municipal power to require prospective developers to pay for direct impacts of their projects. For example, a developer who wishes to subdivide land for residential use must first build the road, water, and sewer systems that will service the parcels before he can sell them. Were it otherwise, the local government might get stuck with these costs.

In an era of diminished federal funds, local officials have been under increasing pressure to look to new development as a potential revenue source; this pressure has been compounded in states which have capped local property tax revenue. Costs of infrastructure which were once borne by the public treasury are being shifted to private developers as "impact fees," at least in hot real estate markets. Local officials have found them politically attractive in part because "impact fees" typically favor current property owners over future ones: the former vote; the latter do not. Moreover, where impact fees are "off-budget" local officials can earmark the funds for specific projects or mitigating measures, without seeming to sacrifice other programs.[16]

Exactions imposed on homebuilders necessarily increase the cost of housing.[17] In recent years, however, some cities have imposed requirements on commercial development in order to promote affordable housing. For example, San Francisco and Boston have made developers of downtown office towers pay fees into a special fund to subsidize housing in other parts of the city.[18] In theory, the exaction is justified because the new commercial development is expected to increase the workforce and thus increase local demand for housing. In practice, they usually have been imposed because developers are seen as having deep pockets. These linkage fees are over and above other charges imposed by the city to mitigate direct impacts around the development site.

In some communities, de facto linkage policies have emerged. In Cambridge, Massachusetts, for example, a proposed linkage ordinance was ultimately voted down after protracted debate, but in its place there is a system of "voluntary linkage payments." Cambridge developers who want favorable treatment on their various permit requests and who hope to expedite the approval policy find it in their interest to volunteer funding the construction of affordable housing units. The amount of contribution is an important item on the overall negotiation agenda.

Some developers actually prefer formal linkage requirements to *ad hoc* systems. In Boston, developers can factor the fixed square foot fee into their pro formas. By contrast, in Cambridge some fear that the city can pick them off, one by one. No developer wants to be caught in a situation in which he or she will have to pay significantly more than competitors.

For all the press attention and political debate it has generated, linkage may offer less than meets the eye. In reality, it is a device with limited applicability. In the many cities where there is far too much vacant office space, developers will not pay higher fees for the privilege of adding to the glut. Hot real estate markets like Boston currently have enough bargaining clout to require such contributions, but ten or fifteen years ago, linkage would have been futile there. What little downtown construction was taking place was due largely to positive incentives that the city was offering to developers. Given the cyclical nature of the real estate industry and of regional economies, the day may come again when cities like Boston will be giving to rather than receiving from downtown developers.

Wherever linkage has been proposed, there has been heated debate over whether there should be any exaction, how large such exactions should be, and how the resulting funds should be applied. Opponents to the policy itself have challenged its legitimacy, arguing that it constitutes a confiscatory tax unfairly singling out new development. Others have attacked the wisdom of linkage, claiming that it will send developers elsewhere and thereby deny the city the benefit of an increased tax and job base.[19] Even among the friends of linkage, there have been bitter fights over where and how linkage funds should best be spent. Housing advocates have to calculate whether the political capital necessary to overcome opposition to linkage may be better spent in promoting other programs.

The Supreme Court Re-examines Zoning

Two recent decisions of the United States Supreme Court leave standing a local government's right to impose exactions and impact fees, but potentially reduce municipal power in regulating development and negotiating approvals. In *Nollan v. California Coastal Commission,*[20] the Court declared impermissible an agency's requirement that a coastal homeowner grant a public easement across his property as the price for getting approvals for substantially expanding his home. In the majority's view, there was no logical connection between the exaction sought (the grant of the easement) and the proposed development (the remodeling of the home); that is, the proposed construction was not going to deprive the public of any physical access it had enjoyed previously. As a consequence, the exaction was tantamount to taking private property without just compensation, and thus unconstitutional.

Opponents of local regulation who initially read *Nollan* as reversing prior exaction cases have probably overestimated its reach. In the future, municipalities will apparently have to demonstrate more clearly the connection between conditions that are imposed on developers and impacts that development can reasonably be expected to have, but in most instances that connection is not hard to establish. *Nollan*'s significance, if any, for linkage fees is still not certain, but it may actually prove easier for some cities to justify exaction of housing impact fees from commercial developers than for some suburbs to defend other requirements and dedications that make residential development expensive.

On the other hand, inclusionary zoning programs—those which require developers of market rate housing to include a percentage of affordable units— may well be vulnerable to attack. Specifically, it is far easier to demonstrate that the creation of new office space stimulates greater housing demand, than it is to establish the nexus between construction of new luxury housing and any *increased* need for affordable housing. A developer could thus contend that the inclusionary zoning requirement, like the access condition in *Nollan* is not directly connected to the impacts of his project.

In a second important land use case, *First English Evangelical Lutheran Church of Glendale v. County of Los Angeles,*[21] the Supreme Court ruled that municipalities which impermissibly impose restrictions on the use of land must pay the owners compensation for the past loss of potential use while the invalid restriction was in force. Until now, the sole remedy of a property owner challenging the constitutionality of a regulation was invalidation of the ordinance; at best, the owner won the right to go forward and build, but he was not compensated for opportunities he lost while the regulation was in place.

The *First English Evangelical* case received a great deal of attention in the popular press, where in some instances it was portrayed as a significant reversal of land use law, a reading that was wrong in theory but could prove right in practice. The *First English Evangelical* decision does not contract in the slightest the broad range of regulatory devices a municipality may use. There are, moreover, relatively few cases in which cities and towns are found to have overstepped those bounds. Yet even so, the small risk of having to pay damages may make local regulators much more cautious in their legislation. If this risk of liability simply disciplined municipalities not to "over-regulate," then no one could quarrel with the decision. It is entirely possible, however, that *First English Evangelical* will cause local land use authorities to draw back much farther, ceding areas of permissible regulation rather than run the risk of lawsuits. Indeed, Justice Stevens, writing in dissent in *First English Evangelical*, warned: "One thing is certain. The Court's decision today will generate a great deal of litigation. Most of it, I believe, will be unproductive. But the mere duty to defend the actions that today's decision will spawn will undoubtedly have a significant adverse impact on the land-use regulatory process."

Read together, the *Nollan* and *First English Evangelical* cases offer causes for optimism and dismay for residential developers and housing advocates. To the limited extent that *Nollan* curtails local authorities from saddling developers with fees and conditions that are not related to their projects, regulatory costs may be reduced somewhat. *First English Evangelical*, in turn, offers even greater encouragement to developers and interest groups who believe that they have been frozen out by exclusionary zoning. In the past, a community that erroneously invoked environmental concerns to block development had little to lose but face when courts struck them down. (Some critics, in fact, believe that communities would establish such barriers in utter disregard of the law, knowing that the time and expense of legal challenge would deter most developers.) Communities tempted to continue this practice may well be chastened by the potential sting of a liability judgment. Developers and property owners, in turn, have been given added incentive to challenge questionable regulations.[22]

For housing interests, however, there is also a decidedly negative side to these two Supreme Court decisions. First, to the extent that *Nollan* reminds local governments that their power to exact is ultimately limited, affirmative attempts to promote affordable housing may be cut back. Well-documented linkage programs may survive scrutiny, but inclusionary zoning may be hard to defend, given *Nollan*'s nexus requirement. It is easier to demonstrate the adverse affect that new commercial development has on housing supply, than it is to do the same for high-end residential construction.[23]

If *Nollan* stood on its own, its effect on local housing initiatives might be modest,[24] but *First English Evangelical* may magnify its impact. A city council that is quite confident that a proposed linkage ordinance is within its authority might still hesitate to enact it, fearful of potential liability, should a court later declare otherwise. *First English Evangelical* creates a strong economic incentive for municipalities to stick only with conventional forms of land use controls and incentives. It may well stifle the implementation of new devices whose legitimacy is yet untested in the courts.

Negotiated Development: A Cautionary Note

The extensive flexibility and discretion in local land use regulation has meant that negotiation is central to the development approval process. To the extent that negotiation is a means through which imaginative solutions can be found to accommodate the needs of different stakeholders, negotiation is a valuable means to important ends. Given the complexity of development, the variability of community needs, and the degree to which unforseeable economic factors expand or control local resources and options, it is hard to believe that a highly codified, rigid system of land use controls could really work in most contemporary American cities and towns.

But though strict *Euclidean* zoning is clearly archaic, negotiated development, as it is currently practiced, also has serious shortcomings. First, it runs counter to most notions of planning. Ad hoc decisions on particular projects may be sensible in their own right, but contradictory and inefficient when taken as a whole.[25] Second, the exercise of discretion sometimes invites abuse; procedures have to be invented to ensure that all parties get treated fairly. Third, the process of negotiation does not redress basic imbalances of power. In disputes over new housing, the developer, abutters, and city officials negotiate, but there is seldom a role for those who would benefit from the development if it is approved. Finally, because it is largely improvised within the traditional adversary process, negotiations are often awkward and inefficient; when creative problem-solving takes place it is usually in spite of the system, not because of it.

In short, the thrust of this section has not been to advocate negotiated development, but rather simply to describe its contours. Any informed attempt to make new housing policy must respond to local land use controls as they are practiced, not simply as they are formally defined in the laws.

Institutionalizing Negotiation in the Approval Process

Emerging Negotiation Theory and Practice

In the past decade, there has been growing interest in finding more efficient and equitable ways of handling disputes, particularly through negotiation and mediation. Research, once confined to collective bargaining and international diplomacy, has now expanded to include virtually every arena in which people have to deal with one another over conflicting agendas. A rich variety of disciplines—among them, psychology, law, anthropology, economics, and sociology—have been employed.[26]

Much of this work is relevant to real estate development disputes generally, and controversies over the siting and regulation of housing in particular. Likewise there are useful lessons in federal experiments using mediation and consensus building to design and implement regulatory policy and to better coordinate intergovernmental responsibilities.[27]

This section describes several policy strategies that have been explicitly aimed at improving the outcomes of development negotiations. They include policies enacted by state legislatures as well as initiatives taken by administrative agencies. Those dealing explicitly with housing policy may be instructive models for other jurisdictions. Other initiatives are sketched because they suggest a way of thinking comprehensively about regulatory reform. The strategies include:

Shifting the balance of bargaining power in development disputes through state legislation. The illustration offered here is the Massachusetts anti-snob zoning act.

Establishing formal ground rules and providing technical support for negotiation. Laws are needed to define who sits at the bargaining table; in hotly contested cases, mediation or arbitration may be required.

Sponsoring a nonadversarial process in which people work toward creative problem-solving. Good intentions are not enough; innovative group decision-making processes can help break impasses.

Actively linking public and private stakeholders and resources. Public-private partnerships may well be essential, particularly if federal housing assistance will be limited.

In short, the policy options summarized below should be considered not only for their substantive content, but for the larger negotiation problems they address.

Enhancing Bargaining Power Through Limited State Preemption: The Massachusetts Anti-Snob Zoning Act

Zoning and kindred regulatory devices are, by definition, exclusionary. While allowing specific land uses in a given zone, they specifically exclude others. Because power is vested at the local level, each community has an incentive to use zoning to attract beneficial uses (such as businesses and clean industry that add to the tax base without consuming many services) but prohibit uses that are seen as costly or undesirable.

From the outset, dense multi-family housing has been subject to such exclusion. Indeed, in *Euclid* Justice Sutherland regarded this as zoning's virtue, not its vice. He echoed the conclusions of reports that "very often the apartment house is a mere parasite, constructed in order to take advantage of the open spaces and attractive surroundings created by the residential character of the district."[28] In their proper places, apartment houses might be unobjectionable, even highly desirable, Sutherland stated, but in single family neighborhoods they "come very near to being nuisances." In subsequent years the Supreme Court has gone to great lengths to avoid even hearing challenges to snob zonings.[29]

Litigants who have taken on exclusionary zoning have fared somewhat better in state courts. Large lot size requirements have been invalidated, for example, in a number of cases where the municipalities could not invoke convincing environmental justifications for the zoning. In the well-known *Mt. Laurel* decisions, the New Jersey Supreme Court more sweepingly declared that the zoning power delegated by the state to cities and towns must be exercised for the welfare of a larger public.[30] Each community has an affirmative obligation to help meet the regional need for housing by classifying a reasonable amount of land for high density residential development. Although the legal principle is clear, its administration by the courts has proven difficult, as parties to the lawsuits fight over what constitutes the regional need and whether a community has done its part.[31]

In Massachusetts, by contrast, the response was legislative, not judicial. Chapter 774, popularly known as the anti-snob zoning act, was enacted in 1969.[32] It applies to all cities and towns that have less than a minimum percentage of low- and moderate-income housing; as a practical matter very few municipalities are exempted from the law's reach.[33]

The law overrides local zoning barriers for qualifying low- and moderate-income housing projects. A city or town can withhold a building permit and related approvals only on serious environmental grounds. A developer whose project has been disapproved has the right to appeal to the state Housing Appeals Committee. In the great majority of such appeals, local permit denials are reversed and the developer's rights to proceed are confirmed. Shortly after the law was passed, the state's Supreme Court upheld the law in the face of home rule and constitutional challenges. Now the HAC's rulings are seldom appealed. The law also establishes a "one-stop" comprehensive permitting process, in which the developer applies to the local Zoning Board of Appeals for all approvals. This consolidation shortens the process significantly, reducing costs for the developer.

Chapter 774 has not solved all of Massachusetts' housing problems, but more than two hundred low- and moderate-income projects with a total of more than eleven thousand units of housing have been built under its provisions; it is generally agreed that the great majority of these projects would not have been constructed if local barriers had been allowed to stand. Although the law partially preempts local authority, municipalities still may block development that has a seriously adverse environmental impact.[34] As a matter of practice, moreover, the state housing appeals committee appears disinclined to overrule permit denials if it has recently forced that same community to accept another affordable housing project. In designing their proposals, developers still have to be mindful of health and safety impacts that are directly related to the project.

In its early years of operation, the law was typically used by developers who were confronting cities and towns hostile to their plans. Going through the comprehensive permit process was often simply a matter of preparing a good record for administrative appeal to the HAC. After the courts upheld the law, however, and after it became clear that the HAC would usually decide in favor of the developer, some municipalities came to realize that they had more to gain through negotiation than they did by steadfastly opposing the issuance of permits. To be sure, developers held most of the cards, but communities learned that they could bargain for concessions (for example, scaling down the project, providing buffer zones, or giving local people priority for the new units) in return for granting the comprehensive permit. Negotiations were not necessarily easy, of course, but when they succeeded, they gave local agencies and citizens more control over the community. Developers, in turn, won the savings of avoiding appeal.

The statute authorizes the HAC only to uphold the local Zoning Board of Appeals findings of significant adverse health and safety impacts, or to order the issuance of the permit as requested by the developer. The HAC may not fashion some middle ground that subjects the permit to added conditions or orders the developer to honor specified municipal regulations. Some observers criticize the law for compelling the state agency to choose between two alternatives, neither of which may be ideal. Others, however, believe that the all-or-nothing nature of appeals actually encourages both sides to negotiate more seriously. Further, it is doubtful that the agency has the time or the resources to take the responsibility for coming up with a better plan; nevertheless, the state authorities apparently give contesting parties informal hints intended to nudge them into settlement.[35]

In recent years, there has been more attention given to so-called "friendly 774s," cases in which communities use the law proactively to create more affordable housing.[36] Local authorities have come to see that in some important respects the law lets them have things both ways. They can avoid the risk of over-development that they might well incur if they allow multi-family or small lot single-family construction across the board, while still maintaining the flexibility of allowing such housing wherever they wish. In this sense, the law allows communities to use the comprehensive permit process to practice spot-zoning. Instead of waiting for a developer to take the initiative, it is even possible for a city or town to identify potential affordable housing sites and to issue a request for proposals. Tax title land or unused municipal property can thus be dedicated to housing without a larger scale—and far more controversial—rezoning.

The Massachusetts law suggests several lessons. First, state preemption is not an all-or-nothing choice. In Massachusetts it was a political struggle to grant the state even this much power; it is unrealistic to expect that this override power could be substantially expanded. Second, streamlining the approval process (in this instance through both comprehensive Board of Zoning Appeals permitting and state administrative review) not only saves time, but also tilts substantive bargaining power by reducing the clout of objectors who practice delay tactics.[37] Third, even after a statute is enacted, it can take some years before judicial and administrative precedent becomes sufficiently clear to the people who must operate within it. The fact that "friendly 774s" did not appear until relatively recently suggests that the learning process takes time for developers, local officials, and other interest groups. Fourth, as developers have become familiar with the process, some are using the 774 system to propose very large scale projects. Local communities have lacked the technical expertise to evaluate such proposals and have had to turn to the state for planning resources.

Finally, experience under this statute confirms the "law of unintended consequences," like the evolution from hostile to friendly 774s. The greatest success of the law may be seen in projects which get built by consensus and which never go through the full appeal process. One recent study reported that 91 percent of the permits approved at the local level resulted in finished projects. By contrast, even when developers succeeded at the state level in overturning local denials, only 69 percent of those projects were actually built.[38] Though the latter number is still good, it does indicate that when community opposition is strong, the delay and changes in circumstances attendant to appeal can kill some projects. Clearly it is in the developer's interest to work things out at the municipal level, if possible.[39]

The statute has had unexpected negative consequences, as well. In the past several years, some large-scale residential developers have attempted to use the Chapter 774 as the Trojan horse for market-rate and even top-end projects. By including the minimum percentage of affordable units, the developers seek to get around local land use regulation. To be sure, even these projects contribute to the expansion of affordable housing stock, but the scale of some of these proposals has been so much larger than what was seen in the past that they potentially saddle communities with legitimate growth management problems. This, in turn, has fueled a political backlash that may prompt revision of the law.

The second negative impact is less visible but perhaps no less important. The existence of the statute may have caused Massachusetts courts to be less sympathetic to exclusionary zoning lawsuits, reasoning that through Chapter 774 the legislature has already struck the appropriate balance between local autonomy and regional responsibility. Although the statute does provide an option for builders willing to pursue a comprehensive permit, it does nothing to encourage communities to create zones in which higher density development can take place as a matter of right. The anti-snob zoning law thus deals only with part of the exclusionary zoning problem, and should not foreclose judicial action.

On balance, the Massachusetts experiment has been a success. Other jurisdictions might tailor their laws differently, but they may see in Chapter 774 an encouraging example of how bargaining power may be shifted through carefully defined state preemption.

Structuring Negotiation: Using Mediation and Arbitration to Site LULUs

It is not enough to shift the bargaining balance to give greater power to affordable housing interests. Equally important is the creation of a negotiation process in which that power is exercised. International diplomats often rely on agreed protocols to guide their discussions, for example. Likewise, an elaborate set of procedures have evolved for collective bargaining between unions and management. By contrast, land use and development disputes have been typically handled through *ad hoc* processes.

Housing policy makers should look carefully at innovative processes used to settle controversies over other kinds of locally unwanted land-uses. A "LULU" is a use that everyone concedes is necessary, but which nobody wants sited in his or her backyard.[40] Prisons, utility plants, and hazardous waste treatment facilities—and affordable housing—are conspicuous examples. Municipalities use their regulatory authority to ban such uses within their borders without having to worry about where else they can be located.

The traditional approach to the LULU problem has been attempted preemption of municipal authority, but local opponents know that if they dig in their heels hard enough, a governor or agency head may abandon the project; in any case, objectors may well be able to delay implementation until a new administration is in office. The siting of locally unwanted housing is, if anything, more difficult than siting other LULUs because the scale of development is much more vast. One or two new prisons may serve the needs of an entire state; in the end only a few communities will shoulder the burden. By contrast, virtually all cities and towns must be involved if a housing shortfall is to be met.[41]

Recent innovations in the location of hazardous waste treatment facilities may offer a model for making the development approval process less adversarial. For example, the Massachusetts Hazardous Waste Facility Siting Act authorizes communities to bargain with prospective developers for compensation in return for hosting such a facility. The compensation can cover direct impacts (such as environmental monitoring, safety equipment, access road repairs, and the like), but also may include payments for library costs, programs for the elderly, or affordable housing, for that matter. Although it virtually eliminates a municipality's right to exclude treatment plants from industrial zones, the law also greatly expands municipal power to demand compensatory payments which would otherwise be regarded as illegal exactions.[42] The important lessons that the siting law can offer for disputes over the construction of affordable housing involve procedure rather than substance.

First, it explicitly acknowledges the importance of negotiation among developers, local agencies, and citizen groups in the approvals process. Instead of setting out extensive regulatory standards, the law lets the parties establish what kind of compensation is appropriate. Second, simply authorizing a city or town to negotiate is not enough. Instead, the law establishes procedures for the creation and composition of a local bargaining committee and sets deadlines for the negotiation. Third, it enables the state to provide technical assistance grants to the local committee so that it can employ its own neutral experts. Finally, if the developer and the community are at an impasse, it provides for mediation, and if that fails then for binding arbitration. Legal appeals are very limited.

Promoting negotiation in the abstract will not work. Housing advocates, local boards, and citizen groups are much more likely to reach accord if they have a context in which to negotiate. State officials contemplating partial preemption of local land use control (as in the "snob-zoning" laws), should be equally attentive to the procedural side of negotiation and define (as the siting law does) what parties are at the pre-bargaining table, when agreements must be reached, and who is available to mediate, if talks break down.

Fostering Creative Solutions: Negotiated Design and Negotiated Investment Strategy

Negotiated development has been with us almost from the time that municipalities assumed regulatory oversight of land use, though usually in the shadow of the formal administrative process. The formalities of public hearings, limits on *ex parte* communications by agency officials, and the need to preserve a record in case of appeal all work to constrain productive problem solving.

In recent years there have been promising attempts to create another process or forum for negotiation over development. One technique, pioneered by Will Fleissig, former director of downtown development of Denver, Colorado, is called negotiated design.[43] In this process, a representative cross-section of parties interested in a particular development site is brought together in an informal setting to state their priorities and explore alternative solutions. Such a group would typically include the developer, immediate neighbors, citizen and business organizations, lenders, and elected officials.

Rather than reacting to a formal development proposal, however, participants are asked to respond to a series of scenarios, none of which is being advocated by any party. Because the proposals are hypothetical, people feel less obliged to exaggerate their support or opposition and are more apt to reveal their underlying interests. Participants gain a truer sense of what is actually feasible and what different stakeholders need. When the process succeeds, the parties are able to create a consensus design that accommodates their varying interests; usually the design is quite different from—and far superior to—any of the hypothetical scenarios. Having won the support of the important players, the plan can more easily be blessed in the formal approval process.

Negotiated design is a particularly appropriate means for handling local disputes over the creation and siting of affordable housing. Many opponents of affordable housing associate it with monolithic and imposing structures, and understandably do not want to live in the shadows of such buildings. There are, however, sensitive architectural alternatives to these stereotypes; negotiated design sessions can result in plans that are in keeping with a single-family neighborhood.[44] Increased density may actually be in keeping with community character, particularly if it is coupled with preservation of nearby open space.[45]

More fundamentally, the negotiated design approach allows stakeholders to reveal their interests and share their knowledge productively. Scenario testing can clarify the relationships between increased density, environmental impacts, financeability, and the ultimate cost of housing, thereby laying the foundation for efficient trade-offs. By contrast, the traditional administrative process creates a dynamic in which heads are counted for or against a specific proposal.

For the most part, the negotiated design process has been used in the context of specific parcels. By contrast, the negotiated investment strategy (NIS), promoted by the Kettering Foundation and others, entails a broader planning effort. Columbus, Ohio; Minneapolis, Minnesota; and Malden, Massachusetts have used NIS to link municipal decision-making on public investments—like sewer extension, school construction, and transportation—to private investment by developers, business, and industry. The strategy is a response to the obvious inefficiencies that occur when intergovernmental decisions are not coordinated with private actions. It is often triggered by a budget allocation issue involving different levels of government or different jurisdictions.[46]

Like negotiated design, NIS involves the convening of diverse interest groups, though here on an even wider scale. The goal is to reach an agreement in which the various public and private players make binding commitments. The task is ambitious. To make the process feasible, the planning horizon is usually short, in the range of three to five years. Even so, agreements usually have to be written so as to allow for a variety of contingencies.

The NIS process could certainly be used to encourage affordable housing on both a municipal and a regional scale, since it provides a forum in which housing advocates can meet with private lenders, community groups, and local politicians to develop basic policy goals which then can be used to guide specific decisions. In 1989 the state of Connecticut sponsored two pilot NIS processes to develop consensus-based housing goals and strategies for the greater Hartford and Bridgeport regions. It is too early to judge success, but negotiation may be an intriguing alternative to New Jersey's judicial intervention and Massachusetts' legislative preemption.

Structuring negotiations over policy design and implementation takes special care.[47] It is critically important to involve all the affected stakeholders. The negotiating parties must be assured, moreover, that if they reach an agreement, it will be implemented and not just treated as a blue-ribbon recommendation. Often the parties will need technical assistance—in the case of a local housing negotiation, perhaps experts in financial analysis, traffic impacts, and environmental design. Where there are many parties, some of whom do not trust one another, a mediator may be needed to avoid impasse; a monitoring system may be necessary to make sure that all commitments are met.

For collaborative ventures to succeed there must be some broadly shared frustration with the conventional planning and approval process. At present, people often oppose specific affordable housing projects because of concern over the long-term precedent they may set. Housing advocates who find themselves perpetually caught up in site-specific disputes should step back and see if those controversies are really symptoms of a planning process that has failed to coordinate economic development, growth management, and expansion of infrastructure and services.

Fostering Creative Solutions Through Public-Private Partnerships

Developers, citizen organizations, government agencies, and institutions wishing to promote affordable housing often find that they lack the resources to do it on their own. Faced with increasing costs of land, labor, and materials on one hand and decreasing federal subsidies and tax benefits on the other, such groups are seeing the advantage of pooling their assets, energy, and political clout.

Alliances of both public and private sector interests have formed spontaneously in a number of cities throughout the country. These efforts have taken a variety of forms, depending on the needs and character of the given community, but these organizations share certain traits.

First, they act as catalysts for putting affordable housing at the top of the local agenda. Second, they provide a forum to educate the general population about affordable housing, how it gets built, and whom it serves. Third, local public-private partnerships are a vehicle for insuring that new housing development meets the needs of a particular community. Fourth, they create a bargaining table for deals in which a city may contribute tax title land, a local bank may facilitate financing, and nonprofit organizations may coordinate social services. Finally, such partnerships serve as a continuing constituency for the provision and maintenance of affordable housing. What is learned in the fashioning of one venture can be used productively in the creation of another.

Strategies for putting together public-private partnerships are described and evaluated elsewhere.[48] It is not necessary to reproduce that material here, but two points deserve brief attention. First, local partnerships have learned that it is virtually impossible to advocate affordable housing without becoming embroiled in broader growth control issues, particularly traffic impacts, groundwater protection, and provision of municipal services. Even though the interest of the partnership may be focused on a particular project on a specific site, other players in the political process will invariably raise growth management concerns. Attempts to narrow the agenda almost never succeed, and often prompt heightened opposition to a project. Like it or not, housing partnerships may have to take the initiative in promoting more comprehensive planning. If the provision of affordable housing is understood as a component of a broader growth management strategy, it is far more likely to win popular support.

The good news is that other interest groups are now also seeing the need to fashion new political alliances if they are to mobilize popular support for their particular goals. Some open space preservationists are working with housing advocates on the state and local levels to make sure that land acquisition programs do not constrain the supply and cost of residential real estate.[49]

The second lesson from the public-private partnership experience in Massachusetts is simple but important. Means are as important as ends. The test of a partnership is not simply whether it can generate imaginative policies and design well-conceived projects, but whether it can get those policies enacted and the projects built. This, in turn, requires considerable political skill and judgment. Fortunately, the growing body of negotiation and consensus-building research offers some guidance for people in the field.[50]

As noted earlier, public-private efforts can arise from local initiatives without state prodding. In Milwaukee, for example, executives from many of that city's prominent businesses came together recognizing that they had a common interest in revitalizing its downtown. Creating the Greater Milwaukee Committee, they developed a broad strategy for stimulating and coordinating new urban investment. An important element of that strategy has been the provision of more housing, particularly for low- and moderate-income families. Not far to Milwaukee's south, the Neighborhood Housing Services of Chicago has persuaded businesses there that it is in their interest to rebuild declining neighborhoods.

Although some cities have successfully improvised public-private partnerships, state and federal governments surely could play a valuable role in promoting and evaluating such programs so that their most effective features can be duplicated in other settings.

The Role of the States in Promoting More Effective Negotiation

States can do more to expedite resolution of local disputes over affordable housing. Legislatures should revise zoning enabling statutes to authorize creative negotiation of the design, scale, and control of affordable housing projects. Reform should particularly focus on the balkanization of local land use control. At present, local planning boards, boards of zoning appeal, conservation commissions, boards of health, and housing authorities often deal with interrelated issues but seldom have a mechanism for coordinating their actions. Indeed, residential developers often find themselves caught in the crossfire between municipal agencies that are administering contradictory policies. Typically such boards operate under state enabling acts; legislatures clearly have the authority to require more integrated planning at the local level.

In addition to creating a negotiating context for the affected stakeholders, states likely have to provide greater technical assistance (legal, financial, and design expertise) to communities coping with affordable housing issues. To the extent that some opposition to affordable housing is grounded in stereotypes about the way it looks and functions, states should support innovative projects that demonstrate how new units can be better knit into the fabric of a community. When possible, moreover, states should provide facilitators or mediators skilled at diagnosing conflict and bringing contentious parties to consensus. Policy has to be better coordinated at the state level, as well, where different agencies involved in housing, social services, finance, and environmental protection often collide. Programs to stimulate job creation, for example, need to take into account housing impacts.

Massachusetts has gone one step further, through its Executive Order 215, which cuts off discretionary state funding to communities which have dragged their heels in allowing affordable housing. The order is part carrot, part stick. Various state agencies can dangle the carrot of possible grants for other projects if residential needs are met, while the department charged with housing can threaten to snatch this aid away if they are not. Executive Order 215 does not apply to basic revenue sharing funds, so this device does not have all the clout that it might; a community does not feel the Order's sting until faced with some substantial public investment.[51]

In many respects, what is needed at both the local and state levels is more effective comprehensive planning. Housing issues are inextricably linked to economic development, growth management, environmental protection, and welfare policies. This is hardly a new plea, of course, but much has been learned since it was first voiced. The experience of states like Oregon and California, which adopted planning programs making affordable housing an important goal, should be instructive for other jurisdictions.[52]

To the extent that new residential development and the resulting growth do impose costs on communities, the question is not simply how those costs can be minimized, but how they can be shared equitably by all those who benefit from expanded housing opportunities. Although most of the costs are local, often much of the benefits are regional. As a consequence, states have a proper role in balancing costs and benefits among those cities and towns that do their share and those that do not.

Implications for Federal Policy Making

The potential federal role in land use regulatory reform is real, but necessarily limited. In theory, the Commerce Clause and other provisions of the Constitution may give Congress the power to preempt local regulation, but as a practical matter traditional municipal prerogatives would be zealously defended from any proposed federal encroachment. Many of the procedural reforms needed to promote greater consensus for affordable housing, moreover, are best undertaken by state or municipal governments.

Affordable housing is a national problem, but it takes quite different forms in different parts of the country. The rapid inflation in housing prices first experienced on the West Coast and more recently felt in the Northeast has not been seen in some other parts of the country. Yet if housing prices are considerably lower in the so-called "rust belt," so is earning power; unemployment is significantly higher. Programs that are appropriate in one place may not be appropriate in another. For example, in hot real estate markets the escalating price of raw land gives first priority to those strategies that allow more dense development; elsewhere these approaches are far less important. Whatever national initiatives are fashioned must take into account these kinds of regional differences.

Even though the most responsibility for land use regulation will remain with states and their political subdivisions, the federal government should act in at least three areas. First, like their state and local counterparts, federal authorities need to coordinate their housing assistance programs and policies. As Sandra Newman and Ann Schnare persuasively argue in chapter 15 of this volume, there is particular need for better coordination of housing and welfare policies, both as they are formulated at the federal level and administered locally. We cannot afford to have programs working at cross-purposes, especially when federal funds are severely limited.

Second, careful thought should be given to making compliance with general housing goals a precondition for federal assistance. A cautious policy would condition the grant of any federal housing funds on a state's or city's willingness to promote regulatory reform; a tougher policy would follow the example of Massachusetts Executive Order 215 and apply to all discretionary federal grants. This policy is well worth exploring, but the problems of designing and implementing it should not be minimized. Consensus would have to be reached first of all on the substantive content of federal housing goals;

zoning which is clearly exclusionary in one region may not really deter middle-income buyers in another. The clout of withholding federal funds would have to be realistically assessed as well; those communities which are the least hospitable to affordable housing may also be the least vulnerable to a cut-off of funding from Washington. Finally, whatever standards were established would have to be broad enough to have the political support of enough states and cities. Regulations that funnel discretionary funds to only a chosen few not only have no chance of passage, but also have very limited national impact. On the other hand, of course, federal agencies which distribute scarce funds must consider where they will do the most good. Cities and states that have promoted negotiated development and public-private partnerships can produce housing far more efficiently than those which have failed to break regulatory impasses.

Third, federal authorities face the specific task of developing protocols for resolving disputes over policies and programs already in place. A prime example for such attention involves federal contracts and use restrictions on government-subsidized rental units, more than a million of which will expire in the next decade.[53] To the extent that funding is available to extend some of these contracts, the government not only must set its priorities, but also establish a renegotiation process. Who, for example, should be at the bargaining table: simply the owner and a government representative, or do tenants, neighbors, community groups, and others have a role? How should such negotiations relate to planning and development efforts in the area; for example, are there regulatory inducements that local officials might offer to persuade an owner to keep his or her property in a subsidized program? What kind of technical and mediating assistance will these cases require? There is a host of such questions. Few are easily answered, but it is clear that they must be resolved on a general policymaking level; it would be enormously wasteful to try to improvise a negotiation process on a case-by-case basis.[54]

Finally, federal policymakers and administrators need to recognize the potential of negotiation and mediation both as means for resolving local disputes between housing developers and their opponents, and as a way of designing and implementing policy itself. The responsibility for housing rests not only with federal, state, and local governments, but with private developers, lenders, community nonprofit groups, and countless other institutions and individuals. A variety of federal agencies have experimented with regulatory reforms intended to reduce the costs of administrative and legal challenges to their rule-making, grant-making, permitting, and enforcement decisions, and also to encourage more effective government action. New approaches like negotiated rule-making, policy dialogues, and collaborative planning hold particular promise in the housing arena, in which so many diverse groups have a stake.

Notes

1. D. Kmiec, "Provision of Affordable Housing—Proposal for a New Zoning Enabling Act," in J. Gailey, ed., *1986 Zoning and Planning Law Handbook* (New York: Clark Boardman Company, Ltd., 1986) 271–289, at 282–283. Kmiec cites the *President's National Urban Policy Report* (Washington: USGPO, 1984) 64. Note that Kmiec cites the most extreme cases.

2. B. Frieden, *The Environmental Protection Hustle* (Cambridge: MIT Press, 1979).

3. In an Everett, Washington demonstration project, a developer saved $10,000 per unit for houses selling in the $70,000 range. Most of the savings were realized through clustering houses and reducing street width. See J. Gailey, ed., *1986 Zoning and Planning Law Handbook,* 14–15.

4. When such calls come from builders and trade organizations, the deregulation lobby is vulnerable to the charge that it is primarily concerned with self-interest and not broader social concerns. Simply relaxing density requirements without imposing other conditions may not produce substantial savings for homeowners, if the resulting value created is captured by the developer. A community that allows multi-family development in an area previously zoned single-family may get all of the negative impacts of greater density without delivering housing to low- and middle-income people. Arguments about trickle-down effects are unlikely to be persuasive.

5. O. Delogu, "Local Land Use Controls: An Idea Whose Time Has Passed," 36 *Maine Law Review* 261 (1984); Pulliam, "Brandeis Brief for Decontrol of Land Use: A Plea for Constitutional Reform," 13 *Sw. W. L. Rev.* 435 (1983); D. Kmiec, "Deregulating Land Use: An Alternative Free Enterprise Development System," 130 *U. Pa. L. Rev.* 28 (1981); G. Lefcoe, "California's Land Planning Requirements: The Case for Deregulation," 54 *S. Cal. L. Rev.* 447 (1981); Ellickson, "Suburban Growth Controls: An Economic and Legal Analysis," 86 *Yale L. J.* 385 (1977).

6. *The Report of the President's Commission on Housing* (Washington: USGPO, 1982), 200 (emphasis added). A municipality would have a much greater burden in establishing that one of its regulations serves a "vital and pressing" interest, as opposed to merely meeting the traditional police power test of "promoting the general welfare."

7. For a somewhat more balanced view, see *Working with the Community: A Developer's Guide* (Washington: ULI, 1985).

8. National Institute of Building Science, "Meeting America's Housing Needs" (Washington: NIBS, 1987) 7.

9. Delogu, "Local Land Use Controls," *1986 Zoning and Planning Law Handbook,* 307–332, at 309.

10. NIBS, "Meeting America's Housing Needs," 13.

11. Even the wave of popular support for federal action to protect the environment was not large enough to keep the national land use bill afloat in the early 1970s.

12. Even development that initially appears to be as-of-right, that is, consistent with the current zoning, may need discretionary permits for other reasons. Resulting negotiation may raise a broad range of issues.

13. *Village of Euclid v. Ambler Realty Co.*, 272 U.S. 365 (1926).

14. Here again some state courts were reluctant to compromise the certainty of strict *Euclidean* zoning, pointing to the difficulty of reviewing the exercise of local discretion, particularly where standards are vague. Nonetheless, special permitting, like variances and rezonings, has become central to the local land use regulation system.

15. The underlying causes of local conflicts over affordable housing and strategies for dealing with them are outlined in "A Handbook: Building Consensus for Affordable Housing," MIT Center for Real Estate Development, Working Paper #7 (Cambridge: CRED, 1987). See also L. Susskind, G. McMahon, and S. Rolley, "Resolving Development Disputes: A Briefing Paper," MIT Center for Real Estate Development, Working Paper #5 (Cambridge: CRED, 1986).

16. Some people are philosophically opposed to off-budget financing even when the expenditures are for "worthy" ends.

17. More precisely, the question is not necessarily one of increasing overall costs, but deciding who bears them: the occupant, the developer, the neighbors, the municipal taxpayers, and so on.

18. It is important to note that housing impact fees imposed on private developers are fundamentally different from so-called parcel-to-parcel linkage programs. In a parcel-to-parcel program, a redevelopment agency holding title to an attractive piece of downtown land requires bidding developers to agree to provide housing also on some other city-controlled parcel, typically one in a depressed neighborhood.

As the owner of the downtown land, the agency is utterly free to attach any conditions to the parcel's disposition. Potential developers who think that the conditions are too onerous simply do not have to bid, but cannot bring a legal challenge. In linking downtown and residential parcels, the redevelopment agency may have to accept less than full value for the prime site in order to induce developers to bid on the whole package. The size of the discount required depends on the local market and the availability of competing sites.

Discounting prime commercial land in order to foster residential development elsewhere may appear needlessly convoluted. It might seem more straightforward for the development agency to maximize its return on the downtown site, then apply the resulting gain as a subsidy for housing on the second parcel. Budgetary and political constraints, however, sometimes force the parcel-to-parcel approach. If surplus gained through downtown redevelopment goes into the general municipal treasury, the agency may have little control over its disposition. Parcel-to-parcel plans (indeed, linkage fees, as well) are really a way of earmarking funds for housing off budget, and thus insulating these funds from claims of other departments and interest groups.

19. For an examination of several linkage programs and an argument that they have limited transferability, see W. Keating, "Linkage Downtown Development to Broader Community Goals," *American Planning Association Journal* (Spring 1986). For a skeptical analysis of the legal underpinnings of linkage, see D. L. Connors and M. E. High, "The Expanding Circle of Exactions: From Dedications to Linkage," 50 *Law and Contemporary Problems* 69 (1987).

20. *Nollan v. California Coastal Commission,* 55 L.W. 5145 (1987).

21. *First English Evangelical Lutheran Church of Glendale v. County of Los Angeles,* 55 L.W. 4782 (1987).

22. In late 1987 the Patton company, a major purchaser and subdivider of raw land, filed a multi-million dollar suit against a small Maine town, claiming that its zoning was too restrictive. The potential damages exceed the entire annual budget of the town and could cost each resident several thousand dollars. The mere risk of such liability has radically shifted bargaining power between developers and town regulators. Developers who rattle the liability sword risk, of course, massive political backlash.

23. Specifically, it is possible to calculate the number of employees in a proposed office tower and from that estimate how many will live within the city, and how many of those, in turn, will be newcomers. Resulting housing demand and its impact

on the local market can thus be plausibly forecast. Even if such estimates cannot be done with certainty, courts are likely to defer to legislative findings.

24. The challenge for local planners will be to identify the specific police power justifications for their regulations and to document their interrelations. If care is taken in the drafting and enactment of local ordinances, municipalities can retain most, if not all, of their traditional powers.

25. For further criticism of negotiated development, see P. Goldberger, *New York Times* and W. H. Whyte, *City, Rediscovering the Center* (New York: Doubleday, 1989).

26. S. Goldberg, E. Green, and F. Sander, *Dispute Resolution* (Boston: Little, Brown, 1985); D. Lax and J. Sebenius, *The Manager as Negotiator* (New York: Free Press, 1986); B. Brown and J. Rubin, *The Social Psychology of Bargaining and Negotiation* (New York: Academic Press, 1975); R. Fisher and W. Ury, *Getting to Yes: How to Negotiate Agreement Without Giving In* (Boston: Houghton-Mifflin, 1981); H. Raiffa, *The Art and Science of Negotiation* (Cambridge: Harvard University Press, 1982).

27. A number of promising experiments are analyzed in *Sourcebook: Federal Agency Use of Alternative Means of Dispute Resolution,* Administrative Conference of the United States (1987).

28. See *Euclid* above.

29. See, for example, *Warth v. Seldin,* 422 U.S. 490 (1975) in which angry dissent by Justice Brennan accuses the majority of manipulating procedural requirements to duck the issue only because of "an indefensible hostility to the claim on the merits." Brennan acknowledged that curtailing a municipality's power to limit residence to those who are white and relatively well off would have "grave sociological and political ramifications," but that did not justify the majority's dismissal of the suit.

30. *Southern Burlington County NAACP v. Township of Mt. Laurel,* 67 N.J. 151, 336 A.2d 713, *cert. denied,* 423 U.S. 808 (1975); and *Southern Burlington County NAACP v. Township of Mt. Laurel,* 161 N.J. Super. 317, 391 A.2d 935 (Super. Ct., Law Div. 1978).

31. Kmiec, "Provision for Affordable Housing," 280–281.

32. The most current assessment of Chapter 774 appears in Cynthia LaCasse, "The Anti-Snob Zoning Law: The Effectiveness of Chapter 774 in Getting Affordable Housing Built," Master's Thesis, Department of Urban Studies and Planning, MIT, 1987.

33. Chapter 774 applies to communities which have not met the threshold criteria of having either 10 percent of the housing stock or 1.5 percent of the land in low- or moderate-income housing.

34. Because the statute partially preempts local authority, it has been controversial from the outset. The law represents a middle ground between traditional local autonomy and sweeping deregulation. As already noted, municipalities can escape its reach entirely by meeting specified goals. No community is required to create multifamily or affordable housing zones; rather, decisions are made on a site specific basis. Finally, as noted in the test, a community can still block a project if there are serious environmental concerns.

35. In practice, the negotiations are a good deal more complex. In addition to dealing with the local authorities and potentially with the state Housing Appeals Committee, the developer must first bargain with the state housing financing agency. Some developers complain that the process of getting state commitments is so time-consuming that whatever advantages come with lower interest rates and other subsidies are more than offset by carrying and opportunity costs. Whether this is true has not

been confirmed, but some of the same developers claim that they jump through the state financing hoops just so that their projects qualify for zoning overrides under Chapter 774.

36. Local observers disagree about whether "friendly 774s" are new or simply that the phenomenon has only recently been recognized.

37. A developer who foresees years of costly litigation may cave in under pressure even if he or she expects to be vindicated ultimately. Shortening the length of appeals thus reduces a developer's vulnerability.

38. In at least some of those cases in which the developer prevailed on appeal but did not build the project, even the more limited delays may have taken their toll. Moreover, in a friendly 774 that is approved at a local level, a city may contribute supplementary resources that probably would not be available in a contested case.

39. See LaCasse, "Anti-Snob Zoning Law."

40. Frank Popper deserves credit for coining this term, which stands for "Locally Undesirable Land Use."

41. One of the policy dilemmas has been whether to promote many small projects or to concentrate on fewer big ones. The former strategy serves the worthy goal of attacking economic, class, and racial segregation, but it invites many battles instead of just a few.

42. L. Bacow and J. Milkey, "Overcoming Local Opposition to Hazardous Waste Facilities: The Massachusetts Approach," *Harvard Environmental Law Review* (June 1982). See also L. Bacow, M. O'Hare, and D. Sanderson, *Facility Siting and Local Opposition* (New York: Van Nostrand, Reinhold, 1983).

43. W. Fleissig, "Negotiated Development," Lincoln Institute of Land Policy, Working Paper #8 (Cambridge: LILP, 1989).

44. See Denise DiPasquale and J. McKellar, "Design Strategies for Affordable Housing," MIT Center for Real Estate Development, Working Paper #8 (Cambridge: CRED, 1987).

45. See J. Mark Schuster et al., "Housing Design and Regional Character" (Cambridge: MIT Department of Urban Studies and Planning, 1989).

46. For a comprehensive description and analysis of public dispute resolution and consensus building, G. Bingham, *Resolving Environmental Disputes: A Decade of Experience* (Washington: Conservation Foundation, 1986); and L. Susskind and G. Cruikshank, *Breaking the Impasse* (New York: Free Press, 1987).

47. See Susskind and Cruikshank, *Breaking the Impasse.*

48. See Wheeler, *Handbook.*

49. The effect of aggressive open space acquisition on the price of remaining developable land has not been conclusively proven. Skeptics who claim that the impact is negligible point to the fact that even in municipalities in which conservation is actively pursued, only a small percentage of the land area is removed from the development market. That point of view assumes, however, a high elasticity of land supply and may ignore the degree to which inflationary expectations get fueled. More rigorous analysis of this point would clarify the extent to which affordable housing advocates and open space preservationists have opposed interests.

50. Interested readers are directed to R. Levitt and J. Kirlin, eds., *Managing Development Through Public/Private Negotiations* (Washington: ULI 1985).

51. This is not to suggest that all of the inconsistencies and conflicts have been worked out of the Massachusetts system. Some developers complain, for example, that requirements that construction workers on state subsidized projects be paid union scale wages significantly drive up the cost of housing. To put it another way, the impact of the subsidy on affordability is diluted if some of it must be applied to production.

Whether housing or wage standards should be given priority may depend on one's viewpoint. What is essential, however, is that policy choices be recognized and resolved intelligently.

52. For a much fuller description of such efforts, see I. D. Terner and T. B. Cook,Chapter 4 in this volume.

53. See P. Clay and J. Wallace,Chapter 12 in this volume.

54. Congress recently required that there be an impact analysis for any federally assisted housing that is about to be released from use restrictions. This requirement buys a little time for tenants and local authorities and in some cases may give them a bargaining chip with the owner. The history of environmental impact analysis is mixed at best, but some experts still believe that a properly conducted process could provide a framework for negotiation. See Susskind and Cruikshank, *Breaking the Impasse*. The same may hold true for housing impact studies.

Chapter 9
The Tax Reform Act of 1986 and Real Estate

Patric H. Hendershott

The Tax Reform Act of 1986 is probably the most anti-investment legislation ever enacted in the United States.[1] While the large increase in corporate taxes to fund personal tax cuts indicates the basic thrust of the legislation, all businesses, not just corporations, are adversely affected. Tax depreciation is less generous for both corporate and noncorporate investments, and investment tax credits are cut for both corporations and noncorporate enterprises. Personal tax changes, too, make investments less profitable. Investment in owner-occupied housing suffers directly from the cut in personal tax rates; other investments are adversely affected by increases in the capital gains tax rate and a general attack on tax shelters. Virtually every imaginable investment is treated less favorably.

This does not necessarily mean that the Tax Act should not have been enacted, although some certainly view the Act's anti-investment character as a major mistake, but it does mean that a partial analysis of its effect on real estate (or any other specific sector) can yield highly misleading results. Given the anti-investment nature of the Tax Act, the aggregate level of investment, and thus interest rates, will tend to be lower. Lower interest rates in turn, will offset some, or, for the less negatively affected investments, all of the direct negative effect of the Tax Act provisions. To account for this, I analyze the impact of the Tax Act's capital provisions on real estate *relative* to other investments. This analysis is largely independent of interest rate changes. I also incorporate a percentage point decline in interest rates when analyzing the impact on owner-occupied housing.

I conclude that real estate activity in the aggregate is not disfavored by the 1986 Tax Act. Within the broad real estate aggregate, however, widely different impacts are evident. Regular rental and commercial activity will be slightly disfavored (modest increases in rents will occur), and historic and old rehabilitation activity will be greatly disfavored. In contrast, owner-occupied housing, far and away the largest component of real estate, is favored, both directly by an interest rate decline and indirectly owing to the increase in rents. Homeownership should increase slightly.

This chapter is divided into three sections and a summary. The first discusses the provisions of the 1986 Tax Act and their likely impact on interest rates. The second provides a rationale for the general pattern of tax law changes in the last decade with a view toward "predicting" future changes. The third reports estimates of the impact of the Tax Act on investment generally and on rental and owner-occupied housing specifically. The final section summarizes the results, highlighting the impacts on low- and moderate-income households, and an appendix explains the calculations presented in the third section.

Briefly, low- and moderate-income owners or potential owners will find costs lowered by 10 to 15 percent, while rents should rise by about 10 percent. The personal tax cuts, which are especially generous for renters, are sufficiently large for married couples and other households with incomes above the poverty line to pay their higher rents. The poor and single renters will suffer a decline in their standard of living.

The 1986 Tax Act and Its Impact on Interest Rates

Investment generally, and housing specifically, is affected by changes in both individual income tax rates and investment incentives. The latter include depreciation schedules, investment tax credits, and rules applied to tax shelters. Legislative changes in each of these areas are described below. The likely interest-rate impact of these provisions is then discussed.

Individual Tax Rate Schedule

The new law replaces the previous 14-bracket tax rate schedule with what is best viewed as a 4-bracket rate schedule. These four rates are 15, 28, 33, and 28 percent. The 33 percent marginal rate reverts to 28 percent when a household's average tax rate on all income above the standard deduction equals 28 percent. That is, the benefits of the zero tax rate on personal exemptions and of the initial 15 percent tax rate are phased out for taxpayers with sufficiently high incomes, the phase-out mechanism being a five percent surcharge—giving the 33 percent marginal rate—on income above a certain level. The new rate schedule took effect in 1988 and has been adjusted for inflation since then.

The Tax Reform Act increased the standard deduction (zero bracket amount) by about a quarter (to $5,000 in 1988) for marrieds filing jointly, by a full two-thirds (to $4,400) for heads of household, and by an eighth (to $3,000) for singles. In 1989, the personal exemption equals $2,000 each for the taxpayer, the taxpayer's spouse, and dependents. The standard deduction

TABLE 9.1   Tax Rate at Which Housing Costs Are Deductible

Income ($1,000)	TENURE CHOICE (AVERAGE)		QUANTITY DEMANDED (MARGINAL)	
	Old law	Tax Reform	Old law	Tax Reform
13–25	.146	.074	.166	.176
25–30	.211	.128	.189	.180
30–50	.279	.242	.251	.184
50–100	.402	.316	.364	.316
100–200	.471	.370	.455	.370

Source: Adapted from P. H. Hendershott, J. R. Follain, and D. C. Ling, "Effects on Real Estate," in J. A. Pechman, ed., *Tax Reform and the U.S. Economy* (Washington: The Brookings Institution, 1987) Table 1.

and the personal exemption amounts are being adjusted annually for inflation beginning in 1989 and 1990, respectively. The substantial increases under the new law are expected to remove 6 million households from the federal income tax rolls.

The reductions in statutory tax rates, including the near doubling of the personal exemption, significantly lower both the average and marginal tax rates at which households deduct housing expenses. Table 9.1 contains some sample calculations for households with different adjusted gross incomes. While the calculations are based on numerous specific assumptions (married couples with two dependents, etc.), the general result—a cut in these tax rates—holds for virtually all households.[2]

The Tax Act also alters the tax rate on capital gains income. The general capital gains exclusion no longer exists. For most households with significant assets other than consumer durables and their residence, the capital gains rate is increased from 20 percent or less to 28 or 33 percent. The effective exemption of capital gains taxation on owner-occupied housing continues unaltered, however. That is, capital gains taxation on owner-occupied housing can be totally postponed upon sale by purchasing another home of at least equal value; in addition, a one-time capital gain of up to $125,000 is excluded from taxation for taxpayers above the age of 55.

Tax Depreciation Schedules and Tax Credits

Under previous law, residential rental property could be depreciated over 19 years using a 175 percent declining balance method with a switch to straight

TABLE 9.2 Tax Depreciation and Investment Tax Credit

	Depr. rate	1985 TAX LAW				TAX REFORM ACT OF 1986				1970s TAX LAW			
		Depr. life	%DB	Tax credit	Basis adj.	Depr. life	%DB	Tax credit	Basis adj.	Depr. life	%DB	Tax credit	Basis adj.
Equipment	.32	3	150	.06	0.5	3	150	0	—	5	200	.033	0
Equipment	.15	5	150	.10	0.5	7	200	0	—	11	200	.096	0
Public utilities	.08	10	150	.10	0.5	15	150	0	—	21	200	.10	0
Public utilities	.05	15	150	.10	0.5	20	150	0	—	32	200	.10	0
Industrial	.03	19	175	0	—	31.5	100	0	—	40	150	0	—
Commercial	.03	19	100	0	—	31.5	100	0	—	40	150	0	—
Residential	.03	19	175	0	—	27.5	100	0	—	32	200	0	—
Historic	.03	19	175	.25	0.5	31.5	100	.20	1.0	40	150	.10	0
Old rehab.	.03	19	175	.20	1.0	31.5	100	.10	1.0	40	150	0	—
Quasi-old rehab.	.03	19	175	.15	1.0	31.5	100	0	—	40	150	0	—

Source: Various Tax Acts

line in about the ninth year. Nonresidential property could use either straight line or the 175 percent declining balance method, but given the severity of the recapture provisions for those who used the accelerated procedure, most nonresidential property was depreciated using straight line. Equipment was depreciated over 3 or 5 years, and public utility structures over 10 or 15 years; 150 percent declining balance with a switch to straight line was applicable to both asset types.

Under the new law, residential rental property is depreciable over 27.5 years and nonresidential property over 31.5 years. The depreciation method is straight line, and the recapture provisions are eliminated. Construction period interest and property tax expenses are added to the basis of the property; consequently, they are amortized over either 27.5 or 31.5 years versus 10 years under previous law. Finally, tax lives for public utility structures are lengthened to 15 or 20 years (still 150 percent DB). While tax lives of equipment are lengthened, a more accelerated method (200 percent DB versus the old 150 percent DB) is available. The net result is roughly no change in the present value of tax depreciation allowances.

Under the old law, tax credits existed for equipment, public utility structures, and rehabilitation expenditures on qualified properties. The latter included historic structures and nonresidential old (over 40 years) and quasi-old (over 30 years) structures. The credits were 10 percent for equipment and public utility structures, 15 percent for quasi-old rehabilitation outlays, 20 percent for old rehabs and 25 percent for historic structures. The depreciation basis was reduced by the full credit for the nonresidential rehabs and by half the credit for equipment and public utility and historic structures.

The new bill removes the credits for equipment, public utility structures, and rehabs of buildings built after 1936. For historic structures, the credit is cut from 25 to 20 percent, and the depreciable basis must now be reduced by the full credit. For old qualifying properties, the credit is lowered from 20 to 10 percent. The depreciation schedules (tax life and depreciation method) and tax credits (including basis adjustment) for ten classes of depreciable assets are listed in Table 9.2 for the 1985 law, the 1986 law, and the pre-ERTA (1970s) law.

Passive Loss Limitations

The Tax Reform Act of 1986 contains multiple attacks on tax shelter activities: (1) the establishment of a new income category (passive income), the losses from which are generally not deductible against other income; (2) a tightening of the limitations on interest expenses; (3) application of the at-risk rules to real estate, but with major exceptions; and (4) an expansion of the individual minimum tax. Because only the passive loss rules could significantly affect housing markets, my discussion is limited to these rules.[3]

For many years, different sources of income have been taxed differently under the federal tax code. For example, until 1981, "unearned" (nonlabor) income was subject to a far higher maximum tax rate than was "earned" or labor income. Also, capital gains have generally been taxed less heavily than other income, owing both to the gains exclusion and deferral until realization. Moreover, portfolio capital losses, while fully deductible against portfolio capital gains, have been deductible against only $3,000 of other income.

The 1986 Act introduces a new income class, passive income, and puts restrictions somewhat analogous to those on portfolio capital losses on passive losses. Passive income includes income generated from business and trade activities in which the taxpayer does not materially participate *and* from rental activities such as real estate. For individuals, partnerships, trusts, and personal service corporations, losses from passive activities can be used to offset income from other passive activities, but not other income (e.g., wages, interest, etc.). Losses that cannot be claimed in a particular year can be "banked" and used to offset passive income in future years. Also, cumulative losses are allowed in full at the time of sale of the property if a gain or loss is recognized.

An important exception applies to "small landlords." Taxpayers who actively manage residential rental investments may deduct up to $25,000 in losses against nonpassive income if their adjusted gross income computed without regard to the losses is less than $100,000. This amount is phased out at the rate of one dollar for two dollars of income for taxpayers with incomes above $100,000, so that no losses are allowed for anyone who earns above $150,000. An identical exemption applies to tax credits in a deduction-equivalent sense; that is, $7,000 in credits is allowed because a $7,000 credit is equivalent to a $25,000 deduction for a taxpayer with a 28 percent tax rate ($25,000 × .28 = $7,000). Active management requires that a taxpayer have at least a 10 percent interest in the property (and not be a limited partner) and be involved in the management of the property on a "substantial and continual" basis.

Two related rationales for the small landlord provision can be provided. The first is based upon uncertainty regarding the true nature of the income from actively-managed properties. With active management, some of the income is earned income and thus should be aggregated with other earned income. The second rationale reflects the difficulties of real estate diversification for small investors attempting to use their management/maintenance skills. Diversification (by geographic area and real estate type) becomes particulary important when passive losses are deductible only against passive gains. Without diversification, large losses can more easily occur. While equity mutual funds allow small equity investors to diversify easily, real estate diversification for small managers/maintainers is impossible because they don't hold enough property.

Other potentially important exceptions to the passive loss rule apply to certain types of corporations. Regular C corporations are not subject to the rule so they will be able to use passive losses to offset both regular and portfolio income of the corporation. Closely held C corporations other than personal service corporations that are subject to the at-risk rules (generally where 5 or fewer individuals own more than 50 percent of the stock) can use passive losses to offset earned income, but not portfolio income (unearned income other than passive income).

When the worse-case *certainty* impact of passive loss rules on rents is computed, that is, the investment earns the expected return with certainty and no passive gains on other investments are available to offset passive losses, the analysis implies little impact. The combination of lengthened tax depreciation and construction period interest and property tax (CPIT) deductions (to 27.5 years), lower interest rates (one percentage point), and higher rents (10 percent) virtually eliminates initial tax losses. Moreover, if passive losses were expected to be greater, as they would be in a higher inflation (and thus interest rate) environment, the financing could/would be restructured. The simplest method would be greater use of equity. Alternatively, debt with equity-kickers (share of asset appreciation or increase in rents) could be used to lower direct interest costs and thus passive losses.

The passive loss rules could still affect market rents, however. While no losses occur when the project "works," significant uncertainty surrounds the net operating income from properties, and losses would occur if this income falls significantly below expectations. If incomes from other projects are not sufficient to offset the passive losses, net losses would not be currently deductible. That is, the passive loss limits increase the riskiness of a real estate investment because the government no longer shares fully in the losses of an unsuccessful investment; rental real estate income earned by proprietors and partnerships is now treated like corporate income, fully taxable if positive, but only banked for future deduction if negative. As a result, investors will raise the required promised (not expected) return on real estate investments. Also acting to raise the required promised return is the reduction in importance of the relatively certain tax depreciation component of real estate investment vis-à-vis the relatively uncertain operating income and cash reversion components.

Tax Reform and Interest Rates

The Tax Reform Act of 1986 has negative direct implications for every type of capital good. Longer depreciation lives raise the investment hurdle rates (annual rental costs) for all structures except owner-occupied housing, and the reduction or elimination of investment tax credits increases hurdle rates for equipment, public utility structures, and rehabilitation projects. Finally, the cut in personal tax rates lowers the demands for depreciable real estate and owner-occupied housing. With the demand for all investment goods falling, interest rates will certainly decline. The magnitude of the decline depends on the interest sensitivities of both the domestic and foreign saving supply and of investment demand itself. Hendershott[4] constructed a model in which total saving is independent of interest rates and the demands for capital are approximately unitary elastic with respect to the rental prices of capital goods. In this model, interest rates have to decline by 1.4 percentage points to offset the negative capital provisions of the Act. That is, rates have to decline by this much to maintain *aggregate* investment at its pre-reform level.

Of course, interest rates will decline less if the supply of saving is reduced, and a reduction might be expected. On the domestic side, the deductibility of contributions to retirement accounts has been limited. IRA contributions for those with established pensions will no longer be deductible for households with incomes above $35,000 (singles) or $50,000 (married couples). Also, the maximum deductible annual contributions to supplemental retirement accounts (401ks) has been lowered from $30,000 to $7,000 (a similar reduction occurs for 403bs). On the foreign side, any reduction in U.S. interest rates reduces returns to foreigners because they pay taxes based on foreign tax schedules, not on U.S. schedules, and thus do not benefit from lower U.S. tax rates. However, international capital flows are not infinitely elastic, and even if they were, the U.S. is sufficiently large that its reduced investment demand would lower the world level of interest rates.

In the calculations reported below, a one (not 1.4) percentage point decline in U.S. interest rates is presumed. Much of the rate decline likely occurred before the actual enactment of the Tax Act. All tax reform plans considered in 1986 proposed elimination of the investment tax credit for equipment and public utility structures retroactive to the beginning of 1986, and the likelihood of some version of tax reform passing was high virtually all year. Thus, the decline in interest rates and the weakness in equipment expenditures experienced in 1986 was partially attributable to the anticipated removal of this provision. Indeed, 75 basis points of a 140 basis point model-calculated decline in interest rates is due solely to the elimination of this credit. Real estate likely benefited from tax-reform induced lower interest rates during much of 1986.

Is There a Rationale Behind Tax Changes in the Last Decade?

The Economic Recovery Tax Act of 1981 (ERTA) contained the most favorable capital investment provisions probably ever enacted: tax lives for all depreciable property were shortened markedly, and capital gains tax rates were lowered sharply owing to the cuts in marginal tax rates. The Tax Reform Act of 1986 more than reverses these aspects of ERTA: tax depreciation is less generous than before 1981, and capital gains tax rates are even higher than before 1978. What brought about this sea change in tax law?

Many explanations for the tax changes exist, most relating to political considerations in one way or another, and politics, in its widest context, certainly shouldn't be denied a major role. However, political considerations do not tell the entire story. The rise in inflation and interest rates in the late 1970s and early 1980s contributed to the investment provisions of ERTA, and the declines since then influenced the form of the provisions in the 1986 Act. Tax depreciation schedules and capital gains rates that look reasonable when inflation is four percent take on a different hue when the tax depreciation base is being eroded at ten percent a year and an overwhelming share of capital gains is pure inflation. Evidence that "inflation affects tax law" is summarized below, and the implications for future tax law changes are drawn.

Tax Depreciation

The 1986 Tax Act represents the fourth change in the depreciation schedule for structures in the past five years. ERTA shortened useful life for a variety of structures from a range of 30 to 40 years to a single 15 years. The tax laws of 1984 and 1985 increased useful life to 18 and then to 19 years. The frequency of these changes suggests that future changes are likely.

Economists argue that tax depreciation should equal real economic depreciation at replacement cost. This criterion implies a quite low (less than 4 percent per year) constant annual depreciation rate for structures but applied to a base indexed to changes in the price level. That is, during inflationary periods, tax depreciation would be backloaded (increased over time), rather than frontloaded as it has always been. Indexation of the basis would result in the present value of tax depreciation being independent of inflation if the discount rate moved one-for-one with the inflation rate.

Legislators obviously have not adopted the economist's explicit indexation recommendation: during the past 15 years tax depreciation has never been less than 6.5 percent in the initial full year and has always declined quickly in subsequent years. However, changes in the tax on useful life of structures over the past decade have been negatively correlated with movements in interest rates and inflation. These useful-life changes have had the effect of offsetting sharp changes in the present value of the tax saving from tax depreciation allowances generated by interest rate movements. For example, ERTA reduced useful life to its lowest level at a time when interest rates were at their peak level, and useful life has increased during the 1980s as interest rates have declined. It appears that legislators have adopted an ad hoc strategy of indexation that involves a change in the tax depreciation schedule in response to changes in the inflation/interest rate environment.[5]

As evidence of this ad hoc strategy, the present value of the tax saving from tax depreciation allowances was computed for various years during the last decade. We began with the relatively low inflation/interest-rate environment of the middle 1970s and then examined the impact of rising inflation (1980–81), the 1981 tax law response (15 versus 30 year useful life), the decrease in inflation and interest rates (1983–84), the 1984 response (15 to 18 year tax life), the further decrease in interest rates/inflation (1986), and finally the Tax Reform Act of 1986.[6] Altogether, seven different combinations of tax law and economic environment were considered. Tax law changes include changes in depreciation policy as well as changes in the marginal tax rate of the marginal investor in real estate.

Under 1976 law, the tax saving from tax depreciation for rental housing was 0.267 per dollar of investment, i.e., the present value of tax depreciation allowances multiplied by the appropriate tax rate equaled 26.7 percent of the original basis.[7] When subsequent increases/decreases in inflation and interest rates lowered/raised the tax saving relative to 26.7 percent, tax legislation systematically altered the tax depreciation schedule to bring the percentage back into line. However, the ERTA of 1981 and the Tax Reform Act of 1986 more than compensated for the earlier increase/decrease in inflation and interest rates. Thus, two cycles for tax depreciation seem to exist, an endogenous response to the inflation/interest-rate cycle and an exogenous "political" cycle. The 1986 Tax Act reflects both of these cycles; depreciation policy under the new law is less generous than any tax-economic combination of the past 10 years (probably of the last 50).

This analysis refers specifically to rental housing, but the same pattern obviously exists for other structures. Moreover, the same pattern likely exists for equipment if one takes the investment tax credit into account (adds it to the present value of depreciation tax saving). While the 1986 Act did not reduce the present value of tax depreciation for equipment, the tax credit was eliminated.

Capital Gains Taxation

After a decade of reductions in the statutory capital gains tax rate (the product of the regular income tax rate and one minus the gains exclusion), the new law sharply increases this rate. For our assumed marginal investor with a regular tax rate of 0.45 (federal and state) under pre-1986 law and 0.36 under the new law, the gains rate doubles from 0.18 to 0.36. This contrasts with the declines in 1978, when the exclusion rate was increased from 50 to 60 percent, and in 1981, when regular tax rate cuts lowered the gains rate further to the 0.18 noted above.

The appropriate tax treatment of capital gains is not obvious. Some would argue that gains should be taxed fully (no exclusion) as they accrue, not upon realization. Others would argue for a favorable treatment, although not necessarily for an exclusion (the deferral advantage of taxation upon realization might be sufficient, at least for long holding periods). Others would opt for the taxation of real gains only, usually accompanied by the deduction of only real interest expense. Our task is not to sort out these issues but only to find a pattern in past legislative behavior regarding capital gains taxation.

Changes in the statutory capital gains tax rate over the last decade are consistent with an effort to maintain a constant tax rate on inflationary gains over a holding period of roughly five years. Thus, accelerating inflation in the late 1970s and early 1980s triggered a cut in the gains rate, while the subsequent disinflation induced an increase in the gains rate.[8] More specifically, the present value of the tax on five years of inflationary gains in the 1976–77 period is 6.7 percent. The increase in inflation to its 1980 level raised the tax to 8.7 percent, assuming no change in tax rates. The cut in the gains rate from 0.25 to 0.18 offset the increase in inflation. Similarly, the fall in inflation during the 1980s cut the inflation tax to 3.1 percent by 1986, and the 1986 increase in the gains tax rate raised the inflation tax back to 6.2 percent.

The Future

The above analysis has clear implications for the future: if the past pattern holds, a reacceleration of inflation will, with some lag, lead to a shortening of depreciation tax lives (and possibly a reintroduction of the investment tax credit) and a cut in the capital gains tax rate. But will the past pattern hold? Possibly not. In the past, inflation has generated an increase in real Federal tax revenues owing largely to bracket creep. Thus, shortening tax lives and cutting capital gains tax rates was easily "financed." With the indexation of personal exemptions and tax brackets, real revenues no longer automatically rise with inflation; making business tax cuts will require explicitly raising other taxes (or borrowing). As a result, the inflation response of tax law is likely to be smaller and to occur with a longer lag. That is, the 1986 Act may represent a permanent shift to a less favorable investment climate in the United States. This bodes well for owner-occupied housing, which is effectively not taxed, but ill for rental housing and other taxed real capital.

The Impact of the 1986 Tax Law Changes

Several questions are relevant to policy makers and housing professionals. For example, how did the Tax Act affect the equilibrium of annual costs and values of owner and rental housing? Also, will owner/rental housing be subsidized relative to other capital goods, namely corporate and noncorporate equipment and structures, and if so, by how much? Put another way, how level will the playing field be across different capital assets under the new law, and is it tilted in favor of or against housing? I begin this section by defining a level playing field and examining the impact of the Tax Act on the slope of the field, and I then discuss the specific impact of the Tax Act on housing.

The Slope of the Playing Field

A level playing field is defined as one in which the net (of depreciation) pretax required returns on all investments are equal. With a level field, the total expected returns from all investments could be maximized. That is, it would not be possible to invest more in one good and an equal amount less in another and increase total expected returns. When one good is subsidized over another by more favorable taxation, the pretax return on the subsidized good is less than that on the unsubsidized good and thus the total expected return to capital is less than it could be. Pretax returns would be increased by substituting more of the unsubsidized goods for the subsidized good, but the tax system prevents such a substitution.

Table 9.3 contains the net pretax required returns under 1985 tax law and the Tax Reform Act of 1986 for three broad classes of assets—corporate, noncorporate real estate, and owner-occupied housing—and numerous sub-categories within these classes (see the Appendix on the specifics of these calculations). As can be seen, under 1985 tax law the tax-favored assets were rehabilitations, equipment, and owner-occupied housing of high income households, and the tax disadvantaged asset was corporate industrial struc-tures. The investment tax credits gave rehabs and corporate equipment their advantage. Corporate investments are generally disfavored by their "double" taxation—taxation at both the business (corporate) and investor (personal) levels.

The 1986 Act cuts back sharply on investment tax credits, creating an almost level playing field within the corporate sector and reducing the advan-tage of rehabilitation. As the change column indicates, the net pretax required returns for rehabilitations and utilities rise by a percentage point and that for equipment rises by over two points. Like points on a mortgage, a given invest-ment credit has a greater impact on annual returns the shorter the maturity/life of the investment. The almost percentage point decline in hurdle rates for owner housing of households with incomes under $30,000 reflects the greater benefit of interest rate declines for those in lower tax brackets (they, rather than the Treasury, gain from the decline in rates). While the interest rate de-cline and tax rate cuts leave the after-tax interest rate roughly constant for high income households, the after-tax rate declines for lower income households. The 1986 Act leveled the playing field within each of the three broad asset categories. Historic rehabs and owner housing for high income households are still favored within their classes, but the advantages are reduced considerably under the 1986 law. The major remaining bias is that against the corporate ownership form.

Calculations have also been performed for pre-ERTA (1970s) tax law, using the same presumed real after-tax interest rate and expected inflation rate. In general, 1986 law is more, not less, favorable to investors than 1970s law, with the exception of corporate equipment and utilities (which had a tax credit then, but not now). Net pretax required returns would be one (rental housing) to two (historic rehabs and industrial structures) percentage points higher. The reason the late 1970s were perceived as a more attractive invest-ment climate than the current environment for both housing and other assets

TABLE 9.3   Net Pretax Required Annual Returns for 1985 and 1986 Law (percent)

	1985	1986 Tax Act	Change
Corporate investments			
Equipment	3.4	5.6	2.2
Utility structures	5.0	6.1	1.1
Industrial structures	6.1	6.2	0.1
Noncorporate real estate			
Commercial	4.6	4.7	0.1
Rental	4.3	4.6	0.3
Rehabilitations			
historic	2.2	3.2	1.0
old	3.0	3.9	0.9
quasi-old	3.4	4.7	1.3
Owner-occupied housing[a]			
13–25	4.7	3.8	−0.9
25–30	4.5	3.7	−0.8
30–50	3.9	3.7	−0.2
50–100	2.9	2.6	−0.3
100–200	2.1	2.3	0.2

Source: See Appendix.
[a] Household income ($1,000, 1986).

is that real after-tax interest rates, not tax statutes, were more attractive then than now.

Rental Housing

In Table 9.3, the net pretax required return for residential rental property was shown to rise from 4.3 percent to 4.6 percent.[9] To obtain an estimate of the percentage increase in rents required to make new investments profitable, I first raise the net rate to a gross rate by adding depreciation, and then convert net operating income to gross rents by adding an estimate of operating expenses. When each of these is 3 percent, the rent-to-value ratio rises from 10.3 percent (4.3 + 3.0 + 3.0) to 10.6 percent, an increase of only 3 percent.

This is too low an estimate of the required percentage rent increase for two reasons. First, the less favorable treatment of construction period interest and taxes has not been accounted for. This change should raise rents by another 3 percent. Second, the possibility of the passive loss limits binding should an investment go bad will raise the required promised return, and thus rents, on real estate investments. A one percent higher equity rate raises rents by another 4 percent. Thus my best estimate of the required percentage increase in residential rents is about 10 percent.[10]

The process by which rents increase in competitive markets is the following. Builders will find it less profitable to invest at the current level of rents with the new tax incentives. The combination of reduced new construction with normal growth in demand and steady obsolescence of the existing stock will eventually generate higher rents for the existing stock.

How quickly will rents rise from the old equilibrium level to the new? The rise will occur most rapidly in fast-growing markets; in markets with high vacancy rates, the tax-induced rent increase will occur only after these high rates are worked off (current rents and occupancy rates get back to their equilibrium level under the previous tax law). A reasonable guess is that it will take three (Columbus, Ohio) to ten (Houston, Texas) years for rents to rise to their new equilibrium level.

In the short run—i.e., before rents have risen to their higher new equilibrium level—the value of existing real estate will be depressed. Consider an investor in early 1987 contemplating purchase of property put in place in 1986. This new investor will face a less generous tax depreciation schedule, a higher capital gains tax rate, a lower marginal tax rate and, possibly, passive loss limitations. The question, then, is how much will this new investor alter his bid for the property relative to his bid under previous law? The standard of comparison is the price of the property that would have made it a zero net present value investment under the old law, assuming that rents were at their equilibrium level.

If rents instantaneously jumped to their new equilibrium level, then value would not decline; the higher rents would compensate exactly for the less generous tax depreciation, lower marginal tax rates, etc. Because rents will not rise instantaneously, value will decline, the magnitude depending on how slowly investors *think* rents will rise to the new equilibrium level. The longer the expected adjustment period, the greater the present value of expected below equilibrium rents, the greater will be the fall in value. A useful analogy can be drawn to the pricing of discount bonds. Bonds sell at a discount when they are earning a below-market coupon (rent). The more the coupon is below market and the longer the bonds are expected to earn the below-market coupon (the longer is the bond's maturity), the lower is the market value relative to par.

Investor expectations of the rental adjustment process should vary with

TABLE 9.4   Estimates of Likely Percentage Property Value Changes (10% Rise in Equilibrium Rents)

	FAST GROWTH		NO GROWTH	
	Total price discount	Discount due to reform	Total price discount	Discount due to reform
Market in equilibrium	−1	−1	−2	−2
10% excess capacity	−5	−4	−9	−7

Source: Adapted from P. H. Hendershott, J. R. Follain, and D. C. Ling, "Effects on Real Estate," in J. A. Pechman, ed., *Tax Reform and the U.S. Economy* (Washington: The Brookings Institution, 1987) 87, Table 4.

both the growth rate of the area and the extent of initial disequilibrium. I consider two growth rates (zero and positive) and two pre-reform states of the market (equilibrium and 10 percent "excess capacity"). In all cases, depreciation or obsolescence is assumed to occur at the rate of 2 percent per year. Thus 10 percent excess capacity or below-market rent would be eliminated in 5 years even with zero growth. The positive growth market is assumed to eliminate 5 percent excess capacity per year, 2 for obsolescence and 3 for growth. Thus 20 percent initially below-market rents, 10 percent due to excess capacity and 10 percent due to tax reform, would be eliminated in 4 years in the high growth area versus 10 years in the no-growth area.

Table 9.4 contains estimates of the percentage value declines in a property purchased in early 1987 owing to a 10 percent increase in equilibrium rents and the failure of actual rents to increase immediately to that level. The first row is for a property that would have had a zero net present value under the old law: in other words, the property is in a market in equilibrium prior to the enactment of the Tax Act. As can be seen, the value decline is a modest one percent in a growth market and two percent in a no-growth market.

Row 2 is the case of 10 percent excess capacity. In these calculations, the total percentage price discount from replacement cost is computed first for the initial disequilibrium and then for the disequilibrium and the 1986 tax act. The difference is attributed to the Tax Act. As can be seen, the value declines are far larger when substantial excess capacity exists. The Tax Act is seen to reduce value, from an already depressed level, by 7 percent in no-growth areas versus only 4 percent in a growth area. The 7 percent is probably the upper bound on value decline. In contrast to the rent increase, the value declines should have occurred instantaneously. Over time, values will rise as rents rise to their new equilibrium level.

These value declines are for sellers of properties in early 1987, not "holders" of properties. Consider the current owner of a new property placed in service in 1986. The value of the investment to this person exceeds that to the 1987 purchaser because this person will be able to use the more generous tax depreciation schedule from previous law (and, if he purchased before October 22, 1986, the passive loss transition rules). The value to an investor not subject to the passive loss rules *rises* by 5 percent even if rents are expected to take 5 years to adjust (the no growth assumption). That is, the present value of the tax saving from the more favorable tax depreciation exceeds the present value of the below-market rents. This suggests a strong disincentive for owners not subject to the passive loss limits to trade properties purchased in 1986. A disincentive to trade also holds for investors not subject to the loss limits who purchased properties in earlier years, but the disincentive is less the earlier the property was purchased because the present value of the tax saving from the more generous depreciation under old law is less.

Owner-Occupied Housing

Current law grants important benefits to homeowners: imputed rental income is not taxed, and capital gains are rarely taxed and then only on a much deferred basis. These benefits automatically accrue to wealthy households who all-equity finance their houses. The deductibility of home mortgage interest ensures that itemizing households who debt finance will also benefit fully from the nontaxation of owner-occupied housing. A consequence of these provisions is that high-income homeowners receive substantial tax subsidies.

The Tax Act of 1986 does not directly alter any of these favorable provisions, but it does affect the after-tax cost of owner-occupied housing. First, the tax rates at which households deduct housing costs or upon which owner equity would be taxed if it were not invested in owner housing are reduced. Second, the pretax level of interest rates will be lower. Furthermore, the combination of changes in owner costs and in market rents will cause some households to shift between renting and owning.

The annual after-tax cost of obtaining one unit of housing capital depends upon the cost of debt, the cost of contributed equity, property taxes, real economic depreciation, expected appreciation, and the tax savings associated with owner-occupied housing. Two costs or "prices" of owner housing are relevant: the average cost, which influences the tenure choice decision; and the marginal cost, which affects the quantity demanded by households that choose to own. The average and marginal costs, respectively, are higher the lower are the average and marginal tax rates at which housing costs are deductible.

Estimates of owner housing costs for households in different income classes under both old law and the Tax Act are contained in the left and middle sections of Table 9.5. The marginal costs are those listed in Table 9.3 plus

TABLE 9.5   Annual After-Tax Cost of Dollar of Owner-Occupied Housing and Percentage Change in Ratio of Owner to Rental Costs, by Income Class

Income ($1,000, 1986)	OLD LAW		TAX ACT OF 1986		Change in cost of owning relative to renting (%)
	Marginal	Average	Marginal	Average	
13–25	.0769	.0788	.0677	.0766	−12
25–30	.0754	.0725	.0673	.0719	−10
30–50	.0687	.0659	.0670	.0619	−15
50–100	.0591	.0540	.0555	.0555	− 7
100–200	.0516	.0500	.0540	.0540	− 2

three percentage points for depreciation (and maintenance). The average costs are computed similarly except the average tax rates listed in Table 9.1 are employed. Households with incomes below about $30,000 will experience about a ten percent decrease in marginal housing costs; households with incomes between $30,000 and $100,000 will experience a five percent decrease; and households with higher incomes will face a 5 percent increase. Thus any tendency toward softer house prices will be confined to the very high end of the market (over $250,000) and will be modest in magnitude.

Average housing costs will decrease slightly for households with incomes below approximately $60,000; households with incomes above about $120,000 will experience a 5 percent increase in costs. The average cost declines are smaller than the marginal declines for lower-income households because the Tax Act both raises the standard deduction and reduces nonhousing-related itemized deductions (sales taxes, consumer interest, etc.), causing more housing deductions of these households to be wasted than was the case under the old law.

Homeownership depends, among other things, on the ratio of the average cost of owning to the cost of renting. The percentage changes in these ratios for households in the various income classes are reported in the last column of Table 9.5. The ratio declines by over 10 percent for households with incomes under $50,000, by about 7 percent for those with incomes between $50,000 and $100,000, and by negligible amounts for households with incomes above $100,000. All currently renting households will find homeownership relatively more attractive than under the old tax law. Given the time lags before rents rise and then before households respond, the resultant increase in ownership will occur quite gradually over the next decade.

Summary

In contrast to the conventional wisdom, real estate activity in the aggregate is not disfavored by the 1986 Tax Act. Within the broad real estate aggregate, however, widely different impacts are to be expected. Regular rental and commercial activity will be slightly disfavored (modest increases in rents should be occurring and declines in values should have occurred), and historic and old rehabilitation activity will be greatly disfavored. In contrast, owner-occupied housing, far and away the largest component of real estate, is favored, both directly by an interest rate decline and indirectly owing to the increase in rents. Home ownership should rise gradually, and the quantity and value of houses should increase slightly, except at the very high end of the market.

The rent increase for residential properties will be about 10 percent with our assumption of a percentage point decline in interest rates. The market value decline caused by tax reform, which should have been greater the longer and further investors thought rents would be below the new equilibrium, is unlikely to have exceeded 4 percent in fast growth markets, even if substantial excess capacity existed before the reform. Moreover, the value of recently-purchased properties *to their current holders* should have increased, as long as the investors did not have negative total passive incomes, because the more generous tax depreciation allowances under old law vis-a-vis new law add more value than the expected below-market rents subtract. In no-growth markets with substantial excess capacity, market value declines could have been as much as 7 percent from already depressed levels. These values will recover as excess capacity is eliminated and rents rise to their new equilibrium level.

Two offsetting factors operate on the after-tax cost of owner-occupied housing. Lower tax rates increase the cost, but lower interest rates decrease it. With a percentage-point interest-rate decline, the after-tax marginal cost will fall by about 10 percent for most households with incomes below $30,000 and rise by about 5 percent for those with incomes above $130,000. Thus, only the highest price houses should have experienced weakness in value. Average housing costs will decrease slightly in this scenario for households with incomes below about $60,000, but increase by 5 percent for those with incomes above twice this level. With the projected increase in rents, homeownership should rise for all income classes, but especially for those with income under $60,000.

The new passive loss limitations are likely to lower significantly the values of loss-motivated partnership deals and of properties in areas where the economics have turned sour (vacancy rates have risen sharply). The limitations should have little impact on new construction and market rents, however. Reduced depreciation write-offs, lower interest rates, and higher rents all act to lower expected passive losses. Moreover, financing can be restructured to include equity-kickers or less debt generally at little loss of value.

So where does this leave low- and moderate-income households? Owners or potential owners are clearly in an improved position. By our estimates, ownership costs for those with $12,500 to $25,000 in income *are* ten percent lower because of the 1986 Tax Act. Rental costs, on the other hand, *will be* about ten percent higher, the increase coming in as short as two years in tight, high growth markets and as long as six to eight years in loose, low growth areas.

Fortunately, lower income households (other than singles) receive greater percentage tax cuts than do higher income households, and renters receive larger cuts than do equal income owners. (Owner housing deductions are less valuable.) As a result, renting married couples and "other" households with incomes of $17,500 to $30,000 will retain two percent more of their adjusted gross incomes.[11] Households with lower incomes who paid taxes under old law will receive larger percentage cuts; for those at the $12,500 level, nearly six percent more income will be retained. Thus, if a household with, say, $20,000 in income spends 25 percent of it on rent, a ten percent increase in rent will take 2.5 percent of their income, but the tax cut will give them two percent more income. Thus 80 percent of the rent increase is "paid for" by the tax cut; because the rent increase occurs over a period of years but the tax cut is fully implemented in 1988, the household is ahead temporarily. Of course, at lower incomes more of income is spent on rent, but then the tax cut is larger. To illustrate, if the household with a $12,500 income spends 40 percent of it on rent, a ten percent increase in rent will take four percent of their income, but the tax cut gives them more than enough additional take home income to pay the rent increase.

When both the rent increase and tax cuts are taken into account, only married couples and other households well under the poverty line will have as much as a percent less income to spend on nonhousing goods. Only such households are a potential problem. If welfare benefit levels were appropriate before passage of the tax act, then they need to be increased. Single renting households, in contrast, did not receive a tax cut and thus will have significantly less income to spend on nonhousing goods. The political consensus appears to have been that singles had been treated too generously under old tax law and thus that they should suffer a relative decline in living standards.

Appendix: The Calculation of Pretax Required Returns

The decision to invest depends on whether the present value of the expected revenue from investment, net of direct operating expenses and indirect taxes, exceeds the outlay on the investment. On marginal investments, the present value will equal the outlay. Put another way, in the absence of taxes, the net operating income from an investment must cover the real interest rate plus depreciation. After allowance for taxation, the equilibrium condition for investment is

$$\rho = (r + d) \frac{1 - k - \tau z}{1 - \tau} \tag{1}$$

where ρ is the marginal product of capital (initial net operating income), r is the real after-tax financing rate, d is the economic depreciation rate, k is the investment tax credit, τ is the business tax rate, and z is the present value of tax depreciation allowances. The right side of equation (1) is the "investment hurdle rate" for a particular asset. The lower the hurdle rate, the greater will be production of the asset and the lower will be the productivity of the marginal investment (ρ). In a "neutral" tax system, $\rho - d$ would be the same for all assets. That is, the net marginal productivity of all investments would be equal at the margin.

The real after-tax financing rate (r) depends on the pre-tax debt rate, the rate at which interest is deductible, the required return on equity (which depends on capital gains taxation), the loan-to-value ratio, and the inflation rate. In general, r is higher for industrial (corporate) structures than for noncorporate real estate because the required equity rate is higher owing to the double taxation of dividends. In general, for noncorporate structures I assume a real after-tax interest rate of 0.0275 both before and after tax reform (the cut in tax rates tends to raise r but a decline in pretax interest rates lowers r); a real rate of 0.0375 is assumed for corporate investments.

The present value of tax depreciation, in the absence of trading, is simply the tax depreciation stream, with the basis adjusted for the tax credit received, discounted by nominal after-tax interest rates:

$$z = (1 - kB) \sum_{t=1}^{L} \frac{\text{TAXD}_t}{[(1 + r)(1 + \pi)]^t} \tag{2}$$

where B is the fraction of the tax credit by which the basis is reduced, TAXD_t is the depreciation in year t, and π is the expected inflation rate, assumed to be 0.045. Tax-based trading will occur if the tax benefits from the trade, τz, exceed the costs of reestablishing the depreciable base, $\beta + \tau_{cg}$, where β is the selling cost and τ_{cg} is the statutory capital gains tax. More formally, if trading every J periods ($J \geq L$) is advantageous, up to T trades, the present value of tax depreciation becomes

$$z' = z + \left[z - \frac{\beta + \tau_{cg}}{\tau} \right] \sum_{j=1}^{T} \left[\frac{1 - d}{1 - r} \right] j'. \tag{2'}$$

As it turns out, trading was advantageous under 1985 law but will not be under the Tax Reform Act of 1986 and was not under 1970s tax law.

In this analysis, we assume that the marginal tax rate of the marginal investor was 0.45 (including state and local income taxes) under old law and 0.36 under new. The 0.0275 real rate and 0.045 expected inflation rate are consistent with a 0.09 percent risk-free interest rate and a 0.023 percent risk premium under old law and a 0.08 percent risk-free rate under new law.

For owner-occupied housing, the τ's in equation (1) are zero (imputed rents are not taxed and no depreciation is deductible for tax purposes). Moreover, the real after-tax financing rate and the value of property tax deductions vary with the household's tax bracket. To make the analysis comparable to that of depreciable properties, we compute the net (of depreciation) marginal product for owner-occupied housing as

$$\rho - d = (1 - \tau)(i - .005) + p - \pi - \tau\tau_p$$
$$= i + p - \pi - \tau(i + \tau_p) - (1 - \tau).005, \tag{3}$$

where i is the nominal debt rate, p is the risk premium, π is the expected inflation rate, τ_p is the property tax rate, and the $(1 - \tau).005$ is the interest rate subsidy received by households with incomes under \$100,000 because of mortgage pass-through programs of the Federal agencies. The same p and π values are used as above, and τ_p is set equal to 0.012. Net required pretax returns ($\rho - d$) are reported in Table 9.3 of the text for a variety of assets both before and after the 1986 Tax Act.

Notes

1. Parts of this paper draw heavily on earlier work with James Follain and David Ling. More specifically, the first two sections respectively are based on P. H. Hendershott, J. R. Follain, and D. C. Ling, "Effects on Real Estate," in J. A. Pechman, ed., *Tax Reform and the U.S. Economy* (Washington: Brookings Institution, 1987) 71–94 and J. R. Follain, P. H. Hendershott, and D. C. Ling, "Understanding the Real Estate Provisions of Tax Reform: Motivation and Impact," *National Tax Journal* 40 (September 1987) 363–372.

2. The households for which calculations are reported are also assumed to have one wage earner and the average fringe benefits and nonhousing itemized deductions of their income classes (based on 1983 SOI data), to own houses of dollar value equal to twice their AGIs and to pay property taxes equal to 1.2 percent of their house values.

3. See Hendershott, Follain, and Ling, "Effects on Real Estate" for a discussion of all the tax shelter changes relevant to real estate.

4. P. H. Hendershott, "Tax Changes and Capital Allocation in the 1980s," in M. Feldstein, ed., *The Effects of Taxation on Capital Formation* (Chicago: University of Chicago Press, 1987).

5. M. Feldstein and L. Summers made a case for cutting taxes on capital income to offset the increase in inflation. See "Inflation and the Taxation of Capital Income in the Corporate Sector," *National Tax Journal* 32 (December 1979) 445–470.

6. Hendershott, Follain, and Ling, "Effects on Real Estate."

7. The weighted average cost of capital is used as a discount rate. It equals $(1 - \tau)i + (1 - \tau^*) \times .03$, where 0.03 is the pretax risk premium and τ^*, a weighted average of the regular income and effective capital tax rate, is the tax rate applied to the premium.

8. M. Feldstein and J. Slemrod made a case for low (or zero) taxation of inflationary gains. See "Inflation and the Excess Taxation of Capital Gains on Corporate Stock," *National Tax Journal* 32 (June 1979) 107–188.

9. As Hendershott, Follain, and Ling note in "Effects on Real Estate," this result is sensitive to both the assumed marginal tax rate of the marginal investor in real estate and the assumed change in interest rates.

10. Some higher estimates that have been obtained are based on a misspecification of the traditional discounted cash flow model (see Follain, Hendershott, and Ling, "Understanding Tax Reform," 368–369).

11. These data have been generously supplied by David Ling. The married couples are assumed to have two dependents and the other household heads to have one. With more dependents, the percentage tax cuts would be greater.

Chapter 10
The Voucher/Production Debate

John C. Weicher

For close to two decades housing policy debates have centered on the broad question of whether to build new housing for the poor or to rely on the existing privately-owned housing stock. This basic issue has been addressed in each of the last three major housing policy studies, dating back to the Kaiser Committee in 1968, and it will undoubtedly be revisited as Congress considers housing policy in the next few years.

Amid continuing debate, both approaches have been employed. New construction was the sole policy until the mid-1960s and has been the dominant policy until recently. Use of the existing housing stock has been growing since the Section 8 program was established in 1974, and it has been the basic policy of the United States since 1983. Some new construction programs continue, however.

The debate and the plurality of programs have resulted in a rich literature on housing policy issues. This chapter summarizes current thinking about the relative merits and problems of the two approaches. It applies consistent criteria to different programs, insofar as possible and applicable. Information is drawn from many sources: program data; formal program evaluations (including the Experimental Housing Allowance Program); independent studies of the programs and evaluations of the evaluations; and analyses of housing market behavior that provide insights into the effects of various programs. Unfortunately, while the literature is indeed voluminous, it is nonetheless true that some important questions have been answered less fully and categorically than is desirable for policy formulation.

The chapter begins with a taxonomy of subsidized housing programs, identifying the important differences among them for policy purposes. It then discusses in turn their effects on assisted households, with regard to housing quality changes and household participation; their effects in housing markets, with special attention to outcomes in different market conditions; and their cost.

The discussion is limited to HUD rental programs, and focuses on those assisting "the poor." It ignores Section 235 and the homeownership components of the Supply Experiment, as well as the Farmers Home Administration programs. It gives little attention to Sections 221 and 236, which were designed to reach people too well off for public housing.

The Programs: From Public Housing to EHAP

Whether to construct new housing or to use existing stock necessarily determines some aspects of the programs. But not all. Programs of both types vary in a number of dimensions. This section classifies current and past programs on the basis of the most important program parameters. The major programs include low-rent public housing; Section 8 New Construction; Section 8 Existing Housing; the Freestanding Housing Voucher; and the Experimental Housing Allowance Program (EHAP) (mainly the Demand and Supply Experiments). The first two are the "new construction" programs (except for the small Section 23 Leased Public Housing Program from 1965 to 1974).

Section 8 New Construction was terminated in 1983, and the housing allowance experiments ended at various dates in the late 1970s. The other programs continue. In recent years additional subsidy commitments have been made primarily in Section 8 Existing Certificates and the voucher demonstration. New construction (primarily the Section 202 program for the elderly) accounted for less than 20 percent of the additional units authorized in 1985 and 1986.

Rehabilitation has been part of both Section 8 programs and the voucher demonstration (separate from the freestanding component). This can create confusion. In most respects, rehab programs are much more akin to new construction than to existing housing programs.

Subsidy Mechanisms

The most important difference between housing programs is whether the subsidy is tied to the unit (project-based) or tied to the household (tenant-based). In all new construction programs, the subsidy is tied to the unit. A decision is made to subsidize a particular project, not a particular household. Units in the project carry a subsidy for any resident; the household receives the benefit of the subsidy while it lives in the unit. Nearly all rehabilitation programs are similar to new construction in this respect, including the Section 8 Moderate Rehabilitation program, which is technically a subprogram under Section 8 Existing Housing. The rental rehabilitation component of the voucher demonstration is an exception. Units have to be rented mainly to low- and moderate-income tenants for a period of seven years; the subsidy stops if higher-income tenants move in. The subsidy can also be tied to the unit in an existing housing program, as in the Section 8 Loan Management/Property Disposition program (LM/PD) of the late 1970s, and the Section 23 Leased Public Housing program.

Subsidies are tied to the household in the Section 8 certificate program, the freestanding voucher, and all components of EHAP. If the subsidized household chooses to move, it can continue to receive assistance. It does not automatically do so; that depends on whether its new home meets program standards. The landlord of the previously occupied unit no longer receives a payment, however, unless another subsidized household chooses to move in.

A related question is whether the household or the local public housing authority (PHA) locates a unit to begin with. In the new construction programs, of course, the agency does. The same is true in the rehabilitation programs and Section 8 LM/PD. In other programs, either is possible. A few households in Section 23 found their own apartments, but most were offered units in buildings that the PHA had already leased. In Section 8 Existing Housing, many PHAs maintain lists of landlords willing to participate, and anecdotal evidence indicates that agencies have found units for some tenants.

The payment mechanism differs among existing housing programs. For both certificates and vouchers, the PHA pays the subsidy to the landlord on behalf of the tenant. In the housing allowance, the payment went to the tenant. This placed more responsibility on the tenant, who had to pay the rent personally every month or face eviction. The experiment thus functioned more like a private market transaction between tenant and landlord. In the absence of housing quality standards, the landlord need not even know that the tenant is being subsidized, though this is unlikely in practice.

Subsidy Formulas

All subsidy programs now condition the subsidy on the tenant's income. Public housing originally subsidized only the capital cost of the unit, with the tenant being responsible for operating costs. This was changed by the Brooke Amendments in the late 1960s and early 1970s, and by court decisions prohibiting PHAs from evicting tenants whose incomes were too low for them to meet the operating costs.

The tenant's required share of income has varied. Originally, when public housing was started, it was 20 percent. It rose during the 1960s as tenant incomes declined, before being capped at 25 percent by the Brooke Amendments. The 25 percent ratio applied to other programs, including Section 8. In 1981, it was raised further to 30 percent, to be phased in over five years. In 1984, Congress increased the deductions from income before calculating the rent/income ratio, effectively rolling back about one-quarter of the 1981 increase.

Programs have different bases for determining the maximum subsidy. Public housing payments are determined by cost—capital costs and operating costs. Maximum operating cost subsidies are based on a formula (the Performance Funding System) that estimates the operating costs of a well-run housing project, given the climate, the characteristics of the units, and other factors. Section 8 subsidies have been determined on the basis of Fair Market

Rents (FMRs)—the cost of living in modest but decent housing in the local housing market. The FMRs have been calculated differently in the New Construction and Existing Housing programs, however. The New Construction FMRs were based on the rents in comparable *new* housing projects, unsubsidized projects of modest design. They could also be adjusted upward to compensate for special factors that raised construction, financing, or management costs. It seems fair to say that in practice, they were based as much on costs as on market rents.

Section 8 Existing FMRs have been set at a percentile of the distribution of rents paid by recent movers for adequate housing within the local market area. Originally they were set at the median rent; in 1984 this was changed to the 45th percentile, excluding new construction. In practice, this has not noticeably changed the FMRs.

The same limit applies to the freestanding voucher. The important difference between the two programs is that, in the certificate program, the FMR imposes a ceiling on rents as well as on subsidies. Thus, tenants cannot rent a unit costing more than a set amount, under that program. With the freestanding voucher, however, the household can rent a more expensive unit and pay the additional amount from its own income, if it chooses to. This should make it easier for households to find satisfactory housing. It should also result in better housing and higher rent/income ratios, on average, since some tenants are likely to choose housing that rents for more than the FMR. The latter outcomes, however, are slightly less likely, because one feature of the voucher can offset the removal of the rent ceiling. If a household can find an acceptable unit renting for less than the FMR, it can keep the difference. In the certificate program, lower rents translate into lower subsidies rather than lower tenant rental payments. Thus to the extent that households take advantage of this "shopping incentive" in the voucher, they enjoy a lower rent burden; and if rents reflect quality, they will live in lower quality housing. (They will still have to meet the Section 8 program quality standards.) In practice, it is likely that the removal of the ceiling will be more important than the shopping incentive, and on balance both rent burdens and housing quality will be higher for voucher recipients than for certificate holders.

The housing allowance experiments used a variety of formulas. The Supply Experiment and one component of the Demand Experiment (the Housing Gap) used an approach similar to the voucher. The other Demand Experiment formula (Percent of Rent) paid the household a fixed percentage of its monthly rent, without reference to the cost of housing in its market area.

Program Coverage

With one exception, housing assistance has never been an entitlement for the poor. Public housing was originally conceived as part of public works, to fight the Depression in the 1930s. The cost of building new housing for all eligible low-income households has been prohibitive. The cost of existing housing has also been too high to make rent subsidies an entitlement, in the view of successive Administrations and Congresses. The only U.S. experience with an entitlement is the Supply Experiment, which offered subsidies to all eligible low-income households in two metropolitan areas, Green Bay and South Bend.

Housing Quality Standards

Also with one exception, all programs have imposed minimum quality standards for subsidized units. The Demand Experiment included several components without physical standards—the Percent of Rent component and some variants of the Housing Gap component, in which program standards were established as a minimum rent level (either "high" or "low"), rather than in physical terms.

Standards have varied between programs, along so many dimensions that it is generally impossible to rank programs by the stringency of their standards. A few conclusions are possible.

First, Section 8 Acceptability Criteria basically require units to meet FHA Minimum Property Standards and applicable state and local codes. The same criteria were applied to both New Construction and Existing Housing units. The freestanding voucher uses these standards as well.

Second, within EHAP, standards were apparently higher in practice in the Demand Experiment than in the Supply Experiment, though this was not intentional. The Demand Experiment standards were based on standards developed by the American Public Health Association; the Supply Experiment, on a model code developed by the Building Officials of America. Unfortunately, it is not possible to compare EHAP and Section 8 standards.[1]

Third, all the programs have set standards that are well above any of the commonly-used measures of "standard" or "adequate" housing that analysts have developed from the broad national housing data bases, such as the decennial Census of Housing and the Annual (now American) Housing Survey. The traditional criterion for substandard housing from the decennial Census— "dilapidated or lacking complete plumbing"—has been superseded since 1970 by more elaborate measures of inadequacy based on the AHS. Several government agencies, including the Congressional Budget Office, the Department of Housing and Urban Development, and the Office of Management and Budget, have constructed these measures. All of them set a higher standard for adequacy than the traditional Census definition, but a lower standard than any program.[2]

Term of Subsidy

The term of the subsidy is not a key parameter. It can easily be varied within any program, without changing other aspects. In practice, the term is important for budgetary purposes, and is also sometimes regarded as an indicator of political commitment to housing.

New construction programs have traditionally been financed by bonds or mortgages, in the same manner as private housing. The term of the subsidy was therefore established as the term of the instrument. In the early 1980s, terms ranged from 20 to 40 years in Section 8; the average was 23 years.[3] Public housing has recently been financed over 30 years. In 1986, however, the financing mechanism was changed; new construction projects in the future will be financed through upfront capital grants, rather than bonds or mortgages. This does not change the cost, in terms of present value, but it simplifies the budgetary accounting; when projects are paid for by bonds over a period of years, the Federal budget for the year that the project is authorized must include budget authority for the total amount of the payments over the full period.

Terms have been much shorter in the existing housing programs. Section 8 certificates carried a 15-year term until 1987, when the term was shortened to five years. The voucher runs for five years. Terms in EHAP varied; three years in the Demand Experiment, five years in the Supply Experiment. In both cases, subsidized households were supposed to be assisted to transfer to the Section 8 Existing Housing program at the end of the experiment, to make the household's response to the subsidy as nearly like its response to an ongoing program as possible.

Mobility Requirements

Households in new construction programs are required to move, by definition. The same has been true in practice for rehabilitation programs. Mobility has not been required in Section 8 Existing Housing, the freestanding voucher, or EHAP. The household can remain in its original unit if the unit meets program standards, or if it is upgraded to meet the standards. Otherwise, the household must move to an acceptable unit in order to receive assistance.

Housing Quality

The most important objective of housing policy has traditionally been to improve housing quality for the poor. In 1949, Congress established the national housing goal of "a decent home in a suitable living environment for every American family." Congress has never formally defined "decent" (or, for that matter, "suitable" or "living environment"), but concern about the housing of the poor and other disadvantaged groups has remained and the goal has been reaffirmed, as for instance in the Housing and Urban Development Act of 1968. The Congressional Joint Committee on Housing in 1948 offered the first and only definition of inadequate housing, concluding that "a reasonable measure" would be "the number of nonfarm units shown by the reports of the Census Bureau to be in need of major repairs, together with all units in urban areas which lack private inside bath and toilet." [4] This definition, expanded to include rural housing, was used by all subsequent housing policy studies through the early 1970s, when the Census Bureau discontinued counting dilapidated units (the successor to units in need of major repairs). The HUD, CBO, and OMB criteria mentioned in the previous section are essentially successors to the traditional Census definition, though they set a higher quality standard.

This history suggests that Congress has usually measured housing problems in terms of a quality standard, and that the objective of housing programs has been to raise housing quality to the standard. This is one way to evaluate housing programs: to set a standard and determine how many households meet it, before and after the program. Another approach is to measure changes in housing quality along a continuum, asking how many households have improved their housing, and by how much. This chapter surveys the evidence of quality improvement on the basis of both concepts.

Congress has been especially concerned about the effectiveness of existing housing programs in improving housing quality. It has been skeptical as to whether the programs are able to reach the people who live in bad housing. It has also been concerned that poor people will not use the subsidies to live in better housing; either they will not choose to do so or they will not be able to do so, because landlords will simply raise rents.

These questions are seldom raised with respect to any of the new construction programs. It is commonly assumed that new projects solve housing quality problems. But they are certainly relevant, at a minimum in order to compare programs. In fact, the answers are not obvious, because from 1968 to 1988 there was no requirement in any housing program that subsidy recipients had to live in bad housing in order to be eligible for assistance. [5] They just had to be poor. Not all poor people live in bad housing.

Current Housing Problems

William Apgar describes the housing condition of the poor in Chapter 2 of this volume. In order to provide a frame of reference for the evaluation of housing programs, however, it is helpful to summarize the most recent data on housing problems among households eligible for assistance (very-low-income renters, those with incomes at 50 percent or less of the area median, adjusted for household size). The data are taken from the AHS for 1987.

Three types of housing problems are commonly identified: low quality; inadequate space; and excessive cost. The 1987 data show that about 15 percent of very-low-income renters lived in inadequate housing, as measured by a criterion developed at HUD over the last decade. Less than five percent lived in adequate housing but were crowded; there was more than one person per room in the housing unit. The majority, 60 percent, lived in adequate housing without crowding, but paid more than 30 percent of their income in order to do so. The remainder, just over 20 percent, experienced none of these problems; many of these households probably lived in subsidized housing. (Some of the households in inadequate or crowded housing also suffered a high rent burden; the tabulations prepared by HUD[6] do not identify households with multiple problems.) The data for 1985 and 1987 are not fully consistent with those for earlier years, but it seems clear that the problems of quality and crowding have been gradually improving, while the problem of affordability has been becoming more serious.

With this housing situation among poor renters, it is by no means obvious that subsidy recipients in any program will automatically be drawn from those living in bad housing.

Achieving Decent Housing

Existing housing programs have often been criticized for failing to serve the people in the worst housing.[7] There is general agreement among analysts of the housing allowance experiments that participation was much lower among these households.[8] The basis for this conclusion is mainly that many households dropped out of the experiment rather than move to better housing, when their current homes failed the initial quality inspection.

Given the current housing conditions of the poor, however, this is perhaps not too surprising. The participation pattern, moreover, has not been unique to existing housing programs. In public housing, for example, HUD program data indicate that only about half of the new tenants during the first half of the 1970s originally lived in substandard housing. The proportion dropped steadily from year to year between 1967 and 1976, the latest year for which this information was published. This is contemporaneous with EHAP, and the proportion of substandard units is similar to the proportion among participating Supply Experiment renters: about half the allowance recipients originally lived in housing that failed the EHAP standards.

The similarity should not be pushed too far. The public housing program definition of "substandard" was not the traditional Census definition, but a more elastic notion based on local housing codes as well. There is no way of determining whether it was comparable to the EHAP standard. Furthermore, there is no information on the housing quality of the universe of eligible households for either program, so there is no basis for comparing participation rates for households by housing quality. The point is not to make precise comparisons, but to indicate that the comparisons should be made.

To my knowledge, there has been only one systematic comparison of housing quality improvements in new construction and existing housing programs. This is the Section 8 evaluation undertaken by Abt Associates for HUD in the late 1970s.[9] This study compared participation rates by the household's original housing quality, between the two programs and between participants and nonparticipants in each program. The study found that each program reached households in bad housing about in proportion to the incidence of these households in the eligible population. Inadequate housing was measured by a standard developed by CBO; households at the eligibility limit (80 percent of area median) could clearly afford to meet the CBO standard without assistance.[10]

Some 24 percent of participants in Section 8 New Construction originally lived in inadequate housing, compared to 21 percent of the eligible population. In the Existing Housing (certificate) program, 19 percent of participants originally lived in bad housing, compared to 19 percent of the eligible population. (The percentages for the eligible populations differ because two additional metropolitan areas were included in the Existing Housing sample.)

The difference in participation rates was on the margin of statistical significance, given the sample sizes. That is, both programs were about equally effective. Section 8 New Construction did a better job in helping people improve their housing, however. Only one percent of households lived in inadequate housing in the program, compared to six percent of certificate holders. The net effect was that 23 percent of assisted households in Section 8 New Construction moved from substandard to standard housing, compared to 13 percent for Section 8 Existing Housing.

This comparison is incomplete because it ignores differences in the willingness to participate in different programs. The existing housing program reaches a broader universe. Any household willing to participate in Section 8 New Construction is willing to move, by definition; certificate holders do not have to move, necessarily.

A more appropriate basis for comparison would be participation rates by housing quality for those households willing to move. Among Section 8 Existing subsidy recipients, this is almost the same as those who did move: 90 percent of those who moved were willing to move, and 90 percent of those who stayed in the same unit were unwilling to move.[11] Some 32 percent of movers originally lived in inadequate housing; 7 percent still did so after they moved; 25 percent, net, moved from substandard to standard housing. These figures are comparable to Section 8 New Construction. But in addition, some households who were willing to move were unable to find units and dropped out of the program; they should be included also. The study does not identify or enumerate these households; they cannot be separated from those who were unwilling to move and dropped out because their current home failed to meet the standards. Evidence from EHAP suggests that a large share of the households dropping out fall into the latter category,[12] but does not allow more precise quantification. A further, probably minor, complication is that both programs have waiting lists; the households receiving assistance are only a sample of the households that want to participate, and they may live in different housing conditions than those on the waiting lists.

The voucher demonstration evaluation indicates essentially similar findings. Among all voucher and certificate holders combined, 30 percent of movers originally lived in inadequate housing.[13] The evaluation does not report how many lived in inadequate housing after moving. It appears also that 30 percent originally lived in inadequate housing among successful voucher and certificate holders who were willing to move; but this figure excludes families that lived with other families to begin with.[14]

The safest conclusion seems to be that Section 8 programs and the voucher did about equally well in helping low-income households upgrade from substandard to standard quality housing. The new construction program may have done slightly better.

Improvement by Program Standards

The Abt evaluation also compared the programs on the basis of the Section 8 quality standards. These standards are much higher than the CBO criterion, and far more households in both programs failed to meet them in their original housing. The failure rates were 64 percent for households in the new construction program, 66 percent for those in existing housing. Section 8 New Construction was much more successful in raising households above the program standards: 11 percent failed them in the new unit, compared to 55 percent of certificate holders.[15] The failure rate in the existing housing program has apparently continued, according to later reports by the HUD Inspector General; however, the violations of program standards are typically minor and the housing units are of generally good quality.[16] It should be noted that these reports are less extensive and less statistically sophisticated than the Abt study.

There is no direct information on the proportion of low-income renters whose units meet the Section 8 standards. But it is possible to make some estimates, by comparing the rental value of Section 8 units to the rent for private housing occupied by the poor, on the reasonable assumption that rent is a good measure of quality. The rent data also provide some insight into the structure of the programs and the effects of alternative quality standards.

The average FMR for the units included in the study sample was $267.[17] The 1979 Annual Housing Survey reports that over 60 percent of unsubsidized rental units in Standard Metropolitan Statistical Areas (SMSAs) had lower rents. Most SMSAs in the study were large; a national study would probably have shown a lower average FMR, more consistent with HUD regulations (FMRs were supposed to be set at the median for standard units occupied by recent movers), and a smaller fraction of renters, perhaps around half, living in housing that failed to meet the Section 8 quality standards. If that rough estimate is correct, then both Section 8 programs succeeded in reaching households whose units failed the program standards.

Program-Induced Quality Changes

One of the most common conclusions about existing housing programs is that they do not result in much quality improvement. Because housing quality has many dimensions—space, facilities, structural condition, location— quality changes are usually measured in practice by changes in rents, either actual changes or changes in the estimated market rental based on the characteristics of the units. Evidence from the Supply Experiment, for example, indicates that assisted households raised the quality of their housing by about 5 to 10 percent.[18] Evidence from the Section 8 Existing Housing Program indicates, if anything, a still smaller effect, around 4 percent or less.[19] Less than 20 percent of the assistance payments in the Supply Experiment went for better housing; the rest was used in effect to buy other goods and services.

One reason for the small improvement is the fact that both programs served so many people who already lived in adequate housing, as measured by program standards. Most of those households chose to continue living in the same unit, with the subsidy. Movers had larger increases in housing quality, about 15 percent in both programs. And in the Supply Experiment, there was modest upgrading in the existing stock—about $250 to $300 worth per unit, in today's dollars, for about one-third of the units that did not originally meet program standards. Moreover, these modest improvements enabled a substantial number of participants to meet the program quality standards; about three-quarters of program participants were living in standard housing after two years, compared to less than half originally.

Comparable data on quality changes for new construction programs are rare. It is common to assume that quality improvements are large and leave it at that. The Abt evaluation, however, did make several comparisons between the Section 8 programs. The study found that housing improvements accounted for about the same share of HUD costs per unit in each program, 40 percent in new construction, 45 percent in existing housing. The remainder went for tenant rent reductions (in effect, tenant purchases of other goods and services), and in the new construction program, program costs that did not result in better housing—that is, rents in excess of market value.[20] These figures omit administrative costs and indirect government costs, which would reduce the share for new construction more than the share for existing housing. Including administrative costs only, for example, housing improvement would account for about 30 percent of per-unit new construction outlays, and about 40 percent in existing housing.[21]

Abt also measured the change in housing quality for individual households. Households in the new construction program enjoyed better housing.

One reason is that the new units were better. The market rent of the typical Section 8 Existing Housing unit was estimated at $265, very close to the FMR, while the typical Section 8 New Construction unit had an estimated market rent of $295—well above the minimum quality standards. The average improvement was about 25 percent for those who moved into new units, compared to 15 percent for movers in the certificate program. The dollar value of the improvement was similarly larger—more than twice as large for households in the new construction program than for certificate holders who moved. Households that did not move showed very little improvement.[22]

Participation

Program effectiveness in serving people who live in bad housing is part of the general question of program participation. Some have argued that new construction programs are inequitable: a minor fraction of the poor are able to live in much better housing, while a large number of equally poor and presumably equally deserving deserving families receive no help at all. Others maintain that participation in existing housing programs is low overall and that the programs do not reach those who have been the subject of special concern.

Participation and Program Standards

The EHAP Supply Experiment, the only entitlement housing program in our history, offered assistance to every eligible household in the two small metropolitan areas of Green Bay and South Bend. It provides the best basis for estimating overall participation in any entitlement program using the existing housing stock.

Somewhat more than half—56 percent—of the low-income renters in these areas wanted to participate in the housing allowance program.[23] Whether this is high or low is a matter of subjective judgment. It is fairly close to the participation rate in Food Stamps, which has a similar income limit.[24] Since 1981, when the Food Stamps income ceiling was lowered to 130 percent of the poverty line (except for households with an elderly member), the participation rate has been about 65 percent.

Actual participation in the housing allowance was much lower, however, because units had to meet the program's quality standards in order for the households to receive the allowance payments. About 75 percent of the interested renters were able and willing to meet the standards, so the overall participation rate was about 42 percent.

The housing standards requirement is unique among low-income benefit programs. Households have to select housing with certain specific attributes in order to participate, whether they value those attributes or not. Food Stamps, by contrast, can be used for any foodstuff (alcohol and tobacco are excluded). Some medical services are not covered by Medicaid, but it is unlikely that program participation is reduced because low-income households would rather have other medical services than those provided by the program.

The standards requirement, however, affects housing program participation; the higher the standard, the fewer the households willing to participate in existing housing programs. This is clearest in the Demand Experiment. It also seems to be a reasonable inference from the comparison of the two experiments.[25] The EHAP Supply Experiment standards were the lowest of any existing housing program; participation rates would be lower if any other program were to be established as an entitlement.

The willingness of low-income households to participate in new construction programs has never been considered an interesting policy question and has never been studied, to my knowledge. The evidence on participation and mobility in both the Demand and Supply Experiments, however, suggests that a significant number of eligible households would not choose to move into a public housing or other subsidized project; they like their neighborhood and they like their present home.[26] About 30 percent of the households in the Demand Experiment were satisfied with their living conditions and made no effort to search for better housing.

Overall Participation in Existing Housing Programs

The ability of households to participate in existing housing programs has been a continual policy concern. Early evidence from Section 8 Existing Housing indicated that less than half of all households that qualified for the program were actually able to find satisfactory housing.[27] The latest evidence from the voucher study, however, is that success rates in Section 8 are now much higher, 60 percent in 1985 and 1986 compared with 45 percent in 1979. The success rate for the voucher is slightly higher, around 65 percent.[28] There are several possible explanations for the improvement. The most plausible are increased experience with the program by landlords, tenants, and PHAs, so that program operations are smoother and more effective; or, alternatively, self-selection by tenants who are likely to succeed. The success rate for the voucher (a new program in 1985) also rose between 1985 and 1986, which is consistent with these explanations. The higher participation rate in the voucher is expected, because the voucher removes the FMR constraint that limits the availability of units in the Section 8 certificate program.

Other possible explanations for the rising participation rate in the certificate program include higher vacancy rates and looser standards. Neither seems to be consistent with the pattern of results.

Minority Participation

Housing policy has long been concerned with the problems of special groups among the poor: minorities, the elderly, and large families, for example.

Some information is available about participation for different groups in different programs. It is surprising to learn that the most recent program participation data available from HUD is for the year 1979, in the last *HUD Statistical Yearbook*.[29] A subsequent HUD staff tabulation indicates that assisted minority households lived more often in public housing than in Section 8 Existing Housing.[30] Both programs served minority households to a greater extent than Section 8 New Construction. In addition, as of 1979, more households with children were being served in Section 8 Existing Housing than in public housing.[31]

These tabulations provide no basis for analyzing or understanding the differences. The best available information comes from the current voucher study, the earlier Abt Section 8 evaluation, and EHAP. Most of this information pertains to existing housing programs, and analysis has centered on racial and ethnic differences in participation.

The main factual conclusion is that minority households participate more frequently than whites in existing housing programs, but this is because many more minority households apply for the programs. Among households that want to participate, fewer blacks and Hispanics are able to find acceptable housing. As of 1979, for example, about half of white certificate holders were successful, compared to just over a quarter of minority households.[32] Success rates have increases substantially for all groups since then, to about 75 percent for white applicants, 60 percent for blacks, and 50 percent for Hispanics.[33] These figures apply to both vouchers and certificates. The only significant difference between the programs is a slightly higher success rate for Hispanics in the voucher program.

Several factors apparently contribute to the different success rates. Evidence from the Demand Experiment indicates that minority households placed a somewhat lower value on housing subsidies than did whites.[34] This is the only attempt to determine the subjective value of housing subsidies to their recipients, and the analysis has not been extended beyond the experimental sites (Pittsburgh and Phoenix). A second factor, interacting with the first and probably more important, is that fewer minority households lived in acceptable housing to begin with, so fewer were able to qualify without moving or upgrading. In all existing housing programs, households that had to move or upgrade have been less likely to participate. This is hardly a satisfactory conclusion, politically or analytically. The differences in initial housing quality have not been studied. Discrimination is an obvious explanation; another could be differences in income within the eligible population.

There are also locational differences. Minority households are concentrated in metropolitan areas that have lower success rates, but within each area (and adjusting for quality differences), minorities have been as successful as whites. In addition, PHAs in places with large minority populations apparently intrepreted the housing quality standards more stringently, at least as of 1979.[35] This pattern has not been studied further.

For policy purposes, the relevant question is: are blacks and Hispanics in bad housing and willing to move served as well by existing housing programs as are whites in the same situation? This question has not been directly answered in the studies to date. The indirect evidence in most cases is consistent with the position that they are equally well served. That is, blacks and Hispanics *per se* have the same success rates as whites, given their initial housing condition and location.

Evidence of racial and ethnic discrimination is reported in the Demand Experiment. Local PHAs can help to overcome this problem. Minority households have been able to participate better when PHAs provide more services to help them find acceptable housing.[36]

Production programs are sometimes favored over existing housing programs because they circumvent the problem of discrimination and directly provide minorities with access to decent housing. Production programs can certainly achieve these objectives, but the record of Section 8 New Construction indicates that success is not automatic.

Through at least 1979, most Section 8 projects were located in neighborhoods with low minority populations and served few minority households; typically they served the white elderly. Minority households were about 15 percent of Section 8 New Construction tenants, compared to about 35 percent of eligible households.[37] The reasons for the failure to serve minority households more effectively have not been systematically studied. In the late 1970s, Section 202 took priority over other Section 8 programs; in some areas little or no money was available for nonelderly housing.[38] But participation rates for elderly minority households were lower than for elderly whites.[39]

Other Special Groups

Differences in participation rates for other groups, like the racial and ethnic differences, mainly reflect differences in the quality of their initial housing. For example, the elderly are better served in existing housing programs than younger households because they live in better housing to begin with; so are small families and families without children, for the same reason. The elderly have also apparently been given the benefit of the doubt in PHA enforcement of housing standards enabling them to qualify more easily, at least in the Section 8 program.[40] Households whose primary income source is welfare also have lower participation rates than households whose income comes from work, partly because the welfare households are larger as well as because of their initial housing situation.

There has been no evidence of differences between certificates and vouchers. Participation rates in the certificate program have risen for all these groups since 1979, and more for nonelderly households than for the elderly.[41] Large households have not been studied separately in the voucher demonstration, so there are no data on the change in their participation rates since 1979.

Market Effects and Effectiveness

This section shifts the focus from the effects of programs on individuals to their effects across a housing market as a whole and between different housing markets.

Rent Inflation

Probably the most common objection to existing housing programs has been that they simply let landlords raise rents without having to provide better housing. This concern was raised at the beginning of EHAP,[42] and every study of existing housing programs has addressed it since then.

The findings are clear-cut. Existing housing subsidies have not resulted in rent inflation. The Supply Experiments should have generated the biggest price increases, because they were entitlement programs. Rent increases in both Green Bay and South Bend were negligible.[43] The Demand Experiment showed a similar pattern, with the exception of one program variant in which the housing standard was established simply at a high minimum rent; in those circumstances the household paid the higher rent without trying to obtain value for the dollar.[44] The Abt Section 8 Existing Housing evaluation found rents for subsidized units to be about 4 to 5 percent above the expected market rent, based on the characteristics of the units,[45] but attributed it to "the fact that recipients paid the normal market rate when they were related to the landlord, as opposed to receiving the discounts usually obtained in such situations."[46] The same circumstances probably explain the very large increases in rents for households with extraordinarily low pre-program rents observed in an earlier certificate evaluation;[47] rents went up by an average of $100 per month in the program for households whose rent was initially less than $50. This is the only instance of apparent rent inflation in any of the program evaluations to date, and it is obviously atypical and irrelevant for most households. Preliminary evidence from the voucher demonstration is that more than half the households that did not move incurred small increases or actual decreases in rent, but the rents were not adjusted for quality changes.[48]

Market Conditions and Program Effectiveness

The effectiveness of existing housing programs in tight housing markets has been a long-standing policy concern. There are several possible problems: lower successful participation rates, less quality improvement and rent inflation—not just for participants, but for all low-income households in the metropolitan area.

"Tight" markets are usually thought of in terms of vacancy rates, but there are other aspects of the market that may be more important. These include the quality of the housing stock and the ability of housing producers to respond to an increase in demand.

The best evidence comes from the EHAP Supply Experiment, where an entitlement housing allowance was tested in two markets. The allowance worked better in the tighter market, Green Bay. The participation rate was higher and the effect on rents throughout the market was equally negligible. Green Bay's housing stock was generally better than South Bend's.

The voucher demonstration study provides some evidence on participation rates in different market conditions, but not as yet on quality improvements or rent changes. Both certificates and vouchers have worked well in a variety of market types. The exceptions are New York and Boston, both classified as tight markets by HUD area offices.[49] New York had successful participation rates in the 30 to 35 percent range for both programs and Boston between 40 and 45 percent. But success rates in two other tight markets, New Haven and Montgomery County in Maryland, were much higher, between 60 and 70 percent. These rates are within the range for much looser markets.

To date, there has been no attempt to analyze the differences between the markets. There are a number of possible explanations for the differences. New York is unique in many ways; it has a long history of rent control and its rental housing stock is of lower quality than other large metropolitan areas. Boston has only recently become a tight housing market; it has an old housing stock. On the other hand, New Haven is an old city as well. Montgomery County has a high-quality housing stock, but it has been subject to local growth controls that probably inhibit new construction. In the absence of further work, these explanations can only be considered speculative.

There have been several models of housing markets developed in order to understand the effect of alternative housing programs without having to put the programs into operation. The model used most extensively for this purpose was constructed at the Urban Institute in the 1970s. The Supply Experiment and the model both show that the quality of the housing stock is more important than the tightness of the market; participation rates are higher in metropolitan areas with a better housing stock, and quality improvement is greater.[50]

A model developed at HUD using actual Secton 8 program data is consistent with the Urban Institute model so far as it goes. This model analyzes rent inflation only, not participation or quality changes; it indicates that some inflation is more likely to occur in markets where the initial housing quality is low, because the demand for better housing as a result of the program is concentrated on a smaller supply of decent housing.[51] Even an entitlement program in an area with a very bad housing stock, however, would result in a rent increase of around five percent, which is not much above the EHAP experience. High vacancy rates reduce the impact.

These are long-run models, analyzing market changes over five to 10 years or even more. In the short run, no program "works" in a tight market. Sudden changes will drive rents up or down until the market or the government can begin to respond. Neither will respond fast enough for those facing large rent increases. The best evidence is that private builders will take perhaps five years to catch up with an unexpectedly tight market.[52] The government is likely to take about as long. Indeed, the slow pace of production has been a constant complaint about subsidized housing programs since at least the Douglas Commission some 20 years ago. Recent experience does not suggest much improvement. In the late 1970s both public housing and Section 8 projects typically took about three years from HUD approval to completion.[53] These figures understate the response time because they leave out the period of time *before* HUD approves a project, which can be considerable.

Before the government can respond effectively to a tight market situation, the market is likely to loosen up. Today's tight markets are not tomorrow's. In the early 1980s, the tight housing markets in the United States were in oil-producing areas, such as Houston and Denver. Now these are depressed markets; the tight markets are in the Northeast. Had the government begun to build public housing projects in Houston and Denver five years ago, those projects would now be coming on-stream when they are unnecessary and even redundant.

Housing Production and Preservation

A major issue with both types of programs has been their effect on the size of the housing stock. It is conceivable that subsidies given directly to low-income households would lead some developers to build housing in the hope that the people who received the subsidy would use it for the new housing. This would be most likely in an entitlement program, such as the EHAP Supply Experiment. Even in these circumstances, however, such a supply response is not really to be expected, and in fact there is no evidence that new low-income housing was built in either Green Bay or South Bend. The question has not been raised for other low-income existing housing programs that are not entitlements, but there is no reason to believe that any of them have generated new units.

Production programs obviously produce housing, but their effect on the housing stock is more complicated. New subsidized construction can displace new private construction that would have occurred in the absence of the subsidy program. The extent of displacement cannot be directly measured with program data; it must be inferred from analysis of the housing market. There have been two serious studies of displacement by Craig Swan and Michael Murray.[54] Both evaluated the effects of the moderate-income programs of the 1960s and 1970s—Sections 221, 235 and 236—and both found no net increase in the housing stock. Virtually all starts under these programs merely replaced unsubsidized starts, because they drew mortgage funds from private lenders who would otherwise have invested in conventional mortgages. Murray also analyzed public housing with somewhat different results. About three-quarters of the new public housing units represented an increase in the housing stock, in the short run; the remaining quarter displaced private construction. Over time, however, private construction fell off, because the new public housing increased the vacancy rate in the existing inventory. Eventually the displacement was nearly 100 percent, and there was little, if any, increase in the total housing stock. The adjustment period is long, however, more than 10 years, and in the interim the housing stock is larger than it would be if no public housing had been built. The difference between public housing and the moderate-income programs resulted from differences in financing; public housing was funded by government rather than private borrowing.

Swan's study ended with 1972 and Murray's with 1977; neither took account of Section 8. One can infer from Murray's analysis that there has been some long-term supply increase, to a lesser extent than for public housing, because both government and private financing mechanisms were used. These results would probably not hold today, however, because the financial system of the United States and especially the housing finance system are very different than they were in the mid-1970s. Differences in the immediate source of funds are probably much less important.

Preserving the existing stock of decent housing has been a goal of existing housing programs. Advocates have believed that tenants' ability to afford decent housing would encourage landlords to maintain their units adequately. This is reasonable, but hard to document, because the effect of better maintenance accumulates over time as repairs are made more or less regularly. There is some evidence from the first two years of the EHAP Supply Experiment on repairs undertaken for subsidized units. Many relatively small repairs did occur, but there is no comparable information for unsubsidized units in these markets. The EHAP data include both owners and renters, and the former can be compared with the Census Survey of Residential Alterations and Repairs. It appears that low-income homeowners in the EHAP sites did make more, and more expensive, repairs than low-income owners in other Midwestern metropolitan areas.[55] A similar analysis has not been undertaken for renters; nor has there been any attempt to analyze experience with existing housing programs in the context of a housing market or a housing maintenance model.

Preservation and maintenance is also a problem in some new construction units. About 15 percent of the current public housing stock needs major modernization;[56] much of the rest needs ongoing maintenance that cannot apparently be funded from tenant rents and operating subsidies. Maintenance problems also exist for some fraction of the Section 221 and 236 units built for moderate-income households.[57]

This limited information does not provide a basis for comparing programs. The point is simply that preserving the housing stock in decent condition is not automatic in new construction programs; it is an important and underappreciated achievement for any housing program.

Neighborhood Changes

Low-income housing programs are frequently considered in a neighborhood context. The location of the housing matters not only for the assisted households themselves but for the communities that they live in. This section considers three types of neighborhood effects that have been public policy issues: racial segregation and integration; economic integration; and neighborhood revitalization.

Promoting residential racial and ethnic integration has been a federal housing policy goal for many years, antedating interest in existing housing programs. The question of whether a housing allowance would contribute to integration was therefore raised when EHAP was begun in the early 1970s, as a counterpart to the issue of effective minority participation. But while federal policymakers were concerned that the allowance would not promote integration, some local groups and citizens were afraid that it would. The Supply Experiment was rejected by suburban officials in two high-minority metropolitan areas who felt that the allowance would help blacks and other minorities move from the central city into predominantly white jurisdictions.[58] In South Bend, the area finally selected, the suburban jurisdictions refused to participate until the experiment had been in operation for more than a year, and the last small town did not join for almost three years.[59]

Neither the hopes nor the fears were justified. Minority (and other) households moved less than expected, and most moves occurred within the neighborhood. There was some tendency for minority households to move out of the worst neighborhood in South Bend, but this had been going on before the experiment began. In the Demand Experiment, assisted black households in Pittsburgh did not move to more integrated neighborhoods, but assisted Hispanic households in Phoenix did, to a modest extent. Most analysts have concluded that the allowance had little, if any, effect on neighborhood racial patterns;[60] at most, it may have slightly accelerated racial mobility patterns already in progress.

The experience has been similar in Section 8 Existing Housing. Black households have been able to move to neighborhoods with a slightly lower minority concentration, on average.[61] (There were too few Hispanic households to offer a basis for any conclusions.) Mobility effects of the voucher, and the most recent certificate data, have not as yet been analyzed.

Minority experience in Section 8 New Construction has been quite different. Most new construction projects have been built in reasonably good city or suburban neighborhoods and have served mainly white elderly households. A disproportionately small number of minority households, again mainly elderly, have participated. Some of them have been able to move from predominantly minority neighborhoods into predominantly white ones, in the process. But the new construction program is probably less effective than the existing housing programs in promoting integration, because it serves so few minority households.[62]

The Abt Section 8 study is the most recent analysis of any new construction program; to my knowledge, there is no comparable study of conventional public housing or other production programs. As part of the EHAP Demand Experiment, however, project location and tenant composition were analyzed in Pittsburgh and Phoenix. The study concluded that high-minority projects were located in high-minority areas and low-minority projects in low-minority areas, for all programs, new and existing alike.[63]

Economic Integration

There is less evidence about economic integration, but the available data tells much the same story. The Abt Section 8 evaluation provides the only information. In the existing housing program, most households already lived in neighborhoods with a relatively low concentration of poverty; on average those who moved located in a slightly better neighborhood.[64] The Section 8 New Construction projects were often located in better neighborhoods, but they did not generate much economic integration. Relatively few households moved into a different neighborhood as a result of moving into a project. Apparently their main effect was to enable elderly couples and individuals to continue living in the same neighborhood, or the same kind of neighborhood, after they retired.[65]

Neighborhood Revitalization

Housing is located·in neighborhoods, and housing and community development programs are inevitably intertwined. One important rationale for federal housing subsidies is that better housing for individual families results in better neighborhoods for all residents, not just those receiving the subsidy.[66] Neighborhood effects have been systematically studied only in the EHAP Supply Experiment, with suggestive but inconclusive results. Modest repairs were made to a large number of housing units. Disproportionately more units were repaired in the neighborhoods with the worst housing. This pattern probably minimizes the possible neighborhood impact; the worst neighborhoods are not the best candidates for revival, even if a large number of housing units are modestly upgraded. It appears that repairs were not widespread enough to reach a critical mass and start any neighborhood on a clear path to revitalization, at least through the end of the experiment.[67] However, many households *thought* that the neighborhood had improved, particularly in neighborhoods with high participation rates.[68] This attitude could eventually result in revitalization in an ongoing voucher program.

Mobility patterns might also contribute to neighborhood changes, if assisted households chose to concentrate in marginal neighborhoods. This did not happen in the Supply Experiment either; in the words of two analysts, reviewing the results, "as a means of transforming neighborhoods, the program impact through moves is so small that it defies measurement." [69]

The Abt Section 8 evaluation did not evaluate neighborhood effects, but the evidence for individual households does not suggest that either program contributed to neighborhood revitalization. There is, however, one recent in-depth study of neighborhood housing markets for Chicago, which addresses the relationship between federal housing programs and neighborhood conditions. The authors concluded that older big-city neighborhoods are better served by existing housing programs; the programs encourage the occupancy and maintenance of the better older housing in the neighborhood. New construction programs, by contrast, weaken the neighborhood by reducing the demand for existing housing, particularly in neighborhoods with declining population.[70]

Housing Program Costs

The relative cost of different housing programs has been a subject of study and debate for two decades. Measuring costs is complicated; comparing measurements for different programs adds further complications. But some conclusions seem well established.

Making Comparisons

The scope of this discussion is limited to housing programs. The chapter does not address "welfare efficiency"—the extent to which poor families would prefer to have cash rather than housing with the same value. It is easy to show that cash is better from the standpoint of the recipient; the household can use the money entirely to buy better housing if it wants, or to buy more food, better clothing, etc., if that is what it prefers. The inefficiency of housing subsidies in this sense applies to all housing programs.

Housing programs have provided housing of widely differing quality. The cost comparisons reported in this section apply as much as possible to housing of the same quality in different programs. In some cases, the difference in quality is an important aspect of the differences between programs; these differences will be discussed where appropriate.

The comparisons attempt to include all the costs of programs, indirect as well as direct. Some programs have lower direct costs than others because of different financing mechanisms. For example, the direct cost of public housing was relatively low because projects were financed by tax-exempt, federally guaranteed bonds. However, the foregone tax revenue was greater than the difference in interest payments on the bonds, so the government as a whole lost money from the tax exemption and the total cost of public housing was higher than necessary.

Most analyses date from the 1970s; a few are slightly earlier or later. Many of the comparisons were developed as contributions to the fundamental housing policy debates of the period, beginning with the work of the Kaiser Committee in the late 1960s and ending with the President's Commission on Housing in the early 1980s. The comparisons are therefore not current, but there is no reason to believe that relative costs have changed significantly. Indeed, HUD policy analysts continue to use calculated costs for the new construction programs as of the early 1980s (updated for inflation) as the basis for estimating costs for the new construction programs now.

Cost Differences

The most important conclusion is that costs of new construction programs are much higher than costs for existing housing. The differences among the various new construction programs are minor by comparison, and the differences between certificates and vouchers are negligible.

One widely-cited estimate is that the total annual cost to the government of Section 8 New Construction was about double the cost of Section 8 Existing Housing.[71] This calculation is based on thorough and sophisticated analysis of the programs. It is still incomplete, however; it omits indirect costs such as tax revenue foregone from tax-exempt financing of some new construction projects. It also omits costs of program administration, but other studies indicate that administrative costs are nearly twice as high for new construction programs, so the differential would be about the same.[72] The cost comparison is not adjusted for housing quality differences, but the study found that new housing was about 10 percent better than existing housing (measured in terms of the rental value of the units). Accounting for quality differences and administrative costs (but not indirect costs), the cost differential was about 50 percent.[73]

These comparisons do not include the tenant's rental payment. The more common approach in the analytical literature is to calculate total costs of the programs, rather than the costs to the government or to the tenant. When tenant contributions are included, the relative cost differential is about 30 percent for the two Section 8 programs. Including administrative costs, the Section 8 Existing Housing program is perhaps 10 to 15 percent more expensive than private unsubsidized housing, so the new construction program is about 40 to 50 percent more expensive than unsubsidized private existing rental housing.

An analogous cost comparison has been employed in evaluations of public housing, where project development costs are compared to costs for unsubsidized housing. As an old long-established program, public housing has been studied more extensively than Section 8. Public housing costs have usually been calculated in comparison to private existing housing rather than to other programs, except in the Demand Experiment. Public housing and Section 8 New Construction appear to be about equally expensive. The central tendency of the analyses is that public housing has been about 25 to 50 percent more expensive than comparable private housing. The range of estimates is wide, partly because different markets have been studied at different times— from 15 percent in New York City in the 1960s[74] to over 100 percent in small towns in North Carolina in the early 1970s.[75] The most recent estimate is about 33 percent, for development costs only.[76] The shift to funding public housing by direct capital grants reduces the importance of other sources of cost differences (such as tax-exempt financing), but the difference in total costs is probably still greater than the difference in development costs.[77]

There are several reasons for the higher cost of subsidized housing. One is technical inefficiency; it is more expensive for the government to build housing, or for private developers to build housing for the government, than for private developers to build private housing.[78] A second reason is that many projects are undertaken when housing market conditions will not justify private construction—when construction costs are high relative to rents. This has been termed "economic inefficiency."[79]

In a long view, construction programs can look less expensive than existing housing. The President's Commission on Housing, for example, found that Section 8 FMRs were higher than public housing annual contributions and operating subsidies combined.[80] The main reason is that the projects were built when costs were lower, in nominal terms. The price level nearly tripled between 1965 and 1982, in an unprecedented peacetime inflation, driving up rents, construction costs, and interest rates. This unforeseen inflation transferred part of the real cost of subsidized housing from the taxpayer to the bondholder. A second factor is quality differences; it seems likely that the public housing units were less desirable than units renting for the FMR.[81]

The voucher study has investigated differences in program cost to the government, but not differences in efficiency. Vouchers cost the government six percent more than certificates in the first year that a family receives assistance, but only two percent more in the second year. The first-year cost difference is statistically significant, the second-year difference is not. The main reason for the higher cost is that voucher recipients may keep any difference between the FMR and their actual rent; the main reason why the costs converge is that annual increases are automatic in the certificate program and optional for the PHA in the voucher program.[82] The cost difference has received substantial press attention; it is minimal, however, compared to the difference between Section 8 New Construction and either program.

Conclusion

Since 1983, the voucher/production debate has been at a standstill. Section 8 Existing Housing—the certificate program—has essentially been the official housing policy of the United States. The Reagan Administration's voucher was only accepted by Congress on a permanent basis in 1988, after five years as a demonstration. A small annual volume of new public housing has been accepted by the Reagan Administration.

The reason for the stalemate is that neither vouchers nor production programs are a panacea, and advocates of both approaches at least implicitly recognize this. Conversely, critics of both approaches have been able to make telling points.

Production programs are expensive and because they are expensive they are inequitable as well. Moreover, production programs have failed to serve their original social purposes. In the 1930s, public housing was seen by urban reformers as a whole Great Society agenda by itself; it would lift the poor out of poverty by providing them with a safer, healthier living environment. This has not happened.

Vouchers seem to be less a housing program than an income transfer program for poor people who already live in decent housing. When EHAP began, most housing economists believed that existing housing subsidies would result in substantial housing improvement. Results have been much more modest.

This paper has attempted to compare new production and existing housing programs on an equal footing—to ask the same questions about each program and answer them on a comparable basis. On that basis, some of the arguments are one-sided and some common perceptions are probably wrong. Most poor people now live in decent housing, although they certainly do not live in luxury. They do not have to live in substandard housing in order to qualify for housing assistance. New construction and existing housing programs are about equally able to reach poor people in bad housing and place them in decent housing. But in addition, each type of program does something else. Existing housing programs serve poor people in decent but expensive housing and solve their rent burden problem; at the same time, they can continue to live in their home and their neighborhood. New construction programs reach poor people in decent housing and enable them to move into still better housing. They enjoy better housing, but their original housing was at least minimally adequate to begin with.

Minority households and other special groups can theoretically be better served in new construction programs. In practice, the record has been uneven. Section 8 New Construction was basically a program for the white elderly and projects were built in better neighborhoods; public housing has been much more a program for urban minorities in minority neighborhoods. Section 8 Existing Housing has served minorities better than the new construction program, and had some modest success in reducing racial and ethnic residential segregation, but many blacks and Hispanics who wanted to participate have been unable to find satisfactory housing. More help for minority households is desirable.

No program works well in tight markets, at least in the short run. New construction programs are notoriously slow; many families are unable to use vouchers or certificates when vacancy rates are low. But few markets remain tight for a long time, unless local governments make housing production unnecessarily expensive.

Vouchers will not result in new housing construction, but they may help preserve the stock of existing decent housing and they may be more effective in strengthening low-income neighborhoods and making them more liveable communities.

Production is much more expensive than vouchers. On a per-dollar basis, existing housing programs help more poor people move from inadequate to decent housing. On a per-dollar basis, both improve housing for subsidy recipients to about the same extent. Neither generates a large improvement for the average household; much of the subsidy in either case goes for other goods and services, higher housing costs, or administrative costs.

Finally, the differences between certificates and vouchers are small in principle and so far seem to be small in practice—especially compared to the intensity of the political argument about them.

* * * *

I would like to thank Cushing Dolbeare and James E. Wallace for comments on an earlier draft.

This paper was written while the author was employed at the American Enterprise Institute, before entering government service. A few factual statements have been updated for publication. The views expressed are the author's own, and not necessarily those of either the American Enterprise Institute or the U.S. Department of Housing and Urban Development.

Notes

1. R. J. Struyk and M. Bendick, Jr., eds., *Housing Vouchers for the Poor: Lessons from a National Experiment* (Washington: Urban Institute Press, 1981) Appendix C.

2. See R. B. Clemmer and J. C. Simonson, "Trends in Substandard Housing 1940–1980," *AREUEA Journal* 10 (Winter 1983) 442–464, for a detailed classification of these quality measures.

3. J. C. Weicher, "Halfway to a Housing Allowance?" in J. C. Weicher, ed., *Maintaining the Safety Net: Income Redistribution Programs in the Reagan Administration* (Washington: American Enterprise Institute, 1984) 86.

4. U.S. Congress, Joint Committee on Housing, *Housing Study and Investigation: Final Majority Report* (Washington: USGPO, March 15, 1948) 9.

5. The 1979 housing act required HUD to give priority to households occupying

substandard housing and those who were involuntarily displaced; the 1983 act added families paying 50 percent or more of their income for rent. A regulation implementing these priorities was promulgated on January 15, 1988.

6. I. Irby, "Housing Quality in 1987," unpublished paper, U.S. Department of Housing and Urban Development, February 1990.

7. U.S. General Accounting Office, *October 1981 Recommendations of The President's Commission on Housing: Issues for Congressional Consideration,* CED-82-42 (Washington: USGPO, February 1982); and National League of Cities, "Housing and Cities, Municipal Perspectives on the Report of the President's Commission on Housing" (Washington: NLC, September 1982).

8. F. de Leeuw, "Comments on the Aaron Paper," in K. L. Bradbury and A. Downs, eds., *Do Housing Allowances Work?* (Washington: Brookings Institution, 1981) 99–106.

9. J. E. Wallace, et al., *Participation and Benefits in the Urban Section 8 Program: New Construction and Existing Housing* (Cambridge, Mass.: Abt Associates, 1981).

10. Analysis of a HUD measure, similar to CBO's, has indicated that about 75 percent of renters could afford housing that met the standard without paying more than 25 to 30 percent of their income for rent. A. Yezer, "The Physical Adequacy and Affordability of Housing in America: Measurements Using the Annual Housing Survey for 1975 and 1977" (Washington: U.S. Department of Housing and Urban Development, Annual Housing Survey Studies, No. 7, June 1981). Households at the current eligibility limit (50 percent of area median income) could probably afford adequate housing; those at the original limit (80 percent) could surely do so, except in unusual circumstances. The HUD measure apparently sets a slightly higher standard (Clemmer and Simonson, "Trends in Substandard Housing"), so the CBO criterion should be affordable as well.

11. Wallace et al., *Participation and Benefits,* 239.

12. F. J. Cronin and D. W. Rasmussen, "Mobility," in Struyk and Bendick, ed., *Housing Vouchers,* 118–119.

13. Mireille L. Leger and Stephen D. Kennedy, *Final Report of the Freestanding Housing Voucher Demonstration* (Cambridge, Mass.: Abt Associates, 1990) Appendix Table B-12, p. APP-58.

14. These are my calculations from Leger and Kennedy, *Final Report,* Tables 3.7.B and 3.10.

15. Wallace et al., *Participation and Benefits,* S-9.

16. The latest of these reports is Office of Inspector General, *Nationwide Audit of the Housing Voucher Program: Phase 1—Extent of Compliance with HUD's Housing Quality Standards* (Washington: HUD, December 1988). The overall characterization of unit quality and violations appears in the Executive Summary.

17. S. D. Kennedy and J. E. Wallace, *An Evaluation of Success Rates in Housing Assistance Programs Using the Existing Housing Stock* (Cambridge, Mass.: Abt Associates, March 1983) 2.

18. I. Lowry, ed., *Experimenting with Housing Allowances* (Cambridge, Mass.: Oelgeschlager, Gunn & Hain, 1983) 144.

19. Wallace et al., *Participation and Benefits,* 330–331.

20. Wallace et al., *Participation and Benefits,* 224, 338.

21. S. D. Kennedy, "What Do We Know About Direct Cash Low-Income Housing Assistance?" paper presented to the October 1986 meeting of the American Evaluation Society (revised version, June 1987).

22. The estimated values of the average improvements were $44, $19, and $5 per household per month, respectively, but these should not be taken as precisely

equivalent numbers. The two measures of housing quality changes discussed in the paragraph are different. The first is based on a comparison of housing occupied by assisted households with that occupied by similar households not receiving assistance; the second is based on a comparison of housing occupied by assisted households, before and after they participated in the program.

23. F. J. Cronin, "Participation in the Experimental Housing Allowance Program," in Struyk and Bendick, eds., *Housing Vouchers,* 79.

24. The income limit for a family of four in the Supply Experiment sites was about 140 percent of the poverty line in Green Bay and about 130 percent in South Bend. The difference occurs because of differences in the cost of standard housing. Net income is not calculated in the same way in Food Stamps and EHAP and there are other differences in eligibility, so participation rates can be expected to differ. (Income limits are taken from M. Bendick, Jr., and A. D. Squire, "The Three Experiments," in Struyk and Bendick, eds., *Housing Vouchers,* 51–75, and the poverty line from the U.S. Bureau of the Census [1975, p. 400].)

25. Cronin, "Participants," 97–100; Lowry, *Experimenting with Housing,* 129–136.

26. J. MacMillan, *Mobility in the Housing Allowance Demand Experiment* (Cambridge, Mass.: Abt Associates, 1980) 82–85; Cronin and Rasmussen, "Mobility," 118–121.

27. President's Commission on Housing, *The Report of the President's Commission on Housing* (Washington: USGPO, 1982) 41.

28. Leger and Kennedy, *Final Report,* 40.

29. U.S. Department of Housing and Urban Development, n.d.

30. P. Burke, "Trends in Subsidized Housing 1974–1981," unpublished paper, HUD, March 1984, 102–113.

31. T. R. Miller and L. Toulmin, "Economic Analysis of Lead Paint Regulations Governing HUD-Assisted and FHA Insured Housing" (Washington: Urban Institute, January 1987) II-2.

32. President's Commission on Housing, *Report,* 41.

33. Kennedy and Wallace, *Evaluation of Success,* 23; Leger and Kennedy, *Final Report,* 184.

34. Cronin, "Participation," 94.

35. Kennedy and Wallace, *Evaluation of Success,* 5.

36. Cronin and Rasmussen, "Mobility," 124–128; Kennedy and Wallace, *Evaluation of Success,* 102–114.

37. Wallace et al., *Participation and Benefits,* Ch. 3.

38. J. C. Weicher, *Housing: Federal Policies and Programs* (Washington: American Enterprise Institute, 1980) 68.

39. Wallace et al., *Participation and Benefits,* 36.

40. Kennedy and Wallace, *Evaluation of Success,* 97–101.

41. Kennedy and Wallace, *Evaluation of Success,* Ch. 2; S. D. Kennedy and M. Finkel, *Report of First Year Findings for the Freestanding Housing Voucher Demonstration* (Washington: HUD, June 1987) Ch. 2.

42. Rand Corporation, *Third Annual Report of the Housing Assistance Supply Experiment,* R-2151-HUD, February 1977, XIV.

43. Lowry, *Experimenting,* 179–185.

44. Kennedy, "Direct Cash Assistance," 20–21.

45. Wallace et al., *Participation and Benefits,* 332–340.

46. Kennedy and Finkel, *First Year Findings,* 25.

47. M. Drury et al., *Lower Income Housing Assistance Program (Section 8):*

Nationwide Evaluation of the Existing Housing Program (Washington: USGPO, November 1978) 60.

48. Kennedy and Finkel, *First Year Findings,* 70–74.

49. Kennedy and Finkel, *First Year Findings,* 45–53.

50. R. J. Struyk, S. A. Marshall and L. J. Ozanne, *Housing Policies for the Urban Poor* (Washington: Urban Institute, 1978). Quality improvement is measured by the change in housing value, not the change in the number of households living in decent housing.

51. H. Hammerman, "The Impact of a Housing Voucher Program on Rent Inflation in 20 SMSAs," unpublished paper, HUD, April 1981.

52. E. O. Olsen, "A Possible Rationale for Government Intervention in Housing: The Slow Adjustment of the Housing Market to its Longrun Equilibrium Position," in *National Housing Policy Review, Housing in the Seventies: Working Papers* 1 (Washington: HUD, 1976) 455–458.

53. Weicher, *Housing,* 66–67.

54. C. Swan, "Housing Subsidies and Housing Starts," *AREUEA Journal* 1 (Fall 1973) 119–140; and M. P. Murray, "Subsidized and Unsubsidized Housing Starts: 1961–1977," *Review of Economics and Statistics* 65 (November 1983) 590–597.

55. J. P. Zais, "Repairs and Maintenance on the Units Occupied by Allowance Recipients," in Struyk and Bendick, eds., *Housing Vouchers,* 203–204.

56. R. J. Struyk, *A New System for Public Housing: Salvaging a National Resource* (Washington: Urban Institute Press, 1980), 37–41.

57. J. R. Heller, Testimony before the Subcommittee on Housing and Community Development, U.S. House of Representatives, March 26, 1987.

58. Rand Corporation, *First Annual Report of the Housing Assistance Supply Experiment,* R-1659-HUD, October 1974, 26–27.

59. Rand Corporation, *Fifth Annual Report of the Housing Assistance Supply Experiment,* R-2434-HUD, June 1979, 71–73.

60. L. J. Ozanne and J. P. Zais, "Communitywide Effects of Housing Allowances," in Struyk and Bendick, eds., *Housing Vouchers,* 227–230.

61. Wallace et al., *Participation and Benefits,* 243–248.

62. Wallace et al., *Participation and Benefits,* 121–128.

63. Wallace et al., *Participation and Benefits,* 96.

64. Wallace et al., *Participation and Benefits,* 255–262.

65. Wallace et al., *Participation and Benefits,* 129–130.

66. J. C. Weicher, "Halfway to a Housing Allowance?" 86.

67. M. L. Isler, "Policy Implications: Moving from Research to Programs," in Struyk and Bendick, eds., *Housing Vouchers,* 279–284; Lowry, *Experimenting,* 206–210.

68. Lowry, *Experimenting,* 210–212.

69. Ozanne and Zais, "Communitywide Effects," 229.

70. R. P. Taub, D. G. Taylor, and J. D. Dunham, *Paths of Neighborhood Change* (Chicago: University of Chicago Press, 1984).

71. Wallace et al., *Participation and Benefits,* 212–228, 325–342; President's Commission on Housing, 12–15.

72. Kennedy, "Direct Cash Assistance," 7–10.

73. It should be made clear that the calculations in this paragraph are my own, not those of Wallace et al. (see *Participation and Benefits*), but they are based on information in the Abt study and easily derived from it.

74. E. O. Olsen and D. M. Barton, "The Benefits and Costs of Public Housing in New York City," *Journal of Public Economics* 20 (1985) 299–332.

75. H. J. Sumka and M. A. Stegman, "An Economic Analysis of Public Housing in Small Cities," *Journal of Regional Science* 18, 3 (1978) 395–410.

76. A. B. Schnare et al., *The Cost of HUD Multifamily Housing Programs: A Comparison of the Development, Financing, and Life Cycle Costs of Section 8, Public Housing, and Other Major HUD Programs* (Washington: HUD, May 1982).

77. The cost literature has been recently reviewed by W. J. Reeder, ("The Benefits and Costs of the Section 8 Existing Housing Program," *Journal of Public Economics* 26 [1985] 349–377); and Kennedy, "Direct Cash Assistance." The National Housing Policy Review in 1973 estimated that public housing was about 17 percent more expensive than private housing, neglecting administrative costs; including them, the difference was about 25 percent (National Housing Policy Review, *Housing in the Seventies* [Washington: USGPO, 1973]).

78. The Turnkey program was originally an exception, but within a few years regulations were established that significantly raised production costs for private builders (I. H. Welfeld, *America's Housing Problem: An Approach to its Solution* [Washington: American Enterprise Institute, 1972]).

79. Kennedy, "Direct Cash Assistance," 11.

80. President's Commission on Housing, Ch. 3.

81. This statement is based on a comparison of the market rents of public housing units as estimated for 1970 by the National Housing Policy Review (*Housing in the Seventies*, Ch. 4) with the average FMR reported for 1979 in the Abt Section 8 evaluation. The FMR was about 30 percent greater, in real terms. The comparison is very imprecise, because each figure is based on a small sample of SMSAs and only two SMSAs were included in both samples.

82. Leger and Kennedy, *Final Report*, 137–149.

Chapter 11
Tax Incentives and Federal Housing Programs: Proposed Principles for the 1990s

Patrick E. Clancy

Investment incentives provided in the tax code have historically been an important stimulus to the housing supply. The current national discussion of future housing programs can only benefit by a thorough consideration of how this stimulus has operated in conjunction with direct assistance programs, how it has been changed by the Tax Reform Act of 1986, and how it could be used most effectively and fairly in the future. This chapter offers a starting point for such a consideration.

One of the preliminary questions faced in this discussion is whether to focus on minor tinkering, where proposals may have a better chance of being taken seriously, or whether to consider more far reaching changes with greater significance but more potential for being dismissed out of hand. In the context of a national reconsideration of the federal government's role in housing, clearly the latter is called for. Then again, it is not the purpose here only to suggest either minor or major changes. Based on my experiences, I will try to lay out the considerations relevant to designing investment incentives and housing programs, and, viewing those considerations in the context of the current likely directions of federal housing efforts, to suggest some parameters for housing and tax policy for the future.

This chapter will consider investment incentives that the tax code provides and their relation to government-supported housing programs for the construction or rehabilitation of housing primarily for people of low and moderate income.[1] It will not seek to deal with tax treatment of existing housing which should be preserved for low- and moderate-income people or with tax treatment of debt financing of low- and moderate-income housing (i.e., tax-exempt bond financing and related matters).

One of the starting points for this discussion is my belief that the inability to meet the basic human shelter needs of everyone in this country is a national scandal. The paper begins also from the hope that, after a dramatic retreat over the last half-dozen years, the federal government is preparing to resume a central role in addressing the problem, though that role will likely be significantly different in many respects from past programs—based upon the current environment of more extensive state and local housing initiatives and severe federal budgetary constraints.

There is another possible approach to the consideration of the tax treatment of housing. Two commentators on one of the earliest tax reform efforts put it this way:

A fundamental problem of income taxation is the proper matching of income and expenses. Clearly the cost of acquiring, constructing, reconstructing or rehabilitating a building is a cost of producing the income from that structure which will be derived over a number of years. A mismatching of income and expenses would occur if these capital costs were written off in the year in which they are incurred.[2]

From the need to create a proper matching of income and expense come depreciation allowances, a variety of rules on the treatment of interest expenses and rules related to the treatment of expenses which are paid from borrowed funds. We will not analyze whether those treatments for housing contained in current law represent the proper matching of income and expense. While leaving that exercise to others, we will assume that current provisions are reasonable and will deal beyond that framework with the advisability and type of investment incentives that have been or should be adopted to modify that basic treatment in the effort to design tax provisions to support affordable housing.

An Historical Perspective

The "beginning of modern times" as far as the structure of the U.S. income tax system is concerned, is marked by the passage of the historic Internal Revenue Code of 1954. Until that time, a simple framework for depreciating a capital asset evenly over its estimated useful life prevailed. Since then, there have been two sixteen-year periods during which the tax treatment of housing for low- and moderate-income households were distinctly different.[3]

From 1954 to 1970, tax provisions allowing for accelerated depreciation over a useful life of as much as 40 years applied to all residential real estate. At the same time, housing programs were more focused on single-family home development, the expansion of FHA insurance programs and public housing development for low-income households.

From 1970 to 1986, the tax treatment of residential rental real estate was consistently improved. In addition, incrementally greater tax benefits were provided for the production of low- and moderate-income housing. Until the last few years of this period, programs that supported privately owned rental housing production were a significant part of the federal housing effort.

The combination of these elements led to the growth of real estate limited partnerships and the establishment and expansion of an investment market-place for individuals who could make substantial use of housing investment incentives. Over this second sixteen-year period, myriad federal housing pro-grams—from Section 221(d)(3) BMIR (Below Market Interest Rate) favor-able mortgage financing to Section 236 mortgage assistance to Section 8 rental assistance—were combined with both generally favorable tax treatment of residential real estate and incremental incentives for low- and moderate-income housing. These incentives included shorter depreciable lives, more favorable recapture, and preferential treatment of construction period interest and taxes. Over much of this period, provisions favored rehabilitation of existing properties over new construction—from the five-year amortization provisions of Section 167(k) of the Internal Revenue Code to the investment tax credit for rehabilitation of historic properties. State housing finance agency activity grew and tax-exempt bond financing for housing expanded. Creative combinations of investment incentives and housing programs burgeoned in major production efforts nationwide that created substantial amounts of new or rehabilitated housing affordable for low- and moderate-income households.

In several instances, combining housing programs and investment incen-tives in particularly lucrative mixtures led to unanticipated high returns for affordable housing development. For example, historic rehabilitation tax cred-its combined with Section 8 substantial rehabilitation assistance often resulted in a significantly higher return than would have been necessary to insure full use of the Section 8 program. At the same time, anticipated results from cer-tain provisions to the tax code failed to be realized. For example, Congress expected that Section 167(k) would encourage housing rehabilitation without other assistance. However, in practice, that provision was used in conjunction with housing programs almost without exception. Throughout this period (1970–1986), no effective coordination of investment incentives and housing programs was achieved.[4]

The Tax Reform Act of 1986 fundamentally altered the tax treatment of residential real estate and the framework and substance of investment incen-tives for affordable housing production. Partly in reaction to the excessive benefits for real estate created in the Economic Recovery Tax Act of 1981, tax treatment of housing and real estate in general was drastically altered. The extension of depreciable building life from 18 to 27 1/2 years, the elimination of accelerated depreciation, severe restrictions on "passive" losses, and the elimination of special capital gains treatment meant that investment in rental housing lost much of its tax-favored status.[5] Combined with this drastic change to the general treatment of rental housing, limited special provision was made for housing targeted to low-income households by means of the low-income housing tax credit. This credit—described in Appendix A of this chapter—for the first time provides a substantial tax incentive targeted exclusively for hous-ing that is reserved for low-income households for an extended time.

Beyond this critical new focus exemplified by the low-income housing tax credit, the Tax Reform Act of 1986 made major changes in three critical respects to the treatment of affordable housing production. First, it dramatically changed the context of affordable housing production. That is, the favorable tax treatment of expenditures on housing units serving low-income people no longer represents modest additional incentives that complement favorable tax treatment of all rental housing, as was the case from 1970 to 1986. Instead, favorable tax treatment exists only for low-income housing units; all other rental housing is treated dramatically differently. The implications of this change in context are quite clear but are only beginning to be felt. Under the current law, unless housing programs overcompensate for this diminished tax support by providing larger direct incentives for non–low-income units, affordable housing will be produced, overwhelmingly, in developments that are all, or almost all, low-income. This will occur for two reasons. First, there is a substantial tax disincentive to create rental housing that does not qualify for the low-income tax credit when the alternative, creating that housing as ownership housing, receives dramatically more favorable tax treatment. And, secondly, because mixing tenure within a development by combining low-income rental housing with moderate and market rate ownership housing significantly increases the complexity of both the financing and the operation of the housing, it is unlikely to be undertaken to any significant extent.

The second dramatic structural change is a change imposed on the market for investors in affordable housing. The investment marketplace built up over the past sixteen years has been virtually eliminated as an investment resource by the passive loss provisions as they are applied to affordable housing ownership and, in only slightly modified form, to the low-income housing tax credit. The reason for this is absolutely clear and incredibly frustrating: the analysis of the distributional effect of the Tax Reform Act of 1986 was based entirely on changes in income tax payments to the Treasury.[6] The result of this narrow perspective is particularly curious in the design of the low-income housing tax credit. With a well designed provision, allowing high income individuals to continue to provide an investment marketplace for housing serving low-income households would result in those upper income taxpayers paying dollars into those investments and reducing their payments to the Treasury. Low-income households would realize savings in housing costs. Since only the reduction in the upper income taxpayers' payments to the Treasury would be reflected in the distributional analyses of the Tax Reform Act, which would not show those taxpayers' investment cost or the low-income households' housing cost savings, Senate Finance Committee and Joint Committee on Taxation staff and members were unprepared to allow the low-income housing tax credit to be exempted from the passive loss restrictions. The anomalous result was that the incentive provided for low-income housing production was unreasonably and severely restricted to a new, untested investment audience: a thin band of middle-income taxpayers able to afford relatively small investments and certain corporations.

The third major change affecting affordable housing incentives was the change in access to these incentives. Historically, investment incentives have been directly accessible without the cost or complexity of governmental allocation. This flexibility and accessibility contrasts with the more rigid bureaucratic requirements for access to direct housing assistance programs. Designers of the low-income housing tax credit, given revenue analyses of various provisions enacted in 1986, faced a perceived problem. The changes in the treatment of rental housing in general and recent reductions in large-scale direct assistance housing programs meant that any low-income housing incentive had to be substantial to be of any use. At the same time, staff were unduly concerned that the cost of such an incentive might exceed their projections. Thus, the amount of low-income housing tax credit that could be used in any state was limited, based on population, with additional use allowed only in connection with tax exempt bond financing, which also was limited in total. Although this increased the potential accuracy of revenue impact estimates for the credit provisions, its negative impacts were far more significant: it resulted in a tax incentive provision that combines the worst features of *both* tax and direct subsidies, the governmental red tape of direct assistance programs and the transaction costs and returns required for private investment.

As important as these limitations, however, is the overall intent reflected in the creation of the low-income housing tax credit: an investment incentive directly targeted to and focused upon housing units that serve households with the greatest need. The establishment of that principle in the course of tax reform represents a major accomplishment and provides a starting point for considering the potential mix of investment incentives and housing programs for the future.

The Characteristics of Investment Incentives

A prime concern in any discussion of tax incentives and housing is what constitutes an appropriate fit between housing programs and investment incentives. To frame the discussion, it is important to look at major characteristics which differentiate tax and direct expenditures.

Tax Expenditures

One of the potential positive features of tax expenditures is that they can be designed to avoid the substantial costs associated with bureaucratic governmental allocation processes necessary for direct expenditure programs. Tax expenditures can also have the positive effect of inducing private investment capital (and the discipline and integrity of the financial marketplace) to meet governmental objectives. This has particularly been the case in affordable housing production over the past 20 years for two reasons. First, to maximize their value, developers have sought to sell interests in tax benefits in their developments to what became a substantial market of high-income individuals accessed through a large private placement network. Secondly, these tax benefits provided the primary component of the owner's return, given severe limits on cash flow in assisted housing developments and restrictions providing for affordable operations over extended periods of time.

Another positive feature of tax expenditures is the potential certainty of benefits. Meeting requirements of the Internal Revenue Code gives access to benefits without a need for receiving an allocation through a governmental process. This reliability can be an important stimulus to a greater volume of productive activity.

Tax expenditures have a large number of potentially negative aspects which must be weighed in considering their use. They are inefficient because only a portion of every dollar spent goes to the purpose of the expenditure with a significant portion going instead to the transaction costs of raising capital and to providing a return on the capital invested. Tax expenditures also have a potential for abuse or misapplication where no direct government oversight is provided. In addition, tax expenditures create greater perceived inequities in the overall income tax system that can undermine the system and introduce a potentially costly complexity into it.

Finally, since tax expenditures are reflected not in governmental appropriations but in reduced income tax collections there is less scrutiny of the expenditure. Recent painstaking estimating and budgeting of tax expenditures has diminished this distinction.

Direct Expenditures

Direct expenditures can be more accurately tailored to achieve specific results. They can also be adjusted to fit local variations more easily than tax provisions. Generally, direct expenditures are more easily quantifiable. The major cost associated with direct expenditures is that they require a governmental bureaucracy for allocation and review of expenditures. Direct expenditures can be designed either as a total resource package for housing production or as separate programs that provide partial support and complement other assistance and financing. Direct expenditures also, clearly, can be designed without the particular inefficiency or potential for misapplication of tax expenditures and do not create real or perceived tax inequities or complexity.

The Need for Investment Incentives

Thoughtful readers will have observed that I have put the cart before the horse thus far. Talk of a fit assumes both direct and tax expenditures are appropriate vehicles for federal housing efforts. It is critical to look hard at whether this assumption is warranted. Consideration of this question must begin where Stanley Surrey, one of the giants of tax policy, concluded his initial comparative analysis almost twenty years ago:

As a generalization, the burden of proof should rest heavily on those proposing the use of the tax incentive method. In any particular situation—certainly any new situation—the first approach should be to explore the various direct expenditure alternatives. Once the most desirable of these alternatives is determined, if one still wishes to consider the tax incentive method for the same substantive program, the question must be what clear advantages can be obtained by using the tax method.[7]

Surrey's treatment of this issue remains the most thoughtful and I will seek to test out my approach in this section against it. Although I agree with Surrey's theoretical view that the advantages of tax incentives could, in a rational world, be designed into direct expenditure programs, I believe that the current environment calls for a mixture of direct and tax expenditures to assist in affordable housing development.

As others have written more recently: "What stands out in the ebb and flow of financial tides is problem succession: old solutions give rise to new problems that are in their turn superseded. No policy instrument is good for all seasons."[8]

Tax incentives. Tax incentives should be utilized as a major part of the federal assistance to affordable housing production for the coming decade for the following reasons:

1. *Reduced bureaucracy and increased flexibility are particularly compelling in an era in which federal assistance is intended to stimulate and complement growing state and local housing initiatives.* Those producing affordable housing can achieve more direct access to assistance with less bureaucratic inefficiency through investment incentives than if the same assistance is provided through direct expenditure. Surrey notes that, in a rational world, if less detailed oversight is appropriate, it can be designed into direct expenditures to as great an extent as into tax expenditures. He is absolutely right in a rational world. In this one, where bureaucratic processes for allocation and oversight of direct funding programs inevitably grow in complexity, providing the equivalent assistance through tax expenditures is one means of avoiding them. This reality is an overwhelming and unalterable one in my view, based upon seventeen years of daily efforts using both an array of direct expenditure and investment incentive programs in producing affordable housing. While a number of recent tax expenditure programs have tended to create substantial bureaucratic requirements, the ability to design these expenditures to be more directly accessible and flexible remains.

In the current environment, a reduced federal bureaucratic presence will complement significantly the substantial role of state and local governments and a variety of housing partnerships, where development initiative, energy, and financial resources are being provided through more localized effort.[9] It is critical for the federal contribution to be as readily accessible and flexible as possible to stimulate as wide a variety of these efforts as possible. In addition, the fact that tax benefits have consistently required and will continue to require direct assistance to make affordable housing production feasible provides a mechanism through which the provider of direct assistance—a federal, state, or local entity—can ensure that tax benefits are efficiently used for their purpose. That is, direct assistance providers are in a position to ensure that the assistance they provide is tailored to be no more than is necessary for development to take place given the availability of investment incentives.

Investment incentives provide a further loosening of the bureaucratic noose for a somewhat more complex reason. Incentives for rental housing are generally bundled together and used by developers to attract additional financing from groups of equity investors reached by structuring projects so that they can be offered in the investment marketplace. The very fact that accomplished developers come to the table supported by the confidence of the marketplace demonstrated through the availability of capital provides assurance to governmental actors that is often critical to loosening what can otherwise become overly rigid and costly bureaucratic underwriting processes.

2. *Tax expenditures for lower-income housing are an important element in achieving a balanced system of tax and direct expenditures for households with a range of incomes.* The current mix of tax and direct expenditures for housing, when looked at in the aggregate, contributes to a housing industry which is operating suboptimally from a public policy perspective. Consistently fewer units are being produced and maintained for lower-income households than were produced in the 1970s; a generally solid housing market in terms of national production is increasingly serving only upper income households in a growing number of areas; increasing numbers of moderate- to middle-income Americans are finding homeownership, their preferred housing choice, unavailable; and increasing numbers of low- and moderate-income households are paying excessive percentages of their income for housing, as production and assistance programs fail to keep pace with demand and prices continue to escalate. It is important that redesign of federal housing efforts be undertaken with a considered view of the total housing market and its strengths and weaknesses and with the full range of tax and direct expenditure programs affecting housing under consideration.

The imbalanced result of current tax and direct expenditures for housing is not surprising when one analyzes the total universe of those expenditures. Tax expenditures for homeownership—primarily the mortgage interest and property tax deductions—which benefit most heavily middle and upper income households currently total almost $50 billion a year.[10] On the other hand, tax expenditures related to rental housing, which more substantially serves low- and moderate-income households, total approximately $8.5 billion a year.[11] Even adding to this figure the entire budget of the Department of Housing and Urban Development—which is approximately $15 billion a year at 1986 and 1987 levels and includes a variety of nonhousing expenditures—it is clear that federal expenditures for housing through direct programs and the Internal Revenue Code are in the aggregate heavily weighted in favor of middle and upper income households.

In his analysis, Surrey asks, "What's lost by using tax incentives?" In reply, he points out the damage to the tax system caused by designing incentives which have disproportionate values to different taxpayers and are inequitable in favor of higher income taxpayers. If we view this issue not from the standpoint only of tax incidence but in the larger context of the tax structure's impact on disposable income, well-designed tax expenditures for affordable housing production can be an important element in balancing the system of tax expenditures for housing in a way that can contribute toward greater equity and less regressivity in the overall impact on disposable incomes.

3. *There is both a necessity and a potential at this juncture to design tax and direct expenditures for housing as part of an overall housing support system.* Surrey's other main concern for what is lost by using tax incentives was with the confusion and complication that results from using both tax and direct expenditures in the same area. He might be prophetic: "These difficulties could perhaps be overcome. Tax committees might refer incentive proposals to the appropriate legislative committees and accept their judgments, or both groups of committees could consider the matter jointly." [12]

With the huge changes made to the tax treatment of housing in the Tax Reform Act of 1986, the work of the housing committees to redesign federal housing efforts for the future can only be effectively carried out by undertaking that redesign with both tax impacts and direct expenditures clearly in mind. Thus, it is essential that tax as well as housing committees ultimately become involved in that redesign. As described below, the Tax Reform Act of 1986 has set the stage for a combined effort of tax and housing committees which can and must be achieved as new programs and policies are developed over the next year.

Direct expenditures. The case scarcely needs to be made for why direct expenditures should remain a critical part of the federal government's role in affordable housing production. Several examples of the important places for direct expenditures in addition to tax expenditures include:

> Where federal assistance is intended to provide the main single source of financing, only direct expenditures can reasonably achieve an adequate level of assistance.

Where state and local governments are unresponsive to low-income residents' needs, some substantial direct assistance is critical to providing resources to those in need.

Where more specific and detailed housing objectives are being served, close government involvement may be necessary to assure that expenditures are directed to meet those specific objectives.

Since there is little disagreement that an array of direct expenditures will continue to be important, this analysis will conclude with the observation that, for the future, it seems appropriate to look at mixtures of tax and direct expenditures. It is therefore relevant to consider a general framework for using tax expenditures.

General Principles: Investment Incentives for the 1990s

In my view, there are six basic principles that should govern use of investment incentives in the production of affordable housing as part of the overall federal housing effort: focus, simplicity, efficiency, accessibility, flexibility, and equity. While a number of these principles are simply different facets of the same character, they are worth separate discussion.

Focus. The Tax Reform Act of 1986 has shifted the treatment of residential real estate to a far less favorable footing. Affordable housing incentives stand out from a context that provides very little tax incentive—and generally a relative disincentive—for the business ownership of real estate. It is proposed that changes over the next few years be focused on providing additional incentives at additional cost only for residential real estate and only where it serves to meet the nation's low- and moderate-income housing needs. In a time of scarce national resources, hardheaded prioritization is critical to provide the assistance needed to live up to the promise of a decent home for every American.

Simplicity. The housing problems of the nation result from a complex mixture of the shelter, income, and human service needs of households and the insufficiency and deterioration of the housing stock. Thus, currently many people face housing problems, from homeless, deinstitutionalized, mentally disabled persons to middle-income, intact families unable to acquire their own single family homes. It is recommended that affordable housing investment incentives be designed as a simple single incentive to assist the production of new or rehabilitated housing, with all types of housing and uses that meet certain affordability criteria treated the same. The low-income housing tax credit—as a single resource in place of the previous, more complex combinations of accelerated depreciation, special amortization for rehabilitation expenses, and the like—represents a step in this direction, although its complexity is greater than necessary.

Efficiency. Investment incentives suffer generally from some inefficiency due to the need to find investors and to provide a return to those investors. The cost of these inefficiencies can be considered a fair one in view of the private investment capital attracted and the value of having a directly accessible assistance resource not entangled in uncertain and bureaucratic allocation processes. Nonetheless, investment incentives need to be designed to minimize both the transaction costs and the proportion of those incentives lost to providing an investment return. To do that, incentives should be available to the widest potential range of personal and corporate sources of capital, so that the demand for incentives is as large as possible. This is critical to ensure that the maximum benefit from these incentives reaches those on whom they are focused: the low-income residents in qualifying developments. The application of the passive loss restrictions to the low-income housing tax credit is an inefficient narrowing of the market for tax incentives which will increase the necessary return and the transaction costs spent in reaching investors.

Incentives targeted to produce housing that is affordable for low-income households—perhaps alone among tax expenditures because they directly benefit low-income households—should be usable by individuals and corporations without limitation. In addition, investment incentives should be based in substantial part on tax credits instead of tax deductions so that the potential use of those incentives has as broad an audience as possible, not only those in the highest tax bracket. Thirdly, interests in housing receiving tax benefits should be transferable as investors' tax positions change—so long as continuing proper use is assured—to avoid the inefficient discounting of prices for the tax risk of an investor's continuing ability to use the benefits fully. Lastly, discounted cash rebates to owners of small affordable housing projects should be considered as a means of eliminating the transaction cost barrier for smaller producers.

Accessibility. Because the level of assistance required to produce affordable housing necessitates aligning tax incentives with other direct resources, the incentives should be directly accessible without the expense of an additional bureaucratic allocation and monitoring process. If investment incentives are made directly accessible to private owners without government involvement, these incentives can be a major vehicle for private investment capital in affordable housing production. Since that production will almost always include direct local, state, and federal assistance, accountability for the appropriate use of resources can be achieved in the design and monitoring of the direct assistance programs, and duplication of bureaucracy can and should be avoided.

Flexibility. The Tax Reform Act of 1986 left little incentive for developing non-low-income rental housing. The investment incentives that are provided for low-income housing are likely to result in creation of rental housing that is all or almost all low-income. Non-low-income development will be done in separate projects with an entirely different financing structure to take advantage of homeowner deductions. The only ways of avoiding this result are if direct assistance programs overcompensate by providing more assistance for non-low-income units—clearly not an appropriate direction—or if developments are done with mixed tenure, providing rental housing for low-income households and ownership housing for non-low-income households. At the same time, there is a growing recognition of the value of creating communities that have people of all incomes within them. However, the importance of concentrating tax expenditures on those in the greatest need militates against providing substantial assistance to developments only partially serving those in need. This problem should be resolved by investments that have some flexibility. This flexibility could be achieved with a proportional system where units serving low-income households could be provided a substantial incentive; units serving moderate-income households would be provided a lesser incentive; and units serving higher-income households would be provided some modest level of incentive when they are created in a development with a substantial percentage of low- and moderate-income units.

Equity. There is a "fiscal illusion," to use Webber and Wildavsky's terminology,[13] that needs to be understood: homeowners, including most middle- and upper-income households, escape taxation on income they use to pay for the substantial portion of their housing costs that go to mortgage interest and real estate tax. Households that rent, which are in much greater proportion low- and moderate-income households, pay income tax on income they spend on rent.[14] Tax expenditures for housing need to be shifted so that their impact on disposable income is at least equal across different income categories, if not in favor of lower-income households. Equity demands as much.

Additionally, the measures taken to balance the tax code treatment of housing for households of different income levels can be sources of revenue to equalize the impacts of tax expenditures for affordable housing production. For example, revenue produced by a cap on mortgage interest deductions for homeowners could offset the revenue cost of additional tax expenditures for affordable housing.

Recommendations

The specific recommendations regarding investment incentives that follow reflect the preceding analysis of principles which should be considered and suggest the way in which housing programs should be tailored to fit with investment incentives.

The Tax Credit

The low-income housing tax credit contained in the Tax Reform Act of 1986 provides a valuable starting point for developing a range of investment incentives for affordable housing production. Its focus on housing units that directly serve low-income people is an important step forward and its design as a credit instead of as a series of tax deductions is more efficient than most past incentives. In light of current housing program realities it provides a good starting point for current deliberations. Based on the preceding analysis, the following changes to the low-income housing credit are recommended [15]:

1. Remove the "cap" on the amount of credit allocated to each state so that, as long as all the requirements are met, the credit can be used without any governmental allocation process. The risk of unanticipated revenue drain occurring from its unrestricted use is not large, and will not be until dramatic increases occur in the direct assistance which is a necessary complement to the credit. Therefore, the cap should be removed, at least until direct assistance levels rise to a point of creating a risk of increased tax expenditure cost beyond authorized revenue impact levels. The concern expressed by some observers regarding potential large credit claims being made by private owners of conventional one- to four-family stock for modest improvements or even just for acquisitions is, in my view, unrealistic. The recapture provisions that require fifteen years of use as low-income housing are so restrictive that use of the credits in such situations is likely to be rare.

Although it is important to remove the cap on the low-income credit to make its use more efficient, it is worth noting that one of the impacts of the cap has been a positive one. By giving states a finite resource to allocate—even though it replaces a previously unlimited resource in the form of accelerated depreciation and other benefits—an environment has been created in which a number of states have viewed this resource as more valuable than the unlimited tax benefit they had before. These states have taken actions they might not otherwise have taken to stimulate affordable housing production in the effort to see this resource fully utilized. To enhance this strong incentive for state and local action, one potential alternative to elimination of the cap might be to allow additional credits without regard to caps where there is a significant direct assistance contribution—for example, ten percent of a development's cost—from a state or local government or charitable organization. If the cap is not eliminated, it is critical to make allocations cumulative from year to year so that the tremendous inefficiency of the rigid annual schedule of the current provisions is mitigated.

2. Remove the sunset date. Already, new development activity designed to create affordable housing and to use the credit runs the risk of being unable to meet the percentage of construction completion deadline for 1989. To avoid killing even the modest level of development activity now working to use the credit, and to provide the kind of certainty of availability that can en-

courage further development activity, the sunset date for the credit should be removed.

3. To broaden the potential market for use of the credit, remove housing units that qualify for the credit from the restrictions on credits and passive losses contained in the legislation. There has been a very modest amount of marketing activity with the credit to date. Opening up the market to moderate-income individuals who can comply with the passive loss restrictions has been difficult and slow. The effort to get corporations to make investments in low-income housing has produced some results—particularly through non-profit sponsors offering a combination of a solid investment and an opportunity to exercise corporate civic responsibility—but the amount of funds raised is greatly exceeded by the time and effort and energy spent raising those funds. The raising of the consciousness of corporate America to the needs of the poor that has accompanied those efforts is a positive outcome. But the only reason that the severe limitations on who can use the credit has not posed major problems is the dramatic decrease in the level of affordable housing production now being undertaken across the country as a result of reductions in federal housing programs. Any significant increase in effort will be stymied by the credit restriction unless a wider, more easily accessible market is available.

4. The credit should remain focused on housing units to serve low-income people, but should be complemented by additional provisions that provide a more flexible framework for mixed-income rental housing development. This recommendation is discussed in greater detail in the following section.

5. Provision should be made for longer term affordability of tax credit subsidized housing units. For an only slightly greater initial return, developers and investors will undertake affordable housing development production with longer term restrictions on its use than the 15-year term provided in the credit legislation. Thus, the future affordability of housing now produced can be assured at a fraction of the cost to replace it or to provide that assurance later. This kind of foresight could avoid the problem currently being faced with expiring use restrictions on developments aided under prior HUD programs.[16] However, changes in this area must be designed carefully if the economic and tax structure of private affordable housing production, finance, and operation are to be maintained.

6. The credit should be usable with any and all forms of federal, state and local assistance. As has been stressed at many points in this discussion, the low-income credit, like incentives before it, can only be used in conjunction with direct assistance; therefore, the notion of restricting the direct assistance that can be used with the credit is inappropriate. Relying on direct assistance providers to insure efficient allocation of direct assistance and to take into account the availability of investment incentives is the far more ap-

propriate way to achieve the intended result of avoiding excessively profitable combinations of investment incentives and housing programs.

Other Investment Incentives

Beyond these changes to the low-income housing tax credit, some degree of investment incentive should be provided for production of units serving moderate-income households, those with incomes from 60 to 80 or even 90 percent of median. Movement in this direction, however, requires maneuvering between rocky shoals. First of all, in a time of scarce resources, it is critical to concentrate resources where the need is greatest. To this end, investment incentives for moderate-income production should be available only in developments where at least an equivalent number of units for low-income households are being created. Thus, some assistance for households with somewhat lesser needs would only be provided where that assistance is a part of making a mixed-income environment viable for low-income households (and potentially acceptable to local governments whose approval is often critical and difficult to obtain).

The other danger is the problem of how it looks to provide attractive investments for upper-income people at the expense of the taxpaying public to benefit a limited percentage of the large class of households with only modest needs. One potential means of dealing with this perceptual problem would be to make investment incentives for moderate-income production themselves taxable benefits so that the problem created by certain individuals or corporations "avoiding tax" is mitigated.[17] Another means of avoiding this problem and perhaps achieving greater efficiency would be to consider providing a tax benefit to a moderate-income renter in lieu of providing the benefit to the owner. Moderate-income households, unlike low-income households, are usually in a position to directly use a moderate level of tax benefit without requiring a rebate provision to insure its full use.

It is a harder question still to assess whether some additional tax benefit should be provided for rental housing for households able to pay market rates in developments with substantial portions of low- and moderate-income households to attract a full mix of incomes. Here, the problems of losing focus and stretching dollars too far become even more significant. At the same time, the need to create viable mixed-income environments and to achieve public support for housing for the poor by doing so means that this issue needs careful consideration. Perhaps seeking a means through HUD insurance programs of simplifying the development and financing of mixed tenure developments, where market-rate and moderate-income housing can be ownership housing, can resolve this problem in a more acceptable fashion.

It is beyond the purview of this discussion to present in detail the array of direct expenditure housing programs which can best reflect the kind of directions for federal housing efforts described here. A critical point needs to be made, however, regarding the structuring of housing programs and their relationship to investment incentives. It is clear that investment incentives alone are unlikely to produce affordable housing. In considering the low-income housing tax credit, as in considering five-year amortization for rehabilitation expenditures 18 years earlier, many tax staffers believed that the credit provided enough benefit by itself to stimulate affordable housing production. There was a great deal of controversy in deliberations on the credit as to how and when and what other assistance resources could or should be used in combination with the credit. Experience to date with the credit, consistent with experience with the rehabilitation provision after 1969 and with the pattern that has prevailed over the past 16 years, makes clear that virtually all tax benefits for affordable housing will be used in conjunction with other direct assistance resources.

Given this pattern, investment incentives should be designed so they can be used with as wide an array of housing programs as might exist. Correspondingly, housing programs should be designed so that they can be used in combination with investment incentives. Further, housing programs should be designed to take into account, as a part of their funding allocation processes, investment incentives available for the housing they support, and to ensure that the level of direct assistance, given those investment incentives, is appropriate and not excessive. That should be done whether the direct assistance is provided through federal, state, or local housing programs. For when direct housing assistance is carefully matched and calibrated to investment incentives, the case for those incentives is most compelling.

The Design Process

The process of designing a range of housing programs and investment incentives that together maximize the federal government's contribution toward meeting the housing needs of lower-income Americans within severe budgetary constraints is clearly a complex one. More important than any substantive recommendations made here is the effort to establish a thought process that weighs, balances, and fits housing programs and investment incentives together as part of an overall coordinated approach. As future housing programs are designed over the coming years, the discussion must include active consideration of investment incentives. At the same time, the Senate Housing and Urban Affairs Subcommittee's work should be informed by the participation of those from the Senate Finance Committee (as well as the Joint Committee on Taxation and the House Ways and Means Committee) whose thinking is critical to the development of any tax changes.

Although the Congressional committee structure and budgetary process make this kind of coordination difficult,[18] the potential for the kind of effective coordination that has not existed in either the design or implementation of housing programs and investment incentives for affordable housing over the past twenty years may now exist. The intense effort of the tax committees in the development of the Tax Reform Act of 1986 to understand housing programs and production and to design an effective investment incentive can be seen as a critical first step. Involving those individuals in the effort initiated by the housing committees, though facing jurisdictional complexities, is clearly both possible and essential to designing future federal housing efforts as the kind of balanced combination of housing programs and investment incentives they need to be.

Recent Congressional activity provides a basis for continued optimism on this score. In recent hearings on the low-income housing tax credit before the Subcommittee on Select Revenue Measures of the House Committee on Ways and Means, the senior minority member of the Senate Subcommittee on Housing and Urban Affairs was one of the leading witnesses. A companion hearing on preserving the stock of low-income housing considered proposed tax legislation to deal in part with expiring use restrictions on federally assisted housing that has both tax and housing subcommittee members' support. The author also had the opportunity to summarize many of the central themes of this discussion at the hearing on the low-income housing tax credit. Both housing and tax committee members and staff are clearly aware of the critical need for coordination in the design of direct housing assistance programs and investment incentives.

Appendix A: A Description of the Low-Income Housing Tax Credit

The Low-Income Housing Tax Credit, created in the Tax Reform Act of 1986, is the key tax benefit available for use in low-income housing investments, and replaces virtually all previously available benefits to low-income housing, including accelerated depreciation, 167(k), and other such programs.[19]

Eligibility

A qualified low-income housing project is one in which:

1. 20% or more of the units are rent restricted and occupied by tenants whose income is 50% or less of median income, or
2. 40% or more of the units are rent restricted and occupied by tenants whose income is 60% or less of median income.

A rent restricted unit is one in which the gross rent does not exceed 30% of the relevant income limitation cited above. (Gross rent does not include federal Section 8 or other state and local rent subsidy payments.)

TABLE 11.1

	REHABILITATION OR RESYNDICATION				NEW CONSTRUCTION	
	Rehab, $> \$2,000/un.$		*Rehab,* $< \$2,000/un.$		*Acquis. cost*	*Construct. cost*
Federally subsidized projects [a]	4%	or	4%	plus	4%	4%
Unsubsidized projects	9%	or	4%	plus	4%	9%

[a] Includes mortgage financing with federally subsidized tax exempt bonds and/or below market rate federal loans or grants for which Eligible Basis is not reduced.

A qualified low-income building is one which:

1. is part of a qualified low-income housing project throughout the 15-year compliance period of the credit, and
2. is subject to new depreciation rules in the Tax Reform Act of 1986, and
3. is placed in service between January 1, 1987 and December 31, 1990.

Credit Amount Calculations

The amount of the annual credit, available for a ten-year period, is calculated according to the following formula:

Eligible Basis $\times$ Applicable Fraction = Qualified Basis

Qualified Basis $\times$ Applicable Percentage = Annual Credit Amount

Eligible Basis is the development cost of a new construction project, less land costs and in some cases, federal subsidies.

Eligible Basis in an existing project would include acquisition costs (excluding land) plus rehabilitation costs, less federal subsidies in some cases.

The Applicable Fraction is the lesser of the ratios of low-income units to total units and low-income floor space to total floor space.

The Applicable Percentage is determined on the basis of project type (i.e., new construction vs. rehabilitation) and by the use of federal subsidies, as shown in Table 11.1. State allocating agencies can allow up to 130% of those applicable amounts in certain limited hard to develop areas or can reduce the amounts for projects deemed not to need this much incentive.

State Credit Limitations

State agencies will allocate credits to projects; allocations are completed during the year in which the project is placed in service. Each state was limited to a total credit cap of $1.25 per capita for the years 1987 through 1989. How-ever, only the first year of a project's credit was counted against the cap. The 4% credits used in tax-exempt bond-financed projects were not subject to the credit cap either, since they were controlled instead by bond caps. As part of a Congressional compromise, the annual credit cap was reduced to $0.97375 per capita for 1990.

Individual Investment Benefit Limitations

No individual investor may claim more than $7,000 per year in the low-income housing credit against salary- or portfolio-generated tax liability, be-cause of limits related to other passive loss restrictions. Additionally, the amount of credit available to individual investors is decreased ratably to 0 as individual income increases from $200,000 to $250,000. Therefore, credit transactions must be oriented to corporations not affected by passive loss re-strictions, or to larger numbers of individual investors, requiring public offer-ings for all but relatively small projects.

Notes

1. This discussion will generally use the terminology "investment incentives" when referring to incentives provided for housing production through the Internal Revenue Code, "housing programs" when referring to housing funding provided through the budget established for the Department of Housing and Urban Development at the federal level and "affordable housing" when referring to housing serving "low-income" (generally incomes below 50–60 percent of median income) and "moderate-income" (generally from 50–60 percent of median to 80 percent of median) households.

2. C. W. Ritter and E. M. Sunley, Jr., "Real Estate and Tax Reform: An Analy-sis and Evaluation of the Real Estate Provisions of the Tax Reform Act of 1969," *Maryland Law Review* XXX.1 (Winter, 1970).

3. An excellent four-page summary of the history of rental housing taxation since 1954 is contained in "Low- and Moderate-Income Housing: Progress, Problems and Prospects" (Washington: The National Association of Homebuilders, 1986) 55–59.

4. One of the best examples of the lack of coordination was Section 1250 of the Internal Revenue Code. This section provided a critical definition of what qualified as low-income housing for favorable tax treatment. The definition specifically referenced certain federal programs and then included a general reference to "similar provisions of state or local laws" which was highly ambiguous and led to a series of questionable applications.

5. In this paper I focus on the tax status of rental housing prior to and after the Tax Reform Act of 1986 rather than the tax status of housing compared to other invest-ments before and after tax reform.

6. Clearly the distributional effect of the Tax Reform Act of 1986 is substantially more regressive than many thought, if one looks at the Act's impact on after-tax or disposable income measures, which are a more comprehensive test of the full impact of the Act.

7. S. S. Surrey et al., eds., *Federal Income Taxation: Cases and Materials* (New York: The Foundation, 1972) I: 272.

8. C. Webber and A. Wildavsky, *A History of Taxation and Expenditure in the Western World* (New York: Simon and Schuster, 1986) 565.

9. Many observers, myself included, feel that the federal role in housing in the 1990s will tend to be flexible in design to energize a wide array of affordable housing producers. Federal assistance should provide strong incentives for state and local participation and adapt to and leverage a variety of capital and assistance resources. Increasing concern for issues of tenure overall and supply limitations in particular markets should be reflected in federal housing programs.

10. Based upon the following five-year estimates of federal tax expenditures prepared by the Joint Committee on Taxation: mortgage interest deduction: $149.8 billion; property tax deduction: $40.3 billion; capital gains deferral on sale of residence: $36.7 billion; capital gains exclusion on sale of residence: $12.2 billion; tax-exempt bonds for homeownership: $7.7 billion. These expenditures total $246.7 billion, or a $49.34 billion average yearly expenditure. "Estimates of Federal Tax Expenditures for Fiscal Years 1988 to 1992," prepared for the Committee on Ways and Means and the Committee on Finance by the Staff of the Joint Committee on Taxation, February 27, 1987.

11. Again from the five-year estimates of federal tax expenditures prepared by the Joint Committee on taxation, tax expenditures over a five-year period for rental housing are as follows: historic rehabilitation tax credit (including substantial expenditures for nonhousing restorations): $8.7 billion; rental housing depreciation: $6.4 billion; credit and loss exclusion for low-income housing: $4.3 billion; tax-exempt bonds for rental housing: $5.0 billion; exclusion from passive loss provision for rental housing: $16.0 billion; credit for rehabilitation expenditures (nonhistoric): $1.9 billion; five-year rehab amortization: $0.1 billion. These expenditures total $42.4 billion, or an average yearly expenditure of $8.48 billion.

12. Surrey, *Federal Income Taxation,* 267.

13. Webber and Wildavsky, *History of Taxation,* 578.

14. To describe this inequity in more precise terms, a homeowner should be taxed on the imputed rental income value of the home. This treatment is also consistent with allowing tax and interest expenses to be deducted. Since the homeowner is not taxed on this imputed rental income, he is in a different position from the owner of rental housing who is taxed on rental income and has only the additional, and currently comparatively minor, value of depreciation to offset this item of income. Thus, an equitable system would provide a tax exempt investment opportunity for the rental housing owner or renter equivalent to the value of the exclusion of imputed rental income to the homeowner, net of the offsetting value of depreciation to the rental housing owner.

15. This chapter was written before the 1989 changes to the tax credit legislation. These changes extended the credit (but for one year only), made carryover of credits possible in somewhat more cases, and extended affordability requirements to thirty years, all consistent with the recommendations here. It also eliminated the income cap for individual investors who can utilize limited amounts of credit, but did not make tax losses on credit investments usable by individuals, and therefore retained the major marketing constraints that severely limit the credit's marketability.

16. See Clay and Wallace in Chapter 12 of this volume.

17. The author owes the general suggestion for making tax benefits for affordable housing themselves taxable to eliminate tax inequities—as well as a number of other thoughtful comments—to Paul R. McDaniel, Professor of Law, Boston College Law School and author, with Stanley Surrey, of *Tax Expenditures* (Cambridge: Harvard University Press, 1985).

18. See Surrey and McDaniel, *Tax Expenditures,* especially Chs. 2 and 3.

19. This appendix has been updated to reflect the 1989 changes.

Chapter 12
Preservation of the Existing Stock of Assisted Private Housing

Phillip L. Clay and James E. Wallace

Traditionally, housing analysts concerned with the poor have been interested in how to produce affordable units for those with limited income. They focused on how to serve different groups among the needy, how to design a subsidy, and production issues such as the best mix of new construction and rehabilitation. Once produced, housing units were counted as permanent resources on which the poor could depend.

However, in the last seven years a number of economic, fiscal, and demographic factors, in combination with provisions of earlier housing legislation have significantly changed the outlook for a large subset of the housing supply for low-income people. Housing resources assumed to be secure are, in fact, not secure. As the number of poor people has increased, the stock of housing traditionally available to them has eroded, both from upgrading for higher income tenants and through disrepair and abandonment.[1] At the same time production of low-cost rental housing has come to a virtual standstill as tax reform has changed the financial groundrules for private developers and the federal government as largely withdrawn from production programs. The essence of the HUD response has been to offer direct assistance (certificates and vouchers) to a few needy tenants. This policy does not expand the inventory of housing units permanently available to the poor and fails to solve the housing problem of many applicants because they are unable to locate a qualifying unit.

A further threat to this tight housing situation and the one this chapter is concerned with is the pending loss through expiration of use restrictions, or through default, of a very large portion of the assisted private housing stock. Perhaps as much as 80 percent of these units may be lost within the next two decades unless steps are taken now to prevent it. When the units were built, mainly in the 1960s, or when they accepted operating subsidies with contractual strings in the 1970s, the possibility that they might revert to market rents when their obligations to restrict tenants and rents expired or that they might go into default seemed far in the future. However, the contract periods are now beginning to run out. Given the continuing need for assisted housing, this potential loss has caused the preservation of this housing to emerge as a major housing policy issue. Policy makers must grapple with the problem and find a solution which is cost-effective and fair both to incumbent tenants and to landlords before too many units are lost.

The first section of this chapter describes the housing options facing low-income households. The specific contractual and tax situations of HUD-insured properties built in the 1960s with federal housing subsidies, those with the earliest expiring use restrictions, are discussed in detail in the following sections of the paper to verify the reality of the threatened loss and to suggest possible means of preventing it. The final section recommends policy initiatives to preserve this housing stock.

Housing Options of the Poor

For its housing needs, the low-income population depends primarily on three sources of rental housing supply: public housing, private unassisted units available at low rents, and federally assisted private housing.

Public Housing

The public housing inventory totals 1.3 million units scattered across the country, though concentrated in a dozen large cities. Public housing residents in recent years increasingly have very low incomes and are dependent on public housing. Unlike earlier generations of public housing tenants who used public housing as a stepping stone to improved private options, they are more likely to remain where they are.[2] Public housing waiting lists—a putative indicator of demand for decent low cost housing—are now sometimes longer than the supply of available public housing units in the area.[3] In Chapter 13 of this volume, Michael Stegman addresses the preservation issue for public housing, including issues related to physical improvements.

Unassisted Private Housing

The private unassisted stock of housing, almost nine million units available at low rents (defined here as $250/month in 1983 dollars), represents a substantial resource for low-income households. While the quality of these units varies considerably, they are important because they provide the largest stock of housing for the poor. In recent years, however, the number of such units has sharply dropped, owing both to upgrading and conversion to units asking higher rents on the one hand, and demolition and abandonment on the other.

During the 1970s, the stock of low-rent units shrank (net) by 18 percent—from 10.8 to 8.8 million units.[4] While a variety of mechanisms collectively referred to as the "shadow market" may yet produce more low-rent units, such housing certainly cannot be constructed and rented privately because poor people cannot pay the rent typically required by the market for a new or rehabilitated unit.[5]

Assisted Private Housing

The poor also depend on 1.952 million units of federally assisted, privately owned housing units developed under a variety of programs, mainly between 1965 and 1982.[6] These units are available to low- and moderate-income tenants at rents not exceeding 30 percent of their income. While the early programs, Section 221 (d)(3) and Section 236, were targeted originally toward moderate-income households, over the years they became important resources for low-income households as well. The current income mix among households in these units reflects that changing dynamic.

In addition to the 1.952 million units with project-based assistance, nearly 800,000 Section 8 Existing certificates and vouchers—tenant-based subsidies—cover part of the rent for private units under short-term contracts.

While these units with various forms of project assistance are privately owned, the terms of their availability and their rents are governed by a variety of contracts and agreements that keep them available to the poor only as long as the contracts are in force. The preservation issue concerns the future of this stock of housing as those contracts and restrictions expire and their owners face the market.

The privately owned, federally subsidized units which are at risk will reach critical contract and financial milestones over the next 15 years. Preservation is not a discrete event to be met once but a process that can be put in place to address a slowly unfolding challenge. The preservation issue is compounded because the units represent an existing resource to be preserved rather than a new housing opportunity on which no individual has a personal claim. In preservation, there are vested interests in the person of incumbent tenants.

Recognition of the imminent threat to low-income housing raises new fears that the gap between the need and the resources will widen, that the regulatory provisions and contracts which have protected the poor in the past will not exist, and that the means the poor have used in the past for self-help (i.e., moving to public or assisted housing, finding a cheap apartment, etc.) will not be applicable. When all the resources available—the assisted units, the public housing units, and the low-rent units—are added up and matched against the low-income population expected in the next 20 years, a substantial widening of the gap between the number of units available and the number of

TABLE 12.1   Number of Housing Units Subject to Potential Prepayments and Section 8 Opt-Outs, 1985–2005

Program	Current stock	Max potential loss
Section 8, New, Sub. Rehab. and Mod Rehab	840,000	696,000
Section 236 and 221(d)(3), BMIR[a]	696,000	334,000
FmHA, Section 515	305,000	305,000
Other FHA	111,000	78,000
Total	1,952,000	1,413,000

[a] Below Market Interest Rate. This category includes properties financed by state housing finance agencies and not insured by HUD.

Source: Kathleen G. Heintz and Ann B. Schnare, "Issues Facing the Assisted Housing Stock" (Washington: The Urban Institute, July, 1987), a paper prepared for the National Low-income Housing Preservation Commission, Exhibit 3, based on compilations of HUD data by the Congressional Budget Office and the General Accounting Office.

households needing them is evident. Though there is debate about the size of the gap, there is no doubt it will widen.[7] This, in short, is the case for adding housing preservation to our housing agenda.

Scope of the Preservation Problem

We can put some numerical parameters on the problem of preserving the stock of assisted private housing. Table 12.1 summarizes the potential loss through the year 2005 of units from the 1.952 million units of existing assisted housing, based on current contract provisions. For the older inventory of HUD subsidy programs (Section 236 and Section 221 (d)(3)) and the Farmers Home Administration rental subsidy program (FmHA Section 515), the table indicates potential losses should owners elect to prepay the project mortgage, when contracts permit, and convert the projects to market use. The HUD Section 8 project-based subsidy program allows owners to "opt out" at the end of subsidy contracts. The table indicates the number of potential conversions of these projects to market uses should the owners elect to take that option and not renew their subsidy contracts.

The numbers in Table 12.1 are meant to suggest the maximum number of losses in each category. Although the contracts of 1,413,000 of the 1,952,000 units are due to expire by the year 2005, there is no claim that 72 percent of the units will surely be lost when contracts permit; however, potential losses through disinvestment and default on financially distressed properties are also possible. It is clear that the risk is large.

Factors Affecting Existing HUD-Insured Housing

Under the sponsorship of the National Corporation of Housing Partnerships and the Ford Foundation and with the endorsement of the Housing Subcommittees of the Senate and House of Representatives, the National Low-Income Housing Preservation Commission (NLIHPC) was formed in the spring of 1987 to address the looming problem of the potential loss of assisted housing units. Backed by a Technical Advisory Group of leading housing policy analysts, the Commission undertook a broad review of the problem. It focused its empirical work on an investigation of the older HUD-insured stock of Section 236 and 221(d)(3) housing through a contract with Abt Associates Inc., of Cambridge, Massachusetts.[8]

The results of the Abt study indicate both the gravity of the problem and possible solutions. The basic contractual and tax aspects affecting these properties are reviewed below. The Commission's empirical findings about threats to this stock and costs of remedies are summarized in the following section.

Use Restrictions

Contracts restricting property uses were generally entered into at the time the project was initially financed or later, when additional operating funds were needed to maintain the project's viability. Two of the older programs for providing assisted housing to low and moderate-income persons provided reduced interest rate mortgages—the Below Market Interest Rate (BMIR) program enacted under Section 221(d)(3) of the Housing Act of 1961 and the Section 236 interest subsidy program enacted in the Housing Act of 1968. In general, nonprofit owner/sponsors of these projects were required to maintain their availability to qualifying low-income households throughout the 40-year life of the mortgage. Projects originally established as nonprofit retain their 40-year obligation even if they were later reconfigured as for-profit projects. For-profit owners in general were obliged to maintain use as assisted housing only for a period of 20 years.

Owners desiring to sell a property before the end of the use restriction period were required to obtain HUD approval for any transfer, and HUD made sure that the new owner took on the use restriction. Owners with use restrictions expiring before the end of the mortgage term, however, can elect to prepay the HUD-insured mortgage and be relieved of the use restrictions running with the mortgage. This option is just now coming due for the first of many projects that will have the option over the next 15 years. Projects financed with below market interest rate bonds issued by state housing finance agencies and having a federal contract for interest subsidy under the Section 236 program were subject only to the use restrictions imposed by the state agencies. Figure 12.1 shows that the number of units in properties eligible to prepay is growing rapidly, reaching a peak in 1994.

Supplementary Subsidy Contracts

The Rent Supplement Program and the Rental Assistance Program provided long-term, 40-year subsidy contracts in connection with the 221(d)(3) program. These 40-year subsidy contracts carried with them a use restriction for the life of the subsidy contract. Many of the latter were converted into shorter term Section 8 subsidies because the current administration, eager to reduce the long-term housing subsidy obligations of the federal government, courted owners having Rent Supplement or Rental Assistance Program subsidy contracts with the offer to replace their 40-year subsidy contracts with Section 8 rental assistance contracts having a maximum period of obligation of 15 years.

Although most owners jumped at this opportunity to create an earlier opportunity for conversion of their projects to market rate, some owners, particularly nonprofit ones, preferred to retain the full-term subsidy contract. One immediate and obvious policy for preserving assisted housing is for HUD to stop providing any further conversions of the older Rent Supplement or Rental Assistance Programs. The remaining opportunity is small though. In a random sample of 300 of these older projects reviewed in the Abt study, fewer than 7 percent (13 out of an original 195 projects) still have a Rent Supplement contract in force.

Another major subsidy now supporting 44 percent of the units in Section 236 and 221(d)(3) properties (according to the Abt sample) is Loan Management Set-Asides (LMSA). These supplementary subsidy contracts were entered into by property owners, especially during the energy crises of the mid-1970s, in order to increase project income and cover operating expenses while limiting the tenant portion of the rents to 30 percent of income. Among the 76 percent of properties with at least some LMSA, the maximum current extent of the contracts reaches the early 1990s for a large group of properties and to the late 1990s for another group. Unless extended beyond their current term, the loss of this subsidy could precipitate a financial crisis for the property owners, leading to default.

Finally, the Flexible Subsidy Program, started in the 1970s, provided mid-life assistance for the physical rehabilitation of deteriorated projects. This program obliged the owners to a 40-year use restriction, as well, independently of any shorter-term restriction attached to the mortgage. For-profit

Figure 12.1 Estimated Number of BMIR and Section 236 Projects With Mortgages Eligible for Prepayment, 1986-2001

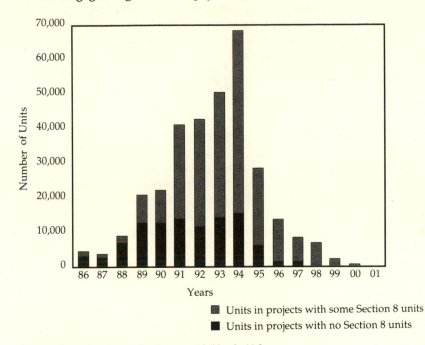

Source: CBO tabulations using data provided by the U.S.
Department of Housing and Urban Development (HUD)
in November 86. Ref. CBO Staff Working Paper "The
Potential Loss of Assisted Housing Units as Certain
Mortgage-Interest Subsidy Programs Mature", March 1987.

projects with initial use restrictions of 20 years were obliged to enter into a 40-year obligation for use as assisted housing upon entering into a Flexible Subsidy contract with HUD.

Tax Law and Resyndication Effects

The tax law changes enacted in the 1981 Economic Recovery Tax Act provided a strong inducement for for-profit owners to sell these older assisted housing projects because new owners could take advantage of very favorable depreciation provisions and the accompanying tax shelter. Of the projects eligible to prepay and convert at the twentieth year, or shortly thereafter, approximately 38 percent, based on the study sample described later, were resyndicated or reconfigured to take advantage of these provisions. These transfers had to have the approval of HUD as a Transfer of Physical Assets (TPA), and HUD usually required some investment in the property to meet capital improvement needs. The typical arrangement was that the buyers paid for their purchase in two components—enough cash that the sellers (primarily the limited partners) could pay their capital gains tax on the sale and a non-amortizing note, usually to the general partner, payable with accrued interest upon sale or at the end of 15 years, the end of the depreciation period. Until stopped by the 1984 Deficit Reduction Tax Act the seller was allowed to claim accrued annual interest as an expense, even though it was not actually paid, and the buyer was allowed to defer reporting the accrued interest until it was actually received.

The resyndication (or restructuring of ownership even if not actually re-syndicated) arrangement created additional depreciable basis in the property, thereby increasing the tax shelter even more, and provided a residual claim against profits of a future sale. This layering of interests in resyndicated projects means that not only the current owners but the holder(s) of the second trust notes also effectively participate in the decision about the disposition of the project at expiration of the use restrictions and again at the time when the second trust note and accrued interest come due either at the point of re-financing or at the balloon payment date (usually 15 years). The obligation of the current owners to pay off the second trust note may itself cause conver-sions to be deferred at least until the balloon payment (a onetime lump sum payment of principal and accrued interest) is due, because sale proceeds would not be sufficient to cover it. This overhang of the balloon payment typi-cally runs from 2 to 12 years past the end of the use restriction attached to the mortgage loan.

It may mean that for these projects there is a built-in financial damper that will inhibit sales until the second trust note is due. At that point, however, the sheer size of this obligation is likely to force a sale by the owners to at-tempt to raise the necessary funds or force the owners to put the project into the hands of the second note holders. Among the properties held by for-profit owners, 40 percent have second notes. These will mature in the period 1997 to 2000 with a peak in 1999. For properties eligible to prepay, this demand will force a prepayment at that point unless another option is more attractive to the second note holders.

Analysis of a Sample of Assisted Projects

The study by Abt Associates for the NLIHPC focused on a sample of 300 projects drawn from the HUD inventory of 236, 221(d)(3) Below-Market In-terest Rate (BMIR) and Market Rate (with Loan Management Set-Aside rental assistance) housing. The study sample was taken from the same sample of projects about which the HUD Office of Policy Development and Research (Hodes, et al.) had earlier obtained data on physical condition and costs of needed repairs.[9] These data, provided to the NLIHPC, were combined with local assessments of the market value of these projects obtained by telephone interviews (the Market Value Survey) conducted by Abt to assess the likely future of these projects based on their type of ownership and market situation.

The problem of possible loss of assisted housing under the Section 236 and 221(d)(3) programs is addressed by considering this older assisted housing in three classes to reflect differences in use restrictions and ownership. (Figures in parentheses are the national totals. Note that because the Commission focused on HUD-insured projects, the 645,000-unit total is a subset of the 696,000-unit total that includes state housing finance agency projects.) These are:

1. nonprofit projects (171,000 units in 1,420 properties);
2. for-profit projects not eligible to prepay—that is, limited dividend projects (for-profit with a restricted cash return, usually 6 percent annually of the initial equity) that have a 40-year use restriction attached (either because they were originally sponsored as a non-profit or have had Flexible Subsidy workouts or continue to have 40-year Rent Supplement contracts) (106,100 units in 820 properties); and
3. for-profit projects eligible to prepay, i.e., with use restrictions only for 20 years (possibly extended somewhat by Loan Management Set-Aside subsidy contracts) (367,500 units in 3,240 properties).

For the first two categories, the preservation issue is whether the properties can survive financially through the full 40-year mortgage term. For the nonprofit projects, the essential financial questions are whether the project has sufficient cash flow to support current expenses and maintain a reserve for repairs and replacements. If not, sponsors are assumed to sell the property under a low-income housing tax credit conversion, using the Low-Income Housing Tax Credit established by the Tax Reform Act of 1986, to avert default. The HUD Policy Development and Research Study by Hodes, et al. made estimates of physical improvement needs of these projects and whether the replacement reserve was adequate for them.

All these types of projects were about equally likely to need funds for physical repairs beyond that available from project replacement reserves and any cash income from the project. About a third of all projects need an average of $600 per unit, over and above project resources, for necessary repairs. The NLIHPC model assumed that whatever funds were needed for repairs were spent, even if that meant owners having to lend the money, at least until the accumulated demands reach $5,000 per unit or forty percent of the capital gains tax payable upon default.

For the nonprofit projects, the NLIHPC model assumed that owners would sustain the project through the full mortgage term (and beyond) as long as the cumulative amount that had to be put into the project for repairs beyond those covered by project income did not exceed $5,000 per unit. If the $5,000 limit was reached, the owners were assumed to attempt a tax credit conversion, if possible, before yielding to the necessity of default.

For the second class of projects, the NLIHPC model assessed the best financial choice of the owners on a discounted present value basis. The after-tax return for each year of project operation and the after-tax returns (or costs) upon sale were discounted to the present at a typical discount rate of 13 percent. Owners were assumed to choose the most profitable discounted value among their choices:

Default

Sell to a low-income housing tax credit conversion

Hold through the mortgage term and sell at market values

The essential financial question faced by the owners is whether there is a positive cash flow after taking care of repair and replacement needs and, if not, whether the prospect of having to pay the capital gains tax upon default makes it worthwhile to put off default for some time. In the event of default on the mortgage, the project owners are regarded for tax purposes as having sold the property at the value of whatever property liabilities are discharged—in this case, primarily the outstanding balance on the HUD-insured mortgage. Because most of these projects will have taken such substantial amounts of depreciation for tax purposes, their basis for tax purposes is quite low. The result is that an effective sale at the mortgage balance constitutes a sizable capital gain (amount by which the mortgage balance exceeds the tax basis of the property), hence a large tax hit that must be paid out of other income of the owners.

For the third class of properties, the owners can consider the option of converting the property to market (unassisted) uses. Whether they choose to do so is conditioned by whether an economically attractive market exists, either for market rate rentals, or condominium conversion, or for some other purpose. The Market Survey data obtained by the NLIHPC provided the judgment of local real estate experts as to the likely market for these projects and the rents or sale prices that might obtain. Properties were assumed to require $5,000 to $25,000 per unit in modernization expenses to reach the estimated market values.

This market information was combined with project information from HUD data files to develop a financial model for analyzing these projects. The model assumes that the for-profit projects used the depreciation allowances that were in effect for the period when the project was originally set up or at the point of change of ownership. To establish reasonable estimates of the tax basis for these projects, the equity portion of the projects and the amounts of second trust notes assumed by partnerships at resyndication were estimated from industry experience provided by the National Corporation for Housing Partnerships.

This financial model was used to evaluate the owners' perspective for the third class of projects, for-profit projects eligible to prepay. These owners are assumed to choose the option that would provide the highest discounted present value of the stream of after-tax annual returns among the following possibilities:

Default immediately

Continue for a period and default

Continue as assisted housing past the use restriction period (possibly transferring the property at some point to another owner operating it as assisted housing)

Sell to an owner able to use the low-income housing tax credit

Convert to market either at the end of the restricted use period (20 years) or within the period up to the point when the balloon payments come due on the second trust note

The results of the NLIHPC model estimates are summarized in Table 12.2 for a 15-year period ending with the year 2002. Only 19 percent of the

TABLE 12.2   Predicted Owner Actions by the Year 2002, Older HUD-insured Assisted Housing[a]

	Default	Prepayment/ market conversion	Operate as is through next 15 years	Total
Nonprofit, not eligible to prepay	68%	—	32%	100%
For profit, not eligible to prepay	73%	—	27%	100%
For profit, eligible to prepay	23%	66%	11%	100%
All types of properties combined	43%	38%	19%	100%
Units	280,000	243,000	122,000	645,000

[a] The model predicts no use of the low-income housing tax credit under current terms: 10-year holding period and availability only through 1989.

Source: National Low-Income Housing Preservation Commission, *Preventing the Disappearance of Low-Income Housing* (Washington: NLIHPC, 1988).

Figure 12.2 Number of Units Affected by Cumulative Prepayments, Cumulative Defaults, Balance Operating as Subsidized – Base Case

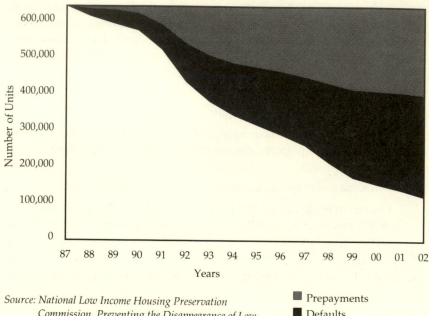

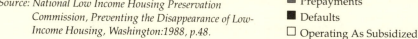

Source: National Low Income Housing Preservation Commission, Preventing the Disappearance of Low-Income Housing, Washington:1988, p.48.

■ Prepayments
■ Defaults
☐ Operating As Subsidized

645,000 units are predicted to remain in the subsidized housing stock at the end of this period; 43 percent are predicted to default and 38 percent to pre-pay. Figure 12.2 from the NLIHPC work shows the predicted timing of these actions over the next 15 years. Serious numbers of defaults and prepayments are predicted in the period when the 20-year use restrictions expire, com-pounded by the end of currently contracted Loan Management Set-Aside subsidies in the early 1990s. Another large drop in the number of units re-maining subsidized is predicted in the 1995 to 2000 period when properties are affected by a combination of loss of currently contracted Loan Manage-ment Set-Asides and by the maturing of the second trust notes on a number of properties. Some 280,000 units are predicted to be lost to defaults and 243,000 to prepayments over this period.

Large numbers of low-income tenants would be affected by such actions. Based on the data collected for the NLIHPC sample of 300 properties, 70 per-cent of the current tenants have incomes under 50 percent of local median income, adjusted for family size, and 83 percent have incomes under 80 per-cent of local median income. The income distributions follow this pattern across all of the categories of predicted owner actions. The problem is grave both in terms of numbers of units and in terms of the tenants who will be affected.

By estimating the investment value of these projects as the basis for owner choices, the NLIHPC model yields an estimate of the amount of money required just to match the market value of a conversion. This amount indicates the financial inducement necessary to dissuade the owner from converting. Presumably if another party offered the same sale price the owners would be indifferent to the source of funds. For example, if a property could be sold for $2 million, $500,000 of which was needed to pay off an outstanding mortgage balance, another offer of $1.5 million and a commitment to take over the mortgage would exactly rival the market option. Additional funds might be necessary to maintain the viability of the project under a restriction to continue as assisted housing. To estimate the supporting subsidies necessary to sustain a property as low-income housing once either default or prepayment had been prevented, the NLIHPC model computed the annual amount of projected operating cash deficit.

Table 12.3 summarizes the NLIHPC results for these estimated costs for preventing defaults and prepayments and sustaining operation as low-income housing. In addition to the direct payments for dealing with defaults or prepayments the table also indicates the NLIHPC estimates for the ongoing subsidies attached to these properties and necessary for their continued operation as low-income housing—interest rate subsidy payments for the Section 236 properties and the Loan Management Set-Aside payments. The combined 15-year total for preserving all 523,000 units at risk is $18.6 billion. If all the annual costs are discounted at a government discount rate (the Commission used the average rate of long-term Treasury bonds, 8.7 percent) and these costs are divided by the 15-year average number of units preserved, the estimated discounted present value for preserving the defaulting properties is $26,000 and for the prepaying properties, $35,000. The 15-year average of units preserved is used to avoid understating per-unit costs; for example, while 280,000 units are projected to be lost to default by the year 2002, the 15-year average number of units that would be in default is 156,000.

Other noneconomic factors could reduce the size of the inducement needed. Owners might reasonably be willing to accept less in exchange for not having to displace tenants or face the ire of local community groups about converting a particular project, as well as avoiding whatever stigma might spread from this project to other development efforts of the owners.

To evaluate the cost-effectiveness of such expenditures it is essential to consider alternatives to preserving these existing subsidized units. At one extreme, tenants in these projects might find long-term rental subsidies for their use in the regular private rental market—such as the housing vouchers or Section 8 certificate programs for tenant-based rental assistance—to be quite ade-

TABLE 12.3   Estimated 15-Year Costs of Preventing Defaults and Prepayments in Older HUD-insured Assisted Housing

	Defaults	*Prepayments*	*Total*
Prevent all defaults and prepayments			
Direct payments	$4.5 billion	$ 6.5 billion	$11.0 billion
Ongoing subsidies	$4.0 billion	$ 3.6 billion	$ 7.6 billion
Total	$8.5 billion	$10.1 billion	$18.6 billion
Total units preserved by 2002	280,000	243,000	523,000
15-year average number of units preserved	156,000	145,000	301,000
Discounted present value/ unit preserved	$26,000	$35,000	
Prevent all but most costly 50,000 units[a]			
Direct payments	$3.3 billion	$ 5.0 billion	$ 8.3 billion
Ongoing subsidies	$3.3 billion	$ 3.1 billion	$ 6.4 billion
Total	$6.6 billion	$ 8.1 billion	$14.7 billion
Total units preserved by 2002	255,000	218,000	473,000
15-year average number of units preserved	131,000	126,000	257,000
Discounted present value/ unit preserved	$22,000	$32,000	
(1) $30,000 vouchers as replacement	$1.7 billion	$ 1.3 billion	$ 3.0 billion
Grand Total	$8.3 billion	$ 9.4 billion	$17.7 billion
(2) $44,000 vouchers as replacement	$2.5 billion	$ 1.9 billion	$ 4.4 billion
Grand Total	$9.1 billion	$10.0 billion	$19.1 billion

[a] Excludes properties with new direct payments per unit greater than $30,000 (DPV) plus $11,000 (DPV) in ongoing Section 236 and Section 8 subsidies.

Source: National Low-Income Housing Commission, *Preventing the Disappearance of Low-income Housing* (Washington: NLIHPC, 1988).

quate. At the other extreme, housing costs might be so high and available rental alternatives so few that the only substitute housing for displaced tenants would be new construction or rehabilitation of replacement subsidized housing.

As a benchmark for the lower cost alternative of providing tenant-based assistance (housing vouchers or Section 8 certificates), the Commission obtained from the Office of Management and Budget and from the Congressional Budget Office estimates of the average national costs of such tenant assistance.

These costs are in the range of the lowest estimates for replacement housing the Commission obtained from government agencies. The Office of Management and Budget provided an estimate of the national first-year costs for Section 8 certificates or Housing Vouchers that amount, over the 15-year horizon used by the Commission, to $30,000 per unit on a discounted present value basis. The first-year figure provided by the Congressional Budget Office yields $44,000 per unit on a discounted present value basis over the 15-year period. If no preservation actions whatever were undertaken but all of the tenants could be protected with tenant-based assistance (Section 8 certificates or Housing Vouchers), the Commission estimates the total 15-year cost would amount to $21 billion—$11 billion for units in defaulting properties and $10 billion in prepaying properties. With the higher estimate for tenant-based assistance from the Congressional Budget Office, this total would rise to $31 billion. The preservation costs estimated by the Commission are thus of the same order as the voucher/certificate alternative.

However, the preservation costs for some projects are higher than the voucher/certificate alternative on a per unit basis. To test a conservative limit on preservation actions, the Commission also made estimates of the costs involved if a cutoff of $30,000 per unit in discounted present value of new, direct payments were made. (Adding the discounted present value of the ongoing Section 236 interest subsidies and LMSA subsidies makes this effective cutoff $41,000 per unit.) The highest per unit costs for preventing defaults and prepayments came to $80,000 in discounted present value terms. Table 3 summarizes the effects of such a cutoff, which has the effect of dealing with 473,000 units or leaving 50,000 to default or prepay. The combined 15-year costs of new, direct payments and ongoing subsidies amount to $14.7 billion.

Whether it is cost-effective to set such a cutoff depends on the alternatives available if there is a public commitment to maintain at least an equivalent number of low-income housing units. If alternative housing could be provided through vouchers or certificates for tenants displaced from properties not preserved, the cost for the vouchers or certificates would be an additional $3 billion, using the OMB figure, making the total 15-year costs for all 523,000 units $17.76 billion. If the voucher or certificate costs for the displacees are more like the $44,000 figure from the Congressional Budget Office, the 15-year costs would be $4.4 billion, yielding a total for all 523,000 households of $19.1 billion—a higher figure than the $18.6 billion for dealing with all defaults and prepayments.

The Commission used a fixed national figure for the tenant-based assistance alternatives. The actual cost of such assistance varies by location so that for some of the properties in the older subsidized stock, the tenant-based assistance may be more cost effective than preserving these older properties. On the other hand, it seems quite possible that the areas in which prepayments are likely also will be areas in which housing costs are high, housing markets are tight, and tenant-based assistance difficult to use. In fact, the most feasible replacement housing may be rehabilitation of substandard units or even new construction, which would rival the highest estimates of costs of preserving these older properties. Project-specific solutions to the problems of default and prepayments appear to be more cost-effective as a means of continuing to provide assisted housing than either vouchers or other alternatives for all but a very few projects.

The Commission tested various broad, self-implemented policies as alternatives to the direct, project-specific approach. Policies such as extending Section 8 contracts beyond their current expirations or expanding and extending the low-income housing tax credit only added 50,000 or fewer units to the 15-year average preserved and at much higher per unit costs than the direct strategy. The Commission noted that current project incomes are on average $100 per month less than the local Fair Market Rents for the Section 8 Existing housing program—the effective limit for contract rents under the Section 8 program. Applying a $100 per month per unit of additional income to the properties preserved an average of 149,000 units more than the no-intervention predictions, leaving 162,000 units for other treatments, and at a cost per unit of $47,000 in discounted present value terms, including the ongoing Section 236 and Section 8 subsidies. The conclusion is that project-specific solutions matched to the economies of each project threatened with default or market conversion are both less costly on a per-unit basis *and* are more likely to preserve a larger number of units.

Remaining Questions

While our research provides a broad outline of the preservation options available, several important questions remain. What type and mix of subsidies are required to preserve the assisted stock? How are the responsibilities (i.e., project workouts, financing, etc.) to be shared between the federal government and state or local government? How do we frame a national policy which takes account of the varied project, market, and owner characteristics that need to be considered? Who will be the new owners of units that go into default? How do we build the capacity of the nonprofit sector to house the poor and how do we build long-term interest in low-income housing on the part of for-profit developers?

In addition, the present research looks at preservation of the older assisted stock. In less than five years, we will have to address the same preservation questions to the newer Section 8 inventory. How do we frame preservation policy to take account, not just of the universe of the older projects, but of this larger universe? (There are 840,000 Section 8 units, compared to fewer than 700,000 in the sample addressed here.)

Conclusions and Challenges

The importance of preservation has been established. Preliminary studies have been done, congressional inquiries have been mounted, advocates of tenants have mobilized, state and local state officials have taken action. A serious national commitment is needed to begin actually addressing the preservation problem.

Some scattered initiatives have already been taken. New York State has placed a moratorium on prepayment of state financed projects. The Massachusetts legislature is considering rent control on all converted units. At the federal level, Title II of the Housing and Community Development Act of 1987, referred to as the Emergency Low-income Housing Preservation Act of 1987, requires advance notice by a sponsor of their intention to prepay (where none existed before), provides for some HUD-negotiated financial incentives to extend the operation of the project as subsidized, and imposes a virtual two-year moratorium on prepayments.

The complexity of the preservation issue requires weighing several interests, including those of incumbent tenants, eligible low- and moderate-income tenants who also might expect to rent the units if they were preserved, owners and sponsors, investors, those who would provide subsidy and other resources, and regulatory interests.

While many questions remain, we believe the specific findings we cite relative to the Section 236 and 221 (d)(3) programs do point toward some basic direction in a preservation policy.

> The federal government should make the commitment to assure the most cost-effective preservation of or substitution for the units determined in this analysis to be at risk.

> There is an important role for state and local government in designing and implementing preservation plans for their jurisdictions. However, the financial responsibility is federal and in the absence of initiatives by state and local government, the federal government should take action.

> Project specific solutions are preferable to general ones or to policies that rely primarily on vouchers.

The solution to the problems of default and prepayment is simple. In the case of default the issue is how best to inject revenues that will take the project out of red ink and put it on a sound footing. We recommend an injection of project-based subsidies that cover operating costs and debt service, including new debt service to cure physical or financial problems. As the NLIHPC report suggests, virtually all of the at-risk units can be saved at lower cost than any other policy option.

In the case of prepayment, the issue is whether we are willing to pay the cost to dissuade owners from market conversions. Many owners will be willing to accept less than this full amount for reasons indicated. We believe that the strategy of direct negotiation with owners is the route to the best arrangement that can be obtained in most cases to both protect units and help present tenants.

In the context of financial restructuring of the projects, it is in the long-term interest of low-income tenants to make sure that the projects are owned by sponsors committed to serving a low-income population. To that end, we believe that preservation policies should encourage the sale of the projects to capable nonprofit owners.

Closing the gap between what the poor can afford and what shelter costs is not likely to be done by the sleight of hand (i.e., limited subsidy, skimpy development budgets, construction shortcuts, or favorable tax provisions) that characterized the older subsidy programs. Indeed, many of the poor cannot afford to pay even the cost of *operation* of decent housing—maintenance, taxes, utilities—if the structure itself were provided at no cost, debt-free. Long-term solutions will require long-term commitments.

Notes

1. See Chapter 2 in this volume by William Apgar for a full discussion of the decrease in the supply of low-cost housing and the increase in the numbers of low-income households in recent years.

2. For an overview of public housing, see generally, Raymond Struyk, *A New System of Public Housing* (Washington: Urban Institute, 1980); and Citizens Housing and Planning Association, *A Research Report: Tenancy and Costs in Public Housing Policies, Attitudes and Case Studies* (Boston: CHAPA, 1986).

3. In a 1985 survey of 8 of the largest public housing authorities, the Council of Large Public Housing Authorities (CLPHA) found that in each case the waiting list was larger than total public housing inventory in those communities. See CLPHA, *Public Housing Today* (Washington: CLPHA, 1986) 6.

4. See National Association of Homebuilders, *Low and Moderate Income Housing: Progress, Problems and Prospects* (Washington: NAHB, 1986) 16.

5. The "shadow market" as used here refers to the formal and informal ways that housing is created from the existing structures by rehabilitating, converting or reclaiming space for residential purposes. This process of adjustment accommodates demand for housing consistent with the resources of those who demand it. For example, lower quality units are created for low income households. For an elaboration of this phenomenon and its impacts over time, see William Baer, "The Shadow Market in Housing," *Scientific American* 255.5 (November 1986) 29–35.

The basic disincentive for private construction of low-rent housing is the substantial reduction in tax benefits to rental housing. Instead of developers relying on tax benefits to supplement return, new rental housing must pass development feasibility and investment tests based on cash flow. Since no costs are reduced, rents must be higher on such housing. When the housing is not subsidized, it means new rental housing is affordable to a smaller band of the income stream, which is also the group who may be able to buy a home. For a discussion of these issues, see National Association of Homebuilders, *Homebuilding after Tax Reform* (Washington: NAHB, 1986). Also see A. Downs, *The Revolution in Real Estate Finance* (Washington: Brookings Institution, 1985).

6. There are presently no major programs adding to this supply of federally assisted units. The leveraged grants and loans under such programs as HODAG are not funded to make major additions to the stock. It is not yet clear whether the Low Income Housing Tax Credit will constitute a substantial incentive to increasing the supply of affordable housing.

7. Clay has projected a gap of 7.8 million units by the year 2003. See P. Clay, *At Risk of Loss: The Endangered Future of Low Income Rental Housing Resources* (Washington: Neighborhood Reinvestment Corp., 1987) 24. The Clay estimate assumes this number if no ameliorative action is taken. HUD estimates that the number in 2003 will be 3.2 million units assuming an annual assistance growth (vouchers, etc.) of 79,000 units. See Memorandum from C. Duncan McRae, HUD Deputy Asst. Secretary to Carl Covitz, HUD, July 1987, 2.

8. The Report of the National Low-Income Housing Preservation Commission, *Preventing the Disappearance of Low Income Housing* (Washington: NLIHPC, 1988).

9. L. Hodes et al., *HUD/FHA Insured Rental Housing: Physical and Financial Condition of Multifamily Properties Insured Before 1975* (Washington: HUD Policy Development and Research, April 1987).

Chapter 13
The Role of Public Housing in a Revitalized National Housing Policy

Michael A. Stegman

It has been said that public housing is unpopular with everybody except those who live in it and those who are waiting to get in. This includes more than 1.3 million families who currently occupy public housing units and nearly 800,000 more who are on the waiting lists of one of the nation's 3,060 local public housing authorities (PHAs).[1]

Despite its seeming unpopularity, public housing accounts for around 5 percent of all rental housing in the nation; for as much as 15 percent of all rental housing in a number of central cities, and a much higher percentage of their low-rent stocks;[2] and the demand continues to grow each year. According to the U.S. Conference of Mayors, last year the demand for assisted low-income housing increased in 88 percent of the cities surveyed, with the average increase in demand a startling 40 percent.[3] The National Association of Housing and Redevelopment Officials (NAHRO) reports that although applications are no longer accepted in a number of cities, public housing waiting lists grew by 16 percent between 1985 and 1986.[4]

Moreover, with just 17,000 vacant units available for rent across the country at any one time, the demand for public housing outstripped the available supply by a ratio of 46:1.[5] HUD argues that the vacancy figure understates the capacity of the public housing stock to house families on the waiting list. A more proper measure is the annual turnover rate that is around 14 percent. This means that almost 200,000 new public housing opportunities become available in any given year.[6] While this is true, public housing waiting lists are also dynamic. Among the 223 PHAs in the NAHRO sample, for example, there were 226,078 new applicants for public housing in 1986 alone.

While the average wait for public housing nationally is around 13 months, for 9 percent of all PHAs the average exceeds 3 years, and in many cities it is much longer than that: 7 years in Atlantic City, New Jersey; 5 years in Winston-Salem, North Carolina and 10 years in Jersey City.[7]

This same imbalance in supply and demand is evident in St. Louis. Of the 13,000 families on that waiting list, almost half (6,400) are waiting for the 1,596 three- and four-bedroom apartments the housing authority operates.[8] In Washington, D.C., one of the many cities that has stopped accepting public housing applications, the waiting list for the District's 11,749 units ranges from 10 months for an efficiency to 11 years for a four-bedroom apartment.[9] In short, especially for low-income families with children, when it comes to queuing up for public housing, waiting lists are "whole lives long."[10]

The following discussion charts a new course for public housing in the framework of a revitalized national low-income housing policy. While a focus on public housing alone may seem too narrow to inform the policy debate, the pending loss, due to expiring use restrictions, of thousands of privately owned, federally assisted units contradicts this view. The national investment in the 1.3 million public housing units that currently exist and the historical importance of the program to those who would be homeless without it assure its continuing importance in the nation's low-income housing future.

In this chapter we will discuss the program's poor public image and show how it differs from the reality of what public housing is and who is served by the program. We will summarize the federal commitment to public housing over the last fifty years and review available data on the cost-effectiveness of alternative deep subsidy production programs (surprisingly, public housing holds its own in this important area). We will propose a reinstatement of the public housing production program and will discuss the condition and costs of modernizing the current stock, a need that stands on a par with increasing production. The economics of public housing operations, including the need to reform the operating subsidy system, will also be examined. Finally, we will deal with recent federal efforts to sell off public housing to tenants. The chapter concludes by assessing the feasibility of the public housing sales program contained in recent legislation, and it offers an alternative approach to providing homeownership opportunities to public housing tenants.

Public Housing: Perception Versus Reality

Because of its crucial role in housing a sizable share of the nation's poor (especially single parent minority poor), the popular image of public housing is overwhelmingly negative. The common perception is that most public housing projects:

consist of large, dense, ugly developments built to minimum design specifications, which are poorly maintained and managed;

contain concentrations of large, minority families with undisciplined children and high crime rates;

are isolated from the surrounding community and have a negative impact upon it.[11]

In reality, however, just 27 percent of all public housing developments are high-rise buildings; 32 percent are garden apartments; 16 percent are low-rise walk-up apartments; and 25 percent are single-family detached or townhouse structures.[12]

Not only do high-rise projects, three-quarters of which are in the largest cities,[13] represent a small proportion of the stock, but the terrible living environments they create led Congress in 1974 to prohibit the construction of high-rise projects for families with children unless there is no practical alternative (Section 6(a), U.S. Housing Act of 1937, as amended).[14] Today, to the extent there is any new public housing development at all, high-rise construction is reserved for projects built expressly for the elderly in highly accessible locations within the community.

Who Lives in Public Housing

Contrary to the common perception, the majority of public housing residents are not welfare-dependent single women with children. As a matter of fact, about 38 percent are elderly, and a "small but growing percentage of public housing is occupied by young and middle-aged single people with some sort of handicap, many of whom would be homeless otherwise." Although a majority of the non-elderly are households with a single parent, a large segment of the all-adult families are married couples without children and some traditional two-parent families as well. Also, despite high rates of welfare dependency among single-parent families, around 42 percent of all non-elderly households in public housing have a wage earner. "The proportion of non-elderly families with working members has always been greatest in New York City (60 percent), yet working families constitute at least 30 percent of this group in Charlotte, Greensboro, Oklahoma City, Rochester and Seattle."[15] See Table 13.1.

Despite this heterogeneity, the families and individuals who live in public housing are generally very poor and have been growing poorer over time. For reasons having to do with changes in the demographic composition of cities and to a lesser degree, to federally mandated changes in tenant assignment policies, applicable income limits, and minimum and ceiling rents, incomes of public housing tenants have fallen significantly in real terms for at least the last thirty years. Between 1950 and 1970, for example, the median income of public housing tenants fell from 64 percent to 37 percent of the national median. And between 1974 and 1981, tenants with incomes between 10 percent and 30 percent of the national median rose from 60 percent to 65 percent of all tenants, while those with incomes over 30 percent of median fell from 36 percent to 31 percent of all public housing tenants.[16]

TABLE 13.1   Working Status and Income of Residents of Public Housing in the United States, 1985–86

	NON-ELDERLY FAMILIES			ALL HOUSEHOLDS		
	Number of families	*Percent working*	*Percent on welfare*	*Number of families*	*Average income ($1986)*	*Average monthly rent ($1986)*
Baltimore	10,916	29%	59%	17,680	5,920	116
Buffalo	2,675	23	59	4,570	5,594	127
Charlotte	2,509	38	45	4,020	5,470	100
Greensboro	1,577	51	27	2,220	6,960	141
Louisville	3,995	24	59	5,580	4,290	85
New York City	106,388	60	39	172,970	10,535	191
Oklahoma City	1,592	34	66	2,990	4,900	89
Philadelphia	16,200	18	70	20,580	6,130	123
Rochester	1,072	41	47	2,400	8,010	174
St. Paul	1,396	27	72	4,145	n.a.	133
Sacramento	1,450	12	66	2,790	n.a.	n.a.
Seattle	2,406	30	64	6,520	5,700	129
National sample		42	50		5,360	96

Source: Council of Large Public Housing Authorities, *Public Housing Today* (September 1986) 12.

It is not surprising to find that public housing tenants as a group had an average income in 1980 of only $6,803. For elderly and/or disabled households, who account for 38 percent of all public housing tenants, incomes were 18 percent lower ($5,557), while for families they were 5 percent higher ($7,169).[17]

Most public housing tenants are racial and ethnic minorities; 38 percent are white, 49 percent are black, and 13 percent are Hispanic and members of other minority groups. However, 85 percent of households in family projects administered by large housing authorities are minority. Contrary to popular opinion, incomes of blacks and whites in public housing are not significantly different and the relative incomes of both groups have fallen since 1950.[18]

Managing Public Housing

Public housing authorities (PHAs) are widely represented throughout the nation, although they are most heavily concentrated in the Southeast (26 percent) and Southwest (27 percent).[19] Contrary to public perception, not all housing authorities are very large. The average PHA manages just 403 units and 87 percent of all PHAs manage fewer than 500 units (Table 13.2). Another 9 percent own and manage between 500 and 1,249 units while the remaining 4 percent manage 1,250 units or more. These latter 140 PHAs manage 60 percent of the nation's public housing stock and the 15 largest PHAs among this group manage 30 percent of the stock. New York City, with 173,000 public housing units, is the largest of the nation's PHAs.

While the smallest housing authorities represent a near majority of PHAs, they collectively control fewer than 6 percent of all public housing units. Just as the misplaced popular image of the public housing program as a collection of monolithic high-rise projects undermines local and national political support for the program, so does this problem affect policy makers. One of the greatest challenges facing HUD and the Congress is promulgating rules, regulations, and laws relating to public housing that can be consistently applied to large- and small-scale programs; new ones and old ones; those located in big cities, suburban communities, and rural areas, and those characterized by densely built high-rise buildings or scattered-site single-family and townhouse-type developments.

TABLE 13.2   Units Managed by Large and Small Public Housing Authorities

PHA size category (units)	Number of PHAs	Percent	Units in category	Percent
Very small (<100)	1,533	46.8	71,716	5.5
Small (100–499)	1,313	40.1	289,371	22.2
Medium (500–1,249)	288	8.8	177,453	13.6
Large (≥1,250)	140	4.3	764,862	58.7
Total	3,274	100.0	1,303,402	100.0

Source: Council of Large Public Housing Authorities, *Public Housing Today* (September 1986) 5.

Production of Public Housing

Despite the ebb and flow of popular and political support for the program over the past 50 years, there are more public housing units in American communities today than any other type of assisted housing. More than four out of every ten units of federally subsidized housing were built under the public housing program. And should the Congress be unable or unwilling to negotiate extensions of the expiring regulatory agreements on hundreds of thousands of Section 8 and other privately owned and federally assisted units that guaranteed their low rent character, public housing's importance as a permanent, community housing resource will loom even larger in the future.

Public Housing Completions

From the time of its inception in 1937 until the 1980s, each successive decade saw more public housing units made ready for occupancy than the decade before. From 1939 to 1949, an average of 15,494 public housing units a year were completed (Table 13.3). As the program gained momentum, annual completions rose 63 percent during the 1950s to 25,202 units, and by another 47 percent during the 1960s, to 36,978 units a year. President Nixon's moratorium on all subsidized housing construction in 1973, and the privatization of low-income housing under the Housing and Community Development Act of 1974, still left the public housing program with enough momentum to end the 1970s with a higher average number of completions per year than in any previous decade (41,249 units, up 12 percent from the 1960s).

Despite unprecedented cuts in all low-income housing programs, the completion of prior year starts and the progression of previous-year reservations through ground-breaking enabled the Reagan administration's early housing record to look pretty good. New public housing starts exceeded 40,000 units a year as recently as 1981, and the ratio of starts to completions was well above unity in both 1980 and 1981. However, as previously approved units moved through the pipeline, with few new reservations behind them, annual completions exceeded the number of new starts for the first time in 1982 and for each year thereafter.

By 1988, public housing starts and completions will be almost in balance, but at substantially reduced levels from eight years earlier. Completions of new public housing units in 1988 will be 45 percent below those in 1980, and starts will be 82 percent lower.

Even at the height of Section 8 construction during the Carter administration, public housing maintained an important share of new assisted housing approvals. From 1976 to 1980, 244,200 public housing units were reserved for funding, which accounted for 13 percent of all HUD subsidized unit reservations. This increased to nearly 17 percent in 1981 and fell to 11 percent in

TABLE 13.3   Low-Income Public Housing Units Made Available for Occupancy
1939–1979

Calendar year	Units made available for occupancy	Per year	Change
1939–1949	170,436	15,494	—
1950–1959	252,015	25,202	+62.6%
1960–1969	369,777	36,978	+46.7%
1970–1979	412,490	41,249	+11.6%
Total	1,204,718	29,383	

Source: 1939–1949 data from *A Decent Home,* The Report of the President's Commission on Urban Housing (Washington: USGPO, 1968) 61; remaining data from *HUD Statistical Yearbook,* 1979.

1982. It was all downhill from 1983. Not only did total reservations fall dramatically, but public housing's share of the assisted housing budget shrank as well. In 1986, new public housing units accounted for less than 3 percent of all assisted housing reservations, which are now mostly in the form of Section 8 certificates and housing vouchers, and are projected to fall to just one percent in 1988. Unless it is revived by a future Congress, the public housing production program has ended.

The Cost-Effectiveness of Public Housing

As momentum builds for the resumption of some form of deep subsidy production, the issue of the relative efficiency of various construction alternatives must be addressed. The available and somewhat conflicting analyses of the cost-effectiveness of public housing construction nevertheless lead us to conclude that although more costly than other forms of subsidized new production, public housing's permanence and proven record of housing the most difficult low-income families warrants its continuation as an important component of our national housing policy.

One of the problems in assessing the cost-effectiveness of various low-income housing programs is disagreement over the components of program cost. For example, most cost analyses of public housing do not include the continuing costs of HUD operating subsidies, which averaged more than $1,200 per unit in 1985; nor do they consider the costs of the modernization program that, at around a billion dollars a year, adds nearly $800 annually to the cost of the average public housing unit.

Historically, construction standards, financing arrangements, and tenant contributions to rent have varied across low-income housing programs, thereby making cost comparisons all the more unreliable. We reviewed cost comparisons from three formal studies that were either carried out or sponsored by a federal agency, plus one back-of-the-envelope assessment by an executive director of a mid-sized PHA in the Southeast.

The GAO report. The first government study, completed in 1976 by the U.S. General Accounting Office, found public housing to be more cost-effective than either the Section 236 or Section 8 programs when both direct and indirect subsidies were considered. The study did not, however, take into account public housing operating subsidies or modernization costs. GAO found that public housing's lower cost was achieved while being built to "higher standards than Section 236." [20]

In the most prescient part of its assessment, GAO analysts found public housing's more permanent low-income character as an asset unmatched by any other form of low-income housing:

In addition to the lower subsidy under public housing, the building is still owned by the housing authority after it is paid off at the end of 40 years. If it has been adequately maintained and modernized, it can continue to provide housing. Other analyses have shown that public housing is more expensive and sometimes conclude that, since the buildings and land are retained and have some residual value, perhaps it is worth the expense. *Our calculations indicate that public housing is the cheaper alternative even before the residual value is considered. We have not tried to estimate this value, since the real value is the continuation of housing services and the freedom from starting new units at the end of 20 years* [emphasis added].[21]

The CBO study. Three years later, in 1979, the Congressional Budget Office (CBO) also found public housing to be the most cost-effective means (though less efficient than Section 8 existing housing) of creating affordable housing. According to the CBO, public housing costs ranged from $2,200 to $2,530 a unit in constant costs per year compared to $2,490 to $3,510 per unit for Section 8 new and substantial rehabilitation housing.[22]

The USR&E study. In 1980, HUD contracted with an independent research firm to compare multifamily program costs, using the FHA-insured unsubsidized program as the baseline against which to measure the cost-effectiveness of alternative production mechanisms. Unlike the earlier studies, Urban Systems Research and Engineering (USR&E) did not assume equal brick and mortar costs per unit for housing built under each program. Rather, the researchers substituted actual development costs for projects built during the period 1974 to 1979 for the hypothetical unit cost figures used by GAO. This enabled USR&E to estimate better the actual costs of various production alternatives.

According to USR&E, per unit construction costs for public housing were around 46 percent greater than those for Section 8 new construction, and almost 60 percent more expensive than for unsubsidized FHA projects. Total development costs for conventional public housing averaged $49.80 per square foot of gross floor space (in 1980 dollars). This compared to $43.89 per square foot for Section 202/8, and $31.87 for unsubsidized FHA projects.[23]

Although USR&E researchers were not able to pinpoint the causes of public housing's higher cost, they suggested that it was probably due more to lack of efficient production management at the housing authority level than it was to higher construction standards:

> While quality differences were shown to be slight for most public housing projects, higher land and site development costs appear to be an important factor in increasing public housing costs. The causes of these markups were difficult to pinpoint but, overall, indicated a need for more careful review and control in this area. In addition, it appears that the large number of uncontrolled budget categories for public housing permits a greater proportion of public housing costs to fall into non-dwelling accounts.[24]

While USR&E's implication is that poor management controls at the PHA level may be largely to blame for public housing's higher development cost, another reason could be that because it houses a disproportionate number of single-parent minority families, decent building sites are hard to find and are very costly. USR&E's reference to higher non-dwelling accounts for public housing could also reflect this same problem. The costs of litigation, site security and other expenses associated with overcoming neighborhood resistance to public housing are charged to non-dwelling accounts. Since no other program assessed by USR&E has tenants similar to those in public housing, a portion of these higher charges may reflect not so much PHA management inefficiencies as it does the costs of housing very-low-income families in a democratic society.

The assessment for St. Petersburg, Florida. Edward White, Jr., Executive Director of the PHA of St. Petersburg, Florida, found in his study—by no means as formal as the others—that, over the long term, public housing is more cost-effective than demand-side programs like housing vouchers. According to Mr. White:

> Jordan Park, the oldest public housing project in St. Petersburg, Florida contains 446 units (all low rise). Since it opened in 1940, it has housed an estimated 10,464 households, an average of one new resident per unit every two years. The average per household subsidy cost at Jordan Park, including debt service and capital improvement grants, has been $387 per year.
>
> Where all of St. Petersburg's traditional public housing units are considered and operating subsidies are included, the annual federal subsidy per unit is still only $1,512. By contrast, federal outlays for the housing voucher program in St. Petersburg are just over $5,000 per year.[25]

With the repeal of most other major HUD production programs and the serious threat to the standing stock of low-income units posed by the pending expiration of subsidy contracts on hundreds of thousands of federally assisted, privately built units, the long-term cost-effectiveness of public housing is now looking better and better.[26] This proposition was emphasized in a June 1987 *New York Times* editorial:

> Where prudently and effectively managed, expensive public housing projects are still providing decent homes after nearly a half century. The long list of successful projects suggests that initial cost is not necessarily the best measure of long-range economy. New public housing should remain in the nation's housing program. But public housing alone cannot fulfill the Congressional promise to give every family a decent, safe home in a suitable living environment.[27]

Modernizing Public Housing

The funding formula for public housing never provided for a capital replacement reserve. HUD responded to the need for capital improvement funds in 1968 by creating the first public housing modernization program. From 1968 to 1978 "modernization funds were provided by HUD, based on priorities established annually in Washington. In some years the priority would be roofs, in others heating facilities, and in still others, energy conservation."[28]

Though tremendously helpful to housing authorities with no other funds to renew their inventories, the way the modernization program was structured made it very hard for PHAs to substantially rehabilitate an entire project needing more comprehensive treatment. Moreover, the piecemeal approach to modernization based on HUD priorities rather than PHA needs was not very cost-effective. "Many times, rehabilitation in the form of replacing all the roofs would be undertaken even if not actually needed because of the PHAs' fear that when roof repairs were needed several years later HUD would have established a different priority."[29]

The Creation of CIAP

In 1980, Congress took constructive steps to deal with that problem by creating the Comprehensive Improvement Assistance Program (CIAP). Under CIAP, public housing authorities are required to develop comprehensive plans to upgrade whole projects and to improve their management capacities.[30] Since 1980, CIAP has financed comprehensive, special purpose, and emergency repairs and replacement work on older projects through loans provided to PHAs by HUD. Upon completion of the modernization work, CIAP loans are forgiven by HUD.

The receipt of a CIAP loan requires the execution of a twenty-year

TABLE 13.4   Age of Public Housing Buildings in
the United States

Age	Percent
Less than 3 years old	10
4–14 years old	32
15–25 years old	25
26–45 years old	31
46 years and older	2
Total	100

Source: Council of Large Public Housing Authorities, *Public Housing Today* (September 1986) 16.

modernization annual contribution contract and guarantees the low-income
character of a modernized public housing project beyond the forty years con-
templated in the original Annual Contributions Contract (ACC). This is one
reason why there is less policy concern about older public housing projects
dropping out of the low-income stock than there is about the pending expiration of subsidy contracts on privately owned, federally assisted projects. Section 9 of the U.S. Housing Act of 1937 also requires that PHAs continue to
use projects as low-income housing for ten years following the end of the year
in which they last receive operating subsidies for a housing project, unless the
secretary of HUD approves the use of the project for other purposes.[31]

The cost of the HUD modernization program has risen substantially over
time. Aggregate funding under the various modernization programs totals
$7.9 billion since 1975, ranging from a low of $707.4 million in 1986 to a
high of $1.26 billion in 1983.[32] Since one-third of all public housing buildings
were built more than twenty-five years ago, and housing authorities operate
under strict financial constraints that prevent them from financing their own
project improvements, modernization needs will substantially increase in the
years ahead (Table 13.4).

Backlogged Needs

A 1987 study of repair and modernization needs within the public housing
stock indicates that, despite large previous federal investment, there is still a
significant unmet need for revitalization of the public housing stock. Abt Associates, the independent contractor retained by HUD to prepare national esti-

mates, has indicated a backlog of modernization needs of at least $21.5 billion.[33] According to Abt, at least $9.5 billion is needed just to repair or replace existing structural, mechanical, and electrical systems; and it would cost another $9.5 billion to upgrade or change existing features of individual housing projects to meet specific HUD standards or to enhance their long term viability.[34] The remaining $2.5 billion would finance necessary cost-effective energy improvements, make more public housing units accessible to the handicapped and eliminate all remaining health problems caused by the presence of lead-based paint in older projects.

While not disputing these various cost estimates, HUD has taken the position that existing modernization standards do not require as much change in project-specific features as implied by the Abt study, and that just $10.7 billion is needed to clear up the backlogged repairs to meet federal regulations.[35] Whether HUD or Abt is correct, or whether the truth lies somewhere in between, the backlog of modernization needs is obviously very substantial.

The Congress must not only deal with the tremendous backlog of deferred modernization needs, but also determine whether and how the "accrual needs" of the nation's nearly 11,000 public housing projects should be treated. "Accrual needs" refer to the rate at which public housing projects physically deteriorate and become obsolete over time. When accurate accrual needs data become available, it will be possible to determine how much a housing authority must save each month to build up sufficient capital reserves to finance a major portion of their own replacement needs.

The necessity of increased federal funding for modernization inevitably raises this issue: given adequate, sufficiently flexible, and long-term funding, do local housing authorities have the ability to plan, manage and carry out a modernization program on the scale required to restore the inventory to usable condition? From Congress's standpoint, the answer is, yes, they do. With only a few exceptions, Congress places the responsibility for slow PHA progress in implementing their modernization programs squarely at HUD's doorstep. Even though CIAP has been a substantial improvement over the past, HUD has established cumbersome procedures designed to second-guess and challenge minute details of each rehabilitation proposal, has failed to fund multi-year proposals on a consistent basis, and has not requested sufficient funds to address the outstanding need.[36]

The House of Representatives Report on the Housing and Community Development Act (HCDA) of 1987 underscored the fact that despite its alleged comprehensiveness, the current system for allocating modernization funds

denies PHAs the flexibility and responsibility essential for setting priorities of capital improvement expenditures weighing the needs of all projects against each other and weighing the options of repairs and maintenance against capital replacement. Because HUD presently decides what to fund and when to fund it, PHAs cannot do rational multiyear planning for the capital improvement needs of the existing public housing inventory now estimated to be worth in excess of $60 billion.[37]

The Post-CIAP Era

The new modernization system created by the Congress in the HCDA will "rely more heavily on the professional judgment of, and provide greater flexibility to the PHAs while assuring individual PHAs of reliable annual funding to meet identifiable needs."[38] It would provide PHAs with modernization funds based on five-year comprehensive plans and annual statements of work. The plan would

assess the physical condition of each public housing project owned or operated by a PHA; describe the physical improvements necessary to rehabilitate such projects; estimate the replacement needs of equipment systems and structural elements projected to be necessary during the 5-year period of the plan; assess the improvements needed to upgrade the management and operation of the public housing agency; and describe a 5-year plan for making the improvements in order to ensure the long-term social and physical viability of the project.[39]

The flow of funds to a PHA sufficient to implement its plans would be contingent upon an annual performance review by HUD to determine that the housing authority is carrying out its modernization activities in a timely manner and that it has the continuing capacity to do so.

The Congressional plan would also rationalize the condition of local inventories with the need for new production. Housing authorities would not be able to lay claim to funds for new production as long as a sizable share of its existing stock was in serious disrepair and no systematic efforts were being made to remedy the situation.

Finally, modernization policies must also be closely related to policies governing the demolition and disposition of public housing. On the one hand, there is justifiable concern among housing advocates that HUD will use the multi-billion dollar estimates of modernization needs to justify a policy of planned shrinkage of the public housing inventory.

On the other hand, a sound future for public housing cannot be built upon a policy that would preserve every public housing building no matter the cost. Selective demolition for density thinning, project reconfiguration to enhance livability, and the disposition of some older projects needing substantial redevelopment (where permanent replacement housing can be financed from net sales proceeds) are all integral parts of an enlightened public housing policy. The key to a fair and equitable disposition policy is ensuring that the replacement housing is for the same group displaced. Replacement of a family project with housing for the elderly is not fair. Nor is the substitution of housing vouchers or Section 8 certificates with five- to ten-year contract terms a fair replacement for a publicly owned low-income housing project.

Tackling Troubled Projects

A recent survey of the nation's 35 largest PHAs conducted by the Council of Large Public Housing Authorities (CLPHA), placed the number of potentially unviable public housing units in excess of 138,000, or 12 percent of the nation's total. All of these are family units in projects that were built an average of thirty-four years ago.[40]

These 40 to 60 seriously troubled family high-rise projects in major cities across the country must be radically altered, reconfigured, or demolished. Not only do those mistakes of the past provide inhumane living environments, but by stereotyping all public housing they cast a long shadow over the program and threaten its very foundation. There is an urgent need to tackle the troubled projects, and a bold initiative to do just that must be the centerpiece of a revived public housing program.

According to CLPHA, most seriously troubled projects have vacancy rates in excess of 15 percent and require an average of $28,000 a unit in capital improvements, for a total cost of $3.8 billion. In a limited number of instances, projects are too far gone to be preserved and should be replaced on economic and humanitarian grounds. In other cases, modernization will require selective demolition of whole projects, the removal of several floors from high-rise buildings, and the reconfiguration of building interiors, which would also reduce the total number of units in the local public housing stock.

Since hundreds and even thousands of units in the most seriously troubled developments are unoccupied, many of them for years, one-for-one replacement is not necessary in all cases. For these PHAs, such a policy would essentially require the local supply of viable public housing units to be increased as a condition for obtaining HUD approval of demolition/disposition plans. Unless funds for public housing production are substantially increased, this requirement makes no sense at all.

Building Toward a Goal

We would suggest that Congress establish a modest annual goal to construct 20,000 new public housing units. Not only is this level of production exceedingly modest based upon demonstrated need, but also when measured against historical standards. We are calling for a level of production in the 1990s that is slightly lower than the average annual level of starts during the 1980s (21,329), and more than one-third below the average number of new public housing starts recorded during the first fifty years of the program's history (29,383). Half of this annual authorization could be allocated for troubled projects to help PHAs raze and reconfigure their inventories of the worst high-rise projects that plague the families forced to live there. Another 5,000 to 7,000 units should be made available through a competitive process to the hundreds of PHAs throughout the country in communities with documented housing shortages and proven development capacities. The remaining 3,000 units are needed just to replace the public housing units now being lost to the inventory each year through demolition or disposition at the local level.[41]

How the special set-aside of new units would be used to resolve the troubled project problem would be determined locally by a special tribunal or commission consisting of public housing tenants, PHA and other local officials, representatives of the state, concerned and knowledgeable citizens, and members of the private development community. The planning framework for this kind of initiative is already contained in those provisions of the Housing and Community Development Act of 1987 dealing with comprehensive modernization, which was signed into law by President Reagan on February 5, 1988.

It is important to emphasize that new public housing development does not have to be of the conventional mold. It could include the redevelopment of existing public housing units currently unsuitable for occupancy; major redevelopment of existing projects currently wholly or mostly vacant; acquisition of private market units, with or without rehabilitation; new construction; acquisition of units built or rehabbed specifically for the housing authority; or acquisition of some units in a larger building or subdivision where the balance of the units are not owned by the PHA.[42]

With their extensive development experience, PHAs could work jointly with neighborhood-based organizations sponsoring new low-income projects that could be built by the PHA and managed by either the housing authority or by the nonprofit.

With as many as 100,000 units in distressed projects to be demolished and replaced under locally prepared redevelopment plans at proposed production and allocation levels, the troubled project initiative would take up to ten years to complete, following an initial planning period.

What Would It Cost?

The most current estimates of public housing development costs contained in the conference report to the 1987 HCDA indicates that a new unit costs $68,857.[43] Therefore, to produce 20,000 units would cost $1.4 billion a year.

Operating Subsidies and Regulations

The 1937 statute creating the public housing program restricted the federal contribution to full debt service. A 1983 report issued by Boston's Citizens Housing and Planning Association states:

The system functioned relatively well for about twenty-five years—a period during which the building stock remained in good condition and the tenant population was composed largely of the working poor. By the mid-1960s, however, significant changes had occurred in the operating environment of many PHAs. The 1949 Housing Act, which prohibited discrimination against welfare recipients and gave priority to those displaced by the Urban Renewal Program, as well as the post-war move to the North by many southern blacks and the move into FHA-insured housing by working families, brought an increasing number of very-low-income families into public housing. With a growing proportion of tenants on low, fixed incomes, an increasing need for social services and the rising cost of maintaining an aging building stock, the rental receipts of PHAs were no longer sufficient to cover the cost of operation. Many housing authorities were forced to raise rents to levels which required tenants to pay a high proportion of their income for shelter, in some cases as much as 80 percent.[44]

Because of this new reality, in 1961 the Congress authorized a $10 monthly special subsidy for each elderly family being housed.[45] Except for the $10 subsidy PHAs had to meet virtually all their operating expenses out of rent receipts. Rather than permitting housing authorities to increase their revenues by raising the maximum income limits for continued occupancy (which would have permitted more working families to stay in public housing), the Housing Act of 1964 extended the $10 monthly subsidy to all families displaced by governmental action. To be eligible for this new subsidy, however, PHAs had to first consume all or most of their operating reserves. Efficiently managed housing authorities that had accrued substantial reserves were penalized, while less efficient PHAs received financial help immediately.[46] This is not the first time, nor would it be the last, that laws or regulations rewarded poor management or eliminated the incentive for sound and efficient local management of public housing.

The Housing Act of 1968 extended the special subsidy to two additional groups: unusually low-income and unusually large families. Also in 1968, HUD promulgated a regulation titled "Tenant Selection and Assignment Policy" that required the selection of families for public housing on a "first come, first served" basis. This severely reduced a PHA's ability to screen tenants and balance income groups and rent-paying abilities among the applicants.[47]

The Housing Act of 1969, containing the first so-called Brooke Amendment, gave rise to HUD's public housing operating subsidy system. The Brooke Amendment protected very-low-income tenants by capping rents at 25 percent of income. In the process, it also had the effect of removing minimum rents in public housing and thereby reducing PHA rental income. To compensate PHAs for this lost revenue, an operating subsidy was authorized, provided once again that the housing authority did not have sufficient operating reserves upon which to draw.

The Performance Funding System

With housing authority operating deficits growing and the subsidy system lacking any restraints on spending or incentives for sound management, a different operating subsidy system had to be devised. In 1971, HUD implemented an operating subsidy system based on an "Interim Funding Formula," which became the forerunner of the current formula-based Performance Funding System (PFS).[48] Implemented in 1975, the PFS is intended to encourage sound housing management practices.

Under PFS, the prototype equation was calibrated by using the average real cost of high-performing PHAs that had been identified in a HUD-sponsored study of public housing management practices.[49] In this system an individual PHA's operating subsidy is calculated as the difference between its expected rental and other income and an estimate of operating costs (called allowable expense level—AEL) that is based on the cost structure of well-managed housing authorities, and an allowable utility expense level. The PHA's actual operating costs never enter the calculation. Theoretically, at least, the better managed a PHA is, the more likely it is that HUD operating subsidies will be sufficient to cover its revenue deficit.

Problems with PFS. There is substantial disagreement over whether the PFS formula accurately reflected the cost structure of "high performance" PHAs. For example, the original PFS equation was designed so that 90 percent of all actual PHA budgets would fall within the range of predicted operating expenses. In fact, only 70 percent actually did. Forty-eight of the large and extra large PHAs were out of range from the start, which suggests that the PFS equation inaccurately modeled the operating environments of a whole class of housing authorities.[50]

Moreover, many large housing authorities argue that, through no fault of their own, their operating environments have changed for the worse since 1975. So even if it once was equitable, the PFS system is no longer an adequate means for determining their operating subsidy needs.

There are other serious flaws in the current system:

1. The PFS formula provides significant negative incentives for PHAs to improve their productivity. They lose the benefit of generating non-rental income, which if retained, would benefit their program. Rather, the benefit of any entrepreneurial activity or even local government contributions to PHA operations, is passed back to the federal government in the form of a reduced PFS allocation. This practice penalizes creative and energetic PHAs and rewards non-creative inefficient housing authorities.[51]
2. PHAs face negative incentives for undertaking energy conservation. If they do not, utility cost deficits are paid by the federal government. If they do, under current rules, they may keep one-half the savings in the current fiscal year and none thereafter. Therefore, for a PHA to recoup its energy conservation investment, it must receive a 200 percent payback in the first year.[52]

3. Changes in state and local mandates are not accounted for as increased expense items under PFS. Requirements of workmen's compensation laws, for example, can exceed the annual adjustment factors allowed in the original base year calculation. HUD only provides "add on" monies for changes in federal legislation or regulations, not state or local adjustments.[53]

4. Under the PFS funding formula, the operating subsidy is partly dependent on a regional cost factor which is the ratio of the cost of living in the PHA's region to the cost of living nationally. This factor can lead to under-funding of selected PHAs located in high cost areas of low cost regions (e.g., the city of Miami).

5. The PFS formula makes no provision for a maintenance replacement reserve. Conditions must deteriorate in a public housing project to the point where modernization is called for before funds for physical improvements become available.

6. The operating subsidy formula does not provide for automatic adjustments when particular components of operating costs increase well beyond their share of total operating costs as established in the base year formula. The current case in point is insurance. In the initial year of PFS, the formula allowed for $1.34 per unit month (PUM) for insurance based upon a survey of operating costs of well-managed PHAs. Since 1975, the amount for insurance provided in the PFS formula has been increased by national inflation factors, bringing the formula-based amount of insurance for FY 1987 to $3.02 PUM. During the spring of 1985, however, the cost of required liability, fire and extended-coverage insurance increased for many PHAs at a rate of 4 to 15 times the 1984 cost. Current estimates are that PHAs paid an average of $10.10 PUM for insurance in FY 1986.

7. The PFS formula does not make adjustments for conditions in the community that have changed since the formula was first introduced. Many PHAs, for example, are now sponsoring security programs due to increases in crime rates in project neighborhoods. These programs are not included in the PFS formula and therefore must be financed from operating receipts or from local sources.[54]

Fine-tuning PFS. Despite the momentum building to change the PFS system, the operative word should be caution. Now that the 1987 HCDA has authorized $1.6 billion in operating subsidies for FY 1988, which approximates full funding of the basic PFS system, it appears there is political consensus over basic PHA operating needs. PFS should be fine-tuned rather than replaced in the next two years. Fine-tuning would be better in the current policy environment because, flawed as it is, the PFS system was designed with the interest of PHAs and their low-income housing mandates at heart. This is in stark contrast to various budget-driven alternatives to PFS such as a fair market operating subsidy system indexed to the cost structure of the private sector that is less encumbered by federal regulations and provides fewer services to low-income tenants.

PFS proposals have been made that would:

increase PHA incentives to raise occupancy levels above the 97 percent benchmark HUD uses to calculate operating subsidy allocations;

reduce PHA incentives that allow units to remain vacant for extended periods of time without loss of subsidy;

encourage energy conservation; and

encourage PHAs to increase non-rental revenues.

All these proposals should be pursued. Also, institution of an appeals process as part of PFS would give PHAs an opportunity to demonstrate to HUD how changes in operating environments during the past fiscal year were not recognized and included in operating subsidy allocations.

Replacing PFS. As indicated above, it has been proposed that PFS be replaced by a fair-market rent (FMR) driven system that would base public housing operating subsidies on the operating and maintenance costs of comparable private-sector housing. In past years this proposal has floundered over disagreement on the definition of comparable private-sector housing; the greater management prerogatives of private landlords in evicting both destructive tenants and those who fail to pay their rents; and the fact that the quantity and quality of tenant services provided by housing authorities are not reflected in the operating cost structure of private landlords.

The President's Commission on Housing suggested in 1982 that public housing authorities should be permitted to charge rents high enough to cover full operating costs. And instead of PHAs receiving operating subsidies, tenants should receive housing vouchers to supplement their rent paying abilities.[55] Tenants would thus be free to use their vouchers to remain in public housing or to move into the private rental market. Competition for tenants would ostensibly increase housing authority incentives for sound management. "Those authorities that are unable to attract a sufficient number of tenants (with or without vouchers) to cover their expenses would be forced to close."[56]

One of the more serious disadvantages of such a program is that some families, due to their race or ethnicity and/or composition, are frequently discriminated against in the private housing market. Large, female-headed households, for example, have an extremely difficult time finding shelter in the private market even if their incomes are adequate. If unprofitable housing authorities were simply allowed to "go out of business," these families might find it almost impossible to find shelter.[57]

The notion of placing PHAs in head-to-head competition with private providers of housing services through a voucher system is conceptually appealing, but it would only make sense after all public housing has been brought up to minimum property standards.

No proposed alternatives to PFS can be shown to meet the legitimate revenue needs of housing authorities in a more equitable and cost-effective manner. They can make no provision, as PFS can, for the fact that "an increase in the number of families with children places different demands on PHA resources, including the need for child care, increased routine maintenance, and possibly increased security.[58]

Nor can an operating subsidy system that is indexed to costs and operating conditions outside of public housing take account of the fact that an aging public housing population "needs more services to assist in maintaining independence of the elderly and [that] security must be increased as the tenants become more vulnerable." [59]

While additional research is conducted to find a more cost-effective and equitable operating subsidy system, some of the problems with PFS can be resolved through negotiations with HUD after actual costs, inflation factors, etc., are known. At the same time HUD can demand more accountability from the most poorly managed PHAs through the development of mandatory workout plans, greater federal oversight and regulations, placement of PHAs under receivership-type arrangements, or the replacement of inept management with other public or private management entities.

Finally, as an economy and efficiency measure, HUD should continue its promising on-going efforts to deregulate the public housing program by exempting PHAs that meet specified performance standards from unnecessary HUD audits, reviews, and other burdensome regulations.

The Burden of Overregulation

Because of the inverse relationship between the size distribution of PHAs and the respective shares of the total units they administer, HUD regulations rarely support both the majority of PHAs and those that manage a majority of the nation's public housing units. In response to serious problems in a handful of large PHAs, HUD all too frequently issues rigid regulations that restrict management prerogatives and impose unnecessary costs on *all* housing authorities no matter how well they are managed.

The relevance of geographic and size-related realities is that the inherent variation across public housing programs, including differences in local political climates and economic and housing market conditions, causes the impact of HUD policies on development, modernization, disposition and demolition, privatization and deregulation to vary a great deal. PHAs are not of a single mind about the pitfalls and promises of various policy and program alternatives. That is why deregulation leading to maximum local flexibility is an absolute necessity.

HUD and the Congress should move aggressively to deregulate the program for housing authorities that meet a demanding set of performance standards, and impose a higher level of federal oversight and workout requirements for seriously troubled programs. The framework for deregulation should be in-depth up-front HUD review and approval of local budgets, followed by effective implementation monitored through a system of annual audits. HUD has made an impressive start toward deregulation by issuing a new handbook on this topic. These positive first steps should be encouraged and the pace of deregulation accelerated. Not only is deregulation consistent with the mood of the country, but it will become an economic necessity in the effort to keep public housing costs under control.

Tenant Participation

HUD believes that tenant involvement in housing authority operations leads to positive program outcomes and that "tenant organizations are generally the best vehicle for achieving effective tenant participation on a regular and sustained basis." [60] To stimulate tenant participation, HUD requires PHAs to provide tenants with information about housing authority operating policies to determine their interest in forming a tenant organization, and to assist in the establishment of such organizations. Resources permitting, PHAs may also provide in-kind and cash assistance to support tenant participation activities. However, outside CIAP, for which tenant participation costs are an eligible item, HUD provides no ongoing financial assistance to PHAs to support these programs.

The extent to which PHA's embrace HUD's tenant participation policies varies inversely with program size. Around 50 percent of all large, and 72 percent of all very large, PHAs have authority-wide resident councils, compared to just 15 percent of small housing authorities (Table 13.5). Larger PHAs are also more likely to have formal agreements with tenants to take over various maintenance and tenant services responsibilities, and to hire tenants on the PHA staff. Such formal arrangements, however, are not very widespread and are almost non-existent in housing authorities that operate fewer than 2,500 units. This latter group represents the vast majority of all PHAs, although a minority of public housing units, and underscores the point made earlier about how difficult it is for federal public housing policies to be applied equally to all PHAs across the country.

Tenant Management

Tenant management of public housing is one of those complicated areas of housing policy about which reasonable people can disagree. Basically, tenant management involves the election of a board of directors from among the tenants themselves, and the training of that board in organizational skills and in

TABLE 13.5 Resident Participation in Public Housing: 1986

| | | PERCENT PHAs WITH PHA-RESIDENT AGREEMENTS | | | AVERAGE NUMBER TENANTS ON STAFF | |
| | *Percent PHAs with tenant* | | | | | |
PHA size[a]	*councils*	*Manage-ment*	*Mainte-nance*	*Services*	*Total*	*Mainte-nance*
Small	15.0	1.3	1.3	1.3	1.0	0.6
Medium	17.1	—	—	—	3.8	3.1
Large	50.9	—	3.8	3.8	10.2	5.6
Very large	71.8	7.9	13.2	15.8	26.4	16.0
Largest 14	100.0	25.0	33.3	25.0	369.2	237.1
All respondents	38.8	3.2	5.6	5.6	28.6	17.9

[a]Key: Small = 1–500 public housing units; medium = 501–1,250 units; large = 1,251–2,500 units; very large = 2,501 or more units, excluding the largest 14 PHAs
Source: National Association of Housing and Redevelopment Officials 1986 Housing Survey

the principles of real estate management. "Major board responsibilities include formulating policy, determining the rules and regulations governing the development, and ensuring that residents can participate in policy-making and operations."[61]

Generally, in tenant-managed projects the routine daily management is carried out by a staff hired from the resident population.[62] HUD used the results of a Department commissioned management audit of a single highly successful tenant management corporation (TMC) in Washington, DC to support its policy position that tenant management results in "significant economic and social benefits, such as reducing the cost of operating public housing, reducing vandalism, and increasing the stake residents have in their housing."[63]

While little systematic research has been conducted on the effectiveness of tenant management, the above audit presents a far more positive view of the outcomes of tenant management than did the independent evaluation of HUD's own $20-million national tenant management demonstration carried out on seven sites from 1977 to 1979. According to the Manpower Development Research Corporation (MDRC),

In most of the public housing developments in the demonstration, tenant management worked just as well as previous management by housing authorities. This suggests that tenants can manage public housing projects effectively under certain conditions attainable in many projects. But it also indicates that at least in the short run, tenant management does not usually produce results markedly superior to those stemming from conventional housing authority management.[64]

In sharp contrast to HUD's assertion of the cost-reducing benefits of tenant management, MDRC concluded that

Specifically, tenant management was not significantly better than housing authority management in terms of individual performance indicators such as average rent collections, vacancy rates, or speed of response to maintenance requests. However, resident satisfaction with overall management was higher in tenant-managed developments than it had been previously, or than it was in other similar conventionally managed developments.[65]

In addition to improperly generalizing the benefits, HUD policy at least implicitly understates the costs of tenant management by not providing the necessary funding to train and otherwise assist tenant management entities to develop the skills required to perform at expected levels of competence. While tenant management generates additional employment opportunities and social benefits such as a sense of personal development among participants, it also incurs significant additional costs, adding from 13 percent to 62 percent to what continued traditional management would have cost in the tenant-managed projects.[66]

Because tenant management is not a panacea to housing authority management problems and was found not to pay for itself in operating costs or other economies, MDRC quite reasonably

concluded that it would be unwise to mandate tenant management of public housing— either requiring it everywhere or prohibiting it everywhere. Rather, individual housing authorities should be able to pursue it if they desire, and if they meet certain preconditions. *HUD should act as a sympathetic respondent to an interest in tenant management expressed locally if it has enough resources to help local housing authorities finance the additional costs involved* (emphasis added).[67]

Congressional interest in tenant management is the highest it has been in a decade. Despite research findings to the contrary, there is a growing sense that tenant management must be an integral element in all plans designed to turn around troubled projects and that it is also an excellent way to prepare public housing residents for the responsibilities of homeownership.

In support of this view, the 1987 Housing and Community Development Act contains a new tenant management initiative and authorizes funding to establish a limited number of resident management corporations at a cost of $100,000 per entity. While backing its belief in tenant management to a greater extent than HUD, the one-time $100,000 grant per site provided in the HCDA pales in comparison to the $743,000 in soft costs that HUD provided to each development in its national tenant management demonstration nearly a decade ago. In short, tenant management programs envisioned in 1987 HCDA are small and under-funded and not likely to become a significant component of future public housing policy.

Privatization of Public Housing

Privatizing public housing through sale to tenants is an idea which has found much support in the Reagan administration and lately in Congress. The sale of public housing to tenants raises three related issues: the primary purpose in creating a public housing sales program; the effects of privatization on the size of the low-income rental stock, and the rights of tenant buyers and non-buyers. Each of these issues is discussed below.

Objective of a Sales Program

In view of its disappointing housing record, it is understandable why Reagan administration critics "are very skeptical of a group of conservative people who are opposed to any kind of social program all of a sudden taking an interest in public housing." [68]

If it is not simply an economy measure, then what policy objective would a public housing sales program support? If the major objective is to expand homeownership opportunities for the poor, then according to Schussheim, selling public housing could make only a small contribution toward that end. After all, "there are only a million and a quarter public housing units in the country against about 16 million very-low-income households with a housing problem of one kind or another." [69]

In addition to the economy motives, a public housing sales program could also

help families in assisted housing break the cycle of dependency and achieve self-sufficiency as homeowners;

offer those who would otherwise be renters all their lives a chance to build equity and have something of value to leave to their children;

build a sense of responsibility and homeowner stake in the community that would lead to neighborhood stability and ultimate improvement; and

provide tenants who are already involved in the management of their public housing projects the opportunity to take the next step to ownership. [70]

While few would argue the merits of these objectives, only the last one that views project ownership as a reward for successful tenant management would seem to require that the sales units come from the public housing inventory.

While a limited-scale public housing sales program may make good policy sense, an even more compelling case can be made for an ownership program that provides upwardly mobile public housing residents opportunities to move out of public housing into homes of their own. Not only would such a program reward ambition and provide incentives for public housing families to improve their economic circumstances, but it would also increase turnover and free public housing units for other families who are now on ever-expanding waiting lists.

The Effects of Privatization on the Low-Income Stock

A large-scale public housing sales program would have three major impacts on the nation's permanent stock of low-income housing. First, it would shrink the rental housing supply. Second, concern has been raised about the long term affordability of the units sold to tenants. The homeownership proposals discussed below do not include the retention of federal operating subsidies or other formal after-sale financial support to homebuyers over the longer term. Finally, concerns have been raised about the long-term implications of selecting the best quality units for sale—the issue of residualization.

If a public housing sales program were to remove the best units from the stock, PHAs would be left with a larger proportion of less attractive and more poorly maintained inventory, and the public image of the program would decline further. Should a sales program also cream off the highest income families in the program, despite reductions in the size of the stock, aggregate federal operating subsidy costs still could rise. This is because "on average, tenants paying the maximum rent in public housing not only cover full operating costs for their units, but pay enough in addition to equal the subsidy amount for an additional unit." [71]

HUD's Public Housing Homeownership Demonstration

The Public Housing Homeownership Demonstration (PHHD) announced by HUD Secretary Samuel R. Pierce on June 5, 1985, represents the latest federal effort to extend homeownership opportunities to low- and moderate-income families. As part of the PHHD, seventeen public housing authorities have been authorized to transfer a total of 1,290 public housing units to tenants at affordable prices.

HUD is leaving it up to the PHA to select the public housing units for sale and to set the prices and terms of sale. HUD will continue to pay the debt service on the outstanding federal bonds that financed the construction and/or subsequent modernization of the units to be sold, thereby allowing PHAs to reduce the sales price to tenants. The amortization of rehabilitation costs beyond those previously financed by HUD, along with all operating costs (including property taxes where applicable, maintenance, and insurance costs) will be the responsibility of the tenant-buyers.

While most PHHD programs will transfer to tenants fee simple interest in their single-family dwellings, at least five of the 17 demonstration programs involve the sale of attached townhouse or multi-family units using the co-operative or condominium form of ownership.

In addition to differences in building type and ownership interest, PHA sales programs vary by number of units to be sold; character of the neighborhoods in which their sales projects are located; extent to which the sales prices are subsidized; financing approaches used; and the income groups served. With respect to the latter, average incomes of tenant buyers who closed on their houses by August 1987 range from a low of $7,900 to more than $26,000, and averaged $17,026.[72]

As of August 1987 a total of 105 units had been transferred to tenants under the PHHD. A total of 43 sales had been closed in the 11 single-family demonstration sites at an average price of $30,158 per unit. Sixty-two multi-family sales had been closed at two sites at an average price in excess of $45,000 per unit.[73]

HUD's public housing homeownership demonstration has been criticized for failure to require replacement housing as part of local sales programs. Nor does the new program adequately deal with the long-term affordability issue. Lower-income homeowners, whether taken singly or as groups organized into cooperatives or condominium associations, do not have the resources to withstand many future-shocks, be they in the form of sharp utility cost increases, or unexpected major repair and replacement needs.

Public Housing Homeownership Under the 1987 HCDA

The Congress recently approved a public housing homeownership program that would sell projects to qualified resident management corporations (RMCs) that have established track records as effective and efficient housing managers.[74] This new public housing homeownership measure permits HUD to set sale prices at levels affordable to the tenants, and PHAs to finance the sales if no other financing is available.

Sales from RMCs to individual public housing tenants would contain restrictions limiting the profits from resale, and these restrictions would apply to all subsequent buyers. The HCDA contains strict housing replacement requirements and very strong protections for tenants not wishing to buy their unit. Finally, the act authorizes HUD to continue paying debt service on the bonds issued to build (and modernize) the project but prohibits the payment of continuing operating subsidies after sale.

Few qualified resident management corporations currently exist, and the HCDA requires three years of proven management excellence before an RMC becomes eligible to purchase its project. Looking at the situation realistically, it will be at least five years before this homeownership program could possibly generate a significant number of sales. Moreover, since Congress failed to authorize a specific level of spending for the sales program, it would seem that Congressional support for public housing homeownership may be a mile wide but only an inch deep.

Another major problem with the 1987 HCDA public housing sales program is that it requires replacement housing on a one-for-one basis, but makes no provision for financing it. Clearly, the 7,000 new public housing units authorized by the act can't meet even a tiny portion of the demonstrated national need for more low-income housing and also replace units sold under local homeownership programs. Unless Congress wants to discourage PHA interest in a sales program by implicitly requiring that replacement housing be provided locally or through state programs, it must authorize substantially more than 7,000 new public housing units a year.

Tenant Considerations

Public housing homeownership programs must balance the interests of buyers and non-buyers. With respect to supporting homebuyers, especially in multi-family projects, carrying out a successful homeownership program is extremely labor-intensive for the PHA. It requires either a substantial allocation of housing authority staff to provide heavy doses of one-on-one counseling and more formal training of co-op and condo boards; or expensive third party contracts to independent service providers.

Rights of non-purchasers. The HCDA program does a thorough job of protecting the rights of non-purchasers. Sensitive to the forced-relocation issue raised by critics of HUD's PHHD, the HCDA goes the extra mile in assuring that the sales initiatives will not interfere with the rights of other families living in public housing. However, the bill blankets continuing renters with so many options and protections as to render most multi-family transfer programs probably infeasible. This is because even highly successful resident management corporations that buy their buildings with a high percentage of nonbuyer tenants will be in for a tough time as landlords, in view of a ban on involuntary relocation, and a permanent loss of operating subsidies. This causes one to question the underlying congressional commitment to a workable public housing homeownership program in the first place.

Foreclosures. Under neither HUD's homeownership demonstration nor the 1987 HCDA would the foreclosure of individual or project mortgages return the housing to the active public housing stock. Nor would a foreclosure provide the families who lose their homes the right to return to public housing as tenants. The Congress should address this downside of the public housing ownership issue by simply permitting buyers to retain priority status on public housing waiting lists in case they cannot make it as homeowners; by accepting foreclosed housing back into the public housing inventory, and thus restoring its eligibility for operating subsidies; or, by having a special set-aside of Section 8 certificates or housing vouchers to help financially troubled homebuyers stave off default.

The necessity of having to deal with the problem of potentially high default rates is made all the more clear by actuarial data on another low-income homeownership program. "The cumulative proportion of foreclosures and assigned mortgages among homebuyers under the original Section 235 program—a group of purchasers with incomes about a third higher than non-elderly public housing families—was 20 percent from 1970–1979." [75]

Up and Out: The Case for Nehemiah

A more promising way that the dream of homeownership can be realized by public housing tenants without compromising the rights of non-purchasers is for the sales units to be separate and distinct from the public housing stock.

The 1987 HCDA authorizes a new lower-income homeownership demonstration called the Nehemiah Housing Opportunity Grants program, which could be tied to the public housing program. Named for the Biblical prophet who rebuilt Jerusalem, the Nehemiah program is based on the highly successful program of a consortium of New York City churches that built 5,000 single-family homes in a devastated area of East Brooklyn. Built on city-owned land by a nonprofit developer with the aid of zero-interest construction loans from the consortium, tax-exempt financing from the state, and $15,000 deferred payment second mortgages from the Urban Development Action Grant program, Nehemiah houses are affordable to the higher-income end of the public housing community.

The HCDA has authorized $150 million for HUD to use in supporting local Nehemiah programs that receive substantial state, local, and private assistance. HUD's participation would come in the form of deferred second mortgages. By strengthening the link between the Nehemiah and public housing programs, distressed inner city neighborhoods could be rebuilt around the anchor of new Nehemiah communities, upwardly mobile tenants of public and other assisted housing would realize their ultimate goal of owning a home, and low-income families now on public housing waiting lists could be housed.

Believing that "a modest downpayment requirement has proven to be a valuable incentive for families wishing to purchase a home," [76] the Congress provides that buyers of Nehemiah houses pay 10 percent in cash at closing. To help public housing tenants accumulate the downpayment needed to buy a Nehemiah house, legislation reimposing ceiling rents could be enacted. By permitting PHAs to set ceiling rents equal to the unsubsidized average operating cost per unit and setting aside in an interest bearing equity account the difference between the ceiling rent and 30 percent of income, a family could build up a modest down payment in relatively short order.

With the average federal share of a Nehemiah house ($15,000) costing less than a quarter as much as the typical public housing unit, it makes economic sense to structure a homeownership program in a way that increases the opportunity for families to move out of the "projects." It probably will also be easier to encourage states, localities and the business community to contribute to local Nehemiah programs than to share the federal burden of building more public housing. Yet a Nehemiah-type sales program for public housing families with homeownership potential would have the same supply-increasing effects as building a comparable number of new public housing units. In fact it should be easier to convince Congress to fund 20,000 sales units for current residents of assisted housing to purchase than to obtain appropriations to build the same number of new public units.

It is also possible to tie resident management to the new homeownership program. Public housing families can obtain the skills they will need as homeowners by participating in a resident management corporation. Rather than the RMC buying its project after three years of capable, efficient management, the project would remain a permanent part of the public housing stock and participating families would "graduate" out of the RMC into their own houses. These successful families would be replaced in the RMC by other aspiring homeowners who are willing to take on self management as a means of preparing themselves for the future.

In this new environment, there is no reason why the housing authority could not participate in the development of Nehemiah housing as an independent sponsor or in conjunction with other neighborhood-based organizations.

Conclusion

From a historical standpoint, low-income housing programs have had very limited life cycles. Starting most recently, the Section 8 production programs lasted about a decade, and the interest subsidy initiatives they replaced were even shorter-lived, and so on down the line. Housing programs also vary in the way they are terminated. Rightly or wrongly, some, like Section 8, became symbols of budget-busting programs and were formally repealed by the Congress in a public show of outrage, while others, like rent supplements, faded quietly from the scene with scarcely a whimper.

Against this backdrop of "housing as fashion," the public housing program stands tall with fifty years of continuity and proud tradition. The permanence of public housing as a community resource for the poor and the stability of local housing authorities that administer the program stand in stark contrast to other housing efforts that have come and gone. Public housing might not be cheap, but neither is it a tax dodge. Public housing authorities might not be as well staffed as we would like, but neither are they shell corporations created merely to receive federally insured mortgage or subsidy contracts. Even the high cost of improving the public housing stock is preferable to the speculation about the number of privately owned low-income projects that will opt out of the system when their subsidy contracts expire.

On the occasion of the fiftieth anniversary of the U.S. Housing Act of 1937, which gave birth to the public housing program, it is fitting to reflect on its successes and failures. More importantly, however, "it is a time to look ahead and set a course of the future." [77] In looking ahead, many will be tempted to recommend radical change for public housing in an effort to bring this rigidly regulated anachronism into the decentralized world of block grants and local self-determination.

While program change and reform are necessary on a variety of fronts as discussed in this paper, history warns us that we should proceed with caution. Public housing has outlived all of its successors for good reason. It was soundly conceived; it continues to meet an urgent public need more cost-effectively than most other programs; and it is capable of significant additional improvement without destroying its basic framework. More importantly, in its fifty-year history public housing has managed to avoid becoming entangled with the housing fads of the day and so has remained alive through the seemingly endless progression of short-lived alphabet-soup-named low-income housing programs.

Notes

1. M. L. Matulef, "This is Public Housing," *Journal of Housing* 44, 5 (September/October 1987) 175.

2. Public housing as a percent of all rental housing was 5 percent or greater in the following central cities: New York (5.6%), Chicago (5.4%), Philadelphia (9.0%), Detroit (5.0%), Baltimore (10.3%), Washington, D.C. (5.9%), Cleveland (8.6%), Boston (8.0%), St. Louis (5.9%), Seattle (5.8%), Atlanta (14.6%). Data are for 1974, 1975 and 1976, from R. Struyk, *A New System for Public Housing: Salvaging a National Resource* (Washington: The Urban Institute, 1980) 14.

3. T. Riordan, "Housekeeping at HUD," *Common Cause Magazine* (March/April 1987) 27.

4. The 1986 NAHRO Housing Survey was sent to a stratified sample of public housing authorities. The sample was structured to represent the eight NAHRO regions and PHAs of every size. The 223 survey responses represented 46 states and the District of Columbia. Responding PHAs manage about 50 percent of the national conventional public housing stock.

5. Matulef, "Public Housing," 179.

6. J. W. Stimpson, Deputy Assistant Secretary for Policy Development, U.S. Department of Housing and Urban Development, correspondence to M. A. Stegman, October 29, 1987.

7. Matulef, "Public Housing," 179.

8. M. Jones, "Housing Voucher Plan is Short-Sighted," *St. Louis Post Dispatch*, March 23 1987.

9. Riordan, "Housekeeping," 27.

10. "Truce in Housing," editorial, *Washington Post*, April 4 1987.

11. Council of Large Public Housing Authorities, *Newsletter*, Washington (February 7 1987) 4.

12. Stimpson, correspondence.

13. Matulef, "Public Housing," 175.

14. Stimpson, correspondence.

15. Council of Large Public Housing Authorities, *Public Housing Today* (September 1986) 13, 15.

16. Citizens Housing and Planning Association, *Tenancy and Costs in Public Housing-Policies, Attitudes and Case Studies* (Boston: CHPA, March 1986).

17. Matulef, "Public Housing," 176.

18. CHPA, *Tenancy and Costs,* 3, 4.

19. Matulef, "Public Housing," 178.

20. U.S. General Accounting Office, *A Comparative Analysis of Subsidized Housing Costs* (Washington: USGAO, July 1976) 7.

21. USGAO, *Subsidized Housing,* 22.

22. Congressional Budget Office, *The Long Term Costs of Lower Housing Assistance Programs* (Washington: USCBO, March 1979) xiii.

23. Urban Systems Research and Engineering, Inc., *The Cost of HUD Multifamily Housing Programs* I (Cambridge: USR&E, May 1982) 4–7.

24. USR&E, *Cost of HUD Multifamily,* 6–7.

25. *Los Angeles Times,* August 17 1987, Part 2, 5.

26. See Chapter 12 by Phillip Clay and James Wallace in this volume and also Congressional Budget Office, "The Potential Loss of Assisted Housing Units as Certain Mortgage Interest Subsidy Programs Mature" (Washington: CBO, March 1987).

27. *New York Times,* June 13 1987.

28. House Committee on Banking, Finance and Urban Affairs, *Housing, Community Development, and Homeless Prevention Act of 1987, Report to Accompany HR-4,* Report 100-122, June 2 1987.

29. House Banking Committee, *Homeless Prevention Report,* 20.

30. House Banking Committee, *Homeless Prevention Report,* 21.

31. Stimpson correspondence.

32. Abt Associates, Inc., *Study of the Modernization Needs of the Public and Indian Housing Stock: National Estimates Report,* draft (Cambridge: Abt Associates, March 1987) 2-1.

33. National Association of Housing and Redevelopment Officials, *NAHRO Monitor* (April 15 1987) 2.

34. *NAHRO Monitor,* 2.

35. *NAHRO Monitor,* 3.

36. House Banking Committee, *Homeless Prevention Report,* 20.

37. House Banking Committee, *Homeless Prevention Report,* 21.

38. House Banking Committee, *Homeless Prevention Report,* 21.

39. House Banking Committee, *Homeless Prevention Report,* 22.

40. Council of Large Public Housing Authorities, *CLPHA Modernization Survey* (Washington: CLPHA, January 29, 1988) 3.

41. Stimpson correspondence.

42. Council of Large Public Housing Authorities, *Proposal for Future Public Housing Development Program,* draft (Washington: CLPHA, September 11 1987) 1.

43. House of Representatives, *HR-4, Housing, Community Development, and Homelessness Prevention Act of 1987,* June 2 1987, 10.

44. W. Sherwood and E. March, *Operating Subsidies for Public Housing: Problems and Options, A Working Paper* (Boston: Citizens Housing and Planning Association, August 1983) 3.

45. A. W. Kuhn, "A Defense for Local Public Housing Operations Against the Criticisms of Poor Management," unpublished, June 15 1987, 3.

46. Kuhn, "Defense," 3.

47. Kuhn, "Defense," 4–5.

48. Kuhn, "Defense," 8.

49. Sherwood and March, *Operating Subsidies,* 6.

50. Sherwood and March, *Operating Subsidies,* 19.

51. NAHRO, *Keeping the Commitment* (Public Housing Performance Funding System, Detailed Substantive Outline, draft), November 23, 1987, 2.

52. NAHRO, *Keeping the Commitment,* 2.

53. NAHRO, *Keeping the Commitment,* 2.

54. Council of Large Public Housing Authorities, *Newsletter,* Washington, July 2 1987.

55. *The Report of the President's Commission on Housing* (Washington: USGPO, 1982) 38.

56. Sherwood and March, *Operating Subsidies,* 54.

57. Sherwood and March, *Operating Subsidies,* 54–55.

58. House of Representatives, *Homeless Prevention Report,* 19.

59. House of Representatives, *Homeless Prevention Report,* 19–20.

60. M. A. Stegman, W. M. Rohe, and R. Quercia, "U.S. Experience with the Privatization of Public Housing," prepared under contract with PADCO, Inc, for USAID, May 1987, 19.

61. Manpower Development Research Corporation, *Final Report of the National Tenant Management Demonstration* (Washington: MDRC, May 1980) xiv.

62. MDRC, *Final Report,* xiv.

63. Stegman, Rohe, and Quercia, *Privatization,* 19.

64. MDRC, *Final Report,* xviii.

65. MDRC, *Final Report,* xviii–xix.

66. MDRC, *Final Report,* xx.

67. MDRC, *Final Report,* xxii–xxiii.

68. CLPHA, *Newsletter,* Feb. 7 1987, 2.

69. M. J. Schussheim, "Selling Public Housing to Tenants: How Feasible?" (Washington: Library of Congress, Congressional Research Service, December 14 1986).

70. Department of Housing and Urban Development, "Issue Paper on the Sale of Public Housing to Tenants" (Washington: HUD, April 1984), 4.

71. HUD, "Sale of Public Housing," 12.

72. W. M. Rohe et al., "Public Housing Homeownership Demonstration Assessment, Background Program Description Report," draft, prepared for U.S. Department of Housing and Urban Development, September 1987, 16.

73. Rohe et al., "Homeownership Demonstration," 16, 22.

74. House Banking Committee, *Homeless Prevention Report,* 27.

75. Schussheim, "Selling Public Housing," 14.

76. House Banking Committee, *Homeless Prevention Report,* 97.

77. M. K. Nenno, "National Association of Housing and Redevelopment Officials," *Journal of Housing* 44, 5 (September/October 1987).

Chapter 14
The Role of Nonprofits in Renewed Federal Housing Efforts

Neil S. Mayer

Nonprofit organizations have been the sponsors, developers, and operators of housing, especially for lower income people, for many years. Often their housing activities have been assisted with federal funds. Nonprofits are significant participants in current major federal housing programs including HUD's Section 202 program (as well as past efforts) and significant competitors for local allocations of CDBG and other monies for housing purposes.

As new housing policies are now shaped, a central issue is the potential role of nonprofits as delivery agents for housing rehabilitation, construction, acquisition, and management programs serving people of limited means. Key questions in shaping nonprofit participation are whether there are substantial roles in housing provision that nonprofits can play especially well; what the current levels of nonprofit capability and performance are in housing production and what this implies; how federal programs can and should be structured to facilitate and take advantage of nonprofit involvement; and what the potential of nonprofits is as actors in a context of expanding—probably gradually expanding—federal housing assistance.

This chapter addresses these issues in detail, examining (in order) why nonprofit housing activity is important, recent performance and production by nonprofits, the impacts of and responses to federal cutbacks, broad principles of housing policy that affect nonprofit activity, the design of housing programs to allow for effective nonprofit participation, and the potential for nonprofit activities within an expanded federal housing agenda.

Because nonprofits are program delivery agents, a wide spectrum of housing programs and program issues affect them; and this discussion necessarily addresses an extensive set of concerns. In choosing its focus, I have unavoidably been arbitrary in including certain matters and neglecting other important ones. I have deliberately confined attention largely to nonprofits that are themselves "developers," actively undertaking the nitty gritty activities of housing construction and rehabilitation projects. I have not discussed nonprofits' work in property acquisition and management or in sponsorship of projects developed by others, nor the specific needs of rural nonprofits.

I approach the issue of nonprofits not from ground zero but as one whose research and experience suggest strongly that nonprofits have an important part to play in increasing the supply of housing for lower income people. In this chapter, I have interpreted evidence of modest but growing nonprofit production levels to suggest potential for further growth with improved and expanded support, where another observer might focus more on the limited scale to date and the difficulties of "scaling up" production and expanding to new geographic areas. The chapter focuses on what past performance promises in terms of nonprofits' potential and on lessons we have learned for reaching that potential by properly shaping federal housing programming.

Potential Gains: Why Do We Care If Nonprofits Produce Housing?

A primary question in thinking about shaping federal programs to assist nonprofit production of affordable housing must be whether there are significant values in having nonprofit, especially community-based nonprofit, organizations be substantial housing producers and users of available federal resources for that purpose. If there are, then we have grounds to pay serious attention to the level of production nonprofits can be expected to handle, ways to build upon and expand their existing capacities, production mechanisms that meet their specific needs, and other issues of policy and program design that affect nonprofit participation. What are the potential advantages of nonprofit housing production that we might wish to reap? I believe they are numerous and important, stemming from the goals nonprofits select and the roles they play in their communities and their projects.

Most nonprofits deliberately and voluntarily target their housing activities to meeting the needs of lower income people who are, by every study of housing costs and conditions, the households in primary need of housing assistance. Nonprofits generally do not need to be regulated by complex program specifications, tightly monitored, or given expensive incentives simply to get them to focus on this population. On the contrary, they systematically pursue the resources necessary to make each project affordable, often in contexts where producing housing for other economic groups is an available, far easier option.[1]

Most nonprofits have *permanent* affordability as a consistent goal for the housing they produce. The nation is confronted currently with the potential for sharp losses in existing federally subsidized, affordable housing as requirements for serving low-income people expire. Nonprofits are willing participants in programs that provide for truly long-run provision of affordable housing, saving us the expense and dislocation of losing and having to replace the already subsidized stock.

Nonprofits are the housing producers most willing (along with Public Housing Authorities) to serve population groups with special needs that increasingly are recognized to predominate among those who require housing assistance, including large families, households headed by women, and the homeless. And they voluntarily target their housing provision efforts to neighborhoods and communities where housing need is greatest but where it is difficult to attract other developers, investors, or owner-operators. Very frequently the absence of other actors has been the impetus for the formation of nonprofits.[2] In other low-income areas with stronger adjacent housing markets, for-profit developers are active but often not in serving the existing low-income population.[3] If we are to expand the supply of decent affordable housing in troubled neighborhoods or rural areas, nonprofits seem likely to remain a central vehicle.

Nonprofits willingly pursue rehabilitation of the existing housing stock, despite the uncertainties and difficulties of many rehabilitation projects. And they carry out adequate maintenance because it is a social goal, even when greater profits might be made by limiting these expenditures, given that subsidized rents may not be adjusted upward in response to better housing quality.

Nonprofits often have the community links and sensitivity that allow them to put together housing projects that have strong support from their neighbors. Such projects can then gain both rapid local approvals and the long-term support needed to limit vandalism and other operations problems.

Because most nonprofits voluntarily serve low-income people and troubled neighborhoods, they do not need costly financial incentives to concentrate their efforts and resources in these directions. They are not actively comparing returns on affordable housing with the returns available in nonresidential projects or luxury housing in other locations, or in other financial markets. They also have access to at least some "social capital" belonging to other investors who are not seeking to maximize their returns. As a result, if they can be assisted in continuing to develop efficient modes of planning and production, nonprofits may be able to produce affordable housing in critical locations at least governmental subsidy cost.

Nonprofits, especially community-based ones such as community development corporations, have as central objectives the overall improvement of their neighborhoods or wider areas. They link housing improvements to job provision, improvements of other facilities and services, changing residents' attitudes and behavior, and other aspects of neighborhood revitalization. But housing rehabilitation and construction are critical components in substance and symbol of those broader efforts. Clearly no other private actors, and rarely the public sector without nonprofit cooperation, are undertaking these broader strategies for revitalization in a systematic way. Enabling nonprofits to carry out and expand their housing functions and to build broader capacity and programming in the process seems a key part of efforts to revitalize distressed neighborhoods and communities for the benefit of their residents.

In addition to these potential advantages, in the last several years nonprofits, in collaboration with local and state governments, foundations, and other supporters and in the absence of substantial federal subsidies, have been major providers of housing for lower income people. They may stand well-prepared relative to other actors, in a significant number of localities, to be principal users of expanded federal aid. Are they realistically capable of playing a significant housing production role? It is to this issue of scale that we now turn.

Performance and Production

Nonprofit development corporations have a specific set of housing roles, focusing on conserving and expanding the stock of housing available to people of limited means, particularly in distressed or gentrifying neighborhoods, rural areas, and certain suburban locations. At the same time the role of many nonprofit developers is wider and more difficult than simply housing provision because of their substantial focus on strengthening neighborhoods and communities through building local institutions and leadership, and providing supportive services and employment. Goals of a purely "big production numbers" kind are both hard to reach and misleading measures of performance, because of the nonprofits' deliberately focused objectives and the inherent difficulties in serving their typical target populations and communities. The question is, do these developers have the ability to provide significant amounts of housing? If policy makers are to consider expanding resources available to nonprofits and tailoring housing programs so that nonprofits can successfully use them, they want evidence that these developers can put resources to effective use on a scale that justifies careful attention to their needs.

There is now a substantial body of evidence, summarized below, that not-for-profit organizations can deliver significant levels of housing production. The evidence furthermore suggests strongly that the scale of results could be much increased with modest and careful expansion of federal resources, given the impressive performance of nonprofits in the recent period of very sharp federal cutbacks in resources that support their work.

While there is no single and complete census of the level of production by nonprofit developers, the evidence that is available shows clearly that not-for-profit housing development is a major force within the context of its objectives. Consider some of the existing measures of activity.

CDC Activity Measured by National Organizations

One important piece of nationwide data comes from the work of the Local Initiatives Support Corporation (LISC). Founded in 1980 with prime impetus from the Ford Foundation, LISC assists community-based nonprofits throughout the country in undertaking housing and economic development projects in partnership with local public and private institutions, largely in distressed areas. LISC draws on corporate and foundation capital and provides assistance primarily in the form of loans or investments rather than grants, loans at preferred terms that provide critical up-front capital to get projects started, or gap financing that allows leveraging of conventional financing and public funds. LISC also helps organize local partnerships among groups of these nonprofit community development corporations (CDCs), private corporations, foundations, and government to pool resources and talents, spread risks, and increase the volume of activity.

LISC began its work just as federal resources for low-income housing and CDC activity were being sharply cut. Yet in seven years of operation, the nonprofit projects it has assisted have produced 11,000 units of new and rehabilitated housing for lower-income people, largely in seriously distressed neighborhoods. Leveraging of LISC resources in housing development projects is more than 11:1, and that ratio has been growing rapidly since the start of operations as the CDCs grow in skill, sophistication, and reputation.[4] By mid-1987 donor contributions to LISC totaled over $103 million and loan repayments and other earnings added another $32 million. LISC has been organizing partnerships to assist CDCs in more than 25 "areas of concentration," deliberately creating the circumstances for further growth in production levels nationwide.

There are also many nonprofits pursuing projects in which LISC resources are not involved. Among these is the Neighborhood Reinvestment Corporation. The NRC, begun with federal funding, works through local nonprofits and with local lenders to provide capital which nonprofits and private homeowners and landlords use to acquire and improve property in areas of moderately (and sometimes more seriously) depressed housing and lending markets. This network of Neighborhood Housing Services (NHS) providers has provided over 13,000 direct loans, totalling more than $110 million, along with technical assistance, in some 240 neighborhoods. Many more loans, from private lenders and local government, have been generated in the same neighborhoods in significant part through the NHS's initiative.[5] Another quite different model, The Enterprise Foundation, which assists nonprofits serving only very low income people, reports nearly 2,400 units of production in its short life.

While each of these organizations is itself an intermediary and catalyst, most of the housing produced and reported here is the direct work of individual local nonprofit developers. (NRC activity is a mix of such direct work and assistance to others.) A recent survey by the National Congress for Community Economic Development suggests that as many as 1,000 nonprofits are producing new and renovated housing. Data from 631 groups showed total production of 125,000 units including over 23,000 units in 1986 and 1987.[6] It is also worth remembering that the highly successful HUD Section 202 program of housing for the elderly has been implemented solely by nonprofit sponsors in this same period at program levels reaching 30,000 units per year. Sponsors varied in the extent of their developer roles.

Local CDC Production

Available evidence of housing activity by nonprofits within individual urban areas and regions suggests that they can make a significant impact in particular locations.

> In Chicago, the 15 active members of the Chicago Rehab Network have more than 1,000 housing units in production.[7]

> In Boston and nearby areas, the nonprofits that work with technical assistance providers at the Greater Boston Community Development Corporation have been producing about 1,000 housing units per year and in 1987 may reach 2,000 units throughout New England. These and other nonprofits within Massachusetts, now numbering about 75,have produced about 7,000 units since 1975 with sharp acceleration in recent years.

> In New York City, the CDCs assisted by LISC have developed 6,800 units in the past and have 1,800 units in the pipeline. Total rehabilitation and construction by New York City neighborhood groups is estimated at 3,000 units of low-income housing annually.

> San Francisco neighborhood housing developers, with a later start than many East Coast counterparts and a very compacted, high cost market have produced between two and three thousand affordable units in recent years.

> Smaller but still promising production levels are shown in other locations such as Cleveland where annual production of 200–400 housing units is significant in a market where very little investment in affordable housing or any other kind is taking place.

A survey including additional cities is just now being reported and should provide increased information that can be used for policy and program planning during 1990.[8]

CDC Scale of Production

Some individual nonprofits and their partners have reached substantial scales of production. One of the very large individual not-for-profit producers of housing, the BRIDGE Housing Corporation, operates in the Northern California region rather than in a single city. This developer typically starts a project with contributed foundation and corporate capital to use for pre-development costs. It targets households with a mix of incomes, often in collaboration with private and/or local CDC partners. Primarily by convincing localities to permit projects of greater density than normal regulation would allow, it earns money on the market rate portions of its developments and applies those funds to subsidize more affordable units within the same projects. Meanwhile, it returns the original predevelopment capital to a pool for re-use. BRIDGE further increases affordability using public funds where available but its projects are not fundamentally dependent upon them.

BRIDGE has been in the production stage since 1983. By 1986 it had participated in production of some 2,500 units of housing, including about 1,000 units that are rented at below market rates. It expects to produce about 1,000 units in 1987 alone, reaching its goal of roughly 5 percent of total new housing production in the area of its operation and becoming one of the ten or so largest developers in Northern California. While this model depends on a strong demand for market rate new construction and is therefore not applicable in many distressed inner city neighborhoods, it offers an important approach to housing provision in areas where affordable housing is in very short supply and demonstrates the ability of properly staffed and funded nonprofits to reach volume production.

Individual nonprofits have also had an important impact within their own local neighborhood areas. In Boston, for example, by the early 1980s Inquilinos Boricuas En Accion (IBA) had produced over 800 units of new and rehabilitated housing within its extremely narrow turf and had had a major impact on the quality of housing within that closely defined area. IBA's housing production, in contrast with that of BRIDGE, is targeted only to low-income residents. In New York City, the first of the large CDCs, Bedford-Stuyvesant Restoration Corporation, has built or renovated over 1,600 housing units and provided mortgage or rehabilitation assistance to nearly 6,000 homeowners. Over 300 organizations report more than 100 units of production.[9]

Furthermore, nonprofit efforts in distressed neighborhoods can lead to sufficient improvement in substance and image to attract private capital to those areas where it was not previously available. Not only is substantial leveraging achieved in the CDCs' own projects, as the LISC experience documents, but capital is drawn into other projects in the same areas.[10] In some rural areas, nonprofits are alone in bringing new housing capital into their communities.

In suburban areas, smaller cities, and more affluent cities without neighborhoods of concentrated low-income households, nonprofits can be the primary groups concerning themselves with the needs of lower income residents. The work of the Mid-Peninsula Housing Coalition on San Francisco Bay's wealthy peninsula, the Rehab Project in Lima, Ohio, and the Santa Barbara Community Housing Corporation provides examples of these important contributions.

Past CDC Performance

Many of the projects and initiatives discussed here were conceived and carried out in the period of sharply declining federal resources, by effectively assembling private funds and public resources from other levels of government and leveraging remaining federal dollars. However, a look at output and especially quality of performance in the earlier period of greater, though still limited, federal programming offers some direct illustration of nonprofit productivity in the context of a collaborative federal role that might be recreated in revised form in the future.

The most detailed published research concerns nonprofit CDCs' performance with assistance from the now-cancelled Neighborhood Self-Help Development (NSHD) program operated by HUD over a single funding cycle in 1980.[11] Grants totaling nearly $14 million were made to 125 CDCs, 99 of them in urban areas, with individual grants of less than $150,000 typically. The grants were designed to provide funds for completing the planning and preparation of already well-defined development projects and/or for part of the expense of actual implementation. In either case, CDCs were expected to obtain other major resources in cash and in kind for the projects, from various public and private sources and from the neighborhoods themselves. Notably, this program largely avoided making grants to the largest and most sophisticated of existing CDCs because many of those were already funded from other sources and because NSHD was intended to support the maturation of smaller and younger organizations. It had to reject several hundred applications for assistance by other organizations operating in the same fields, given its funding limitations.

Seventy-three of the 99 urban CDCs evaluated included some housing rehabilitation in their projects—either exclusively or as part of mixed-goal efforts. These projects produced 1,808 units of rehabilitated housing by the time the study ended, with 41 of the 73 projects still underway at that time. Completed projects reached over 83 percent of their originally planned housing rehabilitation production goals, and CDCs still at work expected to do at least that well. If final performance simply mirrored the accomplishments of the finished projects, the 73 projects produced nearly 3,000 units, more than 40 units per project. Twelve projects included new construction, with a goal of 665 total units. Despite very sharp increases in interest rates and decreases in federal production subsidies in the very period when these projects moved to final financing, finished projects produced 56 percent of expected housing units. Units then under construction raised the total production to 360 (about the same percentage of planned units as for finished projects). In sum, the small first-year program helped CDCs to produce some 3,000 plus units of housing, in projects of typically 40–50 units, with grant recipients achieving a very high percentage of intended outputs in the face of difficult conditions.

These production figures do not count other simultaneous projects by the same CDCs, their supporting neighborhood revitalization activities, and the concurrent work of other non-NSHD CDCs.

The NSHD funds were successfully leveraged by grantees, at a median ratio of over 3:1 and an average ratio three times that high, from many private and public sources. The average leveraging achieved was almost precisely that projected in CDC grant proposals.[12] Even in that earlier period of greater federal funding availability, almost two-thirds of the CDCs used private funds totaling over $31 million in their projects. Private sources provided about one-quarter of total funds, and private lenders most frequently were the single largest source of funding.

At least equally important, the NSHD CDCs systematically delivered the housing they developed to low-income people currently residing in their communities. Most of the organizations operated in severely distressed neighborhoods and the others provided affordable low-income housing in hot and gentrifying markets. Furthermore, they performed this role virtually alone. The NSHD study tried to identify any similar efforts in comparable neighborhoods by other actors, to make performance comparisons. The effort to find comparable actors proved fruitless.[13] CDCs are performing a role in housing provision that other investors and developers choose to avoid, an avoidance that is frequently a spur to CDC direct project action.

Available evidence indicates that CDCs and similar nonprofits are continuing their records of effective performance in the 1980s. A recent evaluation of a sample of LISC-assisted organizations showed that they were successful in meeting their output goals in 86 percent of their housing projects (and the other 14 percent were qualified successes), and three-quarters of the projects reached anticipated financial objectives.[14]

What we find then is a substantial and growing body of current housing production by nonprofits, employing mostly private and local or state public resources, often in complex partnerships and combinations. Not every nonprofit organization or nonprofit project succeeds. But the available evidence is that nonprofits can and do stick to their difficult work and still produce significant levels of housing, when enough resources are available to make production of low-income housing economically feasible for any institution. The activity is of significant scale and widespread, but as yet neither massive in relation to national goals nor at all uniform across regions and local areas.

Nonprofits have now had the experience of carrying out their housing and neighborhood revitalization activities in collaboration with private and local and state government actors, with the assistance of important intermediating institutions (including but by no means limited to the LISC example). One might anticipate that by carefully restoring an appropriate federal role in support of nonprofits and low-income housing in a way that supports and enhances the participation of these other actors and builds on the nonprofits' own accumulating expertise, policy makers could generate production, performance, and leveraging by nonprofits that well exceeds the results of past strategies. Notably, nonprofits would be building on a base of experience and pre-existing supporting relationships. This contrasts with 1960s experiences with Section 221 and Section 236 in which many nonprofit "developers" were indeed nonprofit organizations, churches for example, but hardly developers by inclination or past practice.

We shall now turn from past performance to a very brief summary of the impacts of seven years of reduced federal support for nonprofit and lower income housing, and then to the issues of how new federal policy and programs can be constructed to enhance the work of nonprofits. Those policy and program issues are critical, because the evidence indicates not that the nonprofit organizations are already fully equipped for massive-scale nationwide production but that they show the potential to be effective delivery agents if federal housing efforts are properly designed.

Impacts of Recent Federal Policy and the Nonprofit Response

Cutbacks in federal programming since 1980 have produced a unique three-level reduction in the nonprofits' ability to deliver affordable housing. During the late 1970s, expanding funding of nonprofit housing organizations and their activities through CDBG and CETA, along with the availability of housing and other project subsidies, had helped to produce a rapid blossoming in numbers of community-based nonprofit development corporations carrying out their own projects.[15] But sharp federal cutbacks undercut this progress on multiple fronts.

First, federal funds that served to pay for part of the basic operations of these nonprofits, for training, technical assistance, junior staff salaries, and other elements of capacity building, and for the pre-development costs of putting projects together were substantially cut. The Community Service Agency's Title VII program for CDCs, which had provided major funding for many of the largest and most productive nonprofits, was cut back and re-oriented, with a particular de-emphasis in the housing area. HUD's new Neighborhood Self-Help Development Program, carefully targeted to pre-development costs and project-capital-matching of younger CDCs, was axed. The much smaller Neighborhood Development Demonstration program, intended to partially replace it, was slow to be funded and implemented. CETA funding, which had earlier paid for significant amounts of nonprofit staffing in various positions, disappeared. CDBG funds, critical for both operations and project capital (especially in housing rehabilitation) fell sharply in real terms, and competition for them grew as other sources of federal aid to cities were eliminated.

Second, federal project subsidies used by nonprofits declined sharply in total funding levels, as of course they did for all developers of housing for lower income people. The demise of the Section 8 program for construction and rehabilitation was naturally the central blow, along with increased pressure on CDBG funds.

Third, the shift in federal housing program composition, even where new programs were initiated, was in important ways harmful or of limited benefit to nonprofits. Relatively shallow subsidies, such as those involved in the Rental Rehabilitation program or HODAG, were in many instances not sufficient by themselves to reach the concentrated low-income target populations in both weak and gentrifying markets. The absence of demand-side subsidies explicitly tied to supplying improved units—as opposed to mobile subsidies tied to households—made rental rehabilitation projects much more difficult to undertake or facilitate, particularly in distressed neighborhoods. Vouchers alone were especially inappropriate to meet needs for housing quality improvements in many nonprofit target areas. Increased tax depreciation benefits, as generous as they were, could not alone produce housing affordable to many nonprofits' clients; and the same applies to the new tax credits.

Together, these three factors curtailed nonprofit delivery of affordable housing and, equally important, interrupted and too often reversed growth in the organizations' delivery capacity. Critical expertise and experience were lost, as operating budgets and program funds fell below levels necessary to retain key staff members and provide them with further training and support.

Nonprofits and their supporters responded in a number of ways to these difficulties. In some cities, they coalesced to pressure local government to increase their share of CDBG and other locally controlled resources such as redevelopment project land and tax incentives. Emerging as virtually the sole providers of lower income housing, they began being looked to by concerned local officials for effective housing delivery. They sought and gained increased access to private foundation and corporate funds. They pressed for new sources of funding and, in places like San Francisco and Boston, were successful in creating "linkage" funds, paid by developers of nonresidential projects. In Chicago, Hartford, and elsewhere they gained new commitments of funds from lending institutions and insurance companies to provide project debt financing. An increased number of nonprofits, with support from technical assistance providers, became sophisticated in using tax-benefit partnerships to raise equity capital for low-income housing, although at some potential cost to very long-term project affordability. They learned to patiently combine multiple forms of funding. As just one example, a large nonprofit project in Cleveland, Lexington Village, combined loan funds from a private lender, three foundations, and LISC; grants from several corporations; tax syndication; a UDAG; CDBG money; and Urban Renewal Bond funds to produce 183 housing units.

Available evidence yields the following pattern of nonprofit response federal cutbacks.[16] Losses of federal funds were extremely heavy in operating and capacity-building, pre-development, and project-subsidy funds, with a reduction in federal support to less than half of previous levels. Funds from private and non-federal public sources did increase, but not in amounts at all sufficient to balance the federal losses. In absolute terms the largest losses were in project subsidy funds, but all categories suffered significant percentage net reductions. On the more positive side, the nonprofits that survived seem to informed observers to be more tightly budgeted and managed, better able to assess the true feasibility of planned projects (by themselves and with competent technical assistance), adept at assembling complex combinations of resources to make projects work, and possessed of greater access to private funds and effective and innovative intermediaries. Many important forms of growth in capacity and expanded housing delivery were derailed by federal cutbacks, but the remaining nonprofit sector seems well poised to make use of measured new forms of assistance, especially if the assistance is properly structured to build upon and take advantage of their recent experience.

Principles of Policy and Program Design

Given the current goals, roles, and recent performance of nonprofits, we can state a number of broad principles about the structuring of federal housing production policy and programs for people of limited means that would greatly help make nonprofits effective participants in them. We can then use these principles to address a set of narrower and more specific issues of program design.

1. *Federal housing production programs should be designed with explicit attention to the needs and abilities of nonprofits* to assure that the programs are made workable for this key set of actors.

Nonprofits are currently playing a significant role in producing housing for lower income people, targeting troubled neighborhoods and hard-to-serve populations, and coupling their own housing activities with neighborhood improvements carried out both by themselves and by other actors enticed into revitalizing. At the same time, nonprofits have needs for program resources that can meet the deep subsidy requirements of their target areas and clientele, effectively augment their on-going resource-gathering, and help them expand their still-limited production levels. A continuing commitment to deliberate program planning to meet these needs is the central requirement for assuring effective nonprofit growth and participation in renewed federal housing efforts. The other principles and specifics of program design recommended here fall within this broad concept.

2. *Housing programs' basic parameters must be in harmony with the specific types of people and situations nonprofits focus on serving.* That means most notably, establishing subsidies sufficiently deep to make feasible projects affordable to people of very limited means. But it also means including rehabilitation (moderate and substantial) and owner-occupancy (where mechanisms to assure long-run service to lower income people are attached) as pro-

gram components eligible for support, with realistic regulatory requirements and flexibility. Carefully crafted provisions of these kinds are necessary both to assist nonprofits to do what they do well and, from a broader policy perspective, to meet a series of critical national objectives for which nonprofits are logical—and sometimes the only available—delivery agents.

3. *Federal housing programs should take advantage of and build upon the advances in developing affordable housing that nonprofits have made in collaboration with nonfederal partners in recent years.* It would be wasteful to now construct a new round of federal programming which, in its attention to national objectives and to relations between federal agencies and housing producers, neglects the progress that these other actors have made in building cooperative mechanisms. If nothing else, it would be inefficiently expensive to lose the financial resources from these other sources, by constructing programs that do not fit neatly with such contributions and provide incentives for their continuation and expansion. Retaining and expanding other actors' participation goes well beyond the issue of collaboration with nonprofits. Encouraging local government cooperation and participation in expanded federal initiatives deserves major policy and program consideration in and of itself.

4. *Federal actions should include programs that are explicitly designed to expand the capacity of nonprofits to effectively undertake housing rehabilitation and construction of affordable housing* and extend their production beyond current limits. Although nonprofits already play critical roles in low-income housing and neighborhood revitalization and their skills, experience, and production have grown over time, there are still significant gaps. For instance, nonprofit capability varies widely by geographic area. Many organizations have as yet operated only on a limited scale of housing production; expanded production levels, for them, will require not only more money but more trained staff and other related capacity-building components. Continuity of funding for these organizations is critical to allow orderly growth with attention to staff retention and management-system building.

Earlier federal programs that served to expand nonprofit capacity have been sharply cut or eliminated. Efforts to assure that new housing production programs are used effectively should include a specific federal contribution to strengthen these key delivery agents, in collaboration with the private sector and state and local governments that have predominated in this area in recent years.

Elements of Policy and Program

Nonprofit developers have quite conventional resource needs: predevelopment funds; "cheap money" to make housing affordable to low-income residents; debt financing; and money for technical assistance, basic operations, and organizational capacity building.

Based on the nature of nonprofit organizations and activities, and the principles stated in the previous section, some specific inferences can be drawn about how federal programs might best contribute to the provision of these needed resources. Many of the issues and choices raised here are also matters for broader consideration in overall federal housing policy. I shall focus on the implications for nonprofits and acknowledge, as appropriate, instances where broader considerations are simultaneously at stake, consistent with the principle that nonprofit needs be explicitly considered in federal housing program design. In many instances, I raise design issues that must be addressed but about whose precise resolution, in terms of the exact structure of funding allocation mechanisms, people with shared objectives may reasonably disagree. I shall address first matters concerning housing production programs per se and then turn to the needs of nonprofits as organizations in the areas of operations and capacity-building.

Production Programs

Deep subsidies. Nonprofits serve low-income people. It is critical, both for nonprofits to do their work and in order to meet national housing goals through any delivery agent, that federal assistance programs provide sufficiently deep subsidies to meet real needs. There is in some quarters, at least implicitly, a mistaken belief that nonprofits can and should work magic in producing affordable housing on a substantial scale without these critical gap-filling subsidies, through hard work at low pay, access to private philanthropy, cooperation with local government, and so forth. This belief is a basis for frustration and failure, as both attention to standard economic feasibility analysis of many current major projects and sometimes painful long-run experience readily reveal. Producing affordable housing on a substantially expanded scale, particularly for the groups nonprofits so systematically serve, fundamentally requires deep forms of federal assistance.

From this perspective it is also critical that major assistance programs be tightly targeted to serving low-income people. Assistance funds will not be sufficient to reach the truly needy if direct and tax expenditures are allocated in substantial part to households at other income levels. A specific element of proper targeting must be that, in rating projects competing for subsidies, projects first be tightly standardized in terms of the income of clients to be served and the period of assured affordability. Projects should not be credited, for example, for leveraging non-federal resources at the expense of income targeting.

Eligible activities. Federal programs need to encompass as eligible activities the specific functions that nonprofits seek to undertake. Substantial and moderate rehabilitation of single- and multi-family homes (including owner-occupied residences) are crucial in many distressed areas and form the heart of nonprofit neighborhood revitalization strategies. While aggregate national data or other considerations may lead some observers to support voucher programs in lieu of rehabilitation or other production programs, the conditions of the distressed communities and rural areas in which many nonprofits work (and the research evidence that vouchers produce little additional investment in housing improvements) indicate that rehabilitation programs, be they supply side or demand subsidies tied to specific units, are critical components to overall housing strategy as well. The need for large-family units must be reflected in rational cost and subsidy differentials for bigger units. In addition, the nonprofits' concentration on local areas of intense need must not be thwarted by regulations aimed at dispersing subsidized housing.

Single-room occupancy units in existing residential hotels, ineligible for aid in many past federal programs, are important housing resources in many nonprofit target areas and their preservation is central to actions to house the homeless. Limited-equity cooperatives are one good mechanism for assuring long-term affordability combined with effective management and maintenance. Both of these housing forms have often been made unworkable within federal program contexts either through neglect or deliberate design. The array of common nonprofit initiatives need to be explicitly "winnowed in" as new programs are designed and expanded, both as categories of eligible activities for major subsidy programs and in terms of other forms of flexibility such as in housing "quality" and "siting" standards.

Capital grants. Subsidy funds might well be provided in the form of up-front capital grants, roughly similar to the HODAG concept but with greater flexibility in terms of project types and the size of subsidies. Such funds would have two particular advantages in assisting nonprofit projects. They could be used to fill financial-feasibility gaps in diverse projects, and they can combine easily with additional resources in the form of land, cheap capital, and technical assistance obtained from other actors. As other resources are available to narrow the affordability gap, the size of federal grant or deferred loan funds can be appropriately reduced, based on conventional project feasibility analysis. Of course, this choice of the basic form of production subsidy turns also on wider issues of the timing of federal budget impact, availability of nonconcessionary loan finance under this and alternative subsidy structures, and the like. If there is desire to spread out budget impacts by providing both up-front funds and demand or supply side continuing subsidies, the key for nonprofit goals of housing improvement is that the latter subsidies be tied to housing units, not households.

Credit for generating funds. Production subsidy programs should give developers explicit credit for generating concessionary project funds (grants, low-interest loans, or land and services in kind), both as a matching requirement and in ranking competing project funding proposals. The relationships non-profits have developed with local and state governments and with philan-thropic organizations and other portions of the private sector, together with the emergence of financial intermediaries like LISC, are generating substantial funds for affordable housing right now. Nonprofits should be given incentives and rewarded for continuing to pursue such funds on an expanding scale.

Matching and crediting provisions, coupled with adequate federal subsidy programs, would also create substantial incentives for other levels of government and the private sector to increase their contributions to affordable housing efforts. Many institutions, especially in the private sector, have been reluctant to contribute to affordable housing projects because their very high per unit subsidy costs seem to dictate very limited results from the modest resources available. And low-interest loans seem to be of little help in achieving affordability without other major sources of cheap capital. The potential to leverage federal funds—at a substantial leveraging ratio—could induce significant increases in other institutions' participation. Note that up-front capital grants lend themselves well to matching.

A significant concern about crediting nonprofit developers for obtaining nonfederal resources, when allocating federal funds, is that in some localities there are few foundations or fiscally well-equipped and cooperative local governments to provide matching funds. One possible approach to this problem is first to allocate a substantial portion of federal funds to geographic areas on the basis of need (as measured by housing conditions, housing costs in relation to income, etc.). One could then further allocate this money to individual projects within these areas on a matching basis in relation to other funds raised. Needy areas would not lose out by being matching-money poor, but within each area matching would be encouraged. The same program would also allocate an additional amount of "bonus funding" to projects based in significant part on their matching accomplishments, either without regard to location or flexibly within larger geographic regions. Either this or some other strategy to deal with potential allocation problems arising from matching requirements is well worth developing further, in order to encourage continued growth in nonfederal support.

Delivery. Whether housing assistance—for instance in the capital grant form suggested here—should be delivered directly to individual developers from the federal government or come as block grants to states and localities for allocation to developers is still an outstanding issue. My own view is that—given the difficulties under block grants of assuring proper targeting to low-income people, maintaining a consistent project rating and quality, and ensuring prompt action to develop low-income housing across the wide range of localities—direct provision to individual developers is preferable. But enough nonprofits have now built credibility and positive relations with localities that a program that provides substantial funding in block grant form, with a separate set-aside for direct competitive federal-government-to-developer funding as well, would also be viable.[17] Any block grant program would itself need federal standards for income-targeting, leveraging, long-term affordability, and the other program elements already outlined for effective nonprofit use.

An extremely important issue is whether to establish a distinct production program for which only nonprofits would be eligible or to give nonprofits access to a broader production program. I believe that on balance the advantage lies with nonprofit access to basic federal production subsidy programming. Nonprofits, at least initially, should have a specific set-aside within the program, based on their unique contributions to permanently affordable housing and the desirability of increasing their production capability—as in the current low-income tax credit. But they should still be able to compete as well for additional funds in the nondesignated pool.

This alternative could accomplish several desirable results. It could allow highly experienced nonprofits access to a much larger pool of funds than would likely be allocated to any nonprofits-only program, while simultaneously assuring the broader range of still-maturing nonprofits a protected funding pot. It would allow for growth in nonprofit participation as more organizations proved able to compete with other developers. It would increase the long-run credibility and visibility of nonprofit developers, as they demonstrate successful participation in a broad national initiative.

The net value of nonprofits participating in the broader program(s) is in significant part dependent, of course, on program design. If the broader program lacks the structural components that match nonprofits' needs and advantages (such as program flexibility, deep subsidy, credit for matching, targeting, and long-term affordability) then it might be better to pursue the creation of a separate program sensitive to the concerns of nonprofits and their clients. I hope that will not be the case and consider the shaping of broad programs to fit with nonprofit development a fundamental recommendation of this paper.

Predevelopment funds. Nonprofit developers have an acute need for predevelopment funds to pay early costs for such items as placing options on potential project sites or preparing initial plans, and to pay somewhat later costs for detailed architectural work or other soft costs of development preparation. Nonprofits generally do not have pools of funds from previous project "profits" to use to undertake new work, and only a few (notably, BRIDGE) have assembled such pools from outside sources. In recent years nonprofit organizations have raised these funds from private foundations and corporations and from local and state government; but if the level of activity they are to undertake is to expand smoothly, nonprofits will need expanded access to predevelopment monies from the federal government as well.

These funds might best be delivered in the form of an add-on to CDBG monies or in a small separate block grant to localities, for use by nonprofits explicitly. Local governments are usually aware of potential projects at an early stage and can allocate pre-development funds promptly. Perhaps a certain share of the predevelopment money might be held in a federal discretionary fund to aid competent but locally unfavored organizations.

In addition, production programs might well provide sufficiently deep subsidies to repay predevelopment costs and leave a small surplus after construction, conditional on its being re-used for predevelopment costs in a future project. That way nonprofit developers could build on their initial successes to establish at least small "revolving" predevelopment pools. Another source of expanded predevelopment funds might be accelerated local recovery of UDAG and CDBG loans, perhaps through the creation of a secondary market for this paper aided by federal insurance or further credit enhancement.[18]

The federal government should require that localities use matching or leveraging of predevelopment monies from other sources as a rating criterion in their fund allocations. Nonprofits have successfully pursued nonfederal predevelopment funds in recent years and should be encouraged to continue to do so.

Debt financing. Federal action is also necessary to assure the availability of debt financing of the portion of project costs not met by capital grants. Nonprofits have been successfully gaining access to private lending, but remaining lender reservations may be increased by a program focused more on initial grants and less on long-term unrestricted operating subsidies. Federal insurance (for lending institutions and/or taxable bonds) or direct lending as used very successfully by nonprofits in the Section 202 program, could be appropriate in various traditional forms. In addition, federal regulators could vigorously support communities' efforts to press lenders for loans for affordable housing within the requirements of the Community Reinvestment Act.

Capacity Building

As indicated earlier, many nonprofits have made substantial progress in producing affordable housing and have developed the capacity for further expansion. There remain, however, significant areas of the country where nonprofit developers are neither numerous, strong, nor experienced; many individual nonprofits show early promise but need to mature in skill and build a track record; more sophisticated organizations still need to increase the number of skilled staff members and sources of financial and technical support required to move to truly large-scale activity. An appropriate goal in restoring a greater federal funding role in housing production is to increase nonprofit capability to deliver housing at a larger scale. In recent years we have learned more about what factors make up this capability,[19] how to assist nonprofits to effectively expand their capacity and how to replicate program initiatives transferred from elsewhere.

Recent research on nonprofit, community-based development has identified several key factors needed to increase capacity. These include a skilled executive director, technical and project skill requirements for key staff members, financial and market analysis capability, a division of responsibilities and skills among a variety of actors, competent bookkeeping and other basic business skills, appropriate roles for citizen boards of directors, a past track record, good relations with outside public and private sources of support, and the ability to respond to difficult and changing environments. We have also learned how nonprofits build these capacities, including elements of recruitment and training, project experience, technical assistance, external actors' collaboration at critical points, and appropriate types and scales of funding as capacity-building and program activity proceed and grow. These lessons suggest the following federal roles.

Operating funds. Nonprofits need increased operating funds to provide financial continuity for core staff members. We know that complete financial independence is the exception for nonprofit organizations serving low-income people. The short supply of operating funds not only burns up nonprofit energy in constant fundraising but also frustrates the key people whose growing expertise is vital to organizational capacity building. A modest level of federal operating funding for a significant number of nonprofits can make a substantial impact (as state funding has in Massachusetts and New York).

Operating funds could be delivered directly to nonprofits from an independent federally sponsored agency such as the National Endowment for Neighborhoods, as proposed by a coalition of nonprofit supporters,[20] or from a restored Neighborhoods office in HUD. In either case, nonprofits should be called upon to assemble matching funds from other sources, with flexibility for organizations in relatively resource-poor environments. The independent endowment approach has the advantage of enabling the endowment agency allocating the federal contribution to actively seek out other private funds itself and be a repository for them.

Local governments, some of which have been reluctant to see direct federal funding of nonprofits in the past, would retain influence through their ability to affect the availability of local matching funds, their control over new predevelopment funds, and some limited sign-off power regarding the harmony of nonprofit goals with local public objectives.

Nonprofits should provide explicit plans for how they will build organizational capacity during the operating grant period. Otherwise capacity building may receive inadequate attention under the pressure of daily project work. At the same time, knowledgeable observers agree that capability grows largely through the process of doing projects. Nonprofits should receive federal operations/capacity-building assistance as they proceed with identifiable projects. Individual organizations could and should be funded on a continuing basis, but to receive such support they would have to show progress both in delivering effective programs and meeting their capacity-building goals.

Funding of intermediaries. A portion of federal assistance for nonprofits' activities should be reserved for certain kinds of productive intermediaries. Of particular value, I believe, are area or regional sources of experienced technical assistance with staff available for day-to-day assistance in carrying out projects. Such intermediaries, well-exemplified by the Greater Boston Community Development Corporation (GBCD) which assists with some 1,000 housing units annually, can increase nonprofit production efficiency (not every nonprofit need have on staff the full range of technical skills), help train people from neighborhood-based nonprofits in development skills, and shorten the time it takes for a nonprofit to move to real housing production.

Also worthy of federal support are intermediaries explicitly devoted to concrete, practical training of people from the low-income communities served by nonprofits. The Development Training Institute in Baltimore is a notable example of such an organization. Related to this technical assistance and training function is the supplying of information about what has worked elsewhere and why. Effective information providers, such as the Community Information Exchange, could be aided in delivering such short-cutting knowledge.

A pool of discretionary funds might also be used to help fund the replication of successful nonprofit-oriented initiatives that contribute to building the potential for a larger scale of accomplishments. Examples include the Chicago Equity Fund in which private and public actors pooled capital for quick and assured availability to local nonprofits, and the Boston-based Hyam Trust's effort (with LISC) to accelerate recycling of social capital by helping to create a secondary market for nonprofit project debt.

It is important to note that at the time this chapter is written, a coalition of housing groups, the National Community Housing Partnership Legislative Working Group, has prepared an outline of legislation for support of nonprofits in housing production and capacity building. Their two-part program, one for production and pre-development, especially for relatively mature nonprofits, and one for capacity building especially among less-sophisticated ones, has many elements in common with the policy and program guidelines I have provided here. There are differences as well, including their preference for a nonprofits-only production program and for funneling most production money through cities and states; but the differences are on points on which neither my views nor those of the members of the Working Group with whom I have spoken are set in concrete. The Working Group's outline provides another very good basis for discussion in terms of the policy and program principles I have stated above. Components of that approach are included in the proposed Community Housing Partnership Act (HR3891).

Realistic Programming and Nonprofit Potential

In an environment of continued budget deficits, existing knowledge of non-profit activities can be used to outline practical standards for the start-up of expanded support for low-income housing programs with nonprofits as key delivery agents.

First, programs that are phased in at a moderate scale—to allow not only for budgetary constraints but also for testing and monitoring to build public/political confidence in new programs—are very much consistent with effective nonprofit participation. Total nonprofit production could be significantly increased through participation in programs funded at levels initially well short of 1970 levels. Phase-in would allow for further capacity building through actual experience with the new programs.

The total cost of any production program would not be greater—indeed might well be smaller per unit of properly targeted housing production—as a result of granting nonprofits a set-aside and also the right to compete for non-set-aside funds. The cost of providing operating/capacity building funds to non-profits would be modest. Even a very broad program that provided $50,000 to each of the nonprofits seriously engaged in housing development could be budgeted initially at perhaps $30 million annually. Predevelopment funds would be expected to be recycled into future projects as permanent financing, limiting that cost in the long run.

Individual nonprofits should be carefully funded for projects of a scale that their experience, capability, and growth curves indicate they can handle. We now have a body of research and analysis that informs us about matching projects to the capacity of nonprofits, and it should be used in funding decisions. There is no need to recapitulate the experience of troubled nonprofit projects under the Section 221 or 236 programs, which were sometimes sponsored by organizations that themselves had no capability for development and management—indeed, perhaps no housing experience or capacity at all.

Nonprofits can later build on their expanding track records to take on larger-scale projects, at the same time that the total funding of new federal programs is expanding from initial levels. This growth process will be greatly enhanced insofar as federal resources are in fact devoted to deliberate capacity building efforts as recommended earlier.

What kind of results over time can we anticipate from the nonprofit sector, assuming federal assistance that meets their resource needs? First, we should expect a rapid burst of production, allowing some minimum period for project planning adjustments to new programs. There already exist several hundred nonprofits with significant experience in housing development, along with many supportive nonfederal financial and technical actors. These organizations, painstakingly at work assembling complex combinations of funds for even small projects, would be freed for prompt action by the availability of adequate federal project subsidies to combine with current state, local, and private resources. To gain this result, it is important that the structure of new programs provide for building on recent local initiatives by offering subsidies in flexible forms (e.g., capital grant), with credit for matching funds.

In some locations, activity will be greatly aided by recent substantial commitment of funds by other national and local organizations. These include, for example, multi-million dollar, multi-year commitments of support for operations and capacity-building by combinations of foundations, LISC, and others in Cleveland, Chicago, and Boston.

In the longer run, there are reasonable grounds for expecting successful growth in productive capacity and actual production. Research evidence indicates that even modest levels of project experience greatly increase the ability of nonprofits to carry out projects effectively. For example, among recipients of NSHD grants, researchers identified substantial capacity growth from just a first housing project, and a halving of the likelihood of less than full project success for organizations with two or more projects under their belts.[21] Similarly, NSHD grantees with a regular staff member who had some development expertise had virtually twice the likelihood of full project success as other nonprofits (who either lacked expertise or relied wholly on outside technical advice). Even limited experience produced similarly sharp increases in nonprofit effectiveness among recipients of LISC assistance.[22]

Federal support for nonprofit housing development likely will induce increases in nonfederal contributions from actors who have been reluctant to take part without it. If the federal government helps to support the replication of innovative local partnerships such as Chicago's Equity Fund or the Boston Housing Partnership, then nonprofit access to other support might grow much more widely.

As nonprofit capacity grows, nonprofits should be able to capture an increasing portion of available federal resources in competitive-award programs, or at least a stable portion of a gradually growing total pot of regular and set-aside funds. If they do not show such strengths—in programs that appropriately reward a combination of performance, targeting, and long-term affordability—then the nonprofit role will simply not grow at a rapid pace.

Perhaps the most difficult process will be to develop nonprofit capacity in the regions and areas of the country where few organizations and little capability presently exist. But it may be that the potential availability of adequate federal resources will serve as a catalyst for development both of nonprofits and of non-federal support in these areas, and release critical private resources, now used in relatively resource-rich areas, to support early nonprofit development in areas of scarcity. That process will take active nurturing by existing institutions and new ones such as a National Endowment for Neighborhoods or HUD Neighborhoods office. Expanding nonprofit housing activity both in current areas of concentration and beyond them—in an environment of substantial and deliberately supportive federal assistance—appears to be a challenge to which many determined and skilled people and organizations would like the opportunity to respond.

In this era of reduced housing resources for low-income people, nonprofit developers can play a critical role in providing permanently affordable housing for those most in need. We now have the opportunity for the first time to couple explicitly supportive federal housing programs with both the increased capacity that nonprofits have developed in recent years and an expanded base of nonfederal support for their work. The proper extent of nonprofits' role in housing low-income people cannot truly be judged until the kinds of federal assistance outlined in this chapter are set in place. Skeptics will be watching for nonprofits to falter in increasing the scale of their activity. I, however, believe that with well-structured policies from Washington, the nonprofit housing sector can effectively take on a much expanded part in production and preservation of affordable housing.

* * * *

In preparing this chapter, I benefited greatly from discussions with and comments from individuals too numerous to list individually but too valuable to neglect.

Notes

1. See the Production and Performance section of this chapter for a brief review of available evidence on this topic.

2. See N. Mayer, *Neighborhood Organizations and Community Development* (Washington: Urban Institute Press, 1984) 54.

3. Mayer, *Neighborhood Organizations*.

4. See Local Initiatives Support Corporation, "Report of Progress" (New York: LISC, 1986), 9; and LISC internal reporting documents for 1987.

5. Memo from William Whiteside, Executive Director, Neighborhood Reinvestment Corporation, November 1987 (data through 1986).

6. National Congress for Community Economic Development, *Against All Odds: the Achievements of Community-Based Development Organizations* (Washington: NCCED, 1989).

7. As summarized in Alice Shabecoff, "Neighborhood Housing: Development Innovations," *Journal of Housing* (July 1987) 105 ff.

8. This survey is being undertaken at the New School of Social Research under the direction of Mitchell Sviridoff and Avis Vidal.

9. NCCED, *Against All Odds*.

10. See Mayer, *Neighborhood Organizations*, 88–90, for evidence.

11. See Mayer, *Neighborhood Organizations*.

12. This is the leveraging ratio for all types of projects together. Housing leveraging was not separately reported in detail but was higher than the overall average.

13. Although we generally know that some similar neighborhoods had Section 8 projects undertaken by private developers or in for-profit and nonprofit partnerships, the study did not uncover them in its intensive visits to 30 sites. The large number of NSHD single-family rehab projects seem unmatched except by other nonprofits.

14. A. Vidal et al., "Key Findings, Stimulating Community Development: An Assessment of LISC" (Cambridge: Harvard University, 1986) 6.

15. See, for example, Pierce and Steinbach, "Corrective Capitalism" (New York: Ford Foundation, 1987) 27.

16. See, for example, L. Salamon, "Serving Community Needs: The Non-Profit Sector in an Era of Governmental Retrenchment," Progress Report #3 (Washington: Urban Institute, September 1983).

17. The draft proposal of the National Community Housing Partnership Working Group takes this form. It includes the important protection for nonprofits that the entire program is designated for use by nonprofits alone—an issue I discuss below in the text.

18. This idea was suggested to me by LISC President Paul Grogan.

19. See Mayer, *Neighborhood Organizations,* ch. 3, 4, and 5, for a comprehensive review of this analysis.

20. J. McNeely et al., Proposed National Endowment for America's Neighborhoods, Xerox (Washington: National Neighborhood Coalition, March 1986). This approach has the advantage of being able to directly promote contribution of matching funds from other sources.

21. Mayer, *Neighborhood Organizations,* 100–115 ff.

22. Vidal et al., "Key Findings," 6.

Chapter 15
Integrating Housing and Welfare Assistance

Sandra J. Newman and Ann B. Schnare

As welfare reform moves to a higher priority on the nation's legislative agenda, housing is conspicuous by its absence.[1] This omission makes little philosophical sense, since the ability to obtain adequate shelter, like the need for food, clothing, and medical care, is at the heart of welfare programs.[2] But the omission also makes little practical sense, since general welfare programs, such as Aid to Families with Dependent Children and Supplemental Security Income, spend essentially as much as HUD on shelter assistance for the poor. Thus, welfare programs embody a significant shelter assistance component—a fact that has generally been ignored in the development of both welfare and housing assistance policies. We argue that reforms to both welfare policy and to housing policy should acknowledge the interrelationship of these two systems. The failure to do so in the past is at least partly responsible for the inequities and inefficiencies of the current approach to shelter assistance.

We begin with a brief status report on the nation's housing problems and policies. We then provide an overview of the two-pronged approach to housing assistance and evaluate it in terms of fairness, efficiency, and success in providing the poor with access to decent and affordable housing. We conclude with a discussion of some general ideas on restructuring the current system and provide rough estimates of the costs of these reforms.

Housing for the Poor: Status and Prospects

There is a large, and by all accounts growing, gap between the demand for and supply of affordable units. In 1983, for example, about 9.7 million renters nationwide had annual incomes below $8,000.[3] Using standard definitions of affordability, such households could afford to spend no more than $200 each month on housing. But in that same year, only 5.3 million units in the U.S. had rents below this level, and 20 percent of these were in substandard condition. Since at least some of the sound, inexpensive units were occupied by richer households, a conservative estimate of the additional units needed, if the poor were to be adequately housed, was 5.5 million.

Given the current status of federal housing policy, it is highly unlikely that these housing needs can be met. Cutbacks initiated under the Reagan administration have virtually eliminated all construction programs. HUD's new commitments for assisted housing have dropped from over $30 billion a year to $10 billion. Existing contracts for assisted units, which typically last for 15 years, will begin to expire in the early 1990s, making current expenditures susceptible to future cuts. In addition, there is substantial uncertainty regarding the future development of low-income units because of the 1986 tax reforms. Finally, although many states have become increasingly active in the housing field as the federal commitment has declined, states acting on their own cannot meet the housing needs of the nation's poor. Traditional means of support—primarily tax-exempt bonds—have become less attractive under federal tax reform and must now compete more directly with other uses of such funds. Thus, as federal tax incentives are replaced with state-administered low-income housing units, states face new responsibilities in the housing field but in most cases with no additional source of funds.

The Two-Pronged Approach to Housing Assistance

The current approach to housing assistance is an interrelated, but largely uncoordinated, mix of direct and indirect subsidies to households and owners of housing projects. HUD now spends around $10 billion a year on assisted housing. Tax advantages associated with the development and rehabilitation of low-income housing under the 1986 tax reform could result in an additional $2.7 billion of subsidies over the next five years, though the full impact of the law is uncertain. However, another source of assistance typically has been overlooked in the formulation of housing policy. Our estimates suggest that the welfare system—through the explicit and implicit shelter allowances provided under Aid to Families with Dependent Children (AFDC), Supplemental Security Income (SSI) and General Assistance (GA)—spends at least $10 billion a year on housing assistance, or about as much as HUD.

In reality, then, there are two streams of government financing of low-income housing—a housing stream and a welfare stream. Government involvement is shared by two federal agencies, HUD and the U.S. Department of Health and Human Services (HHS), and a multiplicity of state and local jurisdictions. But their approaches are uncoordinated and potentially overlapping. Furthermore, there are stark disparities in the amount of shelter assistance that the systems provide: similar people are not treated similarly. This two-pronged approach to shelter assistance, through a mix of income maintenance and housing programs, raises serious questions regarding the efficiency, equity and overall effectiveness of the existing system.

Efficiency

At a minimum, the involvement of two federal agencies and many states and localities in the provision of shelter assistance raises the possibility of inefficiency. If these agencies served different populations or goals, the two-pronged approach might well be justified. But inefficiencies could arise if the goals were distinct but inconsistent, or if either the goals or the clienteles overlapped. Recent shifts in HUD assistance policies suggest that the latter two characterizations are most appropriate.

Federal involvement in low-income housing began in the depression years with the creation of the Public Housing Program. Up until the mid-1970s, the primary goal of this and other assistance programs was to increase the supply of standard housing through a variety of approaches involving slum clearance, construction and rehabilitation. However, following the Nixon Administration's moratorium on housing programs in 1973, a very different strategy was introduced: providing housing certificates to qualified households renting units from the existing stock.

By the early 1980s, essentially all new construction and rehabilitation programs were terminated, leaving the cash certificate for existing housing as HUD's main assistance approach.

Public assistance programs administered by HHS in combination with the states, such as AFDC, also provide cash grants to eligible households. While the way in which these grants are spent is typically unrestricted, the standard of need on which the grant is based represents each state's estimate of the cost of basic necessities, including shelter. Thus, regardless of the exact amount that recipients spend on housing, the parallel to the current HUD approach seems clear: cash assistance to low-income households to cover shelter costs of housing from the standing stock.

There is also considerable overlap in the recipients of the two types of aid. As shown in Table 15.1, in 1983 about 22 percent of the welfare population also received a housing subsidy. Some 4.6 million households were receiving income assistance alone; 2.1 million were receiving housing subsidies, but not income assistance; and 1.3 million were receiving both types of aid. Viewed from the housing perspective, roughly 38 percent of housing assistance recipients were on welfare. But the representation of HHS clientele among HUD assistance recipients has undoubtedly increased since 1983 because housing programs are increasingly targeted to very low-income households. Thus, a larger share of the estimated 4 million households living in assisted housing in 1986 were probably also welfare recipients.[4]

Equity

Under the major income maintenance programs, geography rather than need plays the major role in determining the amount of shelter assistance that an

TABLE 15.1   U.S. Households by Type of Assistance, 1983 (millions)

Total receiving income assistance	5,864
Total receiving housing assistance	3,392
Type of assistance (unduplicated counts): Income assistance only	4,568
Housing assistance only	2,096
Both income and housing assistance	1,296
Total receiving income and/or housing assistance	7,960

1. Estimates based on the 1983 National American Housing Survey.
2. Total unweighted number of observations = 5,307.

individual or family receives. Depending on whether shelter subsidies are explicit or embedded in a consolidated grant, based on a realistic need standard that is updated regularly and funded fully, adjusted for such variables as family size and high versus low cost areas within the jurisdictions, welfare recipients will either receive shelter payments that afford them decent housing or not. Under AFDC, shelter allowances covered less than 50 percent of the Fair Market Rent (FMR) in 34 states; the comparable figure for SSI is 13 states, and for GA, 17 jurisdictions. On average, as shown in Table 15.2, neither AFDC, SSI, nor GA provide shelter payments that equal the cost of standard quality housing as measured by HUD's Fair Market Rents: AFDC shelter payments represent only 49 percent of the applicable FMR, while SSI and GA allowances hover around 66 percent of the FMR. The table also shows two additional patterns: variation in the generosity of shelter payments between the different programs, but consistency in that the lowest payment levels always occur in the South.

A final pattern (not shown here) that also underscores the inequities inherent in the shelter component of welfare programs emerges from comparing the shelter allowances recipients receive to their *actual* housing expenditures. On average, recipients actually spend between 17 percent and 262 percent more than the applicable shelter payment they receive from the welfare system. Of the three programs, AFDC payments are by far the most inconsistent with actual housing costs: even in the most generous region, the West, actual expenditures are nearly 60 percent *greater* than AFDC's shelter payment. The argument that these higher expenditures for housing represent a discretionary choice by AFDC recipients to spend more on housing is not convincing since these households have high rates of housing problems, such as crowding and physical deficiencies, as will be discussed later.

TABLE 15.2 Comparison of Shelter Payment Adequacy Under AFDC, SSI, and GA (1984–85)

	Shelter payment ($)	Fair market rent ($)	Shelter payment as % of fair market rent
AFDC 4-person family			
Northeast	178	301	59
North Central	138	266	52
South	76	278	27
West	208	326	64
Weighted average:	144	289	50
SSI single-person household			
Northeast	144	208	69
North Central	117	180	65
South	109	180	61
West	157	236	67
Weighted average:	127	198	64
GA single-person household			
Northeast	149	208	77
North Central	114	180	62
South	76	180	34
West	145	236	60
Weighted average:	129	198	68

1. Estimates based on interviews with state and local welfare officials and official HUD Fair Market Rents.

2. AFDC shelter payment calculations assume national distribution of family size for each state.

3. Regional and national AFDC averages were computed by weighing each state's shelter payment and shelter payment : FMR ratio by the state's average monthly caseload.

4. Regional and national SSI averages were computed by weighing each state's shelter payment and shelter payment : FMR ratio by the state's total caseload.

5. SSI shelter payments and shelter payment : FMR ratio calculations are based on a combination of the 33 percent reduction in the Federal payment (the amount SSI is reduced when a recipient lives in another person's household) with the specific adjustment made by each state that provided supplementary SSI payments.

6. Regional and national GA averages were computed by weighing each state's shelter payment and shelter payment : FMR ratio by the state's average monthly recipients.

7. 2-bedroom FMRs are used for AFDC, while 0-bedroom FMRs are used for SSI and GA.

With the exception of a handful of states, states that generously fund shelter subsidies in one welfare program are not more likely to generously fund them all.[5] But some states do emerge as consistently generous. Among these, California and New York are particularly noteworthy as they are also the states with the largest recipient populations. Since these states' fiscal dependency ratios (i.e., the ratio of the poverty population to the non-poverty population) are no lower than the mean for all states, it can be argued that their higher shelter allocations are a reasonable reflection of their generosity. In contrast, fiscal capacity rather than generosity may have more to do with the low shelter allocations of states like Arkansas and Mississippi, which have fiscal dependency ratios that are much higher than average.

In contrast to the shelter component of general welfare programs, HUD programs are designed to insure that recipients obtain standard housing regardless of location and to provide subsidies up to the full amount of the FMR. Unlike the welfare programs, however, households are assisted on a "first come, first served" basis, so only a fraction of the eligible population can be served.[6] Although, as noted, housing subsidies are targeted to very low-income households, there were 2.8 million renters on welfare in 1983 who did not receive housing assistance, but who had incomes just as low as those receiving multiple subsidies. Roughly 1.3 million of these welfare recipients had annual incomes below $5,000.

Effectiveness

A primary measure of effectiveness in shelter assistance programs is the degree to which recipients gain access to decent and affordable units. As a first approximation, it is fair to say that housing assistance programs are effective since the very large majority of recipients receive decent and affordable dwellings. In contrast, as shown in Table 15.3, 46 percent of all "welfare only" households[7] in 1983 spent more than half of their income on housing, 13 percent were overcrowded, and 29 percent lived in physically substandard units.[8] These rates are between two and four times as great as for housing assistance recipients.

Overall, eight out of every 10 households with income assistance, but no housing program subsidies, had one of these housing problems. These differential housing outcomes of housing subsidies versus welfare assistance are generalizable to different household types (i.e., households with children, elderly-headed households, and other non-elderly households).

But these rates are national aggregates which can hide substantial variation. One obvious source of variation is the *generosity* of the shelter payment provided under welfare programs: if welfare recipients in jurisdictions that provide more generous shelter allowances experience better housing outcomes (i.e., lower rates of crowding, housing cost burdens, and physically deficient housing units), then a strong case could be made for simply increasing shelter

TABLE 15.3   Housing Outcomes by Type of Assistance 1983 (percent)

	Total receiving income assist.	Total receiving housing assist.	Income assist. only	Housing assist. only	Income & housing assist.
Affordability					
% paying >30% of income for housing	62.6	39.6	66.8	34.0	48.7
% paying >50% of income for housing	41.6	19.6	45.5	13.7	29.0
Crowding					
% in unit with >1 person per room	12.1	6.2	13.3	5.2	7.7
Quality					
% substandard	24.8	8.0	28.5	5.8	11.7

Source: Estimates based on the 1983 National American Housing Survey. Categories as in Table 15.1.

payments under welfare as a way of improving the housing conditions of welfare participants.

To look more closely at the effects of shelter payment generosity on housing outcomes of welfare recipients, we examined the housing conditions of the "welfare only" population living in 25 of the largest metropolitan areas in the U.S. relative to the generosity of their shelter payments.[9] There is no simple relationship between the housing conditions of welfare recipients (measured by the presence of at least one housing problem) and the overall generosity of the area's welfare system in relation to the cost of standard housing (measured by the ratio of the welfare shelter allowance to the applicable FMR).[10] For example, New York City has the highest overall incidence of housing needs despite its relatively generous payment standard. At the other extreme, households in Denver fare relatively well, despite the fact that payments are relatively low. The same conclusion emerges if one considers specific types of housing problems. Our analyses (not shown here) of the relationship between generosity and each of the three different measures of housing need—crowding, affordability, and quality—produced no instance in which housing need was significantly correlated with the generosity of the local shelter allowance. Other factors, such as the cost and quality of the housing stock, exercise a stronger influence on the housing situation of welfare recipients in any given market. Thus, welfare recipients in metropolitan areas with generous shelter allowances often fare no better than the average welfare recipient nationwide. As a result, many communities are spending relatively large sums of money with little, if any, tangible return on their higher investments.

This pattern is wholly consistent with the findings of other research. Both the income maintenance and housing allowance experiments conducted by the federal government in the 1970s found that unrestricted cash grants to impoverished households had only a minimal effect on their housing conditions.[11] Thus, while increasing welfare grants may well be warranted on other grounds, simply increasing the shelter allowance in the absence of any other housing-related actions will not have a significant impact on the housing conditions of the poor.

Directions for a Restructured Shelter Subsidy

What should a restructured shelter assistance policy look like? While the details are complex and will require additional work, we can identify some general directions for a restructured approach. As already alluded to, a key principle of shelter policy reform is that unearmarked cash grants alone, unless they are very generous, are unlikely to result in improved housing conditions for the poor. If positive housing outcomes are the goals of housing policy, then earmarked assistance makes more sense.

Reducing Inequities

A restructured approach must be more equitable than the one it replaces. Neither the welfare system nor the housing system ranks high on equity grounds. Under welfare, there is an enormous variation in shelter payments that is unrelated to need. Some welfare programs are more generous than others but even within programs, geography rather than need is a key determinant of payment adequacy. Under housing programs, almost the same number of equally needy households do not receive assistance as the number that do.

Even in the absence of more radical restructuring, then, the inequities in the current system need to be addressed. One option would be to reduce or eliminate the regional disparities in welfare payments. Benefit standards in the less generous areas would be raised to a level that insures a minimal standard of living for program recipients regardless of location. This general theme has been echoed in recent proposals addressing disparities in AFDC payment levels. Focusing on the housing component of welfare assistance only strengthens the call for reform.

While the appropriate level of this new, standardized assistance is subject to debate, shelter allowances under the major welfare programs would have to be raised by an average of between 50 and 100 percent to meet the Fair Market Rent standards employed by HUD. Our data suggest that this increase would cost about $10 billion a year.

In particular, 78 percent of the welfare population, or about 4.6 million households, did not participate in housing programs. A housing voucher currently costs about $3800 per year, which means that the gross cost of serving this group would be roughly $17.4 billion a year. However, since the welfare system already spends about $10 billion a year on shelter allowances, the net cost would be lower. If 78 percent of these indirect subsidies are going to the "welfare only" population, the costs of raising their shelter allowances to the levels that HUD uses would drop to about $9.6 billion per year (i.e., $17.4 billion for the new vouchers less $7.8 billion of existing assistance).

Although these estimates are extremely crude, they imply that if HUD continued to serve a significant number of recipients who were not on welfare, this modification would require an increase in total expenditures on housing assistance (including indirect subsidies available through welfare) of roughly 50 percent.

But reducing the regional disparities in payment standards will not be enough to insure equity under the current system. Some income-eligible families would still receive both welfare shelter grants and HUD subsidies. Others, equally needy, would still receive only welfare. Resolving these problems will undoubtedly require a more efficient system for providing housing subsidies to the poor.

Improving Efficiency

A key requirement for increasing efficiency is the closer coordination between housing and welfare policy, funding, and personnel. Of course, *real* coordination between two programs with different constituencies and vested interests is very difficult. But it is hard to see how the current inadequacies can be corrected if the two systems are addressed separately.

While serious efforts at coordination would have to involve all aspects of the two systems, implementation could take many forms. Funding, for example, could be restructured by merging the two separate streams of housing assistance dollars and channeling them in a manner that achieves minimally decent housing for eligible households.

The fragmented administration of these housing subsidies also needs to be rationalized. In its simplest form, this means that either the housing system or the welfare system must be vested with the primary administrative responsibility for these housing dollars. It is difficult to judge whether it is better to locate the administration of these funds in the welfare or in the housing system. At first glance, however, HUD and its network of local Public Housing Authorities (PHAs) seem to be the more attractive choice since this would capitalize on an existing and well-tested infrastructure. In contrast, welfare caseworkers are notoriously overburdened and often have little housing expertise.

A number of communities have taken some initial steps to coordinate housing and welfare goals, funding, and administration. For example, welfare departments in a few communities have attempted to address the housing needs of their clientele by tying AFDC shelter allowances to local code enforcement efforts and the rehabilitation of substandard housing. AFDC Emergency Assistance has also been used in this way in some jurisdictions.[12] These types of initiatives could have been expanded considerably under Section 191 of H.R. 4, the House version of the 1987 Housing Act, which contains a restatement of the so-called McKinney Demonstration. (This amendment first appeared in the Housing and Urban-Rural Recovery Act of 1983, section 225.) One purpose of this demonstration was to offer the incentive of federal matching dollars to states willing to experiment with ways of rehabilitating housing for AFDC families while assuring that these units would remain affordable to these families. Relatively little is known about the widespread replicability or administrative costs of such approaches. Funding the McKinney Demonstration, coupled with evaluation studies of the various state initiatives, could have closed these information gaps. Unfortunately, the final version of the 1987 Housing Act deleted the McKinney demonstration provision.

Increasing Flexibility

A third important element of a redesigned shelter subsidy system is flexibility. HUD's almost exclusive reliance on demand subsidies in the form of vouchers may be insufficient to improve the housing conditions of the most needy. Households living in deficient housing may find it difficult to convince their landlords to make the necessary repairs, may find the emotional or financial price of moving too high, or may find it difficult to locate an acceptable unit in areas with a housing shortage. As a result, the program may have the perverse effect of excluding the very households and markets it is trying to serve.

Evidence from the federal housing allowance experiment largely supports this hypothesis. The extent of upgrading induced by the experiment was relatively modest and, for the most part, restricted to minor repairs. As a result, households in units that failed quality standards typically were forced to move in order to qualify for the allowance. Thus, while housing allowances clearly worked for the majority of households, participation rates tended to be lower among those who initially lived in substandard housing, an outcome that one observer has likened to a health program that is restricted to the healthy.[13]

Theoretically, raising the purchasing power of low-income households to a level that would provide a reasonable rate of return should eventually produce an adequate supply of housing even in areas where the initial stock is relatively poor. But in the short term, the supply of housing is relatively slow to change. Thus, despite their higher cost, there may be a need for some highly targeted supply-side subsidies to deal with the worst segments of the housing stock. Other assistance approaches that could be linked to the voucher strategy, such as housing counseling or moving subsidies, might also be needed in some locations.

A strategy must also be devised to assist households who, for a variety of personal and unpredictable reasons, simply cannot find a unit that meets program standards. Obviously, such households cannot be denied assistance. One option would be to develop a two-tiered payment system that would distinguish between households living in standard and substandard units, but provide some assistance to all income-eligible. For example, a minimal shelter allowance could be available to all recipients, but only households in units that met program standards would receive the full subsidy amount. If the lower payment standard were about the same as the current national average (about 60 percent of the FMR), the program's costs would probably drop to about $7 billion per year.[14]

Supporting the Costs

While the key changes that must be made to develop a more equitable and effective shelter subsidy system are fairly clear, funding mechanics to support the costs of such reforms are much less obvious. As noted, we estimate that raising the shelter allowance to the local FMR would increase expenditures by between $7 billion and $10 billion a year. Presumably, such a change would not occur unless it were part of a broader effort to standardize payment levels. As a result, total expenditures would be even higher.

Some economies undoubtedly could be achieved by more effectively utilizing general welfare monies that currently are available to low-income housing. Incentives, such as the federal match written into the McKinney Demonstration, could be devised to encourage the use of AFDC shelter allowances and Emergency Assistance dollars to support the rehabilitation of substandard housing instead of the operation of welfare hotels. This strategy would create a permanent resource of the community at little or no additional cost. Likewise, raising existing shelter allowances to levels somewhat below the applicable FMRs would reduce the overall costs of reform and still address the inequities of the current system.[15] Such a step must be taken cautiously, however. While HUD's existing quality and payment standards may be too high for an entitlement program, a significant reduction would ultimately jeopardize housing goals. Finally, HUD assistance could be redirected to serve a higher proportion of the welfare population. In 1983, only about 38 percent of the households in assisted housing also received income assistance, a pattern which may in part reflect the more liberal eligibility requirements that existed prior to the Reagan years.[16] Yet, even if participation in HUD programs were restricted to households on welfare, our estimates suggest that only about 58 percent of that population could be served.[17] Furthermore, the target would take years to achieve since it would have to be accomplished through normal turnover. Because housing needs are not synonymous with the receipt of income assistance, such an approach is neither practical nor politically feasible.

Reinstating a Commitment to Low-Income Housing

The foregoing discussion is based on the assumption that housing goals remain a part of the nation's public policy agenda. Judging by the events of the last several years, it is not at all clear that this assumption is correct. There has not been a federal housing act for six years, virtually all HUD construction subsidy programs have been terminated, funding for existing demand-side programs is meager, and the 1986 tax reform legislation makes the future of private sector involvement in the provision of low-income housing uncertain at best.

We believe there is a case to be made for housing policy, and for earmarked housing assistance in particular. This case rests on several factors: the inequities and inefficiencies of the current two-pronged system; the greater effectiveness of housing programs at achieving housing goals; the realization that transfer payments for housing are substantially different than income transfers; and, most fundamentally, the motivations that underlie society's support for programs that assist the poor. We believe this case is compelling.

*   *   *   *

The research reported in this paper was funded by a grant from the Ford Foundation.

Notes

1. This paper draws heavily on a research report by the authors entitled *Subsidizing Shelter: The Relationship between Welfare and Housing Assistance*, vols. 1 and 2 (Washington: Urban Institute Press, 1988). The major findings are presented in volume 1. State-by-state statistics on AFDC, and GA payment standards are presented in volume 2.

2. P. Starr, "Health Care for the Poor: The Past Twenty Years," in S. Danziger and D. Weinberg, eds., *Fighting Poverty: What Works and What Doesn't* (Cambridge: Harvard University Press, 1986).

3. 1983 was the latest year for which the requisite national data were available for the various analyses reported in this paper.

4. It should be noted that multiple subsidies are targeted to the most needy segment of the population: average incomes of households receiving only a housing subsidy or income assistance alone were somewhat more than $9,000, compared to roughly $5,000 for those receiving both housing and income assistance.

5. As an aside, since there is no tendency for the more generously funded programs to be those for which federal matching dollars are available, there is also no

basis for concern that the presence of a federal match has a non-neutral effect on state funding decisions.

6. In general, eligibility for public housing and Section 8 rent assistance is determined by household income. Households that meet income eligibility criteria are placed on a public housing or Section 8 waiting list. Other conditions of the eligible households are ascertained before priorities are determined. Local housing authorities determine "preferences" based on applicants' current housing conditions. These preferences include the following: without housing; about to be without housing; and in substandard housing. Local housing authorities may take other conditions into consideration before assigning priority, so long as the conditions are consistent with the objectives of Title IV of the Civil Rights Act of 1964.

7. "Welfare only" households are those who only receive income assistance but no housing assistance.

8. Units have been classified as "substandard" or deficient if they fail to meet housing quality standards similar to those used by HUD to define adequate housing. See Newman and Schnare, *Subsidizing Shelter,* Appendix E.

9. We relied on the 1982 and 1983 SMSA data from the American Housing Survey, which were the latest files available at the time of our analysis. While these SMSAs are not purported to represent the nation's SMSAs, they provide sufficient variation in the key variable of interest—generosity of payment standard—for a preliminary search for the answer to our question: Do generous jurisdictions produce the best housing outcomes for welfare recipients?

10. Since these metropolitan data do not identify the specific source of assistance payments, the welfare population had to be treated as a homogeneous group. The "shelter allowances" in the analysis are thus weighted averages of the specific payment standards under each of the three welfare programs, where the weights reflect the relative importance of the different programs within each site. In addition, the ratio of the shelter allowance to the FMR is a weighted average of the separate ratios for each of the three welfare programs. For further technical details, see Newman and Schnare, *Subsidizing Shelter.*

11. K. Bradbury and A. Downs, eds., *Do Housing Allowances Work?* (Washington: Brookings Institution, 1986).

12. E. Rosenbaum, "Linking Housing and Human Services Systems: New Methods in the Provision of Permanent Housing for Homeless Persons," NAHRO Issue Paper (Washington: NAHRO, 1986).

13. F. deLeeuw, "Comments by Frank deLeeuw on the Aaron Paper," in K. Bradbury and A. Downs, eds., *Do Housing Allowances Work?, 99-106.*

14. This estimate assumes that participation rates would be similar to those observed in the housing allowance experiment, which were 70 percent for renters and 76 percent for owners. Since 61 percent of the "welfare only" population are renters, this implies an average participation rate of 72 percent, which would reduce the estimated costs of a voucher-like program to about $6.9 billion (72 percent of the total cost with 100 percent participation). This estimate is similar to the $7.4 billion figure derived by H. Katsura and R. Struyk, "Shelter Supplements for Welfare Recipients," Urban Institute Working Paper #3112-12 (Washington: The Urban Institute, 1984), using a different methodology and a different data set.

15. Since, in 1986, the FMR was lowered to the 45th percentile from the 50th (i.e., the median rent), over time our estimate of the cost of raising the shelter grant to the FMR would overstate the true cost.

16. Up until that time, households with incomes less than 80 percent of the area median (or about 200 percent of the poverty line) were eligible for HUD assistance. In

1981, this cutoff was dropped to 50 percent, a standard that is more in line with traditional income maintenance programs.

17. Using the 1983 estimates, this assumes that the assistance provided to the "housing only" population of 2.1 million households would be transferred to a subset of the 4.6 million "welfare only" population, reducing the number of welfare households without housing assistance to 3.4 million. Under this assumption, program costs would drop to between $3 billion and $4 billion per year.

Chapter 16
Housing and the Homeless

Langley C. Keyes

In the course of the 1980s, the plight of the homeless has been transformed from an issue articulated by a small group of human service advocates in scattered central cities to an issue of sufficient national concern to generate one of the few pieces of social welfare legislation to gain support from the Reagan Administration. That homelessness is an issue whose time has come is symbolized by the Stewart B. McKinney Homeless Assistance Act signed into law by the President on July 22, 1987. Whatever one's view of the Act's substantive content and financial commitment, the fact that it exists as national legislation is testament to the power of the issue and the political competence of its advocates.

With the President's signature, the Reagan Administration demonstrated either conversion to the Act's logic or acknowledgment of the political costs of vetoing legislation carrying a ringing mandate from both House and Senate. Whatever the ultimate reason, by its support the Administration dramatically altered its public view of homelessness. To accept the McKinney Act is to affirm that homelessness is more than an issue of state and local concern and that it poses a moral imperative warranting federal leadership. Arguments about the number of homeless, their characteristics and the seriousness of the problem—issues which had pitted Administration officials against a wide spectrum of advocates for a federal presence—were at least publicly silenced by the passage of the legislation.

The Act's initial price tag was not great by federal standards: roughly a billion dollars over a two year period. It has been described by the National Coalition of the Homeless, one of the architects of its political success, as a "modest start . . . (which) barely begins to address the enormity of the problem."[1] However, the Act's stance towards homelessness and its specific substantive and procedural remedies potentially set a precedent for the future role of the federal government in the issue. It is that precedent, as it relates to housing, with which this paper is concerned.

A central question is whether the McKinney Act is the opening gun in a reassertion of federal engagement in the social agenda or simply a one-shot effort to appease the broad spectrum of interests coalesced around the homeless issue. The answer will be worked out in the political arena in the coming months as the Bush Administration settles on a response. However, an understanding of how the Act has framed the housing and shelter elements of homelessness and of the role posited for the federal government in dealing with those elements may provide an insight into the political dynamics and policy considerations that lie ahead as the entire federal housing agenda comes under intensive review.

Framing the Homeless Issue from a Housing Perspective

The following section steps back from the specifics of the McKinney Act to establish a conceptual framework for looking at the housing issues of the homeless. That framework provides the structure in which to locate the shelter elements of the Act itself.

Such a framework has three elements: (1) the characteristics of the homeless population, (2) the dynamics of the housing market relevant to homelessness, and (3) the stages of homelessness.

The Characteristics of the Homeless Population

Whatever distinctions they may have in social, economic, and family characteristics, age and past history, homeless people share one thing in common: they are unable to maintain or find access to public or private housing stock and as a consequence find themselves on the street. In some housing markets, such people will stay on the street, in an abandoned building or bus station. In areas that have developed an organized response to homelessness, they will eventually end up in a homeless shelter or hotel.

Neither shelters nor hotels represent a long-term solution to the plight of people who have fallen out of the housing market. A fundamental goal, then, is to get these families and individuals out of their temporary accommodations and into permanent housing, a necessary if often not sufficient condition to "solving" the plight of homelessness.

In meeting the challenge of locating permanent housing for such households, a central question from the housing perspective is, what, if anything, in addition to a roof over their head, do the households need once they have moved out of the shelter? What kinds of support services—psychological, job training, educational, for example—will they require to ensure that they can "make it" in the housing market on a permanent basis?

The homeless, both individuals and families, can be categorized in terms of the response to that question: the extent to which they need *something* in addition to housing if they are not to find themselves back on the street.

The following categories, in reality more like a continuum, are presented in terms of the expanding degree to which need for service is linked to need for housing.

The economic homeless are those households who are out in the street simply because they cannot find an affordable place to live. They are victims of a tightening housing market. While their lives may be in turmoil, that turmoil is a function of being without a home. It may be the case that if they don't find a place to live and keep getting shuttled from shelter to shelter, they or members of their family will be in need of help to deal with increasing anxiety, depression, school problems and the like. But for right now, a decent home and a suitable living environment which they can afford will put them back on track. This category, generally families with children, has been dubbed the "new homeless" by the media to contrast it with the other two categories which represent more traditional definitions of homelessness.

The situational homeless are households who enter the ranks of the homeless for more than economic reasons. They are people whose lives are conflicted and who find themselves on the street because they are fleeing from some dangerous or traumatic situation—a battering husband, abusing parents—or personal disorganization that renders them incapable of managing the demands of finding and maintaining housing. These families, often single women with children, require more than financial resources to pay for a housing unit. They need help in their struggle to put their lives together. The head of household is often a person who has moved frequently, been involved in more than one disastrous domestic situation and whose children are at risk. Short on skills, long on hard times and disordered lives, such individuals require a supportive environment in which to gather their resources and sort out their existence to become sufficiently independent, to survive in the housing market on their own. Many argue that failure to provide such help in a sustained manner will result in the family being back on the street, the victim once again of domestic violence, disorganization, and eviction.

The distinction between the situational and the economic homeless is not always clear cut and is often the basis for debate.[2] From the perspective of those advocates who see the plight of the homeless as essentially a housing problem, focusing on the social disorganization of the situational homeless blames the victim and labels the families the problem while obscuring the central fact that these are households under conditions of enormous stress. Get them a housing unit, the argument runs, and most if not all of their problems will disappear.

Would that it were that simple, say those less convinced that housing per se can transform deeply troubled lives and who reason as follows: these situationally homeless families have long histories of abuse, battering, depression and disfunctioning. They are, in social work terminology, "multi-problem" families. It is not enough simply to put them back into the housing market and forget about them. They need ongoing help, the kind and duration of which is open for discussion.

The debate about the solution to the problems of the situational homeless is a reformulation of a long standing issue between housers and social service workers about the impact of good housing on peoples' lives and the problem of "problem people." Where one draws the line between the economic and situational homeless depends, then, on where one stands in that debate.

The chronic homeless are represented for the most part by individuals rather than families who because of substance abuse or mental illness are unable to find a stable niche in the housing market. The group includes most of the bag ladies and the vagrants, the disoriented individuals historically described as "street people."

The deinstitutionalized (or if they are young enough, never institutionalized) mentally ill are the homeless for whom there is universal recognition that housing is not enough. Moving people out of mental hospitals into housing without the necessary services and community-based mental health facilities solved one problem but created another. Housing is necessary; but so is some level of service. And it is the continuity of that service need that distinguishes the chronic homeless from the situational homeless. The chronic mentally ill may over time require less intense levels of service; but they will almost always need help of some kind, unlike the situational homeless who are presumed to move beyond the need for support other than financial or housing subsidy.[3]

There is much debate about the distribution of the homeless population among the three categories described above, and about which of the categories are expanding. Several years ago the "news" was that "many of the homeless people wandering the streets in American cities and crowding into emergency shelters are mentally ill."[4] Shortly thereafter, Ellen Bassuk's study of households living in shelters in Massachusetts highlighted the homeless children, battered wives and "the breakdown of the family"[5] that contribute to what I have called the situational homeless. More recently the "new homeless" have been emphasized as intact families who find themselves on the street for the first time, priced out of even the worst housing.[6]

One major conclusion can be drawn without arguing the merits of the many profiles of local homeless populations.[7] The distribution of a given homeless population among the three categories differs from area to area. The United States Conference of Mayors' December 1986 survey of homelessness in 25 cities makes the point that the profile "varies significantly" in the surveyed cities. While the average distribution found by the survey is 72 percent singles and 28 percent families, individual cities range in profile from 85 percent single males in Charleston to 76 percent families in New York City.

While 29 percent is the average figure for homeless considered mentally ill, the percentage at the local level goes from 60 percent in Louisville to 2 percent in Yonkers.[8]

One can argue endlessly about the statistical veracity of the figures, the definition of mental illness employed at the local level, overlapping categories, and so on. But the fundamental point is that the distribution of the homeless among the three categories of homelessness must be determined at the level of the local housing market area. There are no simple formulas. Given the definitional debates that permeate any discussion of the three categories discussed here, there will be dispute even within a given area as to the character of the homeless population.

Looking ahead, the size of the future homeless population and the distribution among the economic, situational, and chronic categories will be a function of:

(1) The extent of market pressure on the low-income housing stock. The greater the demand for low cost housing, the greater the likelihood there will be more economic homeless and that they will comprise a larger percentage of the total.

(2) The relative success of rehousing programs for the chronic homeless, particularly the extent to which permanent housing is found in the community (or back in the hospital) for deinstitutionalized or the never-institutionalized chronically mentally ill, an issue discussed in Chapter 17 of this volume by Newman and Struyk.

While the majority of the homeless population at present continues to be single people in the chronic or situational categories, there is general agreement among careful observers that the characteristics of the homeless population have changed in recent years,[9] and that family homelessness, generally women with children, has grown in absolute and relative numbers. While various studies put the current family homelessness percentage at somewhere around a quarter of the total,[10] the critical issues are the characteristics of its future trajectory: the increase in the number of homeless families and their distribution between the situational and economic homeless.

In the last years of the Reagan Administration a significant difference existed between the perception of the Mayors' study, referred to earlier, and the Department of Housing and Urban Development (HUD) on this issue.[11] HUD's view was that "family homelessness is most often caused by *personal* crises." [12] It is the problem-filled nature of the lives of the families involved that has precipitated their homelessness. Conversely, the central thrust of the Mayors' report is that a diminishing number of low-income rental units and insufficient income are the driving forces behind much family homelessness. The Mayors did not minimize the importance of mental illness, abuse, and domestic violence, but rather gave less weight to personal crises as the root cause of the problem.

In determining policies and programs it is critical which of these viewpoints best describes the characteristics of a locality's homeless family population. If HUD is right, then homeless families are on the street for much more than economic causes. They are suffering from a complex of personal problems—drugs, alcohol, violence, or trouble with the law—that has precipitated their expulsion from housing. Not all people who pay exorbitant amounts of their income for rent end up with no place to live; and the difference between those who do and those who do not must be some cluster of personal issues that defines these households as the "situational homeless." Personal transformation must occur if people are not to be homeless again.

The Mayors' argument is that the precipitating event to homelessness has more to do with the inexorable workings of the economic system plus bad luck, unexpected expenses, a lost job, or condo conversion. Economic help should alleviate much of this homelessness.

This debate about the characteristics of homeless families is being carried on in states and localities where homeless policies and programs are put in place. As we analyze the characteristics of households being served and what is effective in helping them, we will have a better understanding of where to draw the line between the situational and the economic homeless.

Homelessness and the Dynamics of the Housing Market

The unifying characteristic of households labeled "homeless" is their failure to find permanent affordable shelter in the market—with or without public subsidy. The private housing market has always been problematic for low-income people. Effective market demand, in other words the ability of a household to pay for shelter, has historically intersected the housing supply curve at a point below the threshold of a socially acceptable standard of housing—which is to say that a low-income household can only afford substandard housing. The gap between what the private housing market is able to produce for effective market demand and the level of housing need based on acceptable physical standards and affordable cost constitutes the arena for public intervention. Since the coming of the New Deal when the federal government first became involved in the issue of housing, the great public debates about housing policy for the poor have centered on the most efficient way to bridge the gap between housing need and effective market demand: how to provide shelter for people who cannot afford to pay for decent housing.

From the perspective of a housing market analyst taking a long view of housing policy, a critical question to ask is: how is the homeless phenomenon qualitatively and quantitatively different from the perennial plight of low-income people in the housing market? Is this homeless issue simply the most recent formulation of a long-standing problem: how can we provide adequate housing for low-income people who cannot afford to pay what the private market demands?

One might argue that little is new about the issues of the homeless and the housing market. The chronic homeless have always had trouble finding shelter. The situational homeless, while less identifiable, have been the long-term concern of social workers and helping professionals, particularly when those households are defined as multi-problem families. The economic homeless have not been with us in large numbers since the years immediately following World War II, and before that during the Great Depression when they were (in Lawrence Friedman's felicitous term) the "submerged middle class" [13] who filled up the nation's public housing developments. If one makes the case that the households "on the street" are only the tip of the homeless iceberg, then the issue becomes an even more familiar theme of how to provide standard housing for people who cannot compete in the private market. "Homelessness" as a proxy for all low-income households with shelter problems is simply the current reformulation of the central issue of housing policy in the United States.

Yet while one can make a case for the applicability of the Preacher's wisdom to the homeless and the housing market, that "there is no remembrance of former things," [14] significant differences do exist between the housing issues facing today's homeless and the traditional challenge of providing housing for low and moderate income people. Several of these differences are a consequence of the particular characteristics of today's housing markets. Others are related to changes in public policy which impinge on the housing needs of the poor.

The housing market factors that bear on homelessness as well as the changes in public policy fueling the problem have been well documented in many articles and conferences and in the hearings leading up to the McKinney Act. [15] There is no need to restate the issues in detail here; however, the conclusions should be summarized. All agree that current homeless problems are exacerbated by: (1) structural changes in local housing markets, (2) the feminization of poverty, (3) the failure to deal with the housing issues of deinstitutionalization, and (4) the fraying of the federal social safety net, particularly support for subsidized housing.

For low-income households, the central reality of the nation's housing market is the decline of affordable units. Two recent observers articulate this fact in their findings. Between 1975 and 1983, the number of rental households earning under $10,000 annually increased by three million. At the same time the number of rental units affordable to those households declined by two million. Two-thirds of the 23 million low-income households currently pay excessive rents or live in physically inadequate structures. [16] Close to 75 percent of all renter households with incomes less than $10,000 continue to live in privately owned, non-subsidized housing. Those households seek to occupy a vanishing resource. Private housing at rents these families can afford continues to be either lost to abandonment or upgraded to serve higher income households. [17]

Specific aspects of loss and upgrading are: the decline of single room occupancy units (SRO) through demolition and upgrading, condominium conversion, and the gentrification of the central city. Whether filtering is up or down, the essential dynamic is laid out in the image of a market inexorably tightening on a group of people in American society who do not have the resources with which to combat that pressure.

The Stages of Homelessness

From a housing policy perspective there are three stages at which efforts can be undertaken to minimize homelessness. Stage I comprises households "at risk" of becoming homeless. Prevention strategies are evolved to keep them from falling out of the market. Stage II is made up of people who have taken the fall and are out on the street. Emergency response strategies in Stage II focus on creating shelter space and service for these households. Stage III covers people who have moved beyond the shelter and have been rehoused. Stabilization policies aim to get people into permanent housing and to prevent, in Peter Marcuse's words, "chain displacement," [18] by working to make sure the household remains in the unit.

A central theme of this stage formulation of homelessness is that the scale and character of the Stage II population is very much a function of what happens in the other two stages: before people become homeless and after they are rehoused.

The following analysis explores: 1. the housing market and institutional dynamics in each stage; 2. the potential policy interventions within each; and 3. the interrelationships of the interventions across the three stages. [19]

Stage I: "At risk" households and prevention. Working to prevent households from falling out of the market in the first instance seems to follow logically from any analysis of the homeless dynamic. With rare exception, no one is better off being in the street (although they may be better off for leaving their previous housing situation). The trauma of homelessness has been well documented. [20] Being out of the housing market means disruption and uncertainty. For households with children, the crowded space of the shelter or hotel is a poor and expensive alternative to permanent housing. To the extent that housing stability can be achieved without first going through the ordeal of homelessness and the ritual of time in the shelter, we must develop means of keeping "at risk" households from falling out of the market.

It is reasonably self-evident that today's "at risk" households are tomorrow's homeless, as are rehoused households that again fall out of the market. Yet to date national attention has focused on Stage II, the period during which people are out in the street or in a shelter. From a media perspective, there is more drama in a picture of a family living in a car or a welfare hotel than there is in a portrait of a household about to be evicted because it cannot afford the rent.[21]

"At risk" households are on the edge for economic and personal reasons. Staying in the housing stock requires of them a series of defensive strategies designed to: (1) pay rent that consumes too much income; (2) deal in conflictual situations with a landlord or family member; (3) put up with crowded or substandard space.

When the rent cannot be paid because it is too high or the unit is condemned or converted, when the tension with the landlord becomes too great or when the pressure of crowded space becomes overbearing, the household finds itself out of the unit. With no readily available housing alternative, the household is on the street or in a shelter.

Prevention strategies are designed to patch up existing situations and keep people in place. They divide into two major categories: financial and service. Financial strategies are of two kinds: those related to marginally increasing the tenant's rent-paying capacity and those providing deep subsidy which would transform the economics of the household's situation. Federal programmatic examples of the marginal strategy are: Emergency Assistance and the federal Emergency Fuel Assistance program. Examples of deep subsidy are Department of Housing and Urban Development Section 8 Certificates and Vouchers.

Service strategies focus on the fact that in addition to the financial burden of the "at risk" household, there are interpersonal issues and conflicts that need to be resolved if households are not to be pushed into Stage II. Those conflicts may be between tenant and landlord or among members of a doubled-up household. Service strategies are represented by legal services for tenants, mediation services to establish communication between tenant and landlord, and access to social services such as daycare or job training.

Prevention strategies which combine marginal increases in the rent-paying capacity of tenants with services geared to mitigate conflict between tenant and landlord and to take pressure off members of a household have the greatest chance of success in housing markets that are not overheated. When vacancies are low or nonexistent, rents are rising rapidly, and condominium conversion is rampant, the most carefully crafted prevention strategies will be up against tough odds, the seeming inexorable workings of the local market. In such settings deep subsidies, like those represented by Section 8 Certificates and Vouchers, appear to be the central means of enabling low-income households to stay in place in the housing stock.

To the degree that vouchers and certificates become the prime means of keeping people in housing, a conflict arises between the use of a scarce and highly valued resource for prevention and its use in Stage II to provide the means of getting a household out of a shelter and into Stage III permanent housing.

The criteria for deciding the distribution of deep subsidies between Stage I and Stage II households are not easily formulated. One can talk about "cost effectiveness" and "greatest leverage" but difficult choices remain. Until there is a universal shelter entitlement program, which is unlikely in the short run, the number of people eligible for significant rent subsidy will outrun the supply of such subsidies. Therefore, a rationing process is required to ensure that the "most needy" in both Stages I and II are served and that deep subsidy is employed as a resource of "last resort"—when all efforts at self-help have been tried. No matter how ingenious the criteria and rigorous the hurdles placed in front of households vying for subsidies, the difficult problem of deciding who is "most worthy, most deserving" of the subsidy will remain. The challenge of allocating scarce resources to a select few from a diverse and needy population is a perennial if wearing one for those who deal with housing subsidies. At minimum, local housing and welfare providers must recognize the connection between Stage I and Stage II efforts; adopt similar criteria for selection; and attempt to educate housing and welfare workers to exhaust all possible alternative strategies of meeting rent payments before going for the deep subsidy.

Stage II: Homeless households and emergency response. Shelter and services are combined in this stage to get people off the street and prepare them for re-entry into the housing system. From the housing perspective, Stage II is a hiatus between a household's efforts to cope in the local housing market. Stage II policy and programmatic issues concern the availability, scale, and duration of temporary accommodation: whether or not there is enough shelter space for homeless households; the character and physical lay-out of that space and its relationship to services and rehousing efforts; and the connection between the shelter, transitional, and permanent housing.

In some areas of the nation, the critical issue in Stage II is the gap between the demand for emergency shelter and the number of available beds. For example, it is reported that Los Angeles has "250 beds for homeless families; the city's social-service groups say they could fill 3000." [22] The December, 1986 survey by the United States Conference for Mayors reported that demand for "emergency shelter increased during 1986 . . . [and] an average of 24 percent of the demand for emergency shelter in the survey cities goes unmet." [23]

In other cities the critical Stage II issue is not solely the number of shelter beds, but the character of that shelter. New York City, for example, distinguishes between entry shelters which "function on an emergency basis to provide immediate shelter" and transitional shelters which "function to provide family accommodations for extended periods of time, . . . until the family can make the move to permanent housing." [24]

Transitional shelter as defined in other cities (and as the term is used in the McKinney Act) applies to housing with supportive services in which families and individuals stay for a limited period of time, during which they get help in preparing to enter the permanent housing market. The question of what constitutes transitional shelter, who is in it for how long, and the nature of its service component, represents a complex subset of issues located between the Stage II and III policy domains.

Stage III: The rehoused households and stabilization. From a housing perspective there are three critical policy issues generated by Stage III: the process by which the homeless regain access to the housing stock (i.e., who helps them and how); the financial assistance available for housing; and the nature and extent of ongoing services to the household. The appropriateness of the rehousing scheme, both in terms of its economics and accompanying service support system, is the key to ensuring that such families don't find themselves back on the street again.

In an ideal system, homeless people would spend limited time in the shelter and quickly be routed to the permanent housing appropriate to their needs. For the economic homeless this means simply access to an affordable unit. For the situational homeless the premise is that some level of services on a temporary basis accompanies the housing. For the chronic homeless, the service element is a built-in aspect of the permanent setting.

To the degree that the economics of rehousing requires subsidies, a key issue in Stage III becomes the depth of the subsidy and the mode of its payment. To the extent that the chronic and situational homeless require services, the provision and funding of services becomes an additional concern.

Stage III remedies are essentially a mirror image of the policy interventions in Stage I. Increasing a household's capacity to pay the rent, whether through "marginal fiddling" or deep subsidy, and connecting that household with the appropriate services is not significantly different whether one is trying to keep the household in place or put it back into the stock. As pointed out earlier, criteria must be developed in each instance to ration the resource and keep the threshold guidelines strict enough to preclude an excessive number of eligible households.

An integrated strategy that dealt with housing issues in all three stages would ensure that in a given housing market area (the definition of which evolves from agreement among housing and social service groups as to the appropriate geographic area) there would be a close working relationship among the various public and private organizations concerned with the housing and service aspects of all three stages. The welfare department, the local public housing authority, the department of social services and community action agencies, as well as the appropriate nonprofit organizations, would be challenged to work out a coordinated set of activities.

Complexities abound in the real world in meeting this model's conceptual aspirations. We will look at these institutional realities when we analyze how the McKinney Act has formulated its agenda and what remains to be done to define the federal role in a comprehensive approach to the shelter dimension of homelessness.

The McKinney Act and Housing the Homeless

Before stepping back to view the housing issues in the McKinney Act through the analytical framework developed in the first section of this paper, one must emphasize that the Act's housing and shelter elements are only a part of a complex piece of social legislation that deals with multiple issues. The Act represents a compendium of programs covering health and mental health care, education, job training, community action, and food assistance.

In addition to funding programs, the Act focuses on coordinating federal efforts to deal with homelessness. Title II sets out an interagency council that has much of the aura of the convener concept developed under the federal Model Cities program of the mid-sixties, by which HUD was authorized to pull together other federal agencies whose funding was to be used in the Model City's area. Working one's way through the new legislation, it is easy to lose the housing market forest and its structural complexity amidst the social service trees that populate the Act.

The McKinney Act articulates a clear view of the nation's homeless problems and Washington's role in dealing with them. In setting out the Act's findings and purpose, Title I expresses that responsibility in language filled with urgency and moral imperative:

The nation faces an immediate and unprecedented crisis due to the lack of shelter for a growing number of individuals and families . . . the problem of homelessness has become more severe and, in the absence of more effective efforts, is expected to become dramatically worse . . . the causes of homelessness are many and complex . . . there is no single simple solution to the problem of homelessness because of the different subpopulations of the homeless . . . States, units of local government, and private voluntary organizations have been unable to meet the basic human needs of all the homeless and, in the absence of greater federal assistance, will be unable to . . . [and] the federal government has a clear responsibility and an existing capacity to fulfill a more effective and responsible role to meet the basic human needs and to engender respect for the human dignity of the homeless.[25]

The Act emphasizes coordination of federal resources "to meet the critically urgent needs of the homeless of the nation . . . [and to] provide funds . . . to assist the homeless."[26] The legislation thus offers more than better management of existing efforts. It recognizes the need to put additional federal resources into the pot.

For all their explicitness, however, there are two ways to read the findings from a housing perspective. One might be designated the "narrow construction" view. It would interpret the findings and purpose of the Act as directed at Stage II of the homeless continuum. From this perspective the central theme that "the nation faces an immediate and unprecedented crisis due to the lack of *shelter* for a growing number of individuals and families"[27] means literally that: the need for an emergency response to get the homeless off the street and to put a roof over their heads.

A "broad construction" view would interpret "shelter" as meaning a permanent solution to the problem of homelessness: in short, housing. The challenge, then, is not just to protect people from the elements but also to get them into a place of their own. Taken one step further, this view includes concern for the "at risk" homeless, for keeping people from falling out of the housing market in the first instance. All three stages of the homeless model become relevant from this perspective.

The McKinney Act itself clearly focuses on the narrow construction, emphasizing as it does the emergency response stage of the homeless continuum. But the Act frames the homeless issue in a way which easily leads to the broad construction interpretation. Once national legislation has acknowledged the urgency of the problem and the federal role in dealing with it, the logic of three homeless stages takes on a life of its own. Political and financial realities, of course, mitigate the programmatic conclusions derived from that logic.

While one can question the relationship between the Act's two-year funding level and the sense of urgency articulated in the findings (a billion dollars is significantly less than the cost of a single aircraft carrier), one must take seriously the explicitness of the findings. The federal government comes out four-square behind the view articulated by the homeless advocates that: (1) there is a singularity about the homeless problem that challenges the "business as usual" view of the housing market; (2) the problem involves more than the traditional street people and includes families with children; (3) diverse housing solutions are necessary to meet differing needs; (4) the problem will get worse without concerned help from all sectors including additional assistance from the federal government.

Prior to the passage of the McKinney Act one could have argued that there were essentially two views of the homeless issue at the national level: that of the homeless advocates and that of the Reagan Administration. The Administration posture historically had been to minimize the magnitude of the problem (300,000 homeless vs. the three million counted by the advocates) while arguing that the vast majority were the chronic homeless. The Administration also defined the issue as a local and state problem about which the federal government was already doing its appropriate best. In a formal sense, with passage of the McKinney Act, the battle over the *nature* of the problem was over.[28] The federal government has essentially accepted the view that the challenge of the growing crisis requires additional help from the federal government. How then does the Act translate its findings into programs? Which

TABLE 16.1   The Three Stages of Homelessness

	Stage I "at risk"	Stage II homeless	Stage III rehoused
Economic homeless	—	Emergency Shelter Grant Program is applicable to all three homeless categories ($220m)[a]	Section 8 SRO ($35m)[a]
Situational homeless	—	Transitional housing ($20–165m)[b]	Permanent Housing for Handicapped Homeless persons ($15–160m)[b]
Chronic homeless	—		Supplemental Assistance for Facilities to Assist the Homeless can be used in Stage II & III for all three homeless categories ($50m)[a]

[a] Authorized funding for the first two years of the legislation.

[b] The Supported Housing Demonstration Program has an *overall* authorization, and a minimum funding level for each of its two programs.

of the homeless at which stages of the homeless continuum are helped and how does the Act frame the relationship of the federal government and its new programs to state and local actors?

The Homeless Served by the McKinney Act

The section of the McKinney Act that deals explicitly with shelter and housing is Title IV: Housing Assistance. The five types of accommodation defined in the title were funded for a total of $520 million over a two-year period and represent over 50 percent of the Act's initial authorization of funds. The five types of accommodation assistance are:

1. *Emergency Shelter Grants Program* makes funding available for the renovation and rehabilitation of buildings to be used as emergency shelters for the homeless. Essential services and some operating costs are also eligible for support.
2. *Supportive Housing Demonstration Program: Transitional Housing* focuses on the development of innovative approaches to transitional housing (housing that facilitates the "transition" of homeless persons back to the housing market) and supportive services.
3. *Supported Housing Demonstration Program: Permanent Housing for Handicapped Homeless Persons* provides assistance in developing community-based long-term housing and supportive services for handicapped persons.
4. *Section 8 Assistance for Single Room Occupancy Dwellings (SRO)* represents a commitment of Section 8 Moderate Rehabilitation Funding for 600–800 new SRO units.
5. *Supplemental Assistance for Facilities to Assist the Homeless* funds innovative community efforts to meet the shelter needs of the homeless and supplements the funding under the other grant programs in Title IV.

Table 16.1 lays out the program elements of Title IV in terms of this paper's typologies.

In the ideal world of policy analysis, the allocation of the Act's financial resources should reflect either the relative distribution of the homeless problem among the three types of homeless populations or be a function of the leverage generated by federal dollars expended at each stage of homelessness. We would know how many of which kind of homeless people exist in the nation's urban and rural areas and the relative impact of the different programmatic initiatives outlined in the Act on those populations. Such rational analysis did not inform the way funding was provided for the various programs, nor does it seem possible that it could have done so, given the financial constraints of the bill, the diversity of opinion as to how many homeless there are nationwide, and the debates as to which homeless category individual households belong.

Yet as the Act is implemented and its programmatic elements evaluated, we will come to know much more about the characteristics of local homeless populations and the impact of housing and service on their lives, as well as the various costs associated with those interventions. Despite the absence of an empirical foundation, the distribution of financial resources under the McKinney Act makes an implicit statement about how the Act's framers viewed the relative significance of both the stages of homelessness and the categories of homelessness. The Act has no prevention strategies to assist people of any category "at risk" of homelessness. The sole recognition of Stage I in the Act is the inclusion of "at risk" status in the definition of a handicapped homeless person.

Homelessness, as defined by the McKinney Act, really begins with households in the street and in need of shelter. Accordingly, the largest single allocation of funds in Title IV is to the Emergency Shelter Grant Program. Transitional housing is "an idea in good currency" and the Act makes a major commitment to the concept which it defines as ". . . a project . . . that has as its purpose facilitating the movement of homeless individuals to independent living within a *reasonable* amount of time" (underlining mine).[29] Transitional housing is something of a hybrid—located between Stages II and III. Title IV focuses on permanent rehousing for a small subset of the economic homeless and a major category of the chronic homeless. The Section 8 Assistance for Single Room Occupancy Dwellings (SRO) is the Act's only program directed explicitly to housing the economic homeless. Here there seems to be a mismatch between the target population and the housing type. In practice, the greatest need for such housing is among either the situational or chronic homeless. In the absence of a service component, the Section 8 will not be of use to them.

Permanent Housing for Handicapped Homeless Persons on the other hand, focuses very much on the service component as an integral part of the program to "address the special needs of persons, such as deinstitutionalized homeless individuals with mental disabilities."[30]

In the months ahead, HUD will be funding a variety of local experiments in sheltering, housing, and servicing homeless people. None will need closer monitoring than the Transitional Housing Program. Transitional housing acknowledges that there are situational homeless who need more than a "little help from their friends" before re-entering the market. In transitional housing those of the situational homeless judged unable to be rehoused without additional help reside for a period in a residential setting where they are provided with a variety of services: job training, education, parenting, and personal care skills training.

Transitional housing takes on much of its current definition from work done with battered women and other victims of domestic abuse in which communal living in small groups has provided a supportive environment and training for these women and their families.[31]

Viewed from another perspective, transitional housing is an old concept. It is derived from ideas used in Europe before the Second World War in which problem families were put together in one residential setting and given a particularly intensive array of social services.[32] The history of these projects, and the theory behind them, is strewn with pitfalls to be avoided as the transitional experiments sponsored by the McKinney Act get underway. Issues to consider are:

1. In Holland, prior to World War II, special residential settings were allocated to "problem families." They were closed down after the War because it became difficult to move people out of them. Rather than being transitional they became housing of last resort for households stigmatized as being incapable of living elsewhere.

   In England through the 1960s, each community had its "sink estate" to which problems families were relegated. In some instances, additional services were provided and rehabilitation was, in theory, pursued. In other situations, the developments were simply collections of people who had been evicted from housing and had no other place to go. Transitional housing can thus become permanent because there is no next stage for the occupants. Without firm access to permanent housing resources, transitional housing cannot live up to its name.

   At present, there is no link between the Transitional Housing Demonstration in the McKinney Act and permanent housing. Without attention to the connection and whatever means it takes to move people into long-term housing, HUD runs the risk of having localities set up transitional housing with no exit—the plight of the British "sink estates."

2. There is not always a one-to-one relationship between people who would benefit from transitional housing and a little structured help and those who will accept it. Often people most in need of help—the most problem-ridden and least likely to survive in the permanent housing market—are the least willing to accept the view that they need an interim period in a supported environment. The issue of control, the capacity and desirability of "requiring" a household to go into transitional housing, can become a hotly debated issue among those working on rehousing homeless people at the state and local level.[33]

   The motivation of individuals going into transitional housing is also complex. The head of household who accepts the regime of the transitional housing as a necessary and self-selected part of her/his rehabilitation has already taken one short step on the road to self-reliance. The household that accepts transitional housing because it is a means of getting out of a temporary shelter and the only way to get access to a Voucher or Certificate is clearly in a different posture with regard to the purpose of the residential setting.

3. NIMBY (not in my backyard) can present major siting problems. Transitional housing developments will stall, particularly if the developments are perceived by neighbors as being for "problem families." The political process by which the programs are worked through at a local level could benefit much from the learning being developed by another controversial type of development, housing for the chronic mentally ill, discussed by Newman and Struyk in Chapter 17.

The above issues are not arguments against undertaking creative experiments that learn from the highly successful examples already existing.[34] They are rather a set of concerns that should be taken seriously by those at the state and local level carrying out the demonstrations, and by HUD as it monitors the process it has set in motion.

The Federal Relationship to State and Local Homeless Initiatives

Title IV of the Act takes as its operating assumption that: (1) local housing markets have different distributions of the homeless among the economic, situational and chronic categories; (2) there is significant variation in the local configurations of public and private institutions servicing the homeless and there is no one "right" organizational structure to deal with the complex of issues; (3) the federal role is essentially to "complement and enhance the available services."[35] While a comprehensive homeless assistance plan (already known as CHAP) is required of each locality and state that wants funding, that plan is described in the legislation as very much dependent on local formulation.

The funding pots in Title IV are a mixture of entitlement and discretionary funds. The entitlement money is driven by the community development block grant formula but is targeted at a specific kind of program: emergency shelter. The discretionary money for which localities and states must compete requires matching funds under the Supportive Housing Demonstration Program, described earlier, and clear evidence of hardship with no supplanting of any non-federal resources.[36]

These federal discretionary funds are seen as a matching piece and an incentive for use of local resources but not as an alternative to such effort. Federal money is not to bail out the locals and the states but to make their resources go further. The federal role in homelessness, then, is to augment the existing local and state structures; to help them work better by providing funding for services and facilities. The federal government also encourages experimentation. The Supportive Housing Demonstration Program focuses on the federal role as innovator and "the lessons that the provision of such housing might have." [37]

The applicants for program elements under Title IV include the states, local government and the nonprofit sector. States have a central role in three of the four subtitles. They must prepare a Comprehensive Homeless Assistance Plan (CHAP) for submission to HUD if they want their nonentitlement communities to benefit from the funding under the Emergency Shelter Grant Program. The states are the prime applicant under the Permanent Housing for the Handicapped Homeless Persons Program and must put up a 50 percent matching grant to get the federal dollars.

This discussion of applicants and funding pots presumes a close working relationship among the nonprofit, state, and local actors. For example, the Permanent Housing for the Handicapped Homeless Persons Program envisages a nonprofit sponsor working with the state in which a locality may put up part of the state's matching share.

The multiple sponsors and the variety of "mix and match" subtitles takes as its underlying premise that there are existing relationships at the local level, "partnership efforts" among state, local, and nonprofit groups, which can be extended and energized by the funding made available under the McKinney Act. Where these partnerships are intact or can be put together, the complexity of the various subtitles and funding pots provides an opportunity rather than creating a problem. Where there is little local or state capacity or desire, it may be difficult for even the most aggressive and entrepreneurial nonprofit organization to make headway.

The discretionary nature of most of Title IV's programs and their emphasis on local and state entrepreneurship and money means that the best grantsmen and those with the matching money will stand to get the awards, Sandra Newman points out: "Very unequal capacities of the different jurisdictions are not recognized and everyone seems to be competing as if they are equal. There is no formula that establishes any progressivity in this funding." [38] Thus, in theory, aggressive rich states with a small homeless problem could beat out poorer, less competent but flooded-with-homeless jurisdictions in the race for funding.

The absence of progressivity may produce this outcome in some instances. But the likelihood is mitigated by two factors. The first is that HUD is surely not going to allow its funds to be swallowed up by only the rich and super-competent. Geographic distribution and attention to relative need is a long-standing concern of federal agencies. Congressional oversight ensures that such is the case with grant-in-aid programs. Secondly, one can argue that it is the economically well-to-do states and localities, with their rising rents, low residential vacancies, and gentrifying central cities, that are most impacted by the homeless problem. Their energy in going after funding is fueled by the urgency of their situation.

The obverse of the argument that the localities with the problem will go after the funding is that some jurisdictions may well choose to avoid seeking Title IV funding because they want to avoid dealing with the homeless problem. Fearful that their neighbors will not do their share, they may reason that to not apply for funding may force the homeless elsewhere.

The analytic arguments which posit why localities will either seek too much funding or not enough are conceptually interesting. HUD will have to monitor its distribution of funds as the various programs under Title IV become operational to ensure that neither construct comes to pass in practice.

Operationally, HUD is in a better position to say no to applicants and to spread its funding in a progressive way than to get the avoiders to apply. If some jurisdictions choose to bypass discretionary federal funding for housing and sheltering homeless people, there is little the agency can do about it.

As with all its program dollars, HUD must find ways of ensuring that its resources are being wisely used. The McKinney Act, focused as it is on getting funding out to deal with what is perceived to be an emergency, does not spend energy developing monitoring or program standards. It looks to the good sense and competence of state and local partnerships to use the funds wisely. For those looking at the process from the states and localities, this is a plus. For those observing from Washington, the latitude may appear excessive.

In its first year of operation, many administrators implementing the Act at the state and local levels found it too complex and too inflexible. A comprehensive approach to just the housing and shelter aspects of the Act, let alone the health, job, and education components, required at least three separate application processes. Rather than allowing localities to determine what combinations of programs were necessary and how best to develop and leverage local funding for them, the housing section, Title IV, has very strict stipulations for local match. For states with sophisticated homeless delivery systems, like New York, New Jersey, and Massachusetts, the Act was too restrictive and failed to give sufficient authority to the states. For states without institutional mechanisms for dealing with homelessness, the Act provided no incentive to get them involved. Thus, issues have emerged about the extent to which McKinney fragments planning for the homeless and complicates the process of application for resources. Recent amendments to the Act, favored by many states, have worked to smooth out some initial bureaucratic hurdles.

The McKinney legislation has been in effect for less than two years. There is at present no national survey of the activity it has generated let alone any evaluation of its effectiveness in coping with the stages of homelessness. What knowledgeable observers conclude, however, is that McKinney has evoked a significant response not only from the sophisticated states and localities deeply concerned with homeless issues before its passage but also in areas of the country where homelessness has not been consistent front page news. National organizations have either come into existence or been refocused on the homeless agenda.

The Council of State Community Affairs Agencies (COSCAA) represents a dramatic example of a state organization which has come to focus on the homeless issue. Traditionally a watchdog of federal funding for state departments of community affairs, particularly the Community Development Block Grant Program, COSCAA has seized upon the McKinney legislation as an area of central concern. The organization has sponsored conferences for its members focusing on aspects of the state homeless agenda: prevention and the relationship between welfare and housing. In addition, COSCAA provided a major leadership role in lobbying to refocus the McKinney legislation after its first year of operation.

Despite the absence of evaluations or in-depth national surveys, sketchy generalizations can be made about the way states are responding to the homeless agenda in the wake of the McKinney Act. The most useful evidence in making these generalizations, beyond conversations with individuals who have an impressionistic sense of how things are going, is a study done by the Urban Institute for HUD and the McKinney-generated Interagency Council on the Homeless. This review of six states, undertaken in the summer of 1988, was to "learn about their activities and programs for the homeless and about state utilization of McKinney Act funds." [39] California, Connecticut, Georgia, New Mexico, Ohio and Wisconsin were chosen for review on the basis that "they were active on the national homeless task force, or . . . had done a good deal with their own resources for the homeless." [40] The following observations about the "state of state homeless initiatives" is derived from the findings of the study filtered through personal observations and discussions with knowledgeable individuals.

Two states, Massachusetts and Connecticut, have taken the lead in developing comprehensive approaches to the issue of homelessness (making an effort to "fill in the boxes," in the terms of the homeless matrix presented in this chapter). Other states have developed coordinated approaches but the leadership for the strategy is seen not in the executive office of the state but rather "the coordinating bodies emerged in response to pressure from the private efforts of advocates and provider coalitions, or in response to the McKinney Act's requirement that states submit a comprehensive Homeless Assistance Plan before being eligible to receive shelter/housing assistance under the Act." [41] California is an example of a state with a broad-gauged homeless strategy which has emerged at the state level due to energy generated initially from outside state government.

States vary widely in the level of their financial commitment to the homeless issue. Among the six states studied by the Urban Institute, the dollar amounts range from $13.83 per resident to $0.12. The states selected for review "were thought to be quite active in programming for the homeless." [42] The relationship between the state social service and housing systems lies at the heart of a comprehensive state policy to deal with the challenge of homelessness. In most instances the social service system has taken the central role in coordinating the relationship—as in California and Massachusetts. In others the gap between the "housers" and the "service people" remains acute, as in New York.

The absence of affordable housing is acknowledged almost universally as "the overarching gap creating homelessness." [43] While there are differing views as to how that affordability should be created—demand side or supply side subsidies or simply income transfers—there is a universal sentiment that help in some form must come from the federal government if the housing affordability agenda is to be taken seriously.

The McKinney legislation is perceived as a great boon to extending the role of the states in dealing with the homeless agenda but it is also seen as providing serious impediments to realization of a comprehensive and innovative state program. Much criticized are McKinney's focus on bricks and mortar for emergency shelters; its extremely limited provisions for operating costs and staffing; "its relative lack of focus on serious prevention efforts; and its patchwork structure of grants, programs and applications . . ." [44] As indicated earlier in the paper, recent amendments to McKinney have eased some of these hurdles, and the legislation is moving slowly in the direction of a modified block grant with increasing focus on state initiatives and leadership (due in no small part to the aggressive lobbying of Congress by COSCAA).

Innovative programs for dealing with the multiple aspects of homelessness exist not only in the states with significant homeless initiatives like Massachusetts, New York, Connecticut, New Jersey, California, and Pennsylvania, but also in states in which the major homeless initiatives lie at the city and county level rather than with the state. Washington and Oregon are cited as examples of states with innovative local leadership absent a strong mandate from the state itself.

In states with low vacancy rates and a tight housing market, the dearth of housing for low-income people is a factor of such compelling significance that it can undermine or seriously limit the efficacy of even the most innovative of comprehensive state approaches to the issue of homelessness. Massachusetts and New York and probably New Jersey and California are examples of situations in which the inexorable working of the housing market, absent federal help in the form of housing subsidies or welfare benefit increases, will either overwhelm the existing system or keep it from "solving" the housing problem of the economic and situational homeless. While affordable housing is not the universal elixir, a high vacancy rate, a soft market, and landlords eager for tenants provide a context in which innovative state programming can begin to deal with the social service aspects of the homeless agenda. For example, the housing market in Massachusetts has softened considerably during the past two years but not sufficiently to accommodate those at the bottom. The innovative state housing agenda, the largest in the country by far on a per capita basis, has been insufficient to keep up with the gap between what low-income people can pay and the rent levels in the private market. Now that budgetary woes have come to Massachusetts in the form of revenue shortfalls there is little chance in the short run that the homeless programmatic agenda will be expanded. Curtailment is more likely to be the case. The advocate community, already mobilized to chastise the state's current efforts, faces even more trying times ahead.

Beyond the McKinney Act: The Future of the Federal Role in Housing the Homeless

The future of federal housing policy for the homeless can be deduced, at least in theory, from the "first principles" represented by the McKinney Act's findings and purposes and the programmatic elements and framing of the federal role in Title IV. It is important to spell out the elements of such a future while recognizing the political and economic realities that will intrude upon the logic of those principles. The "findings and purposes" section of the Act articulates the federal government's responsibility for participating in a problem presenting "an immediate and unprecedented crisis" which "in the absence of more effective efforts is expected to become dramatically worse."[45]

The future size of the homeless population and its distribution among the economic, situational, and chronic categories will be a function of forces which, in the words of the McKinney Act, are "many and complex." The Act itself is an effort on the part of the federal government to keep the size of that population from becoming "dramatically" worse. But as has been pointed out, the pressures that push people into the street are beyond the domain of the Act as currently constituted.

The Act takes a "narrow construction" view of shelter and homelessness which translates into a focus on Stage II emergency response and selective Stage III initiatives for the situational and chronic homeless. Yet the longer one tries to solve the problem of homelessness at the emergency response stage, the more the "broad construction" view of shelter inevitably arises. From the perspective of that view, Stage I and Stage III housing issues become critical, for the future scale and character of homelessness in the United States is going to be determined by how successful we are at keeping "at risk" households in the housing stock and at rehousing them permanently when they do end up in shelters.

In the following section we look at the future federal role in dealing with homelessness through the broad construction lens implicit in the McKinney Act's language. That view focuses on four major issues: 1. the "at risk" homeless and prevention strategies; 2. single chronic and situational homeless people; 3. the role and scope of low-income housing subsidies in prevention and rehousing; and 4. the federal relationship to state and local homeless initiatives.

The "At Risk" Homeless and Prevention Strategies

Throughout this chapter we have underlined the importance of keeping "at risk" households from falling out of the market. In part this emphasis follows from the logic that prevention is a better way of doing business than dealing with households once they are on the street. But in addition to logic, the focus on prevention derives from the success prevention efforts have had in various parts of the country and the need to extend their utility through more focused federal support.

New York City, Massachusetts, and New Jersey present examples of how organizational energy and program dollars can be focused on homeless prevention strategies. In Massachusetts, keeping people in their existing housing is the mission of the Housing Services program run by the state's Executive Office of Communities and Development. The program funds community organizations with expertise in housing to mediate tenant-landlord disputes. Housing Services is predicated on the assumption that many issues that arise between tenants and landlords can be worked through with professional help. The local Housing Service entities, Community Action Agencies, and regional nonprofit housing organizations also work to gain private landlord acceptance of the state public housing leasing program and other programs which can help keep rents down and thus keep low-income tenants in the units.

In Massachusetts, the federally-funded Emergency Assistance (EA) Program administered by the Department of Public Welfare (DPW) can be utilized by AFDC households for first month rent downpayments and security deposits, and to help defray the cost of rent and utility arrearages. An aggressive DPW worker can thus use EA to extend the financial resources of a low-income client. Given the disparity between the AFDC allowance and rent levels in many of Massachusetts' market areas, this bridging represents a monumental challenge.

A study done by the Massachusetts DPW found that in a significant number of the state's housing markets, public and private organizations were working together in a "housing network" to successfully prevent "at risk" households from falling out of the market. The formal institutional relationship varied at the local level among the offices of the state's Departments of Public Welfare and Social Services, the Community Action Agencies, the local housing authority, and other nonprofit organizations. Critical to a successful homeless prevention and rehousing effort was the extent of cooperation and mutually shared goals.[46]

In New York City, the Human Resources Administration has "developed a more responsive procedure for emergency intervention to head off evictions,"[47] and the City has established several offices providing protective services for adults and evictions assistance. While there are many recommendations for extending and improving the New York City prevention system, the significance of financial and service strategies organized to keep at-risk people in place is part of the local calculation, particularly among homeless advocacy groups. The New Jersey Prevention of Homelessness Act, passed in 1984, provides the means whereby "families can get short-term loans and grants to help pay rents or mortgages." To date the program is estimated to have "helped 10,000 people avoid eviction."[48]

Variations on these efforts can be replicated in other states. The key to successful approaches is not the organizational form or who is in charge but rather the existence of a self-conscious effort to coordinate local activity focused on the prevention end of the homeless continuum.

In the spirit of locally formulated strategies espoused by the McKinney Act, the federal role in homeless prevention should be (1) to feed money and ideas into ongoing state and local mechanisms to extend local capacity; (2) to help areas learn from each other's experience; (3) to provide incentives for coordinated behavior in housing markets where housing networks focused on prevention do not currently exist; and (4) to encourage those networks to link health and mental health programs and social services at the local level as critical elements in a homeless prevention strategy.

Beyond broadening the McKinney Act to cover Stage I households at risk of homelessness carried out by amendments to the Act in 1988, attention needs to be focused on the creative use of the welfare system, particularly Emergency Assistance (EA), for prevention. Emergency assistance has been a key element in the Massachusetts Stage I strategy and is recommended for more extensive use in New York City. EA is an extremely flexible vehicle which is aggressively administered and "can be used for any emergency affecting families."[49] States vary widely in their use of EA and certainly in their use of it for comprehensive prevention strategies. How creatively it is employed at the local welfare office is a function of how aggressively the state welfare system pushes it. The level of state energy in turn can be influenced by federal policy.

The issue of EA and its role in homeless prevention is not central to the discussion of the relationship between the welfare and the housing systems undertaken in the chapter in this book by Newman and Schnare. While welfare reform and its relationship to housing assistance is the overriding issue, at the marginal level, without any radical reshuffling of the two systems, EA could be utilized in a more entrepreneurial way if tied into Stage I prevention strategies. The institutional refocusing necessary to carry off such a self-conscious shift in federal policy warrants serious exploration *whatever* the outcome of the larger welfare and housing agenda.

Two additional administrative aspects of the welfare system are worth mentioning in the context of local coordination: protective payment and the character of the relationship with the public housing authority. Protective payment, the direct payment of a welfare client's rent to a public or private landlord, is a practice which generates great debate. Some see the approach as infantilizing welfare clients and removing their rights and sense of responsibility. Others view protective payment as the logical way of dealing with a problematic situation: without such guarantee of payment the landlord is likely to put the household out on the street.[50] While the protective payment approach can be abused, when properly handled it represents a useful tool in the homeless prevention or rehousing kit. The bargaining position of a housing service worker with a landlord is greatly enhanced if direct payment of the rent is among the negotiating items. Protective payment should be carefully considered as part of a comprehensive prevention strategy.

Where protective payments are used, it is critical that the welfare check pay for a unit that is in reasonable physical condition and to which responsible landlord services are delivered. How a minimal threshold of quality is defined and its maintenance assured will vary from area to area. Once again, what is critical is not the organizational form or which agency carries out the inspections, but rather that the issue of standards be addressed and institutionalized in the local homeless prevention and rehousing system.

A positive and communicative relationship between the welfare department and the local housing authority is a critical element in preventing situational homelessness. When a household is evicted from public housing for failure to pay rent, something has gone awry in the prevention strategy. At the street level, where policy is actually carried out (or some would say formulated), the relationship between the housing authority and the welfare office is often nonexistent or hostile.

The specific administrative and regulatory devices by which the federal government gets local housing authorities and welfare offices to better coordinate their activities, to create a better "early warning system" for potential homelessness among the public housing population, is an item that an expanded McKinney Act Interagency Council could put on its agenda. That there are good models of cooperation at the local level is clear.[51] Federal encouragement can steer other local agencies in this direction if there is a more self-conscious effort at the national level to recognize the importance of connection among federally funded entities at the local level in evolving coordinated prevention strategies.

As the next discussion makes clear, more deep subsidies are a critical component of prevention and rehousing strategies. But better use of the organizations, services, and financial resources already in the field is a critical step in evolving those strategies. In a world of limited federal resources, coordination of institutional agenda ought to be at the center of any extended federal agenda for dealing with the stages of homelessness.

Single Chronic and Situational Homeless People

While the McKinney rehousing net is cast broadly in terms of the three categories of homeless, there is one large group that remains essentially outside its scope—nonelderly single persons, mostly men—who fall within the chronic and situational categories. These individuals do not have the access either to the public welfare or to subsidized housing systems available to the homeless elderly or families.[52] Even where they might be eligible, "many of the homeless chronically mentally ill deny their mental illness and thus would not even attempt to establish their eligibility for preference for admission to [HUD] assisted housing programs."[53]

Because of their involvement with substance abuse—alcohol or drugs—or their problematic behavior, they are not tenants that private or public landlords would readily accept even if they were eligible for subsidized housing. The emergence and growth of the new homeless, the economic and situational families, should not obscure the hard reality that a large percentage of those on the street and in the shelters are and will continue to be nonelderly, multiproblem individuals for whom solutions are hard to come by and expensive to implement. They will be the people whom local homeless systems will first ignore when the pressure mounts to demonstrate "success" in placing and maintaining people in permanent housing. James Stimpson of HUD states that "over time, federally-funded programs for the homeless may not indeed be able to be used to meet the needs of the most dysfunctional among the single homeless."[54]

The challenge to policy makers is to learn from the implementation of the various elements of the McKinney Act, in conjunction with local initiatives, how to deal with this most difficult group of people; and to ensure that federal resources and guidelines extend the local public and private capacity to take on the problem of the single chronic and situational homeless.

The Role and Scope of Low-Income Housing Subsidies in Homeless Prevention and Rehousing

So far our discussion has not addressed the issue of deep housing subsidies in an overall prevention strategy. It has dealt with ways the existing system can be "fiddled on the margin." In the terms of the model of Stage I strategies laid out in Part I, it focuses on services, better coordination, and marginal financial resources. Yet the reality is that *some* deep subsidy resources have to be included as a resource in Stage I and Stage III efforts. One should not oversell the capacity of coordinated work at the local level to keep all "at risk" households in the stock.

How successful even the most entrepreneurial of local networks can be (and therefore how much the flow of people into the street and shelters can be reduced) will be a function ultimately of the cost of housing in local markets and people's capacity to pay for it. Better use of existing resources and a more coordinated local effort represent critical initiatives and show great promise for slowing down the tide of homelessness. But without additional subsidy, the impact of even the most creative prevention network will be marginal in situations where: 1. low-income housing stock continues to filter up to higher income groups or down and out of the market altogether; 2. the buying power of low-income households is not increased to pay for those rents.

Put baldly, prevention and rehousing strategies can do a great deal by better use of existing service and financial programs provided by the federal government and carried out at the local level. But to be ultimately effective those strategies require financial resources to fill the gap between what low-income people can pay and the prices of units dictated by the market. The Massachusetts prevention and rehousing system, for example, is deeply dependent on the existence of a state equivalent of Section 8 which provides "deep subsidy" to many families to enable them to get out of the shelters and into permanent housing.

In Chapter 2 of this book, William Apgar looks at the issue of housing demographics: the dimensions of the need for low rent housing and its availability. The details of his findings are important in determining the extent and depth of pressure in local markets on low-income households. The drift of his conclusions were expressed in his recent testimony before the Senate Subcommittee on Housing and Urban Affairs when he stated that: "Absent . . . concerted action, there is every reason to project further deterioration in the housing situation of the nation's renter population and further increase (in) the number of homeless individuals and families in the years ahead." [55] Apgar is suggesting that for purely economic reasons without greater efforts to subsidize people in place, the ranks of the homeless will increase.

In their recent study, "Homelessness and the Low-Income Housing Crisis," the National Low Income Housing Coalition addresses the issue of the housing gap facing low-income people and underlines the importance of the future of the expiring use restrictions on HUD-subsidized stock, an issue taken up by Clay and Wallace in Chapter 12. In addition, the Coalition report addresses the impermanency of Section 8 contracts, a topic also discussed elsewhere in this book. Newman and Schnare (Chapter 17) raise fundamental questions about the relationship between the federal welfare and housing subsidy systems and the need not only for additional funding but also administrative and programmatic reform to gain better efficiency, equity, and effectiveness from those resources currently allocated to shelter.

The point here is both to underline the critical nature of the subsidy issue in relationship to homelessness and to indicate that the shape and size of future need for it is addressed from a variety of perspectives in other chapters.

The Federal Relationship to State and Local Homeless Initiatives

As pointed out in Part II, the McKinney Act posits a role for the federal government which: (1) recognizes local formulation of the character and scope of the homeless problem and the solutions to it; (2) combines entitlement with discretionary funding; (3) presumes that states, localities, and nonprofit sponsors will be working in partnership efforts using federal funding as only one piece of locally-generated and funded shelter and housing initiatives. The Act combines a strong statement of federal purpose and concern with a flexible approach to how that concern is worked out at the state and local level. It is a mix and match of options designed to give local, state, and public and private actors room to craft appropriate local responses.

Taking the long view of federal housing policy, the McKinney Act, as modified over the past two years, represents a middle ground between the top-down explicitness of the Housing Act of 1968, for example, with its massive commitment of federal resources to the low-income housing agenda, and the Reagan administration's move to minimize the federal role in attacking the gap between the housing need of low-income people and effective market demand.

Extending the philosophy of the McKinney Act to the "broad construction" view of shelter (i.e., low-income housing) results in a federal role which: (1) looks to localities and states to initiate strategies for dealing with their "at risk" and rehoused populations; (2) encourages the development of public/private partnerships to be worked out at the state and local levels; (3) makes some combination of entitlement and discretionary funds (mix and match) available to carry out local plans; and (4) presumes that the federal dollars are but a part of a combination of state and local public and private funding in which the federal mix of supply and demand subsidies would differ from state to state and area to area.

Historically, the role of the federal government in assisting low-income households has fluctuated from the made-in-Washington cookie cutter programs like Section 221, Section 236, and Section 8 federal rental housing subsidy programs to the total-local-option represented by revenue sharing and, to a modified degree, by the block grant. The thrust of the McKinney approach is to combine a strong sense of federal purpose and intent with a variety of opportunities for local and state entitlement and entrepreneurship. As the debates about the future role of the federal government in the subsidization of low-income housing moves forward, it is well worth exploring the ramifications of this "middle way" for future federal engagement.

Ultimately the critical issue about the federal role in State I and Stage III homeless prevention and rehousing will come down to the amount of money

Washington is prepared to allocate. Yet as the size of that funding looms over the discussion, it is important to bear in mind that *how* the federal government allocates to low-income households is critical in maximizing the efficiency and equity in the use of the funds provided. Ultimately the degree to which the homeless tide is indeed stemmed will depend on the careful crafting of local strategies working synergistically with the federal resources made available for the cause.

Notes

1. National Coalition for the Homeless, "A Briefing Paper for Presidential Candidates" (Washington, no date), 1.

2. See "Childhood Without a Home," *Boston Phoenix,* January 21 1986, for a graphic statement of that debate.

3. In Massachusetts, for example, the Department of Mental Health distinguishes among four levels of chronic mental illness. The type of service varies with the level of intensity; but at all four the premise is that continuity and consistency of service is a central component of any community housing effort.

4. E. Bassuk, "The Homeless Problem," *Scientific American* (July 1984) 40.

5. E. Bassuk, "The Feminization of Homelessness: Homeless Families in Boston Shelters," address given at Shelter Inc., June 11 1985.

6. N. Karlen et al., "Homeless Kids, Forgotten Faces," *Newsweek,* January 6 1986, 20.

7. J. Erickson and C. Wilhelm, eds., *Housing the Homeless* (New Brunswick, N.J.: Rutgers University Press, 1986) has a section of articles and excerpts entitled, "The Importance of Numbers," in which the different methodological perspectives of the Reagan Administration as reflected by the Department of Housing and Urban Development and the "homeless advocates" are displayed. While the methodological problems of a "right count of the right category" are formidible, the difficulty is enhanced by the ideological lens through which those doing the counting record the population(s). See also J. Conason, "Body Count: How the Reagan Administration Hides the Homeless," *Village Voice,* December 3 1985, 25; and "The Homeless: Who, Where, and How Many," *National Journal,* August 9 1986.

8. U.S. Conference of Mayors, "The Continued Growth of Hunger, Homelessness and Poverty in America's Cities: 1986" (Washington: USGPO, December 1986) 15.

9. U.S. Mayors, "Growth of Hunger," 16.

10. Statement of J. W. Stimpson, Deputy Assistant Secretary for Policy Development, U.S. Department of Housing and Urban Development, before Senate Subcommittee on Housing and Urban Affairs, January 29 1987, 5.

11. The precise figure varies depending on the city and the study. A HUD study says 21 percent. A Chicago study says 22–28 percent (see Stimpson, Statement, January 1987). The Mayor's Study (cited above) says 28 percent (15).

12. Stimpson, Statement, January 1987, 5, 17.

13. L. Friedman, *Government and Slum Housing* (Chicago: Rand McNally, 1968).

14. The full quotation is: "Is there anything whereof it may be said, see, this is new? It hath already been of old time, which was before us. There is no remembrance of former things." Ecclesiastes 1: 10–11.

15. See "Hearings before the Subcommittee on Housing and Urban Affairs" January 29, 1987, for a summary of the housing issues as presented from a variety of

perspectives. See also National Coalition for the Homeless, "Briefing Paper," and National Low Income Coalition "Homelessness and the Low-Income Housing Crisis" (Washington: NLIC, no date).

16. National Association of Housing Redevelopment Officials, "Position Papers: Overview" (Washington: NAHRO, 1987).

17. W. Apgar, "The Declining Supply of Low Cost Rental Housing," Testimony presented to the U.S. Senate Subcommittee on Housing and Urban Affairs, June 5 1987.

18. P. Marcuse, as quoted in National Coalition for the Homeless et al., "Stemming the Tide of Displacement" (Washington: NCH, September 1986) 5.

19. The concept of stages and policy intervention appropriate to each is derived from my work with Nancy Kaufman and her formulation of these issues in Massachusetts when she was Assistant Secretary in the Executive Office of Human Services.

20. The National Coalition for the Homeless, the Community Service Society of New York, and the Massachusetts Coalition for the Homeless are among the organizations that have published vivid documentation on the impact on peoples' lives of being on the street. Ellen Bassuk's "Feminization of Homelessness" is another example.

21. A study of three months of newspapers in 1985 determined that of the articles the *New York Times* ran on homelessness during the period "Only 12 percent mentioned permanent housing options for the homeless. A meager 8 percent made any mention of the previous housing of those who were homeless . . ." (N.C.H., "Stemming the Tide," 24).

22. *New York Times,* July 12 1987.

23. U.S. Mayors, "Growth of Hunger," 1.

24. Community Service Society of New York, "Alternatives to the Welfare Hotel" (New York: CSSNY, 1987) 1, 14.

25. Stewart B. McKinney Homeless Assistance Act, Sec. 102.

26. McKinney Act, Sec. 102.

27. McKinney Act, Sec. 102.

28. This is not strictly the case. Maneuvers by the Reagan Administration in 1988 to cut back on funding for the McKinney Act indicate continued opposition to the role assigned the federal government by the Act.

29. McKinney Act (422)(12)(a).

30. McKinney Act (422)(13).

31. See Women's Institute for Housing and Economic Development, "A Manual on Transitional Housing" (Boston, WIHED, 1986).

32. Keyes, interviews in Holland, March 1978 (from unpublished manuscript, "The Problem of Problem People," 1982).

33. This has certainly been the case in Massachusetts where the issue of required service and required transitional housing has been skirmished over between those who see the requirement as a necessary element in a rehousing strategy and those who see it as controlling and arbitrary.

34. Women's Institute, "Manual on Transitional Housing."

35. McKinney Act (401)(b)(4).

36. McKinney Act (421)(2)(4).

37. McKinney Act (425)(b)(2)(A).

38. Sandra Newman, Conference on MIT Housing Policy Project, November 9 1987, Washington D.C.

39. Burt and Cohen, "State Activities and Programs for the Homeless: A Review of Six States" (Washington: The Urban Institute, September 1988) 1.

40. Burt and Cohen, "State Activities."

41. Burt and Cohen, "State Activities," 116.

42. Burt and Cohen, "State Activities."

43. Burt and Cohen, "State Activities," 117.

44. Burt and Cohen, "State Activities."

45. McKinney Act, Sec. 102.

46. Keyes et al. "The Use of Emergency Assistance in Homeless Prevention: The Department of Public Welfare Area Office Housing System" (xeroxed paper), December 1986.

47. N.C.H., "Stemming the Tide of Displacement," 74.

48. National Center for Policy Alternatives, "Ways and Means" (Washington: NCPA, Fall 1986), 6.

49. NCPA, "Ways and Means".

50. See L. Grollman, "Homeless Prevention of AFDC Families," thesis, Master of City Planning, MIT, 1987, for an extended and thoughtful analysis of the issue.

51. Grollman, "Homeless Prevention."

52. I am indebted to James Stimpson of HUD for pointing out the importance of this category of homeless people and the ways in which they are currently left out of the federal welfare and housing systems.

53. J. Stimpson, Conference on MIT Housing Policy Project, November 9 1987, Washington, DC.

54. Stimpson, Conference.

55. Apgar, "Declining Supply."

Chapter 17
Housing and Supportive Services: Federal Policy for the Frail Elderly and Chronically Mentally Ill

Sandra J. Newman and Raymond J. Struyk

A prominent feature of housing policy in the United States has been the attention given to households with special housing needs that are not effectively met by regular market processes. This chapter deals with two populations that are clearly in this category: the frail elderly and the chronically mentally ill (CMI). The lack of adequate market response in providing housing for these populations seems to be due to a combination of insufficient demand (in two senses: some households lack adequate incomes to pay for the needed housing bundle, and in a given local housing market the number of households with these attributes may be insufficient to warrant special attention by suppliers) and a lack of experience with these groups by developers which has discouraged them from entering these markets.

These populations have in common the need for supportive services and, in some cases, special environmental features (e.g., wheelchair access) in order to sustain independent living. They also share the goal of living as independently as possible in the least restrictive setting, a goal which is viewed as enhancing the quality of their lives and potentially their functional abilities.

At the same time, these populations differ in important ways. First, although both require assistance and care, the nature of these supports differ in degree and kind. In general, the frail elderly require moderate levels of care on a daily basis while many of the CMI may need very little care most of the time but intense help on an episodic basis. In addition, even in the presence of appropriate supports, the potential for disruptive or acting out behavior by the CMI may require different approaches to housing assistance.

Second, many of the CMI are young adults: in 1980, the median age of a sample of CMI participating in the National Institute of Mental Health's Community Support Program (a comprehensive community service system for the

CMI) was estimated at 42 years.[1] The age difference between the CMI and the frail elderly translates into fundamental differences in interests and needs, including those concerning social interaction and stimulation.

Third, because the CMI have a chronic illness, their need for assistance is life-long rather than short-term. While the frail elderly also require potentially life-long assistance, the younger median age of the CMI means that they could continue to be assistance recipients for virtually their entire adult lives.

A fourth difference between these two groups is the potential role of informal support systems. While recent studies such as the 1982 National Long-Term Care Survey confirm that the large majority of the frail elderly in the community have an informal support system consisting of relatives and friends, this may not be the case for many of the CMI. Thus, the formal system is likely to bear the full burden of assistance for many in this population.

Fifth, community opposition is also more likely to be a force to be reckoned with in locating housing for the CMI in contrast to housing for the elderly. As a first approximation, housing for the elderly is considered an attractive land use, while housing for the CMI is not. Communities welcome and even seek out the former, but resist the latter, primarily because of expected adverse effects on property values, neighborhood safety, and tranquility.[2] According to one former state mental health agency staff member, siting homes for the CMI is about as difficult as siting prisons.[3]

Finally, in contrast to current thinking on housing policy for the frail elderly, where there is general agreement on appropriate directions with the main debate focused on issues of targeting and income eligibility, there is much greater controversy even over fundamentals regarding housing assistance for the CMI.

The broad similarities in the housing needs of these groups and in the general approaches for addressing them persuaded us to discuss them in the same chapter, but their diversity requires that the details of the two populations be discussed separately. Consequently, the remaining two sections present information about the housing needs, policies, gaps, and options for the frail elderly and CMI, respectively.

Two broad themes unify and fortify our considerations of the appropriate role of housing assistance in addressing the need of these two groups. Housing is a critical element in the long-term care system, even if it is often not recognized as such by health-oriented analysts and policymakers. Housing-based options—such as congregate housing for the frail elderly—should be considered as an appropriate level of care for some persons (households) in the long-term care system. Increased coordination between housing-based and LTC-based assistance to these populations is essential. It is incorrect to view the funding for housing assistance in isolation from the broader federal budget. If use of housing-based options for the CMI or the frail elderly results in lower overall federal costs and reduced health expenditures in particular, then some of the savings should go to fund housing assistance. Where housing based solutions are efficient and effective they should be expanded.

We recognize that the divisions of responsibility within the Congress militates against an approach which cuts across lines of committee jurisdiction. Nevertheless, we believe that the benefits for these long-term care populations and the improved rationality of the assistance system will be sufficient to make joint action attractive to both the housing and finance committees.

The Frail Elderly

The frail elderly—persons at serious risk of institutionalization unless they receive support services—are a significant and increasing share of all elderly today. Accurately defining the number of persons in this group is difficult because of measuring problems and the compensating role caregivers play.

Overall about 9 percent of the elderly need help in basic physical activities because of a chronic health problem. Applying the same rate to households means that in 1985 about 1.65 million elderly-headed households had a member at some risk of institutionalization.[4] Recent analysis of the determinants of persons entering nursing homes indicates that those elderly needing help with toileting and getting in or out of bed or a chair are much more at risk than others with less acute activity limitations.[5] If we use this criterion, then in 1985, about 400,000 persons in elderly-headed households were at relatively great risk of being institutionalized. To this figure should be added those who have mental problems which make it difficult for them to remain at home. Overall, a round figure of 500,000 of those at relatively great risk seems reasonable.

The number of households headed by an elderly person will be fairly stable until the baby boom generation reaches retirement beginning in the early 21st century, after which the number will accelerate sharply. Despite the near term stability, the incidence of those at relatively great risk will increase to about 700,000 by the year 2000 because of the increasing importance of those over age 75 among all the elderly.[6] Moreover, even this number will be swelled by the increased numbers of those over 75 living alone—a group at considerable risk of institutionalization. Note that these are persons at risk beyond those who would be in institutions if current levels of community support are not diminished. By any standard, this is a large number of households, equivalent to 35 percent of all elderly households currently living in federally assisted housing.[7]

Many of those at risk of being institutionalized can remain in the community if they receive varying levels and types of non-medical supportive services where they live. Such services can include meals, housekeeping, chore services, personal care and recreational services, and social and emotional support. In general, of course, these services are provided by family members and friends; but 18 percent of a sample of persons with chronic health problems institutionalized over a recent two year period and 12 percent of those who remained in the community relied primarily on paid assistance for such supportive services.[8] In the years ahead, with higher women's labor force participation rates and fewer children available to give informal care, the need for formal support services will inevitably rise.

The challenge is to design cost-effective programs for providing these services to the frail elderly. A review of current housing programs of the federal and state governments for providing such assistance follows. Because the focus is on the frail elderly, many new living arrangements which provide limited support services—such as group homes, accessory apartments, and house matching—are excluded. We then describe and assess some additional options in which housing assistance plays a key role in providing long-term care in the community. A key feature of housing policy for the frail elderly and long-term care policy is the lack of coordination between the two, particularly at the federal level.

Housing with Support Services

Housing with support services currently comes in three forms, all of which involve subsidized housing projects.[9] The first type consists of projects specially designed for use by physically impaired persons. Even if no additional services are provided, such living environments may enable people to remain in the community, although there is no hard evidence on this point. As far as we know, there is no accurate count of such specially designed units in the subsidized inventory; a reasonable guess of the number in the federal inventory might be 400,000. There is also no information on the number of these units that are in fact occupied by persons who take advantage of their special features. But the absence of any requirement that such units be occupied by people with functional impairments suggests that their use by those needing such environments could be improved.

The second type of program provides support services to people living in government-subsidized housing (specially designed or not). At the federal level, no funding for such services at housing projects is specifically appropriated by Congress. Local agencies—housing, social, and health agencies—identify elderly people who need these services and try to arrange for them generally using state-funded programs or those funded by the Department of Health and Human Services. Housing projects must compete directly with other projects for the available services.

Housing projects occupied exclusively by the elderly are good "targets of opportunity" for providers of support and limited health services, because they make it easy to identify the people requiring services and increase the efficiency with which the services are delivered. Data gathered on the services available at a large sample of elderly-only public housing and Section 202 projects[10] as part of the evaluation of the demonstration Congregate Housing Services Program suggest that such arrangements are fairly common. The problem with them, of course, is the uncertainty about continued funding for these services; in addition, managers of housing projects tend to accept the services available, as opposed to providing those most needed. Various data suggest similar arrangements exist for state-supported housing projects.[11]

Finally, there are the small Congregate Housing Services Programs (CHSP). The federal CHSP program has operated in 60 public housing and Section 202 projects, with about 1,800 persons receiving support services under the program[12]; some expansion is likely under the 1987 housing legislation. Participation is supposed to be limited to people who genuinely need the services. The service bundle has consisted of a mandatory component of twice-a-day meals and options under which services are tailored to the individual resident's needs.[13] To participate in the program, each applicant's needs are assessed by a Professional Assessment Committee and determined to be sufficient to warrant such care. Possibly the most distinctive characteristic of the program is that funding for both housing assistance and support services comes from the Department of Housing and Urban Development (HUD), thus solving the often difficult problem of patching together funding for support services at the local level.

The key measure of success of the CHSP is whether it effectively delays the need for institutional placement of program participants. At the end of the demonstration period, there was no significant difference in the rate at which participants and controls were permanently placed in institutions, but there was a difference in the rate at which the two groups were temporarily institutionalized over the period: 15 percent of experimentals versus 23 percent of controls.[14] These findings, on their face, do not argue for enactment of a major congregate housing program. Still, analysts need to consider several problems with the demonstration and evaluation designs in reaching a balanced judgment about congregate housing.[15] We believe that a great deal was learned from the demonstration which should be used to design a follow-on demonstration structured to overcome the initial problems.

Several states have also launched congregate housing programs. A recent survey lists 10 states as offering programs that meet the general definition of congregate facilities.[16] A typical pattern is for the units to be in newly built projects which were financed by state housing bonds and insured under the FHA 221 (d)(4) program. Projects are almost always "mixed income," with a requirement that at least 20 percent of the units be set aside for lower income households. While most states provide full units in their projects, Massachusetts employs a shared living concept under which the tenant has his or her own bedroom, and the shared living environment includes at least two of the following: community space, kitchen facilities, dining facilities, and bathing facilities. Under these programs state agencies coordinate the provision of support services with the state housing agency, generally using some sort of memorandum of understanding to codify the arrangements. Like their federal counterparts, the state programs are all small at this point.[17]

Several recent developments at the federal level indicate the future direction that national housing assistance policy for the frail elderly may take. First, since 1980 the number of additional households assisted each year has dropped dramatically, and the composition of the units for which funding has been provided has shifted sharply away from newly constructed projects toward rent supplements or housing vouchers; funds are being appropriated only for the elderly and handicapped (under the Section 202 program). Hence, project-based alternatives for developing specially designed housing are waning. Moreover, the Reagan administration is fighting any additional experimentation with congregate services, but the Congress has continued to expand a small program.

There has been some recent movement toward using rent supplements (Section 8 existing housing assistance certificates and housing vouchers) in more supportive living arrangements. Congress authorized two initiatives in 1983 that HUD is now implementing: the use of rent supplements in "single room occupancy" (SRO) housing and the use of rent supplements in shared living arrangements. While important as indicators of greater imagination in using existing programmatic tools, the level of supportive services in these arrangements is very likely insufficient to assist the frail elderly.

Housing in Relation to Long-Term Care Policy

Housing and long-term care policies in the United States are not formally coordinated; indeed, even the informal linkages are tenuous. Basically, the United States has no articulated long-term care policy. The centerpiece of involvement by the federal government—as measured by expenditures—is the system of payments made under the Medicaid program, principally for nursing home care for people unable to pay for such care themselves. Under Medicaid's eligibility rules in the 1970s, some persons who needed long-term care could become eligible for it only if they entered a nursing home; even for persons already eligible for Medicaid, nursing home care was often the only long-term care service available.

Board and care facilities have been the major exception to the placement of the frail elderly in intermediate care facilities (ICF). Board and care arrangements are favored by states because they offer a much cheaper alternative to ICFs. Many residents receive financial assistance to live in board and care facilities through the Supplemental Security Income Program (SSI) (particularly through state supplements to SSI) rather than Medicaid.

A prime example of the creative use of SSI funds in this way is New

York's Enriched Housing Program, operated by the state's Department of Social Services. Eligible participants receive SSI payments equivalent to those for persons in domiciliary care facilities. The program is explicitly targeted at the frail elderly; and a private nonprofit or public agency is responsible for selecting residents, securing suitable housing, and providing required services. A variety of residential settings—ranging from shared living to independent units in a congregate facility—are permitted under the program.[18]

Federal legislation enacted in 1981 and 1985 began restructuring long-term care coverage; these changes reflect a growing recognition that continued reliance on nursing home care as the primary service option is neither economically wise nor socially desirable. The new legislation allows the states—which have primary administrative responsibility for Medicaid and must share the cost of services provided—much more latitude in using community-based options to provide long-term care. This shift in emphasis away from institutional care makes housing a more important component in the overall service package.

Current law offers two ways[19] to expand the degree of community-based services: (1) through the creative use of coverage options in the state Medicaid plans (i.e., the states' basic program of assistance) and (2) through the Section 2176 "waiver program,"[20] in which the states can apply to the Health Care Financing Administration (HCFA) for permission to substitute such services for institution-based services. Personal care is the primary type of service that can be added under the first option, and by 1984 some 20 states were doing so. The principal advantage of this approach is that states can provide these services without any special permission from HCFA.

Under the waiver option, the primary criterion HCFA uses in judging the application is whether the cost of providing the community-based care will be no greater than the cost for institutional services. If a waiver is granted, the states can then provide a much wider array of services and define the target groups eligible for different types of services more flexibly than under the first option. The most common services provided are case management, homemaker services, personal care, adult day care, and rehabilitation. Some states also cover modifications to the dwelling (such as grab bars and ramps) and installation of emergency response systems. As of 1984, 38 states had waiver programs in operation.

Community-based programs have found it difficult to prove that they are cost-effective. The key stumbling block, as revealed by a series of experimental programs,[21] has been an inability to define the target population correctly. Even though programs have applied strict disability criteria in determining eligibility for community-based services, persons with severe functional impairments are still at relatively low risk of institutional placement. Some combination of informal and formal services is sufficient to keep them at home. One effective way to identify people who are at risk is to draw recipients of these services from applicants for admission to nursing homes. Although this screening device may seem extreme, it is the only one to date that has proven effective.

This finding clearly has implications for housing programs being designed to provide cost-effective services to the frail elderly. We already noted the poor results of the Congregate Housing Services Program in this area, in part because of inadequate screening of the recipient population. The so-called targeting issue certainly will have to be addressed in designing new housing initiatives.

Future Policies

In considering future policies for assisting the frail elderly remaining in the community, it is useful to distinguish between housing-based and long-term care-based (LTC-based) options. Under the former, the package of assistance combines supportive services with a housing-based solution. The CHSP is a clear example. In the LTC-based model, housing assistance is added as necessary to community-based long-term care assistance. Below we first review three housing-based and then three LTC-based options. The perspective for most of the options reviewed is that of serving lower-income households— those eligible to receive housing assistance payments under current criteria— although some options are geared more to higher-income households.

Housing-Based Options

Congregate Housing Services Program. The results of the evaluation of the CHSP demonstration (reviewed earlier) did not indicate that the form of congregate housing demonstrated in the project was cost-effective in delaying institutionalization. Even so, we listed several reasons why a redesigned program would probably meet the minimum efficiency criterion of assisted households having lower rates of institutionalization than frail elderly not receiving assistance. (Later we discuss the more demanding criterion of the program resulting in lower overall costs, after allowing for some households who would not have been institutionalized receiving benefits.)

An important question concerns the cost of CHSP services. We can provide some general orders of magnitude on costs. In 1985, the monthly cost of supportive services received by CHSP participants—both those directly paid for by the program and matching services provided by the housing facility— was about $340. We can derive an approximate cost of the housing services and housing subsidies involved by assuming that (a) the income of the elderly receiving this assistance was the same as that of all elderly receiving housing assistance, and (b) the cost in public housing and Section 202 projects was the same as the average outlays under the entire Section 8 program. Under these assumptions, total rent was $430 per month and federal outlays were $274 per month.[22] Thus, the full cost of services was $770 and the subsidy portion was $614 per month.

In contrast, intermediate care facilities are estimated to cost about $45 per day or $1,350 per month. Residents receive assistance through Medicaid and pay all their income except $35 per month for this care. We estimated the monthly cost of Medicaid to the government to be $890.[23] Hence, the difference in resource cost per month between a CHSP unit and nursing home care is about $580 (1350 − 770). However, the difference in subsidy levels is only $276 (890 − 614) owing to the much higher participant contribution to the intermediate care facility. It would be even smaller if the income of ICF Medicaid beneficiaries were as large as those for housing assistance recipients.

For program expansion, the large stock of specially adapted housing in the assisted inventory offers an important pool of units that could be efficiently and quickly converted to congregate facilities under a CHSP-type program.

Congregate Housing Certificate Program (CHCP). Under the CHCP an eligible household would receive a certificate entitling the holder to occupy a unit in a congregate housing project that provides independent living with the necessary non-medical support services, such as some community-provided meals and chore and recreation services. The voucher would cover the cost of housing and support services. Households might contribute 50 to 60 percent of their incomes toward the cost, because housing, some meals, and other services are included.

The projects would be privately developed, financed, owned, and operated. Vouchers would be usable only in the projects (not at home), both to take advantage of economies of scale that result from service provision to many users at one location and to control the substitution of government for family-provided help that would occur in a more dispersed arrangement.[24] Projects would be encouraged to serve voucher holders as well as "market rate" households. Eligibility for vouchers would be restricted to persons who meet the income criteria for housing assistance and are judged to be at high risk of institutionalization. The importance of the "at risk" criterion was noted earlier in the general discussion of the cost-effectiveness of community-based long-term care. The program would be open to households who were either owners or renters at the time they applied.

The costs for congregate care are for a facility providing the following package of services: basic shelter; full congregate meals; basic sundry household items; self-administered laundry; specialized transportation (door-to-door service, eight round trips per month); and heavy housekeeping (eight hours per month). This is a fairly intensive set of services but the level is in keeping with the frail population to be served. Heumann estimates that this bundle of services would cost about $900 per month to provide, assuming that the facilities were built in 1985 (a very conservative assumption).[25] If the income of occupants is the same as that of the "average" elderly recipient of housing subsidies, and the occupants contribute half of their income to cover these services, the subsidy per month would be $589. The total resource cost per month of service at the congregate facility ($900) is higher than the CHSP ($700) because new housing units are being employed exclusively; but it is lower than the cost of the ICF ($1,350). The cost to the government (subsidy), however, is a bit less than that for CHSP ($589 vs. $614) and considerably below the ICF's subsidy of $890. If the tenant's contribution in the congregate facility were not set at 50 percent of gross income but kept at the 30 percent rate for housing assistance, however, the subsidies for the CHCP package and intermediate care would be quite similar.

Are suppliers likely to respond by providing additional congregate facilities? The experience with Medicaid and Medicare clearly indicates that the health care industry can respond with alacrity to changes in program incentives. The general evidence on the responsiveness of housing suppliers also indicates that supply will be forthcoming if the incentives are right. Certainly a small program could be accommodated with existing facilities. However, a program of intermediate size might present some problems because suppliers would have to develop new facilities to respond to demand with no guarantee that demand would actually be sufficient to support the facility.

Targeting and State Interest in Congregate Housing

Before turning to other options, two additional points about congregate housing as a substitute for nursing home care are in order. The first concerns the precision of targeting in the use of congregate facilities required to make congregate housing more cost effective than nursing home placements. In other words, what is the maximum margin of error in selecting low-income tenants for congregate facilities, in order for congregate care to still cost no more for each person who is actually being kept out of a nursing home?

Table 17.1 displays some illustrative figures which address this point. The monthly savings in government subsidies per person in a congregate facility compared to a nursing home ranges from $276 to $431, depending on the congregate costs and tenant contribution rate selected. Compared to the $890 monthly subsidy cost for a nursing home, these figures imply that if nursing homes only contain those needing this level of services, then congregate facilities can serve an extra 45 to 94 persons for every 100 who would otherwise be in a nursing home and still be cost effective. If we relax the assumption about targeting efficiency in nursing homes to 80 percent—i.e., 20 percent of the occupants are assumed to need a lower level of care—then between 53 and 113 "extra" persons could be served in congregate facilities and the overall cost not be greater than that of nursing homes per person properly treated.

These figures may suggest that the targeting requirements on congregate facilities are not very stringent. To the contrary, as noted, the results of vari-

TABLE 17.1   Targeting Requirements for Congregate Subsidies to be Less than
Nursing Home Subsidies

	CHSP		CHCP
	$t = .30$[a]	$t = .55$[a]	$t = .55$[a]
Subsidies			
Nursing home	$890	$890	$890
Congregate facility	614	459	589
Difference	276	431	301
Targeting rate for "break even" [b]			
Perfect nursing home targeting	1.45	1.94	1.51
80 percent nursing home targeting efficiency[c]	1.53	2.13	1.61

[a]Effective contribution rates, making allowance for adjustments to incomes, are .25
and .50 of gross incomes.
[b]Nursing home subsidy/congregate facility subsidy.
[c]Assumes that those not needing nursing home care are placed in congregate facilities.

ous demonstrations of community-based, long-term care as well as those of
the CHSP demonstration indicate that it is extremely difficult to target long-
term care services provided in the community to those who are truly at risk of
being institutionalized. In these terms, the requirements just listed are very
demanding.

The second point concerns the interest of the states in a congregate housing program. States share the cost of Medicaid with the federal government,
with matching rates ranging from 22 to 50 percent, with almost all being in
the 30 to 50 percent range.[26] On the other hand, they do not share in the cost of
federal housing assistance, including congregate services. This presumably
creates a strong interest on the part of the states in federal congregate housing,
if congregate services do delay institutionalization.

It follows that if congregate housing services could be demonstrated
effective in reducing institutionalization, then the states should be willing to
share in the cost of a federal congregate housing program. Table 17.2 shows
the dollar amounts per month and the matching rates (the share of nursing
home subsidies) that states could be willing to pay for congregate housing service units under different assumptions about the state Medicaid matching rate
and the target efficiency of the congregate program. So, for example, a state
with a 30 percent matching rate would be willing to pay up to $214 per month
for a congregate unit, if it believes that 80 percent of the time the congregate
unit will contain a person who would otherwise have been in a nursing home.

TABLE 17.2   Maximum State Contribution to Congregate Services Program Under Different State Medicaid Matching Rates and Congregate Target Efficiency

	MMR = .25	MMR = .30	MMR = .50
Monthly dollar amounts[a]			
"Break even" targeting[c]	$222	$267	$445
Targeting at 80% of "break even"	178	214	356
Targeting at 50% of "break even"	107	134	222
Matching rates[b]			
"Break even" matching	.25	.30	.50
Targeting at 80% of "break even"	.20	.24	.40
Targeting at 50% of "break even"	.12	.15	.25

[a] Matching rates applied to the $890 per month nursing home subsidy figure used in the text.

[b] Share of total (state plus federal) Medicaid subsidies states would be willing to pay for congregate services.

[c] "Break even" targeting rates shown in Table 17.1 for perfect nursing home targeting.

These estimates are somewhat stylized because of the restriction in recent years on nursing home bed supply, but in the main we believe they provide a valid illustration.[27] Clearly, if the states were willing to make such contributions, the attractiveness of a congregate program to the Congress would be dramatically enhanced.

Continuing Care Retirement Communities

A continuing care retirement community[28] (CCRC), or life care community, is a long-term care alternative providing a package of services, including housing, health care, and social services. A CCRC has four particular characteristics:

1. It provides independent living units—either apartments, rooms, or cottages.
2. It guarantees a range of health care and social services, which may include intermediate or skilled nursing care, usually on the premises.
3. It requires some sort of prepayment.
4. It offers a contract that describes the obligations of the tenant and the provider for a term of several years or life.

The concept of life care was developed to provide the elderly with independent living and to give them the security of guaranteed, affordable health care. This arrangement is a form of self-insurance.

Today most communities require payments of both an entrance fee and a monthly service charge. According to a careful study of the finances of CCRCs,[29] the average entrance fee in 1981 was $35,000; 80 percent are in the range of $13,000 to $65,000. The monthly fee averaged $550. The fees vary with the type of housing selected and the number of occupants per unit. CCRCs also take advantage of Medicare and Medicaid programs when possible in paying for health services.

Recently Cohen et al. have analyzed the share of the elderly who could afford various long-term care options, depending on the share of discretionary income they were prepared to spend on long-term care premiums.[30] Their results, summarized in Table 17.3, show that under 5 percent of all elderly could afford to live in a CCRC.

CCRCs reduce the risk to the insurer by screening prospective residents

TABLE 17.3   Proportion of Elderly Who Can Afford Different Long-Term Care Models, Given Willingness to Spend Alternative Amounts of Discretionary Resources (1984)[a]

	LIVING ARRANGEMENTS AND SHARE OF INCOME FOR PAYMENT					
	Married couples[b]		*Individuals*		*All persons*	
Option and monthly payment	*10%*	*25%*[c]	*10%*	*25%*	*10%*	*25%*
Continuing care retirement comm.						
$500–699	<5	<5	<5	14	<5	<5
700+	<5	<5	<5	14	<5	<5
Social HMOs						
$25–49	63	83	48	81	57	82
50–100	63	83	33	48	50	68
Life care at home						
$80–124	26	63	33	48	29	57
125–175	15	63	33	33	23	50

[a] Elderly are those age 65 or above.

[b] Assumes that each couple will pay twice the amount of a single individual.

[c] Percentage of discretionary income devoted to LTC payments.

Source: M. Cohen, E. Tell, J. Greenberg, and S. Wallack, "The Financial Capacity of the Elderly to Insure for Long-Term Care," *The Gerontologist* 27,4(1987) 494–502, Table 6.

for some preexisting health problems. They also require the households to have a certain amount of assets or monthly income.[31]

Obviously the most intriguing point about life care communities is how they manage the financial risk of guaranteeing health services under what is predominantly a prepayment fee structure. Most have managed the risk quite successfully. Analysis by a group at the Heller Graduate School at Brandeis University concluded that after age 65, CCRC residents are 1.5 times more likely than the general population to enter a nursing home at some point in their lifetime but the length of stay per admission differs dramatically.[32] For CCRC residents, the median and mean length of stay per admission is 28 and 179 days, respectively, compared with 72 and 462 days for the general elderly.

These findings suggest that nursing homes in CCRCs are used more extensively for short-term recuperative care than in the general community. Hence, the case management and the availability of alternatives to the nursing home in many life care communities appear to enable more appropriate use.[33]

From our perspective, continuing care retirement communities, with their ability to manage successfully the risk of intensive use of long-term care services, deserve more attention as a market-based option. As noted earlier, these communities cater to a clientele in the higher-income brackets. We see no need to attempt to make these communities serve lower-income households as well.[34]

LTC-Based Options

The next options to be discussed are of interest because of the possibility that those middle-income households who purchase one of the newly developed private insurance plans against the risk of long-term care expenses may, through expenditures on co-payments or full payments when benefit limits on some services are exceeded, liquidate their assets to meet their expenses under the plan. These households could then be eligible for housing assistance.

It is in the interest of government to assure participating households of the availability of housing assistance, so as to encourage them to purchase insurance which dramatically reduces government risk of bearing their long-term care costs. Moreover, Newman has documented that elderly households with a physically impaired member have a significantly higher likelihood of living in substandard housing or spending an excessive share of their income on housing.[35] Hence, such households are good targets for housing assistance.

All of the options described below are in their infancy or childhood. We believe this is the ideal time for bold action on the part of the housing community to join forces with the health community in refining them.

Life Care at Home (LCAH). This and the following option—Social Health Maintenance Organizations—are new long-term care insurance and service delivery models.[36] LCAH combines the financial and health security of a

CCRC with the freedom and independence of living at home. LCAH retains the risk-pooling for long-term care and provides benefits and guarantees similar to CCRCs, including unlimited nursing home care, to subscribers who continue to live in their own homes instead of moving to a campus. By eliminating the campus component, program costs are substantially lowered and more individuals can participate.

The LCAH chronic care benefit package includes all levels of nursing care, personal care, home health and homemaker services, in-home electronic monitoring, respite and day care, and in-home meals. LCAH is expected to cost about $5,000 to $10,000 in entry fees and between $150 and $200 in monthly fees, depending upon age and martial status at entry and on the benefit package. As shown in the final row of figures in Table 17.3, an LCAH cost of $150 per month (after the entry fee) would be affordable to about 15 percent of married couples and 33 percent of individuals, if these households were willing to spend 10 percent of their discretionary income for these premiums. The fraction of households that could "afford" the LCAH would grow considerably if they were willing to spend 25 percent of their discretionary income in this way.

LCAHs would manage risk using the same techniques employed by CCRCs and Health Maintenance Organizations (HMOs): entrance requirements, strong case management, benefit limits, and some cost-sharing. It is through the cost-sharing arrangements that moderate income households who join the program may become eligible for housing assistance by drawing down on their assets to make their co-payments.

As suggested earlier, households joining LCAHs could be given priority in receiving housing assistance in order to encourage them to participate in these programs and thus avoid long-term care payments by government on their behalf. These households would receive a Section 8 Existing payment, with the payment standard determined by the size of unit (number of bedrooms) for which they qualify. For homeowners, an imputation of the income from home equity would be made and added to the household's actual income, thereby reducing its housing assistance payment consistent with the way that other non-income-producing assets are treated in the Section 8 program.[37] Participation would be contingent upon the housing unit passing the Housing Quality Standards of the Section 8 program.

Currently, the first Life Care at Home demonstration project is being launched in Philadelphia under the title of the "Jeanes/Foulkeways Life Care at Home Plan."

Social/Health Maintenance Organizations (S/HMO). This model can be thought of as an option to the LCAH just described which relies on established HMOs as the service provider. Under this model, a single provider organization assumes responsibility for a full range of ambulatory, acute inpatient, nursing home, home health, and personal care services under a prospectively determined fixed budget. Key aspects of this arrangement are the consolidation of health and long-term care under case management in one delivery system and the corresponding consolidated financial risk for the provider organization.

Participants are recruited from the HMO's usual service area through normal marketing techniques. As shown in Table 17.3, S/HMOs are the cheapest of the long-term care options being considered here, with a majority of elderly households able to afford participation using only 10 percent of their discretionary income.[38] Still, S/HMOs involve significant co-payments and benefit limitations. Again, if households make heavy use of the LTC services, they may well become income eligible for housing assistance.

Presently, there are four S/HMO demonstration programs which began operations in the spring of 1985; they have a current (spring, 1987) total enrollment of over 11,000 Medicare beneficiaries. (The Health Care Financing Administration has provided a waiver of some standard Medicare regulations for the demonstration.) Each site has enrolled memberships that are representative of the general Medicare beneficiary population. Thus far, the sites all appear to be doing well in managing care use and keeping costs within the targeted levels. It is doubtful that many participants are income eligible for housing assistance at this time.

Section 2176 Medicaid Waiver. We have already talked briefly about these waivers. Compared to Life Care at Home and the S/HMOs, the waiver program is both mature and large in volume of households assisted. There is little more to say at this point, except that the principles outlined earlier about making Section 8 housing assistance payments available to these households apply here with equal force. Of course, in this case a much larger share of participants will be income eligible for housing assistance because they are all already receiving Medicaid payments.

Summary

In providing the housing assistance component of housing cum support services package to the frail elderly, the key distinction is between approaches that are housing-based and those that are LTC-based. Congregate housing is viewed as the most promising housing-based approach. For congregate housing—either in the CHSP or certificate version—to be successful, the difficult issue of sharply targeting assistance on those truly at risk of institutionalization must be confronted. Likewise, the richness and composition of the bundle of support services provided must be carefully monitored both to improve program effectiveness and to keep costs in line. If these challenges can be met successfully, then the states should have strong interest in creating a joint federal-state congregate housing program, since a good congregate program will reduce their overall long-term care costs by keeping persons out of nursing homes and off the Medicaid rolls.

In contrast, under LTC-based options the principal problem is assuring that those who become eligible for housing assistance receive it. Housing assistance would certainly help sustain households in the community as well as meet the specific objectives of housing programs. Again, it may be possible to reduce the share of total subsidies that must be funded from the housing assistance budget. The argument for funds being contributed by the human service agencies is particularly strong when the households receiving housing assistance have purchased private insurance against the expenses of long-term care. In such cases, the federal liability for long-term care is sharply reduced, and housing assistance will be provided in some cases in which the individual would have been institutionalized in the absence of such insurance. While the exact form of cost sharing would have to be worked out, the principle is clear.

Thus, the dominant theme to emerge from this analysis is the need for stronger working relationships to evolve between the Department of Housing and Urban Development and its state counterparts on the one hand and federal and state health and human services agencies on the other. There appear to be genuine possibilities for cost savings and improved services from such coordination of long-term services.

Community-Based Systems for the Chronically Mentally Ill

The chronically mentally ill (CMI) are individuals with serious and long-term mental disorders that impair their capacity for self-care, interpersonal relationships, and work or schooling. These impairments usually necessitate prolonged mental health care.[39] While many of the CMI tend to experience periodic crises, most are able to function relatively well for long periods of time when appropriate supports are available. In contrast to a previous era when the majority of the CMI spent most of their lives in mental hospitals, it is estimated that today, between two-thirds and four-fifths of the 1.5 to 2.5 million CMI live most of their lives in the community.[40] Those community-resident CMI who are inadequately housed, along with those who may be inappropriately located in hospitals and nursing homes, are the target group for government housing policy. Although precise estimates are not available, one expert has suggested that this group includes nearly 200,000 persons.[41]

Housing Policy and the Chronically Mentally Ill: State vs. Federal Roles

Primary responsibility for the provision of services to the CMI has virtually always belonged to the states, with the federal government playing a secondary role.[42] Housing is certainly a case in point.

State housing activities for the CMI take three main forms: First, 34 states fund supplementary SSI programs that subsidize the costs of living in special housing settings, such as board and care homes, adult foster care homes or other types of community residential facilities[43] (Social Security Administration, 1986). In general, these environments provide tenants with room, board, and some degree of assistance with personal care and protective oversight. Estimates of the number of CMI living in these environments run as high as 300,000 to 400,000.[44]

Second, a number of states directly fund residences for the CMI. For instance, some states have floated bonds to create housing for the CMI; a prime example is Rhode Island where voters have approved 11 bond issues in the last 18 years for this purpose.[45] In other states, such as Colorado, the housing finance agency has set aside a portion of its reserves for construction or permanent financing to develop housing for "special needs" groups.[46] And in many states, the Department of Mental Health owns and operates special residences for the CMI.

Finally, state mental health dollars that fund local (often county) mental health boards and community mental health centers have been used to establish housing for the CMI.

Federal housing activity specifically targeted on the CMI has been limited. While there is no hard evidence on the number of Section 8 units (be they existing, rehabilitated or newly constructed) for the CMI, impressionistic accounts suggest that this number is extremely limited. This is not surprising since the federal housing assistance program that has been touted as the main vehicle for the CMI—Section 202/8—has only authorized an annual average of 450 units for the CMI between FY1982 and FY1985.[47] Even under the most generous assumptions of the number of federally subsidized units developed for the CMI during the last 10 years, the coverage rate of federal programs would hardly reach 1 percent of the CMI population.[48] The comparable rates for the elderly and for families are much higher.

Since states have historically assumed the primary responsibility for filling the housing and related service needs of the CMI, it is legitimate to ask why the federal government should increase its involvement. The main arguments revolve around issues of equity. First, as just noted, the CMI have been underserved by federal housing assistance programs. There are probably a number of reasons why this has occurred: the relatively small size of the population in need which makes it easier to overlook and harder to advocate for; the perception that developing or managing units occupied by the CMI will be fraught with problems (e.g., community opposition, zoning restrictions, the need for on-site, 24-hour supervision, and other obstacles that raise development or management costs); the absence of strong links between the mental health system and the housing system which has prevented mental health professionals from accessing federal housing subsidies for their clients; and, perhaps most importantly, the courts' decision that the Secretary of HUD and the PHAs can refuse to integrate CMI individuals in federally assisted developments with other eligible housing assistance recipients without violating the rights of the CMI to equal protection.[49]

The basis of the court rulings is concern with the availability of necessary supportive services for the CMI which are viewed as different in both degree and kind from those required by other groups. But the practical effects are severe: apparently the CMI can be excluded from all except project-based, 100 percent CMI developments, such as Section 202 complexes or Independent Group Residences (IGRs) where Section 8 Certificates are applied, thereby drastically reducing the number of assisted housing units the CMI can compete for.[50] While the prevailing view among mental health professionals clearly supports the courts' and HUD's concern regarding the availability of appropriate services, the implication that these service needs can only be satisfied in project-based developments is open to debate, as will be discussed later.[51]

An additional equity argument for a larger federal role is the great variation in per capita mental health expenditures across states and, more significantly, the quality of community-based state mental health programs, including housing.[52] The federal government has a legitimate interest in assuring that eligible populations receive at least a basic level of service. This principle may apply with extra force when the eligible population is also a particularly vulnerable one, with special needs that arise for reasons beyond the individual's control. Most entitlement programs (e.g., AFDC, SSI) are structured with this principle in mind; the federal government funds a basic benefit level for all eligible individuals in these programs. But because this benefit floor does not distinguish between eligibles with fundamentally different needs, it is insufficient to cover the special residential or service requirements of populations such as the CMI.

While there may have been the expectation, in the early days of these programs, that states would provide adequate coverage for special needs through special state supplement programs, the actual extent and nature of such coverage varies widely. The SSI program offers one example. It provides basic income assistance to a large share of the CMI (estimates run as high as 50 percent): seven states provide no supplement of any kind; an additional nine do not provide supplements that apply to populations such as the CMI; and there is great variation in the generosity of payments among the 34 states that do provide applicable supplements.[53]

It is not surprising, therefore, that with some notable exceptions, there is continuing concern about the adequacy of residential facilities such as domiciliaries or board and care homes, many of which receive funding via SSI and house a substantial number of CMI individuals.[54] The question of the appropriate federal role regarding board and care homes has surfaced several times over the past 10 years; and, in 1976, the Keys Amendment was added to the Social Security Act in an effort to ensure that such homes would provide adequate settings and services.[55] But continuing problems suggest that policy responses, to date, have been inadequate. For this reason, both the House and Senate Committees on Aging have recently asked the General Accounting Office to study the current status of board and care, with a view toward potentially redefining the federal role.

Concerns about providing basic levels of service and about equitable treatment also come into play when one reviews state housing activities. While there are no estimates of the number of housing units that the states have either directly or indirectly established for the CMI, there is little doubt that such units do not come close to satisfying need. Several states have recently documented the number of CMI whose residential needs are not being met.[56] More gripping evidence is the estimated 25–40 percent of the homeless who are reported to be mentally ill (in absolute terms, somewhere between 63,000 and 200,000 persons, depending on the estimated homeless population.)[57]

These arguments undoubtedly were part of the justification for three different HUD demonstration projects for the CMI that the Department has launched since 1978:

(1) The Section 202/8 Demonstration, which ran from 1978 through 1980. Roughly 2500 CMI individuals were housed in either group homes (average size = 6 units) or independent living complexes (average size = 11 units) under this program. In addition to Section 202 loans for the development of the units and Section 8 rental subsidies, the Health Care Financing Administration (HCFA) provided Medicaid waivers to cover the costs of a broad range of community mental health services not normally reimbursable by Medicaid.

(2) The Transitional Housing Demonstration, first authorized in 1986 with $5 million in funding but renewed and expanded to roughly $60 million in 1987 as Section 421 of H.R. 558, the Homeless Assistance Act. This program provides no-interest loans of up to $200,000 for the acquisition and rehabilitation of housing, as well as funds for technical assistance and operating cost subsidies for up to five years. The target populations include the deinstitutionalized homeless and other homeless individuals with mental disabilities. Support services eligible for the operating cost subsidy include mental health services.[58]

(3) The provision of 125 Section 8 Certificates explicitly earmarked for the CMI to each of the nine cities participating in the CMI Demonstration Program sponsored jointly by the Robert Wood Johnson Foundation and HUD. This program began in 1986 and will continue for five years. Part of the motivation for it was the view that the shortage of appropriate, affordable housing has been an important deterrent to expanding community-based services for the CMI.[59]

Divergent Views on the CMI's Housing Needs and Implications for Policy

It is probably no accident that the chronology of the first and third approaches represented in the federal demonstrations to foster the CMI's access to adequate housing parallels the general shift in HUD programs for subsidizing supply to subsidizing the consumer.[60] But these strategies also capture the different points of view on how best to meet the housing needs of the CMI. In order to evaluate the relative benefits of these housing strategies for the CMI, we must first identify the housing and related needs of this population.

There is wide agreement that the CMI comprise a heterogeneous group of individuals with different levels and types of impairment and, therefore, different service requirements. Several schemes have been developed to classify these needs according to the intensity of assistance required.[61] The Massachusetts "level of need" model, for example, defines the following five levels:

Level I   Persons who require intensive medical and psychiatric interventions and support in a secure environment.

Level II   Persons who need continuous and intensive long-term care.

Level III Persons who may need intermittent or continuous long-term care.

Level IV   Persons who may need intermittent or continuous long-term care.[62]

Level V   Persons requiring ongoing support services, but who are capable of living independently.

As noted, the existence of a range of needs such as that embodied by the Massachusetts scheme is not at issue. Instead, the debate centers around how these needs can best be met and, particularly, in what type of residential setting.

There are two main points of view in this debate. On the one hand, what may be characterized as the traditional view translates these different levels of need first into a continuum of the degree of staff supervision and structure that the CMI client needs, and second, into a continuum of residential settings where these support services can be provided with some degree of cost efficiency. Thus, Level I of the Massachusetts model may take the form of transitional housing, possibly located on state hospital grounds, where 24-hour staff is available, and intensive medical and psychiatric treatment can be provided in a secure setting. In contrast, Level V might translate into an apartment in the community with solid and continuous links between the individual and a system of mental health care.

The more radical "normalization" perspective holds a very different view. Although this perspective acknowledges (albeit tentatively) the need for intensive service settings such as group homes for those with the most intensive need for service (Level I), it rejects any form of facility-based residences for the rest of the CMI population.[63] According to this view, for all but the severely mentally ill, the need for adequate housing should be disentangled from the need for services.[64] In this way, the housing needs of the CMI become the same as those of the rest of the population, and the emphasis shifts to providing decent and safe housing in "normal settings." Implicitly, then, the normalization perspective defines the appropriate role of housing policy to be the same for the CMI as for any other population group: to assure that those with low incomes live in decent and safe dwellings. The need for services is to be satisfied on a case-by-case basis, ranging from the delivery of some services to the individual at home to linking the individual with community services.

Advocates of full normalization believe that separating the setting from the services would result in several beneficial outcomes: the CMI would become more integrated into their communities; the stigma, discrimination, and community opposition to special residences for the mentally ill would be abated; and the individual would live in a homelike, noninstitutional environment.

Finally, the normalization view addresses one of the fundamental weaknesses of the continuum approach, namely, that residents move from one setting to another as their service needs change. In many housing programs for the CMI across the country, this principle has been translated into explicit limits on the length of time a resident is allowed to stay at a particular residential level. There are two major problems with this approach. First, moving from one house to another is a traumatic and disruptive event for most people; to require potentially frequent moves by the CMI makes little sense. Second, some individuals may not make sufficient progress to move to the next residential level within the specified time limits.

Each of these perspective has strengths and weaknesses. Perhaps the main advantage of the traditional, residential continuum approach is the greater cost efficiency in service delivery. This is the case not only when on-site staff is required, but also when service providers must travel to the site because transportation costs constitute such a large fraction of the cost of service delivery. Problems with the institutional or dehumanizing atmosphere in some of these settings, or with time limits on stays, may be weaknesses in implementation rather than concept: time limits can be removed, and features that connote an institutional setting can be eliminated. Difficulties with stigma and community integration, however, may be more fundamental; but, in the absence of any empirical evidence on the extent of these problems for the CMI in normalized settings, it is unclear whether these problems arise under that approach as well.

It is difficult to argue against the principles that guide the normalization perspective. Each individual has maximal freedom of choice in deciding where to live and for what length of time since this decision does not determine whether or not needed services will be available. In addition, there appears to be total flexibility in the types of services used and where they are delivered. Instead, the main weakness of this model is how much it is likely to cost. In the absence of any concentration of individuals with similar needs, there are no economies of scale in delivering services to those who require assistance on site.

Unfortunately, as noted earlier, there is no empirical literature on the normalization approach. Thus, we have no basis for judging not only the absolute cost of this approach but more importantly, how these costs compare to the beneficial outcomes that may be derived by the CMI who participate. Nor do we have any insight into such practical concerns as difficulties in getting landlords to rent units to the CMI or the incidence of disruptive behavior by CMI tenants which might create substantial problems for other tenants. To the extent that some of the nine sites participating in the CMI Demonstration Program adopt a normalization strategy, the housing component of the evaluation of this demonstration should be able to fill this void in empirical evidence. In fact, if otherwise comparable sites adopt different housing strategies, the evaluation should be able to compare the relative benefits and costs of each and under what circumstances (i.e., client characteristics and site characteristics) each works best.

Future Directions for Federal Housing Policy for the CMI

Even without a more solid body of evidence, and without choosing between a facility-based, residential continuum approach or a full normalization approach, we can identify a few guiding principles for a workable federal housing strategy for the CMI. These requirements do not address such fundamental questions as how to increase the share of housing assistance received by the CMI, how to forge stronger links between the housing and mental health systems, or what housing strategies might be best suited to the large population of treatment-resistant, young adult CMI. But they do answer the question: if a federal housing policy were to be developed for the CMI, what would its key elements be?

First, although much greater communication and coordination between HUD and relevant mental health agencies are absolutely essential, as will be clear in a moment, HUD should be allowed to do what it does best, namely, administer federal housing policy. In practical terms, this means that whatever specific housing programs are ultimately developed for the CMI, HUD and its personnel would be concerned with such matters as housing quality standards, financial soundness of developments, tenant income certifications, and residential management. The one exception to HUD's traditional activities concerns the area of eligibility and targeting. For most housing assistance applicants, the primary entry criteria include income and family size. For the

CMI (like the frail elderly), however, additional information is required on the individual's ability to live in the housing unit and his or her plan of care.[65] Since HUD has no expertise in the mental health field, these health and service-related aspects of certification must be handled by mental health professionals.

Thus, a second component of policy would be that the mental health system (e.g., community mental health centers) would hold full responsibility for linking the CMI to the federal housing assistance program(s) that may be developed, targeting for HUD those CMI for whom the particular program is suitable, and providing HUD with certification that the individual is participating in an appropriate system of mental health care. This system should cover a range of support services including full case management, 24-hour crisis intervention to respond quickly to episodes of acute disturbance, assistance in instrumental activities of daily living (e.g., laundry, shopping, managing money), and general monitoring. Such a system of care is analogous to the special features that must be present in housing for the physically handicapped: it is the "ramp" that makes the dwelling suitable for a CMI resident (Stein, 1987).

Current organization and financing arrangements offer both an opportunity and a challenge to implementing this general policy approach. The existing system lends itself to a sharing of responsibility by the federal and state governments since there is a fairly clear division of functions and financing for housing (primarily federal) versus services (primarily state). But it is also this separation of functions and resources that creates the need for coordination.

Beyond these generic elements of a workable federal housing strategy, several additional suggestions regarding specific approaches may deserve attention. First, facility-based settings such as board and care homes do not fall within the purview of federal housing policy. Yet, such settings house more than 300,000 CMI. They are often in dire need of physical rehabilitation and usually receive part of their support from SSI payments which vary greatly in generosity across the country. Such settings may warrant special priority for housing rehabilitation dollars.[66]

Second, to the extent that the facility-based approach persists, serious efforts should be made to normalize these settings. This can be done, for example, by prohibiting institutional features both in design and in operations.

Third, housing finance agencies and housing developments receiving subsidies from HUD should be encouraged to use their accumulated reserves to provide the CMI with greater access to federal housing assistance.

Notes

1. H. H. Goldman, "Long-Term Care for the Chronically Mentally Ill," Working Paper 1466-23 (Washington: Urban Institute, 1983).
2. L. Steinman, "The Effect of Land Use Restrictions on the Establishment of

Community Residences for the Disabled: A National Survey," *The Urban Lawyer* 19,1 (1987); D. Lauber, *Impacts on the Surrounding Neighborhood of Group Homes for Persons with Development Disabilities* (Springfield, IL: Paper prepared for the Governor's Planning Council on Developmental Disabilities, 1986).

3. A. Schectman, Discussant comments presented at Housing Policy Project Meeting, U.S. Capitol, Washington, 1987.

4. Average incidence rates for these two problems were calculated from data for 1979 in B. Feller, "Americans Needing Help to Function at Home," *NCHS Advance Data* 92 (1983). There is no clear pattern of changes in morbidity rates among the elderly; so use of these data is reasonable. On the lack of trends, see J. F. Fries, "Aging, Natural Death and the Compression of Morbidity," *New England Journal of Medicine* (1983) 130–135; D. P. Rice and J. Feldman, "Living Longer in the United States: Demographic Changes and Health Needs of the Elderly," *Milbank Memorial Fund Quarterly/Health and Society* 61,3 (1983) 362–396; L. M. Verbrugge, "Longer Life but Worsening Health?" *Milbank Memorial Fund Quarterly/Health and Society* 62,3 (1984) 475–515; E. Palmore, "Trends in Health of the Aged," *The Gerontologist* 26,3 (1986) 298–301; K. Manton and B. Soldo, "Dynamics of Health Changes in the Oldest of the Old," *Milbank Memorial Fund Quarterly/Health and Society* 63,2 (1985) 206–285.

5. S. Newman, M. Rice, and R. Struyk, *Overwhelming Odds: Caregiving and the Risk of Institutionalization* (Washington: Urban Institute Project Report, draft, 1987).

6. The same incidence rates used in the preceding paragraph have been applied to standard projections of households by age of household head in the year 2000 prepared by the Bureau of the Census; this yielded 550,000. The incremental 150,000 corresponds to the rough increment made to the 1985 figures.

7. R. Struyk, M. Turner, and M. Ueno, *Future U.S. Housing Policy: Meeting the Demographic Challenge* (Washington: Urban Institute Project Report 3608, 1987) Table 5.4.

8. Newman, Rice, and Struyk, *Overwhelming Odds*, Annex B.

9. Not discussed here but an important element in overall federal activity is the FHA insurance for supportive housing projects. The range of the type of projects covered was expanded by 1983 legislation.

10. The Section 202 program is one in which specially designed housing is developed by nonprofit sponsors for occupancy by elderly households and households with a physically handicapped member. Federal subsidies are provided in the form of direct loans which carry below-market interest rates and, in recent years, through rental assistance payments, available under the Section 8 program for all occupants who are eligible to receive them.

11. R. Thielen, M. Tiven, and B. Ryther, *State Initiatives in Elderly Housing* (Washington: Council of State Housing Agencies and National Association of State Units on Aging, 1986).

12. J. S. Nachison, "Who Pays? The Congregate Housing Question," *Generations* (1985 Spring) 33–35.

13. The service bundle requirements have recently been reduced to a single meal service per day.

14. S. Sherwood, N. Morris, C. C. Sherwood, S. Morris, E. Bernstein, and E. Gorstein, *Final Report of the Evaluation of Congregate Housing Services Program* (Boston: Hebrew Rehabilitation Center for the Aging, 1985) Table IV.2.

15. Four points are particularly important:

    a. The population served by the program was not restricted to people who were vulnerable to institutionalization, according to the definition employed in the evaluation; also, the share of participants who were vulnerable varied considerably from project to project.

b. The CHSP was structured around the provision of twice-a-day meals, a service that many of the participants neither needed nor especially wanted. Hence, many of the services provided would not have been expected to affect institutionalization rates.

c. Many of the control projects offered fairly rich service environments themselves. Thus the comparison was not between no services available to residents and CHSP, but rather between some services (which varied sharply among projects) and more and possibly better-tailored services.

d. The observation period may have been too short, given the kind of program and control projects employed in the demonstration. Even with all the problems just listed, some significant effects may have been evident over another year or two. (Alternatively, if a short observation period was to be employed, better measures of health status should have been employed in addition to the relatively crude institutionalization rate measure.)

16. Thielen, Tiven, and Ryther, *State Initiatives*.

17. For more details on the Massachusetts program see A. S. Anthony, "Statement," in *Sheltering America's Aged: Options for Housing and Services,* Hearing Before the Special Committee on Aging, United States Senate (Washington: USGPO, April 23 1984); Building Diagnostics, Inc., *Congregate Housing for Older People: An Effective Alternative* (Boston: Building Diagnostics, Inc., Report to the Massachusetts Department of Elder Affairs, 1984).

18. For more information see Third Age Center, *An Evaluation of an Innovative Program for Older Persons Sponsored by the New York Department of Social Services* (New York: Third Age Center, 1982).

19. These options are detailed in B. Burwell, "Home and Community-Based Care Options Under Medicaid," in R. Curtis and I. Hill, eds., *Affording Access to Quality Care* (Washington: National Governors Association, Center for Policy Research, 1986).

20. Section 2176 (of the Omnibus Budget Reconciliation Act of 1981) Home and Community-Based Medicaid Waiver program.

21. W. Weissert, "Seven Reasons Why It Is So Difficult to Make Community-Based Long-Term Care Cost-Effective," *Health Services Research* 20,4 (1985) 423–433, gives a good summary of these results and a general discussion as to why cost-effectiveness has been so difficult to attain in community-based programs.

22. The figures on CHSP services were provided by J. Nachison for 1986 and were deflated to 1985 using the CPI. The income data for elderly housing assistance recipients is for 1984, from U.S. Bureau of the Census, "Characteristics of Households and Persons Receiving Selected Noncash Benefits: 1984," *Current Population Reports* (Washington: USGPO), updated to 1985 using the CPI. Section 8 outlays are from HUD budget documents.

23. Based on the mean average daily rate (unweighted) for 27 states reporting amounts for 1984 in National Governors Association, *A Catalogue of State Medicaid Program Changes, 1984–85* (Washington: NGA Center for Policy Research, 1986). The 1985 value was obtained by increasing the 1984 amount by 7 percent.

24. Reliance on private providers also means lower federal short-term commitments of budget authority to finance the construction of projects than are necessary under the traditional programs.

25. The difference in cost between this package and one that also provides laundry service, heavy and light housekeeping services, personal care (eight hours per month), and nursing care (four hours per month) is estimated to be about $100 per month. L. Heumann, *A Cost Comparison of Congregate Housing and Long-Term Care Facilities in the Mid-West* (Urbana: University of Illinois, Housing Research and Development Department, 1985) 57, Table 15.

26. M. K. Nenno, J. S. Nachison, and E. Anderson, in "Support Services for Frail Elderly or Handicapped Persons Living in Government-Assisted Housing," *Public Law Forum* 5,2 (1986) 69–84; first pointed out states' interest in this area. Matching rates are from J. Holahan and J. Cohen, *Medicaid: The Trade-Off between Cost Containment and Access to Care* (Washington: Urban Institute Press, 1986) 22, Table 8.

27. Some analysts contend that the type of savings to states discussed in the text would not occur because the limitation on nursing home bed supply in effect over the past several years means that there is an excess demand for these beds. Hence, delaying the institutionalization of some elderly would simply mean that others would occupy the nursing home beds. We think that this explanation is too simple a description of what is really happening. In particular, there are very important differences among states in current practices, which point to a more complex situation and one in which savings are possible from the provision of congregate housing services. First, while the supply of nursing home beds per elderly person has declined in many states over the 1981–1985 period, it has expanded in fifteen; in four states it has increased by more than 25 percent. So at least in these states, the excess demand explanation is questionable. Second, lack of nursing home beds in those states where the shortage is a binding constraint is producing other costs of long-term care such as: (a) delays in the release of patients from acute care facilities because nursing home placements cannot be found (a powerful effect of this type has been documented in ongoing analysis at the Urban Institute); (b) because more very frail elderly are at home, rather than in nursing homes where a higher level of care is available, acute care facilities are being used more intensely; (c) states may be using the S.2176 Medicaid waivers to effectively circumvent the nursing home bed limits by authorizing equivalent care (at approximately equivalent cost) in the community. The first two cost increases (a and b), which are very large on a day-per-use basis, are borne by Medicare, in which the states are not required to contribute; but the federal government has a definite interest in reducing these costs. On the other hand, states do share in the costs of the S.2176 waiver program under the Medicaid program; and currently about three-fourths of all states have received such waivers.

28. This section draws heavily on S. Williams, "Long-Term Care Alternatives: Continuing Care Retirement Communities," *Journal of Housing for the Elderly* 3, 1&2 (1985) 15–33.

29. H. E. Winkelvoss and A V. Powell, *Continuing Care Retirement Communities* (Homewood, IL: Richard D. Irwin, Inc., 1984).

30. M. Cohen, E. Tell, J. Greenberg, and S. Wallack, "The Financial Capacity of the Elderly to Insure for Long-Term Care," *The Gerontologist* 27,4 (1987) 494–502.

31. Most life care communities have been established in the past 20 years; in 1983 there were about 300 CCRCs in the United States. Estimates of the number of persons housed in CCRCs range from 55,000 to 100,000. An additional 1,000 to 1,500 communities may be in operation by the year 2000, accommodating about 2 percent of the elderly.

32. S. Wallack, *Designing Less Costly Continuing Care Retirement Communities* (Waltham, MA: Heller School, Brandeis University, Final Report to the Robert

Wood Johnson Foundation, 1986); Cohen, Tell, Greenberg, Wallack, "Financial Capacity of the Elderly," 494–502; C. E. Bishop, "Use of Nursing Care in Continuing Care Retirement Communities" (Waltham, MA: Heller School, Brandeis University, 1985).

33. In a larger analysis of 207 CCRCs, researchers found that lower rates of nursing home use were related to the community's ability to admit noncontract patients to nursing care (enabling them to add market-rate nursing home fees to total revenue when beds are not filled by contract residents) and the presence of a full versus a limited guarantee. This suggests that strong control by management on the use of nursing home services yields significant cost reductions per resident.

34. Modest federal action might be appropriate in one area, however. A key factor in the continued growth of these facilities is that they retain the confidence of the public. That confidence would be severely damaged by the insolvency of several communities, with the attendant loss by the residents. To guard against this possibility, the federal government could examine the procedures that states use to oversee the financial soundness of those communities and recommend any appropriate improvements. See F. E. Netting and C. C. Wilson, "Current Legislation Concerning Life Care and Continuing Care Contracts," *The Gerontologist* 27,5 (October 1987) 645–651, on these points.

35. S. Newman, "Housing and Long-Term Care: The Suitability of the Elderly's Housing to the Provision of In-Home Services," *The Gerontologist* 25,1 (1985) 35–40.

36. This section draws heavily on E. Tell, M. Cohen, and S. Wallack (forthcoming), "Life Care at Home: A New Long-Term Care Finance and Delivery Option," including some quotation from the abstract.

37. This is the same procedure used for homeowners who participated in the Housing Allowance Supply Experiment.

38. For details see J. Greenberg, W. Leutz, and R. Abrams, "The National Social Health Maintenance Organization Demonstration," *Journal of Ambulatory Care Management* 8,4 (1985) 32–61; and Greenlick, M., "Highlights of the Social HMO Demonstration," Statement to the Subcommittee on Health and Long-Term Care, House Committee on Aging, February 17 1987, Washington: USGPO.

39. H. H. Goldman and R. W. Manderscheid, "Chronic Mental Disorder in the United States," in NIMH, ed., *Mental Health United States: 1987* (Rockville, MD: NIMH, to appear).

40. HHS, *National Plan for the Chronically Mentally Ill* (Washington: HHS, 1980); P. J. Carling, "Housing Status and Needs of the 'Chronically Mentally Ill' Population: A Briefing Paper" (Burlington, Vermont: University of Vermont, Department of Psychology, 1984); HHS-HUD, "Federal Efforts to Respond to the Shelter and Basic Living Needs of Chronically Mentally Ill Individuals" (Washington: HUD, 1983); E. F. Torrey and S. M. Wolfe, *Care of the Seriously Mentally Ill: A Rating of State Programs* (Washington: Public Citizen Health Research Group, 1986); and Goldman and Mandersheid, "Chronic Mental Disorder." Estimates of the number of CMI in the population vary because of differences in definition and difficulties in identifying the population that is chronically mentally ill.

41. Carling, "Housing Status."

42. Torrey and Wolfe, *Care of the Seriously Mentally Ill.*

43. Social Security Administration, *The Supplemental Security Income Program for the Aged, Blind, and Disabled* (Baltimore: SSA, 1986).

44. HHS, *National Plan for the Chronically Mentally Ill* (Washington: HHS, 1980); and Torrey and Wolfe, *Care of the Seriously Mentally Ill.*

45. Torrey and Wolfe, *Care of the Seriously Mentally Ill.*

46. Colorado Housing Finance Authority, "Special Needs Housing Fund Guidelines" (Denver: CHEA, undated).

47. HUD, Office of Assisted Housing, "The Tentative Funding Comparisons of Section 202 Program and Projects for the Handicapped" (Washington: HUD, undated).

48. Carling, "Housing Status" and Goldman, "Long-Term Care."

49. 540 F. Supp. 1300 (D.C.M.J. 1982); 607 F. Supp. 428 (DCNY 1985).

50. While these court decisions involved Section 202 projects, their applicability to Section 8 shared housing or IGRs seems likely.

51. See, for example, B. A. Stroul, *Crisis Residential Services in a Community Support System* (Rockville, MD: NIMH, 1987); and L. I. Stein and M. A. Test, "Alternatives to Mental Health Hospital Treatment" in *Archives of General Psychiatry* 37 (1980) 392–397.

52. Torrey and Wolfe, *Care of the Seriously Mentally Ill.*

53. R. Frank, Personal Communication, September 1987; Social Security Administration, *Supplemental Security Income Program.*

54. S. Segal and U. Aviram, *The Mentally Ill in Community-Based Sheltered Care* (New York: Wiley & Sons, 1978); and N. Dittmar et al., *Board and Care for Elderly and Mentally Disabled Populations* (Washington: U.S. Department of Commerce, National Technical Information Service, 1983).

55. HHS-HUD, "Federal Efforts to Respond."

56. See, For example, Commonwealth of Massachusetts, *ACTION PLAN: A Comprehensive Plan to Improve Services for Chronically Mentally Ill Persons* (Boston: Commonwealth of Massachusetts, 1985); and Ohio Department of Mental Health, *Final Report* (Columbus: ODMH, 1986).

57. HUD Estimates that the number of homeless is between 250,000 and 550,000. The estimated proportion who are mentally ill is reported in L. H. Aiken, S. A. Somers, and M. F. Shore, "Private Foundations in Health Affairs: A Case Study of the Development of a National Initiative for the Chronically Mentally Ill," *American Psychologist* 41 (1986) 1290–95.

58. *Housing and Development Reporter* (Boston: Warren, Gorham & Lamont, Inc., September 7 1987).

59. The Robert Wood Johnson Foundation, *The Robert Wood Johnson Foundation Program for the Chronically Mentally Ill* (Princeton, NJ: RWJF, 1986).

60. The transitional housing demonstration combines elements of both approaches.

61. D. L. Shern, N. Z. Wilson, R. H. Ellis, D. A. Bartsch, and A. S. Coen, "Planning a Continuum of Residential/Service Settings for the Chronically Mentally Ill: The Colorado Experience," *Community Mental Health Journal* 22,3 (1986); Massachusetts *ACTION PLAN;* and American Psychiatric Association, "A Typology of Community Residential Services" (Washington: APA, 1982).

62. III and IV refer to the same intensity of service need but differ in staffing and residential requirements because of underlying variations in their respective populations.

63. P. J. Carling, *Meeting the Housing and Residential Service Needs of Persons with Severe Psychiatric Disabilities: An Overview of Principles, Services* (Burlington: University of Vermont, Department of Psychology, 1985).

64. Aside from the different thrust of this view relative to the traditional, residential continuum perspective, this separation of services from setting runs counter to current thinking regarding housing policy for the frail elderly. As discussed earlier in this paper, there is general agreement that closer links between housing and long-term

care services need to be fostered, including arrangements for on-site provision of services. In addition, both Section 202/8 and congregate housing, which are both facility-based residences, have been quite successful. There are, of course, fundamental differences between the CMI and the frail elderly, as noted at the outset of this paper.

65. Similar information is also routinely required of elderly applicants to project-based housing assistance programs such as Section 202/8 and is provided by Professional Assessment Committees for residents in the Congregate Housing Services Program.

66. The more fundamental problem of inconsistent SSI payments is addressed in Chapter 15 by Sandra Newman and Ann Schnare in their discussion of the relationship between housing assistance and welfare also in this volume.

Contributors

William C. Apgar, Jr. is Associate Professor at the John F. Kennedy School of Government of Harvard University and Associate Director of Harvard's Joint Center for Housing Studies.

Patrick E. Clancy is Executive Director of The Community Builders, formerly Greater Boston Community Development, and has been with the organization since receiving his degree from Harvard Law School in 1971. The Community Builders, a nonprofit corporation working with neighborhood-based organizations, has developed more than 5,000 affordable housing units in the Northeast.

Phillip L. Clay is Associate Professor in the Department of Urban Studies and Planning of the Massachusetts Institute of Technology. He was formerly Assistant Director of the MIT-Harvard Joint Center for Urban Studies and currently does research on housing policy, especially on the role of the nonprofit developer.

Thomas B. Cook is Director of Housing and Land Use for the Bay Area Council, a business-sponsored regional public affairs organization based in San Francisco. He graduated from Dartmouth College and holds a Master's degree in City Planning from the University of California at Berkeley.

Denise DiPasquale is Visiting Assistant Professor at the John F. Kennedy School of Government of Harvard University and a Research Fellow at Harvard's Joint Center for Housing Studies.

Anthony Downs is Senior Fellow at the Brookings Institution in Washington, D.C. Previously, for 18 years he was a member and then Chairman of the Real Estate Research Corporation of Chicago, a nationwide consulting firm.

George C. Galster is Professor of Economics and Chairperson of Urban Studies at the College of Wooster in Wooster, Ohio. He has published widely in the field of housing discrimination and served on the Working Group conducting HUD's Housing Discrimination Survey in 1988–89. He earned his Ph.D. at MIT.

Patric H. Hendershott is Professor of Finance and holder of the Galbreath Chair in Real Estate at the Ohio State University in Columbus. He is also a Research Associate of the National Bureau of Economic Research and editor of the *Journal of the American Real Estate and Urban Economics Association*.

Langley C. Keyes is Professor in the Department of Urban Studies and Planning of the Massachusetts Institute of Technology.

Michael J. Lea is Senior Vice President and Chief Investment Officer of the Imperial Corporation of America in San Diego and its subsidiaries.

David O. Maxwell, a recognized leader in the development of U.S. housing policy, is the Chairman and Chief Executive Officer of Fannie Mae (Federal National Mortgage Association), the nation's largest investor in home mortgages. Previously, he was Chairman of Ticor Mortgage Insurance Co. and served as general counsel at the Department of Housing and Urban Development.

Neil S. Mayer is Director of the Office of Economic Development in Berkeley, California. His professional interests focus on housing and economic development efforts to assist low-income people and communities. He has written extensively on community-based development.

Sandra J. Newman is Associate Director for Research, Institute for Policy Studies, Johns Hopkins University, and Research Professor in the Department of Geography and Environmental Engineering. In addition to the analysis of housing needs and housing policy, her research focuses on long-term care. She holds a Ph.D. in Urban Planning from New York University.

James W. Rouse is Chairman and Chief Executive Officer of The Enterprise Foundation and The Enterprise Development Company. He was formerly Chairman and Chief Executive Officer of The Rouse Company.

Ann B. Schnare is Vice President for Housing and Real Estate at ICF, Inc. She is an economist specializing in housing market analysis and policy research and holds a Ph.D. in Economics from Harvard University.

Michael A. Stegman is Professor and Chairman of the Department of City and Regional Planning at the University of North Carolina at Chapel Hill. Among his current research projects are an evaluation of public housing ownership programs and an assessment of the social and economic impacts of home ownership on lower income families.

Raymond J. Struyk is Senior Research Associate at the Urban Institute in Washington, D.C. He works extensively on issues of housing for the elderly, particularly the relationship between housing and long-term care policy.

Ian Donald Terner is President of BRIDGE Housing Corp., a nonprofit housing developer active in the San Francisco Bay area. Previously he was Director of Housing and Community Development for the State of California. He holds a B.A., M.C.P., and Ph.D. from Harvard University in Architectural Sciences and City Planning.

James E. Wallace is Deputy Manager for the Housing and Labor Economics Area at Abt Associates Inc., in Cambridge. He served as the technical director for the National Low-Income Housing Preservation Commission. He holds a Ph.D. in Urban Studies and Planning from MIT.

John C. Weicher is currently Assistant Secretary for Policy Development and Research at the Department of Housing and Urban Development, on leave from the American Enterprise Institute where he holds the F. K. Weyerhaeuser Chair in Public Policy Research.

Michael Wheeler is Visiting Professor in the Department of Urban Studies and Planning of the Massachusetts Institute of Technology and Director of Research at the MIT Center for Real Estate Development. He has written widely in the areas of negotiation and dispute resolution.

Index